Pessimism of the Intellect, Optimism of the Will

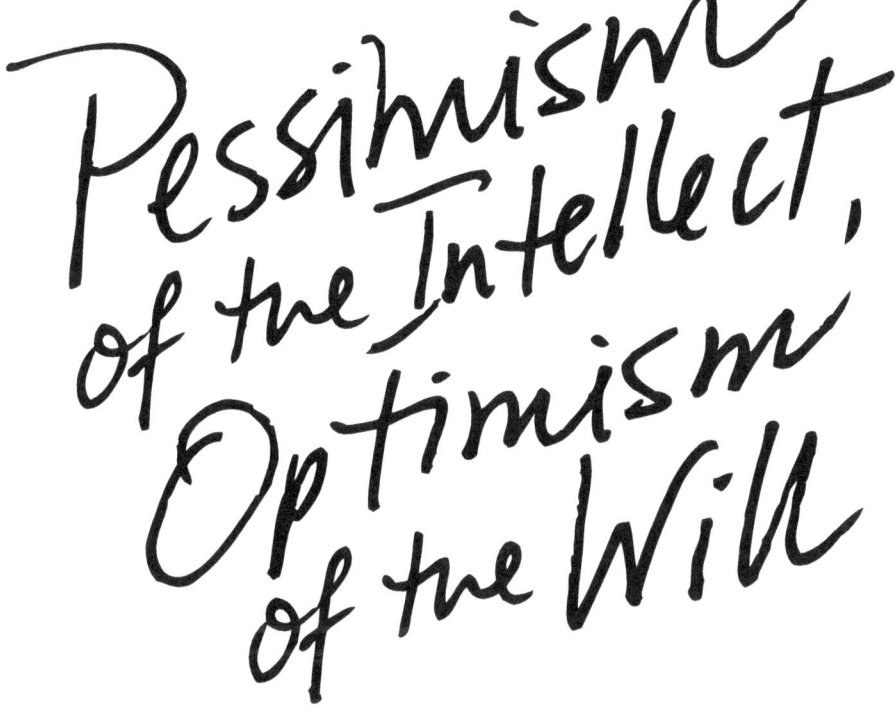

Pessimism of the Intellect, Optimism of the Will

THE POLITICAL PHILOSOPHY OF KAI NIELSEN

Edited by David Rondel and Alex Sager

UNIVERSITY OF
CALGARY
PRESS

© 2012 David Rondel and Alex Sager

University of Calgary Press
2500 University Drive NW
Calgary, Alberta
Canada T2N 1N4
www.uofcpress.com

This book is available as an ebook which is licensed under a Creative Commons license.
The publisher should be contacted for any commercial use that falls outside the terms of that license.

LIBRARY AND ARCHIVES CANADA CATALOGUING IN PUBLICATION

Nielsen, Kai
      Pessimism of the intellect, optimism of the will : the political philosophy of Kai Nielsen / edited by David Rondel and Alex Sager.

Includes bibliographical references and index. Issued also in electronic formats.
ISBN 978-1-55238-530-2

      1. Political science—Philosophy. I. Rondel, David, 1978– II. Sager, Alexander E. (Alexander Edward) III. Title.

JA71.N52 2012   320.01   C2012-904817-8

The University of Calgary Press acknowledges the support of the Government of Alberta through the Alberta Multimedia Development Fund for our publications. We acknowledge the financial support of the Government of Canada through the Canada Book Fund for our publishing activities. We acknowledge the financial support of the Canada Council for the Arts for our publishing program.

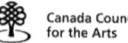

Cover Photo: *Policman Watching Over the Demonstrators* © Srdjan Srdjanov (istockphoto.com)
Cover design, page design, and typesetting by Melina Cusano.

TABLE OF CONTENTS

Preface		vii
Sources		ix
Introduction		
	Kai Nielsen's Political Philosophy: A Critical Introduction and Overview	xi
I. Metaphilosophy: Critical Theory and Wide-Reflective Equilibrium		
1	On Finding One's Feet in Philosophy: From Wittgenstein to Marx	1
2	Metaphilosophy, Pragmatism, and a Kind of Critical Theory: Nielsen and Rorty	15
3	On There Being Wide Reflective Equilibria: Why It Is Important to Put It in the Plural	41
4	The Global Crisis of Values: The Poverty of Moral Philosophy	75
II. Egalitarianism and Socialism		
5	On the Choice between Reform and Revolution	125
6	Justice and Modes of Production: Allen Wood's "The Marxian Critique of Justice" Revisited	151
7	Class and Justice	167
8	Radical Egalitarian Justice: Justice as Equality	193
9	Radical Egalitarianism Revisited: On Going beyond the Difference Principle	213
III. Cosmopolitanism, Nationalism, and Global Justice		
10	Is Global Justice Impossible?	265
11	Liberal Nationalism, Liberal Democracies, and Secession	301
12	Cosmopolitan Nationalism	349
13	World Government: A Cosmopolitan Imperative?	373
Afterword: An Interview with Kai Nielsen on Political Philosophy		401
Selected Writings by Kai Nielsen		437
Bibliography		445
Index		469

PREFACE

This collection is a tribute to Kai Nielsen. We both had the opportunity to study with Kai at Concordia University in Montreal. Kai introduced Alex to political philosophy as an undergraduate and served as co-supervisor for his doctoral dissertation at the University of Calgary. David completed his M.A. at Concordia University under Kai's supervision. As it was for many of his other students, Kai's Friday afternoon office hours were a memorable highlight in our education. As a professor, Kai was available to anyone eager for serious discussion on politics, political philosophy, metaphilosophy, or religion. His office hours were a forum of philosophy at its best, where one was judged not on academic credentials but on the quality of one's arguments.

Kai advised us throughout the preparation of this manuscript, but ultimately believed that an author's judgment of his or her own work is often not the most reliable. He was adamant therefore that the selection of texts rested with us. Nonetheless, we followed many of his suggestions and we are grateful for his advice.

We would also like to thank the John King for his support of the project and for the care he took in editing the manuscript. We are also indebted to Noah Sharpsteen for his work formatting the manuscript and to Pam White for acquiring permission to reprint the articles. The preparation of the index was supported with a grant provided by the office of the Dean of Arts, Ryerson University. We would like to thank Thomas Posie for his work on the index.

David Rondel and Alex Sager

SOURCES

The essays in this volume previously appeared in the following publications:

"On Finding One's Feet in Philosophy: From Wittgenstein to Marx," *Metaphilosophy* 16, no. 1 (1985): 1–11.

"Metaphilosophy, Pragmatism and a Kind of Critical Theory: Kai Nielsen and Richard Rorty," *Philosophical Papers* 36, no. 1 (2007): 119–50.

"On There Being Wide Reflective Equilibria: Why it is Important to Put it in the Plural," *Windsor Yearbook of Access to Justice* 26, no. 2 (2009): 219–51.

"The Global Crisis of Values: The Poverty of Moral Philosophy." In *Philosophy and World Problems*, edited by John McMurtry. Oxford: Encyclopedia of Life Support Systems (EOLSS) developed under the auspices of UNESCO.

"On the Choice between Reform and Revolution." *Inquiry* 14, no. 1 (1971): 271–95.

"Justice and Modes of Production: Allen Wood's 'The Marxian Critique of Justice' Revisited." In *Norms and Values: Essays on the Work of Virginia Held*, edited by Joram G. Heber and Mark S. Halfon, 267–81 (Lanham, MD: Rowman & Littlefield, 1998).

"Class and Justice." In *Justice and Economic Distribution*, edited by John Arthur and William H. Shaw, 225–45 (Englewood Cliffs, NJ: Prentice-Hall, 1978).

"Radical Egalitarian Justice: Justice as Equality." *Social Theory and Practice* 5, no. 2 (1979): 209–26.

"Radical Egalitarianism Revisited: On Going beyond the Difference Principle." *Windsor Yearbook of Access to Justice* 15 (1996): 121–48.

"Is Global Justice Impossible?" *Res Publica* 4, no. 2 (1998): 131–66. (Republished with kind permission from Springer Science+Business Media B.V.)

"Liberal Nationalism, Liberal Democracies, and Secession." *University of Toronto Law Journal* 48, no. 2 (1998): 253–95. (Reprinted with permission from University of Toronto Press Incorporated; www.ntpjournals.com)

"Cosmopolitan Nationalism." *The Monist* 82, no. 3 (1999): 446–68. (Copyright © *The Monist: An International Quarterly Journal of General Philosophical Inquiry*, Open Court Publishing Company, Chicago, Illinois. Reprinted by permission.)

"World Government: A Cosmopolitan Imperative." Originally published in French as: "Un gouvernement mondial : un impérative cosmopolite?" In *Le cosmopolitisme : Enjeux et débats contemporains*, edited by Ryoa Chung and Geneviève Nootens, 119–150 (Montreal: Presses de l'Université de Montréal, 2010).

INTRODUCTION

Kai Nielsen's Political Philosophy: A Critical Introduction and Overview

> I pass now to what the philosophy of liberalism would be were its inheritance of absolutism eliminated. In the first place, such liberalism knows that an individual is nothing fixed, given ready-made. It is something achieved, and achieved not in isolation but with the aid and support of conditions, cultural and physical: – including in "cultural," economic, legal and political institutions as well as science and art. Liberalism knows that social conditions may restrict, distort and almost prevent the development of individuality. It therefore takes an active interest in the working of social institutions that have a bearing, positive or negative, upon the growth of individuals who shall be rugged in fact and not merely in abstract theory. It is as much interested in the positive construction of favourable institutions, legal, political and economic as it is in removing abuses and overt oppressions.
>
> – John Dewey, "The Future of Liberalism"[1]

Kai Nielsen describes himself as a liberal socialist cosmopolitan nationalist.[2] He is the first to admit that the self-description is a mouthful, if not an outright contradiction. Egalitarian, analytic Marxian, critical theorist, and pragmatist might also be added to this jumble, complicating matters even further. Our aim in this introduction is to demonstrate how these disparate commitments come to form a thoughtful and attractive stance in political philosophy. More generally, we attempt to prepare the ground for the essays that follow by sketching some of the details of Nielsen's views along with the intellectual context in which they are couched. The introduction is in three main parts, corresponding roughly to the three sections of the volume. First, we set out some of Nielsen's metaphilosophical views and the significance they have for his political philosophy. In the second section, we discuss Nielsen's egalitarianism and socialism, emphasizing in particular how the former grounds the latter, and, inversely, how Nielsen regards socialism (of a particular non-dogmatic stripe) as the real-world normative upshot of a philosophical belief in equality. In the final section, we turn to questions of global justice and Nielsen's views on cosmopolitanism, nationalism, and multiculturalism. In particular, we set out his account of the political and economic institutions required by justice and his defence of secession for liberal nations based on democratic self-determination.

I. METAPHILOSOPHY, CRITICAL THEORY, AND WIDE REFLECTIVE EQUILIBRIUM

Throughout his long and productive career, Kai Nielsen has returned, consistently and in a wide range of contexts, to questions about the practical role of philosophy.[3] More than most philosophers, he has wrestled with questions about philosophy's role in intellectual culture. What is philosophy and what might it yet become?[4] To what may it plausibly aspire? Such questions are for Nielsen among the most interesting and exciting ones philosophers can grapple with, even if the human impact of other social, political, and economic questions is more urgent and, thus, more deserving of intellectual attention.[5]

Nielsen's keen interest in metaphilosophy is in many ways the upshot of having come of age philosophically against the backdrop of logical positivism in American philosophy departments and, later, the 1953 publication of Ludwig Wittgenstein's *Philosophical Investigations*. Nielsen was twenty-seven years old when the *Investigations* appeared posthumously, and Wittgenstein's bold "therapeutic" enterprise – his attempt to show the "fly the way out of the fly-bottle"[6] – has had a lasting and profound impact on Nielsen's thinking. Much like Stanley Cavell, Donald Davidson, Hilary Putnam, Richard Rorty, and other philosophers of his generation, Nielsen learned how to think about philosophy in Wittgenstein's wake.[7]

Nielsen believes that it is not (and cannot) be the business of philosophy to locate timeless essences and objective truths (where "objective truths" are take to mean something like "mind or language independent truths"). Philosophy cannot hope to penetrate mere appearances and arrive at a synoptic vision of how things truly are.[8] "There is no such thing," Nielsen has it, as "the one true or uniquely adequate description of the world."[9] On Nielsen's view, this does not entail a general skepticism, nihilism, or relativism. There are still better and worse ways of thinking about things – though, of course, "better" and "worse" here will invariably be to some extent time and context dependent.

With the later Wittgenstein and the logical positivists, Nielsen rejects metaphysics on the grounds that metaphysical propositions are nonsense (or "cackle" as J.L. Austin put it).[10] It is human practices all the way down. There is no method with which to evaluate our current practices by reference to something that is not itself just one more practice. Even our most abstract theorizing – about the universe, the nature of mind, truth, goodness, rationality, and so on – is itself just more human practices, differing only in complexity perhaps from the other practices we seek to evaluate. As Nielsen puts it, "We can gain no Archimedean point or skyhook – no 'moment of transcendence' – to appraise our practices. We have no understanding of how to think outside or beyond our practices."[11] We are here like the sailors on Neurath's boat, bound to replace the wooden planks of our vessel (incrementally, in a piecemeal fashion) always while aboard it. The fundamental error of metaphysics, then, is that it aspires to a perspective *outside all human practices*, a point of view untainted by contingent social and linguistic norms. Metaphysics seeks (impossibly) what Thomas Nagel calls "The View from Nowhere" and there is, Nielsen has it, no such perspective to be had.

> We are language-using animals with our practices firmly embedded in the world – where else could they be embedded? – which is not identifiable apart from these practices. And we do not have questions external to the framework and questions

> internal to the framework that are in any fundamental sense different kinds of questions, for we have no inner/outer distinction. There is no intelligible question about how mind or language hooks on to the world. Both are part of the world. Where else could they be? What we always have is part of the world interacting with other parts of the world.[12]

Such pronouncements get their purchase from (among other things) the anti-representationalism to which Nielsen is firmly committed. Nielsen rejects the idea that language "represents" the world, and the corollary that true propositions are *made true* by their faithful fit – their "correspondence" – with reality. It may seem counter-intuitive to think in this way (one often hears contemporary analytic philosophers speak of their "realist intuitions"), but Nielsen, child of logical positivism that he is, has little time for the philosophical theses – realism, representationalism, and the correspondence theory of truth – to which such intuitions typically give rise. The main problem, he thinks, is a verificationist one: it is that we lack a clear idea of what it would mean for bits of language – sentences, propositions, "marks and noises," as Rorty has referred to them – to stand in relations of "fit" or "correspondence" with bits of non-language (the world). In what could such relations consist? What criterion or method of verification might we consult in order to distinguish (supposedly) accurate representations from their inaccurate counterparts? If there is no way to get between language and its object in order to differentiate between the two, we must give up the idea that some of our beliefs correspond to a non-linguistic reality while others fail to achieve this correspondence. As Rorty hyperbolically put the point, we must give up the idea of "Nature's Own Language" – the idea that the world favours certain descriptions of itself over others. "The world does not speak," Nielsen is fond of saying, "only we do." In short, absent some criterion for success in having achieved an "accurate representation of reality," there is no choice but to conclude that, while we may (and do) enjoy causal touch with the world, no good sense can be attributed to the view that we interact with the world *representationally*.[13]

One might wonder how (or if) such metaphilosophical views have shaped Nielsen's political-philosophical thinking. Nielsen has at times denied that philosophy and politics are tightly or necessarily linked, suggesting that the connections between one's views on such philosophical topics as the nature of truth, knowledge, rationality, and morality and one's political commitments are looser than many people suppose. The idea is that philosophy turns on a separate normative axle from politics, that there is ample space for political disagreement among philosophers with otherwise similar metaphilosophical views.[14] On the one hand, many thinkers with whom Nielsen is in broad political agreement – G. A. Cohen or Andrew Levine, say – find many of the metaphilosophical views to which Nielsen is committed hopelessly wrongheaded. On the other hand, as the example of Richard Rorty, a New Deal liberal, confirms, general agreement on metaphilosophical matters is no guarantee of general agreement on political matters. "Rorty ... should not be so spooked by the ghost of 'grand theory,'" Nielsen has remarked, "that [he continues] to ignore the careful and politically relevant work of analytical Marxians such as G. A. Cohen, John Roemer, Erik Olin Wright, Andrew Levine, and David Schweickart."[15] Even so, and whatever is to be made of the connections between philosophy and politics in general, it is instructive to see how the metaphilosophical theses to which Nielsen is committed and his political philosophy are made to hang together.

While Nielsen is skeptical about "grand theory," and while he rejects philosophy as a foundational discipline,[16] he thinks philosophy can assist us in making sense of the world – where "making sense of" is taken historically, contextually, and fallibilistically – and provide us with a vision for how it could be improved. The echoes here of Marx's eleventh thesis on Feuerbach – "The philosophers have only *interpreted* the world ... the point, however, is to *change* it"[17] – is by no means accidental. Nielsen believes that, "after the demise of the tradition," there remains an important role for a kind of *critical theory*. Such a theory borrows selectively from the Frankfurt school – from Adorno, Horkheimer, and, importantly, Marcuse and Habermas – but it is above all distinctly "Marxian" in character.[18] Such a critical theory, Nielsen explains,

> identifies with working-class interests and seeks to sharpen them in ways that will lead to the end of class society, and to the liberation of working people from domination and subservience.... It seeks to show how workers, and others as well,

are dominated and forced into conditions of subordination and sometimes even servitude by the workings of the capitalist system, including the domination of the rest of society by the capitalist class.[19]

Marxian critical theory is thus an empirical theory with an emancipatory intent.[20] While it aims to provide an accurate (causal, empirical) account of things, its research program is animated by a decidedly normative perspective.

There are connections between a critical theory of the sort sketched above and Nielsen's interest in wide reflective equilibrium (WRE) that are worth examining more closely.[21] Just as Marxian critical theory represents the most promising mode of social criticism after the eschatological certainty of earlier Marxian thinkers has been set aside, WRE names the most promising method of justification after the great foundationalist expectations of earlier philosophers have been eschewed.[22] If we accept that there are no deep normative foundations to which we can turn when seeking to justify our moral and political beliefs, the best we can hope for is to bring our moral intuitions, principles, and best empirical studies into wide reflective equilibrium.

> WRE is a coherentist method of justification. It starts with a society's ... most firmly held specific particular considered judgments or considered convictions and seeks to forge them into a consistent and coherent whole along with other considered judgments (judgments at all levels of generality) and as well with other relevant beliefs that are generally reasonably, uncontestedly, and widely held in the society.[23]

On Nielsen's view, in short, Marxian critical theory and WRE are products of the same metaphilosophical picture: both reject the pretensions of Philosophy (big P) in favour of the fallibilist, contextualist, and historicist (though non-relativistic and deeply reflective) orientation constitutive of Wilfrid Sellars's (small p) philosophy. Just as the conclusions of an emancipatory critical theory are subject to revision and correction, so too shall "no wide reflective equilibrium ... be unconditionally final: the 'last word' written in stone."[24] We cannot look around our own corner (as Nietzsche put it) to "anticipate the deeper changes in consciousness, not in our own community and certainly not in any other.... Eternal vigilance is no guarantee of eternity."[25] Taking Marxian critical theory and WRE seriously suggests that there is no point in rendering final pronouncements on normative matters in advance or *a priori*. Both suggest that complex social, political, and economic problems cannot be worked out from the comfort of the armchair – that observation, experiment, historical knowledge, and contextual sensitivity are indispensable. We philosophers may hanker for something more grandiose, for the ability to meditate about normative questions from the point of view of eternity, from *nowhere*. For better or worse, Nielsen regards that as an impossible aspiration. The world is always in flux, the future always open and uncertain.

Marxian critical theory and WRE shouldn't be regarded as consolation prizes or as philosophies of retreat. As Rorty well put the point, "We should not regret our inability to perform a feat which no one has any idea how to perform."[26] We have no choice but to muddle along, gather evidence, test our claims, correct our errors, keep an open mind, and try to have our beliefs and commitments cohere with each other in some kind of justificatory web.

2. EGALITARIANISM AND SOCIALISM

Like most people who think of themselves as egalitarians, Nielsen's belief in political equality has its roots in a conviction about the equal moral worth of human beings, *viz.*, everyone's life matters equally; no one's life matters more than anyone else's. This conviction does not by itself recommend a scheme of distributive justice: it says little or nothing about the kind of political arrangements entailed by a commitment to equality, nor about *which* substantive things (if any) people should have equal amounts of. Rather, it bolsters the moral conviction that when we abstract from our own personal points of view, when we see the world "as if from a great height, in abstraction from the engagement [we] have with this life because it is [ours],"[27] we cannot but conclude that everyone's life matters and matters equally. To be sure, this conclusion will not resonate with everyone. As is the case with all fundamental moral commitments, moreover, it is difficult to imagine how a debate about its truth might be settled without either party – egalitarian and skeptic alike – eventually claiming something like Martin Luther's "Here I stand; I can do no other."

Like most contemporary Anglophone political philosophers, Nielsen regards John Rawls as a pivotal figure. Indeed, Nielsen places Rawls alongside Aristotle and Hobbes as history's most important political philosophers.[28] Despite his deep appreciation of and admiration for Rawls's work, his critical engagement with Rawls's theory of justice represents one of Nielsen's most important contributions to the academic literature on egalitarianism. Nielsen differs from Rawls in two important respects. First, he has argued that Rawls's theory of justice is insufficiently egalitarian, in large part because on Nielsen's reading Rawls's "difference principle" implies some sort of class stratification.[29] (Nielsen has recently weakened this claim; see below.) Secondly – and this is importantly related to Nielsen's first line of criticism – Rawls has remained for the most part noncommittal about the economic and social institutions that would properly implement his principles of justice, thus demonstrating an insensitivity to the point that institutions must be appraised in part by the extent to which they contribute to class divisions.

As is well known, Rawls's highly influential difference principle (that social and economic inequalities be arranged to the greatest benefit of the least advantaged) is designed to be sensitive to those situations in which an egalitarian redistribution removes, or would be thought to remove, the incentive for people to work harder or deploy their talents efficiently. The idea, plainly put, is that intelligent, reasonably altruistic young people who have a choice of career would not submit to the rigours of medical school and practice, say, without superior compensation.[30] Many dismiss any form of egalitarianism that goes beyond the difference principle as absurd. After all, it would lead to everyone, *including* the worst off group, being worse off.

How does Nielsen's egalitarianism go beyond Rawls's difference principle? As we have already seen, Nielsen begins with the principle that everyone's life matters equally. Egalitarianism comes in many forms – there are many ways in which a concern for equality can rear its head, and many dimensions along which people can be made equal. Like Rawls, moreover, Nielsen regards equality as an extrinsic value: equality is not valuable in itself; it is valuable only because it represents a necessary (though insufficient) condition for people to exercise their autonomy and to satisfy their needs:

> [A]s far as reasonably possible, conditions should be brought into existence or, where in existence, sustained, which make for an equal satisfaction of the needs of everyone at the highest level of need satisfaction for each compatible with the needs of everyone being so treated.[31]

From the principle that everyone's life matters equally and the ideal of achieving universal autonomy and need satisfaction, Nielsen concludes that equality of condition, particularly equality of wealth, is what egalitarian justice requires.[32] Nielsen argues that, where such equality of condition does not prevail, social hierarchies will arise as a matter of course. Such hierarchies in turn (and in practice) create power asymmetries that will invariably contribute to the violation of the principle of the basic moral equality of all persons with which we began. A genuinely free society, therefore, must also be an egalitarian society. It must not only provide people with equal rights, opportunities, and liberties but also with substantial material equality so that no members can use their greater share of resources to coerce or oppress others.[33] Under capitalism, Nielsen believes that class divisions will continue to structure society, leading to unequal power relations between the owners of the means of production and the workers. Nielsen argues on this basis that an egalitarian society will also be a socialist society defined by, among other things, the common ownership of the means or the *principal* means of production.

It can be plausibly argued that the difference principle accommodates Nielsen's concerns, given the assumption that, properly understood, it would permit more autonomy and satisfy more needs than a more strictly egalitarian principle. It is important to keep in mind here that Rawls believes that primary goods – "all purpose means" such as rights and liberties, powers and opportunities, income and wealth that every person is expected to want whatever the plans of her or his life – are the proper metric of distributive justice.[34]

In his reply to Norman Daniels in *Reason and Emancipation*, Nielsen allows a conditional reading of the difference principle that states "If certain incentives work to make the worst-off as well-off as possible, then it would be irrational to reject them in favor of strict equality, once we rule out envy."[35] Under this reading of the difference principle, inequality can only be justified *if it is necessary.*

This concession brings Nielsen closer to Rawls. Rawls has often been interpreted as offering a justification for welfare state capitalism with its provisions for unemployment, social security, as well as substantial public goods such as universal health care.[36] It comes as a surprise to many that John Rawls himself claims that "justice as fairness" is compatible with and requires either democratic socialism or a property-owning democracy.[37] The nature of a property-owning democracy is somewhat indeterminate, but it surely and minimally requires significant government interference to ensure that the ownership of the means of production is fair among citizens.[38]

Do Nielsen's criticisms of Rawls miss the mark then? One difference that remains is that Nielsen's response to the "equality of what" question (in light of *what* should egalitarians redistribute goods and resources?) is much broader and includes welfare or well-being along with primary goods and/or capabilities. Nielsen advocates a form of equality of *result* or *outcome* – grounded in what Nielsen has referred to as his "weak consequentialism" according to which the morality of an action is judged *at least in part* by its consequences.[39] He is inclined to think that, when people's needs have been met, we ought to continue to aspire to an equal satisfaction of *wants*.[40]

Another fundamental difference between Nielsen and Rawls involves their understanding and employment of wide reflective equilibrium (WRE). Rawls excludes from wide reflective equilibrium controversial metaphysical, epistemological, and scientific theories. The argument in *A Theory of Justice* proceeds independently of specific facts about the society of the choosers behind the 'veil of ignorance' – indeed, they know neither the type of society they live in nor their place in history. Rawls does not employ reflective equilibrium as a form of critical theory nor does he admit ideological theories or disputed views about economics, imperialism, human nature, class, gender, or race.

In contrast, Nielsen writes,

But the elements that go into *wide* reflective equilibrium, if thought through carefully, burst asunder all autonomous conceptions of moral philosophy, redefining moral philosophy in such a way that it becomes a part of a general conception of critical theory tendering an emancipatory approach to human problems (including moral problems) that remains systematically empirical-cum-theoretical, where moral theory and social theory come to be closely integrated into the human sciences."[41]

Nielsen's egalitarianism is based largely on his analysis of capitalism and what he takes to be its inevitable harms.[42] His domain of inquiry is not the principles of justice for *only* liberal societies, but rather justice for *any* society. This requires an appeal to controversial claims about economics, sociology, human nature, and naturalism. For example: "Many people's beliefs are distorted by ideology and adaptive preferences." "Market socialism can efficiently allocate goods." "Workplace democracy can provide the basis for an efficient and more humane economic system." "Human beings are capable of rejecting the urge to dominate each other and can develop a large scale, classless society." "Naturalism is the most reasonable view about the nature of reality." Reasonable people reject all of these claims. Nielsen's socialism is central to his views; Rawls, to the extent that he might be thought a socialist, makes socialism a relatively minor part of his system.

Another key difference is to be found in their attitudes towards ideal theory. Nielsen has on many occasions engaged in ideal theory, but with considerably more ambivalence than Rawls. Rawls believes that there is a properly philosophical task that involves organizing our intuitions, considered judgments, and moral principles within the scope of moral theory. Nielsen holds that any boundary between moral philosophy and other disciplines is a convention that should be analyzed and rejected if it is without practical import, if it does not contribute to improving the world. Many of the recondite debates engaged in by ideal theorists turn out, he thinks, to be superfluous:

[I]n the realm of ideal theory ... liberals and radicals, social democrats and socialists, can, rather extensively, join forces. When we turn ... to the real world and to a consideration of the

> thick texture of facts and conceptualizations of political sociology, history, and political economy, I would argue ... that the prospects for an extensive equality of condition which also carries with it autonomy – equal autonomy for all – and fraternity are, as near as we can be, to being impossible without socialism and that socialism ... must, to be acceptable, be some form of market socialism.[43]

Socialism is a dirty word in many circles, either identified with violent, despotic planned economies or considered to be an economically unworkable ideal the attempted implementation of which would cause widespread misery. Indeed, Nielsen cites Andrew Levine to the effect that "actually existing socialism is capitalism's best argument in defense of itself."[44] Many political philosophers are egalitarians; far fewer are socialists. Nielsen's socialism is yet more radical in arguing that there is a continuum between reform and revolution.[45] In cases where the injustice and misery is great enough and the probability of long-term success sufficient, violent revolution can be justified.[46] In a revealing autobiographical remark, Nielsen writes:

> ... by the time I began to teach I had settled down into something like Deweyan social democracy. I thought that if we would hold on to our brains and be patient, we in North America, and eventually in the world, could in time end up like Sweden. The Vietnam War changed that. It was an eye-opener for me. In being part at that time of the internal resistance in the United States, I became convinced that such liberal reformist measures would never work, and *slowly* I became a Marxist, or, as I would now prefer to call it, a Marxian.[47]

There are two parts to Nielsen's support for socialism. First, he supports the plausibility of G. A. Cohen's reconstruction of historical materialism in *Karl Marx's Theory of History: A Defense*.[48] Cohen's version of historical materialism presents an empirical, non-teleological theory that purports to show how society may develop. Cohen holds that a society's productive forces determine its economic structure (this is referred to as the "primacy thesis"); its economic structure further influences the superstructure, most notably the legal and political institutions. The "development thesis" claims that productive forces tend to develop over time. (Nielsen follows Joshua Cohen in holding that the historical record falsifies the developmental thesis when applied to particular societies, but argues that it may hold when applied to the history of humankind as a whole).[49] The endogenous growth of human productive power and technological change provides reasons for a particular trajectory of history. Nielsen does not believe that the modes of production sustaining today's capitalist societies must push us toward socialism, but he does believe that this is a possibility worth striving toward.

The second ground for the feasibility and desirability of socialism is the possibility of a functioning, democratic, market socialism. Nielsen follows John Roemer and David Schweickart's proposals for market socialism. We cannot undertake a full description (let alone a defence) of the most developed accounts of market socialism here. However, most versions of market socialism require the public ownership of the major means of production and the democratic organization of firms in which workers elect managers. Firms compete for customers and may go out of business if they fail to operate efficiently. Businesses are taxed and the government uses these funds to provide public goods not allocated by the market, as well as to promote investment. Nielsen allows the private ownership of small businesses in cases where the owner is also a worker.[50]

Though we do not know how market socialism would fare if implemented (the chasm between theory and practice is wide here), Nielsen makes a persuasive case that it is an institutional ideal worth seriously considering and, more importantly, worth experimenting with. Analytic Marxism and advocacy for socialism largely disappeared after the break-up of the Soviet Union in 1989 and the supposed global triumph of liberal democracy. The last twenty years have shown that history did not end and that the apparent demise of socialism was perhaps prematurely declared. The Washington Consensus has done a great deal of damage in the developing world and even the IMF has distanced itself from "one-size-fits-all" demands that states open their countries to free trade, privatization, and the implementation of austerity plans. The global recession that began with the U.S. sub-prime mortgage fiasco has made clear the need for more oversight in the financial markets. In the United States, the comparative lack of a safety net for the unemployed and uninsured is evident to many. Most proposals look backward to welfare state capitalism. Philosophers like Nielsen by contrast provide an ideal to look forward to.

3. COSMOPOLITANISM, NATIONALISM, AND GLOBAL JUSTICE

In his 1985 book, *Equality and Liberty*, Nielsen writes, "The principles of radical egalitarian justice I have articulated are meant to apply globally and not just to particular societies."[51] A significant part of his work over the last twenty-five years has involved defending and elaborating on this claim, culminating in the papers collected in *Globalization and Justice*. At the same time, Nielsen confesses that he sometimes feels "that it is indecent to talk about global justice or engage in exercises setting out principles of global justice."[52] Much academic work on global justice, he sometimes complains, needlessly transforms banal truisms and moral platitudes into highly technical, arcane debates, replete with the requisite jargon and distinctions.

Absolute poverty afflicts hundreds of millions of people who don't have enough to eat and lack access to clean drinking water or basic vaccines. Young children are forced to abandon their school and work to support their families. Refugees flee murderous regimes while the most powerful members of the international community stand by idly, unwilling to do more than sustain – and only barely – the survivors in UNHCR camps.

That there are human beings living such miserable, humiliating lives is shameful; that we inhabit a world of obscene inequality makes such injustices more shameful still. The wealthiest quintile of the world's population commands more than 90 per cent of the global income while the poorest quintile survives on roughly 0.25 per cent.[53] More than 1 billion people subsist on less than one dollar per day, and roughly the same number of people lack access to clean water. The United Nations Development Programme estimates that roughly 1.3 billion people – almost one fifth of the world's population – live below the poverty line.[54] Nearly 800 million people do not have enough food, and about 500 million people are chronically malnourished. More than 10 million children – 98 per cent of them from the planet's poorest countries – die each year before their fifth birthday for reasons directly attributable to extreme poverty.

Statistics like these are horrifying. The disparity between the "haves" and the "have-nots" is greater today than ever before.[55] Unthinkable human misery has persisted in a time of unprecedented opulence. Even *within* affluent societies, some people's life prospects are radically inferior to other people's life prospects. Some people enjoy the resources, freedoms, and opportunities a real chance at a good life requires; many more do not. That so much in this world is horribly wrong is evident to anyone who cares to look.

In recent years, Nielsen has often compared the world to a pig-sty in his writings. Though he has few illusions about the so-called Marxist regimes and their atrocities, the collapse of socialism as a guiding ideal in much of the world depresses him. Some on the left – including, ambivalently, Nielsen himself – find hope with Hugo Chávez, but Venezuela's social reforms, it is worth stressing, have depended heavily on high oil prices. Moreover, Chávez has increasingly curtailed the judiciary and media and squashed opposition to his "Bolivarian" revolution.[56] For Nielsen, as for Rorty, the left is the party of hope.[57] Without a vision of a better world to work toward, however, hope dwindles. Our title for this collection, *Pessimism of the Intellect, Optimism of the Will*, comes from the Italian Marxist Antonio Gramsci.[58] Nielsen's vision of the world is grim, yet his politics are optimistic – some would say utopian. But without a vision of a better world to work toward hope dwindles.

What then is the value of sophisticated philosophical inquiry? Nielsen's answer is that philosophical inquiry, conceived along contemporary disciplinary lines, is of limited value. On Nielsen's view, moral *theory* is unlikely to be of much help. However, a critical theory employing *wide* reflective equilibrium that includes not only our moral intuitions but also scientific and social scientific research may allow philosophers to become public intellectuals. His work has increasingly moved in this direction. At Concordia University in Montreal, the assigned readings for Nielsen's 2003 seminar on "Globalization, Imperialism, and Global Justice" included David Harvey's *The New Imperialism*, Jan Aart Scholte's *Globalization: A Critical Introduction*, Richard Falk's *The Declining World Order*, and Thomas Pogge's *World Poverty and Human Rights*. Of the four, only Pogge has a philosophical background, and he has increasingly collaborated with economists and moved in the direction of providing policy recommendations.[59]

Despite the increasingly practical nature of his analysis, Nielsen's account does contain many philosophical arguments and positions. To begin, he is a cosmopolitan. Cosmopolitans hold that every human being is of equal moral worth. More controversially, they contend that justice applies globally, not merely within the nation, state, ethnic group, or similar association. We have duties of justice to all humans, irrespective of individuals' group membership (though this does not rule out some special associative duties owed to compatriots and others). Though cosmopolitanism has attracted many supporters over the last decade or so, it is still a relatively controversial position.[60] Philosophers such as Thomas Nagel, David Miller, and Michael Blake have argued that the conditions that give rise to claims of justice do not occur on a global level.[61]

None of these philosophers deny that there are moral duties to alleviate absolute poverty. Compassion and a regard for people's common humanity serve here as a ground for eliminating misery. What they deny is that such duties are rightly characterized as duties of *justice*, in principle enforceable through the use of coercion. Indeed, Nagel, Miller, and Blake endorse egalitarian justice *within* societies but explicitly deny that the imperatives of distributive justice apply between societies. On their view, the necessary institutional arrangements that give rise to claims of justice simply do not occur outside of the state.

Such theorists endorse a version of what Richard Arneson calls "sufficientarianism," a version of the doctrine that what *really* ought to trouble egalitarians is not inequality as such but the poor absolute condition of those at the bottom.[62] As long as everybody has a decent quality of life, the comparative squalor of some states to their opulent neighbours is not by itself *unjust*.

Nielsen has not weighed in on this debate at any length, though it is clear that he believes that egalitarianism does extend beyond borders. He is one of the few theorists who has argued in favour of a world government on the grounds that this would provide the conditions for global egalitarianism that many critics claim is currently lacking. It is likely, too, that he considers these debates somewhat superfluous given the miserable state of the world. A good deal of philosophical work on global justice is conducted at a high level of abstraction. Philosophers are content to follow Rawls in doing "ideal theory," articulating the principles of justice that would be used to guide the institutions of the best feasible society. They regard substantial policy recommendations as beyond their competence (often rightly so!) but wrongly think that their moral principles can float free of detailed engagement with the way the world actually works.

Nielsen dedicates *Globalization and Justice* to the anti-globalization movement and writes: "May it flourish, grow, and win." Nielsen reported on the protests against the 2001 Summit of the Americas in Quebec City. He may well have been the only protestor in his seventies near the wall and police that shielded the political and business elites from criticism.[63]

Nielsen's target is not globalization *per se*, but *capitalist* globalization, particularly the form that has taken place under the "Washington Consensus."

> What anti-globalizers are really set against (whether they recognize it or not) is imperialism, and most particularly capitalist imperialism and the imperialists' use of globalization increasingly to exploit people, though some people are exploited more harshly than others – for example, Colombian poor workers more harshly than Danish poor workers. Capitalism's relentless pursuit of surplus accumulation, a persistent and tenacious pursuit of profit, is endemic to it.[64]

Globalization is likely unavoidable and in many respects positive. New technologies and ideas do enormous good and the opportunity to travel broadens many people's range of freedoms. Yet Nielsen believes that there is considerable evidence that capitalism not only harms people but because of its very structure must continue to harm people. A just world for Nielsen will invariably be a socialist world:

> Socialism is and always has been an internationalist movement. Socialism may, of course, start in one country or at nearly the same time in a cluster of countries, but it can never be stable or be what it aspires to be until it is worldwide.[65]

The driving force behind capitalism is the maximization of profits, quite independently of the intentions of individual capitalists: the very nature of the system eliminates competitors who sacrifice profits for social goods. Moreover, capitalists use state governments and international organizations such as the World Bank and IMF to further their interests, entering markets and overriding the efforts of national governments to provide alternative economic arrangements or a social safety net. Nielsen accepts what he calls a weak version of the *capitalist domination thesis*: capitalist economic systems have a strong influence on societies' political institutions (as well as their cultural institutions).

Contemporary cosmopolitans for the most part eschew socialism as either unfeasible or undesirable. Nielsen addresses this concern in a commentary on Charles Beitz and Henry Shue's seminal works on global justice: "[their analysis] looks at the world as if capitalism and a capitalist world order did not exist and then talks about international justice independently of the facts about imperialism, exploitation, class division, the imperatives of capitalism and the like."[66]

According to Nielsen,

> We will not get beyond an ideological understanding of how global justice requires a north/south redistribution, and what that redistribution is to consist in, if we see the issue as simply a conflict between affluent nation states and poor ones and do not understand it in terms of capitalist domination rooted in the imperatives of the capitalist mode of production.[67]

What would global market socialism look like? Global socialism would be built on the wealth produced by capitalism. It would use markets for allocation, but the guiding principle for production would not be profit but rather human need (and not the needs created by the advertising industry).[68] There would be a democratic form of collective ownership and a division of powers, many devolving to nation-states, municipalities or worker-controlled firms with feedback mechanisms between levels. Global socialism would require a form of world governance. Nielsen himself suggests we could have a world federation of nations built out of a reformed General Assembly.

For a clear idea of Nielsen's views about a just global institutional structure, we must discuss his liberal nationalism. Nielsen is a Quebec separatist and a liberal nationalist,[69] but also holds that "[his] commitment to nationalism and, under certain conditions, secession, takes second place to [his] Marxian internationalism or, if you will, cosmopolitanism."[70] Despite the priority of cosmopolitanism, Nielsen believes that the two do not in fact conflict but rather complement each other. Cosmopolitans should be liberal nationalists. A just global institutional structure will be organized in a way that permits the self-determination of nations.

How are the two seemingly conflicting ideals of national self-determination and cosmopolitanism reconciled? Nielsen defends the paradoxical claim that cosmopolitans ought to be sympathetic to liberal nationalist projects. National self-government provides an effective forum for democracy, as well as a key source of identity for most people. Indeed, cultural membership and group identity should be thought of as Rawlsian "primary goods," a position for which Will Kymlicka has argued. Furthermore, *liberal* nationalism in the actual world provides a better basis for cosmopolitanism and global justice than versions of cosmopolitanism that are non-nationalist or anti-nationalist. As a result, Nielsen supports a presumptive moral right for a liberal nation to secede from the state if the majority of the citizens clearly express a preference to do so.

Nielsen denies that his commitment to nationalism arose from his affiliation with the Quebec sovereignty movement. Rather, he locates it in his reading of Isaiah Berlin's *Vico and Herder* and in Herder himself[71]:

> The Enlightenment, and Marxism as one of its heirs, has seen very well indeed how tradition and local attachments fetter us. It took, as a way of counterbalancing that, Herder to show us the importance of local attachments in enabling us to find significance in our lives and to sustain that sense of significance. He showed us how we could have that without falling into cultural chauvinism.[72]

When Herder's insight is generalized to contemporary times, national identity becomes a universal good arising from the need for self-definition:

> Self-definition is an indispensable condition for human flourishing. But self-definition involves, though it, of course, involves much more than this, seeing ourselves as New Zealanders, Dutch, Irish, Ghanaian, Canadians, or whatever. Or at least this sense of national identity has come into being with the establishment of industrial societies. And in all societies that we know anything about, group identity is important. It is plausible to regard national identity as a form of group identity appropriate to, and functional for, modern industrial societies.[73]

Cosmopolitans, on Nielsen's account, must not only recognize the equal moral worth of humankind and exhibit common concern for its well-being, they ought also to take an active interest and pleasure in the diversity of human cultures. Cosmopolitanism can take a moral form according to which every human being matters equally but remain neutral with regard to institutional arrangements. Or it can prescribe specific institutions for its realization such as increased centralized power (e.g., in the UN), or, in Nielsen's case, a plurality of liberal nations within a world state. Since national identity matters to most people, cosmopolitans should prescribe nationalism as long as it remains compatible with cosmopolitan ideals. Furthermore, under present conditions, nations play a fundamental role in guaranteeing democracy as the primary forum under which people can achieve self-government. The qualification is that only *liberal* nations are compatible with cosmopolitanism.

The consequence is that when a majority of members within a liberal nation vote to secede, they have a right to do so. Nielsen likens this right to no-fault divorce. It is important to understand how radical Nielsen's view is, its similarities to what many sovereigntists maintain notwithstanding. For example, it contradicts the Supreme Court of Canada's opinion *Reference re Secession of Quebec* ([1998] 2 S.C.R. 217).[74] Most theorists argue that secession should be difficult since it often leads to violence and the widespread violation of human rights. Nielsen denies this holds when liberal nations secede from liberal democracies.

Notably, only *nations* have a right to secession. Nielsen follows David Miller in defining nations as historical communities that share a common history, language, and culture, as

> a group of people who recognize one another as belonging to the same political community, acknowledge special obligations to each other, and either have or aspire to political autonomy in virtue of the characteristics they believe they share, such as a common history, attachment to a geographical place and to a public culture that differentiates them from their neighbours.[75]

Nielsen rejects the partition of Quebec because Anglophones and Allophones in Quebec do not constitute a distinct nation.[76] What distinguishes nations from ethnic minorities (composed of immigrant groups) and national minorities (who do not aspire to form their own political community) is their territorial and political nature. Nations of course rise and fall, but when they do exist, they aspire to some form of self-government. They need not wish to form their own state and, indeed, this is unfeasible in the case of many smaller nations who lack the infrastructure to support a viable state. But they *may* aspire to statehood and when they do, they should have this right:

> ... we should realize that in our state system, given the present strategic importance of nations, democracy is best attained or approximated by a liberal nationalism or by a people, generally with social liberal commitments – socialist or social democratic commitments – that will carry with it a cosmopolitanism organized in a nation-state or a multi-nation-state, which will be nationalistic if their nations are threatened or insecure. Both realize democracy more adequately than other forms of political liberalism, including its anti-nationalist cosmopolitan forms.[77]

Nielsen's global socialism and his cosmopolitan nationalism raise some concerns. One question is how Nielsen reconciles his arguments for liberal nationalism with his ideal of a world government that would be a federalist, constitutional democracy. Some form of world government is needed to ensure that justice is upheld in the international sphere. Max Weber's understanding of the state as holding a monopoly on the legitimate use of violence over a territory is important here. Without some means of enforcing rules, there is little hope for a stable and just international regime. Powerful states will renege on their agreements when it suits their leaders, genocide will continue in regions of little geopolitical consequence, the global poor will remain voiceless in their penury. However, an *effective* form of global government may not sit easily with the self-determination of liberal nations. There is something to the fear of some Quebec sovereigntists that even the status of a "distinct nation" as a federal system may undermine the shared political culture that motivates secession.

Turning now to socialism in general, rather than an aspect of Québécois political culture, we should note that it requires robust participatory or deliberative democracy at a grassroots level. It requires a democratic *culture* as much as it requires democratic institutions and procedures. As Nielsen conceives of it, socialism relies on a conception of *homo politicus*: people will take an active interest in collectively running their political and working lives. What happens when local and global interests conflict? On the one hand, considerable local control is necessary both because of the limits of information (local people have a better understanding of their needs and resources) and because of the desirability of democracy. On the other hand, what is good for the locals is not necessary good for humanity.

Consider the vast difference in resources around the world. What would happen if Saudi Arabians, Russians, or Canadians, say, wanted to keep their resources for their own populations, unless they received significant payment? Would the reformed General Assembly arrive at a decision and send in an occupying force if the Canadians resisted? No doubt there are reasonable solutions in many cases, but the pluralism that characterizes most contemporary states will be less tractable on a global level. There is powerful evidence that robust democracy and the desire to contribute to the common good relies in part on the relative homogeneity of the population.[78]

Finally, there is a tension between Nielsen's pragmatism and his *global* socialism. Pragmatists favour – or ought to favour – experimentation in the arena of social and political affairs. As a matter of fact, we don't know what a democratic, market socialist society will be like at the level of the nation-state, let alone at the global level. Nielsen is surely correct that we should construct reasonable social theories that attempt to explain how, for instance, market socialism can work. But theory will come up against the world in unpredictable, perhaps appalling ways. This might suggest that we should not aspire to global socialism until we have more reliable evidence that it is feasible and desirable at the level of the nation-state.

Global poverty is enormously complicated and its causes are sometimes counterintuitive.[79] Nielsen in many places suggests that what is required is the redistribution of wealth from the North to the South. As he well knows, this is too simple, even if the message that *some* action on the part of the privileged is necessary. It ignores the vices of an international aid bureaucracy beholden, not to the people it is supposed to help, but to wealthy private and public funders with their own agendas. It overlooks the possibility that food aid can undermine local agriculture, creating dependence. Most damningly, it risks dismissing the possibility of *capitalist* solutions such as microloans or the removal of trade barriers such as agricultural subsidies and tariffs. One of the most successful means of lifting people out of poverty is microcredit.[80] But this is a *capitalist* strategy – a strategy employed *within* a capitalist economy – that provides the poor with access to private property.[81]

Capitalism is a complex, flexible economic system, and we should be careful to distinguish between the capitalism of William Blake's satanic mills and the nineteenth-century robber barons which dominated American industry and the capitalism of much of the developed world. This isn't to claim that contemporary developed democracies approach an ideal of the just state. Rather, it is a demand for sensitivity to detail and nuance to the range of possible economic systems, including so-called mixed economies.

We do not suggest that Nielsen has not or cannot respond to these concerns. Unfortunately, while Nielsen at times resembles Dewey or Rorty in rejecting theory and advocating practical measures, he in many respects remains a highly abstract theorist. He is somebody who has dedicated most of his life to philosophy. Readers will look in vain in his books and essays for detailed analyses of the economic and sociological literature. Instead, they will find careful, often compelling philosophical arguments, but relatively little in terms of specific evidence.

This is perhaps to be expected. Nielsen has given cogent reasons for moving beyond the traditional disciplinary barriers set by twentieth-century analytic philosophy. His work provides an ideal for philosophical practice: it liberates younger philosophers from the strictures of insular, professional philosophy. Best of all, he leaves work to be done toward articulating an empirically informed, coherent account of a better world, uninhibited by the strictures of professionalized philosophy. The legacy of a political philosopher is not so much in the solutions offered but in the problems posed and the paths opened for further investigation. It remains to be seen whether greater numbers of political philosophers will move still further away from (big-P) Philosophy's abstraction and generalization and instead acquire the tools to do, as well as evaluate, social science.[82]

A NOTE ON THE SELECTION OF THESE PAPERS

Toward the end of an unusually long meeting in the University of Calgary philosophy department, Nielsen's colleague Thomas Hurka is said to have quipped: "I'd like to state for the record that during this meeting Kai has completed a monograph, four articles, and an edited collection." Nielsen's legendarily voluminous productivity is partially accounted for by what he has called his "compulsive busyness."

Selecting thirteen papers from Nielsen's over four hundred publications is a difficult task. This volume offers a selection of what we judge to be Kai Nielsen's best work in political philosophy. We acknowledge at the outset that different papers could have been chosen. Whether another set of essays would have been more illuminating, more representative of Nielsen's political-philosophical vision as a whole, or superior in some other respect, we can only leave to readers to decide.

Two aspects of Nielsen's work in political philosophy posed a further challenge to our editorial task. First, there is some repetition and overlap among Nielsen's political essays: his ideas have changed over time; emphases have shifted; criticisms have been modified and sharpened; positions have been restated and reframed; claims and arguments have been expressed in new and different ways. This raised for us a number of difficult questions: Should we include Nielsen's most recent papers on a particular issue or topic? Should we opt instead for the papers Nielsen himself thinks best or most edifying on that topic? Or should we rather let our decisions be guided by the critical attention some of his essays have enjoyed?

The second major editorial challenge we faced – a challenge closely related to, and perhaps even the corollary of, the first – stemmed from our judgment that there is no definitive paper people ought to read if they want to know (in a nutshell, as it were) what Nielsen thinks about equality, wide reflective equilibrium, critical theory, global justice, socialism, and other topics that he has discussed repeatedly over the years. In the end, no collection could have assuaged all of these complications. There are simply too many papers to select from, and too many plausible criteria against which to select them.

Our main goal in selecting the papers we did was to give readers an idea of the scope of Nielsen's contribution in political philosophy, as well as to provide the intellectual context to appreciate its significance. We have tried to include papers that fully state Nielsen's views on the topics discussed in the introduction and have for the most part selected papers that have not appeared in previous collections. There is also an emphasis on recent publications, particularly when Nielsen's views have evolved over time. We hope that the volume will demonstrate the breadth of Nielsen's political-philosophical writings and the eclectic mélange of sources and influences from which they draw.[83]

Above all, our aim is that the essays collected here show how Nielsen's ideas in political philosophy hang together, how they come to constitute an original, elegant, and mutually reinforcing whole. We seek to show how Nielsen's political philosophy represents a humane vision guided by the conviction that human beings can rationally administer their own affairs in accordance with their best ideals and most worthy values.

Notes

1. Address at the twenty-fourth annual meeting of the American Philosophical Association, Eastern Division, New York University, December 28, 1934. It is reprinted in Dewey, *The Later Works of John Dewey*, 292–99.

2. Nielsen, "Toward a Liberal Socialist Cosmopolitan Nationalism," 437–63.

3. We confine our discussion here mainly to Nielsen's work from the eighties up to the present. However, it is worth noting that Nielsen was a leading proponent, along with Stephen Toulmin, of the so-called good-reasons approach. See Nielsen, "Class Conflict, Marxism, and the Good-Reasons Approach," 89–112. There is a clear link between Nielsen's earlier work on the "good-reasons approach" and his later ruminations on wide reflective equilibrium and critical theory. See Nielsen, "The 'Good Reasons Approach' and 'Ontological Justifications' of Morality," 116–30. Unfortunately, a full elaboration of these connections takes us beyond the scope of this introduction.

4. For Nielsen's sustained treatment of these issues, see Nielsen, *After the Demise of the Tradition* and *On Transforming Philosophy*. Also see Nielsen, *Marxism and the Moral Point of View*. An abbreviated list of other papers include "On Finding One's Feet in Philosophy" (included here); "The Poverty of Moral Philosophy" (included here); the essays in parts two and three of Nielsen, *Naturalism without Foundations*; "On Needing a Moral Theory"; and "The Very Idea of a Critical Theory."

5. Nielsen has remarked that he should have liked to dedicate more time and intellectual energy to metaphilosophical topics but feels that his effort is better spent in the service of moral and political causes such as equality, socialism, global justice, and human emancipation. Spending too much time on metaphilosophical questions would be like "fiddling while Rome burns."

6. Wittgenstein, *Philosophical Investigations*, 309.

7. The influence of John Dewey should not be overlooked, though Dewey plays a less significant role than Wittgenstein or Rorty. See Nielsen, "Dewey's Conception of Philosophy," 110–34.

8. There is nothing inherently problematic about an appearance/reality distinction. Ordinary people make use of such a distinction without difficulty all the time. As Nielsen might say, this sort of distinction only becomes problematic when it becomes metaphysical, when philosophers take it as their unique task to view the world "under the aspect of eternity."

9. Nielsen, "Metaphilosophy, Pragmatism and a Kind of Critical Theory," 126.

10. Not all repudiations of metaphysics rely on the claim that metaphysical propositions are nonsensical. This is significant since Nielsen sometimes lumps together his rejection of metaphysics with other philosopher's views in ways that obscure important differences. When Nielsen writes, for instance, "It is clear that, like Wittgenstein, J.L. Austin, Burton

Dreben, the logical positivists, Richard Rorty, and, in effect, W.V.O. Quine and Donald Davidson, I reject metaphysics regarding it as nonsense." Nielsen, *Atheism and Philosophy*, 10–11. It is easy to get the (erroneous) impression that all of these philosophers reject metaphysics in the same way and for the same reasons. To consider only the example of Richard Rorty, it is not that metaphysics is nonsense *per se*. Rather, on Rorty's view, metaphysics is a language game (or series of language games) that has outlived its utility, one we would do well, therefore, to eschew.

11 Nielsen, "Metaphilosophy, Pragmatism and a Kind of Critical Theory," 122.

12 Nielsen, *Wittgensteinian Fideism?*, 327. As Hilary Putnam says, in a passage which amplifies what Nielsen says here,"[E]lements of what we call 'language' or 'mind' penetrate so deeply into what we call 'reality' that the very project of representing ourselves as being 'mappers' of something 'language independent' is fatally compromised from the start. Like Relativism, but in a different way, Realism is an impossible attempt to view the word from Nowhere." H. Putnam, *Realism with a Human Face*, 28.

13 Whether and to what extent Nielsen considers himself a nominalist (à la Goodman, Rorty, or Foucault) is not entirely clear. Still, one imagines that he would express considerable sympathy with Richard Rorty when he writes, "none of us antirepresentationalists have ever doubted that most things in the universe are causally independent of us. What we question is whether they are representationally independent of us. For X to be representationally independent of us is for X to have an intrinsic feature (a feature that it has under any and every description) such that it is better described by some of our terms rather than others." Rorty, *Truth and Progress*, 86.

14 Consider, as Nielsen notes, that "One can be an anti-foundationalist and a consistent and plausible one (e.g., Nietzsche or Burke) and still not be a political liberal and one could make a reasonable case for political liberalism, as J.S. Mill and Kant did in their time and C.I. Lewis did in ours, while remaining a foundationalist."

15 Nielsen, "Taking Rorty Seriously," 504.

16 Nielsen would be quick to remind us that "philosophy" is an academic discipline formed by the exigencies of the modern university and bureaucratic power struggles within the humanities and social sciences. It is questionable whether people included in the philosophical canon up through the nineteenth century would recognize philosophy as currently practised. Readers might wish to ask themselves whether they can recognize a common denominator shared by Aristotle, Kierkegaard, Kripke, Heidegger, Rawls, Foucault, and David Lewis that makes them all practitioners of a single, coherent discipline.

17 See Marx, "Theses on Feuerbach," 145.

18 Nielsen prefers the designation "Marxian" to "Marxist." The former picks out someone broadly committed to the approach and moral-political vision of Marx, whereas the latter denotes a dogmatic follower. To

put the point by way of an analogy, almost everyone working in biology today is a "Darwinian" but very few (if any) are "Darwinists." As Nielsen explains: "I regard Marx and Engels, and Rosa Luxemburg as well, as master thinkers of modernity. Much of my thinking has been formed and sustained by them. But I use 'analytic Marxian' advisedly, on analogy with 'Darwinian' rather than 'Darwinist.' Modern biologists are overwhelmingly Darwinian, but they are not 'Darwinists.' They realized – and how could it be otherwise with a broad-ranging scientific account – that Darwin was wrong about many things. But their very way of thinking was deeply formed by Darwin and they regard him as a scientific giant." Nielsen, "Socialism and Egalitarian Justice" In *Globalization and Justice*.

19 Nielsen, "Analytic Marxism: A Form of Critical Theory," 131. An earlier and shorter version of this article appears as Nielsen, "Analytic Marxism Streamlined," 79–89.

20 For those who worry that the phrase "empirical theory with an emancipatory intent" reveals a deep confusion of "is" and "ought," it is helpful to recall that Nielsen, following Hilary Putnam in particular, denies the rigid bifurcation of facts and values. Nielsen thinks that it is sometimes possible to derive a moral (though not a logical) 'ought' from an 'is.'

21 See Nielsen: "On There Being Wide Reflective Equilibria," (in this volume); "In Defense of Wide Reflective Equilibrium"; "Philosophy within the Limits of Wide Reflective Equilibrium Alone"; and "How to Proceed in Social Philosophy."

22 Indeed, one of Nielsen's main worries about critical theories of the Frankfurt school is that they often remain beholden to the synoptic ambitions of Classical Marxists, "[they] have been grand, sweeping theories of society with a wide scope, giving us programmatic schemes of an all-encompassing sort. But analytical Marxism maintains a disengaged character and self-consciously modest and critical stance." Nielsen, *Globalization and Justice*, 122.

23 Nielsen, "On There Being Wide Reflective Equilibria" (in this volume, 41).

24 Ibid., 43.

25 Walzer, *Spheres of Justice*, 319.

26 Rorty, *Philosophy and the Mirror of Nature*, 340.

27 Nagel, *The View from Nowhere*, 216.

28 See Nielsen's reply to Norman Daniels's, "Nielsen and Rawls on Egalitarianism," 294. This pronouncement came out of a conversation with G. A. Cohen, who takes Plato (not Aristotle) as the most significant political thinker of antiquity. Cohen has recently written: "I believe that at most two books in the history of Western political philosophy have a claim to be regarded as greater than *A Theory of Justice*: Plato's *Republic* and Hobbes's *Leviathan*." G. A. Cohen, *Rescuing Justice and Equality*, 11.

29 See Nielsen, "On the Very Possibility of a Classless Society," 191–208. Macpherson has been an important influence on Nielsen's criticisms of Rawls.

30 For important criticisms of Rawls's so-called incentive argument for

inequality, see G. A. Cohen, *Rescuing Justice and Equality.*

31 Nielsen, "Radical Egalitarianism Revisited," 181.

32 It is important to point out that Nielsen does not endorse the untenable view that each citizen be afforded equal shares of money. One need only quickly reflect on what money is, how it works, and what it is for, to see the incoherence of that ideal. As Walzer writes, "We may dream of a society where everyone has the same amount of money. But we know that money equally distributed at twelve noon of a Sunday will have been unequally redistributed before the week is out. Some people will save it, and others will invest it, and still others would spend it (and they will do so in different ways)." Walzer, *Spheres of Justice,* xi. Indeed, money exists precisely to make just these kinds of transactions possible. It wouldn't be money if those who had it were not permitted to save, invest, and spend it. When Nielsen endorses equality of wealth, then, he has in mind the more radical (and socialist) idea of each person sharing equally in their society's productive forces and sharing equally in the fruits of those productive forces. Nielsen's "equality of wealth" needs to be understood against the background of this radical socialist transformation.

33 See Nielsen: "Radical Egalitarian Justice," and "Radical Egalitarianism Revisited." Also see Nielsen, "On Liberty and Equality."

34 Rawls depicts these goods as "all-purpose means" in the sense that, "They are things which it is supposed a rational man wants whatever else he wants. Regardless of what an individual's rational plans are in detail, it is assumed that there are various things which he would prefer more of rather than less. With more of these goods men can generally be assured of greater success in carrying out their intentions and in advancing their ends, whatever these ends may be." Rawls, *A Theory of Justice,* 92

35 Daniels, "Nielsen and Rawls on Egalitarianism," 283.

36 C.B. Macpherson drew this conclusion in *Democratic Theory,* 77–94; and "Rawls' Models of Man and Society," 341–47. Cf. Nielsen, "On the Very Possibility of a Classless Society."

37 Rawls, *Justice as Fairness: A Restatement,* 139; also see Rawls, *A Theory of Justice,* 239–42.

38 See Freeman, *Rawls,* 226–35.

39 See Nielsen: "Rights and Consequences: It All Depends," and "There Is No Dilemma of Dirty Hands." Also see Barry, *Liberty and Justice: Essays in Political Theory,* 2.

40 See Nielsen, "Impediments to Radical Egalitarianism."

41 Nielsen, *After the Demise of the Tradition,* 232.

42 See, for example, Nielsen, "Nozick and Socialism: Some Sociological Critiques," 222. "Nozick is utterly – or so one would judge from reading *Anarchy, State, and Utopia* – innocent about power and particularly about the way a drive for power works in our societies. That is to say, he is utterly innocent about the capitalist system. His account requires him to assume that those bent on accumulating wealth, and with that wealth unavoidably power, will restrain

43 Nielsen, "Radical Egalitarianism Revisited," 186.

44 Nielsen, "State Bureaucratic Socialism and Freedom." He cites Levine, *Arguing for Socialism*.

45 Nielsen: "On the Choice between Reform and Revolution," and "On Justifying Revolution."

46 Nielsen: "On Justifying Violence," "On Terrorism and Political Assassination," "Political Violence and Ideological Mystification," and "On the Moral Justification of State Terrorism."

47 Nielsen, "Reply to Andrew Levine and David Schweickart," 202.

48 G. A. Cohen, *Karl Marx's Theory of History*. For Nielsen's writings on historical materialism, see Nielsen, "On Taking Historical Materialism Seriously"; "If Historical Materialism Is True, Does Morality Totter?"; "Afterword: Remarks on the Roots of Progress"; "Reply to Andrew Levine and David Schweickart on Marx and Marxism."

49 See Joshua Cohen, "G. A. Cohen: Marx's Theory of History"; and Nielsen, "On Taking Historical Materialism Seriously."

50 See Roemer, *A Future for Socialism*; Schweickart, *Against Capitalism*; and Schweickart, *After Capitalism*. Roemer's version of market socialism in particular is one about which Nielsen has expressed his enthusiasm. Briefly, Roemer's proposal involves "two kinds of money." One is used for the purchase of ordinary goods, while the other "coupon" currency can only be used for buying shares of mutual funds in companies. Only coupons can be used to purchase shares of mutual funds, not money. Only mutual funds can purchase shares of public firms, using coupons. An equal share of coupons is distributed to each member of society upon reaching the age of majority, and while citizens are free to trade their stock in mutual funds for stock in other mutual funds, they cannot liquidate their portfolios (cf. Roemer 1993, 96). Plainly, since coupons and mutual funds can only be traded with other coupons and mutual funds, each citizen will necessarily hold a (profit-sharing) stake in the country's firms, whether they want to or not. The coupon system, Roemer explains, "is meant to endow each adult citizen with a stream of income during his lifetime, his transient property right in the nation's 'public' firms. Only during his lifetime does a citizen have an entitlement to the profits of firms. Because shares can be purchased only with coupons, and coupons cannot be sold by citizens for money, rich citizens will not generally own more shares than poor citizens." Putting aside the proposal's many intricacies, Roemer's version of market socialism is designed to preserve the efficiency of free-market capitalism – as with capitalism, the assigned task of firms under this scheme is to maximize profits within the limits of the law – while honouring the quintessentially Marxian (egalitarian) dictate according to which the primary means of production be publicly owned, by citizens in common. The main ambition, says Roemer, is to provide a "future for socialism" – "to sketch blueprints for a feasible socialism, to provide a basis, once again, for daring to believe

in the dream." Roemer, *A Future for Socialism*, 124.

51 Nielsen, *Equality and Liberty*, 291.

52 Nielsen, "Is Global Justice Impossible?," 131.

53 See Pogge, "The Bounds of Nationalism," for a more detailed analysis of this calculation.

54 The "poverty line" is defined as "that income or expenditure level below which a minimum, nutritionally adequate diet plus essential non-food requirements are not affordable." See the United Nations Development Program, Human Development Report 1996, 20. All other statistics are cited from the 2005 edition of the same report.

55 As the 2000 United Nations Human Development Report explains: "Global inequalities in income increased in the twentieth century by orders of magnitude out of proportion to anything experienced before. The distance between the incomes of the richest and poorest country was about 3 to 1 in 1820, 35 to 1 in 1950, 44 to 1 in 1973 and 72 to 1 in 1992." See Nussbaum, *Frontiers of Justice*, 224.

56 See Vivanco and Wilkinson, "Hugo Chávez versus Human Rights." Also see Human Rights Watch, *Political Intolerance and Lost Opportunities for Advancing Human Rights in Venezuela*. http://www.hrw.org/sites/default/files/reports/venezuela0908web.pdf. Also, see Lomnitz and Sánchez, "United by Hate: The Uses of Anti-Semitism in Chávez's Venezuela."

57 Nielsen borrows this phrase from Richard Rorty. "The Left, by definition, is the party of hope. It insists that our nation [and indeed, our world] remains unachieved." Rorty, *Achieving Our Country*, 14.

58 In a December 19, 1929 letter from prison, Gramsci writes, "I'm a pessimist because of intelligence, but an optimist because of will." (Gramsci 2011) The phrase also appears in *Passoto e presente* and *Ordine Nuovo* (Gramsci 1971, n. 75). Gramsci attributes the phrase to the French writer Romain Rolland. Nielsen often refers to Gramsci's phrase to reconcile his socialist convictions with his pessimism about the social, political, and economic status quo. It appears in "Is Global Justice Possible?" and he makes mention of it in the interview published in this collection.

59 See, e.g., Hollis and Pogge, "The Health Impact Fund: Making New Medicines Accessible to All."

60 Some recent defences include: Nussbaum et al., *For Love of Country*; Jones, *Global Justice: Defending Cosmopolitanism*; Singer, *One World: The Ethics of Globalization*; Kok-Chor Tan, *Justice without Borders*; and Appiah, *Cosmopolitanism: Ethics in a World of Strangers*.

61 Nagel, "The Problem of Global Justice"; D. Miller, "Justice and Global Inequality"; D. Miller, "Against Global Egalitarianism"; and Blake, "Distributive Justice, State Coercion, and Autonomy."

62 Arneson, "Why Justice Requires Transfers to Offset Income and Wealth Inequalities." Also see Frankfurt, "Equality as a Moral Ideal."

63 Footage of the protests is captured in Jennifer Abbott and Joel Bakan's film "The Corporation."

64 Nielsen, "Globalization as a Tool for Imperialism," 191.

65 Nielsen, "Response to My Critics," 148.

66 Nielsen, "Ideal and Non-Ideal Theory," 37.

67 Nielsen, "Global Justice and the Imperatives of Capitalism," 608–10.

68 See Galbraith, *The Affluent Society*.

69 See Nielsen, "Secession: The Case of Quebec," 29–43, for a defence.

70 Nielsen, "Reply to Michel Seymour," 393.

71 See Herder, *Another Philosophy of History and Selected Political Writings*; and Berlin, "Herder and the Enlightenment."

72 Nielsen, "Cultural Identity and Self-Definition," 383. Also see Nielsen, "Undistorted Discourse, Ethnicity, and the Problem of Self-Definition."

73 Nielsen, "Liberal Nationalism, Liberal Democracies, and Secession," 261.

74 Available at http://csc.lexum.umontreal.ca/en/1998/1998rcs2-217/1998rcs2-217.html. Also see Buchanan, "The Quebec Secession Issue: Democracy, Minority Rights, and the Rule of Law," 238–71.

75 D. Miller, "Secession and the Principle of Nationality," 266.

76 Nielsen, "Against Partition."

77 Nielsen, "Toward a Liberal Socialist Cosmopolitan Nationalism," 451–52.

78 E.g., Robert D. Putnam, "E Pluribus Unum."

79 A very small sample of the literature includes, Amartya Sen, *Development as Freedom*; P. Collier, *The Bottom Billion*; Sachs, *The End of Poverty*; Stiglitz, *Making Globalization Work*; and Easterly, *The White Man's Burden*.

80 Muhammad Yunnus and the Grameen bank won the Nobel Peace Prize in 2006. See Yunnus, *Banker to the Poor*.

81 See Alison Benjamin, "Dollar a Week Bank Is Still a Success."

82 For a sampling of political thinkers whose work should be read broadly along these lines, see, among others, Anderson, *Value in Ethics and Economics*; Beitz, *Political Equality*; A. Phillips, *Which Equalities Matter?*; Shapiro, *Democratic Justice*; Walzer, *Thinking Politically*; and Young, *Inclusion and Democracy*.

83 On his own eclectic mélange of sources and influences, Nielsen writes: "My own predilection is for the work of Karl Marx and John Dewey (as different as they are from one another) and my predilection among our contemporaries is principally for the work of, and to work myself in the light of, *perhaps* the unstable – even an overly eclectic – mix of Amartya Sen with a toss of John Rawls, Brian Barry, and G. A. Cohen thrown in, and, in other ways, and for different purposes, of Edward Said, David Harvey, and Noam Chomsky, and with something of Ludwig Wittgenstein's and Richard Rorty's metaphilosophy and historicism." Nielsen, "The Global Crisis of Values: The Poverty of Moral Philosophy" (in this volume, 79).

Part 1

METAPHILOSOPHY: CRITICAL THEORY AND WIDE-REFLECTIVE EQUILIBRIUM

On Finding One's Feet
in Philosophy:
From Wittgenstein to Marx

I

This address will be resolutely metaphilosophical. It will reflect some of my ambivalence about philosophy. Perhaps more than most people whose conceptions of philosophy were formed in the first two decades following the Second World War, I have my difficulties about the point of doing philosophy, remain ambivalent about what it can and cannot do and remain unsure about what it should try to be. I am both depressed and astounded at the complacency with which so many philosophers view philosophy. They seem to have no awareness of how marginal our discipline has become or, at the very least, is felt to be by many people (including intelligentsia) outside of philosophy.[1]

I shall try to confront these things and ask, knowing what we know now and standing where we stand, what philosophy can plausibly be and what it ought to be or at least try to be. To proceed in any reasonable way here, we need to say something about what philosophy has been in our recent history and how well its research projects have panned out.

This, of course, is a vast subject and a tendentious one. It is plain that anyone who sets out to talk about it in a way which is not utterly platitudinous will skew her discussion in a certain way, perhaps skew it so badly that many of the key issues get begged at the outset. I think one way of offsetting that to a certain extent is to begin in a rather autobiographical way and to indicate something of the philosophers and ways of doing and viewing philosophy that have formed me. That would be rather self-indulgent, if it were not reasonable to believe that what I say about myself also in part narrates a history that is not, among my generation, so terribly unique to me and that in that narrative there may be an object lesson. So I shall start by being autobiographical.

Around 1950, when I was finishing my dissertation, the ideas of the post-*Tractatus* Wittgenstein and something related, but a little more pedestrian, namely what was variously called Oxford philosophy or ordinary language philosophy, rapidly and extensively penetrated the whole of the English-speaking philosophical world. It came first through Oxford philosophy (principally Ryle) and through the reading of typescript copies of *The Blue Book* and *The Brown Book* and two collections of articles by John Wisdom. (I still remember the exhilaration I felt when in one sitting I read *The Blue Book* with the sense that scales were falling from my eyes.) A little later the *Philosophical Investigations* became available to us. It was excitedly discussed and, indeed, by many of the older professors even bitterly discussed. Their ways of doing things were already rather set and they felt challenged. For me it turned around my philosophical outlook and practice. This manifested itself in three ways: first, it confirmed and – or so it seemed to me – strikingly vindicated my setting aside of metaphysics and epistemology. That was something my initial philosophical interests predisposed me toward and an earlier study of pragmatism and a little later of logical empiricism had reinforced. But the study of Wittgenstein stamped it in thoroughly.

Secondly, Wittgenstein turned me away from the study of logic and what was then called ideal language philosophy. Just prior to the onslaught of Wittgenstein, I had, in the course of writing my thesis, come under the influence of C.I. Lewis and Rudolf Carnap. While it seemed to me what was significant in their work was done quite without the use of logical techniques, their authority was such that I thought, much against my inclinations, that I somehow should use such techniques, though I could not, for the life of me, see how the use of them would further the resolution or the dissolution of any philosophical question I was interested in. Wittgenstein (along with

Moore, Wisdom, Waismann, and Austin) put an end to all that. I came to see how we could do something rigorous and conceptual without engaging in what seemed to me the pointless activities of logic. It wasn't regimented ideal languages we needed, what we needed was to command a sufficiently clear view of the workings of our own language so that we could break philosophical perplexities where they emerged from our misunderstandings of the workings of our language. We operated *with* our language well enough, in the standard contexts, but we, around certain philosophical issues, fell into perplexity when we tried to operate *upon* it. (Of course, most philosophers caught in such perplexities would not see it that way. To make it apparent that their philosophical perplexities were about the workings of their language was a central task for a Wittgensteinian philosopher.)

The third, and I suspect the most important, turn-around Wittgenstein forced on me was, for a time, to shift the whole emphasis of my work in ethics. I was trying, at the time I started to study Wittgenstein, to work out a defence of the emotive theory of ethics against its more rationalistic critics and indeed even against more sympathetic critics such as Hare and Nowell-Smith. I thought, and still think, that Stevenson's and Hägerström's accounts are more powerful than is usually realized, though I also thought at the time that their accounts were approximately right. The study of Wittgenstein and ordinary language philosophy changed that. We should, I came to think, worry less about the logical status of evaluative utterances and come to concentrate more, in the specific contexts of morality and of politics, on what made something a good reason in ethics. We should worry less about what "good" means and concentrate more on what good reasons are and on the underlying structure of moral reasoning. I saw Toulmin, Findlay, Baier and myself, and in his very early work, Rawls as well, as trying to carry out a very analogous project in moral philosophy to the work done by Wittgenstein and Wisdom in philosophical psychology, the philosophy of mind and the philosophy of language.[2] And I expected similar things to be done in legal, social, and political philosophy. (Hart seemed to be paving the way here.)

Much of that seems very distant to me now, but it informed all my earlier work in ethics and, with a good spicing of something of logical empiricism, my work in the philosophy of religion as well. Some of this, of course, is idiosyncratic to me, but much of this turning away from ideal language philosophy and developing Wittgensteinian techniques is common to philosophers of my generation.

II

After that I slowly began to get out of step with the philosophical *Weltgeist*. This happened gradually and without an iconoclastic intent on my part. But, all the same, it became a reality.

Wittgenstein did not study language systematically. He did not set out to construct a philosophy of language, he did not try to utilize the results of linguistics or to contribute to the development of linguistics or to integrate philosophy and linguistics. Instead, he sought, by reminding us of how language actually works in particular contexts, where there is actual philosophical perplexity, to break the spell that a mistaken picture of language can come to have on us. But this does not require an alternative theory, though it does require that we develop a cultivated ear for the workings of our language and that we do have a good feel for philosophical problems. However, under the influence of Austin in England and under the quite different influence of Quine and Chomsky in North America (influences which were themselves diverse), philosophy began to take a different turn. At first Austin seemed like a more exacting, less programmatic and less exciting Wittgenstein, but as his search for the performative petered out in the last third of *How To Do Things with Words*, it became clear that Austin's analysis no longer tied itself to identifiable philosophical problems and developed instead an interest in language for its own sake that would better transfer itself to linguistics. And where such work did stick with a philosophical problem, as in Paul Ziff's *Semantical Analysis*, it became evident enough, as the book was inspected carefully, that Ziff's analysis of "good" did not require the elaborate linguistic paraphernalia he deployed to do the job. I found myself, as work like this unfolded, thoroughly out of sympathy with the turn to linguistics in the 60's and the 70's. It seemed to me, and it still seems to me, to have never felt the bite of what Wittgenstein was on to about the role of language in philosophical activity. In any event, it seemed to me to be a wrong turning and I ignored it after its initial developments.

Instead, I cultivated my garden by continuing my work in moral philosophy, though with less and less concern about the logical status of what I was doing or with whether I was making what Wittgenstein would call "grammatical remarks" or with whether I was doing normative ethics or metaethics or about whether philosophers could properly do normative ethics. Once those demarcations seemed to me terribly important to make. I once thought that to progress in thinking about morality, to be clear about what we were doing when we did philosophy, we needed to be clear about such boundary questions. But slowly that belief withered away. Instead I simply tried to think about moral and, increasingly, political questions as carefully as I could, utilizing a very minimal philosophical vocabulary though I did continue to attend, where relevant, to the workings of our language and to draw contextually pertinent distinctions where they were, as they frequently were, enlightening. (That is something I learned from Moore, Wittgenstein, and Austin, though I could have learned it from Sidgwick or Broad, though the latter does it rather pedantically and sometimes to excess.)

Quine, and later Sellars and Davidson, hove onto the scene. My ordinary language philosophy predilections and my convictions that Wittgenstein had dealt a death-blow to ideal language philosophy made me, I am now sorry to say, utterly unreceptive to that way of doing philosophy. I thought of it, say until about ten years ago, as a cluster of (philosophically speaking) reactionary steps turning the clock back, missing utterly the philosophical revolution Wittgenstein had made and even many of what I took to be the revolutionary advances made by the logical empiricists. Quine only muddied or pedanticized things with his use of logic. *(Methods of Logic* was one thing, *Word and Object* another.) And, or so I once thought, Grice and Strawson had utterly demolished that foolishness of not trying to draw a significant distinction between the analytic and synthetic.

So it seemed to me that analytical philosophy of the 60's and 70's had taken a retrograde turning and had utterly lost the insights of the Wittgensteinian revolution. The history of philosophy was studied in the same old way again, except that logical techniques were now used more frequently in the elucidation of the classical texts. There was an extensive preoccupation with the philosophy of logic and philosophy of language and Wittgenstein's philosophy of philosophy utterly dropped out, and instead we wondered if we understood what "use" meant in Wittgenstein or we scholasticized the private language argument. It was felt by not a few that it was no better to talk about use than to talk about meaning. *Perhaps* this concentration on the philosophy of logic and the philosophy of language helped us get clear about logic and language and (if there is such a thing) about the foundations of mathematics. But it helped us very little in thinking about distinctively philosophical problems. Philosophy of science (as distinct from the history of science) was similarly implicated and similarly moribund. Only the philosophy of mind seemed at least to progress, though even there, in the hands of some, it turns arcane and small-scale, satisfying the passion of not a few philosophers to play around with puzzles. (Indeed, that seems to be the whole of it for some philosophers.)

Mainstream moral philosophy and social philosophy were similarly moribund, often drawing distinctions to no particular purpose and often doing little more than aping in the domain of the moral a once-fashionable philosophy of language. (In metaethics you get the deployment of a philosophy of language of the previous decade.)

I tried in the early 60's, while also studying Stuart Hampshire's *Thought and Action*, to have a go at the then reigning Continentals. But, while I greatly admired and still do admire much of Sartre's and Merleau-Ponty's political stances, and have sometimes found their political writings insightful, I found what Hare once called their big books impenetrable and replete with all the very kind of metaphysical nonsense that the logical empiricists rightly taught us to reject. *(Perhaps* there is good metaphysics as well as bad, but their sort of metaphysics is surely not it.) I am prepared to believe that their work here might with patience be demythologized. Moreover, I suspect that what they are trying to do is very important indeed, particularly when what they are trying to do is contrasted with the aims of the puzzle solvers, but their obscurity and indiscipline is so formidable that I for one do not have the stomach for the demythologization.

III

Two events occurred in the 60's, one external to philosophy and the other internal to its development, which had a considerable influence on philosophy. The first was the Vietnam War and the second was the publication in 1970 of John Rawls's *A Theory of Justice*. The Vietnam War, and in particular the students' reactions to the war, forced philosophers to try to think in a hard way about political morality and political and social problems. This was most obvious in the United States but it held for us [in Canada] and for the Europeans as well.

We also came to see straight off that we were not very well equipped to do so. The most underdeveloped side of analytical philosophy was political philosophy. Moreover, its right hand, moral philosophy, had been so exclusively metaethical that philosophers found, though the spirit was often willing, that they in fact had very little to say. Even the kind of piecemeal social analysis that we are now accustomed to seeing in *Inquiry*, *Philosophy and Public Affairs*, and *Ethics* was something that had to be recreated. Sometimes we managed to say some things worthy of attention, but generally we lacked the ability that our Continental colleagues had to put them into a framework where we could see that these discrete analyses might add up to something and give us a broader understanding of social life and politics.

John Rawls's *A Theory of Justice* brought back to English-speaking philosophy the tradition of systematic and holistic socio-political philosophy. It was also the first book written in English on moral and political thought during the post-War era which received extensive attention outside of philosophy. It also gave us a sense of how we could systematically do moral and social philosophy with discipline and sophistication and how, as well, in doing so we could set aside questions of metaethics or the analysis of moral concepts. We didn't have to answer questions about the logical status of moral utterances, whether we could derive an ought from an is, whether and how moral utterances could be true or false, what was the meaning of "moral" or even of "justice" in order to pursue, even at a very fundamental level, moral and social theory. He also, both by the fiction of the original position and by his appeal to considered judgments in wide reflective equilibrium, has given us an attractive consensus model of justification that will survive the death of foundationalism. This way of proceeding will also survive the rejection of Rawls's particular principles of justice, the recognition that an Archimedean point of the sort he seeks is not to be had and the realization that the contractarian method has a liberal bias and an unrealistic political sociology.

I have in various ways and in various places criticized Rawls, but it also seems to me that he has shown us how philosophy and indeed social philosophy can forge ahead.³ His work is miles ahead of the orthodox linguistic analysis characteristic of Hare, Stevenson, and Foot, but it is also a clear advance over the good reasons approach, which in reality always remained too descriptive of the moral point of view.

Richard Rorty has said that, while Rawls's work is a considerable achievement, there is nothing distinctively philosophical about it. It could just as well have been written by an economist, a political scientist, a lawyer, or the like. I think that that is an exaggeration, but there is merit in it all the same. Certainly, to have written *A Theory of Justice* would have taken an economist or political scientist who had a very extensive familiarity, indeed, with the history of moral and social thought. There is also clearly in Rawls's work the mark of Quine's rejection of any substantial version of the analytic/synthetic distinction, Goodman's anti-foundationalist consensus model of justification, and a philosophical sophistication concerning what proof could come to in philosophy. There is an understanding here that only a philosopher is likely to have. While an economist or a political scientist, unless she was philosophically sophisticated, would not be likely to have those conceptions in mind, still something very much like them might well be implicit in her procedures so that the account she would construct might well be in substance very much like Rawls's. That is to say, a Rawls-like structure could very well have been written by an economist or political scientist innocent of everything philosophical except the history of moral theory.

However, it is *that* that is behind Rorty's exaggeration. No analytic/synthetic distinction is utilized by Rawls, in effect segregating philosophy and moral theory to the domain of conceptual analysis, no claim to any distinctive *philosophical* knowledge is made (whatever that might mean), and no allegedly powerful philosophical analytical tools are appealed to as would have come natural to a Reichenbach, Quine, or Dummett. There is nothing in Rawls's account, either in the actual substantive structure of his account or in its methodology, that is distinctively philosophical. Indeed, most of it is something which more likely could have come from someone with Marx's, Weber's, or Durkheim's training than from someone trained like R.M. Hare, Peter Geach, John Searle, Gilbert Harman, or Phillipia Foot.

(The Quine and Goodman things mentioned above are hardly distinctively philosophical.)

I think this turn of Rawls's, along with the demise of substantial versions of the analytic/synthetic distinction, the rejection of any appeal to the given, the undermining of correspondence theories of truth that go beyond Tarskian minimalism and the recognition of the unassailability of historicist claims about knowledge, give philosophy, now much less clearly distinct from the human sciences, the possibility of new directions. (I shall return to this in a moment.) But we also see again the depth and pervasiveness of the destruction of foundationalism in philosophy.

I am not very impressed by Richard Rorty's positive turns in philosophy, and it seems to me that what he says about both hermeneutics and truth is slapdash. But I do think he is substantially right in his remarks about the centrality of Wittgenstein and Dewey and about how Quine and Sellars led us to similar results from inside traditional analytical philosophy. That belief was reflected in my remarks in the previous paragraph. The core of Rorty's critique comes to an undermining of the whole classical enterprise of epistemology, the rejection of foundationalism and a non-platitudinous essentialism, the rejection of any belief that there could be any plausible inquiry bearing the title "the conceptual foundations" of so and so or any conceptual analysis which could give us the analysis of anything so that we could have some distinctive philosophical categories which would have some privileged place in the critique of culture, including the analysis of science, law, morality, or common sense. Conceptual or linguistic analysis cannot deliver in the way that at least classic analytic philosophy thought it could, and the critique of culture that the various traditions of "perennial philosophy" thought they could achieve has also been decisively undermined. Wittgenstein, Dewey, and (Rorty claims) Heidegger have so turned philosophy around. Where such a deep intellectual revolution has taken place, it is hardly surprising that we have been such a long time in seeing that this is what has happened. After all, such changes are threatening to us and our defence mechanisms immediately go up. But I do think Rorty has correctly narrated the history of what I, and many others, intuitively felt that Wittgenstein had done with swift, bold, ironic strokes, when we first read him and what Dewey earlier did in a different way and in a very different idiom. (Perhaps what made me so receptive to Wittgenstein was the very deep impact the reading of Dewey had made on me when I was an undergraduate and how in some muted way it survived the impact of logical empiricism and linguistic analysis.)

But when Rorty goes positive he gets both slapdash and too effete. There is too much a shrug of the shoulders, anything goes, attitude. As an attitude about how to structure universities in our cultural context, that is fine, but, as a procedure about what kind of conversation of humankind philosophy should try to be, it is a cop-out. But what then can we do after the demise of logical empiricism and programmatic linguistic analysis? Can there be anything like the recovery in philosophy that Dewey sought? Perhaps not, perhaps philosophy is doomed to become an increasingly marginal discipline as the de-mystification of the world proceeds apace. It could become simply a narrow specialist's inquiry. If someone wants to know about deontic logic of rigid designators, it could deliver up answers. But unless such considerations can be put in a wider context, it just is a specialist's inquiry.

Perhaps philosophy is not so utterly doomed to become just somebody's little speciality. (You do kidney transplants. I do deontic logic.) Dewey, famously, said that philosophy begins to recover itself when the problems of men become the problems of philosophers, and Rawls, eschewing the techniques of linguistic analysis, and utilizing all kinds of empirical claims (including claims from the social sciences), constructed in a reasonably rigorous way a holistic moral theory that not only characterized our moral capacities but made, in a systematic way, normative claims that were closely linked with social theory.

Still, if we can get something more than what Rawls gives us that doesn't turn into obscurantism or ideology, we, if we believe in the possibility of this move, will believe that Rawls's theory is too much just descriptive of our moral capacities. We want, if such a thing is possible, a moral and social theory that can produce a critique of culture, a critique of society, and a critique of ideology. It should, as well, be somehow a descriptive-explanatory-interpretive account. It should enable us to come to better understand who we are, who we were, and who we might possibly become. But it should also have a critical-emancipatory thrust. It should help us to see more adequately who we might better become and what kind of a society would not only be a more just society, but also, since justice is not the whole of social assessment, a more truly human society. Beyond that, such a theory should help us as well to better understand the mechanics for the achievement of those things. It should not only paint a picture of human emancipation; it should as well give us at least a nascent theory of such a society, namely something which in general terms describes what such a society should look like, explains how it could come to be and sustain itself, and gives a justification of the claim that such a society is indeed a better society and indeed a society that could rightly be called a truly human society. Perhaps, as the logical empiricist and linguistic philosophers thought, nobody can possibly pull off anything like this. Neither philosophy nor anything else which would be reasonably clearheaded ought to aspire to such heights.

Surely such aspirations run well beyond anything that Rawls has. He gives us an account of our moral capacities and provides a rationale for liberalism and for our traditional democracies, but he does not go beyond that to provide a critique of culture or an all-out defence against alternatives to liberal society. He gives a rationale for liberal welfare state capitalism, but he does not show it to be superior to Marxism or anarchism or for that matter to a reflective elitism and the societies that go with these conceptions. It is some assessment here of what we could say one way or another that we should like to have if we could get it.

If Rorty is roughly right in his critique of an epistemologically based philosopher's self-image, we cannot get it from a foundationalist social theory. We can no more go the route of *moral* epistemology's foundationalist quest than we can take an epistemological turn more generally. We can't go the way of Price, Hume, or Hägerström.

I think, however, that there is another route that might conceivably pay off if it were really tried. It is a route Rorty utterly ignores for all his sensitivity to alternatives. Let me state it indirectly. Both in our time and in the late nineteenth century, the great synthesizing and interpretative accounts of our social life, which were once done by philosophers such as Hobbes, Locke, Smith, Condercet, Hume, Kant, and Hegel, came to be done by holistic social scientists such as Marx, Weber, and Durkheim. What we once got from *Leviathan* we now get from them. We get a holistic interpretive-explanatory-critical account of society. It will, Max Weber's official *wertfrei* stance to the contrary notwithstanding, be descriptive, explanatory, and critically normative.

What exactly we are trying to do in doing these things in a holistic theory is not clear. We have to build the ship while we are aboard by both doing this kind of theorizing and, at the same time, reflectively assessing, or at least pondering on, what it is we are doing. The social sciences are shot through not only with obscurity but with distorting ideology and, not infrequently, ideological apologetic, sometimes apparent and deliberate, more frequently and more insidiously hidden and unwitting. Yet, it is these human sciences that tell us, if anything tells us, who we are and were, and who we might hopefully and reasonably become.

What is vital to see is that here we have something that cuts across many standard conceptualizations of disciplines, including philosophy and sociology. There is room here for, among other things, the traditional analytic underlabourer conception of philosophy, for sometimes what needs to be done with historically powerful theories, either before or as we go on constructing new critical theories as our own alternatives to the classical theories, is to do what G. A. Cohen brilliantly does for Marx and Charles Taylor for Hegel.[4] We need, that is, to present a rational reconstruction of a historically influential and important work that might plausibly be believed to contain more than a modicum of truth. There we will be presenting a tidier version of the classical version. And there classical style clarifications are perfectly in order: techniques for drawing relevant distinctions by noting ambiguities, possibilities, finding more perspicuous formulations and the like. Here we take a leaf from the practices of Broad, Wittgenstein, and Austin, but it mainly comes to being very sensitive about the workings of our language, and Rorty is dead right in saying against Reichenbach that in doing this we should not claim that we have at hand, are on the verge of getting or needing, any powerful analytical tools.[5] What we need is a good understanding of the theory we are reconstructing, as well as the alternatives to it and a fine ability to draw distinctions rooted in our natural languages. We do indeed assemble reminders for a particular purpose. Here Cohen's practice in analyzing and critiquing Marx is very revealing. It brilliantly translates into the concrete what I have just been talking about.[6]

However, philosophy, done in the mode I am advocating, wants to do something more as part of a systematic critical theory. But what that will come to is not clear. I think, following Quine here and not Wittgenstein, that we should just proceed, using whatever is at hand, and trying to be as clear as we reasonably can, with holistic social theory construction which we, in turn, repeatedly relate to an at least putatively emancipatory practice without worrying overly whether what we are doing is philosophy, sociology, economics, social history, social criticism, or whatever. Worry about whether what we are saying is true, well-warranted, important, how it connects with other things we are saying, and the like. But do not ask if it is philosophy and do not ask, à la Wittgenstein in the last part of the *Investigations*, if our remarks are grammatical remarks and thus properly philosophical. Ask, instead, if they are tolerably clear, if there are good grounds for believing them, and whether, if true, they are important – particularly for giving us a grip on who we are and were, and who we are to become. If we can do something like that with some tolerable rigour we will plainly have done something worthwhile. Whether we want to go on to call it philosophy will not matter at all. *If* it is not philosophy, it is something more important than philosophy that ought to replace philosophy's traditional cultural role. But I also do not see why we should not say that it is a central element in philosophy: what philosophy should be when it gets reconstructed.

Notes

1 Worsley, *Marx and Marxism*.

2 Nielsen, "The Functions of Moral Discourse"; "Justification and Moral Reasoning"; "Good Reasons in Ethics"; "Appraising Doing the Thing Done"; "The Good Reasons Approach Revisited"; and "Moral Truth."

3 Nielsen, "Methodological Interlude"; "Radical Egalitarian Justice"; "Impediments to Radical Egalitarianism"; and "Class and Justice," all in *Equality and Liberty*, 13–99.

4 See G. A. Cohen, *Karl Marx's Theory of History*. See also Charles Taylor, *Hegel*; and *Hegel and Modern Society*.

5 Rorty, *Consequences of Pragmatism*.

6 G. A. Cohen, "Reply to Four Critics," 195–221.

Metaphilosophy, Pragmatism, and a Kind of Critical Theory: Nielsen and Rorty

I

Metaphilosophy is not meta to philosophy. It is itself philosophy about philosophy: philosophizing about what philosophy is, has been, can be, should be, what the point (if any) of it is, what its relation to our lives can be or should be, and what its relevance to thought about and action concerning the institutions of our society and to even the very structure of societies can be and even should be. Philosophy has given us visions of what society and our lives should be, though this is not, of course, all that it does. Yet some philosophers have it that this is a practice philosophy should abjure. Metaphilosophy, among other things, grapples with this.

Richard Rorty has a cluster of well-thought-out and perspicuously articulated, well-known metaphilosophical views. These views in some circles are much admired while in still wider circles they are (if not just ignored) much derided. I, though not uncritically, am on the admiring side.[1] I will bring out here something of what I take to be the attraction and viability of his metaphilosophical views, views which, in a somewhat different characterization, I largely share. That done, I shall turn to his opposition to critical theory and, more broadly, to his opposition to even moderately theorizing our views about society and political life.[2] I shall argue that there is a plausible case to be made on the other side. I shall argue (*pace* Rorty) that we can and should (though with caution) theorize about society and politics and that there is a non-rationalistic form of critical theory that merits our attention – that yields an attractive emancipatory account of society.[3]

To put my cards on the table, making a blunt and stark capsule articulation of my views:

(1) In metaphilosophy I am roughly a Wittgensteinian therapist.

(2) In what Rorty and Burton Dreben as well call "Big P Philosophy" – Philosophy asking questions about the *nature* of certain normative notions such as "truth," "justice," "rationality," and "goodness" in the hope thereby of better acting in accordance with such norms – I take a Wittgensteinian therapeutic turn.

(3) I try instead to do *p*hilosophy in a much less problematical sense of philosophy which Rorty has called the little-*p* sense in which "philosophy" comes to mean simply what Wilfrid Sellars called "an attempt to see how things, in the broadest possible sense of the term, hang together in the broadest possible sense of the term."[4] I try to philosophize, roughly after the fashion of John Dewey and John Rawls in their own distinctive ways, carrying as little baggage from *P*hilosophy – as little metaphysical, epistemological, metaphilosophical, or metaethical baggage as possible.

(4) Finally, I try to do philosophy – something I call critical theory – as social theory and social critique, including what has been called ideology-critique after the fashion (broadly speaking) of Marx, Gramsci, and the analytical Marxists.

There is considerable overlap between (3) and (4), and I hardly think of (4) as philosophy at all but as social theory misleadingly called "the Philosophy of Karl Marx" or "the Philosophy of Antonio Gramsci," though perhaps sometimes so calling it doesn't do any harm. Moreover, while through most of my life I was unfortunately preoccupied with the "demarcation problem,"[5] I have come to think like Quine (though somewhat ambivalently) that what gets classified as philosophy and what not should be of more interest to librarians than philosophers. But for good or for ill I have tried to do those four things which it might be useful to classify in that way. Obsession with the demarcation problem – certainly a metaphilosophical issue – would be a (5). But (5) is something I would now set aside.

II

I am skeptical concerning whether we can gain anything with any considerable substance – have any knowledge or understanding – that transcends a historicist perspective. Like Rorty, I do not think this implies a general skepticism, nihilism, or relativism, though it might imply something like Hume's mitigated skepticism (i.e., a resolute fallibilism).[6] But it does imply that we are not going to gain a context-transcending understanding of anything substantial. We cannot, that is, overleap history. We can gain no Archimedean point or skyhook – no "moment of transcendence" – to appraise our practices. We have no understanding of how to think outside or beyond our practices, though we can, relying on our practices, repair the ship at sea, and we can make modest idealizations of our practices that can sometimes lead to an improvement of them. The pragmatists, including Quine, are right: fallibilism rather than a thorough skepticism or relativism, is the name of the game. Moreover, I think Michael Williams is correct in thinking that fallibilism and Hume's *mitigated* skepticism come in the end to much the same thing.[7]

So, broadly speaking, I agree with Rorty against Jürgen Habermas, Thomas McCarthy, and Christine Korsgaard in rejecting unconditionality, namely the belief that there are some beliefs or arguments that are unconditionally valid, that just must be accepted by anyone who would be rational regardless of context.[8] There is nothing substantive that just must be accepted at any time and place whatever beliefs, interests, desires, stances, or social practices one has come to have. We will never get anything (at least non-platitudinously) like that. We may have a few Peircian acritical beliefs (e.g., fire burns, people die, water is wet, things change), but that is all. Justification is time-, place-, and context-dependent. If to espouse critical theory is to accept unconditionally, universal validity (as anything other than a purely formal device), transcendental arguments, quasi-transcendental arguments, or context-independent arguments, then I am no critical theorist. Rorty and I are at one over critical theory *so construed*. The kind of critical theory I espouse is articulated in my *Globalization and Justice* and most programmatically articulated in Chapters I–III.

"Enlightenment rationalism" is not pleonastic. I am not an "Enlightenment rationalist" or any other kind of rationalist. But I also think the Enlightenment is not a dead artifact of an earlier time. I believe a better world is possible and that we need not and should not live in the hell we live in now. I not only believe there is a lot of *unnecessary* suffering, unhappiness, and alienation now but that in many respects the world we live in now – our social orders – can and should (*pace* Rorty) without mythology or obfuscation or reification be characterized as irrational. I believe in the possibility of moral progress and the possibility of economic progress. I believe in the irrationality of religion (though some denominations are more irrational than others), and I believe that with more education and more social wealth we could well come to do without religion. And I believe that some social orders are more reasonable and more productive of happiness than others. In short, I believe in most of the various beliefs of the Enlightenment, but I see no need – or indeed any desirability – of tying such beliefs into the usual rationalistic beliefs that typically go with it or indeed into any rationalistic beliefs. So far, some perhaps contentious or misleading unessential phraseology aside, and my willingness to ascribe irrationality to some societies aside, Rorty and I are one.

There are other things that we both agree about: (1) We do not think that some arguments are *intrinsically* better than others. Justification is always to a reasonably determinate audience for a reasonably determinate purpose and is always time- and place-dependent; (2) there is no *natural order of reasons*; (3) there is nothing more immutable about our present ways of doing and viewing things than our past ways; (4) truth is not a goal of inquiry or the goal of anything else; (5) there are no interest-free and context-free criteria of unity, coherence, and completeness; and (6) the source of our moral obligations are our historically conditioned social practices. (Indeed we might even drop talk of "obligation" from our moral repertoire.)

Contrasting my views, as expressed above, and his views of what "philosophers might do after they give up on metaphysics and epistemology," as Rorty has it, his idea about "what comes after the demise of the tradition" is roughly "historical narrative and utopian proposals, [while mine is] roughly critical theory."[9] That is quite right provided two things are kept in mind: (1) that my way of doing critical theory not be conceived as a Kantian-Habermasian enterprise, that is, it not be conceived as the search for the unconditional via a search for universal validity, some deeply embedded modalities or in any other way; and (2) that philosophy can be a narrative philosophy doing cultural history *and* a critical theory which is both a narrative philosophy and a problem-solving philosophy integrally melded. Problems are solved in the context of a cultural and intellectual history clearly displayed and argued for. In this way problem-solving has a context *and* keeps narrative philosophy from just being story-telling – setting out what some anthropologists call just so stories; in simple terms, my type of critical theory seeks rather to give narratives with historical and empirical constraints. We should remember Dewey's slogan according to which philosophy recovers itself when philosophers worry less about the problems of philosophers and turn their attention instead to the problems of human beings. Rorty actually attempts to do this himself. Any adequate narrative *philosophy* must be a narrative philosophy *and* a problem-solving philosophy.

But how does this add up – or does it add up – to philosophy as critical theory? A narrative philosophy need not be a critical theory, and Rorty would think that a critical theory is *too theoretical to be useful*. But the way I conceive of critical theory out of the Marxian tradition, this does not seem to me to be so. I should put some flesh on those bones.[10]

As narrative philosophy is, as Rorty puts it, a "meld of moral philosophy and social and intellectual history," so critical theory should also involve critical intellectuals – those who with a critical consciousness would speak truth to power – practising their vocation, namely engaging in a meld of social criticism and ideology-critique, social and economic theory and history, and political and moral theory after roughly the fashion of Rawls, Levine, Scanlon, Geuss, and Daniels. It would utilize narrative philosophy as characterized by Rorty, but in using the various forms of narrative critique just mentioned it would provide a critical edge that purely narrative philosophy lacks. (But remember sometimes certain perspicuous descriptions undermine or on the other hand underpin certain moral beliefs.) It would not only show us what our cultural history has been, is now, and perhaps is going to be, but teach us to look at these narratives with a critical eye: to try to weed out the just so stories. It would help us (among other things) to take note of mystifications and to spot trends that can have very harmful effects and trends that can have liberating effects. There are a lot of narratives around. Practising what I call "critical theory" would help us to pick out narratives that are more plausible – have greater warranted assertability – than others. It would indeed not give us the one true or uniquely adequate description of the world. There is no such thing. It would not give us a narrative that was universally valid and unassailably true. Again there is no such thing. But it perhaps could, if we work very hard at seeking clarity, accuracy, and sincerity, yield some sorting out of narratives giving us ones we could reflectively and knowledgeably endorse as for the time the most adequate account or at least more adequate than the run of the mill accounts.[11]

The wider and more diverse the groups of people in conversation with each other, probing each other's views and convictions, the more likely we are to get, for a time, a more adequate view of things. We never get anything which is final – the "last word" – but we can, with luck, get something that for a time is compellingly reasonable to believe and do. Critical theory melded with narrative accounts is more adequate than narrative accounts alone. Moreover, in practice critical theories have been narrative accounts though accounts carrying too much Kantian transcendental baggage with them.

Rorty argues that there is not much that philosophy more traditionally conceived can do here. Perhaps, as I would conjecture, some of the social sciences including history and social geography can do something useful, but not philosophy.[12] (Presumably here Rorty means Philosophy.) Appealing to grand philosophical categories either metaphysical (ontological) or epistemological will not much help us to understand how society is developing, what fundamental social structures there are and what they are like, or what our fundamental political options are and which are the more attractive. As Rorty puts it, "Discussion in such areas as epistemology, philosophy of language, philosophy of mind, and philosophy of science is not easily made relevant to spotting sociopolitical trends, nor to the construction of safeguards against the dangers such trends foretell."[13]

III

We philosophers are likely to think that we are specialists in the elucidation of rationality. But, even *if* we are, that won't help much in setting forth a critical theory. The same is true of other regulative ideals such as truth, completeness, coherent unity, or coherence taken apart from particular contexts. These philosophical categories yield nothing thick enough to serve as criteria for social critique. Rorty remarks that, "Gadamer seems to me quite right in saying that one context's domination is another context's liberation. And that the ideas of complete freedom from domination and complete independence of context are empty."[14] And he adds that, "Foucault seems to me quite right in suggesting that history will always reveal domination hiding behind Enlightenment."[15] Neither philosophers of the genteel tradition, analytic philosophers, nor non-analytic continental philosophers command special techniques that enable them to function as critics of culture. Neither philosophers nor anyone else have super-concepts that enable them to clarify ordinary concepts. Philosophers of any sort have a very limited role to play in critical theory, limited to things like cleaning the Augean stable, making suggestions about broad outlooks, and (perhaps) clarifying *sans* super-concepts contested concepts – uses of words not free from historical change – deployed in critical theory. But I could and indeed do accept such a critique of Philosophy and still say in articulating critical theory, as I conceive of it, that it is not another Philosophy but a *successor* subject to Philosophy after the demise of the tradition that can do some critical and emancipatory work. What I think critical theory can do, without getting (as Habermas does) in the old Philosophical stew, in spite of his talk of post-metaphysical philosophy, is to articulate a critical account of society that is empirically, historically, geographically, and sociologically based and that yields some measure of objectivity (or, if you will, so as to not reify objectivity, the intersubjectivity of wide reflective equilibrium).[16]

Rorty would retort that critical theory with its utilization of sociology yields no such new objectivity. We still have *over-theorization* along with the naive scientific belief that social science can save us. Perhaps nothing can save us, but certainly no discipline can. If we think critical theory can, we are just spitting into the wind. What we need here is not more theory but more openness, more experimentation, more conversation with different people with different slants or takes on things, more democracy, more freedom to broaden our horizons, and the like. We should be more like Foucault and less like Habermas and kick the theory fetish.

Certainly we should have that openness and I think Rorty's, as well as Foucault's, distrust of theory is a very salutary thing. We should particularly be skeptical of grand theory in the social studies. Perhaps there is no such thing as a *science of society*. Yet we can learn a lot from Marx, Weber, Durkheim, Polanyi, and Keynes. Rorty, for example, applauds Marx for his prophetic and inspirational value. In this he throws him in with the poet Shelley. But their values and take on things are very different. Moreover, Hitler prophesied and inspired as well. Many a "Big Mouth" has prophesied and inspired. Even George W. Bush, to my incredulity and dismay, has done so. It isn't his inspirational and prophetic side that makes Marx valuable, or Weber, Durkheim, Polanyi, or Keynes. And it is not *just* that Marx (as well as Habermas and Foucault) "are imaginative and well read trend-spotters," though that is valuable. "Marx," Rorty remarks, "warned us against such trends as the tendency of the modern state to become the executive committees of the bourgeoisie, and the increasing ability of capitalism to immiserate the proletariat by maintaining a reserve army of the unemployed."[17] Similarly, Habermas was a trend-spotter when he spoke of the "colonization of the life-world" as was Foucault when he spoke of the "medicalization of the sexual life." But these trend-spotting remarks, unless they are to function only as inspirational propaganda, must be backed up, as they are, by Marx, Weber, Habermas, Polanyi, and Foucault, with reliable empirical accounts including theory-rooted observations and argument-rooted theoretical elaboration entwined in narratives. Foucault's trend-spotting account is less theory-elaborated than Marx's or Habermas's, but it isn't a theoretically innocent characterization without interpretive conceptualization and argument either. And Marx's and Habermas's trend-spotting remarks are comprehensively theoretically elaborated. Some of this theory can and should be excised. But not all of it should be. It is not irrelevant that we sometimes have good reason to believe that what is claimed to be trend-spotting, is not *just* trend-spotting, but actually captures something that is the case; that gives us some insight into how societies work. This requires confirmation and something like coherently putting the pieces together, utilizing something like wide reflective equilibrium, critically attending to alternative accounts, and intelligently and thoughtfully attending to objections. This is what it is for an account to have intellectual force. Nothing here, of course, will be the last word. But this is just to acknowledge fallibilism. And some accounts (e.g., Marx's, Habermas's, Gramsci's, and Foucault's) are so fallibilistically backed up. They are not giving us just so stories or making prophesies. Or at the very least they are not just telling stories or making prophecies.

IV

Rorty will say that there can be better and worse narratives, though none, of course, have "the final say," but, he would add, we are better off here with *just good journalism* than with *Philosophy*. (Sometimes some types of good films and types of good literature serve a similar function.) Theory, Rorty claims, just gets in the way.[18] Good journalistic accounts, good films, and good narrative literature are by contrast indispensable. But – so I claim – they are not sufficient by themselves. Moreover, there is journalism and journalism; films and films. I spoke above of "good journalism" but some may balk at that. They shouldn't. As Noam Chomsky allegedly does, I grind my teeth at a not-inconsiderable amount of journalism occurring in even such prestigious papers as *The New York Times*, *The Globe and Mail*, and *The New York Herald Tribune* (and these are good newspapers compared to many others). But in spite of the fact that I at least think I recognize a lot of the writing there to be ideologically slanted, I realize we usually get a fairer, more thorough, more accurate, and better account of things there than in the tabloids. It may well be that all newspapers are in some way or another ideologically slanted or, if you will, to some extent socio-politically slanted. But still there is journalism and journalism. I would put more trust in *Le Devoir* than *Le Journal de Montréal* or even *L'Express*. Some might say that expresses political bias on my part, but it would be hard to say that if, wanting views that were reasonably objective, I restricted my comparison to *Le Devoir* and the tabloid *Le Journal de Montréal*. If I see someone reading *Figaro* I will surmise that person is right-leaning (though probably intelligently so), and if I see instead someone reading *Le Monde* I will guess she is more left-leaning or at least more liberal. Similar things are true if I am in Germany and I see someone reading the *Frankfurter Allgemeine* or the *Frankfurter Rundschau* or in the UK and I see a person reading *The Times of London* or *The Guardian*. In those situations as well, I make similar conjectures to those I make concerning Quebec newspapers. What I want to emphasize here is that: (a) none of these major newspapers is just a propaganda sheet; (b) they are all responsible newspapers; (c) they contain some good journalism; and (d) they all present *a political* perspective, though surely somewhat different political perspectives; moreover, they can all have their failings in the way Chomsky vividly details. Similar things are even more true of more general socio-political-economic journals. I like to read *Le Monde Diplomatique*. My conservative friends like to read *The Economist*. I have read *The Economist* often enough to know it is not a mere right-wing political rag, and I think just a little attention to *Le Monde Diplomatique* would convince a fair-minded conservative that it is not merely a moderately leftish rag. Yet I think I get a better picture of what is going on in the world from *Le Monde Diplomatique* than from *The Economist* and my conservative friends think just the opposite. Who, if anyone, is more nearly right concerning which journal usually comes closer to "telling it like it is"? Is there anyone, or can anyone, justifiably say: "Is there anything like a reasonable approximation to telling it like it is here?" Contestable as such claims are, is it implausible to think such claims cannot be justifiably made? Without abandoning fallibilism I think they can.

Journalists in such publications are typically well-educated and sometimes have lived in the area they standardly report on for a long time and know the local language. Their reporting seeks to be accurate while unavoidably remaining interpretive and almost invariably has a somewhat distinctive political orientation. We can also see (usually by reading between the lines) that their reportage has in its background the study of at least some of the great socio-political theorists. They, of course, need good empirical evidence and they need to ascertain how (if they do) the referred things fit together. They, if they will be responsible, cannot make up stories. That they sometimes do, as Chomsky shows, reveals that even such accounts are not always responsible. The journalists need, when they are being responsible, to make interpretations which are not off-the-wall. In providing us with informed and probing interpretations of specific matters, they and we both need a reasonably good understanding of background matters – an understanding of the general socio-political-economic background and some understanding of social-political theory, including crucially some understanding of what I have called critical theory. Good journalism is, of course, crucial, but so (*pace* Rorty) is a good empirically based theoretical understanding of society, e.g., Marx, Weber, or Polanyi. Something that is difficult but not impossible to have and it need not be so politically biased that it either blocks our understanding or paralyzes our determination to act. I agree with Rorty that journalists typically should carry on their investigations and reportage "without using either the jargon of the social sciences or that of philosophy."[19] But that is another matter.

Rorty is right that *philosophy* – particularly big-*P* Philosophy – is not of much help here except perhaps in teaching us to be cautious and attentive to nuances, to respect clarity, and to teach us to make (in many situations) distinctions. (Sometimes there is the making of too many distinctions, e.g., C. D. Broad on egoism.) But Rorty is also right in believing that Marx, Habermas, and Foucault will not have been assisted in their trend-spotting from having read Kant's *Critique of Pure Reason* or more generally most of what we study in studying *P*hilosophy. These things, whatever their distinctive merits, will not help us in gaining a greater socio-political awareness and, I would add, a better grasp of what I have called critical theory.[20]

V

I think Rorty and I will continue to disagree in part about the importance of theory in socio-political matters. I say "in part" because I am usually on Rorty's side in the discussion of such matters both with standard analytical political philosophers, Habermasian critical theorists, and some of my Marxian comrades. This is particularly true of those Jon Elster has dubbed Marxist Fundamentalists. I think, to put it crudely, that philosophers and many other intellectuals tend to greatly overemphasize the importance of theory. I'm not enthusiastic about post-modernism, or even very informed about it, but I agree with Rorty that many philosophers, even good philosophers (e.g., Daniel Dennett and Akeel Bilgrami), get too Colonel Blimpish about post-modernism. That notwithstanding, I have tried to do a little something here to convince Rorty (as well as others) that figures like Marx, Keynes, Weber, Durkheim, and Polyani have been – and continue to be – of considerable importance to us and not principally as prophets and inspirers and that something called critical theory is an important *successor* to Philosophy.

To translate this continued disagreement between us into the concrete let me discuss where we disagree politically. Rorty rightly says, "Nielsen and I share the same political theory for the achievement of most goals."[21] We both want an egalitarian, classless, nonracist, genderless, nonhomophobic, nonstatus-ridden world – a world, as George Orwell put it, where there is no bowing and scraping. Still we importantly differ. *Rorty is a social democrat believing that the advancement of socialism is not possible, while I am a socialist believing that socialism is both possible and desirable.* Neither of us believes socialism is inevitable, and I am even skeptical enough to think (on my more depressed days) that it may not even probably, however it is labelled, get on the historical agenda again. Still I hope and think it is possible and should be struggled for. We need to take our chances in our rough and troubled world. Rorty contrariwise thinks that the struggle to achieve socialism is both hopeless and unfeasible. What we should hope for, he has it, is a capitalist society with a human face, the most egalitarian, classless, nonracist, nonhomophobic, nonsexist, nonstatus-ridden society that we can attain compatible with (what, so he believes, we cannot avoid anyway without doing even more damage) a capitalist ordering of our social life and economy. He might be for socialism if he thought it were achievable without tyranny, stultifying bureaucracy, and considerable inefficiency, and I might reluctantly acquiesce in the kind of capitalism that he wants (a social democratic capitalism) if it proves to be the closest that we could get to egalitarianism, classlessness, nonstatusism, nonracism, nonsexism, nonhomophobiaism and to (putting it generally) people being less brutalized and coming to have more control over their own lives. And *if* I came to believe that with what can come to pass for socialism we will get none of these things and added to it an inefficient tyranny and a stultifying bureaucracy, then I would acquiesce in the ideal of a Rorty-style capitalism and abandon my socialism. There would be nothing else to decently do if, as Rorty thinks, we would get the world of Josef Stalin or his lesser tyrannical followers rather than that of Rosa Luxemburg. I don't take that road because I believe that we would get none of these bad things if socialism came into existence in a society that could sustain it (e.g., a society of considerable wealth, such as in our own rich capitalist democracies, and a society with a secure liberal democratic tradition). Moreover, with the shift in such conditions to a socialist society we would get good things that capitalism even with a human face could not provide. I think such a socialist society, and eventually such a world, can come to be, and that *only* such a society could be classless (if any society could), thoroughly democratic (with both economic [workplace] democracy and extensive political democracy), and thoroughly egalitarian. That is why I am a socialist and why I think that Rorty, believing that anything like that is impossible, remains a social democrat. I have argued against Rorty on that, arguing that such a socialist world is possible (briefly) in my "Taking Rorty Seriously" and more extensively in Chapter 5 of my *Globalization and Justice*.[22]

I shall return only to that part of my argument that contests Rorty's claim that *theoretical considerations* are of *scant* importance here, being wheels that turn no machinery even where we are trying to decide whether we, if we are egalitarians and want (as Rorty does) a classless society, should go for socialism or social democracy. I do not claim that theoretical issues are decisive; indeed, I think nothing concerning anything substantive is going to be decisive and particularly *nothing is going to be decisive over such issues that are so important to our lives*. But I do not think that all theoretical considerations are idle wheels here turning no machinery.

Socialists, and most particularly Marxists, Rorty tells us, put too much trust in theory and particularly in grand social theory: a theory that would make plain the underlying structure and necessary (factually necessary) development of society. There is, he plausibly claims, no such "science of society." Belief in one leads us into metaphysical nonsense or at least to confusions, to dogmatism, and to arbitrariness. There is nothing like so-called "scientific socialism." There is nothing here that is actually scientific in any straightforward sense of the term.

The intellectual Left generally, and Fundamentalist Marxists in particular, are, as Rorty puts it, "dominated by the notion that we need a theoretical understanding of our historical situation, a social theory which reveals the key to future development, and a strategy which integrates everything with everything."[23] The Soviet experiment has, Rorty claims, abundantly shown us that in a modern dynamic economy answering to people's needs, a socialism *without markets* will not work. It is inefficient and features a stifling bureaucracy. It cannot obtain goods and services when they are needed and where they are needed. It cannot be innovative and produce things that people want. People in such a world will not adequately get either what they need or want.

Rorty also stresses that there is a strong tendency for a socialist society to either not be democratic at all or to be minimally insecurely democratic.[24] Worse still, what has been taken to be the Marxist tradition, by some people, is a tradition, Rorty remarks, "that is covered with filth because of the governments that have called themselves Marxist."[25] Think, for example, of Romania when it had a communist regime or now of North Korea. Marx, Engels, and Luxemburg had good intentions, but they assumed too easily that, after such a class-based revolution, democracy would still rather easily come into being and be sustained. They thought that, victorious in a class-based civil war, we could and would move from a socialist society with little in the way of democratic traditions to a fully democratic socialist society: a society with both an economic democracy and a political democracy. But that was unrealistic and it did not happen.

VI

Rorty from such considerations concludes that an efficient and democratic socialist society, let alone a world, is not in the cards. I have argued that he has not made his case.[26] But here I want to argue that, whether or not he has made his case, both he and his opponents appeal to theoretical considerations and that we cannot reasonably argue for or argue against socialism without them. Having good moral intuitions, having careful descriptions, having strong commitments, and being on the side of "the good guys" and against "the bad guys" is not enough. We can and should do without grand philosophical narratives, including philosophical metanarratives. Going for these grand philosophical narratives, we have Hegel and Leo Strauss but not analytical Marxists or some other Marxists (Gramsci, for example) or people like Weber, Keynes, Durkheim, or Polyani. Analytical Marxists (whom Rorty utterly ignores) avoid such grand *a priori* and teleological roads; instead (as we shall see in the next section), they construct accounts of historical materialism that are empirically testable, that give us a causal account (sometimes a functional account which is also a causal account) of epochal social change, have clearly articulated concepts of class, and show us both that and why we have class and strata in our societies and how and why capitalist societies, no matter how human their faces come to be with social democracy, will – indeed must – remain class societies.

Furthermore (*pace* classical Marxists but with minimal changes in Marxist theory), they – think of the work of Alec Nove, David Schweickart, and John Roemer – have given us carefully articulated models of market socialism that could feasibly be a matter of social experiment in societies evolving from the rich capitalist democracies.[27] As in modern capitalist societies, a market socialist society would have in its economic life *both* market and plan working together. A market socialism could even have – indeed would have – central planning. But what it cannot have, and be even minimally efficient, in complex societies, is a command/administrative *allocation* system (which should not be confused with central planning). Such an allocation system does not work for modern industrial societies. But central planning in an economic regime that has markets is another matter. Central planning pervasively exists in capitalist societies and it could, and would, exist in socialist societies as well (including market socialist societies). But such societies would not be consumerist societies, societies with a market orientation. Markets would have the limited function of being used for efficient allocation of goods, services and labour. This does not add up to the market society that orthodox Marxists rightly decry.

VII

In his discussion of socialism, Rorty contents himself with saying socialism didn't work in the past so why should we expect it to work now? But this simply ignores the above theoretical considerations and ignores the classical Marxist claim that socialism piggybacks on developed capitalism. Socialism, the claim goes, is only stably possible in a world with societies that are wealthy industrial societies – societies historically growing out of capitalism – and are as well societies that have a firmly established tradition of liberal democracy. Socialism could not work in the Third World unless the First World was socialist or clearly on the way to becoming socialist. As Rosa Luxemburg recognized, the Russian Revolution was doomed when the Russian Revolution did not extend to the West and, as G. A. Cohen has well argued, if the Soviet Union had *not* collapsed, historical materialism would have been refuted or at least infirmed, not confirmed. Without extensive capitalist development somewhere in the world, we will not get socialism. We *may* not get it anyway, but we will not get it without a developed capitalism being transformed (perhaps in revolution) into socialism. A Second World country *might* ignite socialism, but unless it rapidly takes root in the First World – the wealthy and powerful capitalist countries – it will burn out or eventually be repressed. I wish it were otherwise, but I agree here with Rosa Luxemburg.

Rorty may think the strong and wealthy capitalist countries – particularly the present-day king-pin, the United States – do not have a fat chance of turning in such a direction. But down the road a decade or so, we *may* be in for some surprises.

There is *nothing inevitable* here. We may have to settle at best for a worldwide Sweden, though I think a genuinely socialist transformation and not just a social democratic one is more likely. Even with capitalism, we may never have anything like a *worldwide* Sweden. Such rich countries *may* depend for their economic viability on some other societies being poor. But be that as it may, these are empirical-*theoretical* issues. Theory has its place here, though – whichever direction the wind blows – the issue surely will not be settled by empirical and theoretical investigations *alone*.

Both Rorty and I agree that the Left is the party of *hope*. I think social democratically that a worldwide Sweden (if it could come to be) would not, to understate it, be such a horror. At least it would be far better than the world of Bush or even for that matter of Romano Prodi and Bill Clinton. But I hope I am not being too *parti-pris* in arguing and hoping that a genuine socialist alternative is possible and not just a social democratic compromise. But whether or not this is pie-in-the-sky-by-and-by will not be decided independently of theoretical considerations and social experiments as well as struggle. Here Rorty engages in theoretical arguments as much as his socialist opponents do. What Rorty is right about – or so I think – is that Philosophy won't be of much help here, particularly grand Philosophy setting forth grand philosophical narratives or metanarratives. But, thank God, there are straight, or relatively straight, empirical-theoretical theories of varying degrees of "grandness" with both empirical and narrative impact. Testing here, as Elliot Sober has well argued, is crucial.[28] The utilization of such theories has not been shown to be so much love's labour lost as Rorty believes.

VIII

So while we both would like to refurbish "the hopes and aspirations of the Enlightenment," we travel down two different roads in so seeking its refurbishment. Rorty "doubts that anything of a theoretical sort will be of much use" in doing so. He is dubious of my claim that the great hope of the Enlightenment was in making rational criticisms of our social institutions and in setting out coherently structured and carefully reasoned alternatives. Well, "rational" is ambiguous but not so ambiguous that we can't make it apparent what is at issue. Moreover, the very idea of *the* great hope is too strong, but *a* crucial great hope is not. We can without wildness hope that a better world is possible and that it is indeed both viable and possibly achievable.[29] Moreover, and here I agree with Rorty, "the great hope of the Enlightenment was to replace those institutions" – the institutions we have inherited from the past – "by institutions that would cause less suffering and would provide greater individual freedom." But we need equality here too. And rational criticism of our institutions is important as well – though not by itself alone – for so is the articulation of perspicuous and emotionally engaging narratives, literature (the arts generally), and accurate description through history, geography, ethnology, and good journalism.[30] (We critical public intellectuals need all of them in our toolbox.) Philosophy, taken as a classification and elucidation of concepts, can sometimes play a perhaps useful *subsidiary* role here. But the central thing is *not* just for intellectuals, Leftist or otherwise, "to inflame our imagination with glorious hopes of the results of a particular institutional change." Franco, Hitler, and Mussolini were rather good at that and so was Thatcher and, rather mystifyingly, so for a time was Bush. We should expect more and something qualitatively different of our intellectuals than that. Part of the task, as Rorty says, is to make proposals, to suggest projects. But they should be reasonable proposals and projects backed up, or at least capable of being backed up, by the sort of considerations that usually make a proposal or project viable and reasonable, and, though both "viable" and "reasonable" are *at least* partly context-dependent, they are not purely emotive or otherwise just non-cognitive. We, as John Rawls shows, can say something about "reasonable" and, by extrapolation, "viable" in determinate contexts.[31]

Neither *P*hilosophy as traditionally conceived nor analytic philosophy have the tools, Rorty and I agree, to enable *P*hilosophers to function effectively (even if they try) as *critics of culture*. We should give up (at least in such a role) on metaphysics and epistemology. Hegel made the right move – though it was too bad he did it in such a constipated way – when he saw philosophy as ancillary to history rather than to either religion or science.[32] But it should also be ancillary to socio-political studies and crucially to social criticism, and this means it is ancillary to its successor – to what it is hopefully transitional to – critical social theory.

Rorty is on the mark when he says: "Not all politically engaged philosophy has been bad philosophy, but a lot of it has been boringly programmatic and tiresomely self-righteous."[33] I know that all too well from fundamentalist Marxists: good political comrades of mine but tiresome philosophers and theorists. But this is true of any type of philosophy or way of doing philosophy, including narrative philosophy. There are plenty of uninspired narratives around. However, it was an important and perceptive thing for Hegel to have said that philosophy is its time held in thought.

IX

In the last half of his "A Response to Kai Nielsen's Proposal for a Transformation of Philosophy," Rorty makes some incisive criticisms of me, some of which I now think are well taken, but they critique some ideas that in my last four books I have set aside.[34] I have come to give up, reluctantly and ambivalently, the idea, common to the classical pragmatists (Peirce and Dewey), the logical positivists, and Bernard Williams, that science has any privileged epistemic or methodological place in our lives. There is nothing special, as far as that is concerned, about science. It has a reasonably specific cluster of jobs to do and if you want to find out what is the best thing to think concerning *these matters* you better trust the relevant science and the relevant beliefs should be fixed by the relevant scientific method. If you want to know if atoms are observable, trust science. If you want to know if the SARS virus jumped from a certain sort of monkey to human beings, trust science (unless it gets politically inspired there). If you want to know why the Earth has been getting warmer for the last twenty years, again, if practitioners do not get politically inspired, trust the relevant science. The answers given by the various scientists in question may be wrong – we never escape fallibilism – but they are (to put it mildly) very likely to be much more reliable than any alternative non-scientific answers. The scientists in their different scientific disciplines have their different beliefs and more or less determinate ways of answering their questions, fixing their beliefs. But (*pace* Dewey, Sidney Hook, and Ernest Nagel) there seems to be nothing so general as *the* scientific method that we can rely on in all domains to fix belief. There are simply somewhat different scientific methods for different disciplines and in many other domains there are other methods, some of them reliable and some less so; perhaps in some domains their methods are not reliable at all. But I have now come to agree with Rorty: there is no single method – nothing like *the* scientific method – putting us uniquely in touch with reality. There are better and worse ways – and perhaps sometimes there is no determinate way – of finding out whether there are blue-jays in Australia, that and why the Earth is getting warmer, if the SARS virus jumped from a determinate type of monkey to human beings, whether in our societies there are classes or only strata, whether capitalist globalization causes more immiseraton than would obtain without it, whether neutrinos have mass, whether the Vikings planted vineyards in Newfoundland, whether expressionism is more complex than impressionism, whether *Anna Karenina* has more verisimilitude than *Madame Bovary*. But none of these inquiries – not even those that belong to physics – puts us in greater touch with reality. We cannot determine something like that for we do not know what we are talking about in talking about reality *full stop* and we have no non-question-begging criteria for determining which (if any) of the various realities we are talking about is the *really real*. (Indeed, what the devil are we talking about in talking about "the really real"?) To privilege physics here (*pace* Bernard Williams) is simply arbitrary.

Rorty is not so far off the point in saying that in *After the Demise of the Tradition* I was still to a certain extent in the grip of a tradition that we both now wish we have transcended. There is no area of culture that is more or less in touch with the non-verbal reality than any other. This does not mean that all texts are caught in a web of texts though no discipline is free of something like texts, i.e., none is transcendent of or to all social practices. I agree with Rorty and Putnam (again *pace* Bernard Williams) that there is no way of knowing what just is there anyway.[35] Indeed, we don't even understand what we are talking about here any more than we understand Kantian *noumena*. Such talk is at best useless and at worst incoherent. Kuhn is right in thinking that progress in science consists in greater problem-solving ability rather than an increased ability to represent or know *the world as it really is*. Here by now Rorty and I are in complete agreement.

X

However, in the last few pages of the above-mentioned article, he rings me in with Habermas's Enlightenment rationalism. When I wrote *After the Demise of the Tradition* I was, at least partially, *unwittingly* caught by such rationalism. But by now my more historicist and contextualist orientation would, even with Wide Reflective Equilibrium (WRE), never let me speak of or assume our ability to take "everything into account," or to believe or even to understand what it would be to have the force of the better argument that would preserve the Enlightenment idea that there is something called Reason "which always sides with the good guys." I do not know what it would be like to take everything into account, to have a unified overarching conception of rationality, to have a completed or final physics or anything else, or of what it is to speak of Reason, and to know that it will always side with the good guys. I once made the terrible mistake of speaking of the *widest* reflective equilibrium.[36] There is no such thing and if there were we wouldn't know when it obtained. There can only be wider equilibria when in a determinate context we are comparing different equilibria for a determinate purpose. When we are in a problematic situation where we have two or more conflicting wide reflective equilibria answering to that problematic situation, we, in trying to see if we could come to a reasonable consensus, seek a wider reflective equilibrium and, if problems remain, we seek a still wider equilibrium. Yet we do not understand (let alone even remotely expect to understand) what it would be like to gain *sans* context a widest equilibrium where in good objective idealist fashion anything is related to everything, where we would have gained the "last word," and seen what Reason, God, or the Absolute requires. There is, of course, no such "dance of the dialectic." We can, as Rorty himself stresses, if we are lucky, converse with ever wider audiences, gain an understanding of and a feel for how more and more people see things, gain greater and ever wider consensuses which are not *mere* consensuses but what we would get by getting our different and conflicting views into – for a time – a wide reflective equilibrium. But such WRE, striving to gain an ever-greater coherence, is sometimes faced with conflicting views. We should *seek* (though we might not get) in such a situation a wider reflective equilibrium that would satisfy the conflicting parties with different wide reflective equilibria where their differences could be reasonably settled without a fight or just an arbitrary decision: something that in *some* situations might obtain. We might get a wide reflective equilibrium that the contending parties could each reflectively endorse when they each had carefully applied the method of wide reflective equilibrium. There is still the need for *endorsement* here, but it is not a blind or arbitrary endorsement but a *reflective* endorsement. It is not that I think, as Rorty thinks that Christine Korsgaard has it, that if you really think things through, if you carefully apply the scientific method or apply WRE, you will always come out on the right, emancipatory side of current political controversies. You still may be on the wrong side, but you will have the best obtainable reasons, for a particular time and in a particular place, to think you are on the right side. What it is reasonable to think or do may always turn out to be false or mistaken. But it is, being in WRE, all the same the best thing to think and do for that time. Rudolph Carnap in 1932 was right: *truth is time-independent but confirmation is time-dependent*. But what we want to know about is not truth (strange as this may sound) but about what the applications of wide reflective equilibrium tell us is the time, place, and context-dependent notion of what we are justified in believing and doing: what we should at a given time and place *take* for truth. We will never get by such a method something that will yield unconditionally universal validity: what we must, for all time, if we follow Reason, believe, and what is the last word. There is nothing like any of these things. Spinoza was wrong about this. But maybe we can get, if we are lucky and persistent, what for a certain people, at a certain time and place, with certain interests, is the more reasonable and desirable thing to do and reflectively endorse. We probably can't even get that. I am perhaps persistently too Whiggish. But some reflective stasis remains an empirical possibility. Our reach must exceed our grasp or what is humanity for?

There should be no forced choice between narrative or problem-solving or theory. All are needed. We need our Balzacs, Zolas, and Dreisers, and we also need our Marxes, Webers, and Durkheims. They both play different but complementary roles in attaining wide reflective equilibria.

Rorty, though he himself appeals to reflective equilibrium, does not think I can get as much out of it as I want to. He remarks (like Nicholas Wolterstorff):

> This is because the bad guys can be as reflectively equilibrious as the good guys. Each side can paste together an equally coherent set of moral convictions, moral principles, and plausible empirical predictions about the results of emancipatory policies. Neither will have much trouble whomping up an empirically based broadly scientific conception of *homo sapiens* an account of human nature to suit their own needs. The racists, the phallocentrists, and the homophobes, for example, are all happy to offer accounts of human nature that dictate that various emancipatory changes should not be attempted.[37]

Surely with some bright spin doctor they can *whomp* them up. But they would have to *whomp* them up. Wide reflective equilibrium forces us to eschew *whomping* and rather to look carefully with an earnest attempt at impartiality at a wide range of considerations. When we do so and carefully reflect on them and take them to heart, we are less likely to be racists, phallocentrists, homophobes, Bushites, or Neofascists. We are less likely to just whomp things up. (Or is one man's careful and honest looking at things another man's whomping?) It is not impossible that a present-day well-educated person will be a racist or a Bushite but it is rather unlikely and rather difficult. It is perhaps no accident that (for example) most of the better educated strata do not oppose same-sex marriage. Yet *perhaps* these things are not a matter of "education" but "indoctrination": just plain social acculturation, what gets drilled into us. Sad tales can be told on all sides and maybe for some ears (but hardly the same ears) with verisimilitude. The Nazis had their sad tales too. And if the Nazis had won the war, conquered the world, and stabilized things, our (what was left of us after the ethnic cleansing had been carried out) children and grandchildren would no doubt be good little Nazis. That is a chilling thought, but where wide reflective equilibrium is functionally in place, or something like it is in place, those things, as damaging as they are, are not likely to persist. It is hard (but not impossible) to be a Black-hater or a Jew-hater if we have a little information about or acquaintance with people. If we come to know the people on the other side of the mountain, it is usually more difficult to hate them.[38] It is much harder for an educated person to believe – really believe – that Jews are a race with a different evolutionary history. Harder, but not, as we sadly know from history, impossible. Wide reflective equilibrium never promised a rose garden where right, or even reasonability, would always triumph or even usually triumph. It did promise a way, fallibilistically, of course, to ascertain what is more likely to be reasonable and right. This will, like all substantive understanding, be for a time and place. What else is new? And while Rorty is right in thinking there is no essence of human nature (or indeed of anything else), we have slowly come to have a not-inconsiderable empirical knowledge of human nature that we can appeal to in wide reflective equilibrium. Lukács was right about this in his dispute with Sartre. If we recognize that contingency and fallibilism is all-pervasive, we will not be surprised that what is right (or the closest thing thereto) does not always prevail or can even always be ascertained. But wide reflective equilibrium will provide us with a way of ascertaining (sometimes successfully) what is most plausibly to be believed at a given time and place to be the right thing to do and what is most plausibly believed to be the best explanation of why that is so. It is not so far from Rorty's enlarging the circle of cooperative and sympathetic understanding.

Surely the society that both Rorty and I would like to see come into existence, replacing the horror that we have now, is "a world in which there is less suffering and more freedom," but that will in considerable part be so because our societies and our world will become more reasonable, less ethnocentric (in the anthropologist's sense), and better educated. With our as a matter of fact worldwide increase in literacy, we get some gain in reasonableness. Human nature is plastic, but *perhaps* not all the way down. We can learn something from the ways we have been and are.[39] Indeed, this will help us ascertan what we might become. Anthropology and contemporary geography – I did not say only these disciplines and I am not forgetting about literature – can teach us something about the ways we have been and are.[40] Ways that are not, or need not be, just giving us just so stories.[41]

Notes

1 See Nielsen, "Pragmatism as Atheoreticism."

2 See Rorty, *Take Care of Freedom and Truth Will Take Care of Itself*; and "A Response to Kai Nielsen's Proposal for a Transformation of Philosophy."

3 See Nielsen, *Globalization and Justice*, 41–138.

4 This is not Wilfrid Sellars's own view of philosophy but what he takes to be an uncontroversial conception of philosophy widely held by philosophers and non-philosophers alike. Besides this, for Sellars, it is crucial to do big-P Philosophy. He developed a distinct kind of scientific realism that is reasonably regarded as Philosophy in the grand old metaphysical style: that is big-P Philosophy. Rorty, by contrast, regards only little-p philosophy as a legitimate enterprise. See Rorty, *Consequences of Pragmatism*, xiv–xvii.

5 Couture and Nielsen, *Méta-Philosophie*, 1–40.

6 Rorty nicely puts how I also take 'historicism' as follows: "By *historicism* I do not mean claims about historical inevitability of the sort Popper rightly criticized in *The Poverty of Historicism*, but rather the idea that our philosophical vocabularies and

problematics are attempts to deal with contingent historical circumstances rather than 'perennial' or 'basic' ones." Rorty, *Take Care of Freedom and Truth Will Take Care of Itself*, 152.

7   Michael Williams, "Rorty on Knowledge and Truth," 61–80.

8   Habermas, "Richard Rorty's Pragmatic Turn," 31–55; McCarthy, *Ideals and Illusions*; Korsgaard, *The Sources of Normativity*.

9   See Rorty, "A Response to Kai Nielsen's Proposal for a Transformation of Philosophy." See also Rorty, "Philosophy as a Transitional Genre."

10 See Nielsen, *Globalization and Justice*, 41–138.

11 Rorty with his anti-representationalism (something I share with him) will *perhaps* not be happy with talk of accuracy here. It looks like it commits one to representationalism. But I think it can be (and should be) de-mythologized away from representationalist epistemology into something that travels philosophically light.

12 See Harvey, "Cosmopolitanism and the Banality of Geographical Evils."

13 Rorty, "Response to Simon Thompson," 52. See also Rorty, "Philosophy as a Transitional Genre."

14 Rorty, "Response to Simon Thompson," 49.

15 Ibid., 49–50. More attention might have been paid to self-reflective or self-referential problems. My historicism as well as Rorty's rules out universal, totalizing interpretations of history. But Rorty reads Foucault as claiming that "history will always reveal domination hiding behind Enlightenment" and I claim (as Rorty would as well) there is no transcending our historical perspective and gaining some absolute universality "rooted in reason." But, one referee notes, are not these examples of the very universal totalizing interpretations of history that we say we eschew? They are not. They are empirical interpretive generalizations that could be infirmed (weakly disconfirmed).

16 See Wright, "A Compass for the Left."

17 Rorty, "Response to Simon Thompson," 51.

18 Rorty, *Against Bosses, Against Oligarchies*, 13–24.

19 Rorty, "Response to Simon Thompson," 51.

20 Ibid., 51–52.

21 Rorty, *Take Care of Freedom and Truth Will Take Care of Itself*.

22 See also Wright, "A Compass for the Left."

23 Rorty, *Against Bosses, Against Oligarchies*, 45.

24 There have been post-capitalist statist societies *calling* themselves socialist. But, as Wright well argues, they are not genuinely socialist societies but non-capitalist statist societies. To properly count as socialist, a society must be democratic. Wright, "A Compass for the Left."

25 Rorty, *Against Bosses, Against Oligarchies*, 21.

26 See Nielsen, *Globalization and Justice*, 191–223.

27 See Nove, *The Economics of Feasible Socialism*; Schweickart, *After Capitalism*; and Roemer, *A Future for Socialism*.

28 See Sober, "Testability."

29 See Wright, "A Compass for the Left."

30 See Harvey, "Cosmopolitanism and the Banality of Geographical Evils"; and Rorty, "Philosophy as a Transitional Genre."

31 See Rawls, *Political Liberalism*, 48–66.

32 See Rorty, "Philosophy as a Transitional Genre."

33 Rorty, *Against Bosses, Against Oligarchies*, 20.

34 See Rorty, "A Response to Kai Nielsen's Proposal for a Transformation of Philosophy."

35 Nielsen, *Naturalism without Foundations*, 418–24.

36 Nielsen: "Relativism and Wide Reflective Equilibrium," 316–33; "Philosophy as Wide Reflective Equilibrium," 3–42; "Wide Reflective Equilibrium without Uniqueness," 23–36; Nevo: "Is there a Widest Equilibrium," 3–22; and "Reflective Equilibrium and the Contemplative Ideal of Knowledge," 22–35.

37 Rorty, *Take Care of Freedom and Truth Will Take Care of Itself*.

38 A referee remarks that he finds implausible my claim that once we know people we are unlikely to hate or oppress them. Perhaps I am being too Whiggish here? It is certainly not an article of faith for me. It is an empirical conjecture of mine. Perhaps it expresses more of a hope than anything else? There is, however, one thing that should be cleared up. I have in mind, in so speaking, situations where people work together and in some degree share a life. (I am not speaking of intimate relations between people.) My conjecture is that when people are together in that kind of social situation and really get to know each other it will be more difficult to hate or oppress each other. But surely that is an empirical matter and my conjecture may be false. It will be a bad day for humanity if it is.

39 It is also thought that I engage in some hand-waving as I finish up, in effect claiming there is a human essence. But I am anti-essentialist to the bone. I agree with Sartre and Rorty about that. I only think, as does Lukács, that there are as a *matter of fact* some properties that are common to and distinctive of all statistically normal featherless bipeds, e.g., being able to speak. But these are factual matters and not something we must have: something that is a kind of metaphysical necessity.

40 Harvey, "Cosmopolitanism and the Banality of Geographical Evils," 529–64.

41 In 1987 I published an essay programmatically articulating philosophy as transformed into a distinctive type of critical social theory that is holistic and already moving in the historicist direction of my later work. It already rejects unconditionally an appeal to what was coming to be called 'a discourse ethics.' It specifies further my conception of the structure of my thoroughly naturalistic critical social theory. See Nielsen, "Philosophy as Critical Theory."

3

On There Being Wide Reflective Equilibria: Why It Is Important to Put It in the Plural

I

I deploy wide reflective equilibrium [WRE] principally as a method of justification for accounts of morality and normative political and social theory. Here I shall be primarily concerned with how to use it where political morality is being thought about. WRE is a coherentist method of justification. It starts with a society's or a cluster of societies' most firmly held specific particular considered judgments or considered convictions and seeks to forge them into a consistent and coherent whole along with other considered judgments (judgments at all levels of generality) and as well with other relevant beliefs that are generally reasonably, uncontestedly, and widely held in the society or cluster of societies with which we are concerned.

It is a coherentist method but with the unique feature – some would say a conflicting feature – that some *initial* credibility is taken to obtain for those considered judgments themselves that we reflectively endorse and take as our starting points. Their initial credibility will gain in strength for those considered judgments when they get winnowed out as we proceed in equilibrating and continue to be reflectively endorsed at the point where (for a time) we make closure. What we continue reflectively to endorse after such an exercise has considerable weight with us. But these initial considered judgments themselves that we reflectively endorse are not like logical atoms or protocol sentences; for in the very fact of being *considered* and being *reflectively* endorsed, they cannot stand alone, and their initial credibility obtains not independently of the relations they have with some other beliefs and convictions. Without that they could not even be *understood* to be something we could consider or to be the result of reflective endorsement. However, without such *initial* credibility, a *purely coherentist* method (assuming – what is problematical – that there could be one) would be subject to the standard objection that views may be as coherent as you like but without having any warrant at all, e.g., the belief systems of Christian Scientists or "flat earthers."

The thing is to seek to maximize the coherence of our moral beliefs and practices by forging them into reflective equilibrium. It should be a wide (broad) reflective equilibrium and not a narrow (partial) one because beyond collecting together moral judgments, moral practices, medium-level moral rules and moral principles into a coherent whole, it also needs to take into account well-justified and widely accepted empirical factual beliefs including beliefs about the functions of morality, the functioning of parts of the social structure (including the economy) relevant to social facts, political realities, and relevant scientific developments. WRE, that is, does not work in a moral or social vacuum. How the world goes is not taken to be irrelevant to how morality goes. We seek an equilibrium which takes into account matters such as I have just mentioned, including ascertaining the extent and intractability of the pluralism in our modern liberal societies and whether and to what extent the comprehensive views extant in our societies (or at least some of them) are reasonable. And where some views are not reasonable, as is most certainly the case, we seek to determine which ones (if any) are such that it would be reasonably possible to (rationally) persuade people holding those unreasonable views to be reasonable, thereby abandoning their unreasonable views and, by doing so, moving us along in the direction of a more well-ordered society. We seek to obtain a consistent cluster of moral, political, uncontroversial factual, and uncontroversial theoretical beliefs that would yield the best available account of what our social situation is, what the reasonable possibilities are in the society, and what is reasonable and desirable to do. As a bit of ideal theory, this is a reasonable thing to say, but whether it has much resonance in the hurly-burly of our moral and political lives is very much another matter.

No WRE will be unconditionally final: the "last word" written in stone. We can be confident that all equilibria will eventually be upset as the world changes, including people's perceptions of the world and their reactions to it. However, the method is *self-correcting*, and it is reasonable to *hope* that, if WRE is applied with care, integrity, and intelligence, later equilibria built on earlier ones will *tend* to be more adequate: that is, render more thoroughly and more perspicuously the consistency and coherence of our moral beliefs and practices. But there is no escaping fallibilism (Hume's mitigated skepticism, if you will), historicism, or finitism. We never get an equilibrium which says it all, which finally sums things up in a way which is complete and yields a moral view of things that is certain and unconditionally valid. We do not even understand, except perhaps in the vaguest terms, what it would be like to get such a thing.

II

Idil Boran and Andrew Lister have launched incisive critiques of my account of WRE. They aim at a place where I may be importantly vulnerable, though I should note in passing that it would *not* make for trouble, as well for the WRE accounts of John Rawls, Norman Daniels, or T.M. Scanlon.[1] It has to do with my rather singular and, as some may regard, my incoherent or at least deeply mistaken, desire to have my Rawls and Richard Rorty too. As a heading to his article, Lister appropriately quotes me as saying, "Moral, social and political philosophy should travel metaphysically and epistemologically light for both Rawlsian and Rortyian reasons which are different but do not conflict."[2] He then challenges the claim that they do not conflict and indeed goes on to add that they do not only conflict but conflict in a revealing and important way.[3] He made the following remark in his critique of my work at a conference held in my honour:

WRE is a nonfoundationalist method of justification in ethics. Two kinds of considerations motivate the development of such a method: a Rortyian denial of the existence of philosophical foundations for knowledge claims and social practices, and a Rawlsian attempt to avoid appeals to controversial religious, metaphysical or philosophical ideas in the justification of social institutions. Nielsen claims that these two motivations do not conflict. However, the Rortyian reason for not making foundationalist claims is that they are indefensible or incoherent, whereas the Rawlsian reason is that they will inevitably be a matter of deep, reasonable controversy for the design of social institutions. The Rawlsian seeks to avoid the whole debate between foundationalism and anti-foundationalism, and so would not defend WRE on Rortyian grounds.[4]

Boran, as well as Lister, rightly claims that the two types of justificatory appeal for WRE are different, and importantly so. Boran is also correct in asserting that if their aims were the same or importantly similar they would be conflicting. She also gives ample evidence that in previous writings I have not kept them properly apart. And she is justified in saying that Rawls would not, and indeed could not, avail himself of the Rortyian justification for appealing to WRE. If he did, Rawls would be violating his own restrictions on justifying political liberalism without making any controversial philosophical claims or moves whatsoever. Rejecting foundationalism and taking an anti-foundationalist or even a non-foundationalist stance is one such controversial claim. Perhaps it is well-justified (indeed, I think it is), but it is controversial. It is metaphysical as Rawls uses "metaphysical" in a broad sense to designate any controversial philosophical view.[5] Rawls, in defending political liberalism and in using WRE to defend it, does not criticize or reject foundationalism or adopt non-foundationalism but just benignly sets aside such issues.

However, WRE is a procedure and it can be used for different purposes. Rawls uses it for one purpose, as described above, and Rorty and I use it for different purposes but purposes that do not conflict with Rawls's. (Indeed, I also use it for Rawls's purposes.) Rawls's deployment of WRE is, I shall argue, safe at home just as he deploys it for *his quite legitimate purposes*.

But his purposes are not the only legitimate purposes for which WRE can be deployed even when only political liberalism is at issue. And some other deployments of WRE do not operate with the same constraints. I shall try to make these dark sayings clear and hopefully persuasive.[6]

It is crucial to recognize, as Burton Dreben has (as well as Norman Daniels and T.M. Scanlon), how Rawls came to have, particularly in *Political Liberalism* and *The Law of Peoples*, a very constrained but creatively determinate purpose.[7] He saw that the extant defences of political liberalism (social democracy, if you will) had internal conflicts: conflicts that its adherents had not been able either to resolve or plausibly dissolve.[8] He set out to present a way of understanding political liberalism that would enable us to see it as something free of those conflicts: free most centrally of conflicts between liberty and equality and of any entrenched conflict between what Constant called the liberties of the ancients and the liberties of the moderns. He also sought to show how there was in political liberalism a conception of tolerance that made sense of political liberals' relations to non-liberal peoples that did not come to ethnocentrically *imposing* liberal views on them. His aim was, taking it as given that political liberalism was an attractive view to which he and many others were committed, to articulate an account of political liberalism that could plausibly be seen to be a consistent and coherent view that was perspicuously displayable. Rawls sought to articulate a view, taking into account the varied comprehensive doctrines of liberals in such democracies, which yielded an "overlapping consensus" concerning our *political* lives together. One very central element of it was to be committed to the toleration of conflicting metaphysical and religious or non-religious comprehensive conceptions of how life is to be lived, *no matter how deep their conflicting metaphysical and religious or non-religious beliefs, as long as, in the very minimal sense Rawls had in mind, these various comprehensive views of the good were reasonable*. If this obtains for them, Rawls argued, they will come to agree on a commonly acceptable family of conceptions of a broadly egalitarian conception of political justice.[9] In achieving such a WRE for his defence of political liberalism he articulated, at least arguably, a view, given the pervasive and intractable debates about liberal democracies, that was a very considerable achievement indeed.[10]

It is very important to see how *minimal* this sense of being reasonable is and how keeping it so is essential for gaining agreement concerning and reflective endorsement of the adequacy of his conception of political liberalism. But it is also important to keep firmly in mind a point Rawls makes himself: that justification is always for a particular audience at a particular time and never for humanity at large.[11] The justification Rawls proffers is for liberals themselves and not for all and sundry. Liberals can come to see that political liberalism is not *ad hoc* and is not a conflicting or (if there is such a thing) an incommensurable jumble but something that hangs together for them in an attractive way. Leaving out "in an attractive way," non-liberals may see that coherence too but since some of their considered judgments are importantly different from Rawls's (or for that matter mine), Rawls's liberal WRE will have little hold on them. They can see its coherence and still shrug their shoulders. Rawls does not try to argue that they are justified in so reacting or that they should not so react or that anything like a justification here is impossible or unimportant. To do that is not what he is trying to do. It is not his kettle of fish. It is not what he set out to accomplish. What he most centrally set out to accomplish, specifically in *Political Liberalism*, is what I have described in this paragraph.

Rawls's justification of political liberalism is an *internal* one, making minimal claims *on those committed to political liberalism* and who accept its orientation and the ethos of its background culture, but who will often have very different comprehensive conceptions of the good. Starting with their considered judgments, concerning which he believes there is a considerable consensus among liberals, Rawls sought to get their views into WRE. He did *not* seek to show (though he also did not deny or affirm that it could be done) that political liberalism could be justified to someone trying to advocate some form of an aristocratic hierarchical society, a Leninist communist society or a fascist society, or to someone trying to advocate a serf or even a slave society. And he did not claim to have arguments sufficient to turn their minds around if they would be reasonable. Rawls was not concerned to present an argument that would require for everyone, if they would be rational, to re-attune their hearts and become political liberals. He, like most of us in our societies, thought some of these non-liberal views, which were also illiberal, were very implausible and in some instances evil. But Rawls did not think that anyone, anywhere, no matter what his situation and particular socialization and culture, would recognize, or have grounds for accepting, justice as fairness or any of the related family of politically liberal conceptions of justice. He was not in the business of answering Calvin or Luther or Nietzsche or Carl Schmitt or Lenin or Marx or fundamentalists of any stripe. He did not say that it could not be done or that it could be done or even that it should be done but rather gave to understand that that was not his task. He sought instead to present political liberalism in a coherent way and to convincingly show how he could make it coherent and plausible even to political liberals aware of the difficulties in extant liberal accounts. To do this he crucially and distinctively deployed WRE. He deployed it in a manner that travelled philosophically light, *taking no positions at all that were philosophically controversial*. He did not deny there may be *a* deep, contested truth or soundness in political liberalism, but responded that the person committed to political liberalism need not invoke or even grasp such a truth or soundness (if indeed there is one) to achieve agreement with other political liberals who hold very different metaphysical and epistemological views. For example, a secularist political liberal could say to a Thomist political liberal,

> Perhaps you are right. There may be natural moral laws rooted in God's reason and they may be the *ultimate* ground for our shared considered judgments. But I, along with a not-inconsiderable number of reasonable others, do not agree with you about that and I, as well as others – reasonable others – even after considerable argument and dialogue, are not very likely to come to agree with you about these *philosophical* matters. But there is agreement between us – between you and me – about a whole host of considered judgments themselves. So wherever the philosophical quest may take us, *for political purposes* – for our attaining a common political rationale for our political liberalism – we can, and should, bracket such controversial philosophical questions. We can for *political purposes* benignly neglect them, even if we, when we are philosophizing, seek to ascertain the truth concerning what we severally and differently and perhaps irreconcilably disagree about concerning what we

are to take to be the deep ultimate basis or lack thereof for our allegiance to political liberalism.

To expect agreement about these controversial *philosophical* matters – in Rawls's terms, metaphysical matters – is utterly unrealistic; but it is not unreasonable or implausible to expect agreement concerning a whole host of commonsense considered convictions and beliefs and about how they fit together.

It is important to recognize, as Rawls stresses himself, and Boran rightly reiterates, that this is not to be confused with a skepticism (a Mackie-type error theory, say) or a Rorty-like anti-foundationalism or Rorty's and my anti-Philosophy philosophy or even (as Rawls commits himself to in his Dewey lectures) a Rawlsian metaethical Kantian constructivism.[12] We simply *bracket* these things when what is at issue is an *internal* political justification of political liberalism in an attempt to make it plausible to people who are already political liberals but worry about its rationale or even its consistency.

However, "being bracketed from" is one thing and "being incompatible with" is another. For his particular purposes – fundamentally political purposes – Rawls cannot appeal to what has been called (I think mistakenly) epistemological/Rortyian reasons or any controversial epistemological reasons or anti-epistemological stance or anything else philosophically controversial. They are not part of the language-game Rawls is playing in defending political liberalism. But a political liberal who wants to answer Carl Schmitt or Aquinas or Mao or Lenin is playing another *importantly different* language-game, also distinctively politically liberal, but for a different but (or so I claim) non-conflicting purpose. To give an *internal* political justification of political liberalism – to show how political liberalism plausibly hangs together – is one thing, and to give an *external* political justification of political liberalism – showing its superiority to hierarchical aristocratic systems or to fascism or Soviet-Union-style communism in *statist* post-capitalism – is another. These tasks are not the same tasks but just different tasks with different ends in view. This is not to show or to say that they stand in conflict or to give any credibility to that claim.

III

With the above I am inching closer to showing how I can consistently and coherently have my Rawls and Rorty too. They are playing different language-games for different purposes but not, for all of that, conflicting purposes, or at least not necessarily conflicting purposes. I did not say "incommensurable" purposes but just "different" purposes. Or to use a different jargon, they, in asking about the justification (perhaps better, "a justification") of political liberalism, have what John Dewey calls different *ends in view*.[13] Rawls wants an *internal* justification of political liberalism showing how it hangs together, how it is a consistent and coherent view meshing with our considered judgments. But he neither affirms nor denies that an *external* justification is possible. Rorty presumably wants the same thing, but he is concerned *as well* with an *external* justification of political liberalism. He is concerned with how, if pushed, political liberalism could respond to a Carl Schmitt or a Lenin. His own examples are Nietzsche and Loyola but the issue remains the same.[14]

Rorty gives his contextualist, historicist, finitist, social practice-oriented, if you will, Wittgensteinian answer.[15] We cannot ever gain, he argues, some standpoint where we can, standing free from any perspective, neutrally assess such matters. It is unintelligible to try to set aside all our social practices and gain a perspective-less view from nowhere – say, Sidgwick's "the point of view of the universe"– a point of view from which we can come to see that some regimes or practices are justified and others are not. (Rawls could not take such views, however, for they are controversial philosophical views and thus for him metaphysical views. He seems in his later thought to be in practice very much a historicist, though he would not say this. He could not acknowledge that, for it would be inconsistent with his eschewing what he takes to be metaphysical views in arguing for political liberalism. That is a way, as Rorty does and as I do, to characterize his views – I think an accurate way – but Rawls need not do so himself in showing how political liberalism hangs together.) But it would be harder for him to defend his characterization of what justification consists in, namely that it is something that obtains for a certain people at a certain time and place and for people with certain interests. That notwithstanding, political liberalism, fascism, Stalinist "communism," Calvinism, the various religious fundamentalisms, are not on the agenda for Rawls. But holders of such deeply illiberal views will return the compliment. For some, the very word "liberal" is a derogatory term. A liberal can, of course, give a bucketful of reasons for rejecting these illiberal views. They are intolerant, fanatical, show a kind of disrespect for persons, an indifference to liberty, cause extensive misery, have (in some instances) irrational conceptions of what the world is like, etc. But such remarks will not faze the illiberal opposition. These reasons are all, they affirm, question-begging. They (depending on what kind of an illiberal is involved) will say these secularly oriented political liberal responses ignore the utter transcendence of God and the unquestionable unchallengeable authority of His law or the wisdom of the Führer and his call for the racial solidarity rooted in "racial science" and the purity of his New Order or the historical reality of the proletariat and the clear practical understanding by them that capitalism will break down of its own internal contradictions, something shown to the proletariat (and only to them) in the turmoil of their everyday life and so on and so on. (This latter is something that Georg Lukács argued).[16]

Political liberals will *not* say or even think, as, when pushed, very far extreme illiberals will, that "I have the right to persecute you because I am right and you are wrong. I have the truth and you do not. My beliefs are true and yours, and importantly and dangerously so, are not, and I must do everything I can to see to it that my views prevail." Moreover, any uncorrupted person, an illiberal could go on to say, can see that or indeed any right-thinking person can see that. Such an extreme illiberal (and they are plentiful) will add: "Given those corrupt views of yours or patently false views of yours, there are no good reasons for being tolerant of you, except perhaps sometimes *tactical reasons* of expediency when the balance of forces outweigh us." Many of them will say (and differently for different illiberal views): "We cannot by any means respect or even tolerate Tutsis, Muslims, Jews, Hindus, Christians, Communists, Fascists, or atheists." Tolerance for illiberals has at best instrumental value and need not be rooted in respect for persons. They may even be so fanatical, as Nazi ideologues were, to believe that some life is unworthy of life. Here the liberal very well may feel with Wittgenstein that justification has come to an end and that his spade is turned. Our views of life and its worth, he may well feel, are so different from those of that collection of illiberals that nothing further can be said.

Other political liberals, John Dewey for example or myself, will think that inquiry and justification never come to a dead stop such that, even after a period of cooling off and reflection, nothing more can *possibly*, relevantly be said. Moreover, if that was so, we could not know that it is so, which is tantamount to saying it never comes to an end. Rorty will say, as I would as well, that whatever "answer" there is, if any, we can never escape fallibilism, perspectivism, historicism, and finitism. There are no giants or gods or an absolute perspective – some view from nowhere, some point of view of the universe. Whatever is said at a given time may be upset at a later time. There is no unconditional validity, no Archimedean point, and no ahistorical perch. There is no escaping perspectivism. (But is this not, however well-justified, to take what Rawls would regard as a metaphysical view? Do we need to do this to show the *coherence* of political liberalism? I think we do). Justification is time-dependent though truth is not. But there is no attaining truth, as distinct from something tentative and time-dependent like warranted assertability, let alone *The Truth*, whatever (if anything) that means. We can only gain, with luck and careful reasoning, warranted assertability for a particular time and place. But we can sometimes get that and that is not without significance. And that is something that we can reasonably commit ourselves to.

Justifications of truth-claims arising from our various inquiries may appear to be, and perhaps actually are, more adequately justified than the ones that came before them or some other purported justifications that are contemporaneous with them. But convergence here is neither inevitable nor assured beyond reasonable doubt. The most we can hope for is the best-justified belief we can get, for the time being. But that, to repeat, is always time- and place-dependent. There is no *history transcendent viewpoint* where we just have the truth or something that is warrantedly assertable *period*.

Many, perhaps most, political liberals will take this to heart and draw the consequences in a way people holding illiberal viewpoints generally do not. Many political liberals may come to see that there is no escaping perspectivism and with it a historicism, finitism, and fallibilism – Hume's mitigated skepticism, if you will. Many political liberals may come with that understanding to see – though some may continue to think this is a bit too extreme – that though we can have reasons for what we do or think they can never be more than historicist/fallibilist reasons. This, of course, is a contestable and contested philosophical position that Rawls, given his own methodological commitments, must bracket as he also must bracket asserting the opposite. They are both what he calls metaphysical views.

Such a historicism shows its head in claims concerning how to argue (if political liberals choose to do so) about the relative merits of political liberalism vis-à-vis the range of illiberal or non-liberal views. We cannot escape assuming this *or* some other contestable philosophical position in arguing with this assortment of illiberals. But Rawls resolutely refuses to take any such argumentative route. But to take such a controversial argumentative route, as Rorty does or I do, in trying to answer the questions concerning how to answer the likes of a Carl Schmitt, does not conflict with Rawls's avoidance of metaphysics (for him, remember, any controversial philosophical view). It is just (to repeat) that they are different things – indeed different things that a consistent political liberal may legitimately do – with different rationales for different purposes. Rawls tries to justify political liberalism *internally* by showing how it can be a consistently, perspicuously, and attractively arranged position without departing from the considered convictions that all political liberals could accept. His aim is to show how political liberalism can be rendered consistent and coherent. I seek in addition to defend it in competition with and from challenges from various illiberal views and particularly from the strongest ones that can be mustered.

It is important to recognize that in both Rawls-type arguments and in Rorty-type arguments for political liberalism "WRE is employed" and "its *core* is the same thing." It is the same procedure. It functions with deeply embedded beliefs and considered judgments at all levels (particularly those most characteristic of the background culture of political liberalism). In doing so, it attempts to forge a consistent and coherent *(perhaps* this comes to the same thing) set of beliefs into a coherent and perspicuously displayed whole that will yield *both* an explanation and a justification of the relevant phenomena. Yet some WREs, while in that respect the same, will be different in having different objectives, sometimes using *partially* different considered judgments and beliefs as "raw material." They will use the same procedures but utilize some different beliefs in their different WREs. This even obtains concerning an attempt to justify political liberalism. Some, as I have said, seek an *internal* justification and some will seek an *external* one, and some, as I do, (perfectly consistently) will seek both. (Those who seek *external* justification will presuppose political liberalism's *internal* coherence.) The considered judgments to be forged into a coherent whole will, in some significant instances, be different depending on which type of justification is at issue. In a Rawls-type justification of political liberalism, all the considered judgments placed in WRE must be philosophically (in his sense metaphysically) neutral and must be acceptable to all those who partake of the *ethos* of political liberalism. Remember this type of justification is an *internal* one attempting to show how political liberalism can be shown to form a consistent, coherent, and attractive whole. The Rorty-type justification will also collect together all the same type of considered judgments but will as well have contested-type philosophical claims to be fitted together with the non-contested considered judgments in that WRE. Those contested philosophical principles are those it is necessary to deploy to relevantly respond to various illiberal or non-liberal claims so as not to just beg the question with them. But both have WRE arguments utilizing a common method. It should also be noted that the various illiberal or non-liberal positions could themselves deploy at least some narrow reflective equilibrium in a consistent way. For them, however, the move to WRE is more problematic. Some such illiberal or non-liberal peoples living under conditions of modernity will have a number of what they regard as well-established theoretical and empirical beliefs and other empirical claims that they would at best have a hard time consistently accommodating in their WRE.[17] This will not be true, or at least less likely to be true, of political liberals. But, ignoring such modernist and enlightenment claims, they *perhaps* could manage coherence as well as a political liberal could if such non-liberals *restrict* themselves to a *narrow* reflective equilibrium. With her WRE the political liberal could appeal to some often-mundane uncontroversial beliefs that illiberals and other non-liberals also accept. But there are beliefs in her WRE which are not compatible with other beliefs or considered judgments of such non-liberals while they are compatible with the full range of the political liberal's views.[18]

We should not forget, moreover, that the method of WRE was also used by Nelson Goodman in epistemology (or what was so labelled).[19] If we balk at such an "epistemology," regarding it as a non-subject, we can easily call it "theory of inquiry" or just plain "inquiry" instead.[20] It was also *in effect* used in the philosophy of science by Quine, and I have used it to attempt to show that at least theistic religions could not, under conditions of modernity, be brought into WRE, for too many theistic religious beliefs conflict with well-established scientific beliefs.[21] We moderns cannot get WRE here.[22] But for Jews, Christians, and Muslims living *in the Middle Ages*, their beliefs could perhaps have been forged into partially different, but not completely different, WREs for each with their distinctive ideas of redemption. Something like this also *may* even be true for isolated and marginalized groups in our time such as the Amish and Hutterites.

However, the general point is that WRE could, and perhaps should, be used for the full range of belief-systems or forms of life or conceptions of things from philosophy of mathematics to thinking about science, religion, morality, politics, and law, to society more generally, to aesthetics. The same core coherentist method – a distinctive procedure – would be applied in all domains. Sometimes what are appealed to are considered judgments, sometimes mathematical truisms, sometimes widely acknowledged empirical data and well-established hypotheses, and, for some peoples in some situations, religious beliefs and doctrines and their associated considered judgments, and sometimes a mix of some of these things. Sometimes WRE seeks only explanation or only justification and sometimes both. But always there is a similar procedure. But to return to Rawls's, Rorty's, and my dispute about political liberalism, there is a difference between some of the sorts of reasons that get appealed to, but there is no conflict between them, *given they have different ends in view*, concerning the justification of political liberalism. Moreover, they all utilize the same core method of WRE. I can consistently have my Rorty and Rawls too.

IV

In the above I have used "reasonable," as does Rawls, Scanlon and Barry, lavishly, *perhaps* too lavishly. I, like Rawls, do not assume or think "the reasonable" can be derived from "the rational" (let alone be identified with it) or that "the rational" is a more basic concept that we need to make sense of "the reasonable." Both concepts are essential in social life or indeed life period. But they have different uses.

I want now to explore a bit of Rawls's use of "the reasonable" for I think it is important not only for its own sake but for understanding what is at issue between Boran and myself. In doing so, I shall bring out an important but neglected aspect of Rawls's thought that helps, if thought through, to further my case that we can and should deploy a case for political liberalism along Rortyian lines in one context as well as to hold steady Rawls's manner of arguing for it in another. Both contexts have their distinctive importance.

In elucidating what he means by "reasonable," Rawls does not "define the reasonable directly," but specifies "two of its basic aspects as *virtues of persons*"[23] [emphasis added]. The first "basic aspect of the reasonable … is the willingness to propose fair terms of cooperation and to abide by them provided others do."[24] Rawls makes it clear that he is not asking people to be suckers. The norms they propose they honestly must believe are "reasonable for everyone to accept and therefore are justifiable to them."[25] And they are prepared to reason with others about them. They are open to the various norms being so proposed and take it as something that must also be open to reasonable others. (Those who are not so open will not in that crucial sense count as "reasonable.") They must, as well, if they are reasonable, be prepared "to discuss the fair terms that others propose."[26] They have the idea that the reasonable is an element of the idea of society as a system of fair cooperation and that its fair terms must be those that are reasonable for all to accept and that they indeed generally will be accepted in liberal societies. This is a crucial part of our very idea of reciprocity.[27] If these conditions are violated, the practice of reasoning together reasonably is off. Someone committed to reasonableness should not make a sucker out of herself or just take the badgering of the unreasonable.

The second basic aspect of "the reasonable," and the most important aspect for the restrictions Rawls puts on the types of claims to be utilized in his distinctive defence of political liberalism, "is the willingness to recognize the burdens of judgment and to accept their consequences for the use of public reason in directing the legitimate exercise of political power in a constitutional regime."[28] We need to get clear about what Rawls calls the *burdens of judgment*, and why it is so important for him, including why it is so important in the rationalization of the limitations he puts on the kinds of arguments we can rightly deploy in arguing for the coherence and plausibility of political liberalism. As background to this, we need to note "two general facts about the public culture of a [democratic] constitutional regime: [regimes which prominently include a political liberalism. They are, first,] the fact of reasonable pluralism and [second,] the fact that this diversity can be overcome only by the oppressive use of state power."[29]

We need to ask why, if we just carefully, honestly, and persistently use with one another all our fair-mindedness, all our intelligence, and our good will, we will not invariably end up in reasonable agreement. Why is what Kierkegaard called Socratism, namely, the belief that all problems have a solution if we just reason about them hard enough and carefully enough, not true? Why are the rationalistic assumptions that motivated rationalist philosophers from Plato to Spinoza not achievable? Why is such reasonable argument among philosophers and other intellectuals so motivated, not something that will usually lead to agreement? Why is it that reasonable persons with integrity, intelligence, and good will still will find agreement often so illusive over the above matters and matters like them? Rawls's explanation of this is crucial for his treatment of political liberalism and for the justification of the restrictions that, as he has it, are to be made by liberals in political arguments of the sort in which he engages.

Reasonable persons, Rawls contends, are persons who have realized what he calls their two moral powers: namely, an understanding of and a capacity for justice, and an understanding of and a capacity to achieve their own rational good. With such a realization of their two moral powers, they, Rawls has it, are free and equal when they are in a constitutional regime and "have an enduring desire to honor fair terms of cooperation and to be fully cooperating members of society."[30] They share, according to Rawls, a common human reason. That is to say they have "similar powers of thought and judgment: they can draw inferences, weigh evidence and balance competing considerations."[31] Yet, try as they will, they often cannot reach agreement over ultimate or crucial matters. They have not been able to do it in the past, and there is precious little reason to believe they will be able to do it in the future.

It is here where Rawls's conception of the *burdens of judgment* comes into prominent play. We speak here of the sources and causes of disagreement between reasonable persons, namely persons who have the two aspects of the reasonable person as basic aspects of their virtue as persons. The account of these burdens must be such that they are fully compatible with, and so do not impugn, the reasonableness of those who disagree over such matters. They can and will often disagree, and continue to disagree, and still remain equally reasonable by Rawls's *minimal* characterization of being reasonable; any tighter standards of reasonability would violate their acting in accordance with the *burdens of judgment*.

What are these *burdens of judgment* and why are they regarded as so important by Rawls? The "sources of reasonable disagreement – the burdens of judgment – among reasonable persons are the many hazards involved in the correct (and conscientious) exercise of our powers of reason and judgment in the ordinary course of political life."[32] Rawls goes on to remark:

> As reasonable and rational we have to make different kinds of judgments. As rational we have to balance our various ends and estimate their appropriate place in our way of life; and doing this confronts us with grave difficulties in making correct judgments of rationality. On the other hand, as reasonable we must assess the strength of peoples' claims, not only against our claims, but against one another, or on our common practices and institutions, all this giving rise to difficulties in our making sound reasonable judgments. In addition, there is the reasonable as it applies to our beliefs and schemes of thought, or the reasonable as appraising our use of our theoretical (and not our moral and practical) powers, and here too we meet the corresponding kinds of difficulties.[33]

Rawls lists the more obvious of these sources of reasonable disagreement. They are all sources of difficulties in arriving at agreement in judgment and yet they are sources compatible with those judging being in Rawls's *minimal* sense fully reasonable. Disagreement in such contexts can, and typically will, be reasonable. They can indeed even be compatible with everyone's being *fully reasonable* in Rawls's minimal sense. The six sources listed by Rawls are as follows:

a. The evidence – empirical and scientific – bearing on the case is conflicting and complex, and thus hard to assess and evaluate.
b. Even where we agree fully about the kinds of considerations that are relevant, we may disagree about their weight, and so arrive at different judgments.
c. To some extent all our concepts, and not only moral and political concepts, are vague and subject to hard cases; and this indeterminacy means that we must rely on judgment and interpretation (and on judgments about interpretations) within some range (not sharply specifiable) where reasonable persons may differ.
d. To some extent (how great we cannot tell) the way we assess evidence and weigh moral and political values is shaped by our total experience, our whole course of life up to now; and our total experiences must always differ. Thus, in a modern society with its numerous offices and positions, its various divisions of labor, its many social groups and their ethnic variety, citizens' total experiences are disparate enough for their judgments to diverge, at least to some degree, on many if not most cases of any significant complexity.
e. Often there are different kinds of normative considerations of different force on both sides of an issue and it is difficult to make an overall assessment.
f. Finally, as we note in referring to Berlin's view, any system of social institutions is limited in the values it can admit so that some selection must be made from the full range of moral and political values that might be realized. This is because any system of institutions has, as it were, a limited social space. In being forced to select among cherished values, or when we hold to several and must restrict each in view of the requirements of the others, we face great difficulties in setting priorities and making adjustments. Many hard decisions may seem to have no clear answer.[34]

It is easy to see why, under such conditions, disagreement among reasonable people will obtain, and repeatedly obtain, and to see as well how reasonable people will often *agree to disagree*. As much as some of these matters over which they differ and agree to differ mean to them, they will be tolerant (hard as it may be sometimes) of even deeply different and sometimes antagonistic views. They will be tolerant where those holding such deeply divergent views from theirs will themselves be tolerant of other deeply divergent views including theirs. Rawls goes on to remark:

> Religious and philosophical doctrines express views of the world and of our life with one another, severally and collectively, as a whole. Our individual and associative points of view, intellectual affinities, and affective attachments, are too diverse, especially in a free society, to enable those doctrines to serve as the basis of lasting and reasoned political agreement. Different conceptions of the world can reasonably be elaborated from different standpoints and diversity arises in part from our distinct perspectives. It is unrealistic – or worse, it arouses mutual suspicion and hostility – to suppose that all our differences are rooted solely in ignorance and perversity, or else in the rivalries for power, status, or economic gain.[35]

It is an inescapable fact that many of our most important judgments are made under conditions where it is not to be expected that conscientious persons with full powers of reason, even after full and free discussion, will arrive at the same conclusion. Socratism or rationalism is simply not on the agenda. Some conflicting reasonable judgments (especially important are those belonging to people's comprehensive doctrines) "may be true, others false; conceivably, all may be false."[36] Indeed, I would add that some may arguably be incoherent. But there will be little agreement on which of these things is which. Rawls goes on to add the significant political liberal point that "these burdens of judgment are of first significance for a democratic idea of tolerance."[37]

Remember that Rawls takes as the second part of being reasonable "recognizing and being willing to bear the consequences of the burdens of judgment."[38] This is crucial for the way Rawls structures his conception of political liberalism and for the constraints required of political liberals over political matters. However, reasonable persons, if they affirm any at all, affirm only reasonable comprehensive doctrines. Reasonable comprehensive doctrines for Rawls have three main features. Firstly, as an exercise of theoretical reason, a reasonable doctrine "organizes and characterizes recognized values so they are compatible with one another and express an intelligible view of the world."[39] Secondly, they also single out, each in its own way, which values are "to count as especially significant and how to balance them when they conflict."[40] In this way there is also an exercise of practical reason. Thirdly, a reasonable comprehensive doctrine "normally belongs to, or draws upon, a tradition of thought and doctrine," though from this it does not follow that it is fixed and unchanging.[41] Traditions, we need to remind ourselves, normally change. And arguably they not only change, but also evolve and do not change arbitrarily and without explanation.[42] Doctrines with these three features are present in "the major religious, philosophical, and moral aspects of human life in a more or less consistent and coherent manner."[43]

Rawls is centrally concerned with not excluding doctrines except where they are clearly incompatible with his *minimal* concept of "the reasonable" itself. "We," he puts it, "avoid excluding doctrines as unreasonable without strong grounds based on clear aspects of the reasonable itself."[44] The thing is to bend over backwards to avoid being arbitrary and exclusive and, above all, to avoid being partisan.

He then makes a set of remarks, including a crucial but little noticed remark in footnote 13 of page 60 in his *Political Liberalism*,[45] that is crucial for the case I have been trying to make about the compatibility of Rortyian-reasons and Rawlsian-reasons. In the passage with which I am principally concerned, Rawls remarks in the body of his text, "Political liberalism counts many familiar and traditional doctrines – religious, philosophical, and moral – as reasonable *even though we could not seriously entertain them for ourselves*, as we think they give excessive weight to some values and fail to allow for the significance of others. A *tighter* criterion is not, however, needed *for the purposes of political liberalism*"[46] [emphasis added]. This passage then refers us to footnote 13:

> Certainly, comprehensive doctrines will themselves, as they present their case in the background culture, urge far tighter standards of reasonableness and truth. Within that culture

[which is not a part of public reason] we may regard many doctrines as plainly unreasonable, or untrue, that we think it correct to count as reasonable by the criterion in the text. That criterion we should see as giving rather minimal conditions appropriate for the aims of political liberalism.[47]

And we should recall that the aims are certain distinctive political aims, and these aims are to articulate a coherent conception of political liberalism that all reasonable *political liberals* – reasonable in the minimal sense that Rawls deploys for these purposes – can agree on even where they are holders of very diverse comprehensive doctrines or no comprehensive doctrines at all. Yet they must be views that by Rawls's minimal criterion of reasonability count as reasonable. No stricter criterion can justifiably be invoked for this purpose. This is all we can expect or indeed have and all we need to attain political *agreement* among political liberals in our present-day intractably pluralist societies. But this is sufficient – or so Rawls argues – to attain civility and political justice: deeply *democratic* political justice in our societies. And this is his aim, and, keeping firmly to it, he sticks with playing that language-game, adhering to the cluster of practices we have characterized him as playing. But these are not the only aims, the only language-games, that political liberals can play and play in the service of political liberalism. *Sometimes* in some situations it is important, in politically arguing, and indeed politically arguing about justice, to deploy a stricter criterion of reasonability for political justice.

I am thinking here of places where we could and should use tighter standards than those we employ in the political contexts Rawls is discussing for the internal justification of political liberalism. I conjecture that in his footnote 13 he was thinking of discussions in seminars, first-class media contexts, intellectual debates in various public but non-state contexts and in private discussions. In all of these contexts, there is no question of parliamentary, legal, or other governmental decisions being taken. They can, of course, influence these decisions, but they are not part of the deliberative process where such decisions are made. Where such political decisions are at issue, at least in most such contexts, I think it is obvious that in a liberal society or indeed in any decent complex society that Rawls's minimal criterion of reasonability should be adhered to. However, there are other public discussions and debates, such as those mentioned above, that are designed to enlighten and not *directly* to lead to governmental or otherwise practical decisions either challenging or supporting the government. I think these public discussions should use a tighter criterion of reasonability. I shall argue that there are contexts, indeed political contexts, in which tighter standards of reasonability in discussions or debates are in order. These might very well include writings, discussions, debates that have an indirect effect, and indeed sometimes a relevant effect, on decisions taken in Parliament and the like. However, when a vote is to be taken and the debate is in Parliament then Rawls's *minimal* criterion must – morally speaking "must" – rule the day. The same is so for court decisions or state executive decisions. But in discussions, writings, debates *leading up to* the debate *before* the discussion and voting in Parliament, tighter criteria than what Rawls uses for political liberalism are often to be used. However, in the context of the actual debate in Parliament concerning what governmental decision to make, the minimal criterion of reasonability must prevail, along with public reason. This should be partly definitive of what is to count as being a politically liberal society. Discussions in a seminar are one thing and debates in Parliament are another. The former should use a tighter criterion of reasonability than the latter.

To illustrate the rationale for what I have been claiming, we might consider the proposal to make same-sex marriage part of the law of the land – a debate we have actually had in Canada in 2005 and South Africans had in their country in 2006. But it could as well have been about abortion, drugs, contraception, and in times past (or in places like Chile, time present) divorce. But debates about same-sex marriage are current, often heated, and taking place not only in Canada and South Africa but also in other liberal democracies. I shall use same-sex marriage as an example to make my point concerning when for political liberalism a minimal criterion/criteria of being reasonable must be employed and when it should not, or at least need not.

Suppose a parliamentarian speaking in Parliament in such a debate gets utterly out of line and says, "We can by no means accept such gay and lesbian cohabitation as marriage, no matter how long and steady their relations have been, for homosexuality is a disgusting, loathsome, and sinful practice that can by no means be tolerated (not to speak of its being sanctified by marriage). Homosexuals should be imprisoned or, if we can bring back the death penalty, executed. Burning lesbians at the stake, though utopian, would not be inappropriate." His or her remarks – remember such a person is speaking in Parliament – should be firmly reproved and simply ignored in the subsequent debate in Parliament. But his or her basic point could be put in a milder form. It is, after all, a hyped-up expression of what by Rawls's own account, using his minimal criterion of "the reasonable," is a reasonable comprehensive view of the good even in present-day politically liberal societies. And remember Rawls reminds us that "in a particular case someone may, of course, affirm a reasonable doctrine in an unreasonable way.... That does not make the doctrine as such unreasonable. A reasonable doctrine is one that can be affirmed in a reasonable way."[48] Suppose another member of Parliament [MP] with the same general views (homosexuality is against God's law) rises in Parliament to say that, though his colleague's expression was, to put it mildly, explosive and to many deeply offensive, still, after all, homosexuality is a sin against God's law and should not be acknowledged as something morally acceptable, let alone sanctified by something that the law being voted on here would, if passed, publicly acknowledge, at least from a legal perspective, homosexuality as being morally acceptable. His view, expressed in that way, is a view that by Rawls's minimal criterion would be regarded as part of what counts as a reasonable comprehensive view.[49] Yet it would carry no weight with most liberals. It would be regarded by many, perhaps most, people as an absurd and rather antique view that we would be well to be without; in so reasoning they are at least implicitly using a stricter criterion of reasonability. But the second parliamentarian's claim expressed as he put it could legitimately be entered into the parliamentary debate using the minimal criterion. Though his claim would have little weight with his more secular-minded colleagues in debate over the proposed law, it still should in turn be pointed out that it is not just a matter of a group of more or less secularly minded political liberals ganging up on certain religious people; for the proposed law, if passed, would plainly not force such a religious person or his church to accept, let alone practice, gay or lesbian marriage. "It's the law of the land," they must acknowledge (if the bill is passed), but they need not (and this is, of course, compatible with the proposed law) become gays or lesbians or accept them in their religious community and their clergy need not marry them. To argue, as some might, that they must, if requested, marry them would violate the conception of tolerance and respect for persons which Rawls and which liberals generally regard as central to liberalism. Moreover, such antique views expressed in the way the second orthodox religious MP expressed them should be allowed into the debate. But in a liberal ethos they would have little influence in parliamentary debate. Moreover, the MP and people with his mindset should be reminded that no one is being required or urged to be gay or lesbian, no one in his congregation is being required to perform such marriages, gays and lesbians could even be expelled – or excommunicated – from the church of which he/she is a member and "true believers" could shun their company. But, as the argument goes, the legal right to marry should be extended to such persons, and they should also have the right to the same public presence as other people, e.g., to teach, to practice medicine, to run for office, to themselves perform marriages if they are (as they can be) in a legal position to do so and the like.

Such a religious person may shun them, it is sad to contemplate, but they may not be *publicly* shunned: their legal, political, and social status should remain the same as that of others. There is no possibility of that *not* being so in a genuinely liberal democracy. (Indeed this is a matter of definition.) Moreover, there are many things we have a moral right to do – such as shunning them – that we should not do. So nothing is being forced on the person with such conservative religious views except to accept, should the legislation be passed, the equal legal, political, and social status of persons he disapproves of because of their particular views concerning homosexuality and because of their own sexual orientation. Persons who have not committed any crime in what is acknowledged as such by law in the liberal society of which he or she is a member cannot be persecuted or legally discriminated against for having the sexual orientation they have.

To the response that homosexuality *should* be made a crime, the reply is that it is not a crime, at least in liberal societies. And in societies such as ours there is certainly no consensus on whether it should be made a crime, and to make it a crime, in any society, would show contempt, or at least a lack of respect, for people with a certain sexual orientation and thus violate one of the deepest commitments of political liberalism, namely respect for persons (all persons) where they have done nothing to harm others. A political liberal could not vote that it be made a crime and still remain a political liberal anymore than she could accept apartheid and be a political liberal.

Here, it *might* be argued, we have considerations which must be backed up with tighter standards of reasonability than Rawls wishes to deploy for his internal arguments for political liberalism. But it should in turn be replied that his minimal standards are sufficient for such an argument. They are considerations that all liberals can rightly acknowledge in the face of what actually comes to, even when not so intended, an illiberal assault on liberalism.

Political liberals are in all sorts of situations, where they have different ends in view than Rawls's, where they can make non-question-begging arguments in response to illiberal alternatives to liberalism of an extensive range of topics, e.g., ethnic nationalist or authoritarian assaults. There is no place, in the face of such critiques, where we must say that nothing further can be relevantly said and that our spades are turned and that is that. However, in spite of what I said above, it looks like there are places – emotionally charged places such as gay marriage and abortion – where *perhaps* political liberals cannot, when pushed, proceed just in terms of Rawls's minimal account of reasonability but must appeal to tighter standards. This seems to be so even in parliamentary debate where public reason should rule the day and even more obviously so in the public forum of civil society in arguing the case for legalizing gay marriage. Arguably, there is over such issues sometimes, perhaps even often, a need to appeal to a tighter criterion.

I want to argue now that this is not so evident as it might at first seem. Let us go back to our moderate, mild-mannered, perhaps just small-conservative parliamentarian. He reminds us that homosexuality is a sin. However, becoming more conciliatory, he reminds us (and more appropriately) that it is so regarded in his church; a church which has many members, some of whom regard themselves as political liberals. Suppose in parliamentary debate a secular-minded Bertrand Russell-admiring MP, following Russell, remarks that "sin" is not a term that is a part of his vocabulary or conceptual scheme. The mild-mannered conservative retorts that for many sincere, conscientious, and sometimes even reflective religious believers, "sin" is very much a part of their vocabulary; and there are even certain denominations – Catholic, some Protestant, some Jewish and Muslim – that regard homosexuality as a sin; and for some denominations their adherents must believe it to be a sin on pain of apostasy. (Of course, for the Russellian MP, "apostasy" will also not be a part of his vocabulary.) To the question "Why it is sinful?", the mild-mannered but orthodox believer will retort that it harms people and rends the fabric of society by making life unstable, undermining the family and family values.

The debate, if not in the Parliament then at least in the parliamentary restaurant, will go on probably in predictable ways. The defender of the acceptability of homosexuality and of the proposed law that gays and lesbians be given same-sex marriage rights will argue that homosexuality does not harm people or at least that there is no good evidence that it does, but what *clearly* does harm people is discrimination, non-recognition, exclusion, and not to be afforded equal citizenship rights or human rights. This in turn will generate the response that it does harm people in other ways. It impedes their psycho-sexual development, for instance. Instead of going for treatment, homosexuals, being accepted in society, may even come to be role models for some. Some children, finding them as role models, may have their psycho-sexual development impeded. The moderately orthodox religious MP, if he is reasonably knowledgeable, may point out that even *some* psychoanalysts, heirs (among other things) of Freud's firm atheism, think that homosexuality is harmful, making it impossible for homosexuals to have a "genital personality" and thus making it impossible for them to become mature, or at least optimally mature, persons.

Most secularly minded persons (and indeed *some* religious persons) will think this all nonsense and indeed harmful nonsense. However, mindful of the burdens of judgment, our Russellian MP might say to his mildly orthodox conservative colleague, "Look you and I are not going to agree about homosexuality, and, most particularly, about whether it is a good thing that the institution of marriage be extended to homosexuals, but we do agree about the deep democratic and liberal value of people being treated with equal respect. That is a deeply shared element in our common liberal view. Just as blacks and whites were not treated with equal respect under apartheid or Jewish and Arab-Israeli citizens are not being treated with equal respect in Israel, so homosexuals and bi-sexual citizens in our society are not treated with equal respect and do not, where the proposed law is not passed, even have equal rights. And you and I as democrats and political liberals cannot accept that." The moderate conservative liberal-leaning MP may rather reluctantly come to accept that argument just as some liberal Catholics have so reacted to the abortion debate. And, if that is so, debate can be conducted and settled in terms of Rawlsian minimalism, WRE, and an appeal to public reason.

However, faced with the above argument, the conservative, but still politically liberal, believer, may stiffen his back and respond, "As much as I care about equal respect for people and equal citizenship rights and liberal democracy, I will not – indeed morally speaking I cannot – set aside or go against the *ex cathedra* proclamation of my church, now frozen into doctrine, namely that homosexuality is a sin, anathema to my faith, which requires that homosexuality, a grave sin, must be categorically rejected and never sanctified legally or otherwise. I agree that that doctrine does undermine equal self-respect and equal citizenship. That deeply distresses me. But the Pontiff speaking *ex cathedra* condemns homosexuality and gay marriage categorically. I *must* believe as a Catholic that what is so proclaimed is absolutely true and categorically must be accepted and must be acted in accordance with. I cannot keep my faith and reject that. And my faith is of overwhelming importance to me. My spade is turned. I can do no other." The Russellian MP may feel that his spade is turned too. He may very well feel that there is no more room for further argument and discussion. But he can also see that the conservative MP is acting in good faith and is, by Rawls's minimal criterion of reasonability, being reasonable.

If dialogue is to go on – if they are to get their spades out of the ground – it *seems* at least that they can no longer rely just on Rawlsian reasons, which travel philosophically light. They have to turn to considering challengeable and deeply challenged world-views. But in a stronger sense of "reasonable" these things can and should be argued. However, perhaps surprisingly and perhaps counter-intuitively, I shall argue that this is not so. I do not deny that, in a stronger sense of "reasonable," these things can be argued. What I deny is that, *for political and legal purposes* in a politically liberal society, they need to be and should be so argued. We can and should stick with our minimal criterion of "reasonable." Am I just stamping my feet?

However, there remain two considerations that should be faced. The first one fits with the overall argument I have been trying to make and the second one ends in a jarring note that I take to raise important considerations to which I do not yet (perhaps I never will) know how to respond. The first consideration claims that the moderate but orthodox believer, wishing to be a political liberal, cannot be one, or at least cannot be a consistent one, if he takes the turn I have just put in his mouth. However, he cannot, it is being claimed, consistently be a political liberal and have the faith he has. He must choose to be consistent. As important as liberal values are to him, he (given his faith) is committed and believes he must remain committed to allowing *ex cathedra* religious doctrines to override his politically liberal beliefs where they conflict. He, that is, abandons his political liberalism where it comes (as it sometimes does) into conflict with such doctrines of his faith. He cannot be a consistent political liberal and have the faith he has. However, this is not true if he accepts, within the bounds of political liberalism, a democratic vote to be overriding even when it runs against what his faith deeply commits him to do. His so acting democratically (accepting the vote) does not require him personally to approve of gay marriage or to go against anything that the Pope says when he is speaking *ex cathedra*. Rather, he is free to accept the vote, in a politically liberal parliament, while remaining free to continue to dissent. He continues to think the Parliament has made a grave mistake. But he finally bows, as all democrats must, to the will of the majority where a clear violation of human rights is not at issue.[50] But he keeps faithful to his own conscience and his own personal way of viewing things and responding to them, e.g., a Catholic priest will not marry gays but accepts, if so goes the vote, that it is the legitimate law of the land and that others may do so. (Is this to say, when push comes to shove, democracy is to outweigh any religious orientation? For a liberal, yes. Is this just stamping one's feet for liberalism?)

The second observation is the more glaring and jarring one, given my account. Suppose a religious person (while remaining devoutly religious) accepts certain key political matters (e.g., same-sex marriage) as valid legislation when it gets a majority vote in the legislature. She accepts this, let us further suppose, as trumping *in that domain* whatever her faith categorically commits her to. Can, given her faith, she consistently do so? I have come rather ambivalently to think so. Even if she can consistently do so, however, will it not then be the case – indeed *can it not but be the case* – that in a deeply pluralistic, modern, extensively secular liberal society, with its embedded political liberalism, that religious views, where they sit uneasily with the orientation of such a society (as they do), will be marginalized? (Note that to be marginalized is not to be excluded.)

Central as such religious convictions are for the faithful to such a religious orientation and no matter how much they are a part of the web of (politically speaking) the lives of these religious persons, they will have to be trumped in a politically liberal society, and indeed inescapably, where they conflict with what is central to political liberalism and entail a policy (as they do) which is in deep conflict with it. This is indeed crucial for political liberalism. But is this not, when all is said and done, if that ever is so, to just *insist* on political liberalism – a kind of stamping one's feet – and is not that itself *not* to show respect for such religious persons? *Maybe* things are more complicated than I have made them out to be? Or than Rawls takes them to be? And does this not make difficulties in WRE when it is taken as a method for rationalizing political liberalism?

Maybe we need *some* foundational beliefs? And indeed, where there is more than one, for them to be hierarchically or lexically ordered. But can that be compatible with a genuinely political liberal view or with modernity? Or even with careful philosophical thought? Is it to ignore what we have learned from Wittgenstein, Neurath, Quine, Sellars, Davidson, Kuhn, Rorty, Brandom, and Michael Williams? What to say here is not obvious to me. *Perhaps* we should stick with a consistent fallibilism and acknowledge that even respect for persons, as morally central as it is for us, should not *always* be the overriding value, as *no value* should have such a status? Sometimes respect for a person or persons A conflicts with respect for a person or persons B. Or so at least it seems? This being so, we must look elsewhere for what is to guide us in such a situation. But even this is not evident. We must take to heart the lesson that we never get unconditionality and that over matters, such as discussed above, it is seldom, if ever, that we even get decisiveness. Even, unpalatable as this sounds, respect for persons is sometimes up for grabs. We see that even here we do not get unconditionality – no place where we must stop, where there is something which we *categorically* must do. This is hard for us to accept – almost humanly impossible for us to accept. Yet is this not what, if we can hold on to our brains, we must conclude? Rationalism as well as traces of religiosity dies hard with us. And there is no "Big Daddy" up there in the sky to save us. We can accept this and still ask what we are to do as believers in equal self-respect for everyone, where respect for A conflicts with respect for B and the conflict is ineradicable. But again, is this ever actually the case? I don't know. But, *if it is*, what should be done? Or are we, in typical philosophical fashion, making up artificial puzzles for ourselves?

To sum up, Rawls and Rorty both are, and I am as well, concerned to defend political liberalism and, in doing so, to deploy WRE.[51] All three of us think that, in engaging in that task, we should set aside metaphysical, epistemological theories and any attachment, at least where political liberalism is at issue, to any particular comprehensive theory of the good. We want in that respect to travel philosophically light. In employing WRE, all three of us consistently stick with its basic procedures. We sometimes in defending political liberalism appeal to different substantive considerations – different reasons – in equilibrating and we have partially different aims in defending it. These reasons are thought not only to be different but some think they are conflicting. This I argue is mistaken because our different WREs are constructed for different purposes. Rawls seeks to give an *internal* justification for political liberalism by showing how its considered convictions and beliefs consistently and coherently (if this does not come to the same thing) hang together. Rorty and I seek that too. But we also seek to give an *external* justification for political liberalism by giving reasons that challenge the counter-claims of illiberal (as well as other non-liberal political accounts) and, as well, give additional reasons other than those showing consistency and coherency for political liberalism that challenge non-liberal views. Rawls shows how political liberalism, which has often been thought to involve conflicting claims, can be articulated in such a manner as to show that it is a coherent and attractive view that can make sense of the most fundamental considered convictions of political liberals as well as many others. It can be set out without conflicting views. He does not try to show how those non-liberal considered convictions that conflict with those politically liberal considered convictions – substantive and not purely procedural convictions – can be responded to by political liberals other than by being ignored. Both Rorty and I argue that it is important to show the superiority of political liberalism to illiberal and other non-liberal views and how we can use WRE to do so in a way that is different from, though non-conflicting with, Rawls's position. Rawls, in short, gives an internal justification of political liberalism while Rorty and I give as well an external justification of political liberalism. Both are legitimate even if different activities. But neither is sufficient without the other for a thorough defence of political liberalism.

Notes

1. Lister, "Wide Reflective Equilibrium" (Nielsen quotes from an earlier, unpublished version of the paper); and Boran, "Are Some Sailors on Neurath's Ship Moral Philosophers?" 261. See also Nielsen's response in *Reason and Emancipation*.
2. Nielsen, "Philosophy as Wide Reflective Equilibrium," 127.
3. Lister, "Wide Reflective Equilibrium."
4. Ibid.
5. Rawls, "Justice as Fairness: Political not Metaphysical," 251.
6. In speaking of 'varied uses of WRE' I mean that this procedure can be deployed for different ends or purposes. It can be used in science, logic, metaethics, epistemology, aesthetics, and even metaphysics, as well as politics, and moral philosophy. It tries to get in these different domains, and articulated in a coherent way, a coherent account in which their various most firmly held beliefs (and in some cases convictions) are shown to fit together consistently and coherently. Where (if at all) a political system (conservatism, political liberalism, a hierarchical corporatism, socialism, communism, fascism) can make a claim to justification, the judgments that for it are its considered beliefs or (in some cases) considered convictions must be forgeable into a consistent and coherent set or whole. This is a necessary but not a sufficient condition for an adequate justification. The considered judgments that get equilibrated must also be thought to have some initial credibility by the people who accept that belief system. And indeed they must have some *initial* credibility, at least for them. Many philosophers (as well as others) will want more. But it is, I believe, an illusion to think that they can get more.
7. Daniels, "Democratic Equality," 241; Dreben, "On Rawls and Political Liberalism," 316; and Scanlon, "Rawls on Justification," 139.
8. Rawls remarks in the preface to the French translation of *A Theory of Justice* that what he calls "justice as fairness" and calls a liberal view would in Europe be called "social democratic, and in some ways as labor." Rawls, "Preface for the French Edition of *A Theory of Justice*," In Rawls, *Collected Papers*, 415–16.
9. Justice as fairness is one member, perhaps the most prominent member, of a family of liberal (social democratic) conceptions of justice. Rawls, "The Idea of Public Reason Revisited,"581.
10. Dreben, "On Rawls and Political Liberalism."
11. Rawls, *A Theory of Justice*, 506–14.
12. 'Anti-Philosophy philosophy' will sound wilfully paradoxical without

some explanation. It rests on a distinction Rorty draws in his book: *Consequences of Pragmatism*, xiv–xix. Rorty writes, "'philosophy' like 'truth' and 'goodness' is ambiguous." A little 'p' 'philosophy' can mean simply what Wilfrid Sellars calls "an attempt to see how things, in the broadest sense of the term, hang together in the broadest sense of the term." Here talk of 'philosophy' is at least reasonably unproblematic and many people – George Elliot or Thomas Hardy, for example – who are normally not thought of as philosophers are in that sense philosophers, and sometimes much more so than some of the professionals. Philosophy (with a big P) denotes something more special such as the metaphysical and epistemological activity characteristic of Plato and Kant as well as their contemporary heirs, such as Kripke and David Lewis. This Rorty regards as a very dubious activity, indeed up for Wittgensteinian dissolution. But whether that is so or not, it remains important to distinguish philosophy and Philosophy. One might be for the former without being for the latter, and if anti-Philosophy philosophy is on the mark, as both Rorty and I think it is, then one should be for undermining Philosophy and for practising philosophy. Wittgenstein to my mind – though he certainly would not say anything so crude – is the best example we have of an 'anti-Philosophy philosopher.' See Nielsen, "Anti-Philosophy philosophy," 149; and Nielsen, *Naturalism without Foundations*, 200–201, n. 1.

13 Dewey, *Human Nature and Conduct*, 223–37.

14 Rorty, *Objectivity, Relativism and Truth*, 175–96.

15 Ibid.

16 Lukács, *History and Class Consciousness*.

17 Nielsen, *Naturalism without Foundations*, 79–155.

18 Ibid.

19 Goodman, *Fact, Fiction, and Forecast*, 65–68.

20 Nevo, "Reflective Equilibrium and the Contemplative Ideal of Knowledge"; Rorty, *Philosophy and the Mirror of Nature*; Nielsen, *After the Demise of the Tradition*, 39–90; and Nielsen, *On Transforming Philosophy*, 85–192.

21 Quine and J.S. Ullian, *The Web of Belief*.

22 Nielsen, *Naturalism without Foundations*, 79–113.

23 Rawls, *Political Liberalism*, 48.

24 Ibid., 54.

25 Ibid., 49.

26 Ibid.

27 Ibid., 49–50.

28 Ibid., 54.

29 Ibid.

30 Ibid., 55.

31 Ibid.

32 Ibid., 55–56.

33 Ibid., 56.

34 Ibid., 56–57.

35 Ibid., 58.

36 Ibid.

37 Ibid.

38 Ibid., 58–59.

39 Ibid., 59.

40 Ibid.

41 Ibid.

42 MacIntyre, *Three Rival Versions of Moral Inquiry*.

43 Rawls, *Political Liberalism*, 59.

44 Ibid.

45 Ibid., 60, n. 13.

46 Ibid., 59–60.

47 Ibid., 60.

48 Ibid., 60, n. 14.

49 Rawls, "The Idea of Public Reason Revisited," 574–615. Boran ignores this distinction between Philosophy and philosophy. See Boran, "Are Some Sailors on Neurath's Boat Moral Philosophers?" But I (*pace* her understanding of me) argue for an anti-Philosophy philosophy. See Nielsen, "Anti-Philosophy philosophy." I eschew Philosophy (metaphysics, epistemology, metaethical theories, normative ethical theories, and normative political theories) not philosophy with its reflective and critical activity, not, as Boran puts it, by saying: "that philosophical reflection should be abandoned in order to be replaced by practically viable forms of thinking." See Boran, "Are Some Sailors on Neurath's Boat Moral Philosophers?" 269. Surely Sellars' conception of philosophy endorses a thorough reflective orientation. What Boran calls normative naturalism is much the same, if not identical with, what I have called social naturalism. Nielsen, *Naturalism*, 25–55. Neither of these doctrines is metaphysical nor, I would argue, make epistemological claims. In that way they remain deeply anti-Philosophical while still being philosophical. Boran is right in saying that WRE is a procedure that is not without an appeal to substantive matters. After all, as Rawls uses it, and as I do, it collects together and utilizes considered judgments. They are matters that are surely substantive. Rawls is insightful here in his reply to Habermas. See Rawls, *Political Liberalism*, 421–33.

50 The politically liberal conservative might respond that such a vote violates human rights. Political liberals, he might continue, can no more make that a 'vote issue' than they can make genocide or slavery a 'vote issue.' Not everything is a vote issue where we (if we are democrats) must bow to the will of the majority. We, while remaining democrats, cannot vote on genocide or anything that violates what is plainly a core human right. But gay marriage is not a matter of human rights. Gay marriage is within the bounds of political liberalism while genocide is not. But *suppose* the Pope, speaking *ex cathedra*, says that gay marriage is a violation of human rights. Does this make it so? Must our conservative political liberal then accept that? Can the Pope, speaking *ex cathedra*, say that $2 + 2 = 5$? Must the conservative political liberal so crucify his intellect if the Pope proclaims that *ex cathedra*? Perhaps he must?

51 I should add parenthetically, so as not to confuse people who know my work, though I will not try to explain it here, that this is perfectly compatible with my socialism. I have at times, somewhat paradoxically, but as I see it perfectly consistently, characterized myself as 'a liberal communist.'

4

The Global Crisis of Values: The Poverty of Moral Philosophy

> [It] takes a lot of things to change the world:
> Anger and Tenacity. Science and indignation,
> The quick initiative, the long reflection,
> The cold patience and infinite perseverance,
> The understanding of the particular case and the
> Understanding of the ensemble;
> Only the lessons of reality can teach us to transform reality.
>
> Bertolt Brecht, *Einverständnis*

INTRODUCTION

We should not think of our contemporary crisis – better, crises – in and of the global, moral, political, and economic order as unique to us, i.e., we present-day human beings. It is not. Crises have always been with us, though the plague waxes and wanes. That said, we also should realize that we are now globally – as it was for a good part of Europe during the Thirty Years War – in a very waxing time. The advent of capitalist globalization, our plundering of the planet, our rapacious consumerism, abetted by our technological capacities to fuel it, has produced, to not put too fine a point on it, a world of degrading and cumulating horror. The pigsty that is now our world very much needs as proper an understanding as we can muster and, equipped with that, a deep transformation. (I do not mean to suggest that

75

we can finish off the first task and then take up the other. From very early on, there should be a shuttling back and forth between the two with what John Dewey would call an experimental attitude.) Don't misunderstand me: I am not defending an atavistic, reactionary attempt in the style of Solzhenitsyn or Heidegger to return to, or, at least, to develop nostalgia for, the past – "a past" – that cannot be replicated or approximated now (if, indeed, that is desirable) and one that perhaps never was. My *general* orientation (though I have a much more analytical way of articulating it) is more in accord with a Marxian orientation with a whiff of Michael Bakunin and something from classical critical theory, principally from Max Horkheimer and Herbert Marcuse.[1] I specify in the body of this text some of the massive but not arcane problems that will correctly be seen as urgent for us if we can come to see our world at all clearly and take what we see to heart. For we inhabitants of a globe that we collectively inhabit (some may say that we in some way own) readily discover to our dismay that our fundamental normative moral-cum-political-cum-economic problems are largely ignored by philosophers and, more importantly and alarmingly, by governments or, where they do respond to them at all, they respond superficially and inadequately. If our governments were individuals we would say they were in a state of psychological denial.

I specify briefly in Section I my core thesis vis-à-vis what I call and contend is the poverty of moral philosophy. It consists in extensively ignoring what I shall specify as the global crisis of values. I then in Section II characterize a key selection of urgent issues for humankind that philosophy has little to say about. I go on to argue, starting in Section III, that these problems, largely ignored by moral and social philosophy and, indeed, philosophy more generally, are problems that philosophy, as it is practised in its various ways, does not have the resources to at all adequately come to grips with. Hence my title: "The Poverty of Moral Philosophy." Yet they are problems that obviously and urgently, humanly speaking, need confronting. We need, if we can, to come to see how we can respond to them, and in doing so come to see how we can transform our world, to see in which direction to go in transforming it so that this obscenity that is ours can be radically transformed into being a reasonable humane social order where the lives of everyone – and as equally as reasonably possible – can to some reasonable degree flourish. But this, if we can manage it at all, will be a long hard slog.

It is natural to feel that this is such a tall order that its attainment cannot even be approximated. The task, it is hard not to feel, is just too great. It would require on our part a deep understanding of life in various conditions spread throughout the world, a knowledge of geography, history, and the social sciences.[2] And, in spite of what I have just said, it would require a knowledge of the history of moral and political philosophical theory; one coming up to and including its contemporary continuations, principally, but not exclusively, as done by John Rawls, Thomas Scanlon, Amartya Sen, Brian Barry, and G. A. Cohen.

Philosophy, as Richard Rorty has perceptively argued, may, seen in its long history, be a *transformational genre*, though what he sees it – and in ways desirably – being transformed into may be somewhat skewed.[3] One important thing concerned with what philosophy may be transformational to is an activity where philosophers see their principal task as that of being critical public intellectuals. Jean-Paul Sartre, Edward Said, and Noam Chomsky have all characterized (though variously) this activity and explained and stressed the important place it has in our cultural life. Moreover, Sartre, Said, and Chomsky have, though again in various ways, wonderfully exemplified such a vocation, involving themselves, with commitment and perseverance, in the fundamental social problems of their time.[4] They offer, in their emancipatory activity, an analysis and critique of their society, spelling out how people, and as well whole classes and societies, are harmed and degraded and how opportunities for human flourishing are crushed. But they have also shown how people have resisted. And they show, as well, something of how this plays out in our society in our own time.

Some philosophers, as well as other intellectuals – philosophers, *pace* Kant, have no privileged position here – become critical examiners of the "human scene" and of the ways we can come more adequately to live and view things. (Note, vis-à-vis one's image of being a philosopher, the difference between seeing oneself as a professional and often *only* as a professional, as the typical philosopher does, and seeing oneself centrally as an intellectual, or part of an intellectual collective, or an intellectual, whether part of an intellectual collective or not, as well as a professional where being a critical public intellectual has pride of place.[5] Which way one goes here shows a lot about one's self-conception and, from that, it can fairly well be predicted what one's typical philosophical activities will be.)

In orienting oneself toward being a critical public intellectual (to be pleonastic), as pompous as this sounds, one would be centrally concerned to come to grips with those both urgent and massive moral-cum-political-cum-economic problems that I shall characterize in Section II. However, faced with them, we are liable to despair. They are just too massive and too complicated for us; intellectuals inculcated in any "expert culture" (a determinate discipline), as analytic philosophy has become, would, though perhaps unwarrantedly, come to feel – could hardly *not* come to feel – faced with these "big problems" that they are *fach idioten* (subject idiots). It was perhaps possible to take a comprehensive perch when Karl Marx or even Max Weber wrote. It was then perhaps possible to have in some reasonable measure an integrated thoroughly comprehensive understanding. But for us now it is hard to believe that is possible. There is just too much to know and things are too complicated. We will end up, if we try for that comprehensive take, as "sweet singers," enunciating – pontificating, if you will – what are little more than platitudes as "great discourses" promising profound truths. It is hard not to become here what Rorty calls an ironist. Or is all this hand-wringing a rationalization for doing nothing?

There are three things I want to say about this. First, with the vocation (in Max Weber's sense) that goes with being a critical public intellectual, there still can, and should be, some division of labour. For example, Leo Panitch (a political economist) makes a different contribution, in method and topic, than Timothy Brennan (a literary scholar), though both are firmly on the Left. Noam Chomsky makes a different contribution than Michel Foucault, Simone de Beauvoir and John-Paul Sartre than Bertrand Russell (their general political agreement notwithstanding), Edward Said and Timothy Brennan than G. A. Cohen and Andrew Levine. With each of these contrastive pairings, their work can, at least arguably, complement each other and still, in places, both methodologically and substantively, be conflicting. Moreover, not all public intellectuals need have the awesome scope of Karl Marx, Max Weber or, in our time, Edward Said or Noam Chomsky. Leo Panitch and Timothy Brennan seemingly lack that scope but are anything but *fach idioten*; in their distinctive ways, they have integrated and comprehensively thought-out views. Moreover, these things admit of degree. Yet they make their contributions to coming to grips with these problems of our time. They importantly enhance our understanding of the world and help focus our political orientation.

Secondly, I want to say that some people living and writing now in some measure do work in a hedgehoggish way on a comparable scale to that of Marx and Weber – who still remain our paradigms – and *some* of them are also foxes. Amartya Sen and David Harvey exemplify both traits and Jürgen Habermas, Michel Foucault, Noam Chomsky, and Edward Said, while perhaps not without their characteristic disciplinary blemishes, have something of the scope that would fully exemplify "being a public intellectual" with the commitments that entails. They, in their different ways, can serve as role models for us as we go in our different ways to try to contribute something to that emancipatory task. Simone Weil and Iris Murdoch point one way, Simone de Beauvoir and Jean-Paul Sartre another, Theodor Adorno and Max Horkheimer another, Edward Said and Timothy Brennan another, Noam Chomsky and Michael Parenti another, Jürgen Habermas and Thomas McCarthy another, David Harvey and Colin Leys another, Martha Nussbaum and Kwame Anthony Appiah another, Joshua Cohen and Thomas Pogge another, and Michel Foucault, building on Nietzsche, still another. These pairs hold very different views and use different methodologies (if that is not too *scientistic* a term for it). Moreover, they sometimes conflict with or talk past one another. (This sometimes obtains both *between* the pairs and – though to a lesser extent – *within* the particular pairings themselves.) That conflict is normally healthy and some of it may get ironed out in the smithy of our intellectual culture as time goes on. Progress here, while not inevitable, is possible.[6]

My own predilection is for the work of Karl Marx and John Dewey (as different as they are from one another) and my predilection among our contemporaries is principally for the work of, and to work myself in the light of, *perhaps* the unstable – even an overly eclectic – mix of Amartya Sen with a toss of John Rawls, Brian Barry, and G. A. Gohen thrown in, and, in other ways, and for different purposes, of Edward Said, David Harvey, and Noam Chomsky, and with something of Ludwig Wittgenstein's and Richard Rorty's metaphilosophy and historicism. Many will think, I believe mistakenly, that this last consideration is a jarring note. I will reply that there are many ways to cook a chicken. This is so, as well, in our emancipatory endeavours and in the vocation – as pompous sounding as it is – of being a critical public intellectual. Perhaps all of these approaches are too cerebral? And to claim that there is some *one* truth and *the* way reveals *hubris*, self-deception, and that we have not taken in the non-skeptical lessons of fallibilism.[7]

With my personal predilections concerning how – treating *philosophy as a transitional genre with a narrative (perhaps illusory) of maturation* – I move from practising philosophy as rather conventionally conceived to being as well a critical public intellectual. (Perhaps, as Ramonet points out, only someone who has gained pre-eminence in some "expert culture" can then turn, in any way that has a chance of success, to playing such a role. There is something to that. But it is a matter of degree, leaving some *lebensraum* for us lesser mortals.) In doing that I find, perhaps surprisingly, both John Rawls and G. A. Cohen play for me a central role in my thought, even though they certainly do not themselves take such a stance concerning philosophy.[8] But they, very probably against their conception of themselves, contribute mightily (though indirectly) to such activities. What strikes me as most crucial is not their conceptions of themselves as philosophers – their (so to speak) "meta-images" of themselves as scholars and philosophers – but what they do or perhaps certain strands of what they do that I find vitally important and appropriate in my own thinking and acting. There are, however, let me repeat, many ways of preparing a chicken (consult any good cookbook). The same goes for the way of engaging in philosophy or whatever it becomes that philosophy transforms itself into (if it does).

I

So much for painting with a broad brush with what, I fear, may be too long and too pretentious-sounding an introduction. So with that behind me, I now turn to my principal topics. I shall argue that we not only can but should carry out our ethical, moral, and normative political thinking without metaphysics – something that is not very controversial – but as well (or so I claim) without epistemology, metaethics, or the familiar baggage of philosophical normative ethical *theory*.[9] I think that it is illusory to accept the traditional belief, at least among most philosophers, that we philosophy professors, or more centrally even the great philosophers of the Tradition, can provide foundations of our moral beliefs or hunt out the deep presuppositions upon which our moral thinking depends and then critically examine them or display the underlying rationale (or lack thereof) of our moral and ethical reasoning. It is illusory to think that if people come to us for help in their quest for how to live their lives or to ascertain what would be a good and just society or what would be a decent, just, and good world order or to ascertain from us – we philosophers – what human flourishing would come to, they will find sustenance. They will (to switch the metaphor) go away empty-handed just as we do ourselves in practising our philosophical art. There is, I claim, little they can learn from us beyond a few platitudes (perhaps articulated a little more clearly than they usually are) and the corrections that can be achieved by some adroit Augean stable cleaning. Stable cleaning, I would acknowledge, is particularly to the point where it has become clear that in trying to come to grips with the great moral-cum-political-cum-economic problems of our lives, we have in one way or another been infected by metaphysical or metaphilosophical maladies such as a belief that there is a great gulf between fact and value such that our values are, and indeed can be, really only the expression of our preferences or of our culturally inculcated preferences. If we stick just to the facts, so such a belief goes, we will never come upon a value. We – doing some Augean stable cleaning – can and should show how such philosophical beliefs can and should be set aside.[10] But beyond such stable cleaning and the assembling of reminders of some truisms – truisms that might in some contexts have been forgotten or repressed or to have become so because of some changes in our world – there is little we philosophers *qua* philosophers can offer our fellow humans concerning the deep and pressing ethical, and moral-cum-political-cum-economic problems that press down on us and have pressed down on others in times past and that will press down on others at some future time. (I link moral-political-economic together because the urgent problems I speak of are such an inextricable mix.)

    I should not be misunderstood. I am not some kind of general skeptic or "value nihilist" or error theorist. I think, for the usual reasons, that epistemological skepticism, moral skepticism, ethical relativism, ethical subjectivism (as well as its country cousin, ethical absolutism) are all absurd doctrines and that even a reasonably competent moral philosopher can point out why. Nor am I deeply skeptical about human rationality or reasonability – Rawls seems to be roughly right about both – and I am not skeptical about the human capacities for moral reasoning or political – including *normative* political – reasoning. What I am skeptical about is the capacity of philosophers, using their expert cultures, to articulate anything that will in any crucial way contribute to our coming to grips with and to resolving the great ethical, moral, and normative political and economic problems that bedevil us – as they in one form or another have bedeviled people during every age and in every clime – and that urgently require what for a time will in some way be a resolution of them, or at least a non-evasive facing of them, yielding a clear, or at least clearer, understanding of them and some guidance as to how to respond to them and to act in the face of them. What we philosophers are good at is only to collapse, as Wittgenstein saw, houses of cards.

I think we learn more about how to come to grips with the problems of life from critical intellectuals – what I have called "public intellectuals" in the Introduction – such as Edward Said, David Harvey, Noam Chomsky, Michel Foucault, Pierre Bourdieu, Richard Falk, Michael Parenti, Leo Panitch, John S. Saul, and Perry and Benedict Anderson than we can from any of our metaethicists or normative ethicists or applied ethics aficionados. We learn more about what stance to take on these demanding ethical, moral, and political issues that must press on any sensitive, reflective, and reasonably informed human being from reading *Le Monde diplomatique* or the *Boston Review* than we can learn from the best of moral philosophers and – among our contemporaries – even the very great ones of our contemporary tradition, namely John Rawls, Thomas Scanlon, Amartya Sen, G. A. Cohen, or Jürgen Habermas. Don't misunderstand me. I am greatly interested in the issues which divide G. A. Cohen and John Rawls or Jürgen Habermas and John Rawls. I continue to wonder how much can be milked out of Sen's capabilities approach. Is it Aristotle all over again without Aristotle's, or for that matter Martha Nussbaum's, essentialism? Can Sen's approach yield a cross-cultural ranking of capabilities that will show us what we really need to find out about what constitutes human flourishing? I am inclined to think, if there is much point in doing something like traditional moral theory at all, that a kind of blend of Rawls and Sen (where their putative conflicts are seen as only apparent, as Norman Daniels persuasively argues) is the best such game in town.[11] But I am very skeptical about whether even they

– doing the things they do so well – help much in coming to grips with the demanding moral-political-economic problems with which we are faced. Perhaps they do not intend to. But this coming to grips with such problems, more importantly than what they do, is principally what we should attend to. Or so I claim. And that is true in spades for our metaethical problems. This does not mean that I scorn metaethical problems, let alone regard them as pseudo-problems or find them uninteresting. They fascinate me. If we lived in even a marginally decent or in a reasonably structured world, there is nothing I would rather do than to come to grips with the problems that divide Peter Railton and Alan Gibbard or Peter Railton and Christine Korsgaard. But in *our world* this seems to me like fiddling while Rome burns. Moreover we shouldn't complacently regard this as just a division of labour. Some labours are much more crucial than others.

II

What are these great moral-political-economic problems that I am talking about and why do I fear that we philosophers can do so little concerning them? We can, as I have already said, sometimes usefully do some preliminary Augean stable cleaning of the messes that sometimes, for some people, stand in the way of genuinely coming to grips with these problems. Sometimes (but not always) this stable cleaning comes to logical corrective guidance as in pointing out conspicuous fallacies of reasoning. But for someone who is not just plainly confused but has deeply caught the philosophy bug (as Wittgenstein himself with intense ambivalence had) we can, as Wittgenstein did on himself, practice on ourselves Wittgensteinian conceptual therapy. But aside from these preliminaries – nay-sayings to some bad philosophy – what have we relevantly to say concerning these (if you will) "existential problems"? There is, as far as I can see, little that we can offer that will give guidance concerning their resolution or even to our facing them without blinkers. We can sometimes usefully say something about keeping metaphysics or theology out of such matters. But there seems little that we can usefully say except these negative things, though sometimes given a certain intellectual climate that is usefully done. But even with that done, the same substantive problems stand before us untouched.

To make this come to life we need to see, translating into the concrete, what are these great moral-political-economic problems (problems which are thoroughly normative, but not only normative), on the one hand, and, on the other, the quite different urgent ethical problems that, as Habermas would put it, are part of our life-world.[12]

First, the moral-political-economic problems (or rather a crucial sampling of them):

1. The environment is degenerating at a frightening rate. What should be done about it? Isn't it obvious that we should do something to halt this degeneration and, as far as we can, to at least in part reverse it? But what can be done about it when such powerhouses as the United States (prominently among some others) refuse to ratify even such a half (perhaps quarter) measure as the Kyoto Protocol and some other countries, such as Canada, renege on even these modest commitments? Facing this political reality, what should critical intellectuals do? Is the only thing we can do to lament it or be ironical about it?

2. Globalization is a reality among us. The extra-territoriality of many operations as well as their environmental effects increasingly, and in a variety of ways, are making it so that the globe is becoming an interrelated space instantaneously linked in which increasingly many of us consciously live our lives with an awareness that, like it or not, we are living in a space-time compression fix.[13] It is becoming less and less an exaggeration for many of us that our world is becoming a global village. Globalization, unless there is some horrendous environmental, economic, or military disaster, is here to stay. *Capitalist* globalization (at least arguably), except for the great multinationals and the elites that own them and/or control them, has been detrimental (and in some places violently so) for a great many people: indeed for the great masses of people.[14] (Think, for example, of the twelve million slaves that now exist in the world.) But globalization without capitalism *could* be liberating and contribute to the well-being of the

masses of people, though the actually existing globalization that we know has exactly the opposite effect. What should be done about it, lamenting it or being ironical or sardonic aside? Does this mean facing and struggling against capitalism? Is there any moral alternative other than to be anti-capitalist? Or is this leftwing irrealism?

3. The United States has become an empire, though an empire without official colonies but with plenty of client states and comprador states. Some think that this empire (on the whole) is a benevolent one.[15] They see U.S. imperial power as liberating and democratizing others. Others think that just the opposite obtains.[16] Is, for example, the United States in Iraq a liberating power or is it an invader and oppressor? Or is it a bit of both? And *if* so, in what proportions? Is Iraq worse off now than it was under Saddam Hussein? (I think these questions almost answer themselves.)

4. If the U.S. Empire, like the British Empire before it, is an imperialism that (on the whole) brings great harm to people, what, given its awesome military superiority in the world, can and should be done? What stand should we critical public intellectuals take towards U.S. imperialism? And what can we do beyond lamenting it? We can show – try to show – to an uninformed or skeptical or even a hostile public in what ways the U.S. is imperialistic and in what ways that imperialism is harmful. But does this require any philosophical expertise? "Philosophical expertise" aside, how do we, with our pitiful marginal media, counter the juggernaut of the mass media which is so adroit at manufacturing consent?

5. What about humanitarian intervention? There are places where it was indeed justified, e.g., for Hitler's Germany and in Rwanda. But in many places it is questionable, e.g., in Kosovo and in Iraq. So when is it justified? Even if the United States, looked at politically, is a hegemon, it cannot just be assumed that even a benign hegemon (supposing there could be one) has a moral duty to act unilaterally – or is even ever justified in doing so. But the United States has so acted. Is that morally

tolerable (though given their awesome power, we seem in some rather unpleasant sense doomed to tolerate it)? Isn't this just more evidence of what an evil imperial power it is? Has there ever been an empire that, everything considered, brought more good than harm? Isn't there a very heavy burden of proof for anyone who would advocate a return to something like the old imperial system?

6. Can – as the U.S. claims for Iraq – a government be a democracy or be democratically elected while it is still under foreign occupation? Even when the people in the occupied territory vote for a government, and even if they can choose (the resistance aside) their own list of candidates and their own parties, is not what is acceptable and what is not determined by the occupying power? Can the "newly elected government" simply tell the occupying power to go home and it be the case that it *must* be obeyed? Would we – or should we – say that the "government" of Vichy, France, or present-day Iraq or Afghanistan is (was) a democracy or democratically elected? And, even if it is largely a pseudo-election and hardly something we could legitimately call "democratic," can such a political procedure *sometimes* be justified, pseudo or not, democratic or not?

7. There is the realistic possibility, as Richard Falk has argued, that the United States is moving to what has been called a post-democracy and that that post-democracy is very possibly a transition to a fascist state where "fascism" is not used just as a slogan but is used in a sense that has been characteristic of uncontroversially acknowledged fascist societies. With its response to terrorism and with its ascendancy to empire and imperialism (though in an Orwellian double-think manner) is it in a transition from a democracy to a police state? Or are the structures of democracy so deeply engrained that they will prevent such a thing from happening? Is talk of a "fascist state" just irresponsible hyperbolic talk or is it a grim and sober possibility?[17]

8. With reference to this last question: what about the media in the United States? It is more and more under neo-conservative guidance (and indeed under neo-conservative *government* guidance). Think (as a paradigm case) of the role of Fox Media vis-à-vis the Bush Administration. The Bush propaganda line, which Fox trumpets, is not so unlike the Inner Party "doublethink" in *1984*: "War is peace," "Control is freedom." There is in the United States something somewhat analogous to what was going on under the junta in Brazil where the foreign-language newspapers and left-wing journals were readily available in Brazil but oppositional Brazilian newspapers and publications were shut down. The junta very well knew that the masses could not read the foreign-language press. So the junta let them circulate, yielding the appearance of press freedom thereby soothing the anxieties of some naïve intellectuals.[18] So in the United States, left-wing and other critical journals circulate. Nobody, for example, (as far as I know) tries to shut down the *Monthly Review* or *New Politics*. But their readership is self-selective and miniscule. So the neo-conservatives, following Bismarck, reason, "Let them babble on as long as they obey. It will have little effect." Indeed, any English reader could read them but practically speaking many of them have no way of even knowing about such alternatives. In that important sense there are no alternatives. But what of the Internet? And there is the popularity of Michael Moore's films and Noam Chomsky's writings and lectures. Am I being too *parti-pris* concerning the George W. Bush administration? Or am I being too deeply pessimistic? Or am I giving a reasonable interpretative description not without its normative force? Or does the fact that it is "an *interpretative* description" inevitably skew it? Or is for any even somewhat complicated social phenomena some interpretation unavoidable? But are there not better and worse interpretative descriptions?[19]

9. What about developmentalism and the development projects that go with it? On the surface, at least, they seem to be a good thing. There are at present great and growing inequalities in

the world and the disparities of wealth and life-conditions for most of its populations are staggering, making the lives of the poor, particularly in the countries of the South, desperate. Under these conditions it would *seem* desirable to have a flood of development aid directed to the South. Yet much of the populace in the South is against it. And in many of these countries their critical intellectuals as well oppose it, as do many left-leaning intelligentsia in the North. And recently the World Bank's own operations evaluations department noted that 75 per cent of the World Bank's African agricultural projects were failures. So what should we think and do about development? Should it be radically modified and if so how? Or should we just junk such projects? The latter seems clearly wrong, but then what should be done?[20]

10. Consider now immigration. Most of the developed capitalist democracies (Italy and Germany, for example) need (for a time at least) a steady flow of immigrants and there are indeed many people in the world whose conditions of life are such that they desperately need to immigrate. However, in most of the places in the rich North, considerable segments of their populations are paranoid and racist about immigration. Yet Britain or Germany would not cease to be British or German with considerably increased immigration. But what of small countries like Iceland, Luxembourg, Ireland, the Netherlands, or New Zealand? Would open borders, or even nearly open borders, undermine the distinctive cultural structures of such countries? Are there not for their citizens some agent-relative prerogatives here? Think of little Iceland, for example. Their culture, and with it their distinctive language, might be swamped with a policy of open borders. Yet the disparities between North and South, between these little but rich countries of the North and the countries of sub-Saharan Africa, are stark. Clearly from a moral point of view something should be done about it. But what? Is the desirability of preserving the distinctiveness of one's culture to trump considerations of what can be done to relieve the often-

hellish life conditions of the peoples of the South? (People, most of whom, it should be noted, would otherwise not wish to leave their homeland.) Does doing what is decent and fair in such situations entail undermining one's own culture? That *seems* morally problematic. Yet other people need desperately to immigrate. To deny them that in the name of cultural preservation is also morally problematic. This desperate need to immigrate should trump cultural preservation. But, most particularly in small countries, with a distinctive language (say, Iceland) and distinctive traditions, cultural preservation – though not cast in stone – is important to preserve as well. Immigrants should come to acknowledge the culture of the host country and they need to be given some incentive to do so. When the immigrants from a very different culture come in considerable numbers, the host country can be expected to change in certain respects. But this change should be slow so as not to disrupt the cultural life of the host country too jarringly. The immigrants should recognize and acknowledge this. But it is reasonable, and need not be undesirable, for the society to change slowly under their influence over a couple of generations. All that notwithstanding, could there not be extensive redistribution of wealth as well without so opening one's borders? If this were done – really seriously done – more people all around would be happier. People, if that is what they want to do, could keep what is distinctive in their native culture *and* others' vital needs could be met and their life conditions made decent and the few who wished to be cultural migrants could travel without upsetting the cultural apple cart and often enrich it by giving it a little innovative character, some hybrid-vigour.

11. Nine and ten particularly point to the vast and growing inequalities that obtain between people in the North and people in the South and within as well both the North and the South themselves. There are vast and growing inequalities between individuals, between strata and between classes. These obtain almost everywhere and they go against the

egalitarian orientation and egalitarian ethos that many liberals and left-leaning people wish for our globe. This has led many (including me) to call for equality in some or all of these domains. Is this, even if desirable, anything but *badly* utopian? Is it even remotely possible in any foreseeable future to design things so that the life-chances of the average citizen of Chad are even remotely equal to the life-chances of the average citizen of Luxembourg? Is it even remotely possible to reasonably struggle for equality across the globe? Some facing this believe that *sufficiency* (measured, perhaps, by some measure of Rawlsian primary goods or Senian capabilities) should be what is to be striven for. We require, it may be thought, a metric for sufficiency or decency. Should this replace the classic ideal of equality which should perhaps either just be dropped or retained merely as a *heuristic*? Or should we retain some substantive idea of the ideal of equality? If, for example, we replace equality with sufficiency, what becomes of the egalitarian ideal of moral equality, namely that the life of everyone matters and matters equally, or of the deeply embedded ideal among egalitarians of the equal worth of all human beings? Or are these things to be regarded as just so much moral rhetoric: something that is without substantive salience? It is not only morally obscene that there are these huge disparities but it seems at least somehow also obscene to blithely chatter on about moral equality or equal moral worth in the face of these pervasive steep disparities when the governments we democratically elect in the North, and continue to tolerate and sometimes support, do precious little about it. There should be no room for complacency or indifference here. (In so remarking am I *just* being moralistic?)

12. Consider now the fact (or perhaps putative fact) that the Westphalian state with its distinctive conception of sovereignty is rapidly becoming a thing of the past and that there is becoming increasingly a need for *some form* of *global governance*. But what form should it take? For a variety of reasons a world state *seems* problematic. But

consider whether, somewhat on the model of Kant, a world federation is so out of the question; say, something like a Swiss cantonal structure adopted for the whole globe. Would that provide the model for a democratic response to the phenomena of capitalist globalization? To translate a bit into the concrete: could the UN be modified so that it could at least approximate a democratic world federation? What form should the restructuring take? It would seem that it should lead to the abolishing or at least radical restructuring of the Security Council. It would take away its power of veto, and most particularly take away the power of a single permanent member to veto any proposal or even for the collectivity of permanent members of the Security Council acting either on consensus or on majority vote to exercise a veto. Perhaps there should be no permanent members either with or without a veto on the Security Council. Perhaps there should be no Security Council at all. There are many possible alternatives here and they should all be carefully considered. And we should *not* just accept, except sometimes in some situations for *real politik* reasons, the most *minimal* changes.

Furthermore, there are the problems concerning the strength and concerning the increasing democratization of the General Assembly. It should be able to override any resolution of the Security Council (assuming there is one) and it should be further democratized. Individual countries' representatives should be elected by the individual states from candidates nominated by their political parties in the usual democratic manner. And to keep terribly small countries, for example the Bahamas, from having the same power in the General Assembly as, say, a huge country like India, there should be something for the General Assembly like the twin houses in the United States. A house with its members elected on a model something like the U.S. House of Representatives and another house with its members elected in some way like the U.S. Senate is elected. But should we say that neither house acting alone should be the final court of appeal? But then there could be deadlocks. Where is the *final* authority? Must we have a *final* authority? Are we, as good Hobbesians, to think that to avoid chaos there must be some final authority? Are we getting artificial philosophical questions here: questions up for Wittgensteinian dissolution or questions that practically speaking can reasonably just be benignly neglected? Or are they importantly pressing?

These are just more or less off the cuff speculations which certainly would need much to be refined, but there should be something like this kind of democratization of the UN to make it function as a genuine global world federation that could break, or at least brake, the power of the great powers, and particularly that of the United States, to dominate the United Nations, making it a tool of the United States or of the great powers taken together. Is this, or something like this, something that could be the basis for a *realistic utopia* or even a functioning world federation? And is the achievement or approximation of this sufficiently possible somewhere down the line to be something worth struggling for? (Think of the pessimism of the intellect and the optimism of the will.) And if sufficiently possible, is it desirable? Am I too entrenched in believing that it obviously is? But we should keep our feet firmly on the ground. How is this world federation to be effective without a system of law that finally could rule the day? (We should not forget the worries of the anarchists here.)[21] And without a strong army under its control, could the proposed world federation be sufficiently sovereign? Talk of divided sovereignty, at different levels, does not seem to address this problem. Kant hasn't replaced Hobbes. Even with the demise of the Westphalian state, we still seem, at least, to have this problem.

Second, cases of ethical (purely ethical?) problems:

13. Consider a young professional starting out on her career and thinking about the kind of life she would like to lead.

She has the ability and the education to become a research professor at a good university and perhaps (if she works very hard) to become something of a superstar. Suppose she likes research and even demanding research but she knows that would require great demands on her time and energy. And she wonders if she wants to live a life like that with such constant demands. Her second alternative is a kind of compromise between the first alternative I have just sketched and a third I shall go on to sketch. The second (the compromise one) is that she will do a modest amount of research and spend more time with her family (if she comes to have one), with friends and with her students and doing other engaging things she also likes. But she can readily predict that she will get frozen at the rank of associate professor and increasingly be assigned more committee work the likes of which she is not particularly fond. Her third alternative is to go to what in the United States is called a community college – in Quebec a CEGEP – where she will not be expected to do any research and, even if she wants to, there would be little time and little in the way of a sustaining atmosphere in which to do it. But she will have lots of interaction with her students and colleagues in a kind of fraternal life and lots of time to devote to her family, to hobbies and the like. Suppose further that the differential salary conditions are of no considerable moment to her; and further yet, that she really has a choice between these three options.

Is there a *right* answer or some objectively better answer as to which one to choose? Is there no way to go which is the most really rational or even a more reasonable way to go? Would it – to put it even stronger – be her duty to choose one over the others? That (in most circumstances) would seem, to put it mildly, rather dubious. But is there an objective answer (or even an intersubjective answer, if there is a difference here) concerning the question of there being one right answer or one answer which is the most rational or reasonable? Is there even anything like a better or worse choice *for her* among the three? Is it possible for us human beings, being the variable people we are, for there to be a way that hard and non-evasive reasoning could come up with what is objectively the best way? That is surely questionable. Moreover, is to look at things in that way to over-intellectualize things, to make such choices too much a matter of what hard reasoning can yield? Can philosophy in any substantial way guide her in making her decision? It is not unreasonable to think not.

14. Consider now things at the other end of life's spectrum. Suppose a person, again an academic, is approaching the age where he can retire. But suppose there is no requirement that he must retire. Suppose he has done a reasonable amount of research and that he continues to enjoy doing it. But there are also a lot of other things he would like to do that are both intellectually and emotionally fulfilling that the demands of research and university life have hitherto left scant time for him to do and that he would like in the last few years of his life to do them. Suppose he is well aware of Shakespeare's ages of man. He wants to carry out research but at a more leisurely pace. But he needs to consider what kind of projects to undertake, what scope they will have and how long they will likely take. He needs to be realistic about how long he will probably be able to carry out effective research *and* to do the other things he wants to do. Again, is there one right answer here or a single reasonable answer for him that he can garner, if he thinks hard enough, carefully enough, and non-evasively enough about it? Can careful reflection (including consulting his emotions as much as his cogitations) be of no use in helping him to make a better or a wiser choice? Still, is it not unreasonable to believe in this case, as in the previous case, that there is *no one such choice that he should make*, let alone something that "reason requires"? Isn't it more plausible to believe there is a range of choices that he with equal, or nearly equal, reasonability can make? And again the central question for this essay: Is there anything that philosophy can contribute in helping him to his decision?

III

I now want to go some way toward showing how philosophy is of little use to us in facing such problems of either the moral-political-economic life or of ethical life, let alone in helping us resolve such problems. Consider first metaethics. I am *not* saying that metaethics is irrelevant to our moral-political-economic or ethical lives *because* anything goes as far as metaethics is concerned. It doesn't. And I am not saying that about the moral and the ethical life either. There are some remarks that are typically called metaethical that would normally be regarded as close to being decisive by people who have carefully attended to them. But note how I have qualified "decisive." This is instanced in what Hilary Putnam has recently called the entanglement of fact and value and in which he has such predecessors as Iris Murdoch, Isaiah Berlin, Philippa Foot, Bernard Williams, John Searle, John McDowell, and Thomas Scanlon among others. Evaluative utterances, including moral and ethical utterances, are usually (perhaps always) a mixture of fact and value. In different situations they may function, on the one hand, more evaluatively or normatively or, on the other hand, and in other situations, more descriptively and interpretatively. My uttering now (2006), "The U.S. treatment of prisoners at Guantanamo is brutal and completely unacceptable" or "Bush's unilateralism is high-handed, dangerous and completely unacceptable" are utterances (well-taken or ill-taken) that are primarily evaluative and normative in most circumstances and standardly have emotive force as well. In contrast, consider an historian's remark "The treatment of the slaves on the ships carrying them over to the Americas from Africa was brutal and their being broken in – prepared to work as slaves – was cruel in the extreme" or an historian's remark "British colonialism in India was patronizing and racist and more concerned with the accumulation of British wealth than for the good of ('the civilizing of') those colonized." Both these sentences in normal contexts at least function more descriptively and interpretatively than evaluatively or normatively and may have no emotive force at all. The last historian's description *may* be a tendentious one but an interpretative description it is. The important point here is that with all these utterances or sentences we have (as Putnam has put it) an entanglement of fact and value: an entanglement of evaluative and normative elements on the one hand and descriptive and interpretative elements on the other. Moreover, it is very difficult, and at least arguably impossible, to unscramble them into purely evaluative or purely descriptive components or into a pure "tellings to" and a pure "tellings that."[22] We might resort to a thinner rather than thicker normative vocabulary, e.g., "good" or "duty" rather than "cruel" or "beastly." Yet the thinner evaluative or normative vocabulary does not capture everything the thicker vocabulary does, and the thicker vocabulary cannot be reduced to the thinner vocabulary without the use of arbitrary *persuasive* re-descriptions or definitions with their at least implicit arbitrary stipulations and reductionisms. Even when we assert "That is just evil" or "That is certainly good," when we look to the *context* and to what the "that" refers to we will find as well as the normative content a descriptive or otherwise factual content. There are, at least arguably, no pure evaluatives or normatives. When the young A. J. Ayer, Rudolf Carnap, and Hans Reichenbach claimed that moral utterances were really just imperatives or really just pure expressions of emotion, they were clearly saying something that was at best false as a little attention to how our language actually functions (a few reminders of how the language-game is played) reveals.

If Carnap et al. say they don't care how our natural languages are used for they are concerned with regimenting an "ideal language" into having a determinate sense of how (among other things) "normative-talk" should be used, this should be looked at with considerable suspicion. When, for example, they are claiming that normative utterances are *really* imperatives, that that is actually their force, the "really" and "actually" tip us off to the fact that arbitrary stipulative persuasive definitions are at work here.[23] They are stipulations and others can make their conflicting stipulations too. Nothing substantive can be legitimately achieved by stipulation and here at least no clarification is achieved either but just an arbitrary reduction accompanied by an equally arbitrary appeal to "ideal language" theory.[24]

This illustrates, what I admitted at the beginning of this essay, that philosophy can sometimes do some useful Augean stable cleaning – when, for instance, our trio of logical positivists say that norms are imperatives (or *really* imperatives) and values are just expressions of emotion (or *really* expressions of emotion) or some economist or political scientist, even more crudely, says that our norms and values are just our preferences or really just that they are very wide of the mark.[25] While what our preferences are is a matter of social-psychological fact, evaluations or imperatives made in the light of our preferences themselves are not matters of fact or at least not purely so. It is an empirical fact that we have certain preferences, but what it is to evaluate or assess them is another matter. To discover what X's preferences are is not to discover what preferences X should have. What is *preferable* is not a matter *just* of what preferences we happen to have. What is preferable *may* well be a matter of what preferences we would have if we were clearly aware of the causes of our actual preferences and of the consequences of having them satisfied and carefully reflected on that and took the matter to heart in a cool hour. But that is a different matter than just saying our values are our preferences.[26] To assimilate values and preferences is an error that a naturalist such as John Dewey never made.

Someone in good Butlerian-Moorian fashion might say, "Facts are facts and expressions of preferences are expressions of preferences and never the twain shall meet and ditto for facts and values. Every thing is what it is and not another thing." But that the two shall never meet is an incoherence for it assumes, against the way our language-games work, that moral and other normative or evaluative utterances can be unscrambled into their normative/evaluative components and into their factual/descriptive components, but that is impossible as again attention to the use of our language reveals.[27] Moreover, it assumes an *essentialism*, something that is very problematic.[28]

This Augean stable cleaning can be accepted, or even not accepted, and either way nothing would be advanced concerning our coming to grips with the real life – the big (if you will) – moral-political-economic problems or the paradigmatic ethical problems of the sort I have described. With all this meta-talk the engine has been idling. And nothing need be evoked called a metaethical *theory* to establish this; just reasonably careful attention to the way our language works. The point of this noticing is in service to a Wittgensteinian therapeutic turn. We can, and should, be thoroughly atheoretical here.[29]

IV

Let us return to and work with my examples (1–14) given in Section II. And remember what I am claiming is that no philosophical *theory* of ethics or morality is needed, required, or even useful for engaging with, let alone resolving, these problems except when some conceptual confusion is blocking seeing those problems clearly. Moreover, there is no philosophical therapy that will enable us to non-evasively set them aside. (In that way they are not at all like traditional philosophical problems.) They are there, and powerfully, in the tangle of our lives, to be in some way responded to.

Let us – in trying to sort these things out – first consider the very key remarks in (3), (4), and (6) about the United States being an empire and an imperialism and about whether it is (or even can be) *as either an empire or an imperialism* a benevolent or benign one bringing freedom, democracy, stability, and progress to the world's peoples or whether it brings suffering and even greater unfreedom than they had previously known before the hegemon came on the scene. Does it, as well, bring increased instability and stagnation yielding anything but progress to those peoples the hegemon has in its imperialist or imperial control? However we answer these questions or whether we refuse to answer them, it is not something that philosophy has much to say about except perhaps for a little preliminary Augean stable cleaning in the service of liberating someone who is (wittingly or unwittingly) *philosophically* entrapped. If, for example, someone says the United States is an empire all right but not an imperialism for we cannot have imperialism without colonies and the United States has no colonies, it can be pointed out that this rests on an arbitrary, restrictive persuasive definition. The United States has client and comprador states galore in its control and milks them, oppresses them, and robs them of their ability to act as they otherwise would. Left to themselves, things would be rather different. With what I call U.S. imperialism these client states are not themselves able to determine much of what they would do, any more than in the classical British, French, Dutch, and Belgian imperialistic empires the colonized were able to, let alone did, determine things for themselves. Much the same thing is going on with U.S. global behaviour that in the past made the British, French, Dutch, and Belgian empires into imperialisms. It is indeed true (in contrast with colonies) that comprador states can fly their own flag, print their own currency, make their own traffic regulations, and such things, but that is about all. It is arbitrary, utilizing implicitly stipulative persuasive definitions, to call those former empires imperialisms and not to call the United States one. The crucial common aspects are that in both cases there is *de facto* control, the undermining of freedom, the employment of oppression, and exploitive extraction – extraction which, as David Harvey aptly argues, often takes the form in our contemporary globalizing world of "accumulation by dispossession."[30]

If the people who claim that you can't have imperialism without colonies stubbornly stick to their arbitrary, restrictive stipulative definition, their interlocutor can well respond,

> All right, I will give you, for the sake of continuing the argument between us, your definition but, whether we call the American empire an imperialism or not, still the so-called non-imperialist empire has the features we both agree would be relevant to denying, *pace* Ignatieff, that it is benign. It controls without democratic mandate and undermines freedom, paradigmatically by oppressing and milking (that is, by being exploitatively extractive of) the societies over which it has sway. It dominates whole peoples. Whether or not these claimed things are so is the significant issue between those who say the U.S. Empire is malevolent and those who deny it. And that is an issue concerning the empirical facts. Something concerning which philosophy (*qua* philosophy, as they say) has little (if anything) to say, except to say that the evaluative expressions which are articulated in support of the claims of one side and the other involve the characteristic entanglement of fact and value that Putnam and others speak of and find their warrant in empirical claims (not positivist or empiricist "*brute* empirical" claims but empirical claims nonetheless.[31]

These are claims that philosophy *qua* philosophy (at least traditionally) is not concerned about and that philosophers (*qua* philosophers) have no expertise in establishing or disestablishing. Philosophers, that is, have no expertise which privileges them more so than others or aids them over others in establishing the *warrantability* of such empirical claims. That Kantian dream of philosophy's role has been demolished: philosophy is not the queen of the sciences or the guardian of culture. There is nothing here that we philosophers can settle or even adjudicate. How such matters are reasonably settled (if they are) depends on who has the best empirical evidence arranged in the most perspicuous and compelling narrative.

I would put my money on those who claim that the United States is an empire that is for the most part malevolent for it *controls* its client states (or so I believe), as did the classical imperialisms, in its own interests and not – its pretensepretence to the contrary notwithstanding – in the interests of "liberating" and "civilizing" the people they control or, if they ever take seriously their own so-called civilizing ideals, they do so only occasionally and incidentally.[32] Moreover, the United States empire increases misery and harm and is exploitatively extractive and accumulative, e.g., the United States wants Iraq's oil and the control of it on their own terms and they want Afghanistan to gain control of Afghanistan's area because it is essential to gain control, and to secure control, of Afghanistan in order for the construction and continued maintenance of a gas line deemed vital to U.S. interests. The Taliban were indeed brutal but the United States tolerates and even sometimes promotes brutal regimes, e.g., Colombia and Chile under Pinochet or, at an earlier time, Saddam Hussein's Iraq, when it serves what the American government takes to be in its own self-interest. Indeed, at an earlier time, the United States supported the Taliban and sponsored Osama bin Laden when it seemed its interests were in the fight to drive out the Soviet Union from Afghanistan.

However, the crucial thing for this essay is not whether I have managed to tell it like it is, or even approximately like it is, but that we have matters here of the utmost moral-political-economic importance concerning which (and arguably quite appropriately) metaphysics, metaethics, epistemology, and normative ethical theory have precious little to say. Our characteristic philosophical activities, that is, have little relevance here. People who have philosophical worries concerning a straightforward examination of these problems can be perhaps unblocked by some philosophical therapy. But that is the sum of our philosophical expertise here. The real work comes with the examination of these empirical issues and the drawing of interpretative and normative conclusions from them. And here philosophers, at least *qua* philosophers, have no special expertise. (If it is said that this is too much in the spirit of positivism, I would respond that not all is dross in positivism.)

Yet all this notwithstanding, critical public intellectuals and many other reflective and informed people with a historical and political sense will understandably be deeply concerned with these issues. They are crucial to the weal and woe of humanity. There can and should also be some ideology-critique here.[33] We should see (or so I would argue) that, U.S. propaganda to the contrary notwithstanding, a government cannot be freely elected and be democratic while its population is under occupation. And to deny that Iraq or Afghanistan is under occupation is either a lie or a self-deception. (That is hardly a *philosophical* truth but it is a truth.)

Let us now turn to the issues raised in (7) and (8) concerning whether, as Richard Falk has carefully argued, there is a reasonable possibility that the United States with its empire and military adventures and with its "war on terrorism" is becoming not only, as Rorty worries, a post-democracy but also a fascist police state as well.[34] Despite its thin pretense to the contrary, its aggressive wars are *not* in self-defence but for regime-change of other countries and control of their territories and peoples. And does not the U.S. government often spread lies about other countries or at least make unsubstantiated statements to rationalize their aggressive acts toward them? With its Patriot Act and Homeland Security Act, with its demonizing of whole peoples, with its round-up of people and their indefinite detention without charge or trial and without access to a lawyer, with its arguing that nations that are not with them are against them, with its violating international law, with its refusal to act under the mandate of the UN concerning issues of war and peace which are not military acts of self-defence, with its equation of the loyalty of its citizens with the unquestioning acceptance of its state policies, with its treatment of some of those it captures in war being in violation of the Geneva Convention, with its torturing them and degrading them in obscene ways and with the Red Cross or Red Crescent having no access to them, we have, with all these things, acts which are characteristic of fascist states. They are fascist acts of a police state or, if you prefer, of a brutal totalitarianism. (After all, it wasn't only fascist regimes that were brutal and totalitarian, but Stalinist and claimed Marxist regimes as well.)[35] Isn't its increasing control of the media – sometimes turning it into something that is often an instrument of government policy and in other instances muzzling the press, making it less and less a purveyor of objective (intersubjective, if you will) information reasonably and impartially articulated – plainly a rejection of press freedom? Indeed the United States attempts to give the illusion of the freedom of the press by allowing marginal media to say pretty much whatever they want, where, as the government well knows, what really counts politically is what gets said on the big radio and T.V. networks and in the major newspapers and newspaper chains. Are these not further marks of a move to something that is fascist (or at least totalitarian) in everything but name?

Perhaps this latter point is overstated in ways that are *parti-pris*. Am I – at least partially – blinkered here? After all (as previously noted), Michael Moore makes his critical and oppositional films and they are widely circulated, widely viewed, and commented on, and Noam Chomsky gives his talks and writes his books that many listen to or read and with which a goodly number largely agree. It is fair enough to remind ourselves that the *New York Times* reported on torture and abuse by U.S. forces in Afghanistan and Iraq. But recall also that *Newsweek* was forced to retract its story about Koran toilet flushing. So to a *certain extent* things go both ways. But note that this awareness of alternatives is mainly for educated university audiences. (Remember here the parallel with Brazil under the junta.)

Such countervailing tendencies notwithstanding, is not the main thrust of U.S. society going in the direction of fascist or totalitarian governance with a, for the most part, docile and uninformed – indeed sometimes *misinformed* – public?[36] This, of course, will and should be contested. But again – and this is what is crucially relevant for us here – the genuine contestation will be on *empirical-cum-interpretative grounds*. *There should be here a careful consideration of which of the resulting narratives have the greater perspicuousness and the strongest interpretative warrant.* I think that here too Augean stable cleaning philosophical activities can sometimes have some preliminary value, but only in exposing some bad philosophy or ideology which has managed to intrude; but for the most part philosophy neither as metaphysics, metaethics, normative ethical theory, nor epistemology has much (if any) role to play over the moral-political-economic issues that are of vast human importance. And it is only at best a little better at the sort of distinctively ethical issues I have mentioned in (13) and (14). With philosophy here we have, at least over such issues, a wheel which turns no machinery.

There is, of course, the need for careful moral reasoning and attention to the facts – facts which are seldom, if ever, "brute facts" – but the moral reasoning here owes little to philosophy. What does count is the moral capacities and capabilities of reflective and informed people, not bamboozled by ideology or for that matter by metaphysics and epistemology. But we should not equate such reflective activities with philosophy. Many people, quite innocent of philosophy, exercise perfectly well these capacities and capabilities. Moreover, you don't have to be a philosopher to be a public intellectual; philosophical consciousness is likely to be only of marginal help here, though a generally good humanistic education helps, in the way being a "subject idiot" (perhaps an expert in some "expert culture") does not. The latter is a form of professional deformation – and *that* can block understanding.

I turn now to (9), (10), and (11), which come face to face with the moral issues created by the vast and increasing inequalities that we see around the globe and which force us, if we are the least bit morally sensitive, to face questions of what should be said and done about them. We have globally *between* societies in all parts of the world (but particularly between North and South) and *in* almost all societies as well staggering and growing inequalities and immiserating disparities in wealth.[37] Millions of people at the bottom of the scale survive on the equivalent of a dollar a day (what I pay for my morning newspaper) and many more survive on the equivalent of two dollars. These people live (if we can call it that) in grinding and numbing poverty and misery, typically without clean water, without even remotely adequate shelter, living in constant hunger and with little (often no) access to medical care. They have little, if any, education. Many of them are illiterate and their children have no or very little access to education. Not infrequently, even when they have formal access to school, they have to be pulled out to work to help keep their families afloat. These impoverished people live a life of misery and often danger that is nasty, brutish, and short while people at the other end of the spectrum live a life of incredible wealth and privilege and, often enough, of power. For them, as is so for many in the rich North, longevity increases from generation to generation. The four richest individuals among them, for example, have greater wealth than the wealth of many poor nations taken together. Many of us, particularly in the North, are not wealthy either but a goodly number of us are reasonably well off; that is, we are reasonably well housed, well fed, the availability of water is almost never an issue for us, all of us are educated (some of us well-educated or reasonably well-educated) and often, though surely not always, secure in our life-conditions, though here, vis-à-vis security or the lack thereof, class counts even in the wealthier societies of the North. There is something not just plainly unfair but grossly obscene about these worldwide disparities in life-conditions. Can this plausibly and reasonably be seen as just emoting on my part?

On *any theory* of justice – even Robert Nozick's – and not just on egalitarian theories, such inequalities are, to understate it, unjust. Indeed it would be a *reductio* of *any* theory of justice to deny it. The only way reasonably to deny it would be to treat it as being like an earthquake or a tsunami as being unavoidable – as something that is just there in the world that cannot even be ameliorated.[38] But that is plainly false. People who deny it or do not acknowledge it are firmly in the grip of a very right-wing ideology. Some people – Thomas Pogge, pre-eminently, but also Peter Singer – have empirically shown us the small redistributions we in the North would have to make to the South to eradicate the grinding poverty that obtains there and, indeed to some not inconsiderable extent, all over the world. (They are re-distributions that we in the rich North as individuals would hardly notice.) The problem is that there is no *political and extensive moral will* to even make the little changes that we would have to make to achieve it. Most people worry instead about the "high taxes" they are paying and their employment security. And politicians, facing elections, have no choice but to cater to them.

There are no philosophical problems here. We know what has to be done to eradicate world poverty and we know that this poverty is both unnecessary and an intolerable evil. If we had to wait for moral theory to establish this, we would never even get started with moral theory. After all, in moral and ethical theory, we must start with our firmest considered judgments.[39] Put otherwise, in the spirit of G. E. Moore's defence of common sense, we can be more confident that extreme poverty is an intolerable evil than we can of *any* theory that would justify our claiming that or explaining that it is evil or, for that matter, that it really is not evil. We also know, *à la* Pogge, that such poverty is not necessary for it could be eradicated by transfers from the rich nations of the North and at relatively little cost to the North.[40]

Such poverty eradication, of course, will not yield equality or even an approximation of it. But we can make redistributive moves to better the life conditions of people, with little cost for peoples of the North, so that, while some will still be the worst off, few, if any, will be so impoverished and living in such misery as they are now. They could have clean water, decent shelter, enough to eat, medical care of at least a rudimentary kind and some education. In these ways, if some such Pogge-like practical redistributive measures are adopted, they will achieve, not the rose garden of equality and equal flourishing, not even justice; but they will achieve something approximating, perhaps actually meeting, sufficiency. Things would be better for vast numbers of people – the now wretched of the earth – and not be extensively worse for anyone else than they are now.

However – and realizing that sufficiency is a sliding notion, sliding with the productive capacities of the world – we should not be complacent if we ever come to achieving something like sufficiency in our poverty eradication efforts. Practically speaking we will/should have achieved something of very considerable importance. With that achievement our world would be less of a hell than it is now and that is not to be sneezed at. But it still could, even then, be a lot better. When we Lefties say a different and better world is possible, we do not mean *just* that Pogge-like sufficiency is possible.

Keeping in mind my above remarks about "the sliding nature of sufficiency," we should realize that what can be done and should be done is partially set – perhaps completely set – by our historical and contextual circumstances. However, with the increase in the productive wealth of the world, once, for example, everyone has a primary education, we should seek to make secondary education universal and once secondary education is universal, we should work to make free access to college education universal and once that is obtained, free access to university education should become universal. Very likely for entrance to university there would need to be some educational requirements, but universities would be open and free to anyone who can meet them. Corrective measures concerning bad background conditions should be put in place that would help all who aspire to university entrance to meet such requirements. Some, even with such help, may not come to acquire such an ability. They should not be admitted.

But we should be very careful in applying this. We should err, if we have the resources to do so, on the side of leniency and give them a fair chance.

We should work along these lines until we would harm ourselves – viewing society as a whole – still more in some other equally, or nearly equal, vital respect or respects by ploughing all that money into, say, university education. To make, and to be justified in making, such a claim does not require philosophical expertise but, for people living in the wake of the Enlightenment, moral reflectiveness, i.e., a taking to head and to heart – what for us – that is, we children of the Enlightenment – is to take the moral point of view.[41] I say "for we children of the Enlightenment," not for everyone of every time and place, for from the latter vantage points there are only moral points of view but nothing like *the* moral point of view. There is no non-question-begging perspective from which, or by use of which, we can escape a historicism here.

However, even from an Enlightenment social liberal perspective, how do we balance or index these various plain social goods? That, at least, looked at abstractly and generally, poses problems, problems that Rawls was particularly sensitive to. *Perhaps* the general indexing problem can be largely bypassed if we take a Deweyan contextual and broadly experimental approach, reasoning in a particular context concerning particular conditions over a specific problematic situation where hard, practical questions (not "questions" that Peirce said emerged from Cartesian "paper doubts") arise about which social good is to have priority at a particular time and place. Where there are contexts where some social goods at least appear to conflict, then we have a problem: a problematic situation to be rectified. (If it can be shown that they do not conflict, no priority needs to be established.) But where they do seem to conflict or perhaps really do conflict we should make "hypotheses" – careful and imaginative conjectures – about what is to be done *in that context* attending (a) to the situational sense of the fairness involved and (b) to the particular weal and woe involved. We *hypothesize* that if such and such is done, then more good for the people affected would obtain than if it were not done – for instance, there would be less suffering in this particular context. This hypothesis could be put to the test. When what it predicts obtains and it still seems unfair or in some way otherwise undesirable when the people involved carefully reflect in that context, then the hypothesis is infirmed. If, alternatively, when what it predicts obtains it does not seem unfair or otherwise undesirable and people come to contentedly live with it, then it is to some degree confirmed. This does not rest just on approvals but on approvals made when certain conditions obtain. People in such contexts are not simply sacrificed for others as might obtain even under a situational utilitarianism or an *unqualified* consequentialism. We suggest (with our conjecture) something specific about what should be done in certain relatively determinate situations for the people involved and try it on with them for fit: try to see how it squares with a consistent ensemble of people's considered judgments. If it does, the hypothesis is confirmed; if not, it is disconfirmed. This is not to make a conjecture, let alone a claim, about how *in all situations* we would index such social goods. Judgments should remain contextual and fallible (subject to revision). But this is something that can yield an intersubjective form of objectivity, perhaps the only form of objectivity that we can get in such domains: perhaps in all domains.

Where do we stop, let us now ask, in our search for sufficiency? Here is where equality treated as a heuristic is important. It points vaguely in the general direction that should be taken. We should note here that the above Deweyan contextualism and historicism can very well leave intact an *ideal* of equality. Still, sticking with a heuristic vaguely characterized in terms of moral equality (the life of everyone matters and matters equally) and the related conception of the equal worth of all human beings, we get something that yields little of *substance*. But it does give us some *sense* of direction, though not very much. Philosophers such as Rawls, Sen, Dworkin, G. A. Cohen, Joshua Cohen, Thomas Scanlon, Brian Barry, and Norman Daniels have done yeoman's work concerning equality here that, *if* it comes to nothing more, helps us to sharpen our heuristic. They have asked the question, "Equality of *what* and for *whom*?" There are sharp and interesting divisions between them. I am inclined to think, as Daniels has carefully argued, that there is an important convergence between the views of Rawls and Sen (two of the most important views) and with this convergence we have a very persuasive normative view indeed.[42] But I am also inclined to something like G. A. Cohen's conflicting, or at least *prima facie* importantly conflicting, view[43] and at the moment I don't know which (if either) road to take in that yellow wood.[44] But I am not trying to enter that wood *here* and I do not need to for purposes of this essay. It is not necessary for ascertaining that the grinding, debilitating, killing poverty that we have in our world is unnecessary.[45] It is not something that is unavoidable like hurricanes are and in reality it is avoidable at no great cost.[46] So, being an unnecessary evil, its wrongness – its plain intolerableness – is there for all of us to recognize and acknowledge and without getting entangled in what Rawls takes to be metaphysics (for him any controversial *philosophical* view).[47]

That notwithstanding, what I am saying is that getting clear about equality of what and in what measure (how much of it) and with what scope (that is for whom) yields ideals of equality that, even if unattainable, are desirable to articulate as *heuristics*. And that together – never forgetting that ought implies can – with ascertaining what in this respect is achievable both domestically and globally, and what is likely to be the case in the foreseeable future, gives us a crucial sense of what is to be done. The *achievability* questions, and at what costs, are clearly empirical questions. Questions of equality of what and how much of it and with what scope are, of course, in some sense normative philosophical questions – I don't say *only* normative questions – and they engage the attention of philosophers of the first rank. But, and this is vital for what is at issue here, these philosophers, in engaging in such investigations, invoke no (or at least need not invoke) metaphysics, epistemology, or metaethics, nor for their analyses do they require any or presuppose any. They travel, as Rawls says – to repeat, using "metaphysics" very broadly to mean any controversial philosophical thesis – metaphysically light.[48] And this is exactly what is to be done. (Is this just confidently proclaiming where I have no grounds for such confidence?)

However, I have left out here mention of "normative ethical *theory*." But, a critic might remark, are not these activities of the Rawls-Senian-Cohenian sort part of some such thing and is that not a distinctive part of philosophy? Only the logical positivists tried, and mistakenly, to limit acceptable philosophical work vis-à-vis morality or ethics to metaethics and indeed to a metaethics narrowly conceived. Still the Rawls-Sen-Cohen-etc. questions cannot be answered, as can questions about the utter unacceptability of current levels of world poverty, by anyone with just a commonsensically accessible sense – as Engels once put it – of common human decency and a little Pogge-style empirical investigation. In arguing that world poverty is unnecessary and immoral, all we need is *sufficiency* criteria and we don't even have to be very exact about that. We do not need, morally and practically speaking, to argue about equality, let alone about whether it has *intrinsic* value. The Rawls-Sen-Cohen-etc. questions concerning equality do require, of course, careful and disciplined moral reflection and conceptual clarity and they require reasonably systematic and empirically reasonable answers. *In this sense* they are normative ethical and are not innocent of theory. A knowledge of something of the history of moral philosophy and of history and of the social sciences, including economics (pruned of positivist preconceptions), is also helpful here.[49] But, as far as I can see, we do not need to know beans about metaphysics, epistemology, metaethics, or perhaps even of systematic normative ethical *theory* (e.g., utilitarianism or perfectionism) to come to grips with the Rawls-Sen-Cohen-type questions. Such considerations are more likely to get in the way by generating all sorts of pseudo-problems and mental cramps or problems which in some sense are genuine enough, but these considerations do not help us with the demanding moral-political-economic problems or with the living ethical problems I have mentioned. Moreover – and this is crucial – to ascertain that and how, without the North having to commit fiscal *hari kari*, we can rid the world of its grinding poverty and misery, we do not need equality (as desirable as that may be) or even justice but just sufficiency at the level and by the means of which Pogge sets out and argues for when he talks about world poverty eradication. And that certainly is to travel in Rawls's sense *philosophically* light. We do not need to invoke any normative ethical theory at all to resolve problems of world poverty. A clear head and certain considered judgments that are part of a culture of a broadly social liberal, generally Enlightenment sort, together with a few well-thought-out considered empirical hypotheses (conjectures) along with an understanding of their expectable implications (such as the Pogge ones) will suffice without getting into arcane philosophical disputes.

This may all well be. But *perhaps* we do need as well to say how extensive this moving in the direction of something like equality can be and should be. Perhaps we should speak only of political equality. We need to consider what determinate kinds we should seek or (more minimally) what kind of decency and to what extent it is morally speaking required for life in this world to be morally tolerable. Or perhaps we should seek something significantly beyond the obscenity that we now have. Politically speaking, perhaps this is all that we can reasonably seek. Will there be, even if we all are (as surely we are not now) children of the Enlightenment, a convergence toward agreement about what would count as a decent world order? Is the obtaining of this something we can reasonably expect, struggle for, and reasonably hope for? There could be agreement that our actual world is swinish and that something can and should be done to make it less so without there being agreement about equality or even about what thorough decency would come to and about whether we could attain both or either. Is it not here *prima facie* (*contra* my thesis) where philosophical arguments about equality are important? I leave this as an open question while continuing to insist that we do not have to come to grips with that while continuing to recognize that the actual and rising inequality and the resulting severe poverty that we see rampant in our world is a plain and unnecessary evil. Here at least we can, and should, travel philosophically light.

V

Let us now turn, as the last of such considerations, to the two *ethical* as distinct from moral-political-economic cases. I follow Rawls and Habermas in distinguishing between *the moral* (having to do with justice, duty, obligation and decency issues about how society or the world should be ordered and how persons should be treated) and *the ethical* (having to do with how to live one's life, what one's life plans should be, what a good life or a good way of living would be). Ethical questions are usually more personal than moral ones, are less given to universal claims; they leave more room for *agent-centred reasons* and *agent-relative prerogatives* and rest more on personal reflective decisions and individual choice. They are deeply about how one should live one's life, how one should relate to particular others and about what choices we should be making in the living of our lives.

I do not claim there is a dichotomy or a sharp division or even a sharp distinction between the moral and the ethical. There is not. There is often a blurred line between them. And I do not claim that there is some dichotomy between "the private" and "the public." There isn't any more than there is a dichotomy between "the is" and "the ought." And, again like "the is" and "the ought," there are issues and questions that do not clearly fit into just one or the other. But there are plenty of paradigm cases of each, i.e., the moral or the ethical. And it is important to be aware of the distinction, albeit sometimes a blurred one, here.

Reflect back on cases (13) and (14), both clear cases of the ethical and distinct from the moral-political-economic cases; (13) was about a young academic making choices and (14) was about the old academic winding down his career and indeed his life and trying to figure out how to spend his last few years. Let me stipulate, just to make matters simpler, that they both are alone and will remain so. They, of course, have the demands their co-nationals, students and colleagues, and people at large make on them. But they stand in no more intimate personal relations. By this I mean they have no grandparents, parents, spouses, children, or kin. The two cases are parallel in many respects, though perhaps not in all. I shall limit myself to treating them in the ways they are alike.

First for individuals, the instances of my two cases, the issues connected with their deciding what to do are what Williams James calls live and momentous. On the one hand, they could make disastrous choices that would make things very bad for them indeed and, on the other hand, there are a good number of more or less desirable choices that would aid in giving some point and happiness to their lives and enhance their human flourishing without negating what they owe to others. However, it is anything but obvious which of these options for choice we described are the best even for them or indeed whether anything is "the best" even for them let alone for anyone in a similar situation. This is one of the reasons, along with respect for their autonomy, that rules out paternalism – perhaps even "soft paternalism" – here. We *may* mildly offer some warning if we can divine that someone is going for a disaster, but that should be a matter of kindness and concern, not a fussy desire to intervene. But, particularly where someone is alone, as we stipulated, if she (or he) persists, we should, typically with sadness, let him or her go to hell on a hay rake if that is what she or he is bent on doing. After all it is *her* life and what she does with it is her business and her business alone as long as she does not harm others or the state which governs her, say by making unnecessary drains on its resources. There is on our part, where in such circumstances someone does something harmful to herself, normally regret and sadness but no skin off anyone else's nose, including our own. So if she persists we should not try to stop her from going her own way except in very extreme cases. Concerning the range of more or less desirable choices for the young academic or the old one, our lips should be closed unless our counsel is asked. And even then we should counsel with discretion and take care not to inadvertently push what would be our own choice among putatively equally reasonable ones. *Respect for persons* requires this.

All ethical principles, beliefs, and practices that are compatible with what political justice requires are acceptable here; they are up for individual discretion and choice, in a way that moral-political-economic principles themselves or at least the fundamental principles of justice for what Rawls calls the basic structure of our society are not. But over questions of the good life anything compatible with our fundamental principles of justice for the basic structure of society – say the two principles of justice as fairness – is acceptable (where these principles of justice themselves are justifiable).[50] But, to repeat, this does not obtain for the principles of justice for the basic structure themselves. So we get a legitimate place for individual choice and respect for all without falling into "bourgeois individualism" or "*laissez faire* individualism."

All that notwithstanding, the idea that there can be no better or worse answers to such ethical questions as we discussed above is mistaken.[51] Since there can be disastrous resolutions there must be better or worse resolutions of such situations, and, that being so, there is good reason to think there can be finer-grained discriminations of better and worse resolutions (ways of living and reacting) *perhaps*, in principle at least, all the way down to a best resolution of such resolutions for a given time and place and for a given personality or type of personality. But, as we saw above, that does not justify or even sanction paternalism. And even if there is a best resolution there is no justifying a demand that this is the resolution we *must* make or have an obligation to make and that we act in a morally untoward way if we do not.

When it is said *au contraire* that there is no one right answer or no best answer, we might be referring to the rather banal fact that people are different and would make different choices in such situations. I think this is indeed so, but even more importantly, we can be taking to head and to heart an important political and moral consideration which is at the heart of political liberalism, namely the centrality of its belief in the equal worth of persons which goes with a requirement of equal respect for all persons which in turn entails that they have the equal right to live their lives in their own way, by their own lights, as long as they respect that in others and do not harm others. Our general fallibilism contributes to this too – Oliver Cromwell's "think man that, in the bowels of Christ, you might be wrong." But it is the notion of the equal worth of all persons – a deep (perhaps even *the* deep) political liberal conviction – that is the most deep-seated reason.[52]

None of this amounts to the moral of my account of the two ethical cases (13 and 14). The moral is that even more obviously than in the moral-political-economic cases metaphysics, epistemology, metaethics, or even normative ethical *theory* plays no role or (more moderately) only a very minor role in helping us to see clearly our way. Those two cases are powerful and not atypical instances of demanding and humanly important ethical problems. But again here none of the standard philosophical activities plays much of a role in their resolution or even in gaining clarity about them. Lest that appear like mere counter-assertion, I put it to you to articulate any place where some issues of metaphysical, epistemological, metaethical, or grand normative ethical theory relevantly intrude into our reasoning concerning a reflective consideration of these ethical problems that are often at the very centre of our individual lives. Specify a way where philosophy, in its strictly or even in other reasonably standard technical senses, plays any role in such reflections. Give me a case (stable cleaning or Wittgensteinian therapy aside) where philosophy plays any role in the hard excruciating deliberations which are characteristic of the ethical life.

Reflectiveness and being informed does, of course, play an important part, but we cannot *identify* reflectiveness and being informed with being philosophical. There are plenty of reflective and informed people around who are not philosophers (most of them are not philosophers) and some of them know or care precious little about philosophy. There is a *colloquial* sense in which anyone in being reflective by that very act could be said to be philosophical, as in "being pensive and reflective she struck a philosophical attitude, came into a philosophical mood." That shows *something* about "philosophy" and "philosophical," but no one is fooled who knows anything about philosophy into thinking that constitutes doing philosophy.

What is most relevant in gaining clarity concerning what is opportune for the reasoning and reflectiveness that goes on in the two above cases (and cases like them) is literature and certain kinds of historical and journalistic narratives as well. And for the literature it is most salient to think of the kinds of reflections generated by a reading of Cervantes, Turgenev, Tolstoy, Dostoevksy, Chekov, Stendhal, Flaubert, Mann, Balzac, Dickens, George Eliot, Hardy, Virginia Wolf, Melville, and O'Neill, to take some important examples. Reading them with any attention at all makes us think about the characters and the situations they are in and about their lives. In ruminating about those characters and their situations, we think of our own lives and the lives of others both concretely and reflectively abstractly. When the young woman struggles to determine what kind of life should go with her desire to be in some sense an academic in a certain discipline to which she is devoted, having the will to carry on research in that discipline and to teach, to direct theses and the like, she is trying to sort out what kind of various options to consider within that discipline and what they involve. Similarly, the old man wanting to complete certain academic projects but also to live in a certain way in his last years is trying to determine his options and their consequences. For both of them, literature could be of considerable moment, aiding them in the making of their very real, but very personal, reflective choices where they engage in this demanding ethical thinking. But I do not see how philosophy – in any tolerably technical sense – would be of much help. Some might say – as some non-philosophers would – that philosophy just is moral and ethical reflection on our situation, i.e., the human condition. But that is just more arbitrary stipulative redefinition. That is not the sort of language-games that philosophers play – or at least typically play – when they philosophize. That they should transform themselves, and think of philosophy as a transformational genre, is another matter altogether. But, in stressing that, I should not deny that many of the great philosophers of the Tradition – the Stoics, Montaigne, Spinoza, for example – had a vision, a distinctive way of viewing the world with a conception of how it should be ordered that will remain worthy of our study and reflection and should remain a part of whatever philosophy should be transformed into.

Am I simply saying – as one critic put it – that philosophy is not useful? I am indeed saying that it is not useful (something that is generally recognized), and I specify in what important senses it is not useful. I am, and crucially, saying something else as well. I am saying that over the most crucial matters of life – something that *may* have driven us to philosophy in the first place – philosophy has very little to say. That is a bitter pill for a moral philosopher to swallow. But, if they would not deceive themselves, it is a pill they have to swallow.[53] However, it loses some of its bitterness when we come to clearly see, and take to heart, this is a skepticism about what philosophy can achieve in this direction and a realization that it need not, indeed should not, be a skepticism about whether reflective and reasonably informed persons, reflecting and reflecting probingly with honesty and integrity, and sometimes a collectivity of people so reflecting together, can make sense of their lives and of their world and indeed to see something of how it could come to be a more humane and more reasonable world. It is not a skepticism, or at least not in any fundamental sense, about that. It is rather a skepticism about the importance of philosophy as it has come to be conceived, and as the Tradition has conceived it, not a "value nihilism" or skepticism about making sense of either life or the *possibilities* of a decent social order.

It isn't that we do not know that good is to be done and evil is to be avoided (Aquinas's utterly empty first principle of the so-called "natural moral law") or that "unnecessary suffering is evil." Of course we know these things. Even Shakespeare's Richard the Third knew them. But we do not need any *theory* to know them – just enculturation into a humane social liberal ethos (what Rawls would call a liberal background culture). And don't tell me that we do not understand what we mean by "humane" or that it is "an essentially contested concept." (We know very well what we mean and there are no *essentially* contested examples.) But knowing the above truisms tells us next to nothing about "real world justice" or even about just plain "real world decency."[54] It does not guide us about what to do and how to live. We also know that it is a plain evil (to put it mildly) that all those (or even any) children die of malnutrition before they reach the age of five. Similarly it is another plain evil that vast numbers of other children live and work in virtual slavery in horrible conditions. If anything is evil these things are. Saying such things are evil is, of course, to make moral judgments with some substantive content. But they are moral judgments that are perfectly unproblematic. Moreover, I am not just being Luddite in saying we do not need theory to know these things are evil. Our sense of this is exacerbated when we come to realize what Thomas Pogge has shown us empirically, namely that how little are the changes we would have to make – minimal changes to the way people in the rich North live – to end such misery – such plain evils – as I have just described. Our anger here is fuelled when we realize that it is clearly "unnecessary suffering": that there is no longer even the slightest excuse for thinking it necessary because unavoidable. The problem is that nothing – or next to nothing – is done about it in the world order in which we live. Only in *that* world is it "necessary." The thing is to get from our global pigsty to something that is at least minimally decent. We do not know *how* to do that (how to bring it about), though we know along general lines *what* needs to be done. Here philosophy, including moral theory in all its varieties, is silent: silent over what most of all we need to understand and over what needs to be done. Brecht was right and Dickens was right too in writing about their epochs' hard times, times that could be ours. They bitterly described things as they were but, still with a hope of a better future, Dickens wrote in his own Victorian manner, "We shall sit with lighter bosoms on the hearth, to see the ashes of our fires turn grey and cold."[55]

Notes

1. Nielsen, *Globalization and Justice*, 41–137.
2. Harvey, "Cosmopolitanism and the Banality of Geographical Evils"; and Said, *Reflections on Exile*, 453–72.
3. Rorty, "Post-Democracy," 3–28.
4. See here Ignacio Ramonet's perceptive remarks in his leader in *Le Monde diplomatique*, 1.
5. Ibid.
6. Kumar, "Progress, Freedom and Human Nature"; and H. Putnam, *Ethics without Ontology*, 96–108.
7. Nielsen, "Pragmatism as Atheoreticism."
8. Rawls, "For the Record."
9. H. Putnam: *The Collapse of the Fact/Value Dichotomy*; and *Ethics without Ontology*.
10. H. Putnam, *Ethics without Ontology*.
11. Daniels, "Equality of What?"
12. Habermas, *Truth and Justification*, 213–36.
13. Harvey, *The Condition of Postmodernity*, 201–326.
14. Nielsen, *Globalization and Justice*, 33–35 and 243–80.
15. Ignatieff, "How to Keep Afghanistan from Falling Apart"; and Ignatieff, "The Burden."
16. Hobsbawm, "America's Imperialist Delusion."
17. Rorty, "Post-Democracy," on post-democracy; and Falk, *The Declining World Order*, 248–52, on fascism.
18. I am not suggesting by this that all intellectuals or even most intellectuals are naïve.

19 Berlin, *Concepts and Categories*, 103–42.

20 Joseph Stiglitz's *Globalization and Its Discontents* is significant here. But also see Ben Fine and Elisa Van Valyenberge's perceptive criticisms in "Correcting Stiglitz."

21 I mean the classical anarchists, e.g., Mikhail Bakunin, and some contemporary continuers of that tradition, e.g., Noam Chomsky.

22 H. Putnam, *The Collapse of the Fact/Value Dichotomy*, 28–45.

23 Stevenson, *Ethics and Language*, 206–26.

24 Nielsen, "Formalists and Informalists."

25 H. Putnam, *The Collapse of the Fact/Value Dichotomy*, 7–27 and 53–77.

26 Hall, *Categorical Analysis*, 106–32.

27 H. Putnam, *The Collapse of the Fact/Value Dichotomy*, 28–43.

28 Rorty, *Philosophy and Social Hope*, 47–71.

29 Nielsen, "Pragmatism as Atheoreticism."

30 Harvey, *The New Imperialism*; and "The 'New' Imperialism," 137–82.

31 H. Putnam, *The Collapse of the Fact/Value Dichotomy*, 28–95.

32 Said, *Culture and Imperialism*.

33 Geuss, *The Idea of a Critical Theory*.

34 See Falk, *The Declining World Order*, 241–52. I have not mentioned terrorism as one of the major problems of our time and it certainly is. That I do not deny nor wish to obscure or downplay. I have written elsewhere about terrorism and stressed there how much the concept needs clarification in the process of de-mystifying its frequent ideological uses. It is crucial to distinguish small group or non-state terrorism such as practised by Al Qaeda and state terrorism such as practised by the United States, the Soviet Union, or some 'rogue states,' e.g., Libya. These different terrorisms are (or were) all to some people a powerful threat. But it is important to ask how much terrorism is linked to imperialism, either as an expression of it or as causally linked to it, and to consider the possibilities of its going away as long as imperialism exists. See Nielsen, "On the Moral Justification of State Terrorism." See also Chomsky, "Simple Truths, Hard Problems."

35 It pains me, as an old and continuing socialist, to have to say this. But the historical record makes this clear. This does not mean, however, that I agree with Elizabeth Anderson that some form of social democratic capitalism is either the best or only game in town. See Anderson, "Interview." In effect, *pace* Anderson, as well as Stiglitz, see Fine and Valyenberge, "Correcting Stiglitz."

36 Chomsky, "Simple Truths, Hard Problems."

37 Pogge, "Information and Priorities of Global Justice," 1–23.

38 Alternatively, it might be said, as the IMF in effect did, that we have here short-term pain for long-term gain. Try telling this to the starving millions, to the parents of those starving children who will die before the age of five, to the many slaves we have in the world, or to the people living in the shanty towns of the Third World (Mexico City or Cape Town, for example) or in the slums of New York

City or Cleveland, particularly when, as Joseph Stiglitz forcefully argues, feasible alternatives, even within the capitalism system, exist. Stiglitz, *Globalization and Its Discontents*, 145–252. To wait for the markets to right themselves to cure things, as Lionel Robbins advised concerning the Great Depression, is to justifiably provoke Keynes's quip that in the long run we are all dead. To speak as I have is not an appeal to pity but, as Marx well saw, an expression of indignation rooted in a sense of gross injustice. *Das Kapital* rages (and rightly) against the extreme injustice of the capitalist world.

39 Daniels, "Equality of What?"; and Nielsen, "On the Moral Justification of State Terrorism," 139–90.

40 Pogge, "Information and Priorities of Global Justice," 1–23.

41 H. Putnam, *Ethics without Ontology*, 89–129; and Nielsen, "Moral Point of View."

42 Daniels, "Equality of What?"

43 G. A. Cohen, *If You're an Egalitarian, How Come You're So Rich?*

44 See here also Tan, "Justice and Personal Pursuits"; and Chambers, "The Politics of Equality."

45 To say 'grinding, debilitating, killing but not evil' is to fail to understand the use of 'grinding,' 'debilitating,' 'killing,' particularly when linked with 'unnecessary,'

46 Pogge, "Information and Priorities of Global Justice," 1–23.

47 Rawls, "Justice as Fairness."

48 Ibid.

49 H. Putnam, *The Collapse of the Fact/Value Dichotomy*, 40–45; and Toulmin, *Return to Reason*, 47–101.

50 These fundamental (basic, central) principles of justice for the basic structure of liberal society themselves are justified when they are in wide reflective equilibrium with the most coherent system of considered judgments, moral rules, widely accepted empirical beliefs and theoretical judgments that people, subscribing to a liberal ethos, can have at a given time in history. (They are not something there just to be intuited, though they can *become* our considered judgments.) I do not think we can escape that historicism (hence the reference to liberal ethos) and that, in effect, I believe, Rawls accepts. That is not relativism or skepticism, let alone nihilism, but a form of fallibilism. Nielsen, "Pragmatism as Atheoreticism." Rawls's fundamental principles of justice are not *First* Principles upon which everything depends – there are none – but the most deeply embedded principles of a coherentist system that is holist, changing, fallibilistic, and historicist. The most coherent such system for a time (if there is one) is the one that at that time is best justified, i.e., is the most coherent. This is tautological, but it reminds us of what justification is. There is nothing that is 'time-transcendent' which we can appeal to. There is no escaping such contingency and such circularity. Rawls, "Justice as Fairness," 286–302; Nielsen, "Philosophy within the Limits of Wide Reflective Equilibrium Alone," and *Naturalism without Foundations*, 169–205.

51 H. Putnam, *The Collapse of the Fact/Value Dichotomy*, 111–34.

52 Larmore, "The Moral Basis of Political Liberalism."

53 In claiming the impoverishment of moral philosophy, it might be said that I have been subsisting on a one-sided diet. If I had attended to some of the *best* work in biomedical ethics instead of the domains I have focused on here, I could *not* have responsibly or reasonably claimed such poverty. I have in mind the work of Allen Buchanan, Dan W. Brock, Norman Daniels, and Daniel Wikler on genetics and justice as well as the work of Arthur Caplan and James Griffin more generally in biomedical ethics. Buchanan et al., *From Chance to Choice*; Brock, "Quality of Life Measures in Health Care and Medical Ethics," 95–132; Griffin, "Commentary on Dan Brock," 133–39. They all work with sophistication, conceptual adroitness, a good command of the relevant facts on the ground, a good command of ethical theory and give an insightful and creative deployment of it to health issues and matters linked. Isn't this a living and impressive counter-example to what I have been claiming about the poverty of moral theory? Perhaps I should cut down the scope of my claims and further clarify them. (1) I was (and am) claiming it for the urgent matters of which I speak in the body of my text. I believe they are the most urgent matters we human beings now face, but they certainly are not the only urgent matters. However, attending, in the way Buchanan et al. do, to questions raised by ethical and moral matters arising from our modern understanding of genetics or quality of life issues is not fiddling while Rome burns. (2) I did not claim (and do not claim) that there is any conceptual or 'transcendental' *necessity* that moral philosophy be so fettered or impoverished over the matters to which I draw our attention. *Perhaps* there is something important that philosophy can contribute here. I certainly do not try to rule it out *a priori*. However, a good dose of skepticism about that (i.e., philosophy's contribution) would not be unhealthy. Our historical track record has not been very impressive here. (3) I am a philosopher and can hardly not start in my work by working with the resources that we philosophers have. I have resolved, for however long it takes me, to do what I can to say something helpful about the issues revolving around globalization, imperialism, and global justice. I shall do this without worrying about whether what I am doing is or is not philosophy. I shall only be concerned about whether what I say is reasonably clear, well-warranted and empirically responsible. It is important here to keep in mind that 'philosophy' is not the name of a natural kind. I shall go on working with tools from wherever I can find them that are most useful for whatever needs to be said concerning these issues. I think that certain social scientists, principally political economists and historians, are better placed than philosophers or literary scholars are here. (But then I remember Bertrand Russell, Edward Said, David Harvey, and Noam Chomsky; things do not always go along disciplinary lines.) However, for much of the work being done here there is little need for philosophical specialties such as Augean stable

cleaning or Wittgensteinian therapy. I cannot but help asking myself, what can I do to put my shoulder to the wheel in some useful manner in what is our common human task concerning these pressing moral-political-economic problems? Is there anything to be done by philosophers, except perhaps to popularize things, to give a simple and clear account of what political economists, historians, and social geographers say about such matters? Yet can they not do that better themselves? We philosophers would like to think there is something different or special that we philosophers can do. But what? Is there anything we can learn here from the way bioethicists such as Buchanan and Daniels have proceeded in the way they have discussed ethical and moral problems posed by genetics? They shuttle back and forth, in a good Rawlsian fashion, between, on the one hand, specific considered judgments in our culture as well as new such judgments generated by specific reflection on matters genetic and, on the other hand, more general moral considerations as well as warranted empirical beliefs including ones that require a good knowledge of genetics. They seek to get these matters into wide reflective equilibrium. In doing those things, they are attending to context and to being empirically responsible utilizing a good knowledge of genetics and a good knowledge of moral philosophy. Bringing these things together may pay off intellectually (probably more on the conceptual side of things). It *seems* at least to work for thinking about the moral implications of genetics. Perhaps it can work for theorizing globalization, imperialism, and empire as well. We will never know until we try. Still deep skepticism here is not unreasonable. It is also salutary to keep in mind what Buchanan et al. take to be the limitations of their project, namely the importance of context and the necessity of providing guidance without trying to give specific policy recommendations. This is vague – perhaps emptiness lurks here – but it is possible that when things are carefully spelled out this will turn out not to be so. Philosophers are there, in the classical tradition of Socrates, to raise difficulties, of course, but it shouldn't turn into *eristic*, resulting in holding up things when the engine is *not* idling. That would be a mere playing with words and indeed fiddling while Rome burns. Too much is at stake for that. Children sometimes ask why once too often. That can be true of philosophers as well. Yet there are crucial 'why' questions that sometimes do not usually get asked. We need to be able to grasp which is which without allowing this inquiry to distract us from the crucial substantive problems at hand.

Alex Sager, in an insightful and instructive note to me, has questioned whether I have not given too much credit to the bioethics crowd. Even such an important book as *From Chance to Choice*, though fascinating on its own account, may not come to much in answering key problems concerning health that are in some ways parallel to the key moral-political-economic problems discussed in the text. They would include crucially a consideration of to what extent technologies (including genetic ones) can be used to alleviate hunger and how they can help us treat disease. These are straightforward empirical issues hardly needing philosophical analysis. They are largely a matter of cost-benefit-risk analysis. For example, if there is good evidence that genetically engineered crops will produce greater quantities of food with little risk (including the well-known ensemble of at least putative bad side effects), then research into genetically engineered crops should be publicly funded and publicly controlled. We can hardly trust companies such as Monsanto with this. Any research that they do and recommendations based on this research must be carefully checked. Their interests are too much at stake to trust them with it. And apart from that, there is always the risk – and this is crucial – that we do not know enough. We must make sure that we are not unwittingly bringing on a catastrophe. However, as complicated as these matters are, they are complicated empirical matters with important moral implications. But philosophy is of little or no help here, beyond some obvious matters of Augean stable cleaning – or so, at least, it seems. The best of the biomedical ethicists do some useful conceptual clarification of ideas (e.g., the disability rights movement). But the importance of biomedical ethics is vastly overrated. Moreover, biomedical ethicists are not asked how biomedical ethics could – or if it could – help respond to the two urgent issues raised above. Biomedical ethicists do not bring to the forefront an important ideological issue. Indeed, they usually proceed as if there were no problems here. A lot of philosophers engaged in talking about public health actually (usually unwittingly) in effect function to legitimize the policies in place. In striving to be relevant and to now suggest anything too out of the ordinary, philosophical sophistication often in effect becomes a tool for reinforcing the *status quo*. This, at least arguably, is more sinister than the poverty of moral philosophy or its irrelevance. Health care is, of course, of vast importance. But we are so far away from providing adequate health care – especially if we regard the matter globally but even if we stick to the wealthy North – that it doesn't require philosophical sophistication to figure out what is wrong. China, for example, has some magnificent hospitals. But they are extremely costly – some two thousand U.S. dollars for a bed for one night – indeed too costly for almost all patients. Indeed they usually cater to very rich foreigners. But most Chinese people have very inadequate health care and some no health care at all. But the health care in Canada, the United States, and Britain is nothing to get enthusiastic about. Most of the real issues here are empirical and the socially important normative issues they raise are unproblematic. The central concern is with what institutions will guarantee: reasonably, high quality *universal* health care.

54 Nielsen, *Globalization and Justice*, 243–80.

55 Someone might claim that this whole essay is one big performative self-contradiction. I am, it might be contended, using moral philosophy to claim that moral philosophy is impoverished. If that isn't a

performative contradiction, the objection might continue, it is very close to one. How can one use something that one believes to be flawed to argue for its being flawed? I seem at least to be unsaying what I am saying. I reject that. I have invoked no moral theory or moral philosophy. I have described something of our world, I hope reasonably accurately, often using thick normative concepts involving a thorough and unscrambled entanglement of fact and value. Putnam, *The Collapse of the Fact/Value Dichotomy*, 28–45; and Berlin, *Concepts and Categories*, 103–42. I have described, and sometimes practised, a bit of Augean stable cleaning and Wittgensteinian conceptual therapy and acknowledged their occasional value. But none of these activities involve invoking or appealing to a moral philosophy or to some metaphysics, epistemology, or metaethical *theory*. I have made some metaethical or metamoral remarks, e.g., talking about the entanglement of fact and value, and I have, as well, made some substantive value judgments. But I have neither utilized nor assumed anything that would constitute either a moral or a metamoral theory or a moral philosophy. I have assembled reminders and reminded us, concerning places that are relevant to what is at hand, how we play some language games. But I have articulated no philosophical moral theory of any kind or any other kind of moral theory. I have not used a moral theory to try to show that moral theory is impoverished. And I have not assumed one, unless not to assume a moral theory is to assume one. But that is pointlessly paradoxical.

I was just putting the finishing touches on this essay when a new issue of *Imprints* arrived. It included an insightful interview with Elizabeth Anderson that, in effect, provides a strong challenge to what I have been saying here. (The only thing I had previously known by her is her masterful "What is the Point of Equality?") Her approach is very like mine, i.e., her Deweyan pragmatism, contextualism, suspicion of freewheeling speculation unconstrained by empirical realities and of ideal theory and above all her insistence that philosophers be empirically responsible and attend carefully to the facts on the ground. She is also concerned with issues with which I have been concerned and has a very similar sense of what must be done. Yet, in a far more substantive way than I think is feasible, she finds a place for philosophy here and makes creative and original suggestions about that. See Anderson, "Interview." *Perhaps*, by proceeding the way she does, she shows that there is genuine work to do for philosophy here. I am not convinced, but it shows that conversation here is not at an end.

Part II

EGALITARIANISM AND SOCIALISM

On the Choice between Reform and Revolution

I

Given the history of this century, it is understandable that there should be both an extensive fear of revolution and a distrust of the efficacy of reform. Yet when one considers such countries as the United States, Rhodesia, and South Africa (not to mention the poorer and savagely exploited parts of the world), it is also becoming increasingly obvious to any tolerably well-informed person who is also humane that a fundamental social transformation of these societies is humanly speaking imperative. And this, of course, thrusts one back on the suspect ideas of revolution and far-reaching social reform. This in turn raises questions about what one is committed to in believing in the moral necessity of radical social transformation. Is one committed to revolution or only to some form of very fundamental social reform? And this in turn naturally provokes the question: What exactly is the difference between them and what is one asking for when one advocates a progressive fundamental or radical social transformation?

Such questions were debated by Kautsky, Bernstein, Lenin, and Luxemburg in another context, but, without even remotely suggesting that what they had to say is irrelevant for us today, I want to look at this cluster of questions afresh. Is the assumed distinction between revolution and fundamental or radical reform only a distinction concerning the means, the instrumentalities, of social change, or does it refer to what is aimed at as well, e.g., *the kind* of change and the extent of change? Is the putative distinction between fundamental or radical reform and revolution a spurious one? And if the distinction is a genuine one, are they on a continuum? And more fundamentally still, if one is committed to seeking and advocating a fundamental social transformation, is one necessarily for revolution? Or, contrariwise, is the working for reform the only reasonable alternative for a humane person? This cluster of questions in turn raises a bevy of more specific questions including such overtly conceptual questions as what is meant by "revolution" and "reform."

To gain some purchase on these issues, it is well to begin by asking: What are we asking for when we ask for a fundamental social transformation or a transformation of society?

If we are committed to a progressive transformation, we are surely asking for an end to human oppression and exploitation. Even if this is only a heuristic ideal and in fact we can only realistically hope to diminish the extent and severity of oppression and human degradation, it still remains a fundamental guiding ideal: It tells us to what we are aiming as far as possible to approximate in any progressive transformation of society. To achieve this transformation all forms of racism, ethnocentrism, chauvinism, and rigid social stratification with its built-in privileges would have to come to an end. Class divisions and alienated labour would have to disappear. This would involve the abolition of the bourgeoisie; that is to say, there could no longer be a capitalist or any other kind of corporate ruling class, a bureaucratic or technocratic elite or establishment. The modes of production in the society would have to be thoroughly socialized so that their underlying rationale is to serve the interests of everyone alike. To be morally acceptable, specific privileges, when they are necessary at all, must be such that they further (typically in an indirect way) this underlying ideal.

The above characterization of what is involved in a progressive transformation of society is for the most part negative. Positively, our characterization will be more vague. As we know from Dante, evil is much easier to characterize than positive good. It is difficult, in talking about such a transformation, to say anything general which is not vague or platitudinous or (what is more likely) both. A progressively transformed society would give people a fuller and more human life. This quasi-tautology unpacks into the claim that people in such a transformed society would attain a liberation in which their full human powers and their creative capacities would be developed in a many-sided way. They would not be one-sided, emotionally or intellectually stunted individuals or academic *Fachidioten*, but would be people capable of managing their affairs, helping in the management of society in the interests of everyone alike, and capable of a wide range of enjoyments and creative activities. And they would not only have these capabilities, they would also be anxious to exercise them. In addition, there would be an end to possessive individualism and a commodity accumulation which goes beyond what humans need and would want when their wants are not artificially stimulated to enhance capitalist enterprise. Rather, there would be a commitment to social equality and to a fair and nearly equal distribution of the available goods and services. In different concrete situations, these different notions, positive and negative, will of course take different specifications and amplifications. But the elasticity of these specifications *is* not endless, since they are bounded by these general but non-formal conceptions. In transforming society our aim should be human freedom (the liberation of human creativity), equality, and the enhancement of human happiness and the avoidance of misery. In our present historical circumstances, this is best achieved in (a) a society founded upon common ownership of the means of production and (b) a society in which everyone participates in the running of their society. To fully exercise our human agency, we need a common culture with a maximum of human participation. Here we have the *leitmotif* for a progressive transformation of society.

For societies to be transformed so that this would be a reality, we would need, even in the most progressive societies, a very considerable institutional change, and in such powerful advanced industrial societies as the United States and Germany, the changes would have to be structural and very profound indeed. Could such a transformation be achieved without a revolution? Before trying to answer this, we need to gain some clarification about what we mean by "revolution" and how it contrasts with "reform" and what the conceptual links are between revolution and violence, for on *some* employments of "revolution" our question would be nearly as silly as "Are all emerald things green?" That is to say, on some readings of "revolution," it may be analytically (or at least in some sense necessarily) true that to be committed to seeking and advocating a fundamental progressive social transformation is to be for revolution.

II

So let us first get some purchase on what is meant by "revolution" and "reform." In doing this it is important to keep in mind that it is only against the background of a belief in progress that it makes sense to speak either of revolution or of reform. To reform is to convert into another and better form; it is, as the O.E.D. puts it, "to free from previous faults or imperfections." We speak of reforming institutions and social arrangements and by this we mean correcting them or improving them by amending or altering them through removing faults, abuses, malpractices, and the like. This implies that one social arrangement or set of social arrangements, or a practice or institution or set of practices or institutions, can be an advance or an improvement over another. But to believe in this is to believe that progress is possible within a limited timespan at least, though this is not sufficient to commit one to the full-fledged conceptions of progress found in Condorcet, Hegel, or Marx. A belief in the viability of revolutionary activity, as is well known and frequently remarked on, is even more obviously linked to a belief in progress. And if a belief in progress was one of the great and persistent illusions of the nineteenth century, then belief in either reform or revolution is belief in an illusion.[1]

One further preliminary. If the usage recorded in current dictionaries is focused on, it is evident enough that "revolution," or "revolutionary," has a negative emotive force while "reform," or "reformer," has a positive emotive force. Given the conventional criteria for "synonym" and "near synonym," the terms "remodel," "reconstruct," "reclaim," "redeem," "regenerate," "correct," "improve," "restore," and "better" all, in certain types of sentence, count as synonyms or near synonyms for "reform" when "reform" is a verb; when "reform" is a noun "correction," "progress," "reconstruction," and "reformation" count as synonyms. Here we clearly see that by definition "to reform" is to do something which at least the reformer takes to be desirable, and, more generally, in many (perhaps most) contexts, "reform" is so employed that something would not as a rule be said within a society to be a reform unless it was thought to be desirable, though "stupid and undesirable reforms" is not a contradiction in terms. The latter are reforms which have somehow misfired and misfired *as reforms*. Furthermore, if the word "reform" is to continue to have a use, reforms regarded as stupid or undesirable must be exceptions and not the rule. If I assert that I have made a reform, I give you to understand that I have done something good. There is, in short, a pronounced positive emotive force to "reform." Only on some uses of "reform," conspicuously where a reformer is equated with a zealot, crusader, or do-gooder, does the term acquire a negative emotive force. By contrast, given the usages assembled in dictionaries, it is evident enough that "revolution" and "revolutionary" typically have a negative emotive force. I approach this in an indirect way.

We are interested in revolution as a socio-political concept, but the word "revolution" has other uses too and in attempting a very general characterization of "revolution," one dictionary tells us that we are talking about "a complete or drastic change of any kind." And when we keep in mind that "revolution" has this wide range of uses, it is worth noting that sometimes "revolution" is equated with "spasm," "convulsion," "revulsion," and "cataclysm." Here we have words that have negative emotive force. This emotive force is evident again in those contexts where "revolution" is equated with "rebellion," "insurrection," "subversion," "destruction," or "disruption," and we have adjectives such as "radical," "extreme," "catastrophic," and "intransigent" linked with revolution and revolutionary. And while it is true that the meanings of "revolution" and "reform" are not yoked to their emotive force, their emotive force is such that, unless one takes pains to account for it and neutralize it in arguments about the justification of revolution, one is at an initial disadvantage in defending revolution.

In order to know what the actual substantive claims of the reformers are, we must consider what their criteria for improvement, bettering, and the like are. Political reform involves legal, educational, economic, and generally institutional correction or improvements. Faults and abuses are corrected. Here what is crucial is to gain some clarity about the actual criteria for improvement, correction, amendment, or making better. In speaking of reforming Germany's archaic university system, for example, are we talking about altering it to respond more efficiently to the needs of a modern industrial state, or do we primarily have in mind altering it so as to extend, sharpen, and systematize critical awareness among the German population, or do we mean something else again? What in such a situation is the amplification of "reform"? But whatever we mean, we are also saying, when we defend educational reform, that we are for improvement in the existing educational structures and not for sweeping them away and replacing them by utterly new structures of a radically different nature. In talking more generally of socio-political reform, which typically would include as one of its crucial components educational reform, we are talking of amending or improving the fundamental institutions, practices, and social arrangements of a society so as to correct and remove, as far as possible, its faults, abuses, or malpractices.

Very typically, in speaking of reform we have in mind changes which apply to specific amendments or alterations of existing social arrangements. They are the type of reforms, aimed, as they are, only at the elimination of specific ills that Karl Popper regards as the sole admissible reforms. They can be handled by intelligent piecemeal social engineering without a challenge to the basic ideology of a culture, and they do not require argument about fundamental human ends or Utopian blueprints for the improvement of humanity's lot. Commitment to reform here makes a ready contrast with revolution. But when we speak, as we do, of "far-reaching political reforms," "fundamental reforms," "sweeping reforms," or "radical reforms," the contrast with revolutionary change is not so clear. I shall return to this point after I have characterized revolution. Political theorists have given us typologies of revolution and many have stressed that there is a single type of socio-political revolution which is of the greatest critical interest when we ask about revolution and reform and about the justification of revolution.[2] This conception of a socio-political revolution is a more specific characterization and specification than the related characterization given in the dictionaries. In the dictionaries the characterization of the relevant sense of "revolution" is that a revolution is a complete overthrow of a government or social system by those previously subject to it, and the substitution of a new government or social system. Paradigms of revolutions are the expulsion of the Stuart dynasty and the transfer of sovereignty to William and Mary, the overthrow of the French monarchy and the establishment of republican government during the French revolution, the American, the Russian, the Chinese, and the Cuban revolutions. But it is of some consequence to see that these are a mixed bag of examples. In particular, the French, Russian, Chinese, and Cuban revolutions are very different – and indeed particularly different in at least one important respect – from the American Revolution and the English revolution of 1688. The former revolutions – indeed the revolutions sometimes called "the Great Revolutions" – are distinguished from the others in that they *altered in a profound sense the social structure of the societies in which the revolution occurred*. When these revolutions were consolidated, the social structure of the societies which were so revolutionized (and sometimes some others as well) were radically altered. But this was not so when the Stuart dynasty was overthrown and William and Mary became the English (and Scottish) sovereigns, and it was not true of the American Revolution. In the last example, there was an overthrow of a government and of colonial rule, but the rebellious colonists only established a government of a slightly different sort. There was no change in basic social structure. The change was quite unlike that from Batista's Cuba to present-day Cuba. With so-called great revolutions there is what has been called a "shock to the foundations of society."[3] Such revolutions, as Karl Kautsky has pointed out, do not come from nowhere. They are like births, sudden in occurring but only possible after a complex development. When they occur there is "a sharp, sudden change in the social location of power," but this change is not one that can occur without certain tolerably determinate conditions obtaining.[4] For there to be a revolution, it is often claimed, there must be widespread misery, deprivation, and exploitation followed by a brief period of rising expectations which, after some minor improvements in the oppressed people's condition, are in turn dashed by a turn of events for the worse. Where there is a despair over the system coupled with a sense that things could be better, the ground for revolutionary activity is being broken; where there is a widespread despairing dissatisfaction with the present social order linked with a conception – often nebulous – of a new social order, where, in Fanon's phrase, we "set afoot a new man," we have conditions – though indeed not sufficient conditions – for revolution.

Where under these conditions a revolution is actually sustained so that a government topples and a new social order is brought into being, we have the type of revolution – a social and political revolution – that is relevant to our discussions of revolution and reform. This sense of "revolution" is properly caught by two political theorists on the Left: C. B. Macpherson and Herbert Marcuse. Macpherson characterizes revolution as

> a transfer of state power by means involving the use or threat of organized unauthorized force, and the subsequent

consolidation of that transferred power, with a view to bringing about a fundamental change in social, economic and political institutions.⁵

In a similar vein Marcuse writes that a revolution is the overthrow of a legal established government and constitution by a social class or movement with the aim of altering the social as well as the political structure.⁶

If we mark the distinction between violent and non-violent radical activity around the refusal of the non-violent radical to injure or (where she or he can help it) tolerate injury to her or his antagonists, we can see that there is no *conceptual* reason why a revolution must be violent, though there may very well be substantial empirical justification for believing that all revolutions of the type characterized above by Macpherson and Marcuse will *in fact* be violent. (It is important to remember here that there are degrees of violence. Revolutions can and do vary in this respect.) Thus on these terms it is a mistake to characterize a social and political revolution in such a way as to make "a non-violent revolution" a contradiction in terms, and thus it is a mistake to define "revolution," as Carl Friedrich does, as "a sudden and violent overthrow of an established political order."⁷

In the extant typologies, the kind of revolution Macpherson and Marcuse have characterized is contrasted with (1) *private palace revolutions*, e.g., the murder of Duncan by Macbeth followed by Macbeth's succession to the throne, (2) *public palace revolutions*, e.g., a *coup d'état* such as the typical South American revolution, (3) *systemic revolutions*, i.e., a change usually through a series of civil wars in the system of state organization (e.g., a city-state system) effecting a wide-ranging cultural community. (Examples are the change in the state system at the time of Pericles to that of the time of Augustus and the fall of the Roman Empire.), and (4) *colonial revolutions* (rebellions) against rule by the government of another country. (The American Revolution is a good example. But when, as in the Algerian revolution, there is also a considerable alteration of social structure, we have not only a colonial revolution, but also a socio-political revolution.) It is this latter kind of revolution – the socio-political revolution – that I am interested in when I ask about the contrast between reform and revolution. It clearly marks off revolutions from military *coups*, palace revolutions, colonial rebellions, and preventative counter-revolutions. It in effect limits "true revolutions" by a reasonable *persuasive* definition to the great social upheavals which bring about lasting and extensive socio-political change.

III

Given this construal, what exactly is the difference between revolution and radical reform? Typical reforms seek to amend, correct, and improve what we already have; they do not seek to destroy it and replace it with something new. In the United States, redistricting, lowering the voting age, guaranteeing an annual income, and weakening the filibuster rule would be reforms, though certainly not sweeping reforms. What would count as radical reform? Suppose – to take a fanciful but instructive example – the constitution of the United States was, through the normal channels, so changed that (1) the United States like England and Canada adopted a parliamentary system, (2) the division between federal and state government was abolished and newly drawn federally administered districts were created, (3) capitalism was abolished and all the major means of production came to be socially owned, and, finally, (4) the new government, together with the educational apparatus of the State, officially declared its support for atheism and socialism. Would such a set of changes in the United States constitute a radical reform or a peaceful revolution?

Surely such a change would be like a reform in that it was accomplished by "going through channels" and by using the legal and political apparatus of the State which was subsequently to be radically transformed. But it is unlike a reform in that, rather than simply improving or correcting the extant institutions and social arrangements, something quite new and different would be brought into being. Moreover, it is like a revolution in that there would have resulted a "radical transformation of the process of government, of the official foundations of sovereignty or legitimacy and of the conception of social order."[8] Yet here we have something which admits of degrees, for in the hypothesized change in the form of the government of the United States we still have a parliamentary system with political parties and the like. *From a certain point of view*, the change could be said to be not very deep – certainly not deep enough to constitute a radical transformation of the official foundations of sovereignty or legitimacy. At this point we have something which is so essentially contested that there is no objectively correct thing to say here. There are paradigms of revolutions and revolutionary acts which could not properly be called "radical reforms," e.g., the Chinese revolution and the Cuban revolution. But, as with so many quite useful concepts, there is no exact cut-off point. There is no precise point where we can show that here there is an end to reformist activity and here the beginning of revolutionary activity. As Wittgenstein in effect points out, we could by stipulation *set up* such a conceptual boundary, but this would settle nothing, for others with equal legitimacy could set up boundaries at other points.

Someone might resist at this juncture and assert that my above example is plainly only an example of radical reform because there is in it no use or threat or organized unauthorized force, and the use or threatened use of such force is a necessary condition for revolutionary change. There is – it might be claimed – a natural boundary; we need not just draw one. But so to argue is in effect to emasculate the concept of radical reform, for surely what it would be natural to characterize as a radical reform would typically – in actual fact perhaps always – involve, through strikes (illegal or otherwise), demonstrations, disruptions, the seizure of factories, or riots, some form of unauthorized pressure to bring about the change in question. The radical reform would come about at least under the threat of the use of unauthorized force, and such deep structural changes as characterized in my example never in fact occur without the threat of force or extreme social disruption. It could, logically speaking, be otherwise, but it isn't. So it still remains true that my hypothesized change in the State apparatus and social structure of the United States could with equal legitimacy be called "a radical or fundamental reform" or "a revolution" or both. We have a *continuum* here and not a clearly demarcated boundary.

In turn it might be replied that a qualitative and important difference does actually reveal itself in my example, namely that with revolution in contrast to radical reform there is and indeed must be an overthrow of a legally established government. And since this cannot be so with a radical reform, it is a mistake to claim that there is no principled difference between radical reform and revolution. But I should reply that where there is extensive breakdown in the functioning of institutions and established ways of doing things, and where a government under the dire threat of violence and total social chaos radically *alters itself*, so that we have a radically different government and set of social arrangements, it is hardly a deviation from a linguistic regularity to say that the legally established government has been overthrown. With Nixon under such extreme pressures, the power of state governments and (consequently) of the South broken, and a self-consciously atheistic and socialist group of ideologists firmly in control, with federal administrative districts rather than States, it would not be unnatural to speak of "the overthrow of the United States government." At the very least, the distinction between "an orderly but radical change in government" and an "overthrow of the government" would not in such circumstances be a clear one.

IV

What I have been concerned to establish so far is that reform and revolution are on a continuum and that, while there is an evident difference between typical reformist activities and revolutionary activities, there is no principled difference between a commitment to a set of radical reforms and a commitment to a socio-political revolution. (I say nothing here of the weaker notion of "a *systemic* revolution"; the difference between it and at least some types of radical reform is even less pronounced.)

It is the rather pervasive but mistaken assumption that "a violent revolution" is a pleonasm that is the principal cause of the belief that there is a principled difference between radical reform and revolution and that if one is committed to one, one cannot consistently also be committed to the other. Moreover to maintain that a "violent revolution" is not a redundancy is not to use "revolution" – as indeed it often is used in current political discussions – loosely.

Having said this, I do not mean to leave the impression that I believe that the question "Revolution or Reform?" is a pseudo-question. What is sensibly at issue when such a question is raised is whether it is more reasonable to adopt the moderate and piecemeal reformist tactics of liberal reformers or whether a commitment to a more radical political stance is in order. Among present-day political theorists – to amplify this question by giving it a local habitation and name – is the more reasonable course to adopt the general strategies of a Karl Popper, Ralf Dahrendorf, or Isaiah Berlin, or are the more radical positions of a Herbert Marcuse, Jürgen Habermas, or Alasdair MacIntyre more plausible? Note that within this liberal/radical division there is considerable room for technical philosophical differences yoked together with practical and theoretical political affinities. Surely MacIntyre is closer to Berlin philosophically than he is to Marcuse, but in political orientation he is closer to Marcuse. What I want now to do is to compare and assess some arguments of Popper and of Marcuse which I believe sharply and paradigmatically bring out many of the core substantive issues that should be argued out when we ask about the justification of an allegiance to either revolution or reform. Both Popper and Marcuse have a considerable corpus of influential theory and they have both been widely commented upon. But I want to focus on a single short but typical essay by each which, particularly when they are juxtaposed, dramatically and succinctly brings out what I take to be some of the central issues in the sometimes choice: reform or revolution. The essays in question are Popper's "Utopia and Violence" and Marcuse's "Ethics and Revolution."[9]

Popper stresses that, besides disagreements in factual belief – in opinion about what is the case – people also disagree because "their interests differ." Where interests clash there is, Popper maintains, no way – where the clash is a fundamental one – of proving or establishing that one interest or set of interests is right and the other or others mistaken. Where there is such a clash, an agent must either seek a reasonable compromise or attempt to destroy or at least undermine the opposing interest.[10] Popper is convinced we should always resort to compromise here rather than to violence. Over questions of fact, by contrast, we must be guided by the weight of empirical evidence, and where there is a divergence concerning the assessment of that evidence, we must all be open-minded fallibilists prepared to listen to argument and prepared to be convinced by an argument that goes contrary to our beliefs. We must eschew all intellectual imperialism and dogmatism. Violence in human affairs can be avoided if people develop and practice an attitude of reasonableness in human affairs. That is to say, in coming to decisions, we must be willing to hear both sides, to realize and take into consideration that one is not likely to make a good judge if one is party to the case, to avoid claims of self-evidence, and to be willing, where interests conflict, to make reasonable compromises.

In adopting this attitude of reasonableness, we must give up all Utopianism, which Popper takes to be a persistent and disastrous rationalistic attitude which rears its head again and again in political theory from Plato to Marx.

We should not forget that Popper means something rather special by "Utopian." A Utopian believes that an action is rational if it takes the best means available to achieve a certain end, and that we can only judge an action to be rational relative to some given end. Thus to determine whether a political action is rational, we must ascertain the final ends of the political change the actor intends to bring about. His political actions will be rational only relative to his ruling ideas of what the State ought to be like. For this reason, as a preliminary to any rational political action "we must [the Utopian believes] first attempt to become as clear as possible about our ultimate political ends."[11] The Utopian then plausibly but (on Popper's view) mistakenly concludes that to act reasonably we need first to determine the State or society we consider the best and then determine the means by which we can most efficiently realize or at least approximate that situation. The rationally mandatory thing to do is first to get clear about our fundamental political ideals. Only in this way, the Utopian believes, can we be reasonable about political actions. We must have, if we would act rationally, "a more or *less* clear and detailed description or blueprint of our ideal state" as well as "a plan or blueprint of the historical path that leads towards this goal."[12] But it is Popper's belief that it is this political rationalism of Utopianism that we must decisively reject, if we would avoid irrationality and violence in human affairs.

We must reject it because we have, Popper would have us believe, no way of rationally ascertaining which set of these focal ends is the most reasonable, or even which to choose reasonably, "for it is impossible to determine ends scientifically."[13] This means, according to Popper, that there is no rational way of choosing between Utopian blueprints for a truly human society. Because of this, a reasonable person will abandon all forms of Utopianism and will avoid "choosing ideal ends of this kind." She will not have any Utopian blueprint – any conception of a truly human society – at all. It is not that she is criticizing particular political ideals as such, but that she is criticizing the kind of political theorizing and organization that would lead to the holding of any ideals of this type at all. They are to be avoided (1) because they cannot be decided on rationally and (2) because the holding of them leads to violence and tyranny and not, as their proponents believe, to human happiness. Thus Popper in effect argues for an end to all ideology and Utopianism. And he counterposes against this a reformism which takes as its procedural rationale: "Work for the elimination of concrete evils rather than for the realization of abstract goods. Do not aim at establishing happiness by political means. Rather aim at the elimination of concrete miseries."[14] Do not try to construct systematic non-native blueprints for human liberation, but engage instead, without articulating ultimate social and political ideals, in practical piecemeal social engineering. "Choose what you consider the most urgent evil of the society in which you live, and try patiently to convince people that we can get rid of it." This means that we should fight for the elimination of hunger, disease, racism, and the like by direct means, e.g., by improved distribution of farm produce, by establishing Medicare, by voter registration in the South, and by establishing non-discriminatory practices in housing and employment. We should work at these problems directly and forget about trying "to realize these aims indirectly by designing and working for a distant ideal of a society which is wholly good."[15] We can reach agreement "on what are the most intolerable evils of our society and on what are the most urgent social reforms," but we cannot reach agreement about Utopian ideals for the radical transformation of our society.[16] We must steadfastly recognize and take to heart the poignant fact that "we cannot make heaven on earth," though we can, if we put aside Utopianism and reason realistically, reasonably hope "to make the world a little less terrible and a little less unjust in each generation."[17]

Marcuse is, in Popper's terms, an arch-Utopian. Unlike Popper, Marcuse believes that objective moral assessments can be made of what Popper calls Utopian blueprints for society, and he argues for an overall normative conception of society. Marcuse believes that the governing criteria here are whether or not a given set of social arrangements make for the greatest possible freedom and greatest possible happiness for man. And it is important to note, vis-à-vis Popper, that in talking of happiness in political contexts, Marcuse has in mind primarily the task of the avoidance of misery. He takes it to be the case that the role of government in the advancement of human welfare and happiness should primarily be to ensure "a life without fear and misery, and a life in peace."[18] So here, in terms of what should be aimed at, the difference between Popper and Marcuse is verbal rather than substantive. Marcuse is also one with Popper in believing that such a radical change as would be involved in a socio-political revolution would bring with it violence, but Popper denies that this revolutionary violence is ever justified, while Marcuse argues that it is *sometimes* justified and asks about the conditions under which it is justified. In this context, it should first be noted, so as not to raise spurious issues, that Marcuse, like any sane and humane person, shares Popper's detestation of violence and with him takes it as one of the foremost human tasks to work for "its reduction and, if possible, for its elimination from human life."[19] This attitude toward violence is, or at least ought to be, a commonplace in the moral life. Radicals and liberals, revolutionaries and reformers, are not divided on this issue. They are not always or even typically divided over the use of violence in the settling of social issues, for Popper sanctions the use of counter-violence against the threat of revolutionary violence. What does divide them is the issue of whether violence is ever justified "as a means for establishing or promoting human freedom and happiness." Popper denies that it is, while Marcuse argues that it is justified when and if certain conditions prevail. (He also argues that as a matter of fact they sometimes prevail.)

What is likely to be forgotten here is that while socio-political revolutions of the type we have been describing have almost invariably involved violence, and that while they permit and, as Marcuse puts it, sometimes even demand "deception, cunning, suppression, destruction of life and property and so on," if there is a demand *prior* to a revolution for fundamental reforms which will substantially increase equality and alleviate misery and degradation through a substantial redistribution of wealth and privileges, then this peaceful demand for fundamental reforms, if it shows promise of gaining momentum, will be met by the privileged classes with violence and attempted suppression. But without persistent advocacy and pressure for such basic reforms, we still have the day-to-day and year-to-year rather unspectacular yet extensive and persistent violence of any exploitative and repressive society. It does not make headlines, as do terrorist bombings, but it is usually more persistent, threatening, destructive, and pernicious. We surely should join with Popper in his detestation of violence, but the issue he fails to face, and one Marcuse squarely faces, is that in such situations violence cannot be avoided. The central relevant question is whether the use of revolutionary violence will, rather than the available alternatives, make for less misery and human degradation overall. The alternatives to violent revolution are (1) pressure for radical reforms or even revolution – since it is not a conceptual truth that a socio-political revolution must be violent – which deliberately always stops short of using violence as a policy, (2) trying to preserve the *status quo,* or (3) advocating and seeking to implement the type of mild, small-scale reforms that are not likely to offend or threaten the bureaucratic establishment sufficiently to provoke counter-revolutionary violence.[20] We certainly, at least on the general ground he appeals to, cannot rightly claim, as Popper in effect does, that revolutionary violence is never justified, or indeed is never something that reasonable and moral people ought to advocate and defend. We must go case by case and look at each situation as it comes before us. It may very well be that in some situations the use of violence as a political instrument will minimize misery and injustice and thus be morally mandatory or at least morally in order.

A standard argument here is that, while sometimes revolutionary violence is justified, it is never justified in a democracy, because in a democracy we have *fair* procedural means for making the needed social transformation through elections, lobbying, uncoerced public advocacy, and the like. But such a response reflects an extraordinarily idealized and naive picture of how bourgeois democracies work. The realistic, and indeed the most reasonable, moral stance is again to keep (1) to the above principle, i.e., that the underlying rationale for political action is to seek a society which will most likely enable all people to achieve the fullest "possible satisfaction of needs under the priority of vital needs and with a minimum of toil, misery and injustice," and (2) to go case by case (p. 145). We need to ask whether, in the long run, less misery, degradation, and injustice will result by going through channels, by playing the game according to the rules the bourgeois democracy sets, rather than by using revolutionary violence. If the answer is yes or even probably yes, then revolutionary violence should not be used, but if resort to revolutionary violence will lessen the total misery, degradation, and injustice, then revolutionary violence is justified and ought to be advocated. There are, as far as I can see, no conceptual barriers or moral barriers which turn this last *prima facie* possibility into either a conceptual or a moral impossibility. And it might very well actually be something which we are morally required to do. Much would depend on the particular bourgeois democracy. What should be said about Sweden might very well not hold for the United States. Much depends on the present level of social equality and justice, on corruption in the society, on ruling-class intransigence, and on the extent to which the democratic procedures actually work or can, by reasonable effort on the part of the oppressed, be made to work, so as to enhance social equality, help achieve liberation for everyone, and lessen misery and injustice.

It is fairly obvious that in capitalist countries such as the United States and Germany the outlook for such a transformation by going through channels and working within the system is very bleak indeed. But it is also true, loud alarms to the contrary notwithstanding, that these countries are hardly in a revolutionary situation, though we have seen with some segments of the population an increase in class consciousness. What the outlook for change here is can hardly be settled in a philosopher's armchair, but once this is recognized and if the above arguments are sound, it should also be recognized that it is equally arbitrary to rule out on general and aprioristic grounds, as Popper and many others do, the use of revolutionary violence as something that cannot be justified.

Marcuse wishes to show, not only that in certain circumstances revolutionary violence is justified, but also that in certain of the great revolutions in the past it was justified. He believes, as Popper does not, that "there are rational criteria for determining the possibilities of human freedom and happiness available to a society in a specific historical situation."[21] Marcuse argues that what constitutes human freedom and the possibilities of human freedom and happiness varies with the historical epoch. "Obviously," Marcuse remarks, "the possibilities of human freedom and happiness in advanced industrial society today are in no way comparable with those available, even theoretically available, at preceding stages of history."[22] But, given this partial historical relativity of what the particular fettering and degrading conditions are from which humanity needs liberation, it remains the case, according to Marcuse, that the great revolutions have, everything considered, reduced toil, misery, and injustice, and so, since none of the historically possible alternatives could match this, these revolutions are on the whole justified.

In thinking about the justification of revolution, we are forced here into admittedly rough historical calculations. On the one hand, we must take into account both the likelihood of Bonapartism or Stalinism in the successor State after a *successful* revolution and the likelihood that this State, whether Stalinist or not, will be brutal and authoritarian and actually harm human liberation more than help it. On the other hand, we must "take into account the sacrifices exacted from the living generations on behalf of the established society, the established law and order, the number of victims made in defense of this society in war and peace, in the struggle for existence individual and national."[23] In addition, we need to ask questions about the intellectual and material resources available to the society and the chances of the revolutionary group being able to utilize them in reducing the sacrifices and the number of victims. Finally, we must keep in mind the very value of the professed values originating in revolutions, e.g., the conception of the inalienable rights of man coming out of the American and French revolutions and the conception of the value of tolerance emerging from the English revolutions.

Popper makes utilitarian calculations too, but he limits them to the more immediate and palpable sources of misery and injustice and deliberately resists taking into account more distant and less easily calculable phenomena. This surely has the advantage of giving us more manageable materials, but it also cuts off morally relevant data which, to the extent that they are determinable at all, should be taken into consideration. In our calculations concerning what we ought to do, we should take it as a relevant consideration that some phenomena are less readily determinable than others, but this does not justify our ignoring the less easily assessable data. By skewing what we will take as relevant material in the way he does, Popper cuts off the very possibility of discovering (1) systematic interconnections between human ills and (2) any (if indeed there are such) deeper casual conditions of the ills he would alleviate. Thus his theory unwittingly plays into the hands of conservative defenders of the *status quo* with which he would not wish to align himself. Marcuse's wider-ranging utilitarian calculations are perfectly capable of taking into account and giving due stress to the phenomena Popper would account for, but they also hold out promise for attaining a more complete, and thus more adequate, account of the relative harm and relative human advantages accruing to different social arrangements.

For Marcuse, and for the revolutionary tradition generally, when violence is justified it is justified by reason in accordance with the overriding end of revolutionary activity, namely "greater freedom for the greater number of people." Popper, too, in spite of his distaste for Utopian blueprints holds this as a guiding rationale, but he never establishes that violence can never be the means to its attainment or that the great revolutions did not extend and enhance human freedom.

It should not be forgotten that the English and French revolutions attained "a demonstrable enlargement of the range *of* human freedom."[24] There is, as Marcuse points out, a general agreement among historians that the English and French revolutions brought about an extensive redistribution of social wealth, "so that previously *less* privileged or unprivileged classes were the beneficiaries of this change, economically and/or politically."[25] Even when we take the subsequent periods of reaction and restoration into the reckoning, it remains true that these revolutions brought about "more liberal governments, a gradual democratization of society and technical progress."[26] When the extent and permanency of this are taken into consideration in our historical calculations, it outweighs the terror and the excesses of these revolutions. That is to say, there is a sound ethical justification for these revolutions, though to say this is not to condone all the actions carried out in their name, for it is a correct grammatical remark with moral overtones to say, as Marcuse does, that "arbitrary violence and cruelty and indiscriminate terror" cannot possibly be justified by any revolutionary situation.[27]

To the argument that the same changes would have come about more gradually but without terror and violence, it should be replied that while this is an empirical *possibility*, it is also only an unfounded speculation. We do not have comparable situations in which the ruling elite of an *Ancien Regime* voluntarily gave up its privileges and desisted from exploitation and repression where it was not true that there were no previous successful revolutions in similarly situated countries to serve as a warning prod that extensive reforms must be made. What we can say with confidence is this: there is the fact of the moral advance of humankind brought on by these great revolutions, and no adequate grounds have been given for believing that in those circumstances – those great turning points of history – advances would have occurred in anything like a comparable way without the use of force against the old order.

V

What we can conclude from our discussion so far is that there have been circumstances in the past and there will no doubt be circumstances in the future in which violence is a morally legitimate instrument for promoting radical transformations in society toward a greater degree of human freedom and happiness. It is toward this conclusion that a critical comparison of Popper and Marcuse leads us.

If what I have argued in the previous section has been for the most part sound, Popper could only defend himself by laying very considerable stress on, and indeed by establishing the soundness of, what I shall call, "the skeptical side" of his thought.

Marcuse assumes, and I do too, the correctness of what should be the morally important truisms that human freedom and human happiness are very great goods and that misery and injustice are plain evils. Popper indeed makes the same assumptions himself; his very passionate rejection of Utopianism is fuelled by emotions rooted in these assumptions. But he does not believe that such value judgments are rationally supportable since they are not scientific claims. (This note is perfectly general: it applies to any fundamental value judgment simply by virtue of its being a fundamental value judgment.) Thus, on Popper's skeptical view, if someone has a Utopian blueprint in which the above moral truisms are not held (respectively) to be very great goods or manifest evils, there is no way of showing, objectively, that that Utopian blueprint is mistaken or unreasonable.

This is hardly the place to argue the general question of moral skepticism and/or some kind of radical non-cognitivism in metaethics. Suffice it to say for this occasion that the main developments in analytic ethics since World War II have put such conceptions very much on the defensive. Popper, pulling against the stream of contemporary ethical theory, writes as if moral skepticism and non-cognitivism were plainly true, though he does not provide any extended argument for them.

Moreover, as MacIntyre has pointed out, *in practice* Popper assumes the objectivity and rationality of certain ideals – general moral ideals very close to Marcuse's and my own – which, if he would consistently apply them, would hardly allow him to shun all ideology in the way he does.[28] That is to say, for Popper the importance of relieving misery and developing the reasonable attitudes of human give and take, the stress on freedom and on the equal right of every person to be self-authoring and self-directing so far as this is compatible with the equal rights of others, are all leading moral ideas which inform many of his political judgments, and together they commit him to a general set of political and moral ideals in accordance with which particular practices, institutions, governments, and societies can and indeed should, if these principles are to mean anything, be appraised. But this is precisely to utilize a Utopian blueprint, and it is this Popper would avoid. Moreover, if he continues to apply this blueprint, the Marcusean arguments for the rational justification of revolution seem at least to be inescapable; and if he rejects reasoning in accordance with these general moral principles and holds steadfastly to an "end of ideology approach," he gets himself into the position where he could have no grounds for rejecting as barbarous and irrational ideologies which he indeed rightly believes to be barbarous and irrational, namely Nazi and other fascist ideologies.

Surely this is a conclusion that Popper does not wish to embrace, and his grounds for not accepting such ideologies turn on some commitment to something very like a form of negative utilitarianism. Yet this saddles him with a set of abstract moral principles which he should, in consistency, regard with distaste as Utopian.

Some tougher "end of ideology" political theorist may really take this "moral-skepticism-side" to heart and argue that even if avoidance of misery and attainment of happiness are great goods, he sees no rational grounds for adopting some principle of equality or fairness and extending such teleological considerations to all people. Whether, he reasons, we should opt for such a universalistic ethic as underlies both Marcuse's and Popper's thinking, is an utterly non-rational matter resting on human preference.

If such a moral skepticism is rationally mandatory, then the very assumptions of progress essential for even Popper's commitment to mild reform are undermined. There can be no justification of reform or revolution, or any other normative principles. It may indeed not be easy to defend any system of overall normative principles, but if it is not *possible* to do so, the whole program of moderate reform and a commitment to reasonableness is undermined. It is only because Popper himself has an unacknowledged but reasonable set of general political moral principles that his "end of ideology approach" does not appear immediately to be an abandonment of any kind of reasoned defence of a set of normative standards or even of the taking of any principled stand at all.

Popper aside, what can we conclude about reform or revolution? There is plainly much injustice and unnecessary misery in the world and the level of human liberation is hardly what it could be. Without even remotely assuming that we can make a kingdom of heaven on earth, a perfectly good society, or anything of that fanciful Utopian order, it is not Quixotic to hope, and rationally work, for a transformation of society in which these ills are greatly lessened and perhaps some of them even altogether eliminated. Such a social order may never come into being, but there is nothing unreasonable about struggling for its achievement.

I have suggested that there can be no reasonable, unequivocal, non-contextual answer to the question, "In struggling for a better social order should we be reformers or revolutionaries?" In the Scandinavian countries, the needed transformation might very well come about gradually through a cluster of small reforms which, taken together, might add up in time to a considerable transformation. In Brazil, the United States, and Argentina, to take some striking examples, this hope seems unrealistic. And while there is a moral need, and a considerable material base, for revolution in Brazil, the United States – the linchpin imperialist power in the Western social system – is at present at any rate hardly a country in which there is a material base for a revolution. Morally speaking, however, the United States is surely in dire need of radical transformation; whether this should be by radical reform or revolution is, if my earlier arguments are sound, an empty question, more a matter of political rhetoric than anything else. What is evident, particularly when one considers the United States in relation to the rest of the world, is that it becomes increasingly obvious, the closer one looks, that very deep structural changes need to be made. It is surely better, everything else being equal, if they can be attained without a violent revolution. But if one considers Vietnam, the plight of African Americans, and America's imperialist policies in the poorer parts of the world, the level of violence is already very high. It is also true, however, that actions which would trigger or even risk a nuclear war are insane. And to work to bring about in a decade or so a revolution in America which would involve something comparable to the Russian or Spanish civil wars is also something morally equivocal (to understate it); but, as we have seen, there are revolutions and revolutions, and there are various levels of violence. What Marcuse has given us are general criteria in accordance with which we can reasonably answer when, humanly speaking, revolutionary violence of a certain kind and at a certain level is justified and when it is not. In many situations it is difficult to tell, though in others (present-day Angola, Mozambique, South Africa, and South Vietnam, for example), it is quite evident that, when revolution has a reasonable chance of success, it is morally justified.

We have also seen that reform and revolution are on a continuum and that there are contexts in which the choice of labels for description of the transformation in question is, ideology and expediency aside, quite immaterial. Moreover, it is important to see, as Rosa Luxemburg did and stressed in the opening paragraphs of her *Reform or Revolution*, that a revolutionary should not oppose piecemeal reforms, though she or he should seek to give them a direction which will lead to a socialist transformation of society. But a vital means for the attainment of a socialist revolution is the attainment of reforms. It is true that reformist measures have sometimes functioned by buying off the working class, but they have also raised their level of expectation, giving people of working class and peasant origins the education and consciousness to escape the bondage of prejudice and ignorance, and, with the rising new working class, reforms together with the transformation of the working force through technology have gradually given this new white collar working class the capacity to govern themselves.[29] Moreover, since I lack the orthodox faith that history is necessarily on the side of socialism, it seems to me that, where it is evident that certain reforms will appreciably improve human conditions, they should be worked for. They are at least small gains in an uncertain world, though this should not freeze us into being satisfied with them. Apocalyptic and quasi-apocalyptic moves are dramatic but rarely politically or morally sound. That is to say, use of the *nach-Hitler-wir* slogan is to be avoided. Working for Hitler's victory over the Social Democrats, even granting they were *ersatz* socialists, was a suicidal way of attempting to build socialism and a truly human society. Similarly rationalized tactics in working for the victory of Reagan – to turn to a much lesser villain – while not suicidal, were counterproductive for progressive forces. Our ability to make long-range social predictions is so slight that it is irrational to develop any long-range confidence about how things must be, and thus it is irrational and indeed morally irresponsible to accept, where we can avoid them, extensive human ills in the hope of realizing long-range social achievements. Noam Chomsky was realistic and responsible when he remarked: "Surely our understanding of the nature of man or of the range of workable social forms is so rudimentary that any far-reaching doctrine must be treated with great scepticism."[30] This does not mean that revolutionary hopes should be abandoned as an opiate of intellectuals, but it should warn a reasonable and humane person away from the dangerous game of hoping for reaction to help produce revolution. Sometimes extremism on the Left paves the way for moderation, but victories for reaction seldom pave the way for socialist revolution. The thing to be done is to work persistently for a socialist transformation of society. Day by day this means supporting all genuinely progressive reforms, even in those contexts in which this will strengthen liberals against conservatives, while working for a broader structural transformation of society by radical peaceful reforms where possible, and by violent revolution where necessary and where the cure is not likely to produce worse ills than the disease. The rub, of course, is to tell in a particular historical situation whether the cure is worse than the disease. This surely takes more than just philosophical sophistication and moral sensitivity; it requires historical, sociological, and economic understanding in depth of the situation that confronts us.

Notes

1. I have tried to give a kind of minimal and demythologized defence of the idea of progress in my "Progress."
2. Rosenstock-Huessy, *Out of Revolution*; Brinton, *The Anatomy of Revolution*; and Pettee, *The Process of Revolution*; and "Revolution-Typology and Process." See also Macpherson, "Revolution and Ideology in the Late Twentieth Century"; Kamenka, "The Concept of a Political Revolution"; and Falk, "World Revolution and International Order." See also Calvert, "Revolution: The Politics of Violence."
3. Schrecker, "Revolution as a Problem in the Philosophy of History," 35.
4. Kamenka, "The Concept of a Political Revolution," 124.
5. Macpherson, "Revolution and Ideology in the Late Twentieth Century," 140.
6. Marcuse, "Ethics and Revolution."
7. Friedrich, "An Introductory Note on Revolution."
8. Kamenka, "The Concept of a Political Revolution," 124.
9. Popper, *Conjectures and Refutations*, 355–63; and Marcuse, "Ethics and Revolution," 133–47.
10. Popper, *Conjectures and Refutations*, 357.
11. Ibid., 358.
12. Ibid.
13. Ibid., 358–59.
14. Ibid., 361.
15. Ibid.
16. Ibid.
17. Ibid., 362.
18. Marcuse, "Ethics and Revolution," 134.
19. Ibid.," 355.
20. For a defence of a revolutionary but principled non-violent stand, see Deming, "Revolution and Equilibrium."
21. Marcuse, "Ethics and Revolution," 135.
22. Ibid., 139.
23. Ibid., 140.
24. Ibid., 143
25. Ibid., 143.
26. IIbid., 143
27. Ibid., 140–41.
28. MacIntyre, "Breaking the Chains of Reason."
29. Mallet, *La nouvelle classe ouvrière*; and Birnbaum, *Toward a Critical Sociology*.
30. Chomsky, "Notes on Anarchism," 32.

6

Justice and Modes of Production: Allen Wood's "The Marxian Critique of Justice" Revisited

Allen Wood in his *Karl Marx* and in a series of articles stretching over a number of years has articulated a fascinating, challenging, well-researched, and well-reasoned interpretation of how we are to understand what Marx has to say about morality and most particularly about justice. It all began with his seminal, and much discussed, 1972 article "The Marxian Critique of Justice."[1] I will, in looking again after the dust of controversy has settled, stick to remarks on that article with a few supplementary glances at his reply to Husani and his article on Marx in the *Encyclopedia of Ethics*.[2] I will not attempt to do "Marxology." It has been some time since I have seriously studied Marx's texts. But I have in the interim thought a lot about Marxianism, particularly analytical Marxianism and the attempt there to develop a sound and appropriately rigorous Marxian critical social theory.[3] Be that what it may, Wood's work, essentially in the history of ideas, has always struck me as both careful and insightful here, as indeed elsewhere, but vis-à-vis Marx and morality, it has also been extensively challenged by a number of other careful, rigorous, and insightful Marx scholars.[4] I will proffer no view here about who, if anyone, has given the most perspicacious interpretation of Marx on this topic. I am half-inclined to think that Marx's remarks here are too scant and scattered for us to be able to be justifiably confident that there can be a Marxological "getting it right *here*," as distinct from what might be said about the canonical portion of Marx where he has a well-worked-out theory, closely integrated into his revolutionary practice. I refer here to his accounts of historical materialism, ideology, class, class

151

struggle, the state dialectics, and the labour theory of value. As Marxians, if that is what we are, as distinct from Marxologists, we should, as G. A. Cohen, John Roemer, and David Schweickart have, set aside the labour theory of value as an albatross around the neck of Marxian theory and, working with the rest of the canon – the part that arguably may turn some machinery, but still is not wedded to these canonical parts as to a set of doctrines – see what we can infer about what a consistent and clearheaded Marxian, who is also knowledgeable about the world, should say concerning justice and morality more generally.

I want to look at Wood's article in that light. To look at it, that is, not as a contribution to Marx scholarship and the history of ideas, which it surely is, but as a contribution to living Marxian social theory. This may not at all have been Wood's intent, but that should not deter us from so looking at it. The account of Marx he articulates is subtle, complicated, systematic, and it breaks new ground. Given that, we will not only want to ask whether it is a sound account of what Marx thought but also whether it is a sound account of morality. Is what he says that Marx says about justice and morality, whether he is right about Marx or not, also approximately what in developing a sound Marxian social theory should be said about justice and morality? (The crucial thing is that it is sound and only secondarily that it is Marxian.) I think Wood, so understood, whether he wants to be so understood or not, has come closer to getting it right than most of his critics have thought, though, when I articulate that, and winnow it a bit, it may seem like I am engaging in the philosopher's familiar penchant for first saying it and then taking it all back. Certainly in at least one place I deeply disagree with Wood about the design of a sound social theory, Marxian or otherwise.

Wood rightly recognizes that Marx is not an economic determinist or a reductionist.[5] Marx is not saying that the only things that are "genuinely real" are economic facts or that social matters, other than economic, including moral, political, or juridical ideas, can be reduced to statements of economic facts or anything of the kind. Rather Marx shares with Hegel and with John Dewey, and in our time with Donald Davidson and Richard Rorty, a thoroughgoing antireductionist holism, contextualism, historicism, and perspectivism, to engage in a fine fit of labeling. Someone sharing that ground will think, as did both Hegel and Marx, and, I believe,

Dewey as well, that it is a very bad, but still a pervasive, mistake to think, as traditionally moral philosophers and political theorists have, that the theorist can treat, as Wood well puts it, "the social as if he, in his sublime rationality, could measure this whole against some ideal of right or justice completely external to it, and could then standing on some Archimedean point adjust social reality to this ideal."[6] No such ahistorical, noncontextual, particular-perspective-free "point of view of reason" or something called "the moral point of view" is attainable.

Moreover, to so reason is to be in the grip of a too molecularist conception of society. When so gripped, we fail to see the integral unity of society – any society you like – where the different social practices and institutions of society are so tightly connected that there is no explaining one or justifying one without reference to some of the others. We need, for example, to see the state and moral and juridical practices as rooted in the material conditions of society, though these material conditions are in turn also affected by these practices, even though the dominant influence runs the other way. But there is no reducing of one thing to another. Still, rights and principles of justice and right should not be taken as fundamental principles that are the highest measure of all social things and on which all other moral beliefs are based.[7] Rather, they should be thought of as elements of a social whole: historically conditioned and situated, and repeatedly changing, in which these conceptions, and the practices that go with them, are neither separable from economic practices and the material conditions of life. More generally, they are not independently assessable. Moreover, it is not the case that these moral beliefs are hierarchically ordered with certain fundamental ones being the ones upon which all the rest are based. Any such ordering is the arbitrary arrangement of a philosopher or theologian or some other intellectual. It will, in its foundationalism, be an ordering that will distort our understanding of morality and moral life. We cannot justifiably take the general philosophical perspective on morality that Henry Sidgwick and G. E. Moore, as well as such deontologists as W. D. Ross and C. D. Broad, urged us to take: a conception that has remained dominant, in spite of Dewey's persistent criticisms of it, until very recently.

The sphere of political authority – the *Staatsrecht* – with its moral and other normative conceptions is, as Wood reads Marx (I think uncontroversially), an expression, a determination, of the prevailing mode of production. Its point of view, the juridical one, and the conceptions of right and justice which express this point of view, are rationally comprehensible only when seen in their proper connection with other determinations of social life and grasped in terms of their role with the prevailing productive mode.[8]

Given the acceptance of such a Marxian holism and contextualism, how should we think about justice and of morality more generally? We should think of it, with its social practices and juridical institutions, as playing a subordinate, dependent role in social life. The elements of morality are not the measure of social rationality that orthodox traditions of moral philosophy take them to be. (Hume here is the one great exception.) Rather what generally speaking is taken to be just and right has a content that fits with, is functional for, and is determined by, or is at least deeply conditioned by, the distinctive mode of production of the society in which such moral reasoning takes place. For the vast majority of people in a society, any society at all, what passes for being just and right, or for that matter good and bad, is what squares with and is functional for the mode of production of that society; what is dysfunctional for it will be taken to be unjust or in some other way wrong or bad. We have in reality no toehold or skyhook that will enable us to "stand outside of our society" – a particular historically determinate society – and to access what in some absolute sense or society-transcendent sense is really right or wrong, just or unjust, good or bad.

Wood does not draw – and I think quite rightly – relativist conclusions from this. Contextualism and historicism are distinct from relativism or at least they can, and typically do, have nonrelativist forms.[9] Wood does, however, draw antimoralist conclusions from it as well as historicist ones. "All juridical forms and principles of justice," he remarks, "are meaningless unless applied to a specific mode of production, and they retain their rational validity only as long as the content they possess and the particular actions to which they apply arise naturally out of and correspond concretely to this productive mode."[10] For a consistent Marxian, Wood has it, the rational validity of any moral belief is "always measured in terms of the prevailing mode of production."[11]

The very last bit aside, which seems to me mistaken or at least an exaggeration, I take such an account to be a perceptive contextualism and historicism. There is no ahistorical, noncontextual perspective from which we can make moral assessments. And it is, as well, a perceptive specification – a more determinate rendering (though also a contestable one) – of that contextualism to a mode of production. It is also – although this is not how Wood views it – at the very least a plausible articulation of a sociology of morals. If you want to find out what moral beliefs will be dominant in a society, such a Marxian approach goes a long way toward providing it and, as well, explains it: making plain an underlying rationale of positive morality (the traditional morality or moralities of a society), revealing their distinctive social functions.

I spoke, in setting out this Marxian view, of its determining what, in a given society, is taken to be or passes for being just or of what is taken to be or passes for being the right thing to do. This, of course, is not itself a moral or normative determination, but a bit of the sociology of morals. It cuts no moral ice itself. But Wood thinks the Marxian account makes a stronger claim. Wood claims that the Marxian account goes beyond the sociology of morals. It claims that among the moral views extant in society, the moral view that fits best with the mode of production of the society is what is actually just in that society at that particular time and with that mode of production in place. To discover which of the various moral views around is most fully functional for a mode of production at given time is to find out what in that context really is right. That is all, Wood has it that Marx has it, that we can coherently mean by speaking of something as right or just. Is this something that a consistent and knowledgeable Marxian must be or even should be committed to? I think not and I will try to show why.

I agree with Wood that Marx thought, and that we should think, that there are no moral principles that are just derivable from reason *à la* Kant, Alan Gewirth, or David Gauthier. There is no such derivation, and further there is no purely rational construction of the right, the just, or the good. And moral truths (if such there be) are not something there in nature or, for that matter, in "supernature." There are no natural moral laws somehow rooted in nature, including human nature. Nor is there any Divine something-we-know-not-what to take its place. This is all mystification, probably without any coherent sense.

It, however, does not follow from this that we cannot have a critical morality or that we can never be in a position critically to appraise the justice or the desirability of a whole mode of production with its, functionally speaking, dependent principles of distribution. Wood has given us no reason to think that Marxians could not consistently and coherently argue from within the Marxian canon that a whole mode of product is unjust or bad. Indeed, from the Marxian perspective, a mode of production could be so unjust or bad that this justifies a revolutionary practice that would begin the undermining of it and, when the circumstances are propitious, justify overthrowing it and setting about the very long task of constructing a distinct and better social formation less riddled with injustices and other evils.[12] There seems to me nothing conceptually untoward, in all contexts humanly impractical or un-Marxian, about so arguing and so viewing things. Indeed Marxian activists or militants do it all the time. Maybe they are mistaken in doing so, but not because of any of the philosophical considerations articulated by Wood or because they really run counter in doing so to Marxian theory. Moreover, it does not require for its coherent assertion the impossible attainment of an ahistorical Archimedean point: some view from nowhere or some "absolute conception" just giving us the "point of view of reason" or of morality *überhaupt*.[13] Rather, assuming, not implausibly, at least a rather minimal sense of right and wrong on the part of most people, ideologically skewed though it will extensively be, we can engage, bootstrapping ourselves along, as we always do anyway, in a coherentist rebuilding of the ship at sea.[14]

There is no reason at all why a Marxian could not, and indeed should not, use, in such a rebuilding, the method of wide and general reflective equilibrium (WRE). In trying to forge such an equilibrium, Marxian theorists should start, not only with their own considered moral convictions, but, as well, and much more importantly, with the firmest considered moral convictions, and other firm normative convictions, pervasive in the society concerning which they are trying to forge this wide and general reflective equilibrium. But in such a forging of a wide and general reflective equilibrium there must also be, at least on the theorist's part, a firm appreciation of the relevant facts, an understanding of the best social science of the time, where, hardly unsurprisingly, for a Marxian theorist, Marxian social science will have (though, of course, fallibalistically so) a prominent, though certainly not an exclusive, place. Taking these elements together, there will also be a reflective consideration of various moral principles and theories (including principles and theories of justice) extant in such societies and in the cultural history to which such societies are heir. They will be reviewed and sometimes tentatively appealed to, in an attempt to see which of them makes the best fit with our firm considered moral convictions and with what we can reasonably believe about the world. We should seek to forge the most coherent fit between such considered moral convictions, other moral considerations, moral theories, social theories, and the facts. In such a context, we should adopt, from among those we have tentatively reviewed, including ones newly constructed and then reviewed, the principles and theories that most clearly rationalize this mélange. The point is to forge a coherent, perspicuously arranged moral and normatively political conception. It would be a moral account that squares best with what we have good reason to believe to be true about our social world and which, taking into account those beliefs about what is the case, squares best with our firmest moral convictions at various levels of abstraction. It would have to be in accordance with well-established facts (non-moral facts, if that is not pleonastic) and with well-established scientific theories, including, centrally, the best established social theories that we have. We would thereby make sense of morality by showing that some of our moral conceptions, including some of our conceptions of justice, are not just a jumble, but rather form a coherent cluster of beliefs and practices fitting with what we know or reasonably believe about the world. Moreover, by having principles constructed in this process that rationalize our moral beliefs and practices – i.e., explain how they fit together and help clearly to display how they, with considerable winnowing, can form a consistent and coherent whole – we thereby show that the moral beliefs that survive such a winnowing are justified. In normative domains at least, this is just what justification comes to. It should, in this context, be remembered that these considered judgments, in the very fact that they are considered judgments, have some initial credibility. Wide and general reflective equilibrium does not fall prey to the standard difficulties of traditional coherence theories. The moral beliefs (among them these considered judgments), including our beliefs about what is just and what is not, that are not filtered out by this process are the justified ones. The others are not.

Sometimes there will be moral convictions that, for a time at least, cannot be gotten into wide reflective equilibrium and most particularly not into wide and general reflective equilibrium. There may be some beliefs – say, beliefs about abortion – concerning which we cannot, for a given stretch of time or perhaps even forever, reach a consensus about, and they cannot be gotten into reflective equilibrium. Yet they are beliefs, standing where we stand now and no doubt will stand for the rest of our lives, that some of us will not abandon. But whatever else we should say about them, we need to realize that beliefs so held are not, and cannot, as long as they are so held, be justified. Perhaps they are (psychologically and sociologically speaking) so deep for us that we cannot abandon them. But we will still know, if we are reasonable, that, so held, we cannot take them to be beliefs that have been justified. But we should not say they are unjustifiable. We have just not been able to justify them. But we know – given wide and general reflective equilibrium – what it would be like for them to be justified. But perhaps we will never in fact – as a contingent matter – be able to justify them. In morals there is no principle of sufficient reason.

In spelling out this method of wide and general reflective equilibrium, to shift gears again, there need be no moralizing activity. We need do nothing to disturb Marxian antimoralists. Rather it spells out how, if we would be reasonable, we should reason.

I did not say, or give to understand in saying, that the principles of morality so constructed and sustained ground moral beliefs or show their foundation. Such foundationalist talk is incompatible with a thoroughgoing holism and contextualism.[15] Moreover, holism and contextualism aside, it has little to be said for it. This nondeductivist, coherentist model of explanation and justification fits well with a Marxian holism, contextualism, and historicism.[16] And it yields a critical morality that is not stuck with saying that what is right, and not merely what generally passes for or is taken to be right, is what is functional for the mode of production and that what is wrong is dysfunctional for it. Sometimes this is so and sometimes it is not; and, even sometimes when it is so, we can – and consistently as Marxians – coherently say that as things stand this is what, practically speaking, should be done, but that we can, and indeed should, conceive of a transformation of society that will yield a better society, including a society that is less unjust. This transformation will actually come about most centrally because of a clash between the extant production relations and the developing forces of production. With the resulting class struggle, this will generate a new mode of production that will unfetter the forces of production, yielding a society that in time will for more people enhance their flourishing and enable the coming into existence of a different system of distribution linked with this changed mode of production. This new system of distribution will make for more human autonomy for more people and with that make not only for a better society but a less unjust society. That it is more just is not, of course, all that we are commending it for. Talk of an enhanced human flourishing gestures at that more. But, along with a lot of other good things, it will also be a more just society than the one that preceded it with its different mode of production and inextricably linked system of distribution.[17] This can be said, and coherently so, in advance of that mode of production's actually coming into existence.

A Mannheimish sociology of knowledge perspective or an error-theorist metamoral perspective would have it that we are here so conceptually imprisoned that we could not even conceive of such states of affairs. But such conceptions are both very tendentious and totally foreign to Marxianism and would, if true, make mishmash out of historical materialism and Marxian conceptions of the ideological functions of morality.[18] It should also be remarked, again shifting focus a bit, that, while there is indeed, with the use of wide reflective equilibrium, an appeal to considered convictions, that need not land us in ethnocentrism or subjectivism or even, in all circumstances, saddle us with a purely class morality or perhaps even a class morality at all. That is so because that very coherentist method subjects, at least in principle, all considered convictions (taken now individually), their initial credibility notwithstanding, to challenge. If they do not fit with our other considered convictions, the best of our consistently held beliefs, including our well-established scientific beliefs and other well-established factual beliefs, including those that expose ideologically distorted beliefs, prominently among them some moral convictions, then they are either to be rejected or amended until they so fit.

Wood's reconstruction of Marx leaves us with a Marxian account of morality that yields merely a positive morality. But a perfectly consistent Marxian account of morality can yield, as well, a critical morality. Moreover, with the use of the method of wide and general reflective equilibrium, there are Marxian accounts that can at least arguably soundly argue that there can be, although there usually are not, accounts of justice, where principles of justice are functioning as genuinely critical conceptions, which are not distorted – or at least not deeply and uncorrectably distorted – by ideology. There can be, and in my view should be, Marxian accounts of justice that argue for a critical moral perspective without (pace Wood) "removing social reality from its theory and social practice from reality."[19]

To such a general line of criticism Wood has responded that to condemn capitalism as unjust "by applying to it standards of justice or right which would be appropriate to some post-capitalist mode of production" would be to condemn it by standards that would "not be rationally applicable to capitalism at all" and thus "any such condemnation would be mistaken, confused and without foundation."[20] But, given the bootstrapping-repairing-the-ship-at-sea conception of wide and general reflective equilibrium, the confusion runs the other way. There is no assumption at all on such a Marxian account of a "vision of post-capitalist society as a kind of eternal structure against which the present state of affairs is to be measured and found wanting."[21] Wood's response misses the mark, for such a normatively critical Marxianism does not treat post-capitalist society as a kind of eternal juridical structure, but as a society that has different stages of development. Capitalism does not in all respects remain the same thing. Societies are continually changing after all, and will, sometimes, as these changes take place, spin from their bosom. Particularly during times of severe class conflict – though not only during those times – people are willing in one way or another to challenge the system and sometimes they consciously recognize the radicalness of what they are doing. One way they can, and will, challenge the system – I did not say the best way – is by articulating different conceptions of justice and indeed sometimes conceptions of justice that, if implemented with their appropriate set of social practices and institutions, would answer more adequately to human interests and needs than the extant conceptions attuned to an earlier time. Perhaps it is a mistake to say the practices are simply replaced *tout court* – although this may sometimes happen – but what is more likely is that we will get a new idealization of the practices. An idealization that comes into competition with the old idealization – the one that up until then (although again this is a historically contingent and changing matter) had been the standard idealization – renders the practice, or sometimes even a whole set of practices, more coherent and in the process upon occasion changes it.

Indeed a new revolutionary idealization may sweep away a whole cluster of previously competing more or less standard idealizations.[22]

Against such a background, such Marxian theorists articulate conceptions of justice which, within the society in which the theorist lives, and internal to its framework, including, of course, its mode of production, function critically to assess rather than to sanctify the relations of production themselves: in our societies the capitalist relations of production. It does this, for crucial starters, by showing how these relations of production conflict with the forces of production of the society more than is necessary (factually and causally necessary). This obtains given the development of the forces of production of the society. The forces of production are fettered by the relations of production, and this in turn impedes in such a situation the maximal meeting of the human needs of most people and, relatedly, it is not conducive to the human flourishing and autonomy for most human beings in that society. Given the state of the productive forces in the society, many people could live better lives – indeed, considerably better lives – than they do now, but they are blocked from being able to do so by the dominant classes of their society – in our situation by the capitalist class. That class sets itself against, and, for the time being successfully blocks, the adoption of new relations of production that match better the developing productive forces than do the extant relations of production. Perhaps this is not injustice, but it is certainly – if Marxians have their facts and their theoretical comprehension of them roughly right – very wrong: something that, morally speaking, people should not have to endure where such endurance is not necessary, as it, as a matter of fact, is not here. The meeting of people's needs and their flourishing in our world in our time is much lower than it need be.[23] As the forces of production develop, so our moral conceptions can develop as well, without our ever being able to stand outside of these historical developments, impossibly trying to overleap history. Indeed, such a "standing outside," for reasons Donald Davidson has made familiar, is – to put it conservatively – probably an incoherent notion.[24]

Finally, this repairing the ship at sea need not be just a reformist tinkering with the system to make it better without trying to topple it, anymore than it was for its initiator, Otto Neurath, who (logical positivist that he was) was also a thoroughgoing revolutionary communist. A consistent Marxian is a revolutionary aiming at, and seeking to aid in bringing about, when the situation is propitious, the overthrow of capitalist society and its replacement by a socialist and, in due time, a communist society. Such activity is not essentially a matter of correcting abuses prevalent in the capitalist system or "rectifying its tragic and irrational injustices," although in some circumstances that is, at best, all that, for the time being, can be done and then not very adequately. But sometimes, in such circumstances, it is worth trying to do. It all depends on what the circumstances are and what the possibilities for change are. Marxianism, where it is, as it always should be, a genuine social science as well as a revolutionary social practice, is also a contextualism and a historicism. But the Marxian, utilizing wide and general reflective equilibrium, and, in that context, in anticipation of the transformation of society that may well be forthcoming, will articulate post-capitalist principles of justice, ranging over a whole mode of production. But these post-capitalist principles of justice are not eternal or ahistorical principles floating free of any possible mode of production and historical development of society. But such a Marxian does not, for all her revolutionary aims, cease being a fallablist. But this (pace Karl Popper) does not limit her activities to reformist tinkering with the system. Moreover, and crucially, a Marxian who articulates such principles is not thereby a Marxian moralist seeking to change the system by showing how bad it is. What is required instead is revolutionary activity with a good understanding of the social structures and the dynamics of the society. Moral-talk will at best play a subsidiary role in revolutionary activity, although sometimes this role may be rather important. But the system instituted soon after the overthrow of capitalism, if it is going to have much of a chance of being effective, initially at least will be a market socialism and that plainly is an example of rebuilding the ship at sea. Perhaps in time market socialism will be replaced by something more adequate, something less like capitalism, with its typical motivations, and answering more adequately to the needs of persons who will have become, as Isaac Deutscher put it, socialist persons.[25] But for now, John Roemer is quite right: we must take people (ourselves included) as they are with all their warts. And in such a situation, at least, it is hardly reasonable to go for more than market socialism. In that way reform and revolution do not stand in opposition. It was, by the way, with such matters among others, that Marx concerned himself in *The Critique of the Gotha Programme*.

However, Wood is right in noting and stressing the Marxian rejection of utopian socialism and moralism. Nothing that I say here is intended to gainsay that. We will not transform a society just by, or even principally by, moralizing. We, however, with a critical normative account that is attentive (as a critical account will have to be) to the actual social practices and the social structures in which the people making the account are embedded, can sometimes do something to help provide some sense of the direction to be taken when taking new directions becomes possible. The mode of production that arguably is coming into being will set the parameters, but within those parameters there is *lebensraum* for different moral principles and conceptions linked to different social practices and, as well, there is room for serious, specific, and concretely oriented moral thinking and action concerning which ones to struggle to bring into existence or over which of them, if any, where in existence, should gain hegemony, with what idealization and with what, if any, modifications. Wood is right that a Marxian should be an antimoralist, but that is perfectly compatible with fallibalistically articulating conceptions and principles for a critical socialist morality. She should, in doing that, articulate principles for assessing whole modes of production and distinctly, within the moral space left within the parameters set by a mode of production, for specifying and arguing for changed and more adequate moral conceptions and practices. The first challenges the whole system, the second, seeking to make some corrections and improvements within the system, will make, if accepted, changes which, if they continue to be pressed and expanded in a certain direction, might in time themselves pose a challenge to the system.

These are things a Marxian can consistently do. And, Marx to the contrary notwithstanding, they need not be an "ideological shuffle," though admittedly many attempts so fizzle. Wood speaks of the "mystification of moral talk."[26] Well, sometimes moral-talk mystifies and sometimes – though less frequently – perhaps it does not. In this way it is disanalogous to religious-talk, which is always mystificatory.[27] A central task of a critical morality, taken as an integral, though a subordinate, part of Marxian social theory and practice, is to sort out when such talk is mystificatory and when it is not. But this critical morality is plainly not to be taken as requiring or even endorsing an independent, free-standing philosophical moral theory. However, a Marxian critical theory of society – something Marx laboured to produce – can and should have a conception of a critical morality as a proper, though subordinate, part. But it surely should not try to be the principal thing or to be that which is taken to move society along. That indeed is moralism, and Wood rightly stresses that Marx contemptuously rejects that and indeed rightly so. If this is what Marx's famous hostility to morality comes to, then we should all be hostile to morality.

Notes

1. Wood, "The Marxian Critique of Justice."
2. Wood, "Marx on Right and Justice"; and Wood, "Marx" in *Encyclopedia of Ethics*, ed. L. C. Becker and C. B. Becker.
3. Nielsen, "Egoism and Relativism"; and Nielsen, "Analytical Marxism."
4. Allen, "Marx and Engels on the Distributive Justice of Capitalism"; G. A. Cohen, "Freedom, Justice and Capitalism"; G. A. Cohen, "Review of Wood's *Karl Marx*"; Elster, *Making Sense of Marx*; Geras, "On Marx and Justice"; Husami, "Marx on Distributive Justice"; Melanson, *A Theory of Moral Personhood in the Thought of Karl Marx*; Nielsen, *Marxism and the Moral Point of View*; Peffer, *Marxism, Morality and Social Justice*; Reiman, "Moral Philosophy"; Young, "Justice and Capitalist Production"; and Young, "Doing Marx Justice."
5. Wood, "The Marxian Critique of Justice," 249–52.
6. Ibid., 270.
7. Ibid., 248.
8. Ibid., 254.
9. Nielsen, "Egoism and Relativism," 5–9.
10. Wood, "The Marxian Critique of Justice," 257–58.
11. Ibid., 256.
12. G. A. Cohen, *Self-Ownership, Freedom, and Equality*; Nielsen, *Marxism and the Moral Point of View*; Peffer, *Marxism, Morality and Social Justice*.
13. Nielsen, *Naturalism without Foundations*, 418–23.
14. Ibid., 57–77.
15. Daniels, *Justice and Justification*; Nielsen, "Engels"; Nielsen, *On Transforming Philosophy*; and Nielsen, *Naturalism without Foundations*.
16. Nielsen, *Marxism and the Moral Point of View*.
17. Young: "Justice and Capitalist Production"; and "Doing Marx Justice"; contrast Wood, "The Marxian Critique of Justice," 270.
18. Nielsen, *Marxism and the Moral Point of View*, 98–116; and Nielsen, "The Concept of Ideology," 146–74.
19. Wood, "The Marxian Critique of Justice," 270.
20. Ibid., 270.
21. Ibid.
22. Rorty, "Idealization, Foundations, and Social Approaches," 333–35.
23. Nielsen, "Global Justice, Capitalism, and the Third World."
24. Davidson, *Inquiries into Truth and Interpretation*.
25. Deutscher, *On Socialist Man*.
26. Wood, "Marx's Immoralism," 133.
27. Nielsen, "Naturalistic Explanations of Religion."

7

Class and Justice

> Liberty, without the commitment to equality … as the history of even the most wealthy capitalist societies reveals, never achieves genuine liberty for all, and threatens its destruction for each, because the people are deprived of real access to practicing liberty, to exercising their rights and assuming their responsibilities in directing their own social and personal affairs. Liberty becomes the power and privilege of the few, an instrument for the manipulation and exploitation of the many. As the mask for narrow self-interest destructive of community and mutuality of social responsibility, liberty divorced from equality discredits genuine liberty itself and places it in jeopardy to disillusion and cynicism. Candid proponents of capitalism no longer make a pretense at honoring the egalitarian tradition. On the contrary, they fear it as the mortal enemy of capitalism. The capitalist class disowned equality in the interests of exercising the liberty associated with their property rights, and tended to reduce liberty, in their elemental loyalties, to their own marketplace activity.
>
> – Martin J. Sklar, "Liberty, Equality, and Socialism"

THE POSSIBILITIES OF CLASSLESSNESS

It has been argued, not implausibly, against those who would tax Rawls with reflecting a conservative/liberal ideological bias, that his account of egalitarian justice is the most egalitarian form of justice it is reasonable to defend.[1] I shall argue against this claim and attempt to articulate in skeletal form a socialist conception of justice, where liberty and equality are treated as indivisible, that is still more egalitarian and at least as reasonable as Rawls's form of egalitarianism.[2] Indeed, it is my belief that if it were to become a core conception guiding the design of our social institutions, it would guarantee more adequately than Rawls's own account the very values (so important to Rawls and indeed to any reflective human being) of equal self-respect, equal liberty, and moral autonomy.

Rawls unreflectively, and without any supporting argument, makes certain problematic assumptions about classes and the possibilities of classlessness. Only if those assumptions are justified will it be the case that Rawls's account is as egalitarian as it is reasonable to be. My arguments shall be that these assumptions are not justified. Rawls has an inadequate conception of what classes are and what classlessness would be. When taken in conjunction with his theory of the primary social goods and the assumptions he makes about human nature, they lead him to adopt a theory of justice which has not been shown to be the uniquely rational one for contractors in the original position to adopt or for fully informed rational and moral agents to adopt after the veil of ignorance is lifted. It is not at all evident that his difference principle provides us with enough equality or, more surprisingly, that his two principles together afford sufficient effective liberty to provide the underlying structural rationale for a perfectly just society.

In this section I shall pose problems about the possibilities of classlessness and its relation to egalitarianism. In the next section I shall discuss, working with a paradigm, class and moral autonomy and Rawls's difference principle, while in the third section I shall discuss liberty and equality and probe the extent and nature of Rawls's commitment to egalitarianism. Finally in the last section I begin a direct argument for a more radical egalitarian conception of justice, requiring classlessness, and seeing equal liberty as being dependent on equality.

Even in societies that Rawls would regard as well-ordered, in which his two principles of justice were satisfied, there could be considerable differences in the life prospects between the advantaged strata of the society and the least well off. Indeed it may very well be that even in a society where the means of production are socially owned, differences in the whole life prospects of people will persist because of the differences in income, status, and authority which remain even after capitalism has been abolished or died the death of a thousand unifying expansions. With differences in status, authority, and income remaining, different groups, differently affected, may find that their whole life prospects are still very different indeed.

We plainly seem to require something very like an industrial society to feed, clothe, etc., our vast and, for the immediate future at least, growing world population. I speak now just of meeting subsistence needs. I do not speak of making the springs of social wealth flow freely and fully. That seems to require a division of labour and, with that division of labour, divisions of people along class lines which deeply affect their life prospects. I grant that it is by no means certain that this is inevitable – particularly when the time comes when there is no longer any private ownership of the means of production – but it is, to put it conservatively, not unreasonable to believe that the division of labour is an inevitable feature of industrially developed societies. Yet it is also not unreasonable to believe that the division of labour could be reduced – that we could and should have far more versatile, many-sided human beings doing more varied work and standing in many different social roles and that we should and could, as well, develop various social devices to ameliorate the inequalities and inequities resulting from the division of labour. It is at least conceivable that a state of affairs could develop where there was a genuine social ownership of the means of production, with democratic control through workers' councils with the gradual transformation of state power into a governmental structure which, as Marx puts it, would come to have only simple administrative functions. In that sense the State could wither away and exploitation of others could end, because there then would be no structural means of transferring to oneself the benefits of the powers of others. Thus, in that very important sense, there would be no classes, i.e., people who are at higher and lower levels, where the higher levels are the result of or the means to exploiting others, extracting from them surplus value. It is in this way and in this sense that class divisions and the existence of classes most deeply and pervasively affect us.[3] It is because of the existence of classes of this sort that the most appalling and extensive inequalities and injustices arise and persist in our social structures. It is vital to know whether in this sense class divisions are inevitable. If the assumption that they are can be successfully challenged, it makes room for the possibility of a more radically egalitarian form of justice than anything Rawls sanctions.

In seeking to articulate the principles of social justice and to attain an Archimedean point for appraising basic social structures, Rawls does not face the questions raised by the existence of social classes. I do not mean to suggest that he regards our actual class-divided societies as basically just or even well on their way to social justice. He eschews the making of such political judgments, but he does think that capitalist societies with their unavoidable class divisions can still be well-ordered societies which are plainly just societies and he would thus be committed to regarding societies in which class divisions and exploitation, in the sense characterized above, are inexpugnable features as still societies which could be perfectly just societies.[4] Rawls takes the existence of classes to be an inevitable feature of social life and he, quite naturally, regards justice as something compatible with that unavoidable social condition.

In thinking about justice and class, two general facts are very important. The first is that in capitalist societies there are deep class divisions and the second is that, barring some incredible catastrophe, the trend to complex industrial societies appears irreversible. This makes classlessness a problematic matter. Yet the very existence of exploiting classes as an integral part of a capitalist order poses evident problems for the attaining of social justice in capitalist societies. I shall argue that because of unjustified assumptions about classes Rawls (a) takes certain disparities in life conditions between different groups of people to be just which are not just or at least have not been shown to be just and appear at least to be very unjust and (b) too easily accepts the belief that capitalism with its class relations can be just.

Capitalist societies are and must remain class-divided societies. Talk of "people's capitalism" is at best fanciful. Rawls is right in seeing class divisions as an unavoidable feature of capitalist societies, but he is mistaken in uncritically accepting the conventional wisdom which maintains that all industrial societies must have class divisions. Rawls, unfortunately, does not examine classes or exploitation. But he does assume, as I remarked initially, the inevitability of classes at least in the sense to be specified in the next two paragraphs.

There is an important sense of "class," developed in the Marxist tradition, concerning which it is by no means evident that classes are inevitable: Rawls largely ignores that conception and generally talks about classes in the way most bourgeois social scientists do, where "class" and "strata" are roughly interchangeable terms. Indeed, Rawls is not clear about what he thinks classes are, but it is evident that he believes that institutionalized inequalities which affect the whole life prospects of human beings are inescapable in complex societies.

My counter is that it has not been shown that a society without classes (cohesive groups) which determine the broad life prospects of their members is an impossibility and that thus Rawls unnecessarily limits the scope of his egalitarian claims. Rawls seems principally to think of a class-divided society as a society with social strata in which there are differences in status, authority, income, and prestige. He believes, plausibly enough, that some differences will persist in any society and thus assumes that classes are inevitable. But such a belief's evident persuasiveness is tied to the identification of class and strata. If, alternatively, we either think of classes, as a Marxist does, essentially in terms of the relationship to the means of production or as cohesive groups between which there are considerable differences in income, prestige, or authority, and because of these differences there are radically different life prospects, it is not so evident that we can safely assume, as Rawls does, that classes are inevitable.

It is not, however, clear that Rawls is committed to denying the possibility of a society without classes in the Marxist sense. After all he admits that it is possible that societies can be both socialist and just. But he does take it to be an inescapable fact that there are and will continue to be classes in the sense that there are and will continue to be institutionally defined cohesive groups whose whole life prospects are importantly different. We cannot design and sustain a society where that will not obtain.

I shall argue that it has not been established that such class divisions are inevitable or that classes in the Marxist sense are inevitable. With these commonly assumed inevitabilities no longer secured, we are not justified, if we believe, as Rawls does, in the equal moral worth of all people, in qualifying egalitarianism and justifying inequalities in the way he does. But there are many challengeable propositions here that require establishment in a somewhat less conditional manner. It is to this that I now turn.

CLASS AND MORAL AUTONOMY

Rawls argues that for conditions of moderate scarcity, the principles of collective action that rational persons would accept in circumstances in which they were disinterested, uninfluenced by a knowledge of their own particular situation, their natural endowments, their individual life plans or aspirations, but in which they did have general social science and psychological information about human nature and society, are (in order of priority) the following: (1) "Each person is to have an equal right to the most extensive total system of equal basic liberties compatible with a similar liberty for all," and (2) "social and economic inequalities are to be arranged so that they are both (a) to the greatest benefit of the least advantaged, consistent with the just savings principle, and (b) attached to offices and positions open to all under conditions of fair equality of opportunity."[5] Now (a) above (the difference principle, i.e., the principle that inequalities to be just must benefit the least advantaged) has been thoroughly criticized, but it remains a distinctive and crucial element in Rawls's account.[6] I do not want to return to that dispute but to consider against the difference principle, in trying to sort out the issue of class and justice, a far less decisive, yet morally and politically more significant candidate counter-example. This example, I shall argue, exhibits how very intractable moral disputes can be and how knowledge and rationality are far less decisive in moral disputes than Rawls and a great many moral philosophers suppose.[7]

Rawls argues that in sufficiently favourable but still only moderately affluent circumstances, where his two principles of justice are taken to be rational ordering principles for the guidance of social relations, it could be the case that justice, and indeed a commitment to morality, would require the acceptance as just, and as through and through morally acceptable, of a not inconsiderable disparity in the total life prospects of the children of entrepreneurs and children of unskilled labourers, even when those children are equally talented, equally energetic, and the like. A just society, he claims, could in such circumstances tolerate such disparities.

It seems to me that such a society could not be a just society, let alone a perfectly just society.[8] There might under certain circumstances be pragmatic reasons of expediency for grudgingly accepting such inequalities as unavoidable. In that way they could, in those circumstances, be *justified inequalities*. When people, whose only relevant difference is that one group had entrepreneurs as parents and the other had unskilled labourers as parents, have, simply because of this difference, life prospects so different that one group's entire life prospects are considerably better than the others, then that difference is unjust.[9] By contrast, Rawls does not direct moral disapprobation toward a society or moral scheme of things which accepts such disparities, not only grudgingly as unfortunate expediencies necessary under certain distinctive circumstances to improve the lot of the most disadvantaged, but as disparities which even a just, well-ordered society could accept. He believes that such a society could still be a just society (perhaps even a perfectly just society). For me, however, the witting acceptance of such disparities just seems evil. It may be an evil that we might in certain circumstances have to accept because we realize that under those circumstances the undermining of that state of affairs will bring about a still greater evil. But it remains an evil all the same. The moral ideal embedded in a conception of a just and truly human society – a perfectly just society – must be to eradicate such differences.

Rawls or a Rawlsian could reply that in making such judgments I am being unnecessarily and mistakenly sentimental and perhaps a little irrational, or at least confused, to boot. It is bad enough that such inequalities in life prospects must exist, but it is still worse by narrowing them to make the children of the unskilled labourers even worse off.[10] It is better and indeed more just to accept the considerable disparities in life prospects and to apply the difference principle. Otherwise, in absolute terms, these children of unskilled labourers will be still worse off. It can never be right or just to knowingly bring about or allow that state of affairs where it could be prevented. To achieve greater equality at such a price is to do something which is itself morally indefensible.

Rawls is, in spite of himself, being too utilitarian here. Talk of increasing the advantages of such a group with lower life prospects is not the only thing which is morally relevant, even in those circumstances where Rawls's principles of justice are to hold in their proper lexical order.[11] Even when it is to their advantage, the working class people in such a circumstance, who are or were children, have had, by the very existence of this extensive disparity, their moral persons assaulted and their self-respect damaged. This is true even if in terms of income and wealth the inequality of opportunity will make them better off, and, in that sense, enhance their opportunities more than they otherwise would be enhanced. That that is not just rhetoric, envy, or resentment can be seen from the fact that they suffer, among other things, with such a loss of equality, the loss of effective equal citizenship.[12] Their continuing to have these formal rights and liberties is cold comfort. Moreover, their effective moral autonomy is undermined by such disparities in power, in their inability to control their life conditions and in their inability (situated as they are) to obtain meaningful work.[13] It is also important to recognize that these disparities are inextricably linked to the different life prospects of children of working class people and the children of the capitalist class and the professional strata whose loyalties by and large are to the capitalist class.

Rawls, it might be thought, could, in turn, respond that there is no actual conflict with his account even if this is so, for, if such conditions obtain, his equal liberty principle would be violated and his principles of justice would not be satisfied after all. For he does claim that "the basic structure is to be arranged to maximize the worth to the least advantaged of the complete scheme of equal liberty shared by all."[14]

However that there is in reality no conflict with his theory is not so clear, for I had in mind the *effective* exercise of the rights of equal citizenship and the *effective* moral autonomy of people, while Rawls seems at least to be talking about something which is more *formal* and which could be satisfied in such a circumstance. By utilizing his putative distinction between liberty and the *worth* of liberty – a distinction effectively criticized by Daniels – Rawls tries to account for what I have been talking about under the rubric "the worth of liberty" and not under the equal liberty principle. But, as Daniels's criticisms have brought to the fore, it is far from evident that anything like this can successfully be maintained.[15] Yet, Rawls might respond that, in arguing as I have above, I have not given sufficient weight to (a) his insistence that fair opportunity requires, not only that no one be formally excluded from a position to which special benefits attach, but also that persons with like talents and inclinations should have like prospects of attaining these benefits "regardless of their initial place in the social system, that is, irrespective of the income class into which they were born," and (b) I neglect that part of his second priority rule which lays it down that "fair opportunity is prior to the *difference* principle" and that any "inequality of opportunity must enhance the opportunities of those with lesser opportunity."[16] Rawls, with a fine moral sense and thorough integrity, seeks to make perspicuous a requirement "which treats everyone equally as a moral person."[17] Moreover, Rawls might add, I am failing to take into consideration his recognition that certain background institutions are necessary for distributive justice. In particular I am forgetting that we need institutions concerned with *transfer* and *distribution*. The institutions concerned with transfer will guarantee a social minimum to the most disadvantaged and will honour the claim to meet basic needs. Taxation will be used by this institution to prevent a concentration of wealth and power which would undermine political liberty and equality of opportunity. Rawls stresses that for principles of justice to be fully satisfied there would have to be a redistribution of income, a wide dispersal of property, and the long-run expectations of the least advantaged would have to be maximized (in a way compatible with the constraints of a fair equality of opportunity and with the constraints of equal liberty). To achieve these things we need institutions of transfer and distribution on employing taxation and the like.

Yet right there, with the very conception that there will, in a well-ordered, perfectly just society, be a *social minimum*, there is the acceptance of class divisions as just, even though the life expectations of some groups are quite different than those of others. While Rawls has the welfare state ideals expressed in the previous paragraph, he also believes that there can be capitalist, and thus class-divided societies, which are well-ordered and in which his principles of justice are satisfied. Yet it is just such societies which have exploitative classes and which, as Rawls himself admits, have class differences which make for the substantial differences in life prospects that we noticed between the children of entrepreneurs and those of unskilled labourers. Rawls thinks such class differences are unavoidable and he thinks that his principles of justice can be satisfied even when they obtain. But then it is difficult to see how in such a circumstance, fair equality of opportunity, on which he also insists, could possibly be realized. How (or even that) Rawls's theory can take a coherent whole here is not evident, but what is evident is that he is applying the difference principle and claiming an inequality is a just one when that claim is very questionable indeed and when it is not at all evident that a person committed, as Rawls is, to a belief in the equal moral worth of all persons should not opt for a more radical form of egalitarianism.

There surely is merit in the claim, pressed by Dworkin, that Rawls seeks to translate into a working conception of distributive justice an egalitarian ideal that everyone be treated equally as moral persons. Yet there is also – and at least equally evidently – the stress in his theory that such disparities as I have discussed could be justified even in a just and well-ordered society.[18] Rawls's writings on this topic are reflectively self-conscious of objections and are often so qualified that it is difficult to make sure how the various parts go together. But there is in Rawls a line of argumentation – one which interprets the difference principle in terms of income rather than other primary goods – to which my counter-example addresses itself. What I have tried to do so far is to show how very much this line of argument conflicts with some tolerably deep sentiments (intuitions, considered judgments) about justice (including, as we have just seen, some of Rawls's other considered judgments).

However, without trying further to sort this out, I think that Rawls has available a still more fundamental reply, namely the reply that class divisions are *inevitable* and that, since rational principles of justice, whatever they may be, must be compatible with the "ought-implies-can maxim," such disparities in life prospects must simply be accepted as something which is just there in the nature of things much in the same way as are differences in natural endowment. Indeed, Rawls suggests that inequalities may be to the benefit of the least advantaged in that they provide incentives to the better off members of society and thereby serve the interests of *all* members. We cannot reasonably complain about them as unjust when it is impossible to do anything about them.

There is an inclination within me to say that, if those are the alternatives, then one should say that the cosmos is unjust. More seriously, and less tendentiously, one can reasonably follow C. B. Macpherson and Benjamin Barber in questioning whether Rawls has done anything more than uncritically and unhistorically assumed the inevitability of there being classes determining differences in whole life prospects.[19] There is, as I remarked earlier, in spite of the length of Rawls's book, no supporting argument at all for this key assumption, and yet it is a governing one in his work and it is the basis for appealing to the ought-implies-can maxim in this context.

It may well be as Rolf Dahrendorf argues, that a certain social stratification is inevitable – that there will be in any complex society some differences in prestige, authority, and income – but there is no good evidence that these differences must result from or result in institutionalized differences in power, including ownership and control of the means of production which will serve as the basis of control and exploitation such that the whole life prospects of people will be radically different.[20] It is where such differences obtain that we have the reality of exploitative classes, but Rawls has done nothing at all to show that such class differences are inevitable such that we would just have to accept – as not unjust, since they are inevitable – the differences in life prospects between the children of entrepreneurs and those of unskilled labourers.

Let us imagine a slight twist in the case I have been considering and suppose that neither disputant believes there is much prospect of achieving classlessness but that one still takes the more egalitarian posture I take and another the Rawlsian position. (Full equality, for the radical egalitarian, now becomes a heuristic ideal to try to approximate.) Yet, given those assumptions about classlessness, is not the Rawlsian position more reasonable and more just? It is, of course, true that there are greater inequalities if we reason in accordance with the difference principle: but the proletarian or lumpenproletarian in such a circumstance is still in a certain plain sense better off – at least in the sense that they have more income. People in such a position also have, it is claimed, the chance, given the way the primary social goods hang together, to achieve a greater self-respect due to the fact that they will have larger incomes and in that way more power than they would otherwise have.[21]

However, in another, and more crucial way, they would have less power and not as great a realization of certain of the primary social goods articulated by Rawls, including most fundamentally the good of self-respect. That can be seen if we reflect on the following. In terms of income and power (mostly buying power) that the income provides, it is true that in the more egalitarian society the most disadvantaged would still be worse off than they would be in the less egalitarian society in which Rawls's difference principle is satisfied. But it is also true that there would, in the greater equality that

that society provides, still be more in the way of effective equal citizenship and in that way a more equal sharing of power and thus a greater basis for realizing the good of self-respect and moral autonomy than in the Rawlsian well-ordered society. In a society in such a circumstance, ordered on Rawls's principles, the least advantaged would have more power *in the sense of more wealth* than they would have in the more egalitarian society, but, in the more egalitarian society, they would have more power in the sense that their equality or at least their greater equality, would make it the case that no one person would have power over another in virtue of his greater wealth and greater consequent control of society. In determining how things are to be ordered, everyone, in a radically egalitarian society, stands in common positions of power or at least in more nearly equal positions of power.

I am not, of course, claiming that as a matter of fact the worst off will, even in the narrowest of economic terms, benefit by a regime of private ownership. Like other socialists, I do not think that, at this historical stage, capitalism benefits the most disadvantaged. Indeed I think it is plain that it does not. In fact I would go beyond that and argue that it hardly can benefit more than 10 per cent of the people in societies such as ours. However, even if some trickle-down theory were correct and it could be shown that the worst off would have greater material benefits under the regime of private ownership of the means of production than in a socialist society, that still would not be sufficient to establish that the capitalist society would be the better or the more just society. In the previous paragraphs I attempted to give some of the reasons for believing that to be so. (I am, of course, speaking, as Rawls is as well, of societies in conditions of moderate scarcity.)

I suspect that, in reflecting on these two possible social orders, some would be more than willing to trade their equal power and consequent equal effective citizenship for greater wealth and some would not. But, particularly given Rawls's own moral methodology, there seem, at least, to be no grounds – no conclusive or even firmly reliable arguments – to push one in one way rather than in another. Reflective and knowledgeable people go in both directions such that it at least appears to be the case that what is the right and through and through just thing to do in such a situation cannot be objectively resolved. And this suggests, and partially confirms, the belief that justice is an essentially contested concept.[22] However, we shall examine in the next section whether this argument can be pushed a little further. Perhaps the disagreement about justice is not all that intractable.

Moreover, this belief could survive a clear recognition on the part of both parties to the dispute that it is unfair that such differences in life prospects exist because there are no morally relevant differences between the children of such entrepreneurs and the children of such unskilled labourers. But the Rawlsian, utilizing the difference principle and taking what is, in effect, a rather utilitarian turn, is committed to saying that this unfairness in such a circumstance does not, everything considered, create an overall injustice, for if the difference principle is not in effect, it will be the case that in such a society, still more harm and a still greater injustice will result for the least advantaged.

LIBERTY AND EQUALITY

Rawls's bedrock argument here is that the inequality in question is just if the equal liberty principle and the fair opportunity principle are not violated and the existence of such inequalities affecting the sons or daughters of unskilled labourers is to the advantage of the most disadvantaged stratum of society.

Suppose these children of unskilled labourers are part of that most disadvantaged stratum. Rawls, as we have seen, could argue that indeed their life prospects, given their situation, are already unfortunate enough and then rhetorically ask whether, given that situation, it is right or just or even humane to make them still worse off by narrowing the equality. Isn't doing that adding insult to injury? This plainly utilitarian argument has considerable force. Yet one can still be inclined to say that such inequalities remain unfair, indeed even somehow grossly unjust. We have two children of equal talent and ability and yet in virtue of their distinct class backgrounds their whole life prospects are very different indeed. One can see the force of the utilitarian considerations which would lead the parents of such children or the children themselves to be resigned to the inequalities, to accept them as the best thing they could get under the circumstances, but why should we think they are *just* distributions?[23]

In a way parallel to the way Rawls himself argues against simply accepting a maximizing of average utility as the most just arrangement, it is possible to argue against Rawls here. Rawls says to the utilitarian that it is a requirement of fairness to consider the interests of everyone alike even when doing so will not produce the greatest utility. To fail to do that is to fail to be fair. I am inclined to respond to Rawls in a similar way by saying that we should – indeed morally speaking must – just reject such acute disparities in life prospects as unfair and unjust even though they do benefit the most disadvantaged. Are not both arguments equally good or equally bad? If we are justified in rejecting utilitarian reasoning in one case, why are we not justified in rejecting it in the other?

It is not, as Rawls claims, envy that is operative here, for one can have the appropriate sense of injustice even if one is not a member of the oppressed and exploited class. One might even be a part of the ruling class – as Engels was – and still feel it. The point is that it offends one's sense of justice. Or perhaps, I should say, to give fewer hostages to fortune it offends my sense of justice and I know it offends the sense of justice of some others as well. I am inclined to say that here Rawls's principles do not match with my considered judgments and the considered judgment of at least some others. Rawls might well counter that they would if we got them into reflective equilibrium. That is, Rawls might claim, if I considered all the facts, the alternative theories, and the principles of rationality, my considered judgments wouldn't be what they are now. It is irrational *not* to accept these inequalities as just or at least as justified.[24]

Such considerations push us back to some basic questions in moral methodology. If there is anything to the above parallelism and both arguments are equally good or equally bad, we still, of course, want to know which they are. Here our considered judgments come into play and, speaking for myself, even when I have utilized the devices linked with what Rawls calls "reflective equilibrium," it remains the case that they are not settled on this issue. I am drawn by the teleological utilitarian considerations: why not, where we can, act in such a manner that we are likely to diminish as much as possible the occurrence of misery and maximize the attainment of happiness or at least (if that does not come to the same thing) the satisfaction of desire? What else, everything considered, could be the better, the more humane thing to do? But I am pulled in the other direction as well, for

I also find myself asking: but are we to do this when this commits us to doing things which are plainly unfair, i.e., when we in effect, whatever our rhetoric, either ignore the interests of certain people, when considering their interests would not contribute toward maximization, or we simply accept as justified, as "all right," given how things are, vast disparities of life prospects between the children – often equally talented and equally intelligent – of entrepreneurs and of unskilled labourers when the difference principle and an equal opportunity principle are satisfied?

Even on reflection with the facts and the consequences of both sets of stratagems before me, vividly and fully, it still strikes me as grossly unfair so to treat the disadvantaged. Yet I can also see the humanity and indeed the rationality in "utilitarian reasoning" here: why allow any more misery or unhappiness than necessary? If closing up the gap between the classes at same determinate point in history results in that, then do not close it. Still I am also inclined to come back, against such utilitarian reasoning concerning such a case, with something (vague as it is) about fairness, human dignity and being in a better position to control one's own life (effective moral autonomy). Moreover, it is not clear that happiness should be so set in opposition to human dignity and a control of one's life as if being happy were independent of these things. But the concept of happiness also has its more familiar sides as well. Perhaps it too is an essentially contested concept.

I think that what is happening here is that very deeply embedded but, in this context, conflicting moral sentiments are being appealed to and our conflicting considered judgments are being matched with these conflicting sentiments.[25] On the side of a socialist conception of justice, more radically egalitarian than Rawls's, we have a clearer recognition of and accounting for the danger to liberty of inequalities of economic power and the effects of concentrated wealth and power under capitalism (particularly modern, monopoly capitalism) on the moral autonomy and sense of moral worth of such disadvantaged people. There is the recognition that, given the realities of social life, we are not justified in believing, as liberals do, that we can rightly treat as separate the political and economic spheres of life and still serve best each person's human flourishing or even, more prosaically, her welfare, by maximizing political freedoms while tolerating extensive economic disparities. Moral autonomy for all, the socialist believes, is simply not possible under such circumstances.

In circumstances of moderate scarcity, Rawls believes that we can and should act in accordance with the difference principle, while still acting in accordance with the equal liberty principle, i.e., the principle laying it down "that each person has an equal right to the most extensive scheme of equal basic liberties compatible with a similar scheme of liberties for all."[26] But talk of the priority of the equal liberty principle over the difference principle should not obscure the fact that in such circumstances reasoning in accordance with the difference principle, even when placed in its proper lexical order, will make for less moral autonomy – and in that crucial sense less liberty – than will reasoning in accordance with the more egalitarian socialist principles. That is so because the socialist always aims at diminishing morally irrelevant inequalities, inequalities in the primary social goods or in basic human goods. With fewer such inequalities, there would be less control of one group over another and thus there would be greater moral autonomy. By contrast, Rawls's difference principle has the unfortunate unintended effect of limiting the scope of his equal liberty principle.

This greater moral autonomy afforded by the socialist principles would most plainly be so if classlessness, or something far closer to classlessness than Rawls allows, were possible. Most crucially, that should be taken to mean the possibility of there being a complex society in which there are no radical differences in life prospects between different groups of people because some have far greater income, power, authority, or prestige than others. Where there is such a class society, there will be less moral autonomy than in a classless society where the more radically egalitarian socialist conceptions can be satisfied. Moreover, in spite of what Rawls may think, what we speak of here is not something which goes "beyond justice," for such considerations concern the fairness of distributions and relations between human beings. So some justification of Rawls's assumption that classlessness is not possible becomes crucial. However, if the division of classes is indeed inevitable, then, perhaps, for those who find a Nozickian trip neither very intellectually challenging nor morally acceptable, a Rawlsian egalitarianism is the best thing that can be had, if one cares about liberty (particularly equal liberty), equality and human well-being. But, given the choices, we ought to be tolerably certain that classlessness is impossible.

Would Rawls be justified in assuming that institutional inequalities rooted in class structures are inevitable? What Rawls must do, to establish that classlessness is impossible or unlikely, is to show that it is impossible or unlikely that a society can come into existence where there are only rather minimal differences in income and authority and where none of the differences that do exist result from, or are the means to, exploiting others. (Note, given its characterization, it is a conceptual impossibility that such an egalitarian society would be authoritarian.) That is, as Macpherson would put it, the society would be so organized that there would be no way to transfer "to oneself for one's own benefit some of the powers of others."[27]

Whatever we may want to say about the division of labour, it is plainly not necessary that there be private ownership of the means of production. Yet it is the private ownership of the means of production which is the principal source of one human being's ability to extract for his own benefit some of the powers of others. Such exploitation is unavoidable in a capitalist organization of society, but there is nothing necessary, given our position in history, about the continued existence of a capitalist social order. Perhaps, as Dahrendorf believes, some social stratification is inevitable, but that is another matter. What we have no good grounds for taking to be a fixed feature of human life is the sorting of human beings into socio-economic classes in which one class will exploit the other. Unless it is a mistake to believe that it is these socio-economic class divisions (or something rather like them in statist societies) which make for such radical differences in life prospects, there is good reason to believe that a form of egalitarianism more radical than Rawls's is both feasible and morally desirable and that the principal human task will be to struggle to attain classlessness.[28]

RADICAL EGALITARIANISM

I want, at this juncture, to make a disclaimer. I do not claim for these views a support in Marx or the Marxist tradition, though I do hope that they are compatible with that tradition. What Marx's or Engels's views are on these matters is subject to considerable debate.[29] They do not systematically treat this subject and indeed they sometimes talk, when justice-talk is at issue, derisively of ideology or false consciousness.[30] To develop any kind of explicit Marxist theory here would require extensive injections of rather contestable interpretation. I will only remark that my radical socialist egalitarianism is in accord with Engels's claim, in a famous passage on the subject in his *Anti-Dühring*, that "the real content of the proletarian demand for equality is the demand for the *abolition* of classes." Significantly, he then goes on to remark that a "demand for equality which goes beyond that, of necessity passes into absurdity," thereby in effect rejecting what have become straw-men forms of "radical egalitarianism" easily knocked about by philosophers.[31] Neither Marx nor Engels was a complete egalitarian in the sense that he thought all human beings should be treated exactly alike in every respect. No thoughtful person, egalitarian or otherwise, believes that everyone old and young, sick and well, introverted and extroverted, should be treated the same in every respect: as if all people had exactly the same interests, aspirations, and needs.

I cannot here specify fully, let alone extensively defend, the form of "social justice" or, as I would prefer to call it, "radical egalitarianism" which I have argued is at least as reasonable as Rawls's account. In fact I would go further than that and contend that it is a superior conception, at least from someone who starts out with moral sentiments similar to those of Rawls, in that it squares better than Rawls's theory, both with what we know about the world (particularly with what we know about the need for meaningful work and the conditions of moral autonomy) and with some of Rawls's deepest insights – insights which led him to reject utilitarianism and to set out his conception of justice as fairness. Here I have in mind his Kantian conception of human beings as members of a kingdom of ends, the weight he gives to moral autonomy, self-respect, equal liberty, and moral community. My contention has been that such things are not achievable under even a liberal capitalist order with its resultant class divisions. Given the way political and economic phenomena interact, liberty and moral autonomy cannot but suffer when there are substantial differences in wealth.[32] It is not only, as is now becoming more generally recognized and apologized for (see the Trilateral Commission's Task Force report: *The Governability of Democracies*), that capitalism is incompatible with equality, it is also incompatible with equal liberty and moral autonomy for all humankind.[33] Equal liberty is impossible without people – all people of normal abilities – being masters of their own lives, but, with the differences in power and control between classes within capitalism, this is impossible for most people.

Furthermore, given the control of the forces of production by one class and the consequent authoritarian allocation of work, meaningful work must be very limited under capitalism. Meaningful work, as Esheté well argues, must be autonomous, though this does not mean that it cannot be cooperative; it must, that is, bear the mark of our own making in the sense of our own planning, thought, and decisions about what is worth doing, making, and having.[34] But this is only possible where there is effective, cooperative, democratically controlled workers' social ownership of the means of production. For anyone who sees the plausibility of Rawls's "Aristotelian principle" or thinks about the conditions of self-respect and thinks carefully about the role of work in life, it should be evident that under a capitalist organization of production these values and with them full moral autonomy are not achievable.

It is a very deep moral assumption of both Rawls's account and my own that all human beings have a right to equal respect and concern in the design of social (including political and economic) institutions. We must, that is, if our normative ethic is to be adequate, and our reactions as moral agents are to answer to that theory, treat all human beings with an equal moral respect. We must regard it as morally required that equal moral concern be given to everyone. What sort of principles of justice do we need to match with that underlying moral assumption and with the related conception that a good society will provide the basis for equal self-respect for all people? Rawls sees that it is true that in bourgeois societies such as those in North America and Western Europe, relative wealth, to a very considerable degree, provides for most people the psychological basis for self-respect. (No claim need be made that these are the only societies so affected.) Given his belief that classlessness is unattainable and that important differences in wealth and power will remain and indeed are important in providing incentives for the accumulation of material wealth, which in turn will better everyone's circumstances, Rawls understandably tries to break the psychological connection between wealth and self-respect. I argued in the earlier sections that there is a tight link between wealth, power, and autonomy and that equal moral autonomy cannot be sustained without something like a very near equality of wealth and power. It is a simple corollary of that to see that equal self-respect cannot be achieved without equal moral autonomy. If that is right, and Rawls is right in assuming that classlessness is impossible, one should draw some rather pessimistic conclusions about the very possibility of a moral order.[35] However, I have argued that we do not have good grounds for rejecting the empirical possibility of classlessness. Given the fundamental moral beliefs that Rawls and I share, I think that in looking for the basis for stabilizing – indeed making it something that could socially flourish – equal self-respect and equal moral autonomy, we should look again at a principle of justice which would stress the need for an equal division of wealth.

I want now to state my more radically egalitarian principle of justice. I shall do so in a somewhat Rawlsian manner for ease of comparison, though I am not particularly enamoured with its formulation and I am confident, if there is anything in it at all, that it will require all sorts of refinements, clarifications, and (no doubt) modifications. Moreover, I do not offer it as a candidate eternal principle of justice, *sub specie aeternitatis*, but rather as a principle of social justice, for conditions of relative abundance (imagine present-day Sweden as the world). This still fits in the upper end of Rawls's situation of moderate scarcity, where considerations of distribution would still be important.[36] For conditions of full abundance, as Marx stressed, questions of distribution would be very secondary indeed.[37]

What I want to capture, in some rough initial way, with my radically egalitarian principle of justice, is a distributive principle committed to *equal division with adjustments for differences in need*. I am under no illusions about its being a magic formula, and much of its plausibility (if it has any) would depend on the reading given to its various constituent elements – a task not to be undertaken here. But I hope the previous discussion has made evident the need to attempt an elucidation of the often cavalierly dismissed principle of radical equality. My formulation has two parts and is expressed as follows:

1. Each person is to have an equal right to the most extensive total system of equal basic liberties and opportunities (including equal opportunities for meaningful work for self-determination and political participation), compatible with a similar treatment of all. (This principle gives expression to a

commitment to attain and/or sustain equal moral autonomy and equal self-respect.)

2. After provisions are made for common social (community) values, for capital overhead to preserve the society's productive capacity and allowances are made for differing unmanipulated needs and preferences, the income and wealth (the common stock of means) is to be so divided that each person will have a right to an equal share.

I am making no claims about priority relations between 1 and 2. I am saying that in a perfectly just society, which is also a relatively abundant society, these two principles will be fully satisfied. It should be noted that such principles can only be so satisfied in a classless society where, in Marx's famous phrase, the free development of each is the condition of the free development of all. Furthermore, such principles require democracy for their realization, taken here to mean "the people's self-determination in political, economic and social affairs" and such a democracy, it is plain to see, requires socialism.[38]

Even in the circumstances where this principle can have a proper application, it is not the case that this is the conception of justice that any rational person would have to adopt who was constrained to reason impartially about what principles of action are collectively rational. I do not believe that my principle, or any other principle, including justice as fairness or average utility, can attain even such an atemporal rational Archimedean point.[39] I do not think that it can be established that there is a set of principles of collective action which are uniquely rational, even in a determinate historical epoch. *A Theory of Justice* is just the latest in a long line of distinguished failures to achieve such an Archimedean point.

What I think can be shown is that in the situation described, for persons with certain moral sentiments, a conception of justice of the type formulated above would be the rational choice. The sentiment I have in mind is the one that leads Rawls to what Ronald Dworkin regards as his deepest moral assumption underlying his commitment to justice as fairness, namely "the assumption of a natural right of all men and women to an equality of concern and respect, a right they possess not in virtue of birth or characteristic or merit or excellence but simply as human beings with the capacity to make plans and give justice."[40] I do not know how anyone could show this belief to be true or self-evident or in any way prove it or show that, if one is through and through rational, one must accept it.[41] I do not think a Nietzschean, a Benthamite, or even an amoralist who rejects it can thereby be shown to be irrational or even, in any way necessarily, to be diminished in his reason. It is a moral belief that I am committed to and I believe Dworkin is right in claiming that Rawls is too. What I am claiming is that, in the circumstances I described, if one is so committed and one has the facts straight, reasons carefully, and takes these reasons to heart, one will be led, not to utilitarianism or to justice as fairness or even to a form of pluralism, but to some such form of radical egalitarianism.[42]

Notes

1. Dworkin, "The Original Position," 533; and Scanlon, "Rawls' Theory of Justice," 1062.

2. It tries to capture in what is, I hope, clear argumentative discourse something of what Marx had in mind with his conception of a classless society where the free development of each is the condition of the free development of all. An account, at core very close to my own but given a more political and historical expression, and closely related to the contemporary political scene, is given by Sklar, "Liberty and Equality, and Socialism," 92–104. Simpson, "Socialist Justice," argues, much more abstractly, to similar conclusions, but I find his argumentation, as distinct from his conclusions and depiction of the liberal/socialist division, obscure.

3. I am here indebted to the work of C. B. Macpherson. His own important critical essays on Rawls have unfortunately been neglected. Macpherson, *Democratic Theory*; and Macpherson, "Rawls's Models of Man and Society." I have in my own "On the Very Possibility of a Classless Society: Rawls, Macpherson, and Revisionist Liberalism" attempted to elucidate and critically assess the force of Macpherson's critique of Rawls. Elizabeth Rapaport, "Classical Liberalism and Rawlsian Revisionism"; and Virginia McDonald, "Rawlsian Contractarianism," both in *New Essays on Contract Theory*, ed. Kai Nielsen and Roger Shiner, have extended and developed, essentially along Macpherson's lines, a socialist critique of contractarianism.

4. Wesley Cooper has spotted some of the inadequacies in Rawls's conception of a perfectly just society. Cooper, "The Perfectly Just Society," 46–55.

5. Rawls, *A Theory of Justice*, 302. That there is, or even can be, such general knowledge of society is challenged by Nowell-Smith, "A Theory of Justice?"; and Wolff, *Understanding Rawls*, chap. 13. A powerful theoretical

underpinning for the kind of claim made impressionistically by Nowell-Smith and Wolff is brilliantly articulated by Charles Taylor, "Interpretation and the Sciences of Man."

6   Wolff, *Understanding Rawls*, 67–71; Barry, *The Liberal Theory of Justice*, 50–51; Copp, "Justice and the Difference Principle"; and the essays by R. M. Hare, David Lyons, and Benjamin Barber in *Reading Rawls*, ed. Norman Daniels.

7   I have, in various ways, argued this against Rawls in several different contexts. Nielsen: "The Choice between Perfectionism and Rawlsian Contractarianism"; "On Philosophic Method"; "The Priority of Liberty Examined"; and "Rawls and Classist Amoralism." It has also been argued in various ways by Lukes, "An Archimedean Point"; and in his "Relativism: Cognitive and Moral"; by Eshete, "Contractarianism and the Scope of Justice"; and by McBride, "Social Theory sub Specie Aeternitatis."

8   It is clear enough that Rawls would regard such a society, in conditions of moderate scarcity, as a well-ordered society, if certain conditions are met. Whether he would say it is a perfectly just society is less clear, though there is at least one passage (p. 102) that suggests that. Cooper, "The Perfectly Just Society," brings out very well the inadequacy of Rawls's conception of a perfectly just society.

9   Joel Feinberg expresses clearly the standard and, as far as I can see, a perfectly adequate rationale for such a belief as follows: "Let us consider why we all agree in rejecting the view that differences in race, sex, IQ or social 'rank' are the grounds of just differences in wealth or income. Part of the answer seems obvious. People cannot by their own voluntary choices determine what skin color, sex or IQ they shall have, or which hereditary caste they shall enter. To make such properties the basis of discrimination between individuals in the distribution of social benefits would be to treat people differently in ways that profoundly affect their lives because of differences for which they have no responsibility. Differences in a given respect are relevant for the aims of distributive justice, then, only if they are differences for which their possessors can be held responsible; properties can be the grounds of just discrimination between persons only if those persons had a fair opportunity to acquire or avoid them." Feinberg, "Economic Justice," 421.

10 Barry, *The Liberal Theory of Justice*, convincingly argues that there are good empirical reasons to doubt whether the narrowing of such inequalities would in fact have the effect of making the worst-off parties still worse off.

11 Yet it is clear enough that Rawls is not insensitive to these problems. Rawls, *A Theory of Justice*, 298–301.

12 Rawls makes far too much play with envy here. Besides envy and jealousy, the disadvantaged, as Rawls recognizes himself, could feel "resentment from a sense that they are unfairly treated." Ibid., 540.

13 Eshete, "Contractarianism and the Scope of Justice."

14 Rawls, *A Theory of Justice*, 205.

15 Daniels, "Equal Liberty and Unequal Worth of Liberty."

16. Rawls, *A Theory of Justice*, 73–74, 275–79, and 512.
17. Ibid., 75.
18. Ibid., 98–102, 511–12, 530–41 (most particularly 534, 536, 537, and 539). See also Rawls, "Distributive Justice," 66–70. For a perceptive discussion of this, see Macpherson, *Democratic Theory*, 88–92.
19. Macpherson, *Democratic Theory*; and Barber in Daniels (ed.), *Reading Rawls*.
20. Dahrendorf, *Essays in the Theory of Society*, 151–78.
21. Benjamin Barber powerfully probes whether they do so hang together. Barber in Daniels (ed.), *Reading Rawls*.
22. This leads us back to the literature cited in note 6.
23. P. Taylor, "Utility and Justice," has very forcefully argued, in a manner plainly influenced by Rawls's root conception of justice as fairness, how distinct questions of justice are from those of utility.
24. Rawls, *A Theory of Justice*, 546. Rawls, as some have thought, seems to have confused "just inequalities" with "justified inequalities." It may not be just to sanction such inequalities, but it may still be justified on utilitarian grounds. It may be one of those cases, *pace* Rawls, where considerations of utility outweigh considerations of justice and where what we should do, through and through, is not identical with what justice requires. To claim this would require a rather considerable change in Rawls's system, but it would give him a rather more plausible justification for his difference principle.
25. I have discussed problems about matching and problems of Rawls's conception of reflective equilibrium in my "On Philosophic Method," 358–68.
26. Rawls, "Some Reasons for the Maximin Criterion," 142.
27. Macpherson, "Rawls's Models of Man and Society," 341.
28. The conception I use of statist societies is clarified, applied, and defended by Stojanovic in his *Between Ideals and Reality*, chap. 3.
29. McBride, "The Concept of Justice in Marx, Engels, and Others"; Goldmann, "Is There a Marxist Sociology?"; Allen, "The Utilitarianism of Marx and Engels"; Brenkert, "Marx and Utilitarianism"; Allen, "Reply to Brenkert's 'Marx and Utilitarianism'"; Tucker, *The Marxian Revolutionary Idea*, chap. 3; Wood, "The Marxian Critique of Justice"; Lerner, "Marxism and Ethical Reasoning"; Nielsen, "Class Conflict, Marxism, and the Good-Reasons Approach"; Allen, "Is Marxism a Philosophy?"; Fried, "Marxism and Justice,"; and Holmstrom, "Exploitation."
30. We need in this context to face questions which arise about moral ideology. See here McBride, "The Concept of Justice in Marx, Engels, and Others"; A. Collier, "Truth and Practice"; and "The Production of Moral Ideology"; Skillen, "Marxism and Morality"; Binns, "Anti-Moralism"; and Corrigan and Sayer, "Moral Relations, Political Economy and Class Struggle."
31. Engels, *Anti-Dühring*, 117–18. For one recent such effort to refute egalitarianism, splendidly made into a straw man, see McCloskey, "A Right to Equality?" Other such efforts include: Nisbet, "The Pursuit of Equality"; Berlin, "Equality"; and Bedau, "Radical Egalitarianism."

32 Simpson, "Socialist Justice," 2.

33 The provisions and ideological transformations of the concept of democracy are interesting to observe in the literature of the Trilateral Commission. See, for example, Crozier et al. (eds.), *The Crisis of Democracy*, and the Trilateral Commission's publication *Trialogue*, particularly the Summer issue 1975, the Winter issue 1975–76, and the Spring issue 1976. Note particularly the writings of Huntington, Crozier, Watanuki, Dahrendorf, and Carli. For trenchantly critical remarks about the Trilateral Commission, see Chomsky, "Trilateral's RX for Crisis: Governability Yes, Democracy No," 10–11.

34 Eshete's comments on work are particularly important here. See Eshete, "Contractarianism and the Scope of Justice," 41–44.

35 These conclusions are drawn about the attainment and sustaining of genuine moral relations in class-divided societies. The steadfast and probing recognition of this is captured in the deepest way in the work of Bertolt Brecht.

36 A rejection of (a) the possibility of attaining such eternal principles and (b) an argument that they are unnecessary for attaining a basis for rational social critique is made by McBride, "Social Theory sub Specie Aetemitatis"; Eshete, "Contractarianism and the Scope of Justice"; and Frankel, "Review Symposium of *Anarchy, State, and Utopia*," 443–50.

37 See Marx's *Critique of the Gotha Programme*. For a perceptive discussion of issues arising from this and of Marx's slogan "From each according to his ability and to each according to his need," see Edward and Onora Nell, "On Justice Under Socialism."

38 Sklar, "Liberty and Equality, and Socialism," 96 and 103. The arguments in the above paragraph, as well as Sklar's essay, should make it evident why my two principles require socialism. We cannot have industrial democracy of the type characterized or classlessness with any kind of capitalist organization of society. There simply will not be democracy in the workplace under capitalism. People will have to sell their labour and they will be controlled by others in their work.

39 My articles cited in note 7 were, in part, directed to establishing this point.

40 Dworkin, "The Original Position," 532.

41 My "Scepticism and Human Rights," was meant to go some of the way toward establishing this. For two more general arguments which provide a theoretical underpinning for such type arguments, see my "Why There Is a Problem about Ethics" and "Principles of Rationality."

42 In this last section I have speculated from, and turned to my own purposes, points often made in different contexts and for different purposes by Sklar, "Liberty and Equality, and Socialism"; Eshete, "Contractarianism and the Scope of Justice"; McBride, "Social Theory sub Specie Aeternitatis"; Shue, "Liberty and Self-Respect"; Crocker, "Equality, Solidarity and Rawls' Maximin"; and D. Phillips, "The Equality Debate," 247–72.

8

Radical Egalitarian Justice: Justice as Equality

Let me say first crudely and over-simply what I want to do. I want to explicate and defend an egalitarian conception of justice both in production and in distribution that is even more egalitarian than John Rawls's conception of justice. In the course of arguing for this I shall argue that such a conception of justice requires, if it is to be anything other than an ideal which turns no machinery, a socialist organization of society. I am well aware that there are a host of very diverse objections that will immediately spring to mind. I shall try to make tolerably clear what I am claiming and why I want to claim it and I shall try to go some way toward at least considering, and, I hope, in some degree meeting, some of the most salient of these objections.

I shall first give four formulations of such a radical egalitarian conception of justice, formulations which, if there is anything like a concept of social justice, capture something of it, though it is more likely that such a way of putting things is not very helpful and what we have here are four conceptualizations of social justice which together articulate what the Left takes social justice to be. I shall follow that with a statement of what I take to be the two most fundamental principles of radical egalitarian justice.

I

Four Conceptions of Radical Egalitarian Justice

(1) Justice in society as a whole ought to be understood as requiring that each person be treated with equal respect irrespective of desert and that each person be entitled to self-respect irrespective of desert.[1]

(2) Justice in society as a whole ought to be understood as requiring that each person be so treated such that we approach, as close as we can, to a condition where everyone will be equal in satisfaction and in such distress as is necessary for achieving our commonly accepted ends.[2]

(3) Justice in society as a whole ought to be understood as a complete equality of the overall level of benefits and burdens of each member of that society.[3]

(4) Justice in society as a whole ought to be understood as a structuring of the institutions of society so that each person can, to the fullest extent compatible with all other people doing likewise, satisfy her/his genuine needs.

These conceptualizations are, of course, vague and in various ways indeterminate. What counts as "genuine needs," "fullest extent," "complete equality of overall level of benefits," "as close as we can," "equal respect," and the like? Much depends on how these notions function and in what kind of a theory they are placed. However, I will not pursue these matters here. I take it, however, that these conceptualizations will help us locate social justice on the conceptual and moral map.

The stress and intent of these egalitarian understandings of the concept of social justice is on the equal treatment of all people in various crucial respects. The emphasis is in attaining social justice, some central equality of condition for everyone. Some egalitarians stress some prized condition such as self-respect or a good life; others, more mundanely, but at least as crucially, stress an overall equal sharing of the various good things and bad things of the society. And such talk of needs postulates a common condition of life that is to be the common property of everyone.

When egalitarians speak of equality they should be understood as asserting that everyone is to be treated equally in certain respects, namely, that there are certain conditions of life that should be theirs. What they should be understood as saying is that all human beings are to be treated equally in respects $F_1, F_2, F_3 \ldots F_n$, where the predicate variable will range over the conditions of life which are thought to be things that all people should have. This is to say that each person has an equal right to them, but it is not to say, or to give to understand, that each person is to have identical or uniform amounts of them. Talking about identical or uniform amounts has no clear sense for respect, self-respect, satisfaction of needs, or attaining the best life of which a person is capable. The equality of condition to be coherently sought is that they all have $F_1, F_2, F_3 \ldots F_n$. Not that they must all have them equally, since for some F's this does not even make sense. Everyone has a right to respect and to an equal respect in that none can be treated as second-class people, but this does not mean that in treating them with respect you treat them in an identical way. In treating with equal respect a baby, a young person, or an enfeebled old man out of his mind on his death-bed, we do not treat them equally, that is, identically or uniformly, but with some kind of not very clearly defined proportional equality.[4] (It is difficult to say what we mean here but we know how to work with the notion.) Similarly, in treating an Andaman Islander and a Bostonian with respect, we do not treat them identically, for what counts as treating someone with respect will not always be the same.

I want now to turn to a statement and elucidation of my egalitarian principles of justice. They are principles of just distribution, and it is important to recognize at the outset that they do not follow from any of my specifications of the concept of social justice. Someone might accept one of those specifications and reject my principles, and someone might accept my principles and reject any or all of those specifications or indeed believe that there is no coherent concept of social justice at all and believe that there are only different conceptualizations of justice that different theorists with different aims propound. But there is, I believe, an elective affinity between my principles and the egalitarian understanding of what the concept specified above involves. I think that if one does take justice in this egalitarian way one will find it reasonable to accept my principles.

I state my principles in a way parallel to Rawls's for ease of comparison. I will briefly compare them with his principles and show why I think an egalitarian or someone committed to Dworkin's underlying belief about the moral equality of persons, as both Rawls and I are, should opt for something closer to my principles than to Rawls's.[5]

Principles of Egalitarian Justice

(1) Each person is to have an equal right to the most extensive total system of equal basic liberties and opportunities (including equal opportunities for meaningful work, for self-determination, and political participation) compatible with a similar treatment of all. (This principle gives expression to a commitment to attain and/or sustain equal moral autonomy and equal self-respect.)

(2) After provisions are made for common social (community) values, for capital overhead to preserve the society's productive capacity and allowances are made for differing unmanipulated needs and preferences, the income and wealth (the common stock of means) is to be so divided that each person will have a right to an equal share. The necessary burdens requisite to enhance well-being are also to be equally shared, subject, of course, to limitations by differing abilities and differing situations (natural environment, not class position).

Principles of Justice as Fairness

(1) Each person is to have an equal right to the most extensive total system of equal basic liberties compatible with a similar system of liberty for all.

(2) Social and economic inequalities are to be arranged so that they are both: (a) to the greatest benefit of the least advantaged, consistent with the just savings principle, and (b) attached to offices and positions open to all under conditions of fair equality of opportunity.[6]

I shall start with a comparison of Rawls's principles and my own, setting out a brief criticism of Rawls's principles as I go along. (I shall be brief here as I have given that criticism at greater length elsewhere).[7] We both, as a glance at our respective first principles of justice makes clear, have an equal liberty principle, though I do not claim the strict priority for mine over my second principle that Rawls does for his. Over the statement of the equal liberty principle, there is no serious difference between us; and I am plainly indebted to Rawls here. The advantage of my principle is that it makes more explicit what is involved in such a commitment to equal liberty than does Rawls's principle. They both give expression to the importance of moral autonomy and to the equality of self-respect, and they both acknowledge the underlying importance of a commitment to a social order where there is an equal concern and respect for all persons. This must show itself in seeing humankind as a community in which we view ourselves as "a republic of equals." This, at the very least, requires an acceptance of each other's moral autonomy and indeed equal moral autonomy. There can be no popes or dictators, no bosses and bossed; any authority that obtains must be rooted in at least some form of hypothetical consent. ("What one would choose if one were …"). The crucial thing about my first principle is its insistence that in a through-and-through just society we must all, if we are not children, mentally defective or senile, be in a position to control the design of our own lives and we must in our collective decisions have the right to an equal say. (The devices for doing this, of course, are numerous and the difficulties in its implementation are staggering. It is here that demanding, concrete socio-political-economic thinking is essential.)

The sharp differences between Rawls and myself come over our second principles of justice. My claim is that, given our mutual commitment to equal self-respect and equal moral autonomy, in conditions of moderate scarcity (conditions similar to those in most of North America, Japan, and much of Europe) equal self-respect and equal moral autonomy require something like my second principle for their attainability. There are circumstances where Rawls's second principle is satisfiable where equal liberty and equal self-respect are not obtainable. In short, I shall argue, his first and second principles clash. Rawls would respond, of course, that, given the lexical priority of the first principle over the second, this just couldn't obtain. But he, on his interpretation of the second principle, allows inequalities which undermine any effective application of the equal liberty principle.

Rawls would argue against a radical egalitarianism such as my own by claiming that "an equal division of all primary goods is irrational in view of the possibility of bettering everyone's circumstances by accepting certain inequalities."[8] The difference principle tells us that if the worst off will be better off – better off in monetary terms – they should accept the inequality. Justice and rationality conspire to require it. The rub, however, is in Rawls's understanding of "better off" or "improving the position" of the worst off. He cashes these notions in purely monetary terms. This prompts the response that either this is too narrow a notion of being "better off" or of "improving your position," or we are not justified in believing that rational agents, who have a tolerably adequate conception of fairness, will always give first priority to being "better off" or "improving their position." They might very well, in conditions of moderate scarcity, recognize other things to be of greater value. Concerning these alternatives, it is well to remark, as Wittgenstein might, "Say what you will, it still doesn't alter the substance of the matter." Either "being better off" is being construed too narrowly by Rawls or it does not always have first priority in deliberations about what is desirable. Indeed Rawls's own notion of the good of self-respect provides us with a jarring conception of what can, in circumstances such as ours, be a conflicting assessment of what is most desirable. Self-respect is for Rawls the most important primary good and it is something which is to be shared equally. In situations of moderate scarcity (relative abundance), we cannot, in Rawls's system trade off a lesser self-respect for more of the other primary goods. But the disparities in power, authority, and autonomy that obtain, even in welfare state capitalism, and are not only allowed but justified by the difference principle, undermine, for the worst off, and indeed for many others as well, their self-respect. Certainly it does not make for a climate of equal self-respect.

Rawls recognizes this as an "unwelcome complication" and tries to show that self-respect need not be undermined or even diminished by the disparities in power and authority allowable in his system by the difference principle. But he concedes that if they did so undermine self-respect the difference principle should be altered.[9] He argues that a well-ordered society, in which his difference principle is in operation, would not be a society in which these inequalities in power, authority, and the ability to direct your own life would, for the worst off, and the strata which are near relatives to them, be particularly visible; hence their self-respect would not be diminished.[10] There would be, as Rawls puts it, a "plurality of associations in a well-ordered society, with their own secure internal life."[11] The more disadvantaged strata will have their various peer groups in which they will find positions that they regard as relevant to their aspirations. These various associations, Rawls remarks, will "tend to divide into ... many noncomparing groups," where "the discrepancies between these divisions" will not attract "the kind of attention which unsettles the lives of those less well-placed."[12] This itself is a tendentious sociological description of life in contemporary class societies. It is in particular very innocent about the nature of work in those societies. Such a view of things could hardly withstand reflection on the facts about work in the twentieth century brought out, for example, in Harry Braverman's *Labor and Monopoly Capital*.

However, even if that were not so and even if Rawl's account here is in some way "telling it like it is," it still reflects an incredible elitism and paternalism. People are to be kept in ignorance and are to moderate their own aspirations and to accept their station and its duties with their respective roles – roles which often will not bear comparing, if self-respect is to be retained. However, they can, if they are so deceived, retain self-respect and society will not be destabilized by their agitation. They will not make comparisons and will unreflectively accept their social roles. Here we not only have elitism and paternalism, we have the ghost of aristocratic justice. Rawls's "realism" here has driven him into what in effect, though I am sure not in intention, is a crass apology for the bourgeois order.

However, Rawls does not retreat here for he sees it as the only acceptable way in which self-respect can be preserved. The equality of self-respect must be preserved or achieved in this way, for we cannot rationally go for a levelling of wealth and status – an alternative way of achieving equal self-respect – because it would be irrational to undermine the incentive value of those limited inequalities of wealth which will produce more goods for all including the worst off. But that appeal, even if the motivational hypothesis behind it is true, begs the question. Some would say – and there are conflicting elements in Rawls's theory which would support them – "Better a greater equality in self-respect than more goods." Even if – indeed particularly if

– that claim is made by the worst off in conditions of moderate scarcity (relative abundance), that claim, as far as anything Rawls has shown, is not irrational, or even less rational, than his worst off chaps sticking with the difference principle. (Even with the links stressed by Rawls between self-respect and liberty and given the priority of liberty, this is also what he should say. Indeed, given Rawls's and Dworkin's own deeply embedded belief that there should be equal respect and concern across persons, it would seem here that the response, "Better a greater equality in self-respect than more goods" would be, morally speaking, more appropriate, though, for reasons that Bertolt Brecht has made unforgettable, we must never forget that we are, in making such a claim, talking about conditions of relative abundance.)

Rawls might counter that he was not talking about our societies but, operating from within his ideal theory, about an "ideal type" called a well-ordered society, where, by definition, there would not be such disparities in authority and power and effective control over one's life. But he also claims that his account is meant (a) to be applicable in the real world and (b) even there to some forms of capitalism. But my point was that his difference principle sanctions inequalities that are harmful to the sense of self-respect of people in the worse-off strata of any capitalist society, actual or realistically possible. They simply, if they are being rational, must accept as justified, disparities in power, wealth, and authority which are harmful to them. Indeed these disparities attack their self-respect through undermining their moral autonomy; in such social conditions, men and women do not have effective control over their own lives. Thus his difference principle, in a way my second more egalitarian principle is not, is in conflict with his first principle and, given Rawls's doctrine of the priority of liberty, should be abandoned.

Rawls tries to square his two principles and provide moral and conceptual space for both liberty and socio-economic inequalities by distinguishing between liberty and the *worth* of liberty. Norman Daniels, in an impressive series of both internal and external criticisms, has, I believe, demolished that defence.[13] So I shall be brief and stick with the simplest and most direct points. Even allowing the coherence and non-arbitrariness of the distinction, it will not help to say that the socio-economic disparities affect the *worth* of liberty but not liberty itself, for a liberty that cannot be exercised is of no value; and, indeed, it is in reality no liberty at all. What is the sense of having something, even assuming it makes sense to say here that you have it, which you cannot exercise? A "liberty" that we cannot effectively exercise, particularly because of some powerful external constraints, is hardly a liberty. Certainly it is of little value. If I have a right to vote but am never allowed to vote, I certainly do not have much of a right. Moreover, a rational contractor, or indeed any thoroughly rational person not bamboozled by ideology, would judge it rational to choose an equal *worth* of liberty, if she judged it rational to choose equal basic liberties. To will the end is to will the necessary means to the end. It is hardly reasonable to opt for equal liberty and then opt for a difference principle which accepts an unequal worth of liberty which, in turn, makes the equal liberty principle inoperable, that is, which makes it impossible for people actually to achieve equal liberty.

I want now to return to Rawls's arguments that equal self-respect in class societies can be achieved when inequalities remain invisible or at least invisible to those who are on the deprived side of the inequality. This hardly accords with Rawls's insistence that the principles of justice are "principles that rational persons with true general beliefs would acknowledge in the original position."[14] As Keat and Miller aptly remark, "a theory is not acceptable if the stability of a society based upon it depends upon the members of that society not knowing its principles and the way in which it is organized."[15] There is, they continue, something morally distressing – they actually say abhorrent – about a theory of justice relying on "the worse-off members of society continuing not to compare their position with that of the better off. This narrowing of reference groups, and the concomitant lowering of expectations, is something which should be a main object of criticism for any theory of justice which claims, as Rawls's does, to be "democratic" and "egalitarian."[16]

My above arguments – as well as the arguments of Keat and Miller and Daniels – should push Rawls, if they are near their mark, in a more egalitarian direction. Specifically, they should require either an abandonment or an extensive modification of his second principle. If the preservation of self-respect is regarded as a conception at the heart of any theory of social justice and is taken, as Rawls would take it, to be directly relevant to questions about the just distribution of primary goods, then it seems that we would be forced to adopt more egalitarian principles of just distribution than Rawls adopts.

II

However, to go in a more egalitarian direction, is not, of course, necessarily to accept my principles. There are no doubt other alternatives. I shall now directly examine my egalitarian principles, starting with an elucidation of my own second principle and then proceeding to a consideration of some of the criticisms that would naturally be made of it. What is now at issue is my second principle:

> After provisions are made for common social (community) values, for capital overhead to preserve the society's productive capacity and allowances are made for differing unmanipulated needs and preferences, the income and wealth (the common stock of means) is to be so divided that each person will have a right to an equal share. The necessary burdens requisite to enhance well-being are also to be equally shared, subject, of course, to limitations by differing abilities and different situations (natural environment, not class position).

A central intent of this principle is to try to reduce inequalities in primary or basic social goods and goods that are the source of or ground for distinctions that give one person power or control over another. All status distinctions should be viewed with suspicion. Everyone should be treated equally as moral persons and, in spite of what will often be rather different moral conduct, everyone should be viewed as having equal moral worth.

The second principle is meant as a tool for attaining a state of affairs where there are no considerable differences in life prospects between different groups of people because some have a far greater income, power, authority, or privilege than others. My second principle tries to distribute the benefits and burden so that they are, as far as is compatible with people having different abilities, equally shared. It does not say that all wealth should be divided equally, like equally dividing up a pie. Unlike such pie-dividing, part of the social product must be used for things that are of collective value, for example, hospitals, schools, roads, clean air, recreation facilities, and the like. And part of it must be used to protect future generations. Another part must be used to preserve the society's productive capacity so that there will be a continuous and adequate supply of goods to be divided. However, all of us – especially those of us who live in an economically authoritarianly controlled capitalist society primarily geared to production for profit and capital accumulation and only secondarily to meeting needs – must be aware of becoming captivated or entrapped by productivism. We need democratically controlled decisions about what is to be produced, who is to produce it, and how much is to be produced. The underlying rationale must be to meet (as fully as possible, as equally as possible, and while allowing for different needs) the needs of all the people. Care must be taken, particularly in the period of transition out of a capitalist society, that the needs referred to are needs people would acknowledge if they were fully aware of the various hidden persuaders operating on them. And the satisfaction of a given person's needs must, as far as possible, be compatible with other people being able to similarly so satisfy their needs.

A similar attitude should be taken toward preferences. People at different ages, in different climates, with different needs and preferences will, in certain respects, need different treatment. However, they all must start with a baseline in which their basic needs are met – needs that they will have in common. (Again what exactly they are and how this is to be ascertained is something which needs careful examination.)

Rawls's notion of primary goods captures something of what they are. What more is required will be a matter of dispute and will vary culturally and historically. However, there is enough of a core here to give us a basis for consensus; and, given an egalitarian understanding of the concept of social justice, there will be a tendency to expand what counts as basic needs. Beyond that, the differing preferences and needs should, as far as possible, be equally satisfied, though what is involved in the rider "as far as possible" is not altogether evident. But it is only fair to give them all a voice. No compossible need should be denied satisfaction where the person with the need wants it satisfied and is well-informed and would continue to want it satisfied even after rational deliberation. Furthermore, giving all people a voice has other worthwhile features. It is evident enough that people are different. These differences are sometimes the source of conflict. Attaching the importance to them that some people do, can, in certain circumstances, be ethnocentric and chauvinistic. But it is also true that these differences are often the source of human enrichment. Both fairness and human flourishing are served by the stress on giving equal play to the satisfaction of all desires that are compossible.

So my second principle of justice is not the same as a principle which directs that a pie be equally divided, though it is like it in its underlying intent, namely, that fairness starts with a presumption of equality and only modifies a strict equal division of whatever is to be divided in order to remain faithful to the underlying intent of equal treatment. For example, both children aren't given skates; one is given skates, which is what she wants, and the other is given snowshoes, which is what she wants. Thus both, by being in a way treated differently, are treated with equal concern for the satisfaction of their preferences. Treating people like this catches a central part of our most elemental sense of what fair treatment comes to.

It should also be noted that my second principle says that each person, subject to the above qualifications, has a right to an equal share. But this does not mean that all or even most people will exercise that right or will feel that they should do so. This is generally true of rights. I have a right to run for office and to make a submission to a federal regulatory agency concerning the running of the CBC. But I have yet even to dream of exercising either of those rights, though I would be very aggrieved if they were taken away, and, in not exercising them, I have done nothing untoward. People, if they are rational, will exercise their rights to shares in primary goods, since having them is necessary to achieving anything else they want, but they will not necessarily demand equal shares and they will surely be very unlikely to demand equal shares of all the goods of the world. People's wants and needs are simply too different for that. I have, or rather should have, an equal right to have fish pudding or a share in the world's stock of bubble gum. *Ceteris paribus*, I have an equal right to as much of either as anyone else, but, not wanting or liking either, I will not demand my equal share.

When needs are at issue, something even stronger should be said. If I need a blood transfusion, I have, *ceteris paribus*, the same right to blood as anyone else. But I must actually need it before I have a right to an equal share or, indeed, to any blood plasma at all. Moreover, people who need blood have an equal right to the amount they require, compatible with others who are also in need having the same treatment; but, before they can have blood at all, they must need it. My wanting it does not give me a right to any of the common stock, let alone an equal share. And, even for the people actually getting the blood, a fair share would probably not be an equal share. Their needs here would probably be too different.

How does justice as equality work where it is impossible to give equal shares? Consider the equal right to have a blood transfusion. Suppose at a given time two people in a remote community both need an immediate transfusion to survive, and suppose it is impossible to give them both a transfusion at that time. There is no way of getting blood of the requisite type and there is no way of dividing up the available plasma and giving them each half or something like that. In order to live, each person needs the whole supply. There can be no equal division here. Still are not some distributions just and others unjust? If there are no relevant differences between the people needing the plasma, the only just thing to do is to follow some procedure like flipping a coin. But there almost always are relevant differences and then we are in a somewhat different ball game.

It might be thought that, even more generally in such a situation, the radical egalitarian should say: "In such a situation a coin should be tossed," but suppose the two people involved were quite similar in all relevant respects except that A had been a frequent donor of blood and B had never given blood. There is certainly a temptation to bring in desert and say that A is entitled to it and B is not. A had done his fair share in a cooperative situation and B had not, so it is only fair that A gets it. (We think of justice not only as equality but also as reciprocity.) Since "ought" implies "can," and since we cannot divide the blood equally, it does not violate my second principle or the conception of justice as equality to so distribute the plasma.

I would not say that to do so is unjust, but also, given my reservations about the whole category of desert, I would hesitate to say that justice requires it. But the central thing to see here is that such a distribution according to desert does not violate my second principle or run counter to justice as equality.

Suppose the individuals involved were A^1 and B^1. They are alike in all relevant respects except that A^1 is a young woman who has three children and who would soon be back in good health after the transfusion, and that B^1 is a woman ninety years of age, severely mentally enfeebled, and without dependants and who would most probably die within the year anyway. It seems to me that the right thing to do under the circumstances is to give the plasma to A^1. Again it does not violate my second principle for an equal division is rationally impossible. But it is not correct to say A^1 deserves it more than B^1 or even, in a straightforward way, needs it more. However, we can relevantly say, because of the children and people who would be affected by the children, that more needs would be satisfied if A^1 gets it than B^1. This is bringing in utilitarian reasoning here, but, whatever we would generally say about utilitarianism as a complete moral theory, it seems to me perfectly appropriate to use such reasoning here. We could also say – and notice the role universalizability and role reversal play here – that, after all, B^1 had lived her life to the full, was now quite incapable of having the experiences and satisfactions that we normally can be expected to prize, and indeed will soon not have any experiences at all, while A^1, by contrast, has much of the fullness of her life before her. Fairness here, since we have to make such a horrible choice, would seem to require that we give the plasma to A^1 or, if "fairness" is not the correct notion here, a certain conception of rightness seems to dictate that, everything considered, that is the right thing to do.

Let me briefly consider a final pair A^2 and B^2. Again they are alike in every respect except that A^2 is the community's only doctor while B^2 is an unemployable hopeless drunk. Both are firm bachelors and they are both middle-aged. B^2 is not likely to change his ways or A^2 to abandon what is a competently and conscientiously done practice. Here, it seems to me, we again quite rightly appeal to social utility – to the overall good of the community – and give the plasma to A^2. Even if, since after all he is the only doctor, A^2 makes the decision himself in his favour, it is still a decision that can be impartially sustained. Again my second principle has not been violated since an equal division is impossible.

I think that all three of those cases – most particularly the last two with their utilitarian rationale – might be resisted because of the feeling that they, after all, violate not my second principle, but, more generally, justice as equality in not giving equal treatment to persons. B, B^1, and B^2 are simply treated as expendable in a utilitarian calculation. They are treated merely as means.

This response seems to me to be mistaken. B, B^1, and B^2 are not being ignored. If the roles were reversed and they had the features of the A they are paired with, then they would get the plasma. They are not being treated differently as *individuals*. We start from a baseline of equality. If there were none of these differences between them, and if there were no other relevant differences, there would be no grounds to choose between them. We could not, from a moral point of view, simply favour *A* because he was *A*. Just as human beings, as moral persons or persons who can become capable of moral agency, we do not distinguish between them. We must treat them equally. In the limiting case, where they are only spatiotemporally distinct, this commitment to equality of treatment is seen most clearly. Morality turns into favouritism and privilege when this commitment is broken or ignored. *Within* morality there is no bypassing it; that is fixed by the very language-game of morality (by what the concept is, if you don't like that idiom).

III

I want to turn now to what is plainly a perfectly natural criticism of my radical egalitarianism. Mihailo Markovic in his *The Contemporary Marx*, while defending a socialist egalitarianism, argues against what he calls "radical egalitarianism."[17] He rightly points out that,

> Marx was quite well aware of natural differences among individuals and of the fact that these will increase in importance when institutions that favour social discrimination and inequality disappear. He is very far from conceiving communism as a rigid egalitarian society in which all individuals would be equally paid and cultivate a uniform style of life.[18]

Markovic then adds – again correctly and importantly – that Marx's conception of equality is focussed on "the demand to abolish class exploitation, that is to abolish capital and wage labour, in the last instance to overcome commodity production and the market as the basic regulator of production."[19] The sensible demand for an equality of condition, he argues, is the demand for the abolition of classes and differentiation by social status. But what, at the end of a historical process, this classless society would look like, Markovic remarks, was left by Marx "in a very vague, general form, susceptible of all kinds of interpretation, misunderstanding and controversy."[20]

Markovic tries to say something a little more precise about this and, at the same time, to distance more clearly his egalitarianism from what he calls radical egalitarianism. He points out that in every society – including the future classless society – "there will be differences among individuals in their abilities, character, gifts, and so forth."[21] Radical egalitarianism, as he understands it, would impose a uniformity which is "incompatible with the aspiration for individual self-realization that remains the very basic objective of all humanist thought, including a Marxist humanism."[22] Such radical egalitarianism, he claims, is destructive of individual freedom: "The realization of different individual potential capacities ... is incompatible with conditions of life that are the same for all."[23] It is, Markovic argues, utterly wrong-headed and contrary to Marx to think that even in a classless society there will not be some inequalities in the way of there being differentiations, not of rank, but of social role and natural capacity. These will continue to exist, for they arise naturally out of different abilities and proclivities. It is impossible to avoid them. But, even if it were not, it would be undesirable to do so. What we must avoid, however, are inequalities which involve any form of domination or economic exploitation, though we must also realize that in a classless society there will remain different social roles. There will remain, and valuably, differentiation and inequality in kind of role; what must be overcome or avoided in a perfectly just society is this differentiation in social role becoming or remaining as well a form of social stratification (an inequality in rank) and particularly a stratification (endemic to complex class societies) involving a political or economic hierarchy.[24] Differing social roles have in the past brought with them privileged status and, with that, power, wealth, and domination. But this, he argues, need not continue to be so with a socialist organization of society, though something of the length of time it takes can be seen from the (1977–79) class struggles in China.[25]

Markovic departs from Marx and Engels in claiming that the abolition of class differences, while necessary for the achievement of equality, is not in itself sufficient. Social stratification (inequalities in rank) on the basis of different social roles is very persistent and has affected hitherto both socialist and capitalist societies. Various kinds of managers, technocrats, and intelligentsia, given the role they play in social life, gain status, prestige, and power. There is a tendency for them to become new elites with a very considerable power in their hands. An egalitarian society would not only be classless, it would also be without social stratification. But it would not be a society without differentiation on the basis of social roles, and it would have people who, as Bakunin put it, would have a kind of natural authority on the basis of sensitivity and understanding and (if this doesn't come to the same thing) on the basis of their moral and intellectual qualities. This would not be a source of political power or control over people; they would, in Markovic's terms, only be an "elite of spirit, of moral authority, of taste."[26] Any other kind of elite is as unacceptable to an egalitarian as is class society or elitist political and economic control. But this egalitarianism, Markovic continues, is quite distinct from a rigid radical egalitarianism which, in "the distribution of goods," would insist on "strict equality of share" and would advocate "conditions of life that are the same for all."[27] In a fully developed classless, unstratified society – the communist society of the future – goods are not distributed according to equality or on the basis of work (some form of merit or entitlement) but according to need.[28]

It should be evident enough that Markovic and I are at cross-purposes here. We use the term "radical egalitarianism" in different ways and for our own purposes, but, labels apart, our egalitarianism is substantially very similar. I stress, in a way he does not, equal division *of wealth with adjustments for differences in need and non-socio-economic circumstance*, and I am a little more nervous than he is, recalling the cultural role of charismatic figures, about even his "elites of the spirit"; but I do not deny that there can be such people and, when they are genuine and flanked by entrenched democratic institutions of a socialist sort, they are desirable elites. But the last difference in particular is very minor. On the major issues a glance at my two radical egalitarian principles should make it evident that I do not want to reduce people to a uniform sameness of condition, such that they all get the same things, do the same things, have the same interests, and in general behave in the same way. That is not what my conception of equal wealth aims at or would result in. I stress the importance of recognizing differences in need and stress that they must be catered to by an equal-distribution principle. This is built into the formulation of my second principle. I also stress that, where we have full abundance, need should be a criterion of distribution, though surely not the sole criterion. I only claim that, once allowances are made for human differences and the like, in a world of moderate scarcity, each individual should have a right to an equal share.

What I am *most* concerned to avoid, and I expect Markovic is too, is not income differentials but inequality in whole life prospects between members of different classes and strata. With such differences, there exists control, domination, and privilege by one group over another, which makes the lives of some groups quite arbitrarily better and more autonomous than those of other groups. Since this is so, there must be, to achieve social justice, a levelling such that a society will come into existence that has neither classes nor strata. This I call a *statusless* society. Essential for there being such a society – not the whole of it but something without which the rest is impossible – is an equality in political and economic power. It is essential for equal autonomy, and equal autonomy in turn provides the rational basis for equal self-respect. This in turn is necessary if there is to obtain a situation in which there is an equal moral concern for and respect of all human beings.

However, I also argue, in a way Markovic does not, that in a socialist reconstruction of society, where the society is one of relative abundance and tending toward classlessness, the underlying general conception should be that of everyone having an equal share.

We should start with this presumption, a presumption showing an equal concern for all human beings, and a belief – rooted in that equal concern – that there should be an equality of the overall level of benefits and burdens. Departures from that initial presumption must be justified first on the basis of differing genuine needs and differing situations (where differences in rank do not count as being in a different situation) and secondly on differing preferences where the first two are satisfied or irrelevant. This, as I have already shown, in a very literal sense, is not to treat everyone the same, and it avoids what I believe is one of the most persistent criticisms of radical egalitarianism, namely that it advocates, or would result in, a grey, uniform world of sameness where human freedom, creativeness, and diversity would be destroyed.

Notes

1. Miller, "Democracy and Social Justice," 1–19.
2. Honderich, *Three Essays on Political Violence*, 37–44.
3. Ake, "Justice as Equality," 69–89.
4. Hook, *Revelation, Reform and Social Justice*, 269–87.
5. Dworkin, *Taking Rights Seriously*, 150–83; Nielsen, "Class and Justice," 225–45.
6. These are, of course, Rawls's principles of justice. See Rawls, *A Theory of Justice*, 302.
7. Nielsen: "Class and Justice," 191–208; and "The Priority of Liberty Examined," 48–59.
8. Rawls, *A Theory of Justice*, 546.
9. Ibid.
10. Ibid., 535.
11. Ibid., 536.
12. Ibid., 536–37.
13. Daniels, "Equal Liberty and Unequal Worth of Liberty."
14. Rawls, *A Theory of Justice*, 547.
15. Keat and Miller, "Understanding Justice," 24.
16. Ibid.
17. Markovic, *The Contemporary Marx*, chap. 7.
18. Ibid., 130.
19. Ibid.
20. Ibid., 131.
21. Ibid., 132.
22. Ibid.
23. Ibid., 137.
24. Ibid., 132.
25. Bettelheim, "The Great Leap Backward," 57–130.
26. Markovic, *Contemporary Marx*, 133.
27. Ibid., 137.
28. Ibid.

9

Radical Egalitarianism Revisited: On Going beyond the Difference Principle

INTRODUCTION

Would-be egalitarians try, where their inclinations are theoretical, to clearly articulate and display a conception of egalitarianism and egalitarian justice that answers to our reflective moral sensibilities (including, of course, our egalitarian sensibilities), that responds to the deep social injustices in our societies, and that proffers an ideal conception of a better and more just society and, beyond that, of a just world. Egalitarians cannot simply be concerned with domestic justice. Moreover, and of course crucially, they attempt to set out a cluster of sound and clear arguments for a morally attractive conception of egalitarianism and egalitarian justice.

In turning to their task, two central questions egalitarians face are *how much equality is enough equality* and *what* are people to have equally or to be equal in. Concerning the latter problem, suppose that issues about the relations of equality to liberty, fraternity, desert, and incentives are resolved, it is at least plausible that the question of *equality of what* would remain. What, if we are to have anything in an equal amount, should we have equal amounts of or be equal in? How much of it should we have and when and why we should limit it would remain – or so it seems natural to suppose – separate issues.

In Part A, I consider how much equality is enough equality. Here I am doing what John Rawls calls *ideal theory*, and in doing that I try to say, abstracting from practicalities, what a perfectly just society would look like in conditions of very considerable abundance, but not so counterfactually abundant that the circumstances of justice (moderate scarcity and limited altruism) do not obtain. Running against what is at least conventional wisdom, if not more, I argue that it is reasonable and morally justified to urge a form of egalitarianism that is stricter than the liberal egalitarianism of John Rawls and Ronald Dworkin and even the socialist egalitarianism of G. A. Cohen. For all three, their egalitarianism is constrained by the difference principle. I too, in circumstances where there are classes, genders, racism, or hierarchical strata, would argue for the difference principle. However, I also argue, in trying to characterize what a perfectly just society and world under ideal conditions would look like, that we should favour a more extensive equality, which I call radical egalitarianism.[1] I am well aware that such conceptions are often rejected out of hand. I face that right at the beginning in Part A, Section I.

I should also say – though it may seem to cut against my pragmatist bent – that it seems to me that these "Platonic enterprises" of ideal theory, whether in the form of my radical egalitarianism or the liberal egalitarianism of Rawls or Dworkin or the anti-egalitarianism of Robert Nozick or David Gauthier, are important enterprises in which to engage. We should do ideal theory in order to gain, free from all strategic questions concerning instrumentalities and the like, a sense of what our practices, institutions, laws, etc., would have to be like to be perfectly just. This gives us a sense of the direction we should ideally go in if we can. We have to know, if we can, and as a matter of informed and plausible conjecture, what can be done, what are the feasible possibilities, and how we can move from the kinds of societies we live in now to genuinely better societies. We need to face hard live political and economic questions concerning what is to be done and what realistically is to be aspired to and fought for. But to help give us a sense of direction – of what it is we would dearly want to see our lives and our world be like – we also need to confront the questions of ideal theory and that is what I limit myself to here. But stopping there is irresponsible, except as a kind of division of labour, where people caught up in common engagement put to best use their special skills.

In Sections II through IV of Part A, I consider, coming a bit closer to earth, the role of merit, desert, entitlement, and incentives. These are often thought, in one way or another and with greater or lesser severity, to restrict how much equality we can reasonably and rightly have. I try to show that none of these considerations undermines either radical egalitarianism or liberal egalitarianism and that, on the liberal side, even Rawls's defence of incentives will not pass muster. On a strict reading of the difference principle, I follow G. A. Cohen in arguing that Rawls's incentive claims are not justified and are not in accordance with the central thrust of his own liberal egalitarianism.[2]

In Part B I turn to the issue not of how much equality, but of *what kind*. I argue on fairly familiar grounds against both resource egalitarianism and welfare egalitarianism. I then turn to a consideration of the equal capabilities of functioning conceptions of equality. Although I criticize such conceptions, while also proceeding from them and building on them, I develop most fully (though still critically) first an "equal effective freedom conception" and then an "equal satisfaction of needs conception." Finally and tentatively, I consider a more complex conception of *equality of what* by combining these last three conceptions with the "primary goods conception." I indicate in my manner of combining them how they compensate for each other's lacunae. I consider whether together they forge a coherent and plausible conception, yielding a more adequate conception of egalitarianism than do the less complex views of *equality of what*. I seek in this essay both to defend egalitarianism against some anti-egalitarian objections and to articulate a perspicuous and sound form of egalitarianism.

In both Parts A and B, I refer to egalitarian aspirations, to egalitarian hopes and aims, to the egalitarian impulse and to the underlying rationale of egalitarianism. Reflection of these notions is not at all sufficient to answer our questions about *equality of what*, how much equality we should have, how equality and liberty go together and what our principles of egalitarian justice should be. But without a good sense of what is involved in having egalitarian aspirations and the like, we will not know where to look in facing and trying to answer these questions. Without a firm sense of egalitarian aspirations, some sense of what the world egalitarians ideally want, and a sense of the underlying rationale of egalitarianism, we will not know what is involved in asking those questions or when we are going in the right direction in our attempts to answer them or even when, after long trying, we have correctly answered them. They are our touchstone for what is involved in our inquiries into what would be an adequate egalitarian theory or account. So, in my account, I frequently return to them.

PART A

I

Let me start by examining some acute remarks of another socialist egalitarian, G. A. Cohen, remarks that in effect cut against my radical egalitarianism. In his "Incentives, Inequality and Community," Cohen argues against a radical egalitarianism or, indeed, any, as he calls them, strict egalitarian conceptions which urge a stricter egalitarianism than that sanctioned by the difference principle, namely the principle "that inequalities are justified when they render badly off people as well off as it is possible for such people to be."[3] He takes, quite rightly, I believe, the difference principle "in its more generous form, in which it allows inequalities that do not help but also do not hurt the worst off."[4]

Socialist egalitarians, Cohen has it, will not find it easy "to set aside the Rawlsian justification of inequality. They cannot just dismiss it, without lending to their own advocacy of equality a fanatical hue which they could not themselves on reflection find attractive."[5] It is often thought to be unreasonable and morally untoward, in order to gain a strict equality, either to make the badly off worse off still, or "to make the badly off no better off, while others are made worse off to no evident purpose."[6] An egalitarian view becomes incoherent or untrue to itself, if, in a world with badly off people, it rejects the difference principle and cleaves "to an egalitarianism of strict equality."[7]

What, Cohen believes, most fundamentally concerns egalitarians is not such fanatical levelling, but the injustice of some people being so badly off when other people are so well off.[8] Egalitarians are not exercised by the fact that some people are just less well off than others. In a world of millionaires and billionaires, in which no one's life is hard, they would not care much, Cohen maintains, about the inequalities between millionaires and billionaires. What exercises them is that in capitalist societies, and the other class societies that preceded them, there is what they take to be unnecessary hardships at the lower end of the social spectrum. There are people badly off, some very badly off, "who, they believe, would be better off under an equalising redistribution."[9] In such a world they want to use the difference principle to spot the inequalities that are acceptable and those that are not. It is a litmus test for justified and unjustified inequalities. Equality, within the limits of the difference principle, is a good thing because, if followed, it would make the badly off better off, indeed as well off as they reasonably could be in such circumstances. But it would not make the well off worse off, when it is not necessary to obtain this end. Reasonable egalitarians do not think that it is "a good thing about equality that it would make the well off worse off."[10] Egalitarians, in short, are not – or at least should not be – motivated by envy.

In a world of reasonable abundance with strata of badly off people, I too accept the difference principle in its more generous form. To spell out in that context an egalitarian conception of social justice is just what is needed. *In such circumstances*, to reject it in the name of a more radical or stricter equality would be wrong, and, indeed, not only wrong, but irrational.

However, we cannot leave things just like that. Egalitarians aspire to a society, indeed a world, of equals: people with equal human rights, equal in power, equal in access to advantage, equal (insofar as this is possible) in whole life prospects. Egalitarians want, as far as that is possible, equal well-being for all at the highest level of well-being it is possible to attain. The egalitarian impulse and aspiration is not *(pace* Cohen) *just* to make the badly off well off, or, if that is not possible, to make them as well off as possible, but to have a world in which there are *no badly off individuals or groups of people*, a world that is not hierarchically stratified (if that is not a pleonasm) along the lines of "the worst off," "the next worse off," "the middlingly situated," "the well off," "the better off," and "the best off." Put in political terms, socialist egalitarians are *socialists* and not welfare state social democrats. In practical terms (and aside from *ideal theory*), in societies situated as even the better off and more progressive of our societies are situated (e.g., Denmark, Holland, Finland, Iceland, Norway, Sweden), radical egalitarians will, vis-à-vis equality, opt for very much the same things that social democrats will opt for: to make the worst off strata of society as well off as they can be. But their underlying aim is to bring about a society of equals: a classless, genderless, non-racist society in which there are, if that is possible, no social strata or at least a society where the necessary strata hierarchies are as minimal as they possibly can be and not the source of some people having power over others. Perhaps that is an ideal impossible to even reasonably approximate, as the radical historian Eugene Genovese, along with many others, would insist, but, it is for egalitarians there as a heuristic.

It is vital to keep firmly in mind that we (Rawls, Cohen, and myself) are in this context doing *ideal theory*. (It is, for example, a completely counterfactual idealization of ideal theory that everyone always acts justly.) We are trying to give an account of basic justice for the design of social institutions and social practices: an ideal blueprint for such societies. Assuming full compliance for the purpose of ideal theory, we are trying to set out the design of a just society. And, where we turn to global justice, we are trying to say what a perfectly just world would look like under conditions of abundance, where the circumstances of justice still obtain, i.e., *moderate* scarcity and limited altruism. We assume, again counterfactually for the purposes of ideal theory, that all people have a sense of justice and consistently act from it. But we do not assume that they are all saints.

II

In such contexts, I do not give more than pragmatic weight to considerations of desert and merit. I do not think that the traditional maxim that justice is giving each person her due is meaningless but that, in articulating principles of *social* justice, we need to specify how the assets, benefits, and burdens are to be distributed in a society and in the world as a whole. We are not seeking, beyond giving parameters, to solve questions of individual justice. We will, in giving that very specification, determine *what is to count as* getting one's due in various circumstances. Talk of giving each her due has no meaning that is independent of such a social construction. Once we have fixed the design of a just society, we will have a sense of what is due individuals in particular contexts, but not before.

Particularly when, like Rawls and Stuart Hampshire, we keep firmly in mind the arbitrariness of social circumstances and genetic inheritance, we will not give merit, desert, or entitlement a central place in our moral firmament.[11] It is not that we are denying free agency. In good compatibilist fashion we recognize that we (some of us more than others) have some control over our lives, that we can and should take responsibility for our lives, and that we have some capacity to forge life plans and to act on them. This is a plain enough sociological fact that any metaphysical theory of free will or hard determinism will have to accommodate if it is to be reasonable. We make, as Marx stressed, our own history, but not under conditions of our own choosing. Some of us are more industrious or skilful than others of us. Some of us can more adequately stick with what we would do or are better able to realize being the sort of persons we want to be or are better at being able to form some tolerably determinate conception of what sort of persons we want to be. Many of us, perhaps most, but not all of us, are rather at sea here. But just a little reflection on the contingency of social and genetic circumstance will give us a firm sense of the "luck of the draw" here. Jane is bright and industrious and Jim is dull and lazy. But the brightness and dullness are largely a matter of genetic inheritance and social circumstance and even the ability to make an effort, to stick with what one decides on, is rooted in some combination of our social and genetic inheritance. When we recognize that and take it to heart, we will discount talk of "moral merit" and, while not denying the depth of human differences, will not have an elitist, meritocratic, anti-egalitarian conception of justice. With such an understanding, there will not be even a tinge left of a Platonic conception of human nature.

III

Desert goes the same way as moral merit or merit *sans phrase* and for much the same reasons. To say that is not to deny that, if Jane finishes her dissertation and Jill does not, that Jane should get her degree and Jill not or that, if Fred is a rapist and Frank is not, that Fred goes to jail and Frank does not. And, if Bill, in fair competition, wins the music competition that he should have his award. That is largely the way things go and that is the way they should go. Whatever we should say about the ultimate determents of human behaviour, life – the ordinary day-to-day social interactions – could hardly go on if things like this did not obtain. Given the contingency of our social and genetic inheritance, this should be recognized but should only be treated as a pragmatic necessity.[12] *It will not go deep and will not affect our belief in the equal moral standing of all human beings.* Recognizing our secular equivalents of "There but for the grace of God go I," we will not, by the evident differences between people that obtain in many ways and in many domains, be jolted from a deeply embedded and considered conviction that the life of everyone matters and matters equally, a conviction that has appropriately been called *moral* equality: the belief in the equal moral standing of all people.[13]

IV

We should not say quite the same thing about entitlements. Entitlements, as Frederick Hayek and Robert Nozick pointed out, are distinct from merit or desert. If my Father, in good legal order, bequeaths me his farm, I am entitled to it whether I deserve it or not, whether I have any "moral merit" or not. I may, being a wastrel, have little or no merit. There are all sorts of entitlements that have nothing at all to do with deservingness or merit. But their being recognized is essential for the smooth running of society and a just society will acknowledge them. But *what* entitlements we have is not a natural fact about us or our society anymore than is what is our due. Rather, what they are, and when they can rightly be overridden, is set out in the design we construct for a just society. Whether any of the following things obtain is socially set: that individuals have an unlimited right to private property, that we all have a right to an equal share in the means of production, that we all are entitled to health care, that we are, if we are poor, entitled to legal aid, that we have a right to vote, that we have a right to equal access to advantage. These things are not natural facts there to be discovered in the world (including the social world) or self-evident truths or even truths there to be intuited or discovered but matters that we design in constructing a conception of a just society. Where what we have designed has come to have an institutional existence, they then become constitutional realities or something dependent on constitutional realities.

In this manner we also determine when entitlements can be rightly overridden. I am entitled to my front lawn if I legitimately own it. But, if there is a pressing need to drive a road through it, by the right of eminent domain, my entitlement is rightly overridden. I am entitled, given Canada's health care system, to a free flu shot but sometimes this right can be overridden if there is not enough serum to go around. There, depending on the supply, it could rightly be decreed that the ill and over seventy-five, say, pre-empt my entitlement.

What entitlements we have and when they can be rightly overridden is fixed by the system of social justice we devise. An egalitarian one seeking a society and a world of equals will *for starters* insist on equal human rights. What entitlements people have, in such a society, will be entitlements which they have had equal opportunity to obtain and will be the same for all when they are relevantly similar (e.g., all children, all those with kidney failure, all university graduates) and when they are in a relevantly similar situation, e.g., if A is entitled to a flu shot then B is too unless there is a relevant difference between A and B or in their situations. But, even in an egalitarian society, not all actual individual entitlements will be the same. If my father legitimately bequeaths me three houses and, if to do so is legal in the society in which I live, as it probably would not be in a thoroughly egalitarian society under conditions of moderate scarcity, they are mine. Your father may have bequeathed you only one house or none at all. So here your entitlements are different than mine. But if it turns out that others have no place to live, it may rightly be fixed by law that two houses can be taken away from me. In this way an entitlement may be overridden in the interests of justice. Constructors of accounts of justice will often argue, and sometimes rightly, for changes in law and sometimes even in the constitution. And, starting from the constitution, but going beyond it, additional argument will have to be made for what justice requires for certain types of difficult and constitutionally unforeseen cases. Indeed, sometimes a whole constitutional system and the political order that goes with it should be swept aside. But that, plainly, is not the usual case. Where, if anywhere, we can get a claim that has both *de facto* and *de jure* legitimacy, is, in such contexts, a very difficult question.[14]

V

I shall now turn to speaking of incentives. The belief that incentives are necessary for the efficient running of an economy is a widely accepted belief in our society. It is widely believed that even the difference principle requires them, if the worst-off strata of the society are to be no more badly off than they must be. John Rawls stresses this need for incentives in the articulation of his liberal egalitarianism.[15] Often in arguing for incentives, issues of desert, merit, and entitlement get mixed in. But, where the argument for incentives is careful, such considerations are set aside *and just the need for incentives is appealed to*. We have then what Cohen calls "a naked ... use of the incentive argument" for giving extra remuneration to the talented rich to get them to work harder and more efficiently than they otherwise would. The result of that will be, where the incentives are arguably justified, that the poor will be better off than they otherwise would be.

Cohen subjects this familiar claim – a set piece in the defence of capitalism, even social democratic welfare state capitalism – to a careful and nuanced criticism. This criticism puts the claim, even in its strong Rawlsian articulation, very much on the defence.[16] I cannot rehearse, let alone critically inspect, Cohen's detailed and careful argument here. But I shall, oversimplifying considerably, give one core part of it which seems to me to be right. (That does not mean, or suggest, that that is the only thing that I think is right in Cohen's account.)

The following argument is likely to be accepted by many people, including most Rawlsian liberal egalitarians:

1. Economic inequalities are justified when they make the worst-off people materially better off.
2. Giving material incentives to the talented rich will cause them to work harder and the result will be that the worst off are materially better off.
3. Therefore such material incentives should be given to the talented rich.

The first premise could be queried – as I queried it in my *Equality and Liberty* – where the society in question is one of considerable abundance. Being materially better off is not all there is to being better off. This fact, for Brechtian reasons, is of little functional importance where the society is poor, or where the worst off (a kind of lumpenproletariat) in a society of considerable wealth are both very poor and very vulnerable. It would, however, be salient in rich societies where even the worst off are not in desperate straits. (I do not say there are any such societies yet, but with advanced social democratic welfare state capitalism we might get some. And perhaps we already have some approximations.) Where there is abundance and a system of firm welfare nets for the poor – it is not the world of *The Three Penny Opera* – the poor might reasonably reject the first premise. They might do so because they realize that, in such circumstances, increased material inequalities, if they are sufficient to cause the desired effect on the talented rich, are likely to lead to increased imbalances in power, increasing the control of the rich over social life. The poor (in such societies not being so terribly poor), prizing autonomy and the gaining of an equal say in how their society is run, might rightly forgo these material advantages.[17]

However, here I want to set that aside and concentrate on the second premise. Suppose the poor – including, of course, the most disadvantaged – ask the rich, "Why do you need material incentives to work harder?" If the reply from the rich is that they are *unable* to work harder without more remuneration, then this response, given that they are already living well, seems at best implausible. If to the further question "Why are you unable to work harder without the extra remuneration?" they answer "It would not be worth our while," the question in turn comes trippingly on the tongue: "Why would it not be worth your while?" Since considerations of merit, desert, or entitlement are not at issue here – a naked use of the incentives argument is being presented – the only answer that the rich person can relevantly give is "Without the extra pay I just do not *feel* like working harder" or "Without more money I have no *intention* of working harder." But why, since *justice* is at issue, is how they *feel* or what their *intentions* are relevant here? If they are really unable to work harder and the second premise is, as matter of inescapable fact, true, then, given an acceptance of the first premise, egalitarians will reluctantly accept the argument. It seems, so viewed, sound enough. But, as Cohen argues, where it is not *ability* but *intentions* that are at issue, then the situation is very different. In such a situation, the second premise is not true as some impersonal sociological or social psychological fact but is *made* true by the *intentional* actions of the talented rich. It rests on what they *prefer* to do or not do.

In some rich capitalist societies (the United States, France, and Canada, for example), there are homeless people. Suppose, in such a circumstance, the homeless ask the rich "Why do you insist on material incentives?" If the rich answer "I have no intention of working harder without extra remuneration so that you can have shelter," the poor will see that the rich *make* the second premise true by their *acting on their intentions*, intentions rooted in their *preferences*. They are already well off and they could work harder without the extra remuneration, and, if they did, the poor would not be as badly off as they are now. They would have shelter and a little more food. Moreover, working harder does not entail that they drive themselves to the limits of their endurance or anything remotely like that. They just need to put in a little more time and a little more effort. The rich show clearly by their attitude and by making the second premise true that they do not care about the poor, or at least do not care very much about them. They also show that they do not (though this is very much like a corollary), no matter what rhetoric they use, care about *moral* equality either. They care very little, if at all, that the life of everyone matters and matters equally. They have no, or at least very little, interest in there being a society of equals. But their not caring about moral equality means that they do not care, or care very little, about justice, given what justice has become in modern societies. They presumably have a sense of justice, but they will not act from their sense of justice – assuming that an essential component for having a sense of justice in our societies is to have a belief in *moral* equality. (This is something that even Nozick will not deny.) If they would be just, they would not *make* the second premise true, but they do make it true. In such circumstances, they show that they really do not care that some people are unnecessarily badly off, while other people, including themselves, are very well off indeed. They are not prepared to act on a strict interpretation of the difference principle, namely that *inequalities are justified only when they render badly off people as well off as it is possible for such people to be.*

We need, as Cohen well puts it:

> [T]o distinguish between inequalities that are necessary, apart from human choice, to make the worst off better off, and inequalities that are necessary to that end only given what some people's intentions are. And this distinction, between, as one might say, intention-relative and intention-independent necessity, generates a question about how we are to take the word "necessary" in John Rawls's difference principle. When he says that inequalities are just if they are necessary to improve the position of the worst off, does he countenance only inequalities that are necessary (to achieve the stated end)

apart from people's intentions, or also, and more liberally (in more than one sense of that term), inequalities such as those that are necessary when talented people lack a certain sort of commitment to equality and are set to act accordingly? We confront here two readings of the difference principle: in its *strict* reading, it counts inequalities as necessary only when they are, strictly, necessary, necessary, that is, apart from people's chosen intentions. In its *lax* reading, it countenances intention-relative, necessities as well. So, for example, if an inequality is needed to make the badly off better off but only *given* that talented producers operate as self-interested market maximisers, then that inequality is endorsed by the lax, but not by the strict, reading of the difference principle.[18]

Justice, at least in a stratified society of abundance, requires the strict reading of the difference principle and this means that to claim the justifiability of incentives is to claim that they are justifiable *as a matter of justice*. But justice requires the impartial consideration of the interests of everyone alike where each is to count for one and none to count for more than one.[19] But, as we have seen above, there is, where the talented rich so reason, no impartial consideration of interests on the part of the rich. From their positions of superior power, they press their superior bargaining power. They have reasons all right, but they are self-interested ones, not ones that could be defended from the perspective of an impartial consideration of interests.

It should be noted that this critique of the use of incentives is not directed at, and does not apply to, extra remuneration for people taking especially unpleasant, demanding, dangerous, or stressful jobs. In such circumstances, the provision of extra money could be justified as balancing up an inequality caused by the very nature of the job. Where workers suffer much more from their jobs than is normally the case, then, in the name of equality, they are rightly given more money or other extra remuneration, such as longer holidays. This could very well apply to miners, to test pilots, to air control officers in airports, to nurses, to bus drivers, to checkout clerks, and the like.

Similar things could be said, and with a similar egalitarian rationale, for extra remuneration for those workers who suffer deprivation during long years of training at little or no remuneration. There is, of course, lots of room for rationalization here, indeed even self-deception. After all, life in graduate school, law school, engineering school, or even medical school is not such bad thing. It's plainly a lot better than pumping gas or working in a supermarket or collecting garbage. But *perhaps* there are genuine cases of this sort.

If, on either of the two grounds discussed above, the talented rich could really make out a case that their work is either so stressful and demanding or that their training required such great sacrifices on their part (including loss of income) that they need some extra remuneration to come out equally with others, then this could be justified and again justified in the name of *equality*. However, it seems to me that here there is a vast amount of rationalization, self-deception, and perhaps other deception as well. It is highly improbable that their work is more stressful and unpleasant than most work at more menial jobs at a much lower wage. And, as for their taking on more responsibilities, what is so bad about that? It goes well with the good of self-respect and nicely squares with Rawls's Aristotelian principle. The very taking on of responsibility enhances their work and with it their lives. It is not something for which they need to be compensated. But the conceptual-cum-moral point still remains. If, contrary to what I have just claimed, they, because of their responsibilities and the demands of their jobs and the like, are disadvantaged, then, in the name of equality, they should have sufficient extra remuneration to bring them up to the level of others. It would be like a test pilot or a miner getting more money. But to think in the general case that anything like this obtains for the talented rich seems to me pure Alice-in-Wonderland. But, whatever should be said about the sociological realities here, *such arguments for extra remuneration do not violate considerations of equality, but are required by them*, and they are quite different from the naked argument for incentives that we have been considering, where the talented rich demand more, not because they are in any way disadvantaged, but simply to gain as much self-interested market maximization as they can. That is just plain immoral.

VI

Unlike Rawls, and like G. A. Cohen and Brian Barry, I do not take, even from the moral point of view, justice to be always overriding any other moral or even prudential or other practical considerations. "Justice," Rawls tells us, "is the first virtue of social institutions" by which he means that "laws and institutions must be reformed or abolished if they are unjust."[20] But sometimes – and here we depart from ideal theory – justice is unattainable and sometimes acting on principles of justice would have horrendous consequences. In such circumstances other non-native considerations override considerations of justice. Morally we must not, in Michael Kohlhass fashion, do justice, though the heavens fall. Sometimes, indeed very often in real-life situations, whatever we do justice is unattainable. Cohen is right in saying that in such a circumstance "we do well to settle for something else."[21] That holds from the moral point of view itself. A critical morality will not hold that considerations of justice are *always* overriding, that justice is absolute with respect to all other considerations.[22] Sometimes utility outweighs justice, just as justice frequently – indeed standardly – trumps utility. It all depends on the circumstances.[23]

This is clearly seen in arguments about incentives. Recall how Cohen distinguishes in talking about the difference principle between *intention-relative* and *intention-independent* necessities and between the lax reading and the strict reading of the difference principle. In considering what inequalities are just inequalities, inequalities necessary to improve the position of the worst off, we are, where considerations of justice take pride of place, only to countenance necessities that are *intention-independent* necessities.[24] But suppose, departing from ideal theory with its conception of full compliance, we look at the real world. Even in our most benign capitalist democracies – to say nothing of such places as the United States, the United Kingdom, France, Canada, Brazil, or Argentina – we find staggering disparities of wealth and social empowerment. Vast numbers of people live thoroughly rotten lives (in Canada one person out of six lives below the poverty line), a similarly large number of others fare badly, while a few are both very well off and some of them are also very powerful. It is clear that it is in the power of the rich (taken collectively) to change this or at least radically to ameliorate it. But it is also perfectly plain – and has been so for a long time – that they will not. Indeed, anyone who expected that would reveal a very considerable naïveté. It is also, as a small part of this problem, quite possible for many of the rich to work, and as well, with as much self-realization from their work, without demanding material incentives. They can do this while still living comfortably and pleasantly. They are *able* to do it, but they are *unwilling*. They just will not. Moreover, at least for now and for the foreseeable future, they are in *stable* situations where they are in positions of power and control. The media, including much of the academic media, as Noam Chomsky so persuasively argues, will provide the conventional wisdom about the necessity of incentives and the like. The poor, and others as well, if they are not hoodwinked by ideology, will recognize that, with few exceptions, the talented rich "lack a certain sort of commitment to equality and are set to act accordingly."[25]

In such circumstances, as a matter of *social policy*, but not of *justice*, it may be very well to go for what Cohen calls the lax reading of the difference principle.[26] The rich will, whatever moral arguments we give them, go for their material advantage. The only conditions under which they will seek to make the badly off better off is where there is a material advantage in it for the rich or at least where there would be no material disadvantage to them. Where no overthrowing the capitalist order is possible or where its results would be predictably still worse, what should be done is to give the talented rich the incentives they need to induce them to put their shoulders to the wheel. Do not go for justice *in such a circumstance*, for to do so is not what will make the worse off better off. It is a bit of "ancient Marxist wisdom that justice is not the first virtue of institutions in conditions of scarcity. Under those conditions a just distribution may be impossible to achieve since powerful people will block it. In that case striving for justice may make everyone worse off."[27] Cohen remarks, and I would echo:

> Along with Nikolai Bukharin, I would have said to the kulaks: "Enrich yourselves!" without supposing (any more than Bukharin did) that I was thereby voicing a demand of justice. If we are concerned about the badly off, then we should sometimes concede incentive, just as we should sometimes satisfy even kidnapper's demands. We are not then acting on the difference principle in its strict interpretation, in which it is a principle of justice governing a society of just people who are inspired by it. We are acting on the lax version of the difference principle which endorses incentives and which has application in societies of the familiar unjust kind. On the assumption

that they are indeed unavoidable, incentive payments may be justified, but it does not follow that no injustice occurs when they are provided.[28]

They are, in such circumstances, *justified* inequalities. But let us not imagine for a moment that they are *just* inequalities. Remember Brecht: Eat first, morality afterwards. (Or better, in Brecht's own language, "*Erst kommt das Fresen dann kommt die Moral.*")

PART B

VII

I now move to another subject. Assuming egalitarian commitments, aspirations, aims, hopes, and attitudes, *what* is there that justice requires that there be *equal* provision for all. In what dimension or respects should people, where this is possible, come to be more equal? What aspects of our condition should count in a fundamental way for us if we are egalitarians? What metric should egalitarians use to establish the extent to which their ideal is realized in a given society? We are back to Amartya Sen's familiar question, *equality of what?*[29] What is the right way to treat people equally?

In asking about *equality of what*, we also need, as Thomas Nagel and Joshua Cohen have well argued, to consider the facts about the normative import of human diversity. Joshua Cohen puts the matter well when he remarks:

> Does a commitment to equality blind us to human differences? Consider some dimensions on which equality may seem attractive: rights, resources, achievements, and happiness. And consider some of the facts of human diversity: people differ in social circumstances, ability and skills, tastes and preferences, and ultimate values. Diversity appears to cause troubles for equality because differences along the latter dimensions preclude simultaneous equalizations on all the former: different skills and the differences of reward they

typically command imply that equal rights will likely translate into unequal material resources, differences of preference and value imply that equal material resources will translate into unequal proportional achievements (measured in terms of those values). A blanket embrace of equality, then, implies blindness to diversity.[30]

In starting a consideration of this cluster of problems, let me give a table of conceptions of egalitarianism. It is a catholic table for well-being, self-realization, human flourishing (to take one cluster) *may* come to mean much the same thing and opportunity for welfare, access to advantage, opportunities to develop capabilities (to take another cluster) *may* also come to much the same thing. But different egalitarian thinkers have utilized one or another of these ideas and there are at least differences in nuance between what is meant. The table illustrates the range of possibilities that are to be considered in facing the question *equality of what*.

One thing that egalitarians have stressed is that, *beyond formal* equality of opportunity, a deep egalitarian aim is to achieve for everyone *equality of condition*. But what this is is not very clear. Where, for example, would it go in the following table of egalitarianisms? Is equality of condition an equality of means or an equality of ends: an equality of opportunity or an equality of result? And does the latter pair come to the same thing as the former pair? It is both or, if the pairs are significantly different, all these four things. We do not have equality of condition until we have some appropriate combination of an adequate specification of both equal means and equal ends or, what is not exactly the same, equal opportunities and equal results or outcomes. (But would the attainment of this blot out the differences of which Joshua Cohen spoke?) But nothing determinate has been said about equality of condition or its elements until we specify and justify claims about which specifications are the most appropriate, and that takes us back to our table.

Table of Conceptions of Egalitarianism

	EQUALITY OF MEANS (Equality of Opportunity)		EQUALITY OF ENDS (Equality of Result)
1.	Equal rights	1.	Equal welfare
2.	Equal primary goods		a) Equal hedonic welfare (equal enjoyment or agreeable states of consciousness)
3.	Equal resources		b) Equal satisfaction of preferences
4.	Equal opportunity for welfare	2.	Equal advantage
5.	Equal access to advantage	3.	Equal capabilities (Equal capacities of functioning)
6.	Equal access to develop capabilities (capacities)	4.	Equal effective freedom
7.	Equal opportunity to achieve effective freedom	5.	Equal satisfaction of needs
8.	Equal opportunity to satisfy needs	6.	Equal satisfaction of critical interests
9.	Equal opportunity for the realization of critical interests	7.	Equal whole life prospects
10.	Equal opportunity for equal whole life prospects	8.	Equal well-being
11.	Equal opportunity to achieve well-being	9.	Equal self-realization
12.	Equal opportunity for obtaining self-realization	10.	Equal human flourishing
13.	Equal opportunity for human flourishing	11.	Equal achievement
14.	Equal opportunity for achievement	12.	Equal respect and self respect
15.	Equal opportunity for sustaining or achieving respect and self-respect		

However, in trying to get a fix on our problem, we should remind ourselves of what the egalitarian aspiration is, if indeed it is one thing.[31] Vague as it is, it is *an equality of condition for all at the highest level achievable of human flourishing that is the underlying ideal of egalitarianism*. We egalitarians, radical or liberal, socialist or social democratic, want everyone to be as well off as they possibly can be, for their lives to go as well as they possibly can go. And our concern, from the impersonal perspective of the moral point of view, is an equal concern for everyone. We want a world of equals in which the life of each and every one will go as well as possible. (This is quite compatible with a clear recognition that different people will – though not, of course, for everything – want and need different things. They will have different projects and some different critical interests. An egalitarian will want to see all the compatible ones realized as well as the incompatible ones where they do not in practice conflict with each other.) We also do not think, as we have already noted in a different context, that it is a good thing about equality that it would make the well off worse off. That is not the kind of equality – an equality with a *meanness* in it – that we want. We just do not want them to be well off at the *expense* of others who are badly off. We do not want them to be in a position where they can exploit those who are less well off and less powerful. If some must be worse off than others, we do not want to make others who are not so badly off worse off than they now are, where doing so will not improve the lot of the worst off. But what we deeply want, as egalitarians – our central heuristic ideal, if you will – is a world in which *everyone* is very well off and there are no worse off or better off, but where everyone is equally well off at the highest well-offness that can be achieved in a world where its potential for the achievement of universal well-offness is high. This, no doubt, is no more than a heuristic, but it is a heuristic that deeply reflects the sentiments of egalitarians.

Where the latter does not obtain, indeed where we are very far from that, if we were effective in going for equality in such a circumstance we might just be spreading the misery around more equally. There doesn't seem to be much point in that and it is anything but clear that fairness requires it, though fairness does indeed require all of us to share burdens (where this can be done) that are rooted in a fair design of our social world or in the inescapable conditions of the world we inhabit. Still, in such a harsh world egalitarians would want to improve the lot of the worst off as much as it can be reasonably improved. But there the vagueness of "reasonably" leaves a lot of *lebensraum*. Perhaps, in such a circumstance, what we should be governed by, to revert for a second to Part A, is to reason in accordance with the lax reading of the difference principle.

However, I do not want to be taken to be insinuating that our world is *this* harsh world. Our world is a harsh world – but it is not *this* harsh world. In our world, the productive forces are developed enough so that we do not have, in going for equality, to spread the misery around. Our harsh world is not only harsh – very harsh – but *unnecessarily* so, given our material and cultural resources (including our store of scientific arid technological expertise). It is not only harsh but *unjustly* harsh in ways that could never be sanctioned by the strict use of the difference principle.[32]

Vague though it is, this is a crucial part of the underlying egalitarian *aspiration*. It will serve as a touchstone for considering, with reference to our table, more determinate and philosophically articulated specifications of what egalitarianism comes to.

VIII

We can start by assuming what even most anti-egalitarians in *modern* societies also assume, namely *moral* equality, i.e., that the life of everyone matters and matters equally, notwithstanding the fact, highlighted by Nietzsche, that people have rather different moral and intellectual capacities and that they make quite variable inputs into their societies. Still we moderns (perhaps *non-rationally*, but not *irrationally*) take them all to be persons of equal moral worth. This might be said to be a common contemporary moral assumption right across the political spectrum from Robert Nozick and David Gauthier on the Right, to John Rawls and Ronald Dworkin in the Centre, to Andrew Levine and G. A. Cohen on the Left. With that belief, we will favour social arrangements that will yield an equal protection of the rights of all human beings and we will, as well, have the belief that the satisfaction of their genuine interests matters and matters equally. We will, however, sometimes disagree about what are interests and, of course, about what are *genuine* interests. And some of us will even be suspicious of such talk. We might think that the very concept of interests is a slippery one while still thinking that it at least gestures at something that each of us, and equally, should have satisfied. But these disagreements notwithstanding, the broad claims made above can be taken as safe background assumptions to make in trying to give an answer to *equality of what*. These are, to repeat, background assumptions of modernity, but I do not say that they cannot be justified by being put into wide reflective equilibrium. Indeed I think they can be so justified.[33]

IX

An adequate conceptualization of *equality of what* cannot simply stick with equal rights, though no acceptable accounting of what people are to be equal in could leave out basic or human rights. But there are many things that at least most believers in moral equality and the equal worth of human beings will regard as in the sway or ambience of their egalitarianism which go beyond the provision of equal rights. There are things which matter to almost all of us, indeed things which matter to us very deeply, which could be a matter of social provision, or at least could be aided by social design. They are things that we have an equal claim to, where they can be provided, which are not a matter of our having rights. (There are, of course, claim rights, but not all claims are such rights claims.) Interesting and challenging work is one; a pleasant and attractive neighbourhood environment is another; a pleasant and non-stressful working environment is still another; attractive parks readily available is yet another. It is easy to multiply examples. Social provision can, though in different ways, make a very considerable difference here. It can make the having of those things more nearly equal and with that enhance the lives of people. But there is no secure sense in speaking of a right to challenging and interesting work or of a right to attractive parks or perhaps even of a right to a non-stressful work environment. But in aiming at equal whole life prospects or at equal human flourishing at the highest levels possible – all crucial parts of the egalitarian aspiration – these will be matters with which egalitarians will be concerned. We will seek their equal provision and equal access to them. And indeed, where this can be done without making other still more vital matters worse than they are, justice requires that this be done.

Moreover, given the fact of unequal talents and capabilities and the like, simply sticking with equal rights will lead to unequal welfare, well-being, and the satisfaction of needs. Given that our underlying aim as egalitarians is the achievement of an equality of condition and, as far as that is possible, equal whole life prospects at the highest level possible, bringing the highest human flourishing for as many people as possible, we plainly cannot remain content with equal rights.

X

The same obtains for equal resources. Given different talents, intelligence, self-discipline, and the like, provision of equal resources will lead to different results. Where all are receiving equal resources, some will flourish much more than others. Resources can be equal, but that will not at all lead to, to say nothing of insuring, the best approximation we can get to equal human flourishing at the highest level of flourishing attainable or the best life possible for as many as possible. Ronald Dworkin, the leading advocate of resource equality, argues that egalitarian justice should ignore welfare comparisons.[34] Put crudely, the attempt to achieve equality should, Dworkin believes, be limited to attempting to ensure everyone equal means (equal resources) for pursuing what will inevitably be their disparate aims and ends. But, while equalizing resources is certainly very central, it is not the only relevant equality consideration.

Suppose a person, or an identifiable group of persons, suffer constantly from dull but persistent headaches. These headaches are not so bad that they affect the person's capacity to work or to normally function in society or even in their family life or other personal relations. They do not diminish their capacities for functioning properly at all, but they are always there causing mild discomfort. A welfare-insensitive, resource-only-respecting egalitarianism could not consistently compensate for the pain and discomfort of those headaches. But an egalitarianism that sought equality of condition or equal life prospects or equal well-being would. (In the case of well-being it most plainly would.) Resource egalitarianism is for this reason, if for no other, inadequate.

It may be right, against welfare egalitarianism, not to compensate people for welfare inequalities that result from their deliberately cultivating expensive tastes. Thus, if Fred cultivates a taste for expensive wines and truffle pasta, there is no need to compensate him so that he can continue his deliberately acquired habit, without loss of equal welfare, where others would suffer a loss of welfare if we were to equal things up. As long as we have any significant scarcities, there is no call for the state or for society to support Fred's costly habit. If Fred can, without stealing from others or swindling them, make do with his equal bundle of resources and continue to support his habit, fine; but he is not entitled to any extra resources so that he might do so, even though this will result in lower welfare (lower preference satisfaction) for Fred.

In contrast, suppose Eric, growing up in an aristocratic and rich French family, as a matter of course without reflection or initially without even noting that they are expensive, comes to like these wines very much, wines that as a matter of fact turn out to be expensive. But, as a matter of fact, he has from early on become habituated to them and has become very partial to them so that now he can hardly change his tastes. Suppose later in a more resource egalitarian society he can no longer, except on rare occasions afford them, yet he misses them. Indeed, his level of enjoyment of life is to some degree lowered by their absence. But in contrast to Fred, he is certainly not responsible for those tastes. He did not set out to cultivate those tastes or form those habits. Still there is no strong call, or *perhaps* any call at all, to compensate him here, since there is no urgency and his critical interests are not adversely affected.[35]

However, resource egalitarianism to the contrary notwithstanding, where the springs of social wealth flow fully and freely, there is *some* reason for egalitarians to compensate him. But these considerations are welfare considerations. We would, as egalitarians, like the lives of everyone to flourish as much as possible. Eric's will not unless he receives extra resources – resources that upset the balance of equal resources – but, as thorough egalitarians, we should be for it, *if* taking those extra resources will not diminish the lives of others.

Consider now a more telling and more common case developed by G. A. Cohen against resource egalitarianism.

People vary in the amount of discomfort which given low temperatures cause them and, consequently, in the volume of resources which they need to alleviate their discomfort. Some people need costly heavy sweaters and a great deal of fuel to achieve an average level of thermal well-being. With respect to warmth, they have what Dworkin calls *expensive tastes*: they need unseemly large doses of resources to achieve an ordinary level of welfare.

They are losers under Dworkin's equality of resources because it sets itself against compensation for expensive tastes.[36]

Cases like this (including my headache case) seem to be decisive against resource egalitarianism, but the last two are not decisive against Ronald Dworkin. He *supplements* and amends his resource egalitarianism – the familiar philosophical phenomenon of first saying it and then taking it all back – by being willing to compensate for *handicaps* but not for tastes or preferences. He thereby in effect goes to a more complex view of appealing to equal capabilities as well as to equal resources. His conception redistributes for handicaps and, in line with that, those who are abnormally cold in winter (cold where most others would not be) are handicapped and so can be, on Dworkin's view, legitimately compensated for their handicap. But this, unless we engage in linguistic legerdemain, is still a departure from the principle of going for equal resources only. People, on Dworkin's account, should "be compensated for shortfalls in their powers, that is, their material resources and mental and physical capacities, but not shortfalls traceable to their tastes and preferences."[37] But, even extending the very notion of resources so that it is meshed with people's capacities and incapacities, it still fails for at least two of the three above counter-examples, as does G. A. Cohen's Tiny-Tim example as well.[38] The egalitarian case for helping the poor with their fuel bills in winter is founded on the *discomfort* they experience and not just on their disablement. Their thermal incapacities would not matter, or at least would not matter very much, if they did not cause them suffering. And, in the persistent dull headache case, the case for redistribution is founded entirely on ill fare considerations, namely the pain their non-disabling or non-incapacitating headaches cause. The same was true in the case of Eric to the extent, in a society of abundance, there is any case for compensating him at all.

Dworkin's "resource egalitarianism" is more nuanced than the straightforward, plain sort, though it achieves nuance by departing from resource egalitarianism. But he is mistaken in thinking an egalitarianism is adequate which compensates for "resource deficiencies only and not also for pain and other ill fare considered as such."[39] People, on Dworkin's account, whose pain and suffering do not diminish their capacity, fall beyond an egalitarian net. But we egalitarians need a bigger and more finely meshed net which includes welfare considerations as well as resource and capability considerations. To not do so, as the above examples and the arguments concerning them show, is just a moral mistake. It does not square with our considered convictions in wide reflective equilibrium. It is not in accordance with our informed reflective moral sensibilities.

XI

However, I do not want the above argument to be taken as giving to understand that welfare egalitarianism is adequate. If anything, it is even more vulnerable than resource egalitarianism as John Rawls, Ronald Dworkin, Thomas Scanlon, Amartya Sen, and G. A. Cohen, among others, have well argued.

By "welfare egalitarianism" I mean what is sometimes called *subjective* welfarism and is frequently just taken to be welfarism *sans phrase* (that is, "subjective welfarism" is taken to be a redundancy). It is the view on my table that has two subspecies: (1) equal hedonic welfare and (2) equal preference satisfaction welfare. The latter, with the demise of hedonism, is by now the more common view. It is to be contrasted with *objective* welfare theories which are cashed in variously in terms of well-being, self-realization, achievement, need, capabilities of functioning, critical interests, human flourishing, and the like. I shall not, following what is by now a rather common convention, call them welfarisms or welfare theories at all, but treat them separately. (However, nothing substantive turns on that bit of putative tidying up.)

The criticisms I trot out below of equal welfare apply equally to the two subspecies of subjective equal welfare (what I shall call equal welfare). As egalitarians we are committed to treating people as equals, but, if that is interpreted as being committed to trying to attain for everyone equal welfare as equal preference satisfaction or equal happiness, we get something which is self-defeating. Preferences and what will make us happy, when coupled with the tendencies we have to adapt to circumstances (psychological fact), lead to counter-egalitarian conclusions. People who are so socialized as to be accustomed to little tend to demand little and so are easily, or at least more easily, satisfied than others more fortunately situated. However, no one with the egalitarian commitment of treating people as equals would believe or accept for a moment that those who have become accustomed to little are thereby entitled to less, or should have less, even though they are as satisfied as those who have greater resources and more opportunities. This flies in the face of everything that egalitarianism is about. (Here is another place where we need to keep in mind our egalitarian aspirations.) To think that they should have less or are entitled to less is paradigmatic of anti-egalitarianism. Yet consistent welfare egalitarianism would commit us to that. That is why it is self-defeating.

There are as well the familiar problems of *offensive* preferences and *expensive* preferences. Equal welfare where it is read, as we are reading it now, either as equal preference satisfaction or equal enjoyment, treats offensive and expensive preferences as having equal moral standing with preferences which are morally inoffensive (not at all morally untoward) when arguably the former should have *no moral weight at all*. (That they should have no weight *at all* is more evident for offensive tastes than for expensive tastes.) *Welfare equality equates preferences which differ radically in moral character*. Some, for example, take pleasure in dominating or torturing others or just batting them around. But these offensive preferences should not count at all in a "calculus of justice." We do not determine what is a just distribution as being a function which includes such preferences. Offensive preferences, at least of the sort that I instanced above, do not count in the metric of justice. The satisfaction some get from discrimination against others, from dominating or belting them around, will not, from a moral point of view, count in a favourable way in ascertaining what is just. (If, contrary to what I said above, we allow them to count they can only count negatively.) That there is more *such* satisfaction in the world is a bad thing, indeed an evil thing, not a good thing. Rather than counting them in with *inoffensive* preferences, they are, from the point of view of justice, and morality more generally, to be condemned. Such preferences have no claim on being satisfied. But they would have to count equally if we were to go for an equality of welfare. Again we have a *reductio* of welfare egalitarianism.

Expensive tastes are also a stumbling block for equality of welfare, but in a somewhat different way and less severely so. (I will argue the point about severity later in this essay. See Section XIV.) The person, as Fred in our previous example, who deliberately cultivates a taste for expensive wines and truffle pasta has preferences which, of course, are not to be condemned or even *per se* to be disapproved of. The satisfaction of his preferences, however, still does not count in recognizing what people in the circumstances of justice (moderate scarcity and limited altruism) may justly claim, though, if we take a welfarist position, these preferences would have to count and count equally with other morally relevant preferences in a welfarist "calculus of justice." But they do not so count and this constitutes still another *reductio* of welfarism. *A* is satisfied with a diet of milk, bread, and beans, to use Rawls's example, while *B* requires expensive wines and exotic dishes and is distraught without them. Welfare egalitarianism is committed to the claim that where doing this will yield an equality of preference satisfaction justice requires that *B* be provided with a higher income than the person with modest tastes until he is equal with her in overall preference satisfaction (welfare). The beans and corn people go down in welfare to equalize welfare to compensate for the people with the expensive tastes. But justice requires no such thing. Indeed it forbids it. So welfare egalitarianism must be mistaken.

Similarly *C* converts resources into welfare more efficiently than *D*. *C* buys groceries at the local market where they are cheaper while *D* goes to the local convenience store, where they are much more expensive because he is too lazy to walk the three blocks to the market. He, of course, is entitled to so use his resources, but he has no claim, if he does so, on additional resources to bring his welfare level up to *C*'s. Let's say that *C* and *D* start with equal resources, but, because *C* converts her resources more efficiently than *D*, where *D*, with a little effort could do likewise, *D* has less welfare than *C*. Welfare egalitarianism must require that *D* be compensated until his welfare is equal to *C*'s, but again this is a *reductio*. Justice does not require such compensation. Indeed it repudiates it. As Rawls stresses, and G. A. Cohen echoes, moral agents have the capacity to assume responsibility for their ends. *D* could have chosen otherwise. (We can, and should be, compatibilist about this and avoid venturing into the "deep waters" of the metaphysics of free will.) Why should *C*, if *D* or others on his behalf were to press for compensation to equalize welfare levels, bear the costs of *D*'s laziness and lack of self-discipline?[40] It is not fair to let other people pay for the readily avoidable wastefulness of others. Here *C* is being exploited by *D*. Egalitarian justice condemns such exploitation. Welfarism is not the right kind of egalitarianism.

Besides these considerations there are the more familiar difficulties, perhaps impossibilities, of making *objective* interpersonal utility comparisons so that we can at all accurately assess what welfare and ill fare so construed come to. However, if a blind person needs a guide-dog or a disabled person a wheelchair, an egalitarian, unless held captive to welfarist ideology, will argue that we should compensate such persons for their *disability*. We will not try to calculate their ill fare, i.e., determine how much they suffer, let alone *exactly* how much they suffer, from their disability, though presumably something is only a disability if it, in one way or another, causes the person who has it some discomfiture (if nothing more than some inconvenience) of some kind. That is a background assumption about what a disability is. Still, the thing to do is to compensate the disability *as such* without trying to calculate just how much having it makes the person with the disability suffer.

This seems to me to be good sturdy common sense, but all the same I am not entirely happy with it. Suppose N needs a guide-dog and M needs a wheelchair (I assume for simplicity that the total costs of the dog and the wheelchair are the same). Moreover, they seem at least to be equally incapacitated by their disability. Suppose further, we do not have enough resources to provide for both N and M, then, if we can get some reasonable sense of it, we need to figure out, or at least shrewdly guess, roughly how much suffering and other discomfiture the two incapacities cause and compensate the one with the greater discomfiture. We should, of course, first make sure, if we can, that they are equally incapacitated. Still, as far as we can tell, they might sometimes be equally incapacitated. Where this obtains, we should try to ascertain which one suffers the greatest discomfiture. If we cannot make objective interpersonal utility comparisons here, we should make subjective ones. Shrewd guesses are all we have to go on. But it is better than nothing. This would be a way – perhaps not the only way – of figuring out, or at least reasonably guessing at, how severe their incapacities are.

In rejecting welfarism we should not throw the baby out with the bath water. Still, that complication notwithstanding, the practice of compensating for the disability as such seems generally a sound one. So we have further reason to believe that, while welfare egalitarianism is indeed an egalitarianism, it is not of the right sort, for it answers the question *equality of what* incorrectly. (The dogma that we cannot make interpersonal utility comparisons at all should not stand in our way here. Sometimes we can make rough comparisons and sometimes they suffice. Anyone who thinks we cannot has never watched with any attention young children playing on a playground. We can get a pretty shrewd idea for many of them which are playing happily and which are not. I am not claiming that this would provide us with anything like a metric, but it does give us something to go on that is not utterly subjective.)

XII

Resource-egalitarianism and welfare-egalitarianism have been centre stage in many recent discussions of egalitarianism and egalitarian justice and understandably so. I have given both of them some play here. However, I actually think some other candidates for responding to the question of *equality of what* are more adequate responses. I cannot here canvass all the candidates in my table, but I will look at what I regard as the more promising candidates. On the *means* side of the table, they are equal primary goods and equal provision of the opportunity to satisfy needs; on the *ends* side, they are equal satisfaction of needs and equal *effective* freedom.

We should also keep in mind that some of the conceptions listed in the table may not be all that different. Equal opportunity for welfare, equal access to advantage, equal provision of opportunities to satisfy needs, equal opportunity to develop capabilities, equal opportunity to achieve effective freedom, equal access to the realization of critical interests *may*, when clarified, be seen to come to much the same thing. It is still an important question which conception (if any of them) more perspicuously captures what we want to say about egalitarian justice and egalitarianism more generally. Similar things obtain on the *ends* side about equal well-being, equal self-realization, equal satisfaction of needs, equal capabilities (equal capabilities of functioning), equal satisfaction of critical interests, equal effective freedom and equal human flourishing. Which if any of these notions, or which combination of them, most adequately captures what we egalitarians are getting at, vaguely, though centrally, when we assert that what we want is *equality of condition* for all humankind?

Some egalitarians might, trying to simplify things (a good thing where it can be done without sweeping important matters under the rug), say that the goal of equality should be to try to approximate as fully as can be done an arrangement of things where the distribution of resources would lead to everyone living equally good lives, where the good lives they would lead would be the best possible lives that human beings could live. We have already seen how, if "equally good lives" is couched in terms of equal enjoyment or equal preference satisfaction that that cannot be the egalitarian aim. It runs against too many of the considered judgments that egalitarians have. Besides, people are too different in their capacities, capabilities, and talents, including their capabilities or capacities for enjoyment, for us to use such a measure of the good life. Some people are just gloomy, others are (like Tiny Tim) happy in all sorts of circumstances (including adverse ones); some are talented and imaginative and have a lot of self-discipline, others are lacking in talent, dull, and not very disciplined. The former often, though as things go now, certainly not always, can find interesting, self-fulfilling work; the latter cannot. We can do *something* by way of altering social conditions to increase the number of the former and decrease the number of the latter. But there still will remain such differences, and many similar differences as well, such that, by any reasonable definition of "better," the lives of some will go better than those of others. All we can do is increase the opportunities for a good life for everyone by making the conditions for its achievement – different though it will be for different persons and across cultures – more propitious. We cannot ensure, or even do much in the way of bringing it about, that everyone will have equally good lives. That is at least an empirical impossibility. We know that they will not. Also, if we go much beyond truisms and get at all detailed, we have no very clear idea about what a good life is. It is without question a deeply contested – I did not say an *essentially* contested – concept. Things get much worse when we try to go to the Good Life. It is entirely reasonable to be thoroughly skeptical about that.

However, we can try to achieve the social conditions where it would be possible, where people are capable of it, or can be aided into becoming capable of it, for their having good lives at the maximum level of *whatever* their variously conceived conceptions of good lives turn out to be, where their various conceptions of a good life would not involve harm to others or a diminishment of their lives. (Here Rawls's insistence is crucial that the admissible conceptions of the good be in accordance with the principles of justice.) Still, this way of seeing things is rather empty for it leaves out entirely the question of *what* it is to have a good life. But dispute about that is legion. In an attempt to make a little more headway here, we shall see if we can gain some more specification of content by turning to the *ends* side of my table. But perhaps we will only be re-packaging familiar difficulties.

Equal well-being might seem the most obvious candidate, but, aside from its being very vague, it arguably, as Amartya Sen contends, needs to be spelled out as a matter of human functionings, if it is to have much in the way of content. A person's well-being is chiefly a matter of such functioning: the beings and doings that that person actually achieves.[41] But this may turn out to be the near blind leading the near blind. Moreover, and distinctly, there are, as Sen perfectly well realizes, many and diverse such functionings and they, or at least some of them, to a certain extent, vary from culture to culture, from sub-culture to sub-culture, and even from person to person. These functionings include satisfying work, friendship, life-expectancy, escapable morbidity, and self-respect. They are plainly a rather heterogeneous lot.[42]

Sen stresses that actual well-being is a matter of such attained states and activities (beings and doings), some of which involve enjoyment or preference satisfaction, but others, whether we value them or not, whether they yield enjoyment or preference satisfaction or not, we still have *reason* to value. So, to ascertain what constitutes our well-being, we need to collect together the many and varied states and activities, rank them in the face of the fact that there are competing views about their importance or their proper scheduling and distinguish between the merely valued and the valuable, so that we can ascertain what people have *reason* to value. Moreover, if we are to get a little more determinate about well-being, we need to go from functioning to *proper* functioning and this leads, or at least seems to lead, to the need to give something like an Aristotelian account of *essential* human powers and their *proper* exercise. But skepticism is in order concerning whether with this Aristotelian trip anything much more definite has been attained that would better anchor an equality of ends than what has been achieved with talk of well-being. Again, it looks like the near blind leading the near blind. Similar problems obtain for the idea of equal human flourishing and equal self-realization.

However, and the above notwithstanding, we should distinguish, as Sen does, well-being, as a matter of attained states and activities, from the freedom to achieve well-being. This *may* come from or be constituted by, as Sen believes, a combination of beings and doings which are within our reach.

This combination, Sen claims, is a person's effective freedom to achieve well-being. It is, in Sen's language, a person's capability of functioning: the different combinations of functionings open to a person. What we should seek, on Sen's conception of proper equality, is *equal access to develop equal capabilities of functioning*. The idea is to approximate as much as possible a world where people are equal with respect to capabilities of functioning. To quote Joshua Cohen's gloss on that: "people who care about equality ... ought to care about ensuring that equally desirable possibilities for functioning lie equally within everyone's grasp, not about ensuring equal means or equal achievements."[43]

Still, many of the previous difficulties return like the repressed. Again, given human differences, we have the problem of how it is possible reasonably to expect that people can be equal – or even nearly so – with respect to capabilities of functioning. And our previous problems about the diversity of the elements and conceptions of well-being transfer to the freedom to achieve well-being, as do problems about determining *proper* human functioning, "desirable possibilities of and for functioning" and, relatedly, how we determine what we have *reason* to value or how we are to distinguish the *desirable* from the merely *desired*, the *valuable* from the merely *valued*.[44]

XIII

I want now to discuss two other views from my table that I think may be useful in answering the question of *equality of what* and which may be free of at least some of the difficulties that I have already discussed. I have in mind, (1) *equal effective freedom* and (2) *equal satisfaction of needs*. Or, more accurately, keeping John Dewey's and Charles Stevenson's emphasis on a continuum of means and ends in mind, the harnessed view (1*) equal opportunities to achieve effective freedom (means) and equal effective freedom (ends) and (2*) equal provision of opportunities for need satisfaction (means) and equal satisfaction of needs (ends). The reason for the harnessing is that the achievement of either end is not even remotely possible unless we have in place the corresponding means. In serious thinking about what is to be done, we, as Dewey never tired of arguing, must have both in mind. We should avoid a specialist's conception which tries, in the grand tradition of moral philosophy, to just fasten on ends.

I shall discuss (1) and (1*) – equal effective freedom – first because it obviously links with Sen's stress on the importance of our ability and our opportunity to achieve equal well-being. Only in (1) and (1*) well-being, at least officially, drops out and the stress is on the importance of our ability and opportunity to achieve effective freedom or autonomy. Autonomy, however, may very well be a central part of what well-being is. On such a conception we should be concerned with the distribution of means (resources, primary goods, opportunities for welfare, access to advantage, opportunities to achieve effective freedom or satisfaction of needs) to the extent that it will be crucially instrumental in achieving an equal distribution of freedom or autonomy. Moreover, to be concerned with effective freedom, as distinct from merely *formal* freedom, is to be concerned with the *worth* of freedom. Those egalitarians, including myself (here we are all Rawlsians), will value not only *formal* freedom, but *effective* freedom (autonomy) as well, if we are concerned with the good of self-respect, with the achieving of equal respect for all human beings and for their being persons with a firm sense of self-respect (that is, for it to be a functional part of their lives) and with an understanding of the value for each person of having that sense. (Here we have a deep Kantian strand in Rawlsian thinking.) Again these matters, whether we are Kantians or not, are central considered convictions of ours.

Such freedom is essential for the dignity of human beings, for sustaining their self-respect, for their taking responsibility for the setting of their ends, for their living meaningful lives and for giving sense to any public affirmation of their equal worth. For these things to obtain in society, and to be equally provided for all, the familiar basic liberties that Rawls stresses must be a stable staple of the society. This is so because people must have them to be able to do the various things they may want to do in the living of their lives. They will have no effective freedom without them and without them there will be no enhancement of their lives.[45]

Effective freedom comes, most essentially, to autonomy. To be autonomous is to be able to direct and control one's life, to be able reflectively to set one's ends, to be able to change them in the light of further reflection, more information, or changed circumstances, to be able to guide one's action by one's own convictions, to be able to form convictions reflectively, to sustain those convictions, and to be able to criticize convictions inherited from one's life-world. With this we gain the capability of modifying them or even rejecting them: capabilities essential for autonomy. More generally, it is to be able to order one's behaviour in accordance with one's understanding of the world and one's reflective wishes: rationally sustainable wishes.

Such autonomy – such effective freedom – is bound up with the good of self-respect. Whatever else well-being, self-realization, and human flourishing come to, autonomy would be a very important part of it, though still not the whole of it. Having control over one's life, having reflectively controlled and ordered desires, being able to act on such desires, in short, being autonomous, is intrinsically good: it is worth wanting and having for its own sake and will be wanted for its own sake by reasonable people. But it is also a fecund instrumental good, empowering one in all sorts of domains of life and enabling one to more effectively live as one wishes as well as to reflectively and intelligently assess one's wishes.

Egalitarians will desire a world in which the whole life prospects of everyone are equal. Without equal autonomy – effective equal freedom – we will not have that. Therefore, the *equality of what* egalitarians should recommend is an equality of effective freedom or, more accurately, equal opportunities to achieve effective freedom with the hope that this would yield equal effective freedom at the highest level possible. Without trying to deny the reality of our interdependence, or to negate its value, and without taking it to be at all in conflict with human autonomy, that is the world that egalitarians want.[46] It is a world in which all interdependent human beings are as autonomous as it is possible for normal human beings to be in ways that do not fail to acknowledge both the reality and value of our interdependence.[47]

An essential means to come within even a country mile of this is to have the provision of equal primary goods and equal opportunities to achieve autonomy (effective freedom). The having of equal autonomy, particularly in a world where people have very different ends, is one way of partially specifying something of what it would be like for everyone to live equally good lives. Here, it seems to me, for the reasons I have given above, we have a more adequate conception of egalitarianism and egalitarian justice than we have with either equality of resources or equality of welfare. (Remember that equality of welfare accounts were accounts of subjective welfare.)

It might in turn be responded, "More adequate, yes, but not as adequate as an egalitarian account could be, for autonomy, though plainly a strategic and fundamental good is not the *sole* good – nothing is – and it is not by itself adequate for spelling out what it would be like for people to live equally good lives." Two people could be equally autonomous and yet the life of one might go much better than the life of the other. That is as evident as anything can be. Such claims about autonomy do not, the claim goes, capture the deepest aspiration of egalitarians which is for *everyone* to be as well off as it is possible for humans to be: for their lives to go as well they can go.

XIV

This takes us back to (2) and (2*) – to equal satisfaction of needs – to see if it can be an improvement on (1) and (1*). This candidate for a more adequate response to *equality of what* comes to urging, for a full egalitarian conception of justice, equal provision of the opportunity to satisfy needs (the means part) in order to achieve equal satisfaction of needs at the highest level possible of needs satisfaction (the ends part). The more *compossible* needs – needs that can be jointly satisfied – we can satisfy, and the fuller, the better. (Note that here, as in the equal effective freedom conception, there is both an equal distribution dimension and a maximizing dimension. For, *whatever* the *what* is that we are to have equally, we are also to have it as extensively as possible and to the fullest degree possible. Thus, if self-realization is what we are to have equally, we are also each to have it as fully as possible.)

So how are we to understand this equality of meeting needs view? First, needs are not to be taken as social constructs but as something there to be discovered of which we can produce lists. Moreover, there can and should be some considerable intersubjective agreement about most of the items on the list and most particularly over some claimed basic needs. One might want to add some items and even want to delete some, but, for the conception to have the desired objectivity, there would at least have to be a rough intersubjective agreement concerning a central core. It is also the case that claims that something is a need are subject to empirical confirmation and disconfirmation. We do not just have to rely on a consensus, no matter how reflective, for we have empirical testing as well, though such testing is, of course, like all testing, theory-laden.

Such egalitarians believe that there should, in a society of considerable abundance and ideally in a similarly abundant world, be constructed and sustained, as far as these things are possible, socio-economic conditions (centrally involving the provision for meeting needs) which will enable everyone, as far as they are physically and psychologically capable of it, to have equal whole life prospects, prospects which are equally desirable. This requires an equal consideration of everyone's needs and a refusal to just regard anyone's needs as simply expendable: as something which does not count or counts for less than anyone else's needs. Each person's needs must have an equal *initial* weight.

I say "an equal initial weight" because consider what is to be done where there is a conflict of needs and they cannot all be met. When we live in a moral world where each is to count for one and none to count for more than one, the need(s) must be met which yield(s) the fullest satisfaction of needs for as many people as possible, given a consideration of the full set of needs and an impartial equal consideration of the needs of all the people involved. In that situation, where the reasoners have been impartial and there still remains an unresolved conflict of needs between the people involved, then something must give. Suppose in a given situation it is impossible to meet both A's need and B's need. Where this is so, we should consider, as well, both A's other needs and B's other needs and, the type and urgency of A's need which conflicts with B's and the type and urgency of B's need which conflicts with A's and both A's and B's other needs as well and the needs of others affected. In going through what may be rather complicated reasoning, we seek the most extensive meeting of equally distributed *compossible* needs that can be had for the above-mentioned people. Where this can be ascertained, or reasonably guessed at, we should go for that. Where it cannot be ascertained, or some reasonable informed guess made concerning it, we should only consider the relevant urgency of A's particular need and B's particular need in relation to their other needs and go for the satisfaction of the need that is the more urgent. Where we cannot even do that, we should consider only A's and B's particular conflicting needs in that specific situation. There we would be limited to considering just the relative urgency of the two particular needs themselves. The most urgent one is the one to be met.

Where not even that can be reasonably guessed at, we have no basis for acting one way rather than another. If a choice must be made as to which need is to be met, then, beyond the fairness of something like a flip of the coin (though following such procedural matters there is important), there is no reason to act in one way rather than in another. Thus, the choice *there* must be arbitrary. Though we must not commit the Sartre-fallacy of thinking that because *some* choices cannot but be arbitrary they all must be.[48] Generally, however, we should seek the most extensive set of equally distributed compossible satisfactions of needs that can be had. That is, we should meet equally, for everyone, as many of their compossible needs as possible. Where there are the material resources and the intellectual skills to pull it off – the resources and the skills to sustain a very high level of the development of the productive forces – we will seek to construct stable institutions and to develop social practices to provide everyone with resources and the social conditions to satisfy their needs at the highest level of need satisfaction that it is possible to achieve.

For this to be a viable conception of egalitarian justice, we must be able to say what needs are, to distinguish types of need, and to provide grounds for believing that our purportedly universal needs are really universal or at least near universal. We must also be able to distinguish basic needs from non-basic needs, to draw a tolerably clear distinction between needs and wants (preferences) and to show why the satisfaction of our non-destructive needs is a good thing. In a rather sketchy way I have tried to show something of this in my "Justice, Equality and Needs."[49] David Braybrooke has tried to do some of it, in considerable detail, in his *Meeting Needs*.[50] I shall concentrate here on the part most essential for making the case, that an appeal to needs is a good candidate answer to the question *equality of what*.

First, a cautionary note. A lot of needs-talk is ideologically inspired and inflated. It is very easy to call anything we very much want a need and a lot of needs claims will not withstand critical inspection. We also should distinguish between *adventitious* needs and *course-of-life* needs. It is the latter that we will focus on and that are important for our argument. *Adventitious* needs, like the need for a really good fly rod or computer, come and go with particular projects. A *course-of-life* need, by contrast, such as the need for exercise, sleep, or food, is such that, as Braybrooke puts it, "every human being may be expected to have it at least at some stage of life."[51]

To spot a need, to speak first of *adventitious* needs only, it is useful to use the relational formula "B needs x in order to y," as in "I need a heavy duty fly rod in order to sport fish for salmon." In contrast, for a basic course-of-life need, the relational formulae occurs distinctly, and in a certain way platitudinously, but also in a way that is philosophically illuminating. It would go like this: "*B* needs food and water in order to live" or "*A* needs exercise in order to function normally or well." But this gives to understand, with their references to survival or to human functioning, that they are basic needs. Moreover, it is also, at least arguably clear, for at least statistically normal cases, that when these things are specified no further question arises in the standard case about the justification of having the need or having it met. Braybrooke puts the matter thus:

> [O]ne cannot sensibly ask, using the language of needs, "Does *N* need to live?" or "Does *N* need to function normally (robustly)?" *N* does not have to explain or justify aiming to live, or aiming to function normally. It is not the only end that he might be expected to have as a moral agent; for one thing it notoriously does not automatically harmonise even with the same end pursued by other agents. However, there is no more fundamental end that he could invoke to explain or justify this one. Being essential to living or to functioning normally may be taken as a criterion of being a basic need. Questions about whether needs are genuine, or well-founded, come to the end of the line when the needs have been connected with life or health.[52]

Here we touch ground in basic course-of-life needs, "some questions about the importance of needs reach firm answer at last."[53] To live or to flourish (if you will, to function well), we must have these things and so we properly call them basic needs. Adventitious needs, by contrast, will vary greatly in terms of the not infrequently very different ends we have or the projects we have, but there is plainly more of a case for ascribing the same course-of-life needs to everybody. Whatever projects they may have, they will require that their course-of-life needs be met. These needs are not project-relative or intention-dependent or preference-dependent.

Can we actually find or construct a minimal list of such basic needs concerning which we can all agree? Abstracting from some well-known lists, Braybrooke gives the following course-of-life needs which are basic. It has two parts. The first part highlights notions about physical functioning. The second part has more to do with our functioning as social beings, though the connections with physical functions make it difficult to draw a hard and fast line between the two parts. However, it is not necessary for our purposes to do so here.

PART ONE

1. The need to have a life-supporting relation to the environment.

2. The need for food and water.

3. The need to excrete.

4. The need for exercise.

5. The need for periodic rest, including sleep.

6. The need (beyond what is covered under the preceding needs) for whatever is indispensable to preserving the body intact in important respects.

PART TWO

1. The need for companionship.

2. The need for education (or its equivalent in primitive societies).

3. The need for social acceptance and recognition.

4. The need for sexual activity.

5. The need to be free from harassment, including not being continually frightened.

This is a handy list, but there is no claim that it is even near to being complete. Indeed, though this list can be extended, there is good reason to believe that it cannot be completed, nor could any list. There may be things about us or our environment, or both, not previously recognized to be necessary which are in fact necessary for us to live and to function well. Indeed, it may sometimes take considerable sophisticated scientific investigation to discover them. If it is so discovered and confirmed, then there is a newly recognized need that will have to go on our list. Since this is always a possibility, we should not conclude that our list or any list is complete. We should be good fallibilists here as elsewhere. That does not mean, however, that we do not have a good working list – indeed, a list which may very well suffice for giving some more robust content to a conception of egalitarianism and egalitarian justice.

The list was constructed by considering what human beings must have if they are to continue to live and function. The list seems, at least, to have gone some considerable way to doing just that. There are many more things that we need: meaningful work, for example, and an interesting cultural environment, relaxation, amusement, challenges, and the like. Relaxation and amusement might well have gone on Braybrooke's list, though not quite so obviously as the ones he did note. The other three are sufficiently important, and so linked with being able to function well, that they should count as needs. They are not, however, so utterly uncontroversial, something that everyone needs to live and function. This being so they would not be the best candidates to be added to a list concerning which we would expect a thorough consensus. These complications aside, Braybrooke's minimal list does give us things which uncontroversially all human beings must have to live well. Here we have an anchor for our *equality of what*.

What is important to stress is that needs generally trump preferences and basic needs in turn trump non-basic needs. I may want to fish a famous Norwegian salmon river. Having that desire, I have at least two adventitious needs which are necessary to satisfy: I need a fly rod to fish salmon and I need an air ticket to get to Norway. I, of course, would not even have these adventitious needs if I did not want to go salmon-fishing in Norway. In that way these needs are dependent on, and have no importance for me, except in the light of my wants: wants that I by no means *must* have. Adventitious needs are dependent on purposes and wants – purposes and wants which some people have and some do not. But suppose I am poor and I do not have money to buy both the food and the clothing I need to live as well as the fly rod I require for salmon-fishing and the airline ticket to get there. Here these basic needs (my need for food and clothing) normally trump my wants with their attendant adventitious needs. This is compounded if I have a family which is dependent on me. This gives my wants and adventitious needs a still lower priority. However, if I am all alone and I know in six months I will die of cancer and I want one last fling – one last doing of what I very much want to do – it might be reasonable for me in this situation not to let my needs trump my wants and to go on the salmon-fishing expedition. Still these course-of-life needs are necessary for my normal functioning, indeed often for functioning at all, for they are necessary for life. We should also keep firmly in mind that, over the course of a life, they are necessary, but surely not sufficient, for flourishing, self-realization, or proper functioning. We may not properly function even with having them firmly met, but we surely will not properly function without their being met. Whatever else we may require, or think we require, we cannot have a condition of human flourishing or a copious life or good life prospects unless these needs are met. We very well may not have such a life, but we cannot have one otherwise. If we really believe that the life of everyone matters and matters equally, we shall, where we have the material abundance and technical expertise to make this possible, seek – and as a matter of justice – to bring about a world in which everyone's needs are so met or at least a world where everyone has an equal opportunity of having their needs so met.

With this specification of needs, we gain some determinate specification of the needs-based egalitarian principle of equality of condition which asserts that, as far as reasonably possible, conditions should be brought into existence or, where in existence, sustained, which make for an equal satisfaction of the needs of everyone at the highest level of need satisfaction for each compatible with the needs of everyone being so treated. (Though we still must allow, as discussed above, for conflicts of needs.)

We can ascertain in some objective fashion what our needs are and social science inquiry, if carefully pursued in these domains, can give us better answers than we have now. There is plenty of common sense that is adequate here, but social science inquiry can usefully supplement it. With the above understanding and utilization of needs, we can give content to our notions of equality of condition and, without trying to reduce talk of good to talk of needs, help provide content to our conception of good lives. If there were to be equal need satisfaction, we would have a good start on what it is for people to have equally good lives, though surely the latter notion is not exhausted by the former. There is more to a good life than the satisfying of needs. Still, to gain equally worthwhile and satisfying lives, or the best approximation we can get of this, people would still have to have lives in which, as far as possible, their needs are met, and met equally, even when they are not the same needs. When that is established – recall we are doing ideal theory – and the springs of social wealth flow very freely, then, after the full meeting of needs, human wants are to be met as well, where this is possible, and met equally – assuming that we can guess what that would be.

There is the hope, under this conception, to so approximate an equality of well-being where that equality is not purchased by lowering the well-being of some capable of greater well-being to compensate those capable of less, but to develop social structures which help each person to attain the most complete well-being of which that person is capable, compatible with everyone being treated in the same manner.

The meeting-of-needs conception gives the most essential *content* to well-being here. Hence the importance of answering *equality of what* in terms of equal satisfaction of needs. But, as can be seen from the foregoing, the meeting-of-needs egalitarianism is supplemented by an attempt to include, but only as a supplement, where needs have been met, an equal satisfaction of *compossible* wants.

Welfarism was sunk by, among other things, the problems of offensive and expensive preferences. But neither is a problem for the account sketched above. For needs normally trump wants and only compossible wants are admissible. Offensive preferences are ruled out on both counts and expensive tastes are given back-burner contingency. Under most, perhaps all, real life conditions, the latter are also ruled out *sans phrase* because compensating for them would lessen both the satisfaction of needs and lessen the total, and fairly distributed, satisfaction of wants. That is compensating for expensive tastes would lessen the possibilities for others to satisfy their wants. To compensate someone for deliberately cultivating expensive tastes is, as we have seen, both unfair and goes against the maximizing thrust of egalitarianism as I conceive of it. But under wildly abundant – counterfactually abundant – conditions, where there are no costs to others, both the equalizing and the maximizing side of egalitarianism favour such compensation. In that counterfactual situation, if the expensive tastes are satisfied, there would still be more preference satisfaction in the world and more equal preference satisfaction as well. The expensive wine lover's life would go better and no other person's life would be hurt or diminished. Only confusion, Puritanism, or meanness (both offensive preferences) would oppose it. Welfarism, as we have seen, is mistaken, but behind welfarism there rests an important consideration. Would it not be a maximally good moral life for all to live in a world where as many people as possible would have as much as possible of whatever it is that they want and would continue to want with good information and where what they as individuals want, and take as legitimate to receive, would be compatible with others satisfying their wants in the same way? Put more simply, but not quite as accurately, would it not be a good thing if as many people as possible were to have as much as possible of whatever they would knowledgeably and reflectively want, where having their wants satisfied does not harm others?[54] We egalitarians want the lives of everyone to go well and equally well and at the highest level of going well achievable. How then could we consistently reject the above "pleasure principle"? Let us beware of the coldness of religious residues. Or, put more flippantly, let us not be Kant's grandparents.

XV

Finally, on a more sober and eclectic note, I want to suggest that we *might* get a still more adequate answer to the *equality of what* question if we combined in an ordered and coherent way some of the conceptions of egalitarianism in my table of conceptions. I have in mind, along with integrating into that conception the limited role for "welfarism" sketched above, to combine the equal satisfaction of needs conception with the equal effective freedom conception, the equal capabilities of functioning conception and the equal primary goods conception.

To start, the equal satisfaction of needs conception with its relatively rich content has at least two plain lacunae: (1) We have no ranking at all of the basic course-of-life needs. We just have a rather heterogeneous list. In trying to get a clearer or more determinate picture of what a good life would come to, we need some ranking and, as well, a perspicuously arranged conception of our various needs. (2) As we have seen, in order to know what a course-of-life need is, we have to know about human functioning. It looks like the equal satisfaction of needs conception presupposes something like a Sen-like conception of capabilities of functioning. Without it, we have no way of determining what course-of-life and basic needs are. However, we also saw that Sen's conception of human functioning was in many ways indeterminate. There are many diverse and conflicting human functionings and the content yielded by such a conception is thin. To make it less so, and more coherent as well, so as to make it more fruitful normatively, it looks like we need to go to some Aristotelian or quasi-Aristotelian conception of the *essential* function or the *proper* functioning of human beings or to some conception of the *essential* powers or capacities or capabilities of human beings. But the difficulties with such essentialism are well known.[55] Sen and Martha Nussbaum as well have done something to de-mythologize such Aristotelianism.[56] But it is still only a partially drained swamp. Perhaps by combining the equal capabilities for functioning view with the equal satisfaction of needs view, we can, from the specification of needs side, give more content to our conception of egalitarian justice and, from the function side, particularly if its conception of proper functioning can be given some determinate and unproblematical sense, get some ranking and rationalizing of our diverse basic needs. This, if it can be done, would yield a more coherent account. Still, and whatever may be the case about the above, an appeal to human functioning seems to be presupposed in the very determination of what are our course-of-life needs.

Coherence along these ranking of needs lines will be further enhanced by integrating the primary goods conception into the needs-and-functioning conception. Primary goods, as Rawls occasionally acknowledges, are needs – course-of-life needs. Moreover, they are our very fundamental needs, things we would have to have to get anything else that we might want. Their provision is absolutely essential for a commodious life: any commodious life. Furthermore, Rawls has also provided an index of primary goods. This will help provide something of the ranking that the satisfaction of needs conception lacks. So, unless this turns out to be a just so story, with its incorporation, we have still another gain in coherency and determinacy.

The equal effective freedom view (very Rawlsian in inspiration) carries that a step further. It, as we have seen, is somewhat, though not excessively, one-sided. Autonomy and self-respect are not the only fundamental goods, but, on Rawls's primary goods conception, and not unreasonably, they are, under conditions of at least modest abundance and security, highest on the index of primary goods. The equal effective freedom view shows why, and so we have with its incorporation yet another gain in coherency and determinacy.

Finally the capability of functioning approach might, in certain limited but vitally important situations, be a useful supplement to the primary goods approach. There are specific situations where the primary goods approach does not work, but where the capability of functioning approach at least seems to work. I have in mind situations of destitution and severe disablement. Let me explain. Standardly the primary goods approach is best for specifying what very basically we must have to live a good life. It points to what are the very essential instrumentalities here. By contrast the capability for functioning approach is normally near to being useless because of its indeterminacy and its severe informational requirements – requiring information for making judgments about capabilities that is simply unavailable. But for certain extreme cases, such as destitution and severe disablement, the capability of functioning approach does enable us to assess what capabilities are wanting and can enable us to see what would be needed in those situations to ensure an equal worth of freedom so that, for the destitute and the severely disabled, we can have some reasonable understanding of what must be done, if anything can be done, to bring them into a condition where they can achieve something approximating equal effective freedom. It is here, where the primary goods approach will, by simply providing the severely disabled and the destitute with equal primary goods, still leave them with a lesser worth of liberty than people with the same primary goods but not so afflicted. People found in the abandoned Nazi concentration camps and children in the Third World who have been severely malnourished over a long period of time will not gain an effective worth of equal effective freedom by simply coming to have primary goods equal to those of others living in normal situations. So provisioned, the disabled and the destitute have the same primary goods, but they cannot do the same things with them. They cannot use them to achieve equal effective freedom. But here, where we can see clearly what the lack of proper functioning is, we can see *what* it is that they need to gain equal effective freedom, and we can know how to correct for it, if it can be corrected, which, in many circumstances, may, to put it minimally, be problematic. So employed, the capacity for functioning account will aid in helping us to come to see more clearly what must be done, where the primary goods approach fails, to move toward enhancing and equalizing the quality of life of certain specifically situated people at the highest level possible compatible with the same possibilities obtained for everyone alike. Still the primary goods approach is what we need in ensuring the equal worth of freedom in the standard cases.

Again, we have by coherently marshalling these conceptions, different as they are, yet still mutually supportive for a common task, attained a greater coherency and determinacy. By so proceeding we have, we hope, moved some distance toward a more adequate, though more complex, account of *equality of what*. That in turn will make our egalitarianism more definite and articulated.[57]

This eclectic approach is only sketchily set out and is not very clearly articulated. I do not have the details at all worked out or, more importantly, even have the project clearly conceptualized. Moreover, like most eclectic approaches, it may very well, when pressed, come apart. It may be too much of an *ad hoc* cobbling of things together in trying to have the best of all things. I throw it out, with considerable hesitation, as a suggestion that might provide a more adequate rationale for both a liberal and a radical egalitarianism.

XVI

I return, as I close, to what I have tried more firmly to achieve. One crucial claim was for, in the ideal case, going beyond the difference principle. The brunt of the argument for going beyond the difference principle and for going from liberal egalitarianism to a radical egalitarianism was worked out in Part A. In Part B, I tried, by contrast, to give determinate content to *what* equality we egalitarians, both liberal and radical, should hope for, and can do so reasonably, given the underlying aspirations and aims of egalitarianism. This is, as I stressed, to work in the realm of *ideal* theory. Here, liberals and radicals, social democrats and socialists, can, rather extensively, join forces. When we turn, as for the most part I did not attempt to turn in this essay, to the real world and to a consideration of the thick texture of facts and conceptualizations of political sociology, history, and political economy, I would argue, as I argued in *Equality and Liberty* and as Andrew Levine did in *Arguing for Socialism* and as Richard Norman did in *Free and Equal*, that the prospects for an extensive equality of condition which also carries with it autonomy – equal autonomy for all – and fraternity are, as near as near can be, to being impossible without socialism and that socialism, as we can see now, must, to be acceptable, be some form of market socialism.[58] With such a socialism we can have both justice and efficiency. If hopes for socialism are impossible, then hopes for an autonomy respecting egalitarianism or indeed for any kind of attractive egalitarianism are dashed. Equality of condition – a world of equals – may be impossible anyway, but it will not be possible without socialism and a socialism that cannot, where it comes into fruition and stabilizes itself, just be a socialism in one country or cluster of countries.

Notes

1. Nielsen, *Equality and Liberty*.
2. G. A. Cohen, "Incentives, Inequality, and Community."
3. Ibid., 265.
4. Ibid., 266 and 268.
5. Ibid., 266.
6. Ibid., 267.
7. Ibid., 268.
8. Ibid., 267.
9. Ibid.
10. Ibid.
11. Hampshire, "A New Philosophy of the Just Society."
12. Nielsen, *Equality and Liberty*, Part III.
13. Hurka, "Perfectionism and Equality."
14. Nielsen, "State, Authority, and Legitimation," 218–50.
15. Rawls, *A Theory of Justice*, 79–82.
16. G. A. Cohen, "Incentives, Inequality and Community."
17. Nielsen, *Equality and Liberty*, 221–35, 244–46, and 296–97.
18. G. A. Cohen, "Incentives, Inequality, and Community," 311.
19. Nielsen, "Justice as a Kind of Impartiality."
20. Rawls, *A Theory of Justice*, 3.
21. G. A. Cohen, "Incentives, Inequality and Community," 327.
22. Wood, "Justice and Class Interests"; and "Marx's Immoralism."
23. Nielsen, *Naturalism without Foundations*, chaps. 7 and 9.
24. G. A. Cohen, "Incentives, Inequality and Community," 311.
25. Ibid.
26. Ibid.
27. Ibid., 327.
28. Ibid., 326.
29. Sen, "Equality of What?"
30. J. Cohen, "Review of Amartya Sen, *Inequality Reexamined*." 275.
31. Daniels, "Equality of What?" 293–96.
32. Nielsen, "Global Justice, Capitalism, and the Third World," 17–34.
33. Nielsen, *Naturalism without Foundations*, chaps. 5 and 8.
34. Dworkin: "Liberal Community"; "What is Equality? Part 1"; "What is Equality? Part 2"; "What is Equality? Part 3"; "What is Equality? Part 4"; and "Foundations of Liberal Equality."
35. Scanlon, "Preference and Urgency."
36. G. A. Cohen, "On the Currency of Egalitarian Justice," 920.
37. Ibid., 921.

38 Ibid., 917–19.
39 Ibid., 921.
40 Rawls, "Social Unity and Primary Goods," 168–69; and G. A. Cohen, "On the Currency of Egalitarian Justice," 913.
41 Sen, *Inequality Reexamined*, 39.
42 Ibid.
43 J. Cohen, "Review of Amartya Sen, *Inequality Reexamined*," 276–77.
44 Hall, *Categorical Analysis*; and Nielsen, "Mill's Proof of Utility."
45 Here Rawls and Sen supplement each other. See J. Cohen, "Review of Amartya Sen *Inequality Reexamined*," 281–88.
46 Nielsen, "Equality of Condition and Self-Ownership," 87–95.
47 See here Baier, "The Need for More than Justice," 41–56; Code, "Second Persons," 357–82; and Nielsen, "Afterword," 383–418, all in Hanen and Nielsen, *Science, Morality, and Feminist Theory*.
48 Falk, *Ought, Reasons, and Morality*, 259–60.
49 Nielsen, "Justice, Equality, and Needs," 211–27.
50 Braybrooke, *Meeting Needs*.
51 Ibid., 29.
52 Ibid., 31.
53 Ibid., 33.
54 Nielsen, "On Liberty and Equality," 121–42.
55 Nielsen, *Ethics without God*, 9–50.
56 Nussbaum and Sen, *The Quality of Life*; and Nussbaum, "Virtue Revised."
57 J. Cohen, "Review of Amartya Sen, *Inequality Reexamined*," 281–88.
58 Roemer, *A Future for Socialism*; Schweickart, *Against Capitalism*; and Wright, *Rethinking Socialism*.

Part III

COSMOPOLITANISM, NATIONALISM, AND GLOBAL JUSTICE

10

Is Global Justice Impossible?

I

I will start with a preamble. I sometimes feel that it is indecent to talk about global justice or engage in exercises setting out principles of global justice. Why such a strong emotional, perhaps even irrational, reaction? Because I ambivalently feel – or sometimes feel – that talk about it – setting out normative accounts of global justice – is at worst hypocritical or self-deceptive and at best empty or ideological. I say "ambivalently" because I sometimes also feel, in conflict with the above, that our very humanity – our sense of common human decency – impels us to try to see this matter through to the end: to come to see that there are requirements of global justice and what they are and to fight through to the end to try to make them prevail. Moreover, it seems to me that we cannot rightly limit ourselves to considerations of domestic justice and that this is particularly true if we are reasonably well-off members of the rich capitalist nations of the world. The facts of interdependence and of the depth of the despoliation, exploitation, and domination of the peoples of the poor nations of the world (often with the connivance of their elites) by the rich capitalist nations will not allow us so to hedge off our considerations of justice simply to a consideration of domestic justice or justice for our compatriots. Except as a simplifying device – as it is for John Rawls – to get some initial purchase on problems of justice, we cannot in good faith so restrict ourselves.

Yet when we face, or try to face, the question, "What is to be done?" lapsing into despair and coming to think such talk of global justice is self-indulgent prattle is very seductive. This need not – and I think should not for most of us – be a matter of feeling guilty. Our circumstances may just turn out to be comparatively fortunate, given where and when we were born. This is not something that we could be responsible for, any more than we could be responsible for being born impoverished or into a welfare-recipient culture. But, while most of us are not guilty, we can quite rightly be full of anguish and anger over the utter disgustingness of it all. Still, "ought implies can" and things are so horrible that we can come despairingly to feel that nothing can be done, the Cato Institute's bland and confident predictions of a bigger, better, more abundant world to the contrary notwithstanding. We may very well find ourselves going on with business as usual, and that can, if we reflect on it, occasion *feelings* of guilt. (We can, of course, feel guilty without being guilty.) But just a little more reflection can lead us to feel that we are being self-indulgent or at least evasive if we so react. If it *really is the case that nothing can be done*, then business as usual is in order. Anything else is just self-flagellation. Indeed it is a hard world. But then it is a hard world and we should stop uselessly and pointlessly wringing our hands and non-evasively come to grips with it, as we come to grips with the facts of our inevitable decline and death, unless we are going to become an Ivan Illich. Do not try to overcome what cannot be overcome. That is both irrational and wrong: irrational obviously and wrong as well because we should direct our energies to matters where there is a possibility that the ill in question can be overcome or at least ameliorated.

Is global injustice, or at least the terrible extent and depth of global injustice, ineradicable? Or can it, on its grand social scale, be overcome or at least to some extent ameliorated? The world – or rather most of it – is very swinish indeed, as even a minimally attentive reading of any good newspaper will make evident. Perhaps, in some local and fortunate areas of the world, we can do something about it. But can we even minimally de-swinify our world: that is, the whole international order? There is, and understandably, both skepticism and deep cynicism concerning that very prospect. Moving from declamation and lament to argument, I shall, after a brief rehearsing of some facts, articulate and examine what I shall call *the state of the world impossibility argument* and *the political will impossibility argument*. They are both arguments, at least partially distinct, for claiming that a just, or even nearly just, global social order is impossible to achieve. One further preliminary. If we stick to what John Rawls calls *ideal theory*, we can articulate a conception of a just global order. Abstracting from everything but the most general empirical considerations and from all questions of instrumentalities about how we could get from where we are now to such a just global order, we can say what a just world would look like and in terms of that we can easily say things about our unjust social world. Here more or less Left Rawlsians such as Thomas Pogge, D.J.A. Richards, Philippe Van Parijs, Brian Barry, Onora O'Neill, Charles Beitz, and Henry Shue have, with varying degrees of definiteness, made a case for something more or less like a global difference principle. That is the principle that social inequalities are justified only if the practices that sanction them, more than any other feasible arrangements, improve the lot of the worst-off strata in the world. I say "more or less Left Rawlsians," for some are more Left and some more Rawlsian than others: Beitz or Richards, say, are more Rawlsian and less Left-leaning than Shue or Van Parijs, but they all set out *ideal* conceptions of global justice and they all advocate something like a global difference principle, which in that important way gives their otherwise varied accounts an egalitarian thrust.

It is partly this commitment to ideal theory that gives talk of global justice its empty look. However, and that notwithstanding, it seems to me necessary both to do ideal theory and to see very clearly its limitations: what it can do; what it cannot do; and, as well, to be aware that it is something that can easily come to have an ideological tilt.[1] What it can do is to give us a sense where in an utterly ideal world we should go. For those of us who are egalitarians, for example, it can spell out for us something of what our egalitarian aspirations and ideals are and at this abstract level yield a more adequate articulation of what we take global justice to be. But we need also to see the limitations of ideal theory and what it cannot do.

In this connection we should note that both Karl Marx and John Dewey, though in different ways, stressed that we should never take ends in isolation from means and that we should be constantly aware of their functional interdependence. If we are at all reasonable, what ends we will advocate – including what principles of global justice – will not be taken independently of considerations concerning both the means by which they can be achieved and questions concerning what the likely effects of acting in accordance with them would be. We need carefully to ask what measures we will need to take for their achievement or approximation. And we will need carefully to consider the human costs of their achievement. When we engage in such inquiries with any attentiveness, it is quite possible that some of the ends we advocate will change, given a better knowledge of the range of feasible means for achieving them and the alternative available ends, together with their comparative attractiveness and the means available for realising them. Similarly, ends that seem to us on reflection desirable will affect the means we will seriously entertain. There are, in short, reciprocal interactions all the way along.

As egalitarians (if that is what we are), to place this consideration in terms of our present problem, we believe that the life of everyone matters and matters equally. We believe, that is, that all people have equal moral standing. We may give this a welfarist reading where we argue that everyone should be equal in satisfaction or that everyone should be equally happy. But when it is pointed out to us that, given human differences, that is impossible, short of drastic and systematic genetic engineering and a careful control of people, and probably not even then, we will move, if we are reasonable, to something like claiming that it should be the case that everyone should have equal initial resources or an equal opportunity for well-being or equal access to the conditions of well-being or that the basic needs of everyone should be equally met or, at least, that the conditions for their being so met be in place. Again this claim (more accurately a family of claims) should be scrutinized in terms of its (their) instrumentalities and in relation to other ends as well. We need in serious moral reflection to distinguish between means and ends, but we also need, as Dewey repeatedly stressed, to consider them together in their functional interactions and interdependence.

So how the world goes, political-economic and natural, and how it can be made to go are crucial matters for us to consider when we are trying to set out the principles of global justice. So, though we should not scorn ideal theory – it can show us what we would ideally want in a world free from obstacles – we are back, and very centrally, in thinking about global justice, to our impossibility arguments: (1) natural (in some sense); and (2) political-economic. I do not, however, want to say that these two impossibility arguments can, or should be, *sharply* separated. That our forests and fish are disappearing is not, of course, independent of past and present political-economic policies. Things could have been different if previous policies had been different and it is plain that they could have been different. But that there are fewer cod today than in 1930 is a fact about cod stocks (something that just is at a particular time a state of affairs there in nature); and that the Spanish systematically over-fish and are supported by their government is at least a putative political and economic fact (a social fact that depends on what human beings will, on what they do, and on what practices are in place). That capitalism encourages the exploitation of the environment is another such social fact, while that global warming occurs is a physical fact: though it is in fact a fact because of certain social facts concerning what people in the past did and are continuing to do. It is not like the eclipse of the moon. It is more like smog over Los Angeles. Nonetheless, I shall discuss separately, for reasons which shall become apparent, impossibility arguments from the physical state of the world now – our plundered planet arguments – and impossibility arguments linked with the capitalist political-economic order – what I call political will impossibility arguments.

II

In the 1980s, I wrote a series of related articles on global justice where I argued that the problems about its at least seeming unachievability were not what they were usually presented as, namely as a bleak matter of factual impossibilities, but rather they were essentially a certain kind of political-economic impossibility, namely impossibilities that were impossibilities only given the capitalist order or an order fundamentally like the capitalist order.[2] Neo-Malthusian arguments were, I argued, in effect nihilistic romanticism parading as tough-minded realism. I argued that there are enough resources around, including food, to reasonably sustain the world's population. The then 10,000 people starving each day – now up to 20,800[3] – was and still is unnecessary. The problem was access to food that was there or could readily be produced and *not*, as was usually thought, that the resources just were not there, so that we needed to engage in a neo-Malthusian Hardinistic triage faced with our allegedly swamping lifeboat earth.[4] What we needed, instead, was a deep change in our socio-economic order. We needed to move from capitalism to a socialism that could meet people's basic needs in a way that was *politically and economically* impossible under capitalism. (There are now the productive powers under capitalism to do it, but capitalist productive *relations* make it impossible. In that way it is economically impossible under *capitalism*. This puts political struggle centre stage.)

However, the problem, I argued, was very real: for the possibilities of achieving socialism were bleak. By now they are – or so at least it seems – even bleaker; and in addition it is widely believed that with socialism we have a system, *pace* Marx and the Marxist tradition, which is not very good at developing the forces of production and at efficiently allocating what has been produced, even when the political will is there and the socialism genuinely democratic. The old problem about the unlikelihood of achieving socialism is there exacerbated by the belief that socialist economies could not achieve the abundance or the distributive efficiency to bring to an end the starvation, malnutrition, and the general impoverishment of the world. It is a world in which billions of people live in terrible conditions, where nothing even nearly like decent life conditions or life chances obtain. Rather our world is, with its present population and resources, a horror of starvation, malnutrition, ill health, grossly unsanitary life conditions, utter lack of security, and short life expectancy. It is a world where about a quarter of the world's population live in destitution. So we are back, or so it seems, where we started. We are faced here with both political-economic impossibility arguments in all their force and with physical (state-of-the-world) impossibility arguments unmet as well. Whatever brought about the physical despoliation of the earth – perhaps it was rampant and unrestrained capitalism – we have by now, the worry goes, reached a point of no return. We are coming to a triage situation in which the earth is rapidly approaching a state where it can no longer sustain us, or at least cannot sustain us in anything like our present numbers and in anything like the present ways in which people in the rich countries live. It might be said that this is true only where the "us" is taken to range over the world's total population. Perhaps, some will say, the earth can, though with reduced expectations, sustain just a fortunate few, while the rest will continue to live, if they live at all, under conditions of extreme poverty and degradation. Socialism or the worldwide hegemony of Scandinavian-style welfare-state capitalism, this neo-Malthusian claim goes, is not, as a matter of cold hard fact, sustainable on a worldwide scale. It is just not on any feasible agenda. The cosmopolitan and egalitarian aspirations of socialism and of social democracy cannot be met. There is no escape from this swinish world of triage. This is just how it will be. Such claims come from many sources and have sometimes been articulated very powerfully. So I need to return to these things.

III

What first needs to be faced is the fact that things have become worse in the world since the collapse of the Berlin Wall, which was supposed to herald such hope for accountable democracies and for improved economies giving rise to better life conditions. Since I wrote that series of articles, the rich have continued to get richer and the poor, including the staggeringly impoverished poor, poorer. The end of communism and the Cold War has not helped that at all. Things just go on getting worse. The gap between the wealthy and the powerful capitalist nations – the only wealthy and powerful nations there are – and the poor nations of the world has grown in almost every dimension: certainly in wealth, power, access to education, to information, to health, to food, to shelter, to security, and to the like. According to a 2010 press release from the Food and Agricultural Organization, 925 million people, 98% of them in developing countries, go to bed hungry. There are human rights disasters all over the place and deteriorating economic conditions for all but a few rich capitalist elites (either capitalists themselves or their major facilitators). Many countries, even *if* they had the political will, cannot provide even basic healthcare. Or at least their governments say they cannot. According to the World Health Organization, in 2005 the Democratic Republic of Congo spent just $17 per capita (PPP international dollars) per year and Liberia spent just $28. What this means is that the health care systems, such as they are in the poorest parts of the world, do not cover the basic needs of their populations as the statistics on child mortality above attest. As this goes on, the United States spent $698,281 million in military expenditures in 2010.[5] It is plain, as plain as anything can be, on almost any conception of justice, even a libertarian one such as Robert Nozick's or a differently conservative one such as P.T. Bauer's, that something has obviously gone very wrong in the distribution of resources. Poor countries with their not infrequently corrupt ruling elites are pressured into buying arms from the wealthy capitalist countries

– states with large and aggressive arms industries – while the populations of these poor countries starve. Moreover, in some of these poor nations the arms they buy are used to oppress their own people. In some countries work camps, prisons, and administrative detention centres exist where hundreds of thousands of people are incarcerated for political reasons, sometimes for as little as speaking their minds. China is a shining example here. Smaller, poorer countries sometimes have similar situations, but not on such a scale. Proportionally, however, they are no better. The comparatively rich and privileged elites in these countries live very well indeed, while the poor – the bulk of the population – live in wretched conditions and are, to sustain the wealth of the elites, exploited and often brutally repressed by them. In all sorts of dimensions, the disparities between the rich and poor countries are staggering, with billions of people living in conditions that are plainly inhuman.

It was my argument in the past, and it is the argument of many others as well, including the very incisive arguments of Onora O'Neill and Thomas Pogge, that this great disparity is unnecessary.[6] Perhaps we cannot get to a global difference principle, but the extent of some of the differentials in the conditions of life is both unnecessary and horribly unjust. Indeed, "unjust" is too weak a word here. It is just plain grossly inhumane, showing a total disregard for the lives of great masses of people. Being (to put it minimally) unnecessary and being what it is (the things we have described above), it is horribly unjust on almost any account of injustice. I have argued, as have O'Neill and Pogge, and I shall argue again here, that it can, at least in its extremes, be rectified and that any halfway decent world order would rectify it.[7] Yet it goes on, and in some ways at an accelerating pace; and there is little prospect, as things stand, that much, if anything, will be done about it.

One response is that only Band-Aid improvements are *possible* given (a) the depletion of our resources and (b) the way people are wired. Together you get a physical-cum-psychological impossibility argument. What I have called the physical impossibility argument (the state of the world impossibility argument) is very often a physical-psychological impossibility argument. But I will continue to call it the physical impossibility argument for short. The better-off people of the world, the claim goes, can be brought to make some sacrifices, but not the massive sacrifices that, it is claimed, would be necessary to yield anything even resembling a just world order.

It is only pious wailing, to no avail and with no point, to lament that. It is like wailing over the occurrence of tornadoes. So we face again the physical impossibility argument.

IV

Proponents of an egalitarian form of global justice, such as myself, seek a moral community that would in certain important ways be identical with our biological species. We want, that is, a world where everyone has equal moral standing. As Richard Rorty writes, we have the project – the long-range ideal – "of distributing the planet's resources in such a way that no human child lacks the opportunities for individual development, the life-chances, available to any other human child."[8] The difference principle gives expression to what would be the best approximation of that in a world with some inescapable social stratification. Against such egalitarianism, the physical impossibility argument has it that anything like an equality of life chances is obviously impossible given how things are in the world and cannot but continue to be. Even if such human equality were, looked at from the point of view of ideal theory, desirable, it is utterly and obviously unfeasible. In 1900, when someone like William James proposed it, it might, just might, have made some sense. Now, the claim goes, it does not. Today there are over 6.8 billion people, depletion of many of the world's fish stocks, and now irreversible anthropogenic climate change. What might once have been possible – just might have been possible – plainly is no longer possible. No foreseeable application of technology or development of productive forces, the argument goes, could make every human family throughout the world "rich enough to give their children anything remotely like the chances that a family in the lucky parts of the world now take for granted for theirs."[9] Where there are a vast number of starving or very malnourished people, and not nearly enough food to go round, the people with the food are not going to share it. If I have purchased a loaf of bread and there are a hundred starving children clamouring for a piece, there is nothing I can do to help them. The most that I can do – performing "moral triage" – is arbitrarily to select a couple of them and, somehow isolating them and myself from the rest (if I can), share it with them or give them all of it. But that, the argument goes, is a microcosm of the macrocosm that is our global situation. That is how we – we fortunate few – in the rich nations must behave with the peoples of the poor nations, and particularly with the peoples of the poorest nations, if we would be at all reasonable.[10]

The physical impossibility argument is that there is no feasible "way to make decent life-chances available to the poorer five billion citizens of the member states of the United Nations."[11] For there to be any chance of doing so at all would require a massive transfer of resources from the members of the wealthy countries to those poor billions. And that those wealthier people will refuse to do. To try to force them, even if justified – as it very well might be if it would work – will not work, for they will resist, and successfully. So even assuming, counterfactually, that there is anyone strategically placed with the will and the means to try to force them, there would be, if such a forcing were attempted, a massive and continued sabotaging of such efforts in all sorts of obvious and not so obvious ways. No such transfer of wealth on a forced basis can be sustained. But, that aside, there plainly is no one with that political will who is in any such strategic position. We have, the argument goes, passed the point of no return in the balance between population and resources. And now, with a vengeance, it is the world of *The Threepenny Opera*. It need not, it is important to keep firmly in mind, be a matter of greed and selfishness on the part of the rich, but rather tough-minded and accurate economic calculation plus a desire to protect their own very fundamental interests and those of their children. This, unless we are going to extend the use of "selfishness," hardly counts as selfishness. But it does show that few people are willing, over a protracted period of time, deeply to sacrifice themselves and those close to them for the great masses of starving or even poor others. Reasonably secure and reasonably well-placed members – such as some of us are or will be – of the great capitalist states of the world are unwilling to make extensive transfers (or even anything resembling them) to the less-well-off even in our own societies, to say nothing of making such transfers to distant and very different and horribly impoverished others. We will not, through educational opportunities and the like, take the steps necessary to give hope to the children of the poor in our midst when doing so for us threatens to deprive our own children of their advantages: the expectation (albeit a diminishing expectation) they have of having a good education followed by a good job. As Rawls would put it, the strains of commitment will break here. It will generally be said that that is too much to ask of people. Transfers to the poor, even within our own societies, are acceptable, as a matter of fact, only as long as they are relatively painless.

This "realism" is gaining strength, so that by now there is a new hard-heartedness, regnant, and at least seemingly growing, in the world. What reason do we have to think that these same people (that is us), and indeed poorer members of the same society as well, will be willing to make the massive transfers of resources to the five billion citizens of the impoverished states of the world? But it is – or so the usual argument goes – transfers of this magnitude that are necessary to just keep those people afloat, to say nothing of achieving the kind of equality of which egalitarians have dreamed. Forget about the difference principle, some might say, and just consider meeting their most basic needs: clean water, enough food to eat, some marginally decent human habitation, and their most basic health care and educational needs. But that, given the magnitude of the problem, it will be argued, is entirely unfeasible. People will not make such transfers and trying to force them to do so will backfire, even if there were anyone willing to try and with the power to initiate such a program.

V

The physical-cum-psychological impossibility argument (the state of the world argument) looks, at least on the face of it, like a strong one. Is there anything, squarely facing that, that can be reasonably said for the possibility of global justice? I think appearances here are deceiving and that when we attend to the empirical facts we will see that there is no technological-cum-psychological imperative built into the very way things must go in the world – the world that we now inhabit – such that continued impoverishment is inescapable, inescapable because, if we try to achieve global justice, or even some approximation of it, our resources must just keep on dwindling with the pressure that populations put on them where people live, as so many of them do, in conditions of utter poverty, conditions often inadequate even to sustain life. It is not the case, however, some popular wisdom to the contrary notwithstanding, that, without a draconian neo-Malthusian triage, we will run out of food and other resources necessary to sustain what could be a minimally decent life for everyone on our planet.[12] Moreover, there need not be to achieve this, as such Rawlsians as Charles Beitz and Henry Shue fear, such deep transfers of wealth from the rich nations to the poor ones that rich nations would have "to commit a kind of financial hara-kiri."[13] To go toward a greater global equality, or at least to gain a world in which people live in security with their most basic needs met, the peoples of the developed world need not impoverish themselves, something they will surely not do, so that we end up just spreading the misery around. (It was this that Marx said would happen if we tried *prematurely* to achieve equality.) Thomas Pogge has made it wonderfully clear, working with and from data provided by the *United Nations Human Development Report of 1996*, that no such impoverishment is necessary. He estimates, using these data, that the richest quintile of the world population has well over 90 per cent of the world income and the poorest quintile 0.25 per cent. This yields a quintile income inequality ratio of around 400:1. Moreover, it takes into account only income and not wealth. If wealth is taken into consideration the inequality is even greater.[14] This shows, as clearly as can be shown, that transfers could easily be made to deeply lessen and even to eradicate world poverty without causing any serious inconvenience at all to the wealthy of the world. It should also be noted that the world's productive forces are already too developed for anything like this impoverishment to be even remotely near to being necessary. It is not our lack of developed productive powers that keeps us from so meeting needs. It is the way we organize social life along with the utterly uncaring attitudes and even short-sightedness of the wealthy and powerful of this world. It is, to put it bluntly, capitalism, and the attitudes that go with it, and not the world, that is the problem. Some will think that to say this is not only blunt, but crude. But, crude or not, is it not true?

Consider, to give flesh to my claim, agriculture and land use as key illustrations of how no such impoverishment of people in the capitalist centre is required to achieve at least a minimal global meeting of the most basic needs of human beings. For the foreseeable future we have plenty of available fertile land. There is in fact the agricultural potential, even without a change in technology, adequately to feed a much larger world population than we actually have.[15] Less than half of the available fertile land in the world is being used for any type of food production.¹⁶ Though everyone knows there are severe famine conditions in Africa (to take a salient example), what is less well known is that African agricultural production has been on the decline for the last forty years, though not because of lack of fertile land or of people who could farm.¹⁷ Domestic food production in Africa is falling, while food, formerly given in aid or imported very cheaply from the great capitalist centres (principally the United States), is now imported from those same centres at prices that a very large number of people in Africa simply cannot afford to pay. Similarly in South America: there is plenty of agriculturally usable land that is not used at all or is very inefficiently under-used. In Brazil, for example, there are privately owned farms, badly under-cultivated, the size of small European states. There is plainly the capacity there adequately to feed their populations and allow for exports as well. If, for example, the *latifundia* system of agriculture were broken up and the land given to landless peasants to intensively cultivate – intensive cultivation being built into their small-scale ways of cultivating – food production would increase enormously.¹⁸ Similar things could be said for the Indian subcontinent. The fact is that in our world there is plenty of food around and much more could be produced. It is a matter, as Amartya Sen has clearly shown, of its distribution and of people not having the money or other entitlements to obtain it.¹⁹ It is not at all a matter of our farmland's being used up (*pace* Hardin and Rorty) and that we have exceeded our carrying capacity.

Moreover, while the cheap imports to Africa were still in the offing in the '50s and the '60s, African peasants were paid very little for their produce and were encouraged to leave their farms and come to newly formed industrial centres in their home countries.²⁰ There was a push in these countries, aided by the transnationals, swiftly to industrialize; and getting the peasants in large numbers into the cities was essential to its success. Large numbers of these peasants moved to the rapidly growing large urban centres of those states trying quickly to industrialize. They were prodded in this direction by the loss of revenue from the farms on which they worked and by the hope of finding work in the industrializing cities. In such circumstances, the lure of food aid or cheap food imports served as a powerful incentive. Moreover, for most of them there was hardly any viable option other than leaving the countryside and moving into the cities. It was there, in the process of such industrialization, where – and necessarily, given its capitalist structure – a new proletariat and a lumpenproletariat were formed. Where before we had relatively self-subsistent agrarian societies, we have come to have, in these African countries, and elsewhere as well, a newly minted proletariat and lumpenproletariat living and working (when they have work) in, to radically understate it, dreary poverty-stricken urban centres, rife with crime and almost every other imaginable social and physical malady.

What we see happening here is the relentless and formidable growth of a global transnational economy penetrating deeply and pervasively, and with a clear capitalist rationale, into the periphery. And it is there in the periphery, for certain kinds of industries, that these ex-peasants are formed into a proletariat or a lumpenproletariat, the latter functioning as a reserve industrial army. Together they provide a cheap, fantastically exploitable, pool of labour for these transnationals. For these industries, like all capitalist enterprises always in search of profits, move from the centre to the periphery in search of a cheap and reliable labour supply; and, in the process, throw people out of work in the capitalist centres and further erode the strength of the labour movement in the developed countries. The logic of capitalist international expansion – what we now call globalization – is indeed acute and has dire consequences for many people in both the centre and periphery.[21]

Under these circumstances, it is hardly surprising that agricultural production in Africa, South America, and elsewhere has declined, with Africa being in the most desperate situation, even with half the unused, but quite usable, farmland in the world.[22] If it were used, Africa could adequately feed itself and also become a large exporter of food. Similar, if not quite so drastic, things can, and should, be said about the Indian subcontinent and South America. We do not know exactly what the carrying capacity of the world is (perhaps the very notion doesn't make much sense), but we do know that we are not about to be in a position where it is reasonable to say that the earth has exceeded it. Garrett Hardin's analogy with a lifeboat provides a vivid metaphor. But it is just a metaphor and a misleading and dangerous one at that.[23]

If we look at the rich capitalist centres and at the poor periphery, or what extensionally comes to pretty much the same thing, the North/South imbalance, it becomes plain that the great disparities here, with their resultant maladies, are principally the result of the workings of a capitalist world economic order. A clear exemplification of that, as we have already in part seen, is the world food economy, particularly in relation to industrialization in the periphery. The stark difference between North and South is apparent in the vast malnutrition and starvation of the South. What we need to recognize, and keep clearly before our minds, is that these famine conditions result from the working of the capitalist economic system in allocating the ability of people to acquire goods, and not from what Mother Earth could provide. The food available to people is principally a matter of income distribution and entitlement. These are things that, in a capitalist system, are fundamentally rooted in workers', and would-be workers', ability to provide, through working, services for which people in their society are willing and able to pay. In the North the rates of involuntary unemployment remain stubbornly high, but they are nothing when compared with the South, where the number of unemployed, or very marginally employed, is staggeringly high – far, far higher, that is, than in the North.

VI

In thinking about the world food economy and the global injustice it generates, we should think about the control of the economies, and with that much of the life of the periphery by the transnational capitalist giants of the centre. In the late '50s and '60s, the United States government, reflecting plainly not only the interests of its big capitalists but of the then-powerful farm lobby as well, developed a policy of food aid to Third World countries. Many of these countries, as we have already noted, were trying rapidly to industrialize, often under the "inspiration" of the transnationals. This food aid, at one and the same time, provided a lot of inexpensive food for a new, and also a very inexpensive, industrial labour force as well as a respite for the American farmers with their – relative to the market – over-production. As we have seen, a new proletariat was being born in what had once been largely peasant societies. An effective midwife here was the food aid and its related policies of the capitalist centre. Previously largely self-sufficient agrarian societies were being turned into agriculturally dependent societies relying on food supplied by the capitalist centres, first in the form of food aid, later for a while sold cheaply under altered market conditions, and now sold at what for those societies are stiff prices, though still of course prices which reflect world market realities. What we have here is a commodification of food and the placing of the Third World countries ever more firmly in the commodity exchange system of the capitalist order.[24] Today, the global food market is dominated by and distorted by a few giant capitalist corporations. Food aid continues to diminish as the capitalist market ever more firmly takes over. The food imports resulting from such capitalist structures continue to create rural unemployment and insecurity. At a *Panos* briefing at the World Food Summit in Rome (November 1996), it was pointed out that those giant corporations and their subsidiary companies will release food only in response to price opportunities, not to need.[25] The World Food Crisis of 2006-2008 and the volatility of food prices that mostly impacts the global poor are documented in the annual "The State of Food Insecurity in the World" reports that emerged from the Rome summit.[26] But this should hardly be surprising. It is simply the application of the tried and true rationale that makes capitalism tick. As it was earlier when the world food order was developing, so it remains an astute way to help make the world safe for the flourishing of capitalism: but it was also, and still is, a way of creating even greater imbalances between North and South – between centre and periphery – and for the creation of the increasingly harsh exploitation of the people of the South, where there exists an enormous labour pool. In such circumstances there is little prospect of the workers being able to force wages up through labour militancy. They are, to understate it, very vulnerable.

Going back a little to gain a sense of how the world food order developed, we can see how things got worse in the '70s compared with what they had been in the '50s and '60s. In the '70s the International Food Order began to come unstuck.[27] By then, in Africa and other parts of the Third World, there were masses of people, most of them previously peasants, who were separated from any direct ties to agriculture, with the great mass of them forming, as I have already remarked, a cheap labour pool. These people lived (and still do) in conditions of very deep poverty and degradation.[28]

In the capitalist centres grain surpluses dwindled (surpluses that previously had been conveniently sent to the Third World) with much of the grain now being sold instead to what was then the Soviet Union. And, with this, food prices soared in the Third World. In fine, the grain aid program of the '50s gradually lost its capitalist rationale. Few of these newly minted proletarians, to say nothing of the lumpenproletarians, got any new entitlements to food or, in the case of even the best-off proletarians, anything like adequate entitlements. Commercial markets, even in the periphery, began to work in the sense that some of the urban workers could now just barely afford to buy food under market conditions. But at the same time many people who had previously had access to inexpensive food, both in the urban centres and in the countryside, continued to have the need for food, but, in the newly emergent market system, no longer had the entitlement. They were, and still are, like the poor Bengalis during the great Bengal famine of 1943–44, described by Amartya Sen, when again there was an adequate amount of food around but millions of people lacked the entitlement to purchase it.[29] They had, that is, no purchasing power or any other means to acquire it. In this situation – to return to Africa and like places, with the by now extensively dismantled local agricultural system and the introduction of a new system of cash-cropping for export to the capitalist centre – massive malnutrition and starvation resulted; and it continues to flourish on an accelerated scale. In short, these maladies are in large measure the result of the way the capitalist mode of production has developed. Under our globalizing capitalist system there are great masses of people in need of food but with little in the way of entitlements to it.

Capitalism, of course, needs a workforce and a workforce that can reproduce itself (though as technology advances the size of the workforce will shrink); but with the newly developed industrial enterprises in the Third World a little starvation and malnutrition will not hurt, will not, that is, deleteriously effect the efficiency of such capitalist production, as long as they have, as they indeed have, a large reserve labour pool to draw upon. Some individual workers or potential workers, particularly if they are "difficult," may just as well starve as long as there are plenty of replacements. Things like this happened with the industrialization of the Western world under capitalism in the nineteenth century. They are now being repeated with all the old savagery in the Third World in the twenty-first.

So we can see, at least as regards food, that what neo-Malthusians such as Garrett Hardin and Joseph Fletcher take to be just a matter of how the modern world must go has no such necessity at all.[30] It is rooted not in life nor in the world nor in just how people are wired, but in political and economic choices that need not have been made.

Though I have not the space to develop it here, basically similar things can be said in respect of pollution, population growth, fish stocks, forests, and the like. We have the know-how significantly to control pollution without committing financial hara-kiri, but we lack the political will to do so.[31] We also have the know-how to manage our forests and our fish stocks so that they can replenish themselves, just as the Thames and the Rhine are coming back to health under improved environmental policies. We have the science in place to limit the pollution here. Moreover, we know the kind and extent of fishing and foresting that also is a major cause of the problem and we know how to fish and forest so that we can keep our forests and fish stocks intact and revive them where they have been depleted. Look at how successfully the Germans have managed their forests for a very long time and then contrast this with the practice in North America. That German forests are now threatened by pollution does not gainsay that. Their forestry practices are not destroying their forests, pollution is. Again there is no inescapable "technological imperative" built into the world which causes our loss of forests and fish. There is nothing there that we cannot halt and much that we can reverse. And, to shift from pollution to population, population growth, as is well known, levels off with increased wealth and security. Again it is a matter of *political will*, as we have also, though less obviously, come to see with global warming, the utterly Neanderthal claims of some US right wing politicians to the contrary notwithstanding. So the first of the great impossibility arguments (the state of the world impossibility argument), the favourite among Neo-Malthusians, is undermined. But, by the very way it was undermined, the political impossibility argument is thereby thrust to the fore, and there, many believe, is the rub.

VII

Transterritorial capitalist enterprises grow relentlessly and seemingly uncontrollably. They pollute massively, as did the old state industries of state socialism, as they vainly tried to compete with these capitalist enterprises.

And governments take only laughable steps to resist. Giant trawlers harvest the seas of the world and checks against them are ineffective. Particularly in the periphery, workers are savagely exploited, with many a would-be worker anxiously waiting in the wings desperately hoping to have the very job where she knows she is going to be savagely exploited. But, she reasons, quite plausibly, at least there is work. With work there is the hope of being able to some extent to ameliorate her destitution and that of her family. What she aspires to is to be able at least to resist what in many instances is such extensive malnutrition that death, or at least an incapacity to work and properly function, is just around the corner. It is difficult for us to imagine the horror of the lives of at least a quarter of the world's population. But it is palpably there and not a figment of our guilty liberal imagination.

Perhaps in some instances – particularly over some environmental issues – capitalist enterprises can be brought to see that there is long-term profit in being more environmentally friendly. For there to be fish and a liveable environment tomorrow, there had better be a more restrained way of fishing and of respecting our environment today and we had also better do something about the pollution of the sea. For there to be forests tomorrow they had better both stop throwing certain pollutants into the air and forest differently today, particularly in North America. But even such an avoidance of what economists call public bads is not so easy for capitalism, given competition and the necessity for reasonably short-term profit maximization. It is worth remembering that for many managers in capitalist firms, the bottom line is to maintain a fairly short-term profit, for they need to keep their shareholders happy. These managers will not think of the long term, if they want to keep their jobs – to say nothing of being upwardly mobile in the managerial scramble. The thing is to make a good showing for about five years and then move on to a more prestigious firm. Taking into account the long term usually does not have a pay-off for them; though here Japanese capitalism, on the one hand, and North American and European capitalism, on the other, are not quite the same – Japanese managers are not quite so vulnerable in this respect. And this may show that the capitalist system has some play here. But, as we saw above, for many managers it does not pay to take the long view. They have to turn out a reasonably quick profit.

However, managers do not have the ultimate control, John Kenneth Galbraith to the contrary notwithstanding. The capitalists themselves do take, and they *might* come to take, a somewhat longer-term view, though still with the same self-interested rationale. After all, acid rain falls on rich and poor alike. To discipline their managers to be more efficient and to make a profit, as now the stock market and the threat of take-overs disciplines them, North American and European capitalists could institute something like the Japanese system of managerial control. If they did they might be able to operate with a more long-term interest in mind and this might lead them to be more environmentally friendly.[32]

Clearly, the best issues for reform within the capitalist system are such environment-related issues. But with the workforce and their conditions of life, it seems to be another thing. Why should those capitalists who exploit children ten hours a day, seven days a week, in their factories stop until, if indeed that happens, the public outcry gets strong enough to hurt their business badly enough to make it no longer profitable to operate under such labour conditions? That has not happened yet and it may not. Meanwhile these small capitalists have some very cheap and malleable workers who will produce efficiently enough what they want. Indeed, there are labourers, including child labourers, in parts of Pakistan, in Haiti, and in parts of Brazil who are in effect slaves, not just what Maxians call wage slaves. And there is a seemingly endless supply of children to use for such work coming from desperately impoverished circumstances where their parents are willing in effect to sell them. Better that, the parents might well reason, than for the children themselves, and the rest of the family with them, to starve. As Marx and Brecht so well understood, and so well depicted, life – particularly under primitive capitalist circumstances – can be very, very grim indeed. My earlier term was 'swinish,' and in fact I see no reason for toning it down except perhaps to conform to current academic conventions. We do not now speak bluntly as philosophers and other intellectuals did in the eighteenth and nineteenth centuries. Think, for vivid and powerful examples, of the language of Hobbes and Marx. Perhaps we should resuscitate this practice.

In the capitalist centre *some* of the workforce requires extensive training: but many industries, particularly the type coming into being in the Third World, do not need such a highly trained and, to some extent, educated workforce. Furthermore, given population growth, there are plenty of people around to hire, even people with, where there is need for such, the requisite distinctive skills. Why – capitalism is not the Salvation Army – should they move to a capitalism with a human face? There seem, some exceptional circumstances aside, to be no grounds for such a move that makes good capitalist sense, a sense where money is the bottom line.

Perhaps, as both Giovanni Arrighi and Eric Hobsbawm in their studies of twentieth-century capitalism have argued, capitalism is in the process of self-destructing. But neither thinks that this is so because the proletariat is capitalism's gravedigger; nor that there is a socialist replacement waiting in the wings.[33] We Marxians used to think that the non-viability of capitalism would lead to socialism, though not without a fight. But this is something we can no longer safely assume. It certainly was never plausible to think it was *inevitable*; that is pure incoherent metaphysics.[34] But it was once plausible to think that it was the likely way things would go after the collapse of capitalism; that the crisis of capitalism, something that was itself likely, would usher in, though not without intense struggle, socialism. But it is now no longer plausible to think even that. What is reasonable – or so I shall argue – is to *hope*, and not utterly utopianly, that that is the way things will go and to *struggle* to make things go that way. Moreover (*pace* Hobsbawm and Arrighi) capitalism, though certainly not eternal, has proved surprisingly adaptable and resilient, surviving many a predicted collapse, and learning from its Marxist critics. In making the case for a socialism that can be attained in the lifetime of some of us and in providing the institutional background for the achievement of global justice, we should keep that fact firmly in mind.

More generally – to fasten clearly on the political impossibility argument – whatever the merits of socialism – and I think they are considerable – in popular consciousness, at least in the great capitalist centres, socialism seems to be a spent force.[35] There seems to be little popular belief, and not much professional and academic belief either, that socialism can replace capitalism and provide the political will that capitalism lacks, though in 2011 there are *some* signs of this changing.

VIII

In trying to see if there can be anything like a good response here, I want at first to proceed indirectly, by saying something that at first may seem counterproductive about a particular development of Marxian theory. Some of us have tried to articulate a "no-bullshit" Marxianism and to provide a conception of a feasible socialism. With this we could try to begin to meet the political impossibility argument. But it is not very likely that anyone is listening, or at least not enough are listening to make any societal difference – the only kind of difference that in these matters counts. Moreover, even when we gain some fleeting attention, the ideal of a feasible socialism will be met with at least considerable skepticism and not infrequently with scorn. There were the good old days when we were thought to be a danger. Now we are often thought to be a joke.

Such a *Weltbild* notwithstanding, I have argued, and continue to argue, like some other analytical Marxians, and not only analytical Marxians, that we have in place a holistic Marxian social scientific theory that remains the best bet in town for theories of such scale.[36] It is plausible, clearly articulated, and systematic. But, like any other social scientific account, it is certainly not written in stone. The very notion of Orthodox Marxism (Georg Lukács to the contrary notwithstanding) is an oxymoron. Indeed, we should refer to our account as Marxian, not Marxist, on analogy with "Darwinian" and "Darwinist." Almost everyone in biology is a Darwinian. No one is a Darwinist. Marxianism is a plausible holistic social scientific theory. Marxism, with its suggestion of "Orthodox Marxism," is a dogma. Marxianism is subject to continued refinement and modification and is not, thankfully, immune from disconfirmation. Moreover, I think such analytical Marxians as G. A. Cohen, Jon Elster, Andrew Levine, David Schweickart, John Roemer, Philippe Van Parijs, and Erik Olin Wright have articulated conceptions of a feasible and normatively sound socialism. It is – being quite explicitly normative – egalitarian and democratic. Their views, of course, are by no means identical, but taking them together we can, occluding some of the differences, gain a common picture of a feasible and humanly attractive socialism backed up by a carefully articulated descriptive-interpretative-explanatory social theory and a careful and plausible normative account. Schweickart and Roemer in particular have carefully developed conceptions of market socialism which, I believe, are of great importance.

However, and this is crucial for our considerations here, the cogency of the reasoning of analytical Marxians is not here the paramount point. The question at issue here – the political impossibility problem – is whether socialism is on the historical agenda or can be put on the historical agenda. It is the question of whether there is any reasonable prospect of achieving socialism in anything like the foreseeable future. The worry is that our accounts are just utopian; socialism with a professorial face. Roemer and Schweickart have shown how very sensible and theoretically workable market socialism is – at least on paper – and how attractive it is as well, at least from where we are now, where, with apologies to Isaac Deutscher's fine vision of things, there are very few socialist persons around. Roemer and Schweickart have shown that market socialism could be both efficient and fair.[37] And they have shown how well it fits with the egalitarian aspirations of socialism and with its democratic commitments. That is all fine. But there are those who will say, and not implausibly, that it still suffers from "a disabling weakness: the absence of any *politics* of a viable socialism."[38] Analytical Marxians seek to argue for economic realism, and in some ways they succeed; but they still suffer, it is argued, from a bad form of *political* utopianism, to wit the advancing of a "desirable goal with little or no specification of its possible constituency, agency or strategy."[39] They have forgotten Marx's stress on the integral relation of theory and practice and his stress, which was also Dewey's, on never attending to ends without a careful attention to means. We should always be reasoning within a means-ends continuum. Roemer sees that, but then in effect ignores it. He remarks, rightly, that "for any end state of a social process to be feasible, a path must exist from here to there, and so at least a rough sketch of possible routes, if not a precise map, may reasonably be asked of someone attempting to describe the final destination."[40] That is exactly right. But neither Roemer nor Schweickart, nor any of us, have provided such a map for our present situation. It is right to say that we need not have a precise map, but we need to have some guidelines concerning how to get from the mess we are in now to a socialist world. Analytical Marxians have provided us with a good understanding of how socialism is to be democratic, and, roughly speaking, the kind of egalitarianism that should be the aspiration for a just world; and they have refuted F. H. Hayek's claim that market socialism is an oxymoron. Roemer, in doing the latter, shows nicely how a market socialism could combine efficiency and equality. But that is all on paper. How do we proceed to institute such a socialism, or any socialism? How do we bring it about in the real world and provide some reasons to believe it could be stable? What do we do to incline people to socialism whose life experiences with what once was really existing socialism do not incline them to socialism; what do we do to receive assent from people in societies such as our own who have been deeply and in various ways inoculated against socialism? The question remains, that is, *how do we now get socialism on the historical agenda?* Admittedly, particularly for the poorest quarter of the world's population, the world is a wretched place; but the *political* impossibility argument still seems very strong. Moreover, where the wretched of the earth have out of the wretchedness of their lives the will to try to construct socialism, they lack the material means necessary for such construction; and where people in the great capitalist centres have the means to do so, they lack the political will. Where they are motivated they cannot and where they can they are not motivated. We have to find a way out of this.

There is another form of political impossibility argument that again raises the haunting spectre for us socialists of the absence in the Roemer/Schweickart type of arguments for market socialism of any *politics* of a viable socialism. I want to state and then consider that argument.[41] A not-inconsiderable part of the ability of capital to increase global inequality, the argument goes, stems from (a) its ability to move freely around the planet seeking out cheap labour and (b) from its ability to restructure (outsourcing now being capitalistically mandatory). The most influential and powerful capitalist enterprises – the key players in the capitalist game – have global scope, structure, and operation.[42] Market socialist solutions such as those of Roemer and Schweickart look suspiciously like socialism in one country or at least one country at a time. Moreover, suppose we were to get a political majority in one country in favour of implementing market socialist changes along something like the lines of the models they propose. If that were in the offing, this political impossibility argument has it, then, well before the fact, there would be capital flight from the country in question with the immediate effect that the country where the wind was blowing in this way would be a little poorer and certainly less secure.

People – great masses of people – would anticipate this and would not vote for these changes. So the institution of a market socialism experiment could not even commence unless it were to be instituted internationally from the start. But there is fat chance of that, so market socialism proposals are in a bad sense utopian after all.

I think that the capital outflow problem would not be that transparent to most voters and, more importantly, to say that it must be international from the start is too strong. But, that notwithstanding, I do accept the spirit of the argument. That is to say, I think that it is right to argue that market socialism, if it is to be a model that could have a stable exemplification, could not be for just one country or small cluster of countries for the reasons – centrally the flight of capital reasons – given above. Indeed shoe factories, or even computer factories, can move around the world, but heavy industry cannot, or at least not so easily. Still, there will in all likelihood be a great flight of capital from a country going socialist. What is essential for market socialism to work is that it come into being in the large and most powerful, as well as the large and more or less powerful, industrial countries, including places like Brazil, Argentina, Chile, South Africa, Russia, India, Vietnam, and China, at approximately the same time. Then there would be no workable place for capitalism to flee to. But it does not seem to me more unlikely (or at the least much more unlikely) that such socialist conceptions of society could not gain support in all such countries – or at least in most of them – at about the same time than that they would catch fire in just a single country; or that, at least after a decade or so of struggle, they might come together on market socialism and give it a real political life. As my scenarios in the next sections will bring out, these societies, as different as some of them are in certain respects, are all subject to similar pressures and their citizens could reasonably be expected to come to have similar aspirations. Moreover, the socialist movement has always been an internationalist movement. A commitment to *market* socialism, as a way socialists intend to proceed (its value being purely instrumental), would be a part of that internationalist movement. Furthermore, the movements in individual countries would gain increased support and reasonability from the knowledge that there were similar movements afoot in other countries and in solidarity with them, a solidarity that would just go with their being socialist. All this is presupposed in the arguments I give and in the scenarios

I articulate below. The more pressing problem, in my estimation, is how to get the project off the ground anywhere.

IX

The political impossibility argument – the general one I stated before the above rather extended aside – not only seems strong: it is strong and I am tortured by it. It is part of what inclines me to think that to speak of global justice is indecent. Not even a simulacrum of it – or so at least it seems – is on the historical agenda. I want in closing to say something, admittedly with not very much confidence, about how perhaps there is after all a way to a feasible and reasonable socialism and how, if that is so, global justice may someday be approximated. (As things stand now there is no hope even remotely to approximate it.) But I do this while ambivalently worrying whether this is just another instance of socialism with a professorial face and a rather moralistic one to boot. But I also remember Antonio Gramsci's famous dictum concerning the pessimism of the intellect and the optimism of the will.

So what possibilities are there for getting from here to there? I shall give an extended scenario, stating what I hope and believe may be some mass political *possibilities* – the only kind of possibilities that can, and indeed should, deliver the goods. I shall describe these various possibilities for different contexts. In giving my scenario here, I shall interlace comments on how a market socialism could effectively come into play in these situations: how it could, and should, find an instantiation in the world (not just in single societies) where the mass phenomena I shall describe are coming into being. That is to say, for it to have an instantiation, the putative mass phenomena I describe must actually be coming into being. I shall describe how, if that is so, there could be an interaction there – an interaction, if you will, between theory and practice. The clear and convincing articulation of what a market socialism and its effective dissemination might be would help sustain the mass phenomena, give them a direction, and help give the people who are part of these mass phenomena a reasonable hope, a confidence and belief that what they are doing makes sense and might very well yield a feasible socialism. There will, that is, emerge, for a critical mass of people struggling for socialism, and including in their ranks intellectuals who construct these models, the conviction that these models are not merely something for intellectuals to play with, but that they provide models for real-life possibilities. They model, that is, something we should and not implausibly will struggle to make the case.

Stated just like that, what I have just said is something of a dark saying. But I shall make it clear, or at least clearer, as I proceed. There are, of course, other scenarios, including many that would continue to push the political impossibility line. Some of them – including most particularly the more pessimistic ones – may be more plausible than mine, delineating more accurately and realistically how things are *likely* to go for us. What I am claiming is that the scenarios I shall describe are in the realm of *empirically reasonable political possibilities*. Political cynicism and despair are so deep that some may not even grant that. But then I would like to know just why what I shall say does not describe a reasonable *possibility*. I did not say it was the most probable possibility; rather, I claim it is a reasonable one, describing something which it is not unreasonable to believe might come to obtain and to reasonably struggle to make obtain. Moreover, if what I shall describe is such a possibility, then it is enough to remind ourselves that we are also, or at least can be, political actors in the world as well as spinners of what we hope are not just-so stories.

In giving my interpretative description I shall divide things up. I shall talk first about Eastern Europe and what once was the Soviet Union, then about Western Europe and North America, and finally about the western side of the Pacific Rim. What we should say about Africa seems to me to be less clear, beyond saying that South Africa and North Africa (particularly Egypt), in spite of all their difficulties, will need to lead the way by providing the spark for, and being in some important ways the motor and the initial sustainer of, the other African states.

In the early 1990s, I hoped that, in what was once part of the old Soviet Empire, there were the prospects of a move to a return to socialism or communism, this time thoroughly democratically rooted. I thought – and this is where theoretical considerations come in – that in some, perhaps all, of those societies, market socialism would have a genuine chance of being tried out. People would want security, including, of course, confidence that their basic needs would be met. But they would not want a return to the rigidities and inefficiencies of the old command economy. Here I thought they might have been receptive to an intelligently and practically set out conception of market socialism. We might have been able to go from Roemer's and Schweickart's theoretical conceptions to real-world social experiments. People, or at least very many of them, were thoroughly fed up with the old Soviet Thermidor. But the new capitalist society had turned out, in ways that most of them hadn't anticipated, to be a nightmare. Indeed, in many ways, though not all, the new free market societies had turned out to be very definitely worse than the really existing socialisms of their not-so-distant past. Fed up with chaos, with promises not being kept, salaries not being paid or becoming meaningless with inflation; and fed up too with crime, violence, the drastic lowering of their standards of living and with the new class of Mafia-style capitalist gangsters emerging into prominence and power, the peoples of the former Soviet Union, or at least many of them, might have been ready for another try at socialism, this time without dictatorship and a command economy, or at least with an economy that is some coherent mixture of market and command, or at least market and plan. If such a social experiment got under way, the people doing the planning, and the general population as well, would no doubt be ready for intelligently articulated plausible market socialist conceptions. The East Europeans (former East Germans, Poles, Hungarians, Bulgarians, etc.) who had seen certain important things in their lives deteriorate since the arrival of freedom, might, while continuing to prize freedom – but no longer (if they ever did) identifying it with economic neo-liberalism – have been open to intelligently worked out conceptions of market socialism. In 2011, this looks at least a diminished prospect in the near term at least for Eastern Europe, though it may obtain in other parts of the world.

What I said then about the ex-Soviet Union was naïve and thoroughly mistaken. For a long time, like Sartre, with thoroughly desirable hopes for a better future, I continued to believe what was an illusion, though not the illusion of the God, or even *a* god, that failed. (We, as I thought then, and think now, have no need for any gods.) What I later hoped for was that the Soviet Union might have morphed into a genuinely socialist social democratic society, a society more like Sweden under Palme's leadership than what the Soviet Union had become. I deplore what the actual morphing of the Soviet Union has become, what it is now: a form of authoritarian state capitalism. After its first few years, the Soviet Union was never anything like a socialist society, let alone a socialist society moving toward a communism that was a long way down the road, but perhaps achievable. The Soviet Union was rather a totalitarian statism, neither socialist nor capitalist, and under Stalin, to use Dewey's phrase, a brutalitarianism. All that said, I still wish, given the conception that Engels, Marx, and Rosa Luxemburg had of communism, for communism without a command economy, though still with central planning. Something like that is in fact not foreign to the most effective stable forms of capitalism, though this is usually unacknowledged.

Market socialism is something that can perhaps give us what is good about both capitalism and the old state socialism while avoiding what is bad about both. It can be efficient while preventing the emergence of a small dominating wealthy capitalist class, while honouring commitments to equality and security and remaining thoroughly democratic. Here may be a place where there is real social space for something like the Schweickart/Roemer models to have a thorough testing, though surely, as Schweickart and Roemer very well realize themselves, their conceptions will no doubt come to be modified in that very testing. We might in time get something like an efficient and thoroughly democratic socialism with an egalitarian orientation and with the genuine commitment of its citizens. A feasible socialism emerging from where we are now and with citizens socialized as we are socialized cannot yield the full measure of egalitarian aspiration. But it can move us in the right direction by moving us to a far greater equality than we have now. It is a socialism for the short term. The long term – if we ever get there – would involve the coming into being of socialist persons.[43] But for now the short term is that for which we must strive. I do not say, let me repeat, that it will happen, but that it could. There is work here for us – that is we radical intellectuals – to do in articulating a clear conception of what socialism can and should be and in tying this conception to the political and economic struggles of our time. We socialists can, and should, forget about a fixation on cultural critique and put our shoulders to the wheel.

I turn next to a mass phenomena conception of what might transpire in the great capitalist centres in Europe, North America, and the Pacific Rim. There – and most particularly in North America – socialism in any form is now standardly taken to be a ridiculous non-starter. It is widely thought that the capitalist winning of the Cold War decisively established that. Socialism is, popular conception has it, anti-democratic and, what is even more fundamental – because it is taken to just go with the system – very inefficient to boot. It is an organization of social life that results in poverty and economic stagnation, the good intentions, including what could be democratic intentions, of socialist planners notwithstanding. It is hard in many (though not all) of these capitalist centres to get a voice for even the mildest social democracy, let alone for socialism, no matter how democratic and market socialist a program it has. (The United States of America, of course, is the most extreme case, with Canada coming to lag not far behind. So as not to lose our balance, it is important to remember that Scandinavia is different. There, of course, social democracy is very strong even when conservative parties get elected.)

Socialism is not something that at present great masses of people are prepared to take seriously (particularly in North America). Why *might* this change? Conservative, liberal, and even mildly social democratic governments – Scandinavia a little bit to the side – have served capitalist interests, though perhaps, for the social democratic ones, sometimes out of the conviction (honourable in itself) that there is no other *feasible* alternative. The genuine social democrats among them just try to tame the beast a little bit.

Let me now give some reasons why this pervasive capitalist orientation might, just might, change. Under capitalist economic policies, people have been told for a long time now that they have to tighten their belts. Above all, we are told, again and again, in capitalist society after society, that we must bring the deficit down. This is a general, and incessantly repeated, capitalist refrain. We cannot continue to live beyond our means and we must realize that there is no such thing as a free lunch. It is not hard to see here who really determines things. This goes on, as one bourgeois government replaces another, with the various mainstream parties always singing, particularly when they are in office and an election is not in the offing, much the same tune and carrying out much the same policies, though some rather more draconically than others. All the while poor people in all these societies find it harder and harder to make ends meet. Moreover, more of them are becoming unemployed or only marginally and insecurely employed. This happens while people in the so-called middle class come to be, with their high tax burden, increasingly set against the poor. But they also see, in addition to their heavy taxation, their salaries, purchasing power, working conditions, and social safety nets all increasingly and relentlessly eroded. Indeed, a not-insignificant number of them are not so securely in the middle class as they used to be able just to assume and this is increasingly becoming true. They may find themselves or their children becoming a part of the poor they deride. In the United States, for example, there is more inequality now than there has been since the 1920s with the U.S. Department of Agricultural reporting 17.2 million households suffering from food insecurity in 2008. There is a slippery slope, down which not a few people are sliding, from lower middle class respectability to poverty. Life for more and more people is becoming more difficult and more insecure. Faced with these things over a number of years, with different governments coming and going, all heavy on promises of a brighter future but short on delivery, perhaps both the poor and the not so poor (but not so wonderfully well off and getting less well off from year to year) may very well stop believing in the excuses of their governments, whose officials are in effect representatives, sometimes more fully, sometimes less, of the capitalist class and who serve their interests. A critical mass of people may stop believing that what they are experiencing is necessary pain for long-term gain and they may begin, in one way or another, to revolt. In 2011, this is growing. How is it, they may very well ask, that we must be so badly off, and so increasingly badly off, in a world where the productive capacities of our societies continue to grow? To say that all the same, that growth notwithstanding, we must continue to make sacrifices for a rather elusive commonweal, will come, more and more and to more and more people, to seem like an economist's deception. It is rather likely that their revolt, in North America at least, will first take the form of siding with right-wing, more or less libertarian parties. Both the militia phenomenon and the tea party phenomenon in the United States are in this respect interesting: that a not-inconsiderable number of people are coming to see their government as the enemy to be struggled against is not insignificant. The Occupy movement's progressive reaction to the tea party signals that things may be changing.

In Europe its form is more likely first to be corporatist: something like Le Pen in France and the neo-fascists in Italy. But, if the Left's reading of social economic realities is near to the mark, and here we share common ground with more or less Keynesian welfare-state liberals, such right-wing programs (whether libertarian or corporatist) will not work. After a few years with such people in power, it will become plain to great masses of people that the Right cannot deliver the goods.

So what it is reasonable to expect is this: the old liberal-conservative *status quo* will fail. When the effects of radical right policies have had the time to sink in, for poor and the middle strata alike – and this after years of false promises from standard conservative/liberal governments – then "the middle class" will no longer be able to believe that things will get better if governments just reign in those welfare bums, cut taxes, and more generally get off people's backs. In such circumstances, "the middle class," along with the poor, may be ready, in some more thorough way, to attune themselves to different options and to come to revolt. Options that are not open to them now will become significant for them. And there is our chance and there is the cash value of Schweickart, Roemer, and others having worked out practically feasible models of market socialism that actually start from where we are now and recommend changes, some of which could rapidly become operative, so as manifestly and immediately to improve the welfare of great masses of people as well as increasing their control over how things go. What now is merely utopian may – and not in any greatly distant future – cease to be so. A pervasive cynicism about politics may very well defeat us; but then again it may not. We are never going to escape contingency here or anywhere else. But movement in a progressive direction is possible. That is why such intellectual work is so important and not just spitting into the wind.

What I have said about North America and Europe should also apply to Japan, Australia, New Zealand, Singapore, Malaysia, Taiwan (if there will still be such a place), and similar countries. There remain China and Indo-China. There we still have what nominally would be called communist systems, bad to very bad on the democratic and egalitarian side, but having nonetheless become societies oriented by leaders who are what would in Mao's time have been called capitalist roaders. But they are (particularly in China) building up their productive powers at a fantastic rate, though at a not-inconsiderable present expense to a good portion of their population, showing clearly how there can be, and indeed under certain circumstances is, exploitation under socialism as well as under capitalism (though it is probably more accurate to characterize China as an authoritarian state capitalism). But there may be no other way to go to make China a wealthy industrial nation that could then – eventually – make socialism a reality. (I am, remember, not saying that this will happen, but only that it could.) It was not only the Mensheviks but Marx himself who stressed that socialism builds on the back of capitalism. Marx did not think this a pretty picture and it certainly was and is not. But without developed productive forces, by trying to go directly for socialism and equality, we can only spread the misery around. As Marx delicately put it, we shall get the same old shit again. However, as China becomes an industrial giant, the Chinese people may begin to demand, and to be in a position to get, genuine socialism and with it genuine democracy. (Indeed, where they are genuine, the two go together like hand and glove.) And, particularly with their long legacy of Marxism, they may very well succeed – though they may repeat Russia's mistake, with their Marxism becoming something of a facade. And then the story for China, and for Indo-China as well, gets longer and more like that of Eastern Europe and what once was the Soviet Union. But the scenario, *contra* the political impossibility argument, still remains fundamentally the same. It will just be, if things so transpire, a longer march for the people of those countries. And something similar could obtain in India with its very large more or less Maoist insurgency.

X

To return now to a more general stance. It has been evident for a long time that the productive forces of the world are sufficiently developed to institute socialism. It is ideology and capitalist political and cultural domination, plus much, though not all, of the history of the Soviet Union and China which make socialism seem both undesirable and completely impossible. Against this background, we get the first impossibility claim, that the very state of the world makes socialist egalitarian aspirations (which, broadly speaking, are also the Rawlsian-Dworkinian-Senian liberal egalitarian aspirations) to a more egalitarian world – where people, with their basic needs met, could be both secure and in control of their lives – impossible. But, as we have seen, this state of the world impossibility claim is false. So what we are left with is the claim of socialism's *political unachievability*. I have tried to sketch a scenario where this is put in question. What is now politically unfeasible could, and in the not-too-distant future, become feasible. However, we should not forget that, speaking globally, even if things go the way my scenario depicts, a lot of inequalities will remain for a long while, and indeed for a while they will be stark inequalities, though not so stark as now. Socialism, as Roemer soberly stresses, will take a long time in its building.[44] But it is vital that we can very soon see something of its progress toward its goal. People have been lied to or told fairy tales far too often and far too long. But that *moving toward* socialism's egalitarian goals can be accomplished. Unlike with psychoanalysis, things do not have to get worse before they get better. Important changes could be made immediately, so that the plight of the worst-off 800 million people in the world would not be so terrible. That can be done, and done, as we have seen, without the wealthier parts of the world impoverishing themselves or even seriously inconveniencing themselves. It would give people hope who now have no hope and it would start us – and with a vivid sense of a start – on the long march to an egalitarian society, where we would no longer feel it is indecent to say, because it is at best so empty and at worst so hypocritical, that people have equal moral standing.

Notes

1. Nielsen, "Ideal and Non-Ideal Theory," 33–41.

2. Nielsen: "On the Need to Politicise Political Morality"; "Global Justice and the Imperatives of Capitalism," 608–10; "Global Justice, Power, and the Logic of Capitalism"; "Global Justice, Capitalism, and the Third World"; "Ideal and Non-Ideal Theory"; "Survival and 'the Ecological Hypothesis'"; "World Government, Security, and Global Justice."

3. You, Jones, and Wardlaw, "Levels & Trends in Child Mortality: Report 2011." This figure represents progress from 1990 when approximately 35,000 children under five died from preventable causes.

4. Hardin, "Lifeboat Ethics." But see, for contrast, O'Neill, "Lifeboat Earth," 262–68.

5. SIPRI Military Expenditure Database.

6. O'Neill, "Justice, Gender, and International Boundaries"; Pogge, "An Egalitarian Law of Peoples."

7. Nielsen, "Global Justice and the Imperatives of Capitalism."

8. Rorty, "Who Are We? Moral Universals and Economic Triage," 20–21.
9. Ibid.
10. Hardin, "Lifeboat Ethics," 7; J. Fletcher, "Give If It Helps but Not If It Hurts."
11. Rorty, "Who Are We? Moral Universals and Economic Triage," 13.
12. Friedmann, "The Political Economy of Food."
13. Shue, "The Burdens of Justice."
14. Pogge, "The Bounds of Nationalism."
15. Friedmann, "The Political Economy of Food," 16.
16. Ibid.
17. Ibid.
18. *Le Monde*, April 23, 1996.
19. Sen, *Poverty and Famines*.
20. Friedmann, "The Political Economy of Food," 16.
21. Ramonet, "Régimes globalitaires," 1.
22. Friedmann, "The Political Economy of Food," 16.
23. Hardin, "Lifeboat Ethics," 7.
24. Friedmann, "The Political Economy of Food," 16.
25. *Manchester Guardian Weekly*, November 17, 1996, 14.
26. The State of Food Insecurity in the World Reports from 1999–2011 are available at http://www.fao.org/publications/sofi/en/
27. Friedmann, "The Political Economy of Food," 16.
28. Singer, *Practical Ethics*, 157–59.
29. Sen, *Poverty and Famines*.
30. Hardin, "Lifeboat Ethics," 14.
31. See my discussion of Hans Magnus Enzensberger's important contribution in "Survival and 'the Ecological Hypothesis.'"
32. Roemer, *Egalitarian Perspectives*, 292–98.
33. Arrighi, *The Long Twentieth Century*; Hobsbawm, *Age of Extremes*.
34. Berlin, *Historical Inevitability*.
35. Nielsen, "Analytical Marxism."
36. Levine, "What is a Marxist Today?"; Nielsen, "Analytical Marxism."
37. Roemer, *A Future for Socialism*; Schweickart, *Against Capitalism*.
38. Elliott, "Balance-sheets and Blueprints," 42.
39. Ibid.
40. Roemer, *A Future for Socialism*, 126.
41. I owe something like this to Jay Drydyk, though I am not holding him to just how I put it.
42. Ramonet, "Régimes globalitaires," 1.
43. Deutscher, *On Socialist Man*.
44. Roemer, *Egalitarian Perspectives*, 322.

11

Liberal Nationalism, Liberal Democracies, and Secession

I

I want to explicate and defend the right of nations to some form of substantial political self-governance. This entails the right in certain circumstances of nations to secession. I shall further argue that we should be more permissive about this than many theoreticians are prepared to acknowledge (among them prominently Allen Buchanan).[1] The *presumptive* right – a right as a matter of political morality – to secession of a nation, where the majority of its citizens clearly express their preference for it, should generally be taken to be unproblematic. *Pace* Buchanan, the burden of proof should be to show that, in some particular circumstance or type of circumstance, this right (being defeasible as all rights are) should be overridden. There is, that is, a presumptive moral right of a nation to secede from a larger multination state or centralized state, should the majority of the members of that nation wish to do so. The burden of proof is not to *establish* that the right to secede is a general standing right, but, on the contrary, against this right to secede, that, for a particular case or range of cases, that this right can be justifiably overridden. That is what in any case must be established, and that is where the burden of proof is. Or so I shall argue.

My argument is that this is the attitude to be taken in liberal democracies, particularly when both the remainder nations and the seceding nations are liberal democracies. In liberal democracies the right of a people to political self-governance, including the right to secession, is so deeply embedded that it cannot be easily overridden. Indeed the case for overriding it would have to be very strong. The step to secession, of course, should not be taken lightly, but a presumptive right to secession on the part of a people should always be acknowledged in a liberal democratic society. Such an acknowledgment is clearly tied to what it is to have a respect for democracy and (*pace* Buchanan) to the egalitarian belief in an equal respect for persons and for autonomy.

I proceed by first setting out my conception of a nation, of nationality, and of liberal nationalism and why I believe that cultural-national membership is of deep significance to individuals in modern industrial societies and how this justifies their establishing some form of political self-governance for nations in such societies even when to do so involves the secession from a state, even a state that is not oppressive. Having set out my case I shall critically examine the powerful case made by Allen Buchanan that there should be no such strong presumption of the right to secession.

II

I shall limit myself to what should be said concerning the liberal democracies of the rich capitalist countries and whatever successor socialist liberal democracies that we might in time come to have. I do this not because I think these are the only societies worth talking about. That would be absurd. I do it because our thinking about nationalism, its justifiability or lack thereof, and of secession should be significantly different when we are talking about such societies than when we are talking about the nations of the former Soviet Union, the former Yugoslavia, or of much of Africa and the Indian subcontinent where often the nationalisms in question are what Carol Prager has aptly called "barbarous nationalisms."[2] Our thinking should be much more contextual than it usually is. There are nationalisms and nationalisms. We must be very cautious about grand-scale generalizations. We should like to have, of course, if such can be had, an account ("theory" may be too grand a word) that we could generalize to cover the whole world. But we need more humble beginnings. There is enough for a particular occasion to be sorted out if we just stick to the rich liberal capitalist democracies. I shall resolutely so restrict myself.

III

There are myriads of definitions or characterizations of "nation" and, for "nation," its not being the name of a natural kind. There is no such thing as there being the correct definition of "nation." But some definitions are more perspicuous and more useful than others. David Miller and Allen Buchanan give closely related conceptualizations (characterizations) that well bring out what a nation is. Miller takes a nation to be "a group of people who recognize one another as belonging to the same community, who acknowledge special obligations to one another, and who aspire to political autonomy – this by virtue of characteristics they believe they share, typically a common history, attachment to a geographical place, and a public culture that differentiates them from their neighbours."[3] Buchanan relatedly, but less fully, characterizes nations as "encompassing cultural groups that associate themselves with a homeland, and in which there is a substantial (though not necessarily unanimous) aspiration for self-government of some kind (though not necessarily for independent statehood)."[4]

Both authors stress the importance of a common culture. Miller speaks of a public culture and Buchanan of an encompassing culture and other authors with related characterizations of nation speak of an organizational culture, a societal culture, or a comprehensive culture. They are all gesturing in the same direction. Often, though not invariably, that encompassing culture carries with it a distinctive language, and, where it does, that language becomes very important to that nation. This is plainly true for the Catalonian, Quebec, and Flemish nations. But a distinctive encompassing or comprehensive culture is essential here, and, as well, for a group to constitute a nation, people in that group must generally have a sense of a common history and an historical attachment to a particular territory which they see as, though sometimes only in aspiration, their homeland in which they will practice some form of political self-governance. There must also be a mutual recognition between the members of a nation of their common membership and a recognition that they owe special obligations to each other that they do not owe to others. The members of any nation will aspire *in some way* to control a portion of the earth's surface. This makes the very idea of a nation, as distinct from some other cultural groups (an ethnic group, for example, made up of immigrants to a country) *inherently* political. They wish to be *maîtres chez nous*, to have political autonomy and some form of self-government. Again that distinguishes a nation from an ethnic group or even a national minority not in search of nationhood. In Quebec, for example, ethnic groups are the various allophone minorities while the national minority is the historically based Anglophone minority.[5]

I spoke above of "in some way" controlling a portion of the earth's surface or of having "some form of self-government" because, given the extensive mix in many places of different peoples on the same territory – often different peoples long resident in the same territory – there are more nations than there are feasible nation-states and for some nations, the Samaritans, the Lapps, the Faeroese – and *perhaps*, as well, for the Kurds, the Welsh, the Catalonians, and the Basques – their nations are too small or too scattered to be viable states. The First Nations in Canada, Quebec, and the United States are very good examples of nations that, while they can and should have some form of self-governance, are arguably too small and too vulnerable to form states. They are plainly nations, but they are either too intermingled with other peoples on the same territory or are too small or too poor or too much without infrastructures to form viable states. But there are weaker forms of self-government short of statehood that could, and indeed should, be theirs.

So nations are inherently political *and* inherently cultural. The nationalism of a nation will give force to both of those aspirations. And these features will mark them off from other groups. Liberals, socialists, and communists, for example, will cut across cultures and across nations. And ethnic groups of immigrants living in a state will normally not aspire to a homeland or to a political community of their own. As immigrants they will seek to adapt to, and in some considerable measure adopt, the public (encompassing or integrating) culture of the country to which they have immigrated. For them the issue is not to form a political community, to say nothing of seceding from the state to which they have immigrated. For them a crucial *desideratum* is to integrate successfully into their new adopted homeland while still preserving something of their ethnic identity.[6] Only if they are for a long time oppressed will they sometimes move, if they are there in sufficient numbers, from being simply an ethnic group to becoming a nation seeking political autonomy. In such a circumstance they *become* a nation for they already have a common culture – a culture which is becoming ghettoized and marginalized in the society to which they have immigrated. More typically, as we go down a generation or two, their culture will gradually wither away to be remembered only occasionally with nostalgia.[7]

National minorities are distinct from both nations and ethnic groups. Like nations they are historically rooted in a state. They are groups, not seeking self-governance, whose historic homeland has been incorporated into a larger state through conquest, colonization, or voluntary federation or they are groups just living, and for a long time, on a territory bordering on or close to the territory of a neighbouring nation or state whose culture they share – for example, Anglophones in Quebec in relation to English-speaking Canada or Francophones in Ontario in relation to Quebec. Indeed, to be a national minority they must be a people living on the territory of another nation while sharing the comprehensive culture of a distinct nation adjacent to or at least close to the territory they inhabit. Moreover, they must be historical peoples, that is peoples who have been there for a long time. But unlike a nation they do not seek political autonomy; they do not seek a form of self-government. They do not see themselves as constituting a political community but seek to insure that their rights are protected and their common culture preserved and respected in the political community of which they are a part. The Lapps in Norway and Sweden are a good example, as are the Swedish-speaking Finns in Finland, the German-speaking Alsatians in France, the German-speaking minorities in the south of Denmark, the Danish-speaking minorities in Flensburg and its surroundings, and the Tyroleans in Italy.

Sometimes the borderline between national minorities and aspiring nations is fragile as the struggles of Tyroleans in the first two decades after the end of the Second World War well illustrate. Still the distinction is an important one to make. In, for example, a sovereign Quebec, the First Nations would remain nations and the immigrants ethnic groups, but the historically rooted Anglophone community would plainly become, what they have always been if we just consider Quebec, a national minority with the distinctive rights of a national minority.[8] They would have rights that ethnic groups would not have, but also, as a national minority, they, without aspirations to nationhood, would not have rights to some form of self-government as, by contrast, the First Nations do. The same thing would obtain for the francophone minorities in the rest of Canada; they are national minorities in Canada in a way the Poles, Germans, and Italians are not. Similarly, the Anglophone minority in a sovereign Quebec would become a national minority while the immigrant groups would not.

IV

I am now in a position to specify what is distinctive about liberal nationalism, principally, but not exclusively, by contrasting it with ethnic nationalism.[9] All nationalisms – liberal nationalisms, ethnic nationalisms, and authoritarian non-ethnic nationalisms (e.g., Argentina, Brazil, Chile, and Spain under their dictatorships) – are cultural *and* political nationalisms. Those things just go with being nationalisms *of any kind*. (A *purely* "civic nationalism" is an oxymoron.) But pressing for the protection of their distinctive cultural institutions, including, where they have a distinct language, their language, does not turn a nationalism into an ethnic nationalism and, as well, seeking to form a state or some other form of political community to work to preserve and enhance their national and cultural identity does not make such nationalists into ethnic nationalists or make them chauvinistic. An ethnic nationalism will be rooted in an ethnic conception of the nation where membership in the nation and citizenship in a state will be rooted in descent. What determines membership or citizenship in an ethnic nation is who your ancestors were, not the language you speak, your cultural attunements, your conception of yourself, where you live or what your loyalties are. This nationalism is exclusionist, xenophobic, backward looking, and deeply anti-liberal. Where it, in some modified form, persists in some otherwise liberal states, for example, Germany, it is an anachronism firmly to be condemned as running against what liberalism and democracy are all about. Where nationalism is rightly despised and condemned, it is either this nationalism or the sometimes jingoistic, non-ethnic nationalism of some authoritarian states (e.g., Chile under Pinochet and Spain under Franco). But liberal nationalism, while remaining cultural and political as all nationalisms are, is none of these things. It is a nationalism which is non-exclusionist. Citizenship is open to anyone, with a landed immigrant status within the territories of these liberal democracies, and immigration is at least reasonably open and is certainly not based on ethnic, racial, or religious grounds. It is, that is, quite independent of descent, race, and ethnic background. Anyone who wishes to have full citizenship and be a part of the nation may, at least in principle, do so if they learn its language, history, and customs, swear allegiance to it, and are willing to abide by its laws.[10] Perhaps in certain difficult circumstances they will have to meet certain educational or other work skill requirements as well. But that is a pragmatic matter determined by hard economic necessities or, in some instances, by questions of space. Still such restrictions in a liberal society, where it is functioning properly as a liberal society, can never be racial, ethnic, or religious. Membership, with the recognition that goes with it, is defined in terms of participation in a common culture, in principle at least open to all, rather than on ethnic grounds. Both the Québécois and the Flemish stress open access to their nations, and they protect the historic rights of their national minorities to have schools, hospitals, and other public services in their languages and the right to use this language in Parliament.

Where a nationalist movement prevails in a *liberal* democratic society, the state will, as will any state, in certain respects privilege the encompassing culture of the nation. But, it will only do so in ways that will at the same time protect the rights of its minorities and indeed protect rights across the board. A central aim of a nationalist movement in a liberal democracy, as well as everywhere else, is to protect, and beyond that, if it can, to insure the flourishing of the culture of the nation that that nationalist movement represents. But, if it is a liberal nationalism, it will not seek to stamp out, or otherwise repress, other cultures and will actively work to preserve the culture and cultural institutions of the First Nations in its midst and of its national minorities. But it will also insist that there be a common cultural currency across the society; it will insist that that common currency (that public culture) be learned by all the children in the society, *perhaps* very isolated native peoples apart. The children will learn the official language of that culture, or if (as in the United States) there is no official language the dominant language, as well as some reasonable bits of its history and customs and come to have some knowledge of its political system and laws. There will, through its educational system, be this form of socialization. This is what a nation-state must do to preserve itself and to keep the society from becoming a Tower of Babel – to keep it, that is, from dissolving as a society.

A liberalism that in the name of state neutrality gained such a neutrality would undermine any form of socialization. It would, if *per impossible* successful, make any kind of society at all impossible. But this socialization, into a culture, some form of which is inevitable, will not – indeed cannot if the state is a liberal democracy – be at the expense of minority rights and cannot turn either the people of its First Nations, its national minorities, or its immigrant citizens into second-class citizens. It cannot do those things and remain a liberal democracy. Its failure here, if that obtains, is a measure of its failure as a liberal democracy.

There is one further thing that needs to be said about a liberal nationalism before I turn to my argument for a general right of secession for such nations, unencumbered by the strong restrictions that Buchanan would place on it. It is not only necessary that a liberal nationalism not be an ethnic nationalism; it must be a reiterated, generalizable nationalism and not a nationalism of the manifest destiny of a chosen people who can run roughshod over other peoples in terms of its allegedly privileged place in history as being the wisest and the best. It must not only be non-exclusionist; it must, as well, not be chauvinist. There can be no favoured *Volk*, no single people destined to have a pre-eminent place in the sun, while the rest are judged, in one degree or another, to be inferior and are placed, if such a chauvinist nationalism can have its way, in a subordinate position. (The nationalism of the white settlers in the former Rhodesia described so graphically by Doris Lessing is a paradigm case.) Rather than a nationalism for God's chosen people, a liberal nationalism will be a *reiterated* nationalism which claims that *all* nations have a right to some form of self-government and the right, and indeed the same right, when certain generalizable conditions prevail, to justifiably secede from the state in which the nation exists in a multination state or in a centralized state which denies its multinational character and in which one nation dominates the other nation or nations in the society. A just social order will be a social order where all peoples – all nations and all national minorities – will have institutions that protect their culture and which will enhance and protect their national and cultural identities.

V

However, this just assumes that the preservation and enhancement of a national-cultural identity, which is also a conception fitting in with a liberal democracy, is something of great importance to human beings. But why should a liberal democracy or people in a liberal democracy care about preserving such an identity? Indeed should they care about preserving their cultural identities? Why not just think in terms of individuals and in terms of what would maximize their secure flourishing, including a commitment to equal respect for all people and, as well, to what would strengthen their self respect? What, as Buchanan asks, is so special about nations and having a robust sense of national identity? Why not, as Andrew Levine and Harry Brighouse ask as well, just be cosmopolitans without any attention to such particularisms?[11]

First a red herring needs to be disposed of. Cosmopolitanism and a caring about a more local identity (something that makes one a member of a particular and, for one, a cherished community) need not at all stand in conflict. One, for example, can be proud of being an Icelander and be very much committed to one's homeland, its traditions, and distinctive culture and be committed to working to see it flourish without being at all chauvinistic about it, thinking that "the Icelanders are the best." One can have such warm feelings about one's nation while also having cosmopolitan interests and commitments. There is, for many people, perhaps for most people, a place where one feels most at home, a place that one longs for after a long absence, and there is, in that particular culture, for many people, a reasonably definite answer to the question, 'Who am I?'[12] But that is perfectly compatible with valuing others without feeling that their traditions are inferior to one's own and with taking an active interest in what goes on in the world. (Moreover, *pace* Martha Nussbaum, it is psychologically impossible at least for most of us to be "free-floating cosmopolitans" with no roots in a particular culture.)[13] If we are to be focused at all we must have roots in a particular culture. To the extent that we get so extensively detached from those roots that we have no attachment to a people or a place, most of us at least will in one way or another suffer psychologically. But we should also not be ethnocentric, cooped up in our particular culture; we should both be cosmopolitans and have particular attachments. We should, that is, be cosmopolitans but *rooted* cosmopolitans.[14]

If we are not to be alienated and disconnected from our cultural environment, we not only need to develop our powers but to have an understanding of who we are. Self-definition is an indispensable condition for human flourishing.[15] But self-definition involves, though it, of course, involves much more than this, seeing ourselves as New Zealanders, Dutch, Irish, Ghanaians, Canadians, or whatever. Or at least this sense of national identity has come into being with the establishment of industrial societies.[16] And, in all societies that we know anything about, group identity is important. It is plausible to regard national identity as a form of group identity appropriate to, and functional for, modern industrial societies.

When a Dane, for example, meets a fellow Dane abroad, there is normally a spontaneous recognition of a common membership in a nation which is not the same as when she meets, for example, a Chilean; though, if she is a liberal democrat, as she is very likely to be given her cultural attunements, equal respect will go to the Chilean and, if she is reflective, she will take an interest in the different life experiences, conceptions of things, and cultural attunements of people with nationalities different than her own. But normally there will be a sense of at-homeness and an affinity with her fellow Danes that is rooted in their having a common culture: the songs they sing, the structure of jokes, the memories of places, a sense of a common history, literary references, political experiences, and the having of all kinds of common forms of intimate ways of living.[17]

Isaiah Berlin has made vivid for us Johann Gottfried Herder's eighteenth-century resistance to Enlightenment *rationalism*.[18] People will suffer and will not flourish where they do not have a secure social identity. Among our very deep needs is the need to belong to a group; to be, that is, a member of some community. But this means, Herder argues, an attachment to local identities and not *just* to humanity in general. But these *Gemeinschaften* are all distinct with their own characteristic shapes and patterns. The members of these communities are formed into a stream of tradition which deeply forms who they are and what they are like both emotionally and intellectually. Berlin puts Herder's conception as follows:

> Human customs, activities, forms of life, art, ideas, were (and must be) of value to men, not in terms of timeless criteria, applicable to all men and societies, irrespective of time and place ... but because they were their own expressions of their local, regional, national life, and spoke to them as they could speak to no other human group.[19]

Since this is the way almost all human beings are, national identity (the form that group identity or social identity takes under conditions of modernity) is vital for human beings in such conditions. Where it is at risk, even with benign intentions, including benign neglect, it is reasonable for people to struggle to preserve it. They are justified in claiming a right to the sustaining of their national identity. Where it is threatened, a people have the right – though, again, as always, a defeasible right – to take steps to preserve it, even if this means secession, so long as they do not violate the rights of others in doing so and so long as they do not cause more suffering and misery all around by doing so – taking into consideration, and equally, people in both the seceding country and in the remainder country. This is both consequentialist and Rawlsian. It looks to the consequences both negative and positive, but the interests of *everyone* and *equally* must be considered as well.[20]

Nations, to summarize, are encompassing cultures associated with a particular territory where there is an aspiration on the part of at least a majority of the members of such encompassing cultures for a homeland and to some form of political self-governance in that homeland. Encompassing cultural groups are cultures which pervade the whole range of an individual's major life activities and which function as an indispensable source of self-identification and self-definition. Moreover, the very existence of such a culture requires social structures and a complex cluster of interdependent institutions. Without this being in place in the lives of human beings, there can be no secure and stable sense of who they are, and, without that, there will be little in the way of human flourishing. Instead people will experience anomie and alienation. These encompassing cultures – these nations – will have a fragile and insecure existence if they do not have a substantial degree of self-government. Moreover, in industrial societies such as our own – the rich constitutional capitalist democracies – such a nation will be most secure when it either has a sovereign state of its own or, as a component nation in a multination state, it is an equal partner in such a state with the other nations. To achieve that may require it to secede from a pseudo-multination state (a state where the component nations are not equal partners) or from some severely centralized state of which it is a part. In a liberal democracy there is a *presumption* that every nation has a right to one or other of these two state forms. This is a *presumption* which is always defeasible and not infrequently defeated. I have discussed some of the considerations that could justify its defeat in particular situations, and I will return to this when I consider Buchanan's critique of such a claimed general right. But in arguing for the right of a nation to such state forms I am not (*pace* Hegel) assuming that states are loveable institutions. They are not. I no more assume this than did Herder who was, unlike Hegel, thoroughly anti-statist. But that unloveableness notwithstanding, we can see from what has been said above that for people to have such a nation-state or multination state is to have something which makes a very deep link with what is required (instrumentally required) to give sense to their lives. When, as sometimes must be the case, their nation, and for good reasons, cannot have a state of its own, there is, as a result, unless it is a secure nation in a genuinely multination state showing equal respect for its component nations, more fragility and anomie in their lives. Their being able to sustain a stable sense of social identity in such a circumstance is more at risk. This is why in liberal democracies – where human rights are protected and there is a general egalitarian ambience – I attach this strong form of political recognition to nations with the hope that circumstances will make it possible, without denying the conditions of a liberal social order, for nations either to have nation-states of their own or to be a component nation in a genuine multination state. It must be a *genuine* multination state and not a pseudo one as are many so-called multination states. There must be an equal respect and equal authority between their different nations and they must all have an unequivocal and clear measure of self-governance and this right to self-government of each component nation must be a matter of mutual acknowledgment between the component nations of the multination state.

VI

Buchanan believes that *sometimes* nations have a right to secede. But his view of when this is so is much more restrictive than my own. He articulates and defends a particular version of what he calls a Remedial Right Only Theory of Secession.[21] For Buchanan, a group has the right to secede only if:

(1.) The physical survival of its members is threatened by actions of the state (as with the policy of the Iraqi government toward Kurds in Iraq) or if it suffers violations of other basic human rights (as with the East Pakistanis who seceded to create Bangladesh in 1970); or

(2.) Its previously sovereign territory was unjustly taken by the state (as with the Baltic Republics).[22]

It must also be the case for the group to have the right to secede "that there be credible guarantees that the new state will respect the human rights of all of its citizens and that it will cooperate in the project of securing other just terms of secession."[23] This includes a fair division of federal properties in the old state, a fair apportioning of the national debt, a negotiated determination of new boundaries, agreed on arrangements for continuing, renegotiating, or terminating treaty obligations and provisions for defence and security.[24] In his classification of types of theories of secession, my account, as distinct from his Remedial Right Only theory, is a variant of a Primary Right theory. It is an account which, as he rightly says, claims that a group constituting a nation "can have a (general) right to secede even if it suffers no injustices, and hence it may have a (general) right to secede from a perfectly just state."[25] Here "just" must be construed in a thoroughly uncontroversial and thus minimal sense, accepted by both theories, that is, in not violating uncontroversial individual moral rights and not engaging in "uncontroversially discriminatory policies toward minorities."[26] My account, as we have seen, also accepts the last set of conditions for the right to secede, for example, credible guarantees that human rights will be respected, boundaries negotiated, a fair division of the national debt made, and the like. I would further add, where after protracted negotiations the seceding state and the remainder state cannot agree about borders and the fair distribution of the national debt or of federal properties and the like, the dispute should be settled in binding arbitration by an international tribunal. It is here (though I do not say only here) where international law is very important. But my account differs from Buchanan's Remedial Right Only theory concerning his first two conditions. It need not be, on my account, that the physical survival of a nation is threatened. It may instead be the case that (1) only its cultural survival is threatened (say, the loss of its language) either as a matter of deliberate policy on the part of the government of the state in which it is embedded or in effect by actions by the larger state not intended to have these threatening effects but which have them all the same; and (2) that, even though it is clearly expressed (as, say, in a referendum), the democratic will of the majority of the people of the nation desiring to secede is not respected by the state where secession is an issue. If either of these things obtain, then the state opposing the secession acts wrongly even though it had not previously acted unjustly. In such a circumstance the seceding state has the right to secede, though always with the proviso that it does not violate the human rights or the civil rights of any of its citizens.

There is here, I argue (*pace* Buchanan), also a *general* right to secede that his account does not acknowledge. Unless we take it, as we well might (but note this would be controversial), that the potential remainder state, in refusing to accept secession under the above conditions, thereby acts unjustly, the seceding nation need not, if we do not accept this, in any of the less controversial and non-question-begging ways, have been treated unjustly by the remainder state. Put more simply but somewhat less accurately, the nation that would secede to form a state of its own need not have, prior to that time, been treated unjustly in the state in which it abides. It is enough on my account that its culture is threatened, though not necessarily by any deliberately repressive actions on the part of the state, such as repression of its language, for example, the historic treatment of the Welsh, Scots, and Irish by the English. The remainder state need not have in any way acted badly to the seceding state for its culture to be threatened. Or even without that, it may be just that the majority of the people of the nation want to secede and vote to secede. Either is sufficient on my account (but not on Buchanan's) to justify secession – provided the human rights of all people in the territory in question are protected. The option for secession may just be an expression, in a properly democratic manner, of a nation's preferences.

I would indeed bite what Buchanan regards as the bullet and "go so far as to recognize a *right* to secede even under conditions in which the state is effectively, indeed flawlessly, performing all of what are usually taken to be the *legitimating functions* of the state."[27] That a nation *has* such a right does not, of course, mean or entail that in such circumstances it should *exercise* that right or even that in all instances it is reasonable to do so. I have the right to run for mayor in Montreal, and it is important that I have that right, but I shall never do so. A people will not in fact secede without reason. So it is unlikely that it will secede from a flawlessly just state. But it is important in a democratic ethos that it have the right to do so. So my view is very much more permissive than Buchanan's.

Buchanan thinks such a permissive view is both dangerous and absurd – being in a very bad sense utopian. I think *au contraire* that it is entailed by a firm and clear commitment to the right, in a democratic society, of a people to be self-governed. That is something which is very central to democracy. The difference between us can be narrowed a bit by noting that Buchanan is giving a general theory of secession for all societies – democratic and undemocratic, liberal and illiberal – while I am only talking about the conditions under which secession is justified when the contending groups are both firmly and resolutely a part of liberal democratic societies and are committed to its values.

Consider in this context Buchanan's Minimal Realist argument for preferring Remedial Right Only theories to Primary Right theories. The former, as he puts it, "places significant constraints on the right to secede, while not ruling out secession *entirely*. No group has a (general) right to secede unless that group suffers what are uncontroversially regarded as injustices and has no reasonable prospect of relief short of secession."[28] Why accept such a very restrictive view that, Buchanan's intentions to the contrary notwithstanding, would *seem* at least to wed us to the *status quo*? Buchanan's reasons are realistic *realpolitik* ones. The majority of secessions, he reminds us, "have resulted in considerable violence, with attendant large-scale violations of human rights and massive destruction of resources."[29] Given this experience we should move in the direction of secession with caution and reluctance. There is another realistic reason as well. When a national minority in a state forges itself into a nation and secedes, this will often, indeed typically, result in a new national minority within the new state. "All too often," as he puts it, "the formerly persecuted become the persecutors."[30] Moreover, frequently "not all members of the seceding group lie within the seceding area, and the result is that those who do not become an even smaller minority and hence even more vulnerable to the discrimination and persecution that fuelled the drive for secession in the first place."[31]

However, it is just here that the restriction in scope concerning arguments for secession is crucial. I only argued about what should be said about secessionist movements in secure liberal democratic societies where all significant segments of the population, including the secessionists, are firmly committed to liberal democratic values. There, secession or not, the "considerable violence," "large-scale violations of human rights," and "destruction of resources" cannot obtain, nor could there be, so long as the liberal state is functioning as a liberal state should, persecution of or discrimination against minority groups new or old, large or small. These things are incompatible with the *very idea of liberal democracy*. And suffering from such injustices need not be the motive for secession in such societies. Without being persecuted, they may wish to secure the protection of their culture or just to be *maîtres chez nous*. A society or cluster of societies, even in the severe strains of conflict over secession, cannot, if they are liberal democratic societies with both sides being committed to such values, engage in wide-ranging violence (indeed even in any violence) or in massive violations of human rights, destruction of resources, persecution, or discrimination. This, if you will, is true by definition. Liberal democrats could not behave in this way and remain liberal democrats. So we lovers of democracy need not, and should not, have such a restrictive theory of secession for *such societies*, a theory which makes, if the recipe is followed, secession very difficult.

Buchanan could reply that I am engaging in a conventionalist's sulk by appealing to what is in effect an absurd ideal theory distant from the real world. It isn't what is entailed by the very idea of a liberal democracy that counts, but what happens in the real world of liberal democracies: the actually existing liberal democracies. But even there, the clash in Northern Ireland deeply involving England aside, liberal democracies have behaved in a manner that conforms rather closely, but not perfectly, to what the very idea of a liberal democracy requires. Consider Norway seceding from

Sweden, Iceland from Denmark, the division (the wisdom of it aside) of Czechoslovakia, the division of Belgium, the devolution of Scotland and Wales. Tensions were (and, where the struggle is still ongoing, are) high and rhetoric and propaganda flowed (or flows, as the case may be) freely, but there was (is) little or no violence, persecution, or human rights violations and certainly no massive destruction of resources. Moreover, as things calmed (calm) down, relationships of reasonable cooperation came (will come) into being. Sweden massed troops on the Norwegian border in 1905. But fortunately sanity prevailed and they did not invade. Now the two countries are good friends living in close cooperative arrangements. There neither was nor will there be with secession in genuine liberal democracies any undermining of the liberal social order or tearing apart of the liberal social fabric. There was in the above previous secessions arguably even a strengthening of it.

The relationships between Ireland and Britain and Spain and the Basques, however, do not fit this model. But with the latter it is not clear that we have stable liberal democracies with the traditions that go with them. And in the case of the struggle in Northern Ireland, it is not at all clear that all the major players are committed to *liberal* democracy. There is indeed a Protestant majority in Northern Ireland, but what is not at all clear is that the Ulster Unionists are committed to *liberal* democracy and the same could be said for some of their adversaries. But, even if we take these to be cases of liberal democracies, though still with old and severe ethnic enmities, slipping into violence and fanaticism in the course of struggles for independence, it remains the case that secessions have peacefully taken place in societies where all the contending forces were more firmly liberal democratic than the ones slipping into violence. There – and they are the more common case in liberal democracies – none of the ill effects predicted by Buchanan followed during or in the wake of secession.

Of course, the existing states in the UN and in the international law establishment will stick together to seek to sustain the idea of the territorial integrity of states, i.e., of the existing states. They are pretty much, in this respect, like an old boys club. And, of course, we do not want a circus of anarchy, but, as a matter of historical fact, states come and go and it is not such a terrible thing if changes occur, particularly if the societies in question are liberal democratic ones with very distinct nations harnessed together rather artificially, and where the flourishing of these nations, or at least the smaller nations, within the umbrella state, could be enhanced by separation and no great harm would accrue to the remainder state by separation. A state should not, and indeed in most instances will not, break up without good reason. And when it does break up, there will always be some dislocation and not all the after-effects will be good. But some of them will be very good indeed. A nation or a people – which before had been treated as a national minority or worse still like an ethnic group – can now be in control of its own destiny as much (and as little) as any nation-state or nation within a genuine multination can be in the modern world.[32] States come and go, and sometimes they break up, perhaps without the conditions that Remedial Right Only theories could sanction obtaining, with no great harm resulting, and arguably sometimes with considerable gain, for example, Iceland from Denmark and Norway from Sweden. If Quebec should secede from Canada, Scotland from Britain, and Wales from Britain, their thoroughly liberal democratic environments staying intact, it is anything but evident that that would not give more people more control over their lives and a fuller self-realization than the continuing of the *status quo*. Moreover, this could obtain without harming others in the remainder state or the minorities in the new state. Quite possibly more good would obtain all around. At the very minimum, this idea should not be rejected out of hand. Perhaps in some of these cases – the case of Wales, for example – it would not be practically feasible. Here we should go case by case. We need careful contextual moral reflection together with a scrupulous empirical examination of the facts of the case. But there is no case at all for the rejection of the putative right to secession on high moral or legal principle. At the very least, none of the dire results that Buchanan believes must just go with secession seem at all to be in the cards in such cases. It looks at least like it is better to go in the more permissive direction of what Buchanan calls Primary Right theories than in the direction of Remedial Right Only theories.

Buchanan could respond that what I have said unfairly makes his account sound more statist and authoritarian than it actually is. Remedial Right Only theories, on his account, "hold that a general right to secession exists only where the group in question has suffered injustices" – things that plainly and uncontroversially have been taken to be injustices.[33] But, Buchanan insists, the qualification "*general*" is critical here. Remedial Right

Only theory allows that there can be *special* rights to secede if the state from which a distinct nation would secede *grants* it the right to secede or if the constitution of the state includes a right to secede or if "the agreement by which the state was initially created out of previously independent political units included the implicit or explicit assumption that secession at a later point was permissible."[34] But this seems to me only marginally less restrictive than a Remedial Right Only theory would be without such riders. It does not give a people even nearly a strong enough right to self-determination – a right that a liberal democratic society, fully respecting individual autonomy and the right of a people to govern themselves, would want to see instituted. For it is still, on Buchanan's account, the constitution or the authoritative will of the government of the state from which a people as a subunit wish to secede or prior political arrangements of that state which determines whether the nation (the subunit) which wishes to secede can legitimately secede. It is not sufficient, on his account, for secession to be legitimate that (1) a people be genuinely a people (that is, a nation in the sense that Buchanan has defined and I have accepted); (2) in a fair democratic vote (as in a referendum with the issue clearly stated), a majority of its members vote for secession; (3) various civic guarantees such as protection of minority rights be firmly in place; and (4) there to be a negotiated settlement on borders, on the division of the national debt, and on joint assets and the like. These are *necessary* conditions for justified secession, and over them Buchanan and I are in agreement. But Buchanan wants *additional conditions* as well. On Buchanan's account, unless a state is flagrantly violating human rights, the political arrangements of the state from which a nation wishes to secede call the tune. That state, unless it is really a rogue state, ultimately determines what can legitimately be done. In that respect his account is statist and authoritarian and very conservative. That a nation can legitimately secede from it is a matter of *noblesse oblige* on the part of that state. But this runs too strongly against very deep considered judgments about democracy and the self-determination of peoples to be acceptable in a liberal democracy where everyone can be expected to play by the democratic rules of the game, for example, no repression, violation of human rights, persecution, negotiating in bad faith, and the like.

    Buchanan, I am confident, would continue to resist by claiming that my account is too utopian and does not meet the conditions of *minimal realism* that any even nearly adequate substantive normative political account must meet. "Primary Right theories," he has remarked, "are not likely to be adopted by the makers of international law because they authorize the dismemberment of states even when those states are perfectly performing what are generally recognized as the legitimating functions of states."[35] Because of this, Buchanan has it, Primary Right theories "represent a direct and profound threat to the territorial integrity of states – even just states."[36] Because states "have a *morally legitimate* interest in maintaining their territorial integrity," they should oppose Primary Right theory.[37]

I grant that liberal democratic states, including (when they come on stream) socialist liberal democratic states, have a morally legitimate interest in maintaining their territorial integrity. But I would certainly not generalize that to all states. The territorial integrity of Indonesia or Burma is not something to which we should give high priority. Moreover, I think that Buchanan exaggerates when he says that Primary Right theory represents a direct and profound threat to the territorial integrity of states. *Theories* seldom have such causal powers. But, even if they did, in the history of societies that are liberal democratic, secessionist movements are not frequent and come into being only where the encompassing culture of a people – the very thing that continues to make them a people – is at risk and they need self-government to protect their encompassing culture. States will, of course, try, and try hard, to keep their territory intact. And they have a morally legitimate interest in doing so. But morally speaking, a people wanting to govern themselves, particularly when their very nationhood is at risk, is standardly, but not invariably, a *morally more stringent claim* than the claim to the territorial integrity of what, at least in effect, is a multination state, though typically, where secessionist struggles arise, a state in fact is not behaving as a multination state should behave, for example, treating each of the component nations with equal respect. This has typically been the case with secessions in liberal democratic societies. Transition has been, and can be expected to be, orderly, though not without bitterness and tension, in both the seceding state and the remainder state, still the generally recognized legitimating functions of the state have remained in place. A paradigmatic example is when Iceland seceded from Denmark. Protection of individuals' rights and the stability of their lives remained firmly in place in Iceland. And, after secession, no partition took place and the two nations (the Danish and the Icelandic), now both nation-states, maintained, without conflict, their respective territorial integrity. Or, more accurately, Iceland's territorial integrity and control was intact. The Icelandic nation had its homeland securely on the territory it claimed and territorial integrity returned to Denmark as well as soon as the Nazi occupiers were driven out – something that was quite independent of the issue of Iceland's secession, though many Danes understandably resented that Iceland seceded when Denmark was under occupation. But that does not substantially touch the reasonableness or justifiability of the secession. Moreover, *pace* Buchanan, the "incentive structure in which it is reasonable for individuals and groups to invest themselves in participating in the fundamental processes of government in a conscientious and co-operative fashion over time" was enhanced in the case of Iceland and not undermined in the case of Denmark.[38] And the case of Iceland and Denmark is not atypical of secession cases which have gone through the works or are in the offing in *liberal democratic societies*.

Buchanan is right in asserting that, in societies that are in the ball park of being just societies, we want the rule of law and the effective enforcement of a legal order to remain intact. But he has his sociology and history wrong. There was no such breakdown with secession in such societies, and it is not reasonable to expect it to happen if Scotland secedes from Britain or Quebec from Canada. After all Scotland/Britain and Quebec/Canada are not Serbia/Bosnia or Russia/Chechnya. Buchanan sees, wherever there is secession, the threat of anarchy, violence, and the stamping on people's rights. But here he is blinkered by a fixation on barbarous nationalisms, but there are nationalisms and nationalisms. Such violence and the like have not happened in *firmly* liberal democratic societies, and it is not plausible to think that it will happen as new cases come on stream, though sometimes some extremist and sensationalist segments of the mass media make it sound as if it might. But that is just irresponsible sensationalist rhetoric. Territorial integrity is a *desideratum*, but, in liberal democratic societies, it does not have nearly the critical weight that Buchanan and traditionally international law have assigned to it. His account, his intentions notwithstanding, has a conservative *status quo* effect.

Buchanan has a further *realpolitik* argument against accounts of secession such as my own. It is my view that, *ceteris paribus*, if a nation becomes capable of having a functioning state of its own in a territory it has historically occupied and where no other nation has a comparable claim on the same territory, then it is a potential subject of the right to secede if a majority of its members so wishes. To this Buchanan responds that that "would encourage even just states to act in ways that would prevent groups from becoming claimants to the right to secede, and this might lead to the perpetration of injustices."[39] He adds: "Clearly, any state that seeks to avoid its own dissolution would have an incentive to implement policies designed to prevent groups from becoming prosperous enough and politically well organized enough to satisfy this condition."[40] A state, he has it, is justified in so acting even if it acts only from the morally legitimate interest of preserving its own territorial integrity.[41]

If we are doing ideal normative political theory, this contention of his is plainly mistaken. Recall we are talking about secession in liberal democracies where the seceding nation and the remainder state are and will continue to be liberal democracies and in the struggle around secession both will be determined to play by liberal democracies' rules. The state from which the seceding nation is seeking to secede indeed has a morally legitimate interest in preserving its own territory but not at the expense of acting unjustly or in some other morally untoward way. A just state, as Buchanan takes it to be, particularly if it is a liberal democratic one, could not, while remaining just, so act as to perpetrate injustice by treating a group so as to deliberately prevent them from becoming prosperous or politically organized. This is to treat them in an uncontroversially morally untoward way that runs flat against that for which a liberal democracy stands. In so treating them, there would be a manipulating of people and not even in any paternalistic manner for their own good. There would be no treating its citizens as moral equals, as ends in themselves, and there would be the deliberate harming of some for *reasons of state*. In this, the reasons of state come to a preserving the state's own territorial integrity at the *expense* of some of its citizens and at the expense of liberal values, for example, autonomy and self-determination. Preserving their own territory is a morally legitimate state function, but not, in the case of a threatened peaceful and democratic secession, where to do so comes at the expense of so harming its citizens and not treating them as having equal moral standing. It also pays scant attention to the democratically determined aspirations of a nation. Such behaviour is not morally acceptable in a liberal democracy. This is particularly starkly wrong when the seceding nation would become a liberal democratic state respecting human rights and the like and where no extensive harm, or in some instances no harm at all, would result to the remainder state as a result of the secession. But this in many instances would be the case. In such situations the remainder state could not be acting rightly in so acting.

It might in turn be replied that while this may be well and good for purely ideal normative theory, it is not for a normative theory in touch with the real world. For such a normative theory, it could be claimed, Buchanan's argument remains intact. In *really existing* liberal democracies, as elsewhere, states will fiercely resist secession and will indeed play dirty pool with actual secessionist movements. And indeed the secessionist movements will respond in kind. It is arguably, though surely *controversially*, the case, that in Canada, for example, the federal government by its policies toward Quebec, has deliberately impoverished Quebec. Montreal, for example, has gone from being a thriving metropolis to being the poorest large city in Canada.[42] But that possibly *parti pris* illustrative point aside, it is very likely that actual liberal states, feeling pressured by secessionist movements, would do, or try to do, just the things Buchanan mentions. They could not, as we have seen, do them and still remain states that were not unjust in any of the uncontroversial ways that Buchanan describes. But, as we cannot expect individuals to be angels, so we cannot expect such rectitude from the people running the governments of liberal democracies either. And we must, to articulate a practical institutional morality, take such facts into consideration.

To this I have two responses. First, we still should for contexts such as this construct an ideal normative political theory – something to *model* ideally what the situation should be – in terms of what would obtain in a perfectly functioning liberal democracy. Thus, where we have a perspicuous constitution, we can clearly see, if we think carefully and take the matter to heart, what we should aim at in such an ideal world (indeed, very much a counterfactual world). With that clearly before us we can then see what accommodations we need to make to the actually existing political and social realities to get an account which here and now could guide policy while remaining the most morally adequate account available. Second, and quite differently, it is not clear that for the rich capitalist liberal democracies, the only reasonably firm democracies we have at present, that the Remedial Right Only theory would be better, or even as good, at deterring such untoward strategic behaviour on the part of such states as would the Primary Right theory. True, the Remedial Right Only theory would offer an incentive for the state to behave more justly, but, where there is a nation in its midst, being treated as a national minority, or even worse as an ethnic group, and it wishes to run its own show, there would remain, Remedial Right Only theory or not, a creditable threat of secession. This being so, the *realpolitik* incentive would remain on the part of the state to design policies to prevent those groups from becoming prosperous enough and politically well-organized enough successfully to take a road to secession. But, where secession is at all a threat to the existing state, there would have to be a sizeable number of people resident in a distinct territory with a keen sense of nationality. This comes close to being a tautology. Moreover, where the state in question is a rich liberal capitalist democracy, some of them would be well-educated and reasonably powerful. They, and others as well, would clearly see the state's actions as manipulative and repressive, and they would respond by more forcefully struggling against it. And seeing the plain injustice of such repressive measures, some people in the existing state, with another nationality, or with no sense of nationality, will come, as well, to be critical of the state's behaviour. In the real world where nations are treated merely as national minorities or just as ethnic groups, we will get struggle and strife and secessionist movements arising no matter what. We should at least know where the heart of the injustice lies. It lies – as ideal theory makes clear – in putting roadblocks on the way of a nation's right of self-determination, including secession, when, in seeking self-determination, that nation does not violate the rights of others and is committed not to treat unfairly those it is seceding from and not to discriminate against its own minorities.

Buchanan also in effect argues that a view such as mine, as any variant of a Primary Right theory, does not take the reasonable path, which has been traditionally favoured in international law, of first trying to accommodate the aspirations for autonomy of a nation by urging, and seeking to put into place, arrangements within a state for it to become a decentralized federalized state: *a genuinely multinational, but still a decentralized, state*. This way of proceeding might very well be able to protect a nation's aspirations for autonomy – remember that autonomy admits of degrees and of kinds – including the having of some form of self-governance, short of nation-state sovereignty, while still keeping the principle, so central in international law and so cherished by states, of the territorial integrity of the state.[43] Since demands for autonomy and some form of self-governance are accommodated in such an arrangement, Primary Right theorists, Buchanan contends, "cannot reply that the presumption in favour of decentralization as opposed to secession gives too much moral weight to the interest of *states* and there is no reason to prefer decentralization to secession."[44] (It is also important to recognize here that self-determination comes in many forms.)[45]

However, *if* the turn to decentralization, rather than secession, prevents nations from flourishing, and stably sustaining themselves in viable regions, then decentralized federalism is a farce: there is little in the way of a genuine self-governance there. However, if the decentralization is very deep – perhaps the cantonal system of Switzerland is an example – then the nations within such a decentralized federalized state would have a very considerable autonomy and a very considerable amount of self-determination. Then whether to go for decentralization or secession would be a real question; and sometimes a decentralized federalism, with its resultant multination state, could very well be the best option. But it would not have the obvious superiority that Buchanan thinks it has, for still, under the decentralized federation, a nation would not have as full a self-governance as it would have with outright secession. But full self-governance has its attractions, but it is also the case that extensive decentralized federation has its attractions. Perhaps between them there is not very much to choose, and *perhaps* they are not so very different, when we see clearly what they would most likely come to be among liberal democracies in an interdependent world. In making, or trying to make, judgments here, we need, as we do in most complex moral situations, to realize that we will need to make trade-offs.

In such situations we need to go very carefully case by case, attending to the details. Still, all that notwithstanding, if my previous arguments against Buchanan have even been near to the mark, namely my arguments that secession in liberal democratic societies would not produce the anarchy, instability, repression, and the weakening of the rule of law that Buchanan believes is very likely to go with secession, then it still seems that the scales are likely usually to be tipped in favour of secession. A nation, forming a nation-state, can have full self-governance – full sovereignty – while still entering into cooperative arrangements with other nation-states. The Scandinavian Union is a good example. The key thing is that the ethos be stably liberal democratic. In such an ethos, secession carries with it no terrors. Peoples will come to have the fullest form of self-governance possible while still being able to enter into cooperative arrangements with each other – arrangements which will enhance the flourishing of the members of each nation.

VII

In his "What's So Special about Nations?" Buchanan, from a different angle, and even more deeply than in his "Theories of Secession," attacks Primary Right theories of secession.[46] If his arguments are sound they completely undermine the account of secession I gave in sections I–VI. I think, however, perhaps not being able to see the mote in my own eye, that their soundness is very much in question. I shall try to show why. I have argued that under conditions of modernity membership in a distinctive nation is critical for one's self-identification and self-definition. Where such local identities are not in place people will experience alienation and will not flourish. There is, if you will, that much truth in communitarian claims. Without nationhood involving necessarily self-governance in some form, people will be psychologically crippled or at least seriously disadvantaged. Questioning the wisdom of what he calls the new-found enthusiasm for national self-determination, Buchanan rejects root and branch such claims and such conceptions.

Again there are several red herrings to be disposed of. First I, and other Primary Right theorists, agree that the doctrine (sometimes called the "nationalist principle") according to which every nation should have its own state is both impractical and dangerous. As I have made plain here, and as others have as well, including Buchanan, there are just too many nations for them all, given the territorial space that is available, to have nation-states of their own.[47] Sometimes nations must be part of a multination state or be in some other way federated or confederated in a larger state and be content with a more limited form of self-governance than they would have if they had a nation-state of their own. But my point was, and is, that this is, in many (but by no means all) circumstances, a *second best* that *sometimes* we must – including morally speaking "must" – just accept. But it is, all the same, a second best that, at least morally speaking, we do not need to accept as what is ideally speaking right. Given the deep importance of nationality to people, where there is territorial space, and where no harm to others ensues, or everything considered a lesser harm ensues, it is at least reasonable to believe that it is better in such circumstances for each nation to have its own state. That is arguably the ideally right thing. That will be an important ingredient in the maximizing of human flourishing all around and to the seeing that the opportunities for it are as fairly distributed as possible. To illustrate by translating into the concrete, places, such as Lebanon or much of the territory that was once Yugoslavia, where people with distinct national identities are so mixed on the same territory, then the only reasonable and decent thing to do is to go for a genuinely multination decentralized state. With enmities firmly in place, these are second-best solutions determined by humanly inescapable social realities. Given the critical importance of nationality for people, where *possible without violating the human rights of minorities* or denying the genuine nationality of anyone in favour of another nationality, each nationality should either have its own nation-state or be, in a genuine multination state, a component nation with *equal moral standing* with the other component nations in that state and with each nation having extensive powers of self-governance. There must, for this not to be an ideological trap for the component nations, be a real empowerment here. Often, given the hard facts of *realpolitik*, neither of these things – neither a nation-state nor a genuine multination state – can, as a matter of fact, be had and then, for the nonce, we must go for a second best by accepting some kind of umbrella state, a pseudo-multination state, perhaps calling itself a multination state, where all the component nations, the *de facto* dominant (usually larger) nation aside, have only rather limited powers of self-governance. This is not a very good second best, and in the long run it will be unstable. It is an arguable point that this is what the Canadian state is now. That possibly partisan point aside, what should be our first choices should be either, depending on the particular circumstances, a nation-state for the nation or the nation being a component nation in a genuine multination state where the component nations genuinely stand as equals. But whether, even *ceteris paribus*, it is better for each nation to have its own nation-state, the claim made in the previous sentence seems at least to be firmly grounded. These are the things a nationalist movement should struggle for. A pseudo-multination state with one nation, sometimes severely, sometimes benignly, paternalistically, running the show is *a very distant* second best. But these considerations, whatever their force, do nothing to show that a nation does not have a *general* right to secession. Often this cannot be – other moral or factual considerations will in certain circumstances override, without abolishing, this right – and then, to repeat, we must go for a second best.

There is a second red herring to be put in the fish disposal unit. In trying to counter what he calls this new-found enthusiasm for national self-determination, Buchanan rightly asserts that "the basis for ascribing the right to secede has nothing to do with nationality *as such*."[48] Sometimes nations have a remedial right to secede but never, he has it, do "nations *as such* have a right" to secede.[49] What he is very concerned to deny – he returns again and again to his "as such" conception in his "What's So Special about Nations" – is the claim that a nation *as such* – that is, *just in virtue of being a nation* – has a right to some substantial form of self-government. As he puts it in summarizing his position, "I have not argued that nations do not have rights of self-determination; only that *as such* nations do not."[50] But his conception here is also a red herring; nations as such, nationalities as such, have no inherent or intrinsic value. Nationalists need not, and should not, flounder about with such murky notions. And a Primary Right theorist need not and indeed should not assume it or so argue. The thrust of my argument was to show the very crucial instrumental value – strategic instrumental value – of nations and nationality for human self-definition and self-identity and with that for human flourishing. I attach no independent value to nations and none to some *reification* "a nation as such" – whatever that is – but rather I attach a central instrumental value to nations and nationality in the realization of human good. (This will be explicated in what follows.) Buchanan's arguments against nations *as such* having a right to secede have no critical force. They are diversionary, directed with no critical force.

A third red herring also needs to be disposed of. I need not – and indeed I do not – regard "nations as cultural groups that *at one time enjoyed self-government*." That is *perhaps* true of most of them, but not of all, and it is certainly not tied up with the definition of what it is for a group to be a nation. So my claim that nations have a right to self-government is not tied to the claim that they once had self-government – as, say, the Baltic states – and subsequently were deprived of it and have a right to have it back. *Suppose* the Québécois never had self-government. Let us say they were first under the French Crown as a colony, then under the British Crown, and finally under the authority of Canada. But that would not diminish one whit their claim to nationhood and self-government. I neither make that assumption nor is one tied up with the very idea of what it is to be a nation that it at one time must have had to have had its own independent state. My contention, rather, is that nations have a non-remedial right (albeit sometimes they have a remedial right as well, though it is a more secondary thing) to self-government and a presumptive non-remedial right to independent statehood. Here, as should be apparent, Buchanan and I, without the diversion of red herrings, square off. I have so far tried to give considerations to favour my Primary Right account over his Remedial Right Only account. There are, however, some distinct and indeed very crucial matters still to be sorted out. The three red herrings disposed of, I turn now to them.

Buchanan develops something he calls his *equal respect objection* to Primary Right theories. It is directed at the claim "that nations *as nations* have the right to self-government (short of independent statehood)."[51] The Primary Right theory makes a stronger claim as well. But it also makes this weaker claim. I did just that when I argued that there are too many nations for them all to have states of their own so that the only thing nations have an unqualified general right to is *some form* of self-government. It is this weaker claim, which could be true even if the stronger claim is false, that Buchanan's equal respect objection is directed against. His objection is that the singling out of "nations *as such* for such rights of self-government," while denying them "to other groups, is morally arbitrary and this arbitrariness violates the principle that persons are to be accorded equal respect."[52]

If the Primary Right theory required the abandonment of equal respect for persons, then the Primary Right theory should instead itself be abandoned. The equal respect principle is a fundamental principle of a liberal society, though it is honoured more in the breach than in the observance in our rich liberal capitalist democracies. But that notwithstanding, it is such a deep considered judgment of ours that, if Primary Right theory required such an abandonment, I, and I expect its other defenders as well, would abandon the Primary Right theory rather than override in our accounts this fundamental principle. The equal respect principle, that is, is a more deeply embedded considered judgment than moral judgments directly linked to the Primary Right theory. But – or so I shall argue – we, that is, Primary Right theorists (if that is what we should call ourselves), are not committed to such moral arbitrariness, and we do not violate the equal-respect-for-persons principle.

For starters, as I have already pointed out, we do not single out nations *as such* for rights of self-government, but we centre on nations because of their key – or, so as not to beg any questions, allegedly key – *instrumental* value in giving people a sense of themselves, something which is essential for their flourishing and their overcoming alienation. That claim may be false – something we will subsequently turn to – but, true or false, it is not morally arbitrary. It claims that every human being under conditions of modernity needs for her secure self-realization a sense of nationality, and that everyone so situated should have a clear sense of nationality if she is to be able to live a good life. That is for us a central reason why we give such moral weight to considerations of nationality. Rather than a violation of the equal-respect-for-persons principle, it is a consideration that is solidly in accordance with it. Equal respect for persons is one of the underlying deep moral motivations for our commitment to nationality.

However, Buchanan could abandon his nation *as such* talk and still forcefully argue that, only instrumental value or not, too much weight is being given on the Primary Right account to nation and nationality. Even in conditions of modernity (perhaps most especially in conditions of modernity), it is not for all people, the argument goes, an indispensable part of their self-definition. In support of this, he brings forth a number of empirical considerations that certainly are deserving of careful consideration. Like Jeremy Waldron, he argues that there are many individuals, particularly in societies such as ours, for whom nationality is not nearly as important as defenders of nationality, including defenders of liberal nationalism, have alleged.[53] Why, Buchanan asks, should "nations – among all the various sources of allegiance and identification – deserve ... [the] very strong form of political recognition" that nationalists and Primary Right theoreticians accord to them?[54] In facing this very forceful question, it is important, however, to keep in mind that my argument for a general non-remedial right of nations to some form of self-governance was limited in scope. While remaining, at least for the purposes of the present essay, agnostic about societies other than liberal democratic ones, I only argued for my Primary Right account for liberal democratic societies under conditions of modernity. But, and here is the sting of Buchanan's argument, and Waldron's as well, it is precisely in such societies that claims like mine, David Miller's, and Yael Tamir's about the socio-psychological centrality of nationality become problematic.[55] In such societies, Buchanan remarks, where

> there is substantial freedom of religion, of expression, and of association pluralism will continue, with new groups and new conceptions of the good evolving over time. Some groups will attract or hold members, flourish for a time, then lose their grip on individuals' allegiances and identities, just as individuals will revise and in some cases abandon their initial conceptions of the good.[56]

Moreover, "there is no uniformity as to the *priorities* persons attach to their multiple identifications. Some think of themselves first as fathers or mothers or members of a family, and second as Swiss, or Americans, or Blacks, or Hispanics, or Christians."[57] Others have different priorities here. There is not nearly a uniform cultural pattern. And, I would add, adding more fuel to Buchanan's fire, that some have these varied allegiances without having the foggiest idea of what priorities they have among them. Others *ambivalently* prioritize things in some contexts in one way and in other contexts prioritize them in another without a sense of how more globally for themselves coherently to order their priorities. And there are still others, probably less frequent in our societies than the varied people I described above, but still there in considerable numbers, whose "primary self-identification is religious or political-ideological."[58] They are frequently thought of as the ideologues among us, and they indeed have to some extent at least set their priorities. (However, doing so does not make one an idealogue.) Finally there are some individuals for whom no *single* identification is more important than any other or at least many diverse others. Being a father, a professor, a socialist, or French is no more or no less important than many of their other identifications and one of these identifications is no more important than others. How in such a world – a world that is our modern world – can we reasonably privilege nationality? Indeed can we rightly privilege nationality?

The point is, I agree, that generally, special purposes apart, we cannot reasonably privilege nationality or, for that matter, anything else. The crucial point to see about our modern societies, and perhaps other societies as well, is that in pluralistic societies nationality will be only one source of identification and allegiance among others, and for some people it will be of little or no importance relative to other sources of identification and allegiance, whether these are cultural or occupational or religious or political or familial.[59]

Given that cluster of sociological facts (and with Buchanan I take them to be facts), and given such a dynamically pluralistic society, to single out nations as the group that is entitled, among the various groups, to self-government is to give, Buchanan has it, a public expression of the conviction that allegiances and identities have a single, true rank order of value, with nationality reposing at the summit. So to confer a special right of self-government on those groups that happen to be nations is to devalue all other allegiances and identifications.[60]

But this is incompatible, Buchanan asserts, with the fundamental liberal principle of equal respect for persons. Moreover, it is incompatible with the liberal assumption that governments are to act as the agent of all its individual citizens. To give such priority to nations, Buchanan avers, "is an insult to the equal status of every citizen whose primary identity and allegiance is other than national and to all who have no single primary identity or allegiance."[61] It is a form of *discrimination*, and as such it "violates the principle of equal respect for persons."[62] And, to move from individuals to groups, it is also the case that groups other than nations, that is, other cultural associations, including prominently religious and political-ideological ones, are sometimes similarly disadvantaged and in effect discriminated against. Here we have a powerful cluster of considerations that must be soundly met if I am to make out my case for secession and for a liberal nationalism.

VIII

The cluster of considerations we have seen Buchanan raising in the last few pages constitutes, I believe, his strongest challenge to the type of liberal nationalist views on secession that I have articulated. It seems to me that a liberal nationalism must acknowledge that in modern societies, with their dynamic pluralisms, not all people give the pride of place to the nation that *some* nationalists assume they do and that, as different as people are, it is not at all evident that without such strong nationalist identifications all people, or perhaps even most people, will suffer anomie.

Is there any kind of reasonable response that can be made to Buchanan compatible with acknowledging this pervasive pluralism? Buchanan suggests one himself only to, after perfunctorily examining it, set it aside. But I think there is more to such a response than he acknowledges. So I shall examine it and extend it a bit. In speaking of a nation we spoke of an *encompassing culture*. What is special about a sense of national identification is that it functions to encompass our other identities "by integrating them and making them cohere together."[63] It is the integrating structure for the other identities. One's sense of family, say, is very strong. One's family life is at the centre of one's life. But the kind of family it is; the language or languages it speaks; the practices that constitute its family life; the various roles and expectations that the members of the family have; the way the family makes social bonds; the way they see themselves in relation to others and the like is very much structured by their particular encompassing culture. They are significantly different if you are a German, an American, an Israeli, or a Mexican. And that difference is felt and appreciated by the members of these various encompassing cultures. One's encompassing culture is very much hooked up with a sense of who one is, and having a sense of who one is is vitally important to everyone. Similar things can be said for those whose political-ideological or religious identifications are thought by them to be their most important identifications. Being a socialist and being in the struggle for workers' emancipation is for many socialist militants, and some other socialists as well, at the very heart of their lives. And being socialist is in the very nature of the case an internationalist matter, but it is not *just* an internationalist matter. The struggles are also, and typically most intensely, close to home if, say, one is French or Chilean, with one's French comrades or Chilean comrades. A sense of one's country remains extremely important. And exactly the same is true for Islamic militants. The worldwide Islamic movement is of vital significance for them, but so are matters close to home. How, for Turks or Afghans, for example, Islam fares in Turkey or in Afghanistan is at the centre of their attention. And being a Turk and being an Afghan structures how in concrete ways your Islamic practices and even conceptions go.

Encompassing culture does not, of course, *equal* language. The Québécois and the French have the same language, but they are different nations, that is, their encompassing culture is not the same. The same is true for Americans and English-speaking Canadians and for the English and the Scots. But all the same Wittgenstein is on the mark when he says that the forms of language are the forms of life. A language is standardly very closely linked with an encompassing culture and an encompassing culture with a language. This comes out very clearly when for a people their language is threatened or thought to be threatened with extinction, displacement, or devaluation. In such circumstances, nationalist feelings and nationalist struggles come into being and broadly across the culture among people with various identifications and various more particular allegiances and from different strata of the society.[64] This seems to me to show how much of an integrating structure nationality (given its intimate, but not invariable, link with language) is in the lives of people. But it does not follow from this (*pace* Buchanan) that it must be, or even should be, at the *summit* of everyone's or even *anyone's* allegiances and identifications or that the nationalist need be claiming that it is. Being a good musician, being a gentle lover, being politically committed, being a kind and caring person, being a good Catholic, being a dedicated teacher, being an active member of one's local community, being a talented dry fly fisherman, and a myriad of other things may be more important to one, sometimes vastly more important to one, than one's nationality, but, for most of these things at least, one's nationality provides the cultural context of choice for these things and the integrating structure for them. How deeply important this cultural context of choice is to one is revealed when one has a sense that one's language, and with that one's encompassing culture, is being threatened. That is too close to the bone – too close to what one is and what one can do – to be accepted with equanimity. But that does not mean that of all one's allegiances and identifications, one's highest one, and the most important one – the one one prizes the most (assuming, what might not be the case, that one has just one) – is one's nationality. Not at all. Sometimes that may be so but certainly not always or even usually. What it does mean is that nationality as encompassing (integrating) culture, or a central part of it, presents the context for the secure realization of our other allegiances and identifications, and that it is one that we would be at a loss to be without.

So there is no question (again *pace* Buchanan) that people whose scheme of values is such that they do not place nationality at the top – something that would be very rare in any case – are taken by consistent liberal nationalists to be less valuable members of the community or are in any way discriminated against. And it is not true that liberal nationalists just rather unwittingly assume that, or to be consistent, must assume it. In a liberal society people are not valued in that hierarchical way, and a liberal nationalism far from requiring it repudiates it. But it does see, in most circumstances, the necessity of preserving the cultural life of the nation of which one is a member and, by generalization, liberal nationalists acknowledge that this holds for the people of other nations as well, for this (the having of such an encompassing culture) provides the cultural context of choice where people, any and all people, can carry out their various life plans. In that way it is very like, and perhaps is, a Rawlsian primary good. Without an encompassing culture – without something which makes us a "we" so that we can know who we are – we could do none of these things, could carry out none of our life plans; we could have no conceptions of the good at all. Being a good musician in many cultural contexts (and particularly in conditions of modernity) is indeed a very international thing, but an individual who is devoted to the task of coming to be a good musician comes to that in a particular culture, the very form it takes for her is not entirely free of that culture, and, more centrally, a person is not only a good musician but a certain kind of person, and that carries with it the stamp of a particular encompassing culture. That stamp should not be seen, and standardly is not seen, as an infliction but as an empowerment and something that gives us a sense of at-homeness in a very big, sometimes alienating, and amazingly diverse world. Each individual needs to have a sense of who she is, and that sense carries with it, though that is not all that self-identification carries with it, a sense of being Dutch, Catalonian, Fijian, Faeroese, and the like. Moreover, nationality is politically important here for it provides the context of choice for people in realizing, and indeed in even being able to form, life plans. Thus nationality – people being members of a nation – is vital in politics without for a moment (*pace* Buchanan) implying or involving nation-worship or claiming that nations have intrinsic or inherent value. Moreover, there is no assumption at all for liberal nationalists that nationality is superior to other allegiances and identities. So liberal nationalism with its stress on the importance of nationality certainly does not come to "an insult to the equal status of every citizen whose primary identity and allegiance is other than national."[65] A government, where it is decent, as indeed it hardly ever is, acts as the agent of the people: that is for *all* individuals under its jurisdiction. But to do so effectively it must, while continuing to respect individual rights, act to preserve the common encompassing culture of a people without which they, both as individuals and as groups, can do nothing, including, repairing the ship at sea. But in continuously repairing the ship at sea there will be a gradual changing of that encompassing culture. Modern societies will standardly be dynamic pluralisms, but that is perfectly compatible with liberal nationalist projects.

It is not that this sense of nationality necessarily, or even typically (once more *pace* Buchanan), provides the primary source of self-identification for everyone. For some their religion will do that, integrating and rendering coherent their identifications and the like. But, as we have seen, religion, in the forms it takes, in its very possibility of arising and being sustainable, requires even more encompassing cultural structures, structures that go with nationality. For example, we worship in a particular way, in a particular language, and with a whole battery of other practices. Think how different in concrete ways the practice of Roman Catholic worship is in very different cultures. And for modern societies it is only where people are secure as a nation, that is, where they have some reasonable measure of self-governance, that the flourishing of their religion and their religious identification can be secure. Think, for example, of Islam, the religion of the Turkish minority, in Bulgaria. Without their proper recognition as a national minority, and with that a protection of their language, Islam would be very insecure in Bulgaria. It is not a sufficient condition for such security, but it is a necessary condition for it. Nationalism, *pace* Buchanan, need not inhibit religion; it sometimes could, for good or for ill, facilitate it.

There is no claim among liberal nationalists that nations are morally primary. The privilege that nations have in the political order is *strategically instrumental*. It is not that in a liberal society the nation sets the moral order of the life of a people; that it tells them what conceptions of the good are legitimate or what life plans are acceptable. And, while I do argue, as Will Kymlicka does as well, that one's culture provides a meaningful context for choice and that without such a context autonomy is impossible, I do not deny that some people can over time, and usually with considerable effort, change their culture (even their encompassing culture), change, that is, their nationality, and that with new cultural materials they will have a new, or partly new, meaningful cultural context of choice.[66] And it is a good thing, as Harry Brighouse has put it, that cultures become in that way permeable.[67] Liberal nationalism neither tells a tale of cultural imprisonment nor entails it. The extensive changing of one's culture is very rare and for most people it is (drastic circumstances aside) impossible, but the possibilities of such change are there for some few privileged people and, as well, though in a very different way, for immigrants and the like where the conditions of their immigration (or its rough equivalent) are very dislocating (the cultural change being great), uncushioned, and only partial. Still, immigrants become Canadians, Americans, Australians, and the like. And it is also true that over time various people, sometimes acting more or less singly and sometimes in concert, do change cultures, even gradually, comprehensive cultures. This usually happens for them with pain, though sometimes also with a sense of liberation. (Two powerful though somewhat different pictures of this wrenching change are given in Upton Sinclair's *The Jungle* and Henry Roth's *Call It Sleep*.) But such change, hopefully as painless as possible, is not something to which the *liberal* nationalist stands opposed. Instead she welcomes it, particularly when it is the sort of which Waldron speaks.

Waldron and Buchanan are right that since these things are so, for some people there is no need for them to maintain their culture of origin. Indeed, by not doing so, or not completely doing so, we might even gain a certain kind of hybrid vigour where people change – more realistically, partially change – their culture. But that does not mean we can be *rootless individuals shorn of all culture*.[68] That is not even intelligible. What a few individuals might become is *poly-national*. They could have an amalgam, stable or unstable, of several national identities. But that would not be to be without nationality providing a context of choice. Poly-nationality is nationality; it is not, what is impossible anyway, to be a rootless individualistic atom shorn of culture. And that cosmopolitan poly-nationality might very well be a very good thing. (Waldron is on to something here.) But many people, as we have seen, can, and indeed are, cosmopolitans while not being poly-national and while having a more standard sense of national identity as (for example) Scots, Ghanaians, Poles, or Finns. I suspect that as a matter of fact the poly-nationality that Waldron speaks of is very rare, and so thinking of oneself may well be fraught with self-deception. But I need not, and do not, deny either that it can occur and that, if it occurs, it could be a good thing – perhaps even a very good thing – or that it could yield hybrid vigour. What I deny is that it is common and that it can be an option for anything more than a small elite. And I deny, as well, that it is a necessary condition for being a thoroughgoing cosmopolitan or for the fullest flourishing that human beings can gain. (We might not have much of an idea about when that would occur. But I leave that aside.) Thus it seems to me of minor political and sociological significance.

What is so special about nations, among the various groups, that entitles them to political self-government and to a presumption, everything else being equal, to statehood (in a nation-state or in a multination state), is that they, in contrast to the other groups, are encompassing (integrating) cultures, located historically on a territory which the people making up the nation regard as their homeland or, if they are in diaspora, aspire to make their homeland and furthermore, and distinctly, that they are of sufficient size and with sufficient infrastructure to be able to carry out the functions of a state. (There is no algorithm here for what constitutes "sufficient size" or "sufficient infrastructure.") Such groups are (a) capable of self-government and (b) everything else being equal can be self-governing because they alone provide a thoroughly secure meaningful cultural context of choice which, in turn, is necessary for autonomy and human flourishing. No other group meets both conditions (a) and (b). The First Nations in Canada and the United States provide *problematic* cases. *Perhaps* they do not meet all these conditions, for example, they *might* lack the size or infrastructure, and thus they might have a right to self-government but not to full self-government, and thus, not to complete sovereignty. Or perhaps it is better (being less paternalistic) to say that they have the right or at least in certain circumstances they have that right, but that it might be unwise for them to *exercise* that right. But it would have to be shown, to deny them full self-government, that the infrastructure could not in time be provided or stimulated by the state in which they now exist or that they were too small or necessarily too weak to be self-governing or that they had no reasonable territorial claim. Non-natives should be very careful about what they are claiming here. We have for too long assumed, and often with self-deception, the white man's paternalistic burden.

IX

There is a final issue to which I shall now turn. It is the claim forcefully made by Buchanan in "Theories of Secession" that Primary Right theories of secession operate in "an institutional vacuum" and in doing so provide us with no guidance to the urgently practical question of what *institutional* responses are ethically appropriate to the secessionist challenges that actually face us. Theories, such as my own, the argument goes, are utopian in a bad sense for they can provide little in the way of moral guidance for the institutional reform of our international institutions, including the most formal of these, the international legal system.[69] Again we members of the chattering classes (of which philosophers are charter members) are constructing useless ideal theories that provide no guidance concerning actual questions of what is to be done.

In taking a more institutional approach to secession, Buchanan contends that we should distinguish between two questions and come to see that they require quite different answers. They are,

(1.) Under what conditions does a group have a moral right to secede, independently of any questions of institutional morality, and in particular apart from any consideration of international legal institutions and their relationship to moral principles?

(2.) Under what conditions should a group be recognized as having a right to secede as a matter of international institutional morality, including a morally defensible system of international law?[70]

His dichotomy, I think, like so many dichotomies, is more confusing than helpful. How, for example, is it possible – conceptually possible, if you will – to float free altogether from institutional morality? Morality, as one of our forms of life, is inescapably institutional such that "a morality free of all institutional constraints" is an oxymoron. But to go on in this vein might be thought to be diversionary nit-picking. So, having registered a protest, I will let Buchanan's dichotomy stand. In doing so I will take him to be saying that persons centring on the first question give scant consideration to how international law works or to the situations and contexts of possibilities of actual states, while those concentrating on the second question put such matters front and centre. Buchanan's claim is that theories of the sort I have articulated, whatever their intuitive attractions, will not continue to remain attractive when serious attempts are made to institutionalize them.[71] "Moral theorizing about secession," he argues, "can provide significant guidance for international legal reform only if it coheres with and builds upon the most morally defensible elements of existing law."[72] Primary Right theories, including my own, do not do that. Thus, even if all my previous criticisms of Buchanan's account were sound, still, as he sees it, my own positive account, since it does not meet this institutional constraint, must be woefully inadequate. A normative theory of secession, the argument goes, which does not take such institutional considerations into account from the very beginning, is just spitting into the wind. It is the idle speculations of some free-floating intellectuals.

Again I shall bite Buchanan's bullet and do precisely what Buchanan thinks I should not be doing. I have argued in this essay for a general moral right to secede under certain conditions and I have spelled out what those conditions are. I have not considered how my normative argument could be incorporated into international legal regimes. And I am not proposing what I am proposing as an international legal right or indeed any kind of legal right. Rather I am saying that if the general moral right I am claiming for liberal democratic societies is indeed such a moral right, then, whether it is actually incorporated into international legal regimes or not, it should be. As things stand, even with a morally progressive understanding of the legal order, if it cannot be taken to be an international legal right, then so be it. Then the international legal system should be altered so that it comes to be in accordance with that moral right. We should not tailor moral or normative political theory and our moral principles to square with the legal system.

It is just such a "high-handed," if not "high-minded," or, I expect Buchanan would think, "light-minded," attitude that Buchanan believes to be thoroughly mistaken, and, if taken seriously, dangerously mistaken. It simply ignores the decisive role of actually existing states as makers of international law and thus does not have even the minimal realism that any adequate normative theory of secession must have.[73] States, as we have seen Buchanan arguing, will stick to a principle of territorial integrity, in the teeth of secessionist challenges; the international legal order, except over the most extreme cases where clear and extensive violations of human rights are involved, and sometimes not even then, will continue to support the *status quo*, that is, the firm territorial integrity of the existing system of nation-states. I have argued against the acceptance of this bit of *realpolitik*, as something which is morally acceptable, as something which is just to be taken as an institutional fact of life not to be subject to critical moral assessment. It yields, to put it minimally, a too-restrictive account of the right to secession and, if accepted, firmly commits us to the *status quo*. Where we limit ourselves, as I have, to secession crises that emerge in liberal democratic societies, it makes secession in those societies too difficult in a way that works against or conflicts with the very deepest constitutive normative commitments of liberal democracies. In societies that are *actually such democracies* (if indeed, except perhaps in what is our ideologically distorted thought, there are any), Primary Right theories, if acted upon, will not create the perverse incentives of which Buchanan speaks; and liberal democratic societies, to the extent they are actually genuinely liberal democratic, will not be so intransigently committed to actually existing borders. There will be, of course, a presumption in favour of these borders, not lightly to be set aside, but where secessionist issues come to the fore in such societies there will be no principle of territorial integrity *über alles* (excepting only the most extreme cases where states, failing to be liberal democratic states, against a people, commit extensive and repeated human-rights violations). I have resisted such territorial integrity *über alles*, arguing that it is a morally arbitrary statist conception.

Buchanan realizes such a response can be made, and he faces it in the last two pages of his "Theories of Secession."[74] He imagines, and I believe rightly so, a Primary Right theorist responding to him by saying that they and Buchanan are simply engaged in two different enterprises. Buchanan, the argument goes, is offering a *non-ideal* institutional theory of the right to secede while the Primary Right theorist is "offering an *ideal*, but nonetheless, institutional theory."[75] Buchanan puts the following words into the Primary Right theorist's mouth. Primary Right theorists, he writes, "are thinking institutionally ... but they are thinking about what international law concerning secession would look like under ideal conditions, where there is perfect compliance with all relevant principles of justice."[76] In such an ideal world none of the untoward consequences Buchanan mentions concerning secession could arise, and so there are no grounds in ideal theory for restricting the right to secede in the way Buchanan does. Ideal theory, being an ideal theory, depicts *counterfactual* conditions, but it does show us what *ideally* would be the best thing, and that shows us what we should do our best to approximate in whatever ways are practicable under real-life conditions.

Buchanan responds by saying that if Primary Right theories "are only defensible under the assumption of perfect compliance with all relevant principles of justice, then they are even less useful for our world than my [that is Buchanan's] criticisms heretofore suggest – especially in the absence of a complete set of principles of justice for domestic and international relations."[77]

This response only seems to have force because Buchanan makes his ideal theory more ideal, and ideal in a rather peculiar way, than the ideal theory that the Primary Right theorists need to deploy. Buchanan builds into his characterization of ideal theory the condition of "perfect compliance with all relevant principles of justice" and then rightly points out that that kind of ideal theory is as useless as Christian Science for providing any guidance in the real world, at least in the context of theorizing about nationalism. But it is utterly gratuitous to foist that condition of perfect compliance onto the Primary Right theorists' conception of an ideal theory or onto any useful conception of an ideal theory. The proper characterization of ideal theory, without that dangler, is that we are articulating an ideal theory, for liberal democratic societies, which involves thinking institutionally about what international law concerning secession would look like under ideal conditions, that is, under conditions in which states in such societies actually behaved in accordance with the moral principles embedded in the very idea of liberal democratic society, for example, respected human rights, were committed to a principle of equal respect for all persons with its prohibitions on exploitation, manipulation, and the like, and where we had, as well, a society committed to achieving and sustaining autonomy and indeed, as much as possible, equal autonomy. This is the counterfactual ideal conception of a liberal democratic society that ideal theory assumes. It says nothing about perfect compliance of individuals or about the invariant behaviour of individuals in that ideal conception of a liberal democratic society.

Setting aside for the purposes of ideal theory construction questions of political sociology, I attempt to give a perspicuous characterization of what an ideal liberal democratic society would be without asking the question whether there is much likelihood that we could have an instantiation of such a society as distinct from something of an approximation of it. I try to give a characterization of what such a society would look like. But nothing need, or should, be said about perfect compliance of individuals or about having "a complete set of principles of justice for domestic and international relations." The former is Christian Science, and with the latter it is not evident that we even understand what we are asking for in asking for such a "complete set" of principles of justice. The ideal theory that the Primary Right theorist needs, just as the ideal theory that Buchanan claims for his own, is open-ended and in various ways indeterminate as any reasonable normative account, ideal or non-ideal, must be. As in the body of my essay my ideal account unfolded, I worked with articulating what it would be for our societies to be liberal democratic societies. I did not assume that any of our societies meet, or as a matter of fact could meet, fully these conditions. And I did not speculate on how close they were likely to come to meeting them. Rather, taking the under-articulated ideal of what it would be for something to meet the ideal embedded in the very idea of a liberal democracy, I tried to more fully articulate it and to ask, if people were reasoning and living according to that idea, what they would say about secession. With these ideas and ideals and on the assumption that this is the kind of society (deliberately idealized) we are talking about, we can come to say, where such liberal democratic principles are generally being adhered to, when secession would be justified and when it wouldn't be. In doing this we do not need to bring in anything about perfect compliance of individuals or about having a complete set of principles of justice both domestic and global.

The world we know is, of course, quite distant from the very idea of a liberal democratic society – our idealized picture. But by clearly seeing what should be done in a world (a counterfactual world) of well-functioning liberal democratic societies, we can, keeping this model firmly in mind, then, taking the hurly-burly real world into account, attend to determining what qualifications would need to be made for a non-ideal theory to articulate the best possible approximation in real-life conditions to what is set out in the ideal theory. We would with the non-ideal theory have a theory saying something about what is to be done in real-life situations in the harsh, hard world that we know. There with such a non-ideal theory we would, as well as attending to the ideal theory, have also to consider what John Dewey called the "means-ends continuum." That is, we would not only have to consider the ideal, but the probabilities and conditions for attaining or at least approximating what the ideal calls for and the costs of such an attainment. But without the ideal theory we would not know in what direction we should try to go in the correcting of our actually existing institutions. An analogy might help. We know that there cannot be such a thing as a frictionless plane, but understanding the idea of it, the conception itself, we gain some idea of in what direction we would have to go to get as little friction as possible. There is no good reason not to believe that Primary Right theories articulate an ideal theory which provides something to be approximated in real-life situations and in doing that provides something of a useful guide for real-life situations. Where we have come as close as possible to the ideals specified in a sound ideal theory, we have the best real-world account we can gain. Our reach, as the old saw goes, must exceed our grasp – or what is heaven for?[78]

Notes

1. Buchanan: *Secession*; "What's So Special about Nations?" 283–310; "Theories of Secession."

2. Prager, "Barbarous Nationalism and the Liberal International Order," 441. For the less frequently noted case of the Indian subcontinent, see MacFacquhar, "India: The Impact of Empire," 26.

3. D. Miller, "Secession and the Principle of Nationality," 266. See also his *On Nationality*.

4. Buchanan, "What's So Special about Nations?" 289.

5. Seymour, "Introduction: Questioning the Ethnic/Civic Dichotomy," 30–61.

6. Kymlicka, *Multicultural Citizenship*; and Nielsen, "Cultural Nationalism, Neither Ethnic nor Civic."

7. Appiah, "The Multiculturalist Misunderstanding."

8. Seymour, "Introduction: Questioning the Ethnic/Civic Dichotomy," 30–61.

9. Nielsen, "Cultural Nationalism," 42–52.

10. I need the qualification "at least in principle" for there are all kinds of practical impediments that require restrictions on immigration: lack of space, lack of resources, and the like. Still that is the ideal to be approximated as fully and reasonably as possible.

11. Levine, "Just Nationalism"; and Brighouse, "Against Nationalism."

12. G. A, Cohen, *History, Labour, and Freedom*, 132–54; and Nielsen, "Socialism and Nationalism."

13. Nussbaum: "Patriotism and Cosmopolitanism," 3–17; and "Reply," 134–44.

14. Appiah, "Cosmopolitan Patriots," 21–9; and Barber, "Constitutional Faith," 30–37. See also M. Cohen, "Rooted Cosmopolitanism."

15. G. A. Cohen, *History, Labour, and Freedom*, 132–54; and Nielsen, "Socialism and Nationalism," 262.

16. Gellner, *Nations and Nationalism*.

17. Nielsen, "Undistorted Discourse, Ethnicity, and the Problem of Self-Definition."

18. Berlin: *Vico and Herder*, 145–216; *Against the Current*, 333–55; and *The Crooked Timber of Humanity*, 238–61.

19. Berlin, *The Crooked Timber of Humanity*, 13.

20. Nielsen, *Naturalism without Foundations*, 207–59.

21. Buchanan: *Secession*, 27–80; and "Theories of Secession," 37.

22. Buchanan, "Theories of Secession," 37.

23. Ibid.

24. Ibid.

25. Ibid., 40.

26. Ibid.

27. Ibid.

28. Ibid., 44 (emphasis added).

29. Ibid., 45–46.

30. Ibid., 45.

31. Ibid.

32. Hobsbawm: *Nations and Nationalism since 1780*; and the Validity of the Nation-State."

33 Buchanan, "Theories of Secession," 36.

34 Ibid. Here Buchanan would need to meet the powerfully articulated arguments of C.R. Sunstein that it would be a mistake for states to build into their constitutions a right to secede. Sunstein, "Constitutionalism and Secession."

35 Ibid., 45.

36 Ibid.

37 Ibid., 46.

38 Ibid., 46–47.

39 Ibid., 52.

40 Ibid.

41 Ibid., 53.

42 Seymour et al., "Quebec Sovereignty," 7–8.

43 Buchanan, *Secession*, 53.

44 Buchanan, "Theories of Secession," 53.

45 Buchanan, *Secession*, 29.

46 Buchanan, "What's So Special about Nations?" 283–310.

47 Buchanan, *Secession*, 48–50.

48 Buchanan, "What's So Special about Nations?" 307 (emphasis added).

49 Ibid., 285–86.

50 Ibid., 290 (emphasis added).

51 Ibid., 291 (emphasis added).

52 Ibid., 293 (emphasis added).

53 Waldron, "Minority Cultures and the Cosmopolitan Option."

54 Buchanan, "What's So Special about Nations?" 300.

55 D. Miller: *On Nationality*; and "Secession and the Principle of Nationality," 261–82. Tamir: *Liberal Nationalism*; and "The Right to National Self-Determination."

56 Buchanan, "What's So Special about Nations?" 293–94.

57 Ibid., 294.

58 Ibid., 295.

59 Ibid.

60 Ibid., 296.

61 Ibid.

62 Ibid.

63 Ibid., 300; and Buchanan, *Secession*, 53.

64 I did not say, however, only in such contexts.

65 Buchanan, "What's So Special about Nations?" 296.

66 Kymlicka, *Multicultural Citizenship*; and Couture, Nielsen, and Seymour, "Liberal Nationalism Both Cosmopolitan and Rooted," 595–650.

67 Brighouse, "Against Nationalism," 365–406.

68 G. A. Cohen, *History, Labour, and Freedom*, 132–54; M. Cohen, "Rooted Cosmopolitanism," 132–54; and Nielsen, "Socialism and Nationalism."

69 Buchanan, "Theories of Secession," 33.

70 Ibid., 31–33.

71 Ibid., 32

72 Ibid.

73 Ibid., 59–60.

74 Ibid., 60–61.

75 Ibid., 60.

76 Ibid., 77.

77 Ibid., 60–61.

78 It is important to see that my defence of a right to secede under the conditions I have described is a claim to a *moral* right. I argue it, that is, as a matter of political morality. I take

no position on whether it should be made a matter of a *constitutional* right of a state. It may very well be that Cass R. Sunstein is right in arguing, "that a right to secede does not belong in a founding document" of a state (any state). Sunstein, "Constitutionalism and Secession," 669. Sunstein has argued very carefully for this, and it may very well be that he is correct. But, as he makes emphatically clear, the soundness of his arguments about no constitutional right to secede neither do anything at all to show that, as he puts it, a subunit of a state might not, as a matter of political morality, be justified in seceding nor was that the aim of his arguments. He could consistently either agree with Buchanan's more restrictive account of when secession is justified or with my more permissive account or with neither. The point is that his arguments about no *constitutional* right to secede are compatible with either position. In turn, I take no position about making the right to secede a constitutional right. That is to say, I am not saying it should be declared by a constitution to be either legal or illegal. Indeed neither should ever be a background presupposition of constitutional thinking. It seems to me instead that the right to secede is a political-moral matter and that the courts of a *state*, including its supreme court, have no business saying either that secession is legal or illegal. What such a court could justifiably assert instead is that domestic courts (the courts of any state) cannot rightly say that it is either. It is rather that they should say, if they say anything at all about this matter, that it is a matter of political morality not within the jurisdiction of the courts of any state

or at least their state. This can be consistently said while still saying that international law can and does speak to this. It does, that is, make judgments about the legality of secession. I have *not* been concerned here with what international law says or doesn't say on this matter, though I have not, of course, denied its competence to so speak. I have instead been concerned with what should be said as a matter of political morality. And I have further argued that when (if ever) this is clearly established international law should tag along. Morality, where it is firmly established, in such circumstances overrides law, not the other way around.

However, here a perceptive remark of an anonymous referee is very much to the point. She points out that in *Loizidou v. Turkey* the 1996 judgment of the European Court of Human Rights reveals an emerging consensus in international law that the right of secession should be interpreted as remedial. This squares with Buchanan's view of the matter. But the referee then goes on to point out that this development is a recent and contested development in international law. Until very recently the right to secession was much more restricted than even that, being restricted to the right of decolonization. Matters concerning the right to secession, the referee goes on to say, are now in a state of transition in international law and we are (*pace* Buchanan) *in no position to say what it usually favours.* Since, that is, the international law of secession is still in transition from no to some right of secession, one cannot confidently say that it usually favours a least drastic means approach. That would be in effect to take a conservative *status quo* position (in effect, a *political* position) and it could not be justifiably claimed to be something determined by "the very logic of international law." Politics, not law, is what largely calls the tune here. Moreover, it is important to keep in mind here that public international law conceives of both general and regional international law. There are, for example, international legal rules that on certain issues apply only between Latin American states. The referee concludes, "Hence Buchanan's view of what states would or would not realistically do may be true for general international legal rules, but not necessarily for rules that might apply to Western liberal democracies. Indeed international legal theorists themselves are now starting to think in terms of international law between liberal states." Given the truth or even just the plausibility of the above considerations, I should concede even less than I have to Buchanan about what a progressive conception of the development of international law commits us to.

But, in any event, I was concerned, first and primarily, to defend a view of the right to secession as a moral right and second, and derivatively, to argue that, if views like mine are clearly established to be sound, that international law, whatever its position now, should adjust itself to such moral views. What is interesting and from my point of view encouraging about the above observations of the referee is that, if they are on the mark, international law may already be starting to move in that more permissive direction. At least that is in the same realm as far as international law is concerned. One last, and quite different, point concerning secession: if *à la* Bentham one objects (mistakenly I believe) to the very idea of moral rights, then talk instead of the *justifiability* of secession. Nothing of any significant substance would be changed, and my arguments would still go through. For an application of the above considerations to Quebec/Canada relations see Neuman, "Par Consention, le Canada Anglais devra reconnaîte du Québec."

Cosmopolitan Nationalism

I

I want, some might say, to have my cake and eat it too for I want to be both a cosmopolitan and a nationalist, and, congruently with that, I think liberals and socialists, depending on the societies in which they live, should be either cosmopolitan nationalists or people in sympathy with liberal nationalist projects where these projects have a legitimate point. This includes people like myself who are liberal socialists committed, as all socialists are, to socialist internationalism and the international solidarity that goes with it.[1] How can – or can? – these things consistently go together? Beyond that consistency being necessary but hardly a sufficient condition for adequacy – why go for cosmopolitan *nationalism*? Why not instead just go straight-out for cosmopolitanism and its internationalist outlook without the dangler "nationalism"?

In facing these questions let me first say what I take desirable – or at least putatively desirable – forms of cosmopolitanism and nationalism to be. It is sometimes said that to be a cosmopolitan is to be a citizen of the world.[2] However, absent a world state, "citizen of the world" must be a metaphor, but it is, as I think Martha Nussbaum evidences, a useful and important metaphor. Still it needs to be said what it is a metaphor of. To be a cosmopolitan – "a citizen of the world" – is to identify with and have a commitment to and a concern for all of humankind and not just for some subunit of it, *and* it is, as well, to have some reasonable understanding of, to prize and to take pleasure in, humankind's vast, and sometimes creative, diversity. It is not just that a cosmopolitan will grudgingly accept, as an intractable fact, the great variety of forms of life, practices, art-forms, languages, religions, cuisines and the like that the world has on offer, but she will take pleasure in the very existence of them, feel at home with a goodly number of them and wish to see them prevail where their prevailing does not harm others. Above all she will take an active interest in them, be reasonably knowledgeable about many of them and wish to see all of them flourish that are respectful of the rights of others, including, of course, alien others.

Someone who was simply an enlightenment humanist, without also being a cosmopolitan, would identify with, be committed to, and show concern for humankind, but it would be on an *assimilationist* model. She would be a One Worlder advocating a single world culture – one globally encompassing culture, including ideally a single language, for all humanity. In contrast with the cosmopolitan, she would wish to see humankind become as much alike as possible with some preferred model in mind as some French and some English Enlightenment figures wished to see the whole world modelled, as the case may be, on enlightened Frenchmen or enlightened Englishmen – to carry the "white man's burden" from one end of the globe to the other. The ideal of such an enlightenment humanist was to have a world of either Frenchmen, Englishman, or Americans or the closest approximation attainable thereto of one or another, depending on which was their preferred ideal model for a proper humanity.

By contrast a cosmopolitan is not so ethnocentric (ideally is not ethnocentric at all) and is a *non-assimilationist* enlightenment humanist. She is a humanist prizing humankind in and for its diversity without denying that in this diversity there is some commonness as well.[3] Moreover, this diversity is not seen as something to be regretted (accepted with a sigh) but is seen as a source of human richness, a richness that enhances our world.

To be a nationalist is to regard nationality as being of deep and desirable human significance and to regard group identity which (or so at least some nationalists believe) takes the form (in the conditions of modernity) of a national identity, as something to be sustained as being necessary for human flourishing and for there to be a good and just polity. This requires not only the protection of individuals but the protection of nations as well, and the guarantee, where this can be had, that they will have some form of self-governance. This self-governance will in the best case take the form of a nation having either a nation-state of its own or being a secure and equal partner in a multi-nation-state with a considerable amount of autonomy of its own, the exact extent of which is to be negotiated between the component nations of the multi-nation state in conditions of fairness as equals.[4]

However, for nationalism to match with cosmopolitanism it must be a liberal nationalism. By "liberal" here I do not mean the neo-liberalism of *laissez-faire* economics and the economic ordering of the world characteristic of capitalist globalization with its associated, severely individualistic libertarian or neo-Hobbesian social philosophies, but a *social* liberalism with its political exemplifications in social democracy or in genuinely democratic socialist societies (e.g., Chile during the time of Allende) and theoretically articulated now (though, of course, variously) by political philosophers such as Isaiah Berlin, Brian Barry, G. A. Cohen, Joshua Cohen, Ronald Dworkin, Jürgen Habermas, Stuart Hampshire, Thomas Nagel, John Rawls, and Amartya Sen and, to reach back into recent history, by John Stuart Mill, T. H. Green, R. H. Tawney, and John Dewey. There is a stress in such liberalism on the virtues of tolerance, on autonomy, on equality, on the protection of human rights, and on the societal non-privileging of any comprehensive conception of the good. Such liberals will emphasize the importance of there being a recognition and a non-ruling out in the public domain of all conceptions of the good that respect human rights and are in accordance with the political principles of justice of such a liberal society. These are principles that, in a broad sense, are egalitarian: prescribing that the life of everyone is to count and to count equally. To give this moral equality substance, there is also the stress that there be a *roughly* equal sharing of resources (though making allowances for incapacities) and a commitment to attaining an equality of the life conditions that would as fully as possible, produce, and for everyone, to the extent that is possible, conditions of human flourishing for each person, taking into considerations their different capacities and capabilities, at the highest level for each person that they as individuals can attain. The idea is to produce conditions of life for everyone that would enable them to have the best life they are capable of having. It is the stress on these substantively egalitarian features that highlights the *social* nature of this liberalism in contrast with the *individualistic* liberalism of Friedrich Hayek, Milton Friedman, Robert Nozick, and David Gauthier.[5]

Such a social liberalism (as does an individualistic liberalism) meshes with cosmopolitanism. The crucial question is whether cosmopolitanism is compatible with a *liberal* nationalism. There are paradigmatic social liberals (Brian Barry, for example) who are robust substantive egalitarians but strong anti-nationalists, and there are cosmopolitans who are social liberals but not nationalists (Martha Nussbaum, for example).[6] I shall argue, by contrast, that the most adequate forms of cosmopolitanism and social liberalism will also be liberal nationalisms or accept liberal nationalisms as legitimate where there is a need for nationalist movements. I shall further argue that the most adequate nationalisms (and thus the most adequate liberal nationalisms) will be both social liberalisms and cosmopolitan.[7]

To argue this I first must specify what liberal nationalism is in line with my characterization of social liberalism. A liberal nationalist will *reiterate* (if you will, recursively define) her nationalism, taking it that, since group identity and cultural membership are key goods for all human beings (arguably, in Rawls's sense a primary good), then it is something that, morally speaking, must *not* be recognized (acknowledged and accepted) *only* for her group but for all human beings. In that respect human beings (the whole bloody lot) are not relevantly different. And if national identity is the form that group identity takes under conditions of modernity, then sustaining or attaining, as the case may be, a secure national identity for the members of a nation should not only obtain for her nation but for all nations in such conditions. This reiteration only assumes the minimal and unproblematic conception of universalizability that if x is good for A then x is good for anyone relevantly like A in situations relevantly like those of A.

A liberal nationalism will not only be reiteratable. It will, as well, be tolerant of all other nationalisms that themselves accept reiteratability and are similarly tolerant. As a social liberalism it will have substantively egalitarian principles of justice that acknowledge the equal human standing of all human beings, the importance of coming to have the necessary means actually to have that equal standing, the necessity of designing programs and policies aimed at achieving that, and to recognize as well the deep value of a commitment to equal respect for all human beings, keeping firmly in mind the considered conviction, deeply embedded in liberal belief, that the life of everyone matters and matters equally.[8] So that that will not become a hollow human mockery, I will also argue for the necessity of there being material conditions for its realization actually in place so that this ideal can become a reality and not simply remain an ideal. Here we do well to follow Rosa Luxemburg.

Keeping that firmly in mind, along with a recognition that cultural membership is a primary good, it should also be stressed that this primary good must (morally speaking "must") be available to everyone. Not making it so available would be arbitrary, for it is something we all need, for, as a primary good, it is something necessary for the meeting of whatever ends or aims we – that is anyone – happen to have.[9] As different as people are in some important respects, they do not differ here. Some income and wealth, health, at least a minimal intelligence, some recognition and acceptance as well as cultural membership are all-purpose means – I did not say that is all they are – necessary for the realization of the various ends that we have and the life plans (whatever they may be) that are ours. Primary goods, in fine, are something we all need. We will not, and morally speaking cannot, privilege (whoever we are) our own people with respect to them but must argue that this egalitarian treatment should obtain for everyone, recognizing that the people of our nation are not relevantly different from anyone else in this respect.

Being inescapably persons living in a certain place at a certain time, with certain attunements, within a certain culture, we should, and probably will, in this domain, direct much of our attention to sustaining conditions favourable (particularly where they are fragile) to the flourishing of our own society, to making continued cultural membership in the nation a secure possibility, without attempting or wishing to lock people into such a membership. We must have a conception of cultural integrity that seeks, within the confines of reiteratability, the flourishing of our particular nation. But that is not because we regard our nation as more important – as our being God's chosen people or the people with the one truly human way of ordering things – but we seek to further the flourishing of our nation, as we hope others will do as well for their nations, because that is where we happen to be and that is where some (though not all) of our very deep attunements are and where many of our commitments lie. And again this is clearly reiteratable and should be reiterated. Nationalists should be reiterative – they should be recursive – about nationalism and this is exactly what the very idea of a liberal nationalism commits the liberal nationalist to be. Their position is closely analogous to the position of parents vis-à-vis their children. Parents have special obligations toward them and they should lovingly care for them without (absurdly and counterproductively) trying lovingly to care for all – or even many – other children and without their having the same obligations to them that they have to their own children. But in acknowledging this and acting on it, they need not – and indeed plainly ought not – to regard their own children as more valuable, more deserving, or being owed (except by them and others close to them) special protection that is not similarly owed to all other children. In both cases, without needing to, or indeed being justified in, narrowing their moral vision, they are acting there on the ground where they are. Morality, as Hegel taught us, must have this concreteness and contextuality. Without it, moral life would be impossible. But this does not mean that morality should be against universalism and by doing so turn itself into tribalism.[10]

Similarly, a liberal nationalist will stress the importance of self-governance for her nation, but not *(pace* Barry's portrayal of nationalism) at the expense of running roughshod over other nations or violating human rights.[11] Just as self-governance is a very central good for her nation, so it is for every other nation as well. All nations, she will recognize, have – the members of the different nations not differing in their needs *here* – an equal claim to this good. Only if she thought, and *with very good grounds*, that they were, even with the aid of a little "affirmative action," *incapable* of self-governance, would she be justified in rejecting this claim to an equal right of all nations to self-governance. But for that not to be an ideological mystification or a rationalization for hanging onto privileges, it must be the case that there really is an incapability there that is not rooted in remediable poverty, ignorance, and exploitation (past or present). "Ought" indeed implies "can," but we have to be careful that the incapacity is not rooted in remediable contingencies. But it is necessary clearly to recognize that it is very unlikely that it could be rooted in anything else.

Tragically, where two nations have a valid claim to the same land – say, the Israelis and the Palestinians – this will lead, as we well know, to very difficult situations where there may be no ideal solution. But for liberal nationalists – and remember my kind of liberal nationalists are *social* liberals – there must be respecting human rights and reasoning in accordance with substantively egalitarian principles of justice, a resolution by a fair compromise respecting equally the interests of everyone involved and discounting any bargaining from positions of superior strength.[12]

Certainly, in practice, that is not how most nationalists have acted. They have not only sought (reasonably and correctly) to protect their nations' interests but to see that they prevail over the interests of other nations and not infrequently at whatever costs to others. But that by definition is not how a liberal nationalist can behave. A liberal nationalist must recognize that all nations are in the same boat here; they all want to protect their own nationhood and see it flourish. But they will also acknowledge, if they are liberal nationalists, that from the moral point of view equal consideration must be given to the interests of every nation and that no nation's interests can be privileged. However rare such a taking of the moral point of view is in real-life politics, however far it is from the dirty world of *realpolitik*, such liberal nationalist behaviour (such a taking of the moral point of view) is compatible with a robust, but reiteratable, nationalism. It is, that is, compatible with the firm valuing of nationality, with each nation seeking (though within the limits of fairness and certainly not at all costs) to protect the integrity of its own nation and to the sustaining of (where it is in place) or the seeking of (where it isn't) some form of self-governance for one's nation. But it is not, of course, compatible with the drive for my nation *über alles*: the running roughshod over other nations, the taking of one's own nation to have a manifest destiny. Hitler was a populist and a nationalist with, at least in his early days, a lot of popular support in Germany and Austria, and even to a certain extent beyond, but he was, to repeat a commonplace (and to very much understate the matter), a nationalist of the wrong sort.[13] If we wish to attain any moral and intellectual clarity, we must not, however, let this unforgettable paradigm, with its many down-scaled present-day barbarous incarnations, block our understanding of the possibilities of a liberal nationalism and a recognition of the occasional reality of their actual exemplifications.[14]

II

Why should a social liberal and a cosmopolitan be a liberal nationalist? I shall argue that, in conditions of modernity, or (if you will) "post-modernity," liberal nationalism (where nationalism has some point) better anchors: (1) self-identity and, with that, increasing the possibilities of human flourishing and (2) more adequately than the other alternatives, giving democratic empowerment to people, thus contributing to their democratic life. All this understood within the bounds of justice as fairness or justice as impartiality, or some improvements on these egalitarian and social liberal conceptions of justice.[15] I now turn to explicating and defending these claims.

I first turn to self-identity (the having a sense of oneself as being a certain kind of person). We human beings have a deeply embedded and ubiquitous interest in something that gets called, perhaps rather pretentiously, self-identification or self-definition.[16] We have a very strong need to retain a sense of who we are and, in the doing of this, we need to see ourselves in terms of a *we*. And, important as this is, it will not suffice *just* to affirm that we are human beings. It will not do to try to root our self-identification *just* to our humanness – what we have in common with *all* other human beings. In trying to gain some adequate sense of who we are, we need a more local identity as well. We need – and this is the cosmopolitan and humanist impulse – to see ourselves as members of the party of humanity, but we also need to have a sense of our particular bonding.[17] Without that, we are, humanly speaking, at sea. Anthony Appiah has well argued that we need, if we are to flourish, to have a keen sense of our local identities.[18] We need, along with whatever cosmopolitan identities we aspire to and, perhaps to some extent attain, also to locate ourselves as members of a particular human community, with its distinctive ways of being and doing. We need to know who we are and how our identity connects us with certain particular others, since, after all, we are not Hobbesian atoms. The very idea of such "cultureless *human* atoms" is incoherent.[19] Cultural membership and group identity is a fundamental need of all human beings. It fits, as Kymlicka has well argued, Rawls's conception of a primary good.[20]

In the complex societies of contemporary life, where the state form is either that of the nation-state or some form of the multi-nation state, our group identity takes the form (though that does not exhaust it) of a national identity. It is a central and inescapable element of our self-definition, of our sense of who we are, even though it sometimes, perhaps often, will play a rather minimal role in our actual conceptualizations of who we are, or in our sense of our moral identity.[21] We may care very much more about our relations with very particular others (our being a father, a spouse, a colleague, a friend) or about our work, our particular political commitments and identities, or about our religion or lack thereof, than we do about our nationality. For me, for example, my political identity, my being a socialist and a social liberal, is much deeper than my sense of nationality as is, as well, my sense of my being (as part of a deep sense of vocation) a critical intellectual (to be pleonastic). But such things, however true they are, do not undermine the nationalist project or show that we do not need, in the societies in which we live, or could plausibly be expected to come to live, a sense of national-identity.[22]

However, this certainly does need an explanation. The liberal nationalist is not saying, or even suggesting, that we should reverse our priorities here and see our sense of nationality as the central thing: the thing that should be most important to us in coming to understand who we are or in setting our life priorities. But to say this is not at all to deny that national identity is not important. Moreover, the weight we should give to considerations of nationality will vary with the security of our nation.[23] The situation is very different for a Basque or a Kurd than it is for a member of a German-speaking or French-speaking Swiss canton (where their cantons as they are are perfectly secure). Similarly, it is very different for the First Nations in Australia, Canada, New Zealand, and the United States than it is for the dominant nations (the settler nations) that surround and dominate these First Nations. It is the elites of the latter and not the First Nations that have a grip on the state apparatus – the state in which the First Nations are embedded. But nothing of what I said above gainsays what I said about nationality and self-identification in modern societies. In such societies as in all modern societies – national identity is a primary good, but in some circumstances it is secure, and in others it is not.

What liberal nationalists are reminding us of is that, in a world of nations embedded in nation-states or multi-nation states, the nation of which we are a part provides the framework in which these other sides of our identities are formed, sustained, conceptualized, and realized. Nations are encompassing cultures, that, in being encompassing, are political communities (though not in Rawls's strong sense of "community") which are almost invariably associated with a homeland (perhaps only an imagined homeland) and which aspire to some form of self-government, though not necessarily to independent statehood.[24] The people in a nation (where they are not in a condition of very deep alienation) recognize themselves as belonging to the same community, as sharing a common history, typically speaking a common language and having a common public culture. These are things which, taken together, differentiate them from their neighbours. Moreover, this is a common culture which structures the way in which their other relations are formed and realized in the nation. How one is a mother, a colleague, a friend, an artist, a nurse, a businessman, a priest, a painter, a postal worker or what not is significantly (sometimes deeply) affected by this comprehensive (organizational) culture. Globalization has not wiped that away. Or perhaps we should say, with a shudder, "at least not yet."

In modern societies such a comprehensive culture is very much in the background of the beings and doings of their members. It provides their cultural context of choice without which they could not make sense of their lives or, to put it more actively, we could not make sense of our lives. For us, situated in the context of modernity, there would be no cultural membership, no group identity, without a sense of nationality structuring it, providing the organizational comprehensive culture framing and sustaining our other identities. Our situation is very different from that of the people living in the stateless societies of medieval Iceland as they are depicted in the *Sagas*. Without our distinctive national identities we would be lost: there is no standing outside these comprehensive cultures and living a life.[25] The very idea of doing this makes no sense at all.[26]

We have, as I have argued, a need – a very deep need – for self-identification and self-definition. In the context of our particular, distinctively historically situated lives, national identity will be a non-negligible part of that, even though it is not a part that in most circumstances we are adverting to, but its import for us will be felt when it is threatened or thought to be threatened. It is something which, at least strategically and instrumentally, is central in the lives of people in modern societies. Nations are not about to wither away, and a post-national identity is not just around the corner.[27] Having a sense of national-identity is a key element, but surely not the sole element, in our retaining a sense of who we are.

Most of us do not change our identities or at least we only change them in superficial ways. Even where we are the exception and not the rule, and we do over time gradually (most of us are not like Saul on the road to Damascus) in good Parfitian style change our identities rather deeply – become rather different persons with different priorities, commitments, different ways of reacting and responding to the world – still, for all of that, we do not, *individualistic* liberalism to the contrary notwithstanding, *just* choose our identities. The identities that we have are normally not even experienced as being matters of choice. Rather, where they change, though typically to some extent marked by our own endeavours, that change is deeply affected by our circumstances – often conflicting circumstances – and our change is not something chosen out of the blue.[28] And even in the case in which individuals change some bits of their ways of being and doing, it is misleading to say that they choose a new identity, that what comes into place is just chosen. Rather, what happens is that an individual in extensively altering her life is responding to a host of things in her culture and environment that affect her, and typically in conflicting ways. In responding to all of these pressures and considerations, she changes some ways in which she lives and how she views herself. But she hardly "chooses herself" or chooses a new identity. As a deeply culturally embedded person (something we all are) she makes, working with what she has, some renovations.

In the standard case, the comprehensive culture of which we are a part, along with (in many instances) even more localized cultural effects, such as our religion (or lack thereof), our ethnic group (if any), our class, our sexual orientation, our more specific political orientation (being a Communist, Libertarian, a Green) provides the cultural context in which we make our choices. But among the choices we make there is no choice of our identities, though we may deliberately, and sometimes reasonably successfully, seek to alter them. But this change will always be within limits, limits hardly specifiable in advance and certainly not rigid. Still, our identities pretty much come with our distinctive socialization. We grow into the world speaking a certain language and, with that language or languages, absorbing a certain culture. In some rare instances, like the two main characters in Andrei Makine's *Le testament français*, people are split between two conflicting comprehensive cultures (in this instance Russian and French) and the people involved are tugged in different directions and develop various blind-spots and ambivalences, but still, as in the above instance, these conflicting national identities are both deeply there, though probably for most such people one is more deeply there than the other. But it is not that such people are without a national identity, have (*pace* Omar Dahbour) their basic-identity in some subunit more local than a nation.[29] But in these rather rare cases their national identity is to some extent a polynational identity. They have, that is, cultural membership in two nations, sometimes with senses of nationality that are at war with each other within their own breasts. Still, they have national identities, though not a single one. It isn't that they have gone *überhaupt* to a "post-national identity."

The crucial thing to see here is that they have not transcended these national identities into some "post-national identity." Moreover, these are unusual cases; in the more standard case as our socialization proceeds, as the comprehensive culture becomes more firmly a part of us as we grow into adolescence – we come, usually, without thinking about such matters very much, to have ("adopt" would make it too voluntaristic) certain customs, ways of looking at things, and characteristic attunements. In Makine-like cases socialization, of course, also goes on, but it comes from two conflicting sources, producing a keen awareness (sometimes mixed with self-deception) of these disparate national identities. In, for example, the case of the narrator in *Le testament français*, his Russianness is much more dominant than he realizes.[30] But my central point is that, both in the typical case and the non-typical case, the national identities are there and deeply embedded. And it is a Nussbaumian cosmopolitan prejudice to think they must be hostile or even enfeebling to cosmopolitanism. These identities, though not as iron bonds, are prime generators of our reflective sense of self, our sense of who we are. We cosmopolitans cannot set aside our local identities as we change our clothes, for they are crucial to our lives, as they are to the life of any person, and hardly voluntary. Part of our identity, something which is inescapable, is particular and local. It can change, and sometimes deeply, but it is still, in one form or another, something which is powerfully there and a locality (a habitation and a home) remains though it may in time come to be a very transformed one. But in certain ways local it will remain. We cannot *just become* citizens of the world. We cannot *simply* be, though it is, normatively speaking, also vitally important *that* we be, of the party of humanity.

The point is that we – or at the very least most of us – have this need for having a particular culturally determinate identity. It is not enough for us to think we are members of the biological species *homo sapiens* or that we just identify (more accurately attempt to identify) with humanity at large without at the same time identifying with some particular subunit of that humanity. It is not enough because we need, as well, whatever our universalistic commitments, to have a sense of who we are. To have this sense is to have some more particular identification, an identification which is, and must be, historically and culturally rooted. We should, of course, be cosmopolitans, but *rooted* cosmopolitans – the only kind that it is in fact possible to be.[31]

To attain clarity and some reasonable moral adequacy, we must firmly recognize that our self-identifications can be, and often are, illusory and ideologically distorted and that either religion or nationalism, or both working together, have been, and not infrequently, the source of such distortion: the source of what Marxists call "false consciousness." But that does not gainsay the Herderian point that we cannot (extreme circumstances apart, and then only in a particular context) *just* relate to our fellow human beings as members of the same biological species. If we are socialists and (to be redundant) cosmopolitans (Stalin's campaign against cosmopolitanism notwithstanding), we may *try* to be something like that. However, if we are tolerably clear-headed, it will not be exactly that, for that is impossible. We will, and rightly, be egalitarians and egalitarians of a robustly substantive sort, and we will take an interest in, and be in solidarity with, the struggles of the various peoples around the world.[32] We will not, *in a fundamental sense*, put our compatriots first.[33] We must be like that – by definition, if you will, must be like that – if we are to be social liberals or socialist cosmopolitans. (The 'or' here is, of course, not exclusive.) But, if in doing this, we try to set aside local attachments, we will impoverish our lives and have as well an impoverished view of the world. We should, of course, struggle to escape ethnocentricity. But ethnocentricity is one thing, local attachments another. If we would be socialists, or more generally social liberals, we need to align our local attachments with cosmopolitan ideals. We need coherently to integrate our local attachments with a universalistic moral point of view that is committed to moral equality.[34] That is to say, to a moral point of view which takes it as settled that the life of everyone matters and matters equally.[35] So, at least in this way, even to be persons, we must have our local attachments as well. Without them, we will have no sense of who we are and we will be unable to have any attachments, including, of course, larger more universalistic attachments.

III

I turn now from arguing for the importance of national identity as providing grounds for claiming that liberal nationalism (where there is a need for it) is the best carrier of cosmopolitanism to arguing for it as furthering democracy more fully than the cosmopolitan alternatives which are not liberal nationalisms.[36] (I speak here of those contexts where there is a need for liberal nationalism. As we have seen, where a nation is secure there is no need for a nationalist movement. But there is still a need on the part of its members to have a good sense of national identity, to be aware of its importance, and it is as well important for the people in such secure nations to recognize the validity of liberal nationalist movements where a nation is insecure.)

There is an impediment to so considering things which I must first discuss. It is both tempting and easy for us, particularly if we live in the rich capitalist democracies, to be cynical about democracy. We will not, if we are reasonable, wish for the abandonment of universal suffrage (or tolerate its abandonment when we can do anything about it) or the abandonment of representative democracy, no matter how much we would wish to see some more participatory elements come on stream. But while so responding, and here we respond as the vast-majority of our fellow citizens do, we can still readily, and consistently with this, come to think of our actually existing democracies as farcical, standing at a very great distance from the attractive conceptions of democracy articulated – and variously articulated – by John Stuart Mill, John Dewey, Joshua Cohen, Frank Cunningham, Andrew Levine, Jürgen Habermas, John Rawls, Klaus Offe, and Michael Walzer. Actually existing democracy largely consists in spending a few seconds marking a ballot or operating (as in the United States) its mechanical equivalent. The democracy that we live with and which controls our political lives consists, for the most part, in doing that and in passively listening to "political discourse" as brief, usually silly, sound-bites on radio or television, of our viewing negotiated and managed unspontaneous "debates" between our major political candidates, of our viewing, hearing, or reading undetailed, unnuanced, and for the most part unreflective media discussion of what gets selected out as "the issues" with little attention to input from the grass roots. There is in our mass democracies, with their staged political events, little concern for actual citizen participation. Indeed it is exactly that that is not wanted. What is desired is just the opposite: a passive and ignorant electorate. Candidates are selected by elites largely, but not entirely, from elites. It is necessary for a candidate with any real chance of winning to have massive campaign funding. And the sources from which much of this money comes is not even remotely democratically determined, though some of the rich capitalist democracies (e.g., the United States) are worse here than others (e.g., Sweden). But generally wealth calls the tune. This, and other things cut from the same cloth, is what democracy is for most citizens of such societies. And things are usually even worse – sometimes much worse – elsewhere. Moreover, things of this sort are reasonably evident to most of the educated population of the rich capitalist democracies. And rather more inarticulately to many others as well, notwithstanding their lousy media sources. But still such knowledge causes no great stir. "So what else is new?" is a not-unlikely reaction.

All that notwithstanding, we would still struggle very hard to keep "the vote," thinking with horror of countries without it or effectively without it, like the old South Africa, the former Soviet Union, or present-day Burma, Kuwait, Saudi Arabia, and Iraq. We are likely to repeat to ourselves, when feeling the force of such considerations, some version of the old saw that democracy is the worst system imaginable except for all the others. Still, if not in its details, at least in its general thrust, something like Noam Chomsky's view of political life in the rich capitalist democracies, and most particularly in the United States, is very compelling.

So the prospects for democracy are bleak and may well be getting bleaker.[37] But, as Antonio Gramsci will not let us forget, we are participants in our world and not just spectators. However cynical we are about democracy, still, if we could have it, or even something which approximates it, we would want something very like what John Dewey persistently portrayed and what John Rawls models with his conception of political liberalism (though we would pay much more attention than he to workplace-democracy and to issues concerning power). There are vast structural differences of power in all our liberal societies. If they are inescapable, there will be little equality in other domains as well, or autonomy either. What anguishes us, and prods us to rethink what is to be done, is our recognition of the great distance our actual democracies are from such conceptions as we find in Dewey and Rawls.

My contention is that in modern industrial ("post-industrial," if you will) societies, cosmopolitan liberal nationalisms can achieve, where nations are insecure, if their projects for society are successful, a more adequate approximation of democracy than their alternatives in such situations. All of our societies are badly off, and their democratic prospects are bleak. They *may* even be getting bleaker, though that is not so sure. But the prospects are a little less bleak for social democratically oriented liberal nationalisms as well as for societies such as Norway and Finland which are secure nation-states (secure in their nationhood and comprehensive culture), and thus in no need of a nationalist agenda and movement.

Democracy is essentially about popular self-governance: about the governance of "we the people."[38] Nation-states and multi-nation states, having nations as component parts, are for us the most likely democratic options. Both are made up of either a nation or of nations. When we speak of a nation we are, as we have seen, speaking of a people organized as a political community.[39] Popular self-governance and sovereignty is, of course, talk about you and me and the rest of us having control over our lives, including very centrally control over, as far as that is humanly possible, what our society is to be like and how it will develop. But, while remaining individuals – what else? – with all the value that accrues to individual autonomy, we are also members of a nation (in some instances nations) and, as we have seen, our very identity is tied up with that. It is as *a people* (a nation) that we primarily exercise *political* self-governance. And it is nations that can claim sovereignty and sometimes have it. In wishing to be *maîtres chez nous*, it is centrally for us as a people (as members of this "we") that we wish to have it, though, as well, we wish to have it (or at least many of us do) for ourselves as individuals. Many of us despair of getting anything like this. We tend to think belief in it is an ideological illusion. But for most of us, if we could have something in that neighbourhood, we would grab it with both hands. It would be of crucial significance for us without at all being the whole of our lives. But while utopia is certainly not around the corner, it is not clear that nothing can be done that would yield a little bit more by way of self-governance than what we now have. And, where nations are at risk, a robust and intelligently designed and carried-out liberal nationalism will further democratic aspirations without at all undermining individual rights.

I will flesh this out a little. Given the strategic importance of nations, democracy is best attained by a liberal nationalism or by a people, generally with social liberal commitments, organized in a nation-state or multi-nation state, which would be nationalistic if their nations were threatened. Both realize democracy more adequately than the other forms of political liberalism, including its anti-nationalist cosmopolitan forms. People are, though, of course variously, *a people*; they always have a group identity and, under conditions of modernity, this takes the form of a national identity. With their distinctive interests and an understanding of their own culture, when they can freely act politically, individually, and as a people, they are more in control of their lives than they otherwise would be. This being so, they can better govern themselves than if they are governed by others (alien others). The same thing obtains where, as the smaller unit in a much larger political unit, they end up, concerning the bargaining and compromises that go on between the bigger and smaller units, having less say than their bigger brothers. This obtains where there are two or more nations of unequal size and strength in a single state which is not a genuinely multi-nation state. This can be overcome, or at least ameliorated, where these nations split into independent nation-states or organize themselves as a genuinely multi-nation state with equal status for each component nation and with significant self-governance for each nation regardless of size as an equal sovereign nation in a multi-national federation. Here we should also recognize, particularly in our interdependent world that there is nothing like "absolute sovereignty."[40]

So with all of democracy's discontents, nations remain crucial to democracy under conditions of modernity – under, that is, foreseeable conditions for us. Where a nation lacks self-governance, where people cannot be *maîtres chez nous*, to that very important extent, democracy is undermined. Where we have a *pseudo-multi-nation* state – Canada is arguably an example – where some of the component nations lack such self-governance and equal status, then, to that extent, democracy is weakened.[41] It is in bad shape anyway, but without, where nations are endangered, the effective ethos of liberal nationalism, it is in even worse shape. A pseudo-multi-nation state cannot help but be a very imperfect democracy in a very imperfectly democratic world – imperfect, for among other reasons, the reasons to which I have just adverted.

To translate into the concrete what I mean by the very imperfectly democratic world faced by nation-states, genuine multi-nation states and pseudo-multi-nation states alike, consider the present situation of Quebec. It is as thoroughly a liberal democratic society as most societies in the rich capitalist democracies and more so than some. Still, to suggest how imperfect as democracies our rich capitalist democracies are, consider the fact that Quebec may gain its independence while still continuing to be ruled by elites (though now by its own governing elites). Moreover, without democracy coming to the workplace, Quebec (like all the other rich capitalist democracies, though some more so than others) will still continue to be dominated by a capitalist class. And democracy may not (most probably will not) be extended to smaller units of people, so urgently argued for by socialist anarchists and "greens," smaller units that would have, where they become active elements in the civil society, the solidarity so essential for democratic life, and which would give us something on which we can build, so that with them we would come to have effective units – or so the belief goes – to resist neo-liberal capitalist globalization.[42] Quebec might gain independence without gaining any of those things. Put more bluntly, Quebec sovereignty, if it becomes a reality in a few years, is not likely to bear any of *those* democratic fruits.

Some think I am being too pessimistic here and that with the somewhat social democratic orientation of some of the key players on the sovereignist side and, more importantly, the actual civil society of Quebec, there might be more resistance to capitalist globalization and the like than I believe is likely. I remain skeptical here, but it is something that we can hope will obtain. However, even *if* my pessimism is a telling it like it is, it does not at all mean that sovereignty would not inch democracy along in Quebec.

Just that, given that it is liberal nationalism that is at issue – as it is – would justify Quebec's secession.[43]

Still, liberal nationalism is not, nor is anything else, a magic wand that will solve all of Quebec's political ills, yielding the full component of democratic life so essential for human flourishing. If in the next few years Quebec gains its independence, it will not carry with it these wonderfully democratic things – things that surely would enhance human flourishing. The most that can be hoped for is that it will move its citizens an inch or so closer to being able to achieve them. But, even without such an inching, it will to some extent advance democracy. If sovereignty is gained in Quebec (and this can and should be generalized to other nations similarly situated), if, that is, its liberal nationalist agenda pays off, it will give a people – and that is what the Québécoise are – a little more control over their lives than they would otherwise have. And that certainly is not nothing.

It is essential to remember here that we have been speaking of a liberal nationalism construed as a social liberal nationalism and not of nationalism *sans phrase*. As a social liberalism, it will, fitting the model of political liberalism profoundly articulated by Joshua Cohen and John Rawls, have a political conception of justice with its determinate principles of justice for our basic institutions and social practices.[44] There are here principles which are designed to protect equal basic liberties for all and, with them, the civil and human rights of individuals. It will, while seeking solidarity as well (something underplayed in our societies), seek a proper balance of equality and liberty while protecting both and seeking to extend them. This model will make us see how very deeply equality and liberty depend on each other. We cannot have one without the other. (This is the central thrust of the work of John Rawls and of central portions of the work of Ronald Dworkin, G. A. Cohen, and Amartya Sen.) This means that the liberties of the ethnic and national minorities in a sovereign nation (sovereign in either their own nation state or in a *genuine* multi-nation state) will be fully respected. They will either actually have full citizenship or have available to them (as immigrants) the unencumbered right, once they have met certain clearly specified conditions, to attain full citizenship. It will also be the case that their civil liberties will be protected, their distinctive ways of life as ethnic minorities respected, their historical rights as national minorities protected, and neither group will in any way be excluded from the life of the nation. This is, if you will, analytic of liberal nationalism. Nationalism cannot be liberal without having all these features. To the very extent that it lacks any of them, it will *not* be a liberal nationalism. Such things are built into the very idea of liberal nationalism.[45] Moreover, liberal nationalism is not just an *idea* in the heads of some intellectuals but has exemplifications (imperfect though they be) in some liberal societies. Scotland, Belgium, Quebec, Catalonia, and Wales come to mind. And Norway, Iceland, and Finland were exemplifications in the past when there was the need for a nationalist agenda in those societies.

I have argued not only for the compatibility of cosmopolitanism and liberal nationalism, I have argued as well that liberal nationalism – as a social and political liberalism – more fully realizes the ideals of cosmopolitanism (where nations are insecure or reasonably believed to be insecure) than a non-nationalist, to say nothing of, an anti-nationalist, cosmopolitanism. Here the idea of a political liberalism, as opposed to neo-liberalism, is important and was stressed. In articulating this liberal nationalism, the role and import of both national identity and the democratic self-governance of nations in enhancing human flourishing was argued for. Cosmopolitan liberal nationalism is not an oxymoron. Quite to the contrary, "a cosmopolitan liberal nationalism" is a pleonasm.

Notes

1. Nielsen, "Socialism and Nationalism."
2. Nussbaum, "Patriotism and Cosmopolitanism."
3. Berlin, *Against the Current*, 333–55; Appiah, "Cosmopolitan Patriots"; and Nussbaum, "Patriotism and Cosmopolitanism."
4. Rawls, *Political Liberalism*, 15–22.
5. Sometimes these individualistic liberals are also libertarians, but not all individualistic liberals would feel comfortable with the label "libertarian," so I use the more inclusive designation.
6. Barry, "Nationalism"; and Nussbaum, "Patriotism and Cosmopolitanism."
7. What I intend by "adequate" here will become clear, I hope, as my argument unfolds. I am generally here speaking of forms that will be adequate from a reflective and informed political and moral point of view: forms that we would, as moral agents, reflectively endorse when we are well informed and being impartial.
8. Nagel, *Mortal Questions*, 105–27.
9. That is the sense that the idea of a primary good has in Rawls's thought.

See Rawls, *A Theory of Justice*, 62 and 92–93: "primary goods … are things which it is supposed a rational man wants whatever else he wants. Regardless of what an individual's rational plans are in detail it is assumed that there are various things which he would prefer more of rather than less. With more of these goods men can generally be assured of greater success in carrying out their intentions and in advancing their ends, whatever these ends may be" (92). A page later Rawls adds "Now the assumption is that, though men's rational plans do have different final ends, they nevertheless all require for their execution certain primary goods, natural and social. Plans differ since individual abilities, circumstances and wants differ; rational plans are adjusted to these contingencies. But whatever one's system of ends, primary goods are necessary means" (93). As he puts it in *Political Liberalism*, primary goods are "general all-purpose means" (188). They are things that we need for whatever it is that we may want to do.

10 O'Neill, *Towards Justice and Virtue*; and Nielsen, "Cosmopolitanism."

11 Barry, "Nationalism."

12 Rawls, *Political Liberalism*, 16–17.

13 Craig, "Hitler the Populist"; and Lukacs, "The Hitler of History."

14 Couture and Nielsen, "Liberal Nationalism Both Cosmopolitan and Rooted," 579–662; Kymlicka, "Misunderstanding Nationalism"; and Nielsen, "Cultural Nationalism, Neither Ethnic nor Civic."

15 Rawls, *A Theory of Justice*; and Barry, *Justice as Impartiality*.

16 Berlin, *The Crooked Timber of Humanity*, 238–61; G. A. Cohen, *History, Labour, and Freedom*, 132–54; and Nielsen, "Socialism and Nationalism."

17 Barber, "Constitutional Faith."

18 Appiah, "Cosmopolitan Patriots."

19 Berlin, *Vico and Herder*.

20 Kymlicka, *Liberalism, Community, and Culture*, 166–69.

21 Rawls, *Political Liberalism*, 30–31.

22 National identity is a central form of group identity in conditions of modernity. But it might be responded that claims about group identity being a primary good sit badly with the above argument in my text. However, I think not, for a primary good is a strategic good. It is something that is necessary for our achieving our aims, but it does not follow from that that it is what we value the most highly, but rather it is something that we, if we are thinking at all clearly, will recognize is necessary (causally necessary) for us to have in order to attain our ends, whatever they are. A primary good is, that is, as I have quoted Rawls saying, a general all-purpose means. But it need not be the case that we see our nationality (our comprehensive cultural membership) as being the most important thing in our lives. Indeed its being so would be very strange. What is strategically central *may* also be an inherent or intrinsic good, but it need not be. I take no position about whether a primary good (any primary good) is also an inherent or intrinsic good. Moreover, it could be an inherent or intrinsic good without being the highest good, if indeed there is such a thing. What it is vital to recognize is that there

would be little in the way of securely realizing our life plans, whatever they are, without cultural membership, without a secure national identity.

23. It is important to keep firmly in mind the difference between (1) the importance that we give (consciously and deliberately) to our national identity and (2) the strategic importance, often unnoticed by people, of national identity in the formation and the sustaining of their personal identities. In speaking of the importance of national identity and of how it is a primary good, we are concerned with (2). That is compatible with people not giving it a high priority in their lives and its not being much of a factor in their *sense* of self. They may well only come to recognize how important it is to them when they are threatened with its loss. I owe this, or something rather like it, to Jocelyne Couture.

24. Rawls, *Political Liberalism*, 42, 146, and 201.

25. Berlin, *Vico and Herder*.

26. Wittgenstein, *On Certainty*; Davidson, *Inquiries into Truth and Interpretation*, 183–93; and Rorty, *Objectivity, Relativism and Truth*, 93–172.

27. It is not crystal clear what is meant by "post-national identity," though I do not think it is bandied about as loosely as "post-modernity." I think "post-national identity" is something like the idea of people coming to have a sense of their being Europeans as distinct from being French, German, Italian, and the like or being Latin Americans (Bolivar's dream) as distinct from being Argentineans. Brazilians, Colombians, Chileans, Cubans, and the like. The idea is that their being (for example) good Europeans is far more important to them than their being good Germans. To have such a sense of identity is to have a post-national identity. The idea seems to me to rest on a false contrast, for why should there be a conflict, for example, between being Dutch and being European? Only if our sense of nationality was non-liberal or the nation state of which we are members is illiberal would there be a necessary or even a presumptive conflict.

28. This might be thought to conflict with my Rawlsian stress on autonomy. People, and as something of their own doing, have their own life-plans, goals, and ideals. And these things are important to them and to their sense of who they are. All of this is true, and importantly so, but it does not contradict or even stand in tension with my claim that we do not choose our identities and that what we are grows out of our circumstances. We are not prisoners of our circumstances, but they provide us with the context of cultural choice. Human beings, Marx well said, make their own history, but not in circumstances of their own choosing. Situated selves and autonomous selves are not alternatives. There is no anti-Rawlsian commitment to communitarianism in what I am saying here.

29. Dahbour, "The Nation-State as a Political Community"; but see Couture and Nielsen, "Liberal Nationalism Both Cosmopolitan and Rooted," 592–612.

30. Tolstoya, "Dreams of My Russian Summers."

31 M. Cohen, "Rooted Cosmopolitanism"; Appiah, "Cosmopolitan Patriots"; and Barber, "Constitutional Faith."

32 Nielsen, *Equality and Liberty*.

33 Pogge, "The Bounds of Nationalism."

34 O'Neill, *Towards Justice and Virtue*.

35 Nagel, *Mortal Questions*, 106–27.

36 One reader has responded in the following way to my argument in II. "Your argument," this reader remarked, "principally shows that even cosmopolitans need local identities, but that we would be better cosmopolitans if we are also liberal nationalists (or will stand in solidarity with liberal nationalists where our own nation is secure and their nation is insecure) is another matter altogether and has not been established by your argument." But, *au contraire*, if my argument is sound that in conditions of modernity, group identity, and with that, local identity, requires national identity, then to show, as the objection accepts, that cosmopolitans need local identities is to show that they need national identities in the circumstances of contemporary industrial or "post-industrial" societies. The only way to have a local identity, or at least a secure one, in such circumstances is to have a national identity.

37 Nielsen, "Reconceptualizing Civil Society for Now."

38 Though we must add as well, as Rawls stresses, the need for a firm constitutional basis with what he calls "constitutional essentials" in place. Rawls, *Political Liberalism*, 165–67.

39 Kymlicka, "Misunderstanding Nationalism."

40 Pogge, "Cosmopolitanism and Sovereignty."

41 It may be that they have a *de jure* equal status, but not a *de facto* equal status, but for the multi-nation state to be a genuine one, the component nations must have both *de jure* and *de facto* equal status. Otherwise talk of equal status is a fraud.

42 Dahbour, "The Nation-State as a Political Community."

43 Nielsen: "Cultural Nationalism, Neither Ethnic nor Civic"; and "Liberal Nationalism, Liberal Democracies, and Secession."

44 J. Cohen: "Democratic Equality"; and "A More Democratic Liberalism"; and Rawls, *Political Liberalism*.

45 It is a blemish on the democracy of the United States that no immigrant can become president of the United States. This means that full citizenship is denied to immigrants, and so there are legally sanctioned grades of citizenship, some full and some not. This hardly becomes any democratic nation and most particularly not a settler nation.

World Government: A Cosmopolitan Imperative?

I

The root idea of cosmopolitanism is the idea that each individual is a citizen of the world and owes allegiance to "the worldwide community" of human beings.[1] The kernel of this idea, originating with the Greek cynics, was developed by and flourished with the Stoics (particularly with the Roman Stoics), and was later transformed by Condorcet and, most particularly, by Kant, who gave it a clearer *institutional* formulation. It retains the central claim of moral cosmopolitanism, namely, that of the equal worth of all persons on the globe and of an equal respect for the greatest of us as well as for the least of us as "life dishes out its very unequal delights." Cosmopolitanism is committed to supporting the very idea of the equal dignity of all persons. This is indeed something that our actual life conditions grossly violate every day, in some parts of the world more grossly than in others. We must not for a moment blink at that. Yet this ideal, distant from the hurly-burly world, rightly remains a central element of a cosmopolitan heuristic. That very root idea of classical cosmopolitanism, again to repeat, already runs beyond a purely moral cosmopolitanism to a political and institutional cosmopolitanism. There is reference to "the worldwide community of human beings" and to the necessity of our having an allegiance to such a community. (I would say, regrettably, "to the so-called worldwide community of human beings" since such a community is only a hope: a utopian ideal. There actually is no such community and perhaps there is not much likelihood of one coming into being.) Moral cosmopolitanism and political cosmopolitanism need not, and should not, conflict. In fact, moral cosmopolitanism must have a political and institutional home. There must be institutional structures in place for its exemplification and implementation.

It is to such political cosmopolitanism that I now turn. There is a vision of the world that goes with and indeed animates this political as well as moral cosmopolitanism. It views all of us featherless bipeds as sisters and brothers and as being equal members in a worldwide community of *aspiration* and *endeavour*. It doesn't commit itself on whether such a community exists or is likely to come to exist. Political cosmopolitans – unless their heads are completely in the air – know very well that there is no actually existing worldwide community or even one waiting in the wings. Indeed, in the violent and brutal world we know, a global world order – what George H. W. Bush called "The New World Order" – may be increasingly, though fortunately not securely, coming into being with a brutal New Imperialism attempting, and in part succeeding, though at great human cost, in implementing that order.[2] But this global order is no global *community*. It is not even a faint anticipation of one. Indeed, it is (except perhaps in propaganda) the denial of what the Stoics, Condorcet, or Kant aspired to. Nothing like this cosmopolitan ideal is moving into sight, though political cosmopolitans can reasonably *hope* that a global community will arise out of a cosmopolitan transformation of our swinish world – arising, if you will, out of our "actually existing cosmopolitanisms," extensively created by the activities of our multinationals with capitalist state support. But for now, a "world community" is a metaphor for a possible world – hopefully, a near possible world. It is hopefully something that will guide us in transforming our world into a humanly habitable place for all of us and not just (but insecurely) for the lucky few. The thing is to sufficiently cash in this hope and to make it into a regulative ideal that we could struggle to make into something that would actually regulate. I mean for it to be something we can reasonably politically struggle to make into a reality both at home (I speak here of the rich capitalist North) and (more urgently) globally, or at least to approximate it to some reasonable degree and provide corrective measures in the South. This will require not just "fine" moralizing (as Marx well recognized) but careful attention to a future-oriented institutional design.

Without that we will get just utopia and not what John Rawls aspired to and called a *realistic* utopia. (Remember, even Bush Jr., who not implausibly could be charged with war crimes, speaks blithely of the equal worth of all human beings. The tides of moral ideology are running very high.)

II

Let us briefly turn to a somewhat fuller specification of a political cosmopolitan's vision of things – a vision which I take to be a useful prolegomenon to seeing the import of the sort of institutional design I shall characterize and defend.

Cosmopolitans have not only been egalitarians and internationalists, and they are not only believers in the possibility and desirability of a world community and strivers to make it a reality (or at least an approximate reality). They are, as well, both *curious about and tolerant of* most of the many ways of living and forms of life and, in view of these differences, advocates of a pluralism – indeed, what Scheffler has called a Heraclitean pluralism – that sometimes goes over into particularism as well.[3] This, if we are not conceptually confused, does not lead to an absurd cultural relativism (perhaps a pleonasm) which says: (i) anything that gets stamped into a culture is right for that culture or at least for those whom it gets stamped into and (ii) we have no cross-cultural criteria for saying such an enculturated view can be mistaken or morally untoward. Thus, translating again into the concrete, if in some culture the majority is regarded not only as having the right view of things but as having the stringent duty to hack to death members of a minority in that culture that the majority despises, it is right for that majority in that culture to do so. It is not only *thought* to be desirable by them, but it *is* desirable for them. Or, to take a somewhat less extreme example, if it is thought in a culture to be necessary and right to educate men but not women, then it is right for that culture to do so. Such views of things are plainly wrong and demonstrably so. They could never get into a wide reflective equilibrium.

There will be a lot of things in a culture – including our own particular culture – that some of us may not much like. When I see people with yarmulkes, big crosses around their necks, or head scarves, I think to myself (perhaps ethnocentrically), "How absurd." But I wouldn't even dream of banning these practices, criticizing them, or ridiculing them. And when in summer I see Catholic nuns or Orthodox Muslim women in their heavy garb or Orthodox Jewish men or Hutterite men with their big beards, heavy dark suits, and big hats, I think how uncomfortable they must be. I think they must be awfully hot. "How absurd," I think, "for them to think it is their moral and religious duty to go around so encumbered." But that's their business, not mine. It is no skin off my bottom. It doesn't make me hot. *Perhaps* it has, in a way I am not aware of, some deep kind of symbolic significance for them. Similar things apply to me. When I see the red flag of communism or the black flag of anarchy flapping in the wind, I am heartened and when I hear *The Internationale* sung, I cry. Most of you probably will think all of this is absurd on my part. However, if we are political cosmopolitans, we will learn to live with such differences, whether we think privately they are absurd or not, and *some* of them sometimes we may even come to appreciate. We slowly and sometimes with difficulty become tolerant of very different people.[4]

Sometimes it is hard for us as when we are in an apartment building and someone slaughters a sheep there during Ramadan or perhaps someone cooks what to us is some foul-smelling dish such as the Swedish *ludfishe* at Christmas or in the summer a neighbour plays rock music when we are trying to read or write in our gardens. But if we are cosmopolitans, we learn to put up with it. The world wasn't made – indeed, it wasn't made at all – for us as particular individuals with our particular ways of doing things and our particular sensibilities. Bach as background music is fine for me while I read or write, but rap is not. But people are different and we all should have some *lebensraum* if we don't harm others. Sometimes inconveniencing or disturbing others does not constitute a harm or at least it is a "minimal harm" that is tolerable and should be tolerated for the sake of others. We must learn to respect the perspectives of others, sometimes very different others. But we must remember that live-and-let-live cuts in both directions. Perhaps he doesn't have to play his rap music quite so loudly.

There are, however, limits to tolerance – limits to the slogan "different places, different customs." There are things we should not tolerate where we can do anything about them and we should speak out against even when we can't. Though where it is terribly dangerous to oppose them, we should cultivate wile. (Think of the Nazi period in Germany or the United States with McCartheyism.) We should develop a good Brechtian sense here. J. S. Mill and John Rawls were right that we should, *ceteris paribus*, only tolerate those who will tolerate others. We shouldn't, that is, *tolerate the intolerant or at least not tolerate their intolerance*. If it is true that the Taliban buried homosexuals alive and banned women doctors from practising, this should not be tolerated, and the U.S. treatment of prisoners held at Guantanamo Bay and its practice of extraordinary rendition should not be tolerated either. All of these things are gross violations of human rights, and they should be resisted where we have the power to do so and disapproved of (though sometimes with wile) where we don't. Where we have genuine violations of human rights, we have plainly something which is morally intolerable, though sometimes there are some things in some situations we can't do anything about.

Sophisticated political cosmopolitans will also be wary of a lot of talk of human rights. It not infrequently is a Sword of Empire; talk of human rights, that is, is sometimes used to sell an aggressive war. It almost makes me ill to hear Bush prattle on about bringing liberty and democracy to the world. We have there crude moral ideology; still many are taken in by it. Some mouth it unwittingly. Simone de Beauvoir recounts in her autobiography that when fleeing on bicycle the Nazi occupation of Paris, she was stopped at a small village already occupied by the Nazis. A young German officer, checking her papers, politely explained to her that, "We Germans have not come here to oppress the French but we come as friends to protect you from the British." Presumably (and incredibly), he sincerely believed it. It is usually the other fellow, we think, who is caught up in ideology and propaganda and not us. But not infrequently that is a delusion. The other guy may well be caught up in an ideology but so unwittingly may we. Consciousness about these matters is hardly ever clear.

Still, Islamic fundamentalism and American imperialism in the actions I mentioned above, and many similar actions, have violated human rights in ways that are plainly intolerable. (Though without power we can do nothing for the time but "tolerate" – live with – the intolerable.) That notwithstanding, tolerance is an extremely important component of political cosmopolitanism. But in being committed to it we should also guard against being gulled.

However, it is not only tolerance that is valued by political cosmopolitans but also curiosity about and concern for quite different, sometimes *radically different*, peoples. A political cosmopolitan will have a bit of the anthropologist's interest and often the novelist's interest as well in foreigners and in human differences and in what are often people's underlying sometimes not so apparent similarities. (Maybe the anthropologist's interest and the novelist's interest come to much the same thing?) People and ways of life are often radically different and sometimes fascinatingly so, though they are not, of course, completely different. If that were the case we could never even understand each other and we could never even come to understand that that was so vis-à-vis others. We would be up against a blank wall. (Philosophical confusion is abundant here.) We would be in a situation similar to that of not understanding what it is like to be a bat.

We are not, however, in such a predicament. All of us – that is we featherless bipeds – have experienced pain and most probably some moments of happiness or at least pleasure. We – or at least most of us – have experienced some moments of kindness towards ourselves and some moments of lack of consideration and maybe even hostility or perhaps even brutality. We could go on and on in that vein. Things like this are recurrent features in all or almost all human life. What these things will specifically consist in will to some degree – sometimes to a considerable degree – vary from culture to culture and situation to situation, but there will always be some overlap.[5] We can go back in history and empathetically understand something of what is going on there – not all of it, but the crucial parts of it. Some of it will often deeply move us and make us aware of our common human links over time and space, e.g., Priam at Achilles' tent in *The Iliad* or Antigone's determination to bury her brother. But parts of the *Iliad* and even more of *The Divine Comedy* are opaque to all but some specialists. Parts of *Moby Dick* are tedious for contemporary readers. Still, people are often very, very different and we political cosmopolitans want to understand those very different others as much as we can; hence, our anthropologist's interest. We want to understand them not so that we can dominate them or help some imperial power dominate them (though that has been done) and not just so (though sometimes we want to do this too) as to scientifically explain them (be able at least to predict their behaviour and figure out what makes them tick) but so as to widen and deepen our understanding of human life, including our own lives.

The cosmopolitan urge and vision is to *cultivate humanity* – to use the title of Martha Nussbaum's fine book on cosmopolitan education.[6] This is an enormous task concerning which we all, if we are honest with ourselves, cannot but feel very inadequate. Yet the cosmopolitan urge is that there be nothing that is alien to us. That is one deep reason why we read the books that we do, view the art that we view, listen to the music that we do, see the films that we see, meet and converse with the people that we meet and seek out and converse with as much across the world as we can manage and why we go metaphorically back in time as we converse with our great dead ancestors when we reflect on what we have read of them or about them. To have such urges is to have a cosmopolitan aspiration and to, with this, have a cosmopolitan vision of life where we seek to gain as much as we can of this human understanding and this sort of human fellow feeling.[7] The human understanding we seek is an empathic understanding – what some psychologists call *verstehen*.

III

Such a setting out of what it is to have a cosmopolitan aspiration gives us something of a clue as to how we, together and over time, can and should articulate a design of a cosmopolitan world. It gives us some idea of what a cosmopolitan world should look like. David Held and his associates give us *something* of that.[8] They speak of cosmopolitan democracy, of a global community, of a global civil society, of divided non-hierarchical sovereignty, and of global governance. There are sometimes some suggestive things here. But too much is too vague and indeterminate to provide much of anything substantive or yield much understanding. There are too many platitudes and obscurities.[9] There is, as I have noted, no global community. There is hardly anything anymore much like national *communities*, particularly in our increasingly contemporary multi-national, multi-ethnic, and multi-linguistic societies. There is little of the social glue that goes with *gemeineschaftliche* societies and little sense of what the sense of "community" is when we speak vapidly as in talk of "the global community" or (though somewhat less so) of "global civil society." And it is unclear what global governance could come to without some form of global state or global federation. But these notions are anathema to Held and company and indeed to most people. Still, the idea of cosmopolitan democracy contains little that is clear without an explanation (which we do not have) of how there could come into being a cosmopolitan government and what could that be if not a world government or a reasonably articulated conception of a global federation? Divided sovereignty sounds a little better, particularly with the *de facto* demise of Westphalian states. There could be a supernational order (say, the UN) with its distinct type of global sovereignty, some remnant of national sovereignty in the nation-states, and municipal sovereignty at least in the big municipalities.[10] Various distinct powers and prerogatives would devolve to each. *But who (if anyone) has the authority or the power to decide how they should devolve and, when these distinct sovereignties come into conflict, as they at least upon occasion will, who is to decide which sovereignty is to prevail? It looks like some form of Hobbesian sovereignty is inescapable.* And in this context should we not take to heart Hobbes's words that "covenants without swords are mere words"? Does sovereign authority, when push comes to shove, come down finally to brute power? Hobbesianism remains challenging.[11]

I published on request (1988) an essay on world government in which I broke ranks with received wisdom and defended a conception of world government.[12] I wrote it in two weeks as I hiked along, thinking about it, on New Zealand's wild western coast on its South Island. After thinking about it all day, I would hole up each night in some usually ramshackle motel-like structure and scribble what I had been thinking while on those hikes. Thomas Pogge was selected to respond to me and when the whole thing came out and I saw his response, I thought that he had simply, and as conclusively as you can get about such matters, demolished my argument.[13] Perhaps in writing what I wrote my brain got too addled from so much time under New Zealand's sun. So I simply stopped thinking about global government and stuck with the received wisdom that we have gained largely from Kant and latterly from Rawls and from Walzer.[14] Then, three or four years ago, some students of mine read the exchange between Pogge and me and tried to persuade me that I was not entirely wrong and that the whole issue of global government, faced as we are with capitalist globalization, standardly in service of imperialism, needed rethinking and to be put back on the political agenda, particularly in the face of the march of economic globalization.[15] I began to think about global government again.

A few weeks ago, I was asked by a publisher to review a book manuscript of a Swedish philosophy professor. The manuscript bore the title *Global Democracy: A Defense*. It is a robust defence of a world government by an author keenly cognizant of the battery of arguments directed against world government and makes crystal clear the feasible options and issues concerning global governance. I urged its publication. In what follows I will make my own blend of his arguments – more accurately, my understanding or perhaps misunderstanding of his arguments – and arguments of my own devising that have been percolating with me since I began to think about world government again. This will give, if near to the mark, some substance – some backbone – to political cosmopolitan arguments: to the political cosmopolitan ideas of cosmopolitan democracy and global governance, and perhaps even to the idea of a global community that are (hopefully) neither ideological in what is standardly taken to be Marx's sense nor so much moralistic mush. (For a sharp deconstruction of moralistic mush, see the writings of another Swedish philosopher of another generation.)[16]

Our world is an ever-increasingly globalized world: a world of capitalist globalization, and, even if the world shifts to a socialist mode of production, we will still have a globalized world, though with an importantly different economic rationale. We, in either event, have or will have a global economy. Barring a new and devastating world war, a series of devastating nuclear terrorist attacks, a prolonged and global economic catastrophe, or an environmental catastrophe – all distressingly real possibilities – globalization in some form will go right on rolling along.[17] This (for the near future) will take a resolutely capitalist form with the advancement of U.S. imperialism either with a neo-conservative/neo-liberal orientation with its bare-knuckled fist of *hard power* or it will consist of a return (more likely in my view) to a more multi-lateral but still neo-liberal capitalist imperialism of a Clintonist sort utilizing principally *soft power* – the fist covered by a velvet glove – that is with hard power always in reserve if needed.[18] Whichever form it takes, it will be committed to a U.S. domination of the world: an imperialism – indeed, a hyper-imperialism – with a global reach.[19] This, to the extent it continues to succeed, retain, and even gain more power, will be a despotic and dangerously tyrannical world government in everything but name.[20] (It may be slowly dismantling itself.)[21]

An invisible-hand response in reaction to American imperialism *could* be the *beginnings* of an emergence of a democratic and socialist world government. A Bolivarian continental democracy in South America has something of a chance of becoming a reality. "South America today, tomorrow the world" is something we might (in spite of its grim historical reminder) chant and *perhaps* not so irresponsibly. People in the North and the South *might* get fed up with their deteriorating conditions. I don't say (regretfully) that this is the most likely empirical possibility or the most likely scenario for the world, but it is an empirical possibility that we on the Left can devoutly hope will become an actuality. It is something for which we can and should struggle.[22]

The world's population, both North and South, seeing that the United States is the hyper-imperialist sole super-power with a military might that the rest of the world, at least taken as separate nation-states, cannot hope to match, *might* (in a few countries at first, sparked by a few thoughtful and resolute militants, but rapidly accelerating) decide to demilitarize. Without the expenditure on the military, a lot of money would be freed up in these countries to improve the social and economic lives of their populations in the North and, as things (if indeed they do) get less desperate for them, of the South as well. Citizens of the United States, seeing right on their borders Canada's and Quebec's standards of living rising while theirs is going down, might increasingly be caused to have a sense vis-à-vis their own country that something is rotten in the kingdom of Denmark. So people in the United States may very well start asking, "Why are we losing out?" It does not take a genius or an economic wizard to see why: it is principally the heavy expenditures by the U.S. government on its military and its addiction to a rather senseless consumerism. It is those expenditures that are the principal cause of the United States losing out economically and socially and now increasingly and to no rational point since the rest of the world will have become extensively demilitarized and consumerism is becoming increasingly senseless.

Still, there is now no military force to stand against the United States. They can practically occupy any country they want, but, as we have seen in Vietnam, Afghanistan, and now dramatically in Iraq, they can't pacify and control the place once they have occupied it. (Even the "practically occupy any country they want" is overstated. It would for them be quite a trick to occupy Russia, China, or India and impossible to pacify them once occupied.) Nevertheless, given U.S. objectives, occupy or try to control they must, but factually they seem not to be able to control even with all their power to shock and awe. Moreover, their economic model and way of life is becoming increasingly less attractive. They produce, both in Iraq and Afghanistan, hatreds and resistances. Indeed, around the world they are becoming increasingly hated or at least disliked. They are more and more seen not as the world's liberators and benefactors but as the world's bully and this notwithstanding extensive U.S. propaganda to the contrary. Yet still the military expenditures just go on (and indeed increasingly so) and U.S. imperialism, both for itself and its minions, continues to seek dominance with more hatred, or at least dislike, directed at the United States. The United States can neither stabilize Iraq to secure its oil and gas nor lose out on the control of Iraq's oil and gas, something that is geopolitically essential to them. They, as the saying goes, are between a rock and a hard place. If, out of desperation, they end up attacking Iran or Pakistan or both, their troubles will only multiply.

U.S. citizens, however, may very well increasingly come to ask about the rationale and the rationality of such military expense or even come to question what they are told – where they are told anything at all – about the rationale for U.S. government behaviour. Where they perhaps have come to believe (after long periods of denial) in an American Empire, they may now cease to believe it is a *benign* empire that it is what Michael Ignatieff has called an *empire lite*.[23] American citizens may come to ask if, after all, that empire is not out to dominate and, in doing so, aggress the world even if the U.S. population loses out economically and socially. What, they may also ask, is the point of that? In my scenario about non-U.S. demilitarization, the United States becomes invulnerable to attack by another country or coalition of countries. But the U.S citizens, coming to see that these countries demilitarize with the result that no one other than the United States has a military force that is anything other than an extended police force, may well draw the conclusion that a United States, armed to the teeth as it is, is irrational and harmful to their own interests as well as the interests of others. The U.S. citizens, that is, may well come to ask if it is necessary to keep up all that military expense when all other countries have demilitarized and, because of that, could not attack the United States. Thus the United States, they might conclude, no longer needs such a massive military force to protect itself. A remarkably low-budget army would suffice. (It might, of course, well be thought that these nations will not demilitarize. China, for example, is arming itself to the teeth and is undertaking joint military exercises with Russia. That does not seem like a move toward demilitarization. The old geopolitical struggle might just go on as it always has with its increasingly horrible wars. But the strategists of these countries, perhaps with pressure from their populations, *may* come to conclude that the United States will have finally learned a lesson and will not be so foolish as to invade them and try to occupy them and with that belief they will convince their governments to be content with a low-budget army and put their energies elsewhere. The effect, if the other nations so behave, on the United States might be roughly the same.)

It will be said, of course, that there would still be the threat of terrorist attacks by non-state terrorist agents such as Al Qaeda. Indeed, this danger (*perhaps* exaggerated) will for a time remain, though a non-imperialist and non-aggressive United States might *over time* erode such terrorist attractions. But in thinking about what to do now, it is not military power that will stop terrorist attacks or at least not most of them. What might, if anything, be a little more successful is an alert and well-informed and internationally connected intelligence service working with similar intelligence services. (But that they can stop all terrorist attacks seems very problematic. Moreover, the United States has been very irrationally ideological over the use of its intelligence service.) It is impossible to make a successful frontal attack on an enemy that neither has a fixed base nor fixed personnel. Even when driven from Afghanistan, they pop up elsewhere and so on and so on. And even if one network is destroyed, others will pop up. The enormous U.S. military force is then like a handcuffed giant.

A more plausible scenario is that the United States needs a military force, terrorist attacks or not, to control the world in its own interests and in the interests of its allies (most of them in varying degrees comprador states). Otherwise, it will eventually lose out to China or Eurasia or, down the road, to India or more likely to a Japanese-Chinese-Indian alliance (bloc) or that of some other group of powers coming on the scene. I am, the criticism could continue, not thinking geopolitically enough and I very much need to. That I need to I readily grant. I am not here giving sufficient attention to the likelihood that, rather than being opposing powers to the United States, China and India will (in this respect) go the way of Japan and Germany vis-à-vis the United States. That is indeed very likely. It may well be the most probable geopolitical scenario. But it is not the only empirical possibility. There is room for struggle and hope.

Taking into consideration – to return to the scenario I am trying to develop – that other countries and blocs have extensively disarmed and that the United States finally does so as well, it can still *perhaps* control the world, but in that situation *to what point*? After all, nobody will be able to control the United States itself or aggress it (other than terroristically) in that situation. And then it won't be acts of state agents. It is like thinking that Canada might attack the United States. It is utterly in the world of fantasy. Given the expense of the U.S. military and the difficulties of control after occupation, wouldn't it be better (more to the United States's advantage) just to give up the whole military project and work (if they must) with soft power, without hard power in the background in case of non-compliance? In circumstances of others' disarmament, would there be any point in U.S. military control? What is to be gained by it? What have they been gaining in their recent military adventures? There are, as Nye has argued (unfortunate as it may be), other ways of working their influence and even their will.[24] (Still, that they will demilitarize or the world will demilitarize is, while possible, still unlikely, given the volume of present arms sales.)[25]

Well, perhaps, if they continue to have a preponderance of multinationals, they will retain economic control? But already they are losing economically and capitalists tend to go where the secure profit is greatest. Moreover, more multinationals are becoming genuine transnationals.[26] Even if they remain multinationals and remain home- (nation-) based, they will still go where the secure profit is and that might be quite distant from the United States. Also, think of the important fact that China produces while the Unites States consumes. What will this do to the U.S. economy down the road a bit? Some think it is the United States's source of continuing strength. But this seems rather far-fetched.

Still, what we might get – indeed, what in some respects we already have – is imperial U.S. political and economic control. We indeed have, and increasingly so, a global capitalist economy. The United States still has a preponderance of the multinationals (a few years ago it was 80%). But more trans-territorials would in a demilitarized world tend to become transnationals as well; not multinationals with their base in one or several nations but genuine transnationals without a national base.[27] With the United States no longer a military giant, the multinationals will no longer need the United States to protect their interests. They can, and rationally will, throw the ladder away. Capitalists, as Marx saw, know no country. They will go where the stable long-range profit is. (Sometimes some of them will even take chances.) They, as long as we have a capitalist order (capitalist modes of production), will continue to dominate but, not being attached to the United States or any country, they will not be interested in having U.S., or Chinese, or Eurasian military domination. They may need a protective country or several countries (the UN could do it) with a police force to keep proletarians and the other poor and marginalized people from making trouble for the capitalist control of things, but nothing remotely like the gigantic military apparatus that the United States now fields. Trans-territorials would not care much about either which country or countries they are linked to nor with which political system or systems so long as security is provided efficiently, cheaply, and capitalized relations are not endangered. The military forces needed for *such* capitalist control would be little more than a hyped-up police force. Moreover, to the extent there is some power from below, the populations of the world will cease to support militarism. (Perhaps people are so jingoistic and so captured by state propaganda that this will not happen. But that they will not be *so* vulnerable to propaganda is a reasonable possibility that is worth struggling to make an actuality.)

Where the other countries of the North have the economic power they have and the social structures that they have, they, without military structures or extensive military structures, will have populations that are better off economically and socially and increasingly more so than the populations of the United States. The U.S. population may come, perhaps slowly, to see the need for their military expenditures to be drastically cut back. By increasing their own social expenditures and by dropping their military expenditures, they, it is reasonable to believe, will increasingly get off the backs of the regions that they now (somewhat brutally) dominate.

Now, as things are and because of that domination, regions that have been producing most of the terrorists will, when the domination and abuse cease and the pressure is taken off them, slowly cease to be hotbeds for terrorism. It won't happen overnight but it is very likely that it will happen. As the Muslim countries become more *maitres chez nous*, terrorism will fall off. There is no quick fix for ending terrorism. Over time, it is plausible to believe, with the end of U.S. imperialism and its aggressive occupations, with an end to its having comprador states (e.g., Saudi Arabia and Pakistan) and an end to hype about terrorism, the United States and these once comprador states will (though in different ways) cease being generators of terrorism. Slowly, with changed conditions, the supply of people willing to be terrorists will dry up or at least lessen. But we are a long way from that yet. All we need to do is think of the condition of the young in the Gaza Strip to recognize that. Moreover, this does not mean that for a time there will not be terrorist attacks on the United States. There is no effective way of stopping that. Still, after all, candidate terrorists are not in it for a joyride except under the greatest of delusions, e.g., bliss in heaven with plenty of willing beautiful virgins. (The sexist nature of this is not lost on me. Unfortunately, it says something about the sexist nature of some strains of Muslim culture and as well of our culture in placing such emphasis on that.) With an abandonment of U.S. domination and the fall of comprador governments, it may not be so easy to capture the tortured imaginations of despairing, desperate people with no hope for a decent life. (Think of the Palestinians in refugee camps in Lebanon.) With some hope for the populations of the Muslim societies, we are not likely to get many suicide bombers. Desperate conditions drive desperate "solutions." *Pace* Michael Walzer, this is not an apology or an excuse for terrorism but an attempt to explain something of it and to suggest some ways of ending it.

It is not possible where the United States has anything like its present military power to have both guns and butter at least where the U.S. population can have as much butter as others in the rich North. (Norway and Sweden are not the United States. People live better lives in these countries.) It is not unreasonable to conjecture and to hope that that cannot but become increasingly evident to the U.S. population so that even the very dullest in the United States will come to see that the United States now does not need guns or at least not so many of them. So let's, many might conclude, go for more butter and a better life for all. I am not so foolish as to think that this is likely to happen, but it is an empirical possibility and, to repeat, something worth struggling for. A better life is possible.[28] It may never occur but it isn't pure utopian fantasy.

Perhaps the other countries (or their extant governments) will not be rational enough to disarm – Stephen Harper is certainly not travelling that road – and perhaps the U.S. population will not be able to see through the barrage of propaganda that will surely be thrown up by the capitalist imperialist order with its leaders that are our rulers. But the East Germans saw through *Neues Deutschland*. Why is it so impossible not to expect the U.S. population, with their increasing economic and social decline, to come to see through their own propaganda? At any rate, there is an opening for non-tyrannical world government coming principally from below.

It also can reasonably be argued that there are global problems to do with war, global injustices, and the natural environment that cannot be solved by individual nation-states but only, if they can be solved at all, by cooperation between states. This can best be done by a world government formed principally to deal with problems that cannot be solved at a nation-state level. As Rawls recognized, democratic states – of nearly equal power I should add – do not go to war with each other. The horrible lessons of two world wars taught the states of Europe not to do that again. And democratic states, it is reasonable to believe, generally will work out their conflicts, however difficult, diplomatically. (They will use soft power, not hard power.) A democratic world government – a democratic federation of nation-states that could grow up in the United Nations in a way I shall describe – would do that through votes in the General Assembly, not through bullets. (We should not be too complacent about democratic states not going to war with each other. By the middle of this century the geopolitical conflicts between blocs of nation-states may get so intense that they will go to war with each other. If that happens we will have an incredible horror. One can hope and half-believe that an awareness of this will hold the conflicting blocs back.)

Problems between individual nation-states – problems analogous to those of the tragedy of the commons – render it impossible for there to be a solution of the most serious environmental problems in a system of Westphalian-style sovereign nation-states. In such a state of global anarchy, each state, and rationally, seeks its own advancement and protection. In doing this, it will frequently beggar its neighbour. Agreements between independent nation-states, where they are rational, can only be of the *modus vivendi* sort. When a state sees what it perceives to be in its own national interests threatened by cooperation, it will back away from cooperation. As in the case of Athens and Melos in Ancient Greece, weak states, like Melos, will end up making a moralistic appeal in a desperate attempt to defend themselves. Will their appeals not predictably fail? What is involved here can only be resolved by breaking out of and by abandoning the system of sovereign Westphalian nation-states or, more reasonably, the atavistic dream of them. Even prisoner's dilemma solutions will not be stable. Nothing will be under a Westphalian framework. However, globalization is already behind the scenes doing this breaking out. But, utopian dreams of globalizers to the contrary notwithstanding, this is hardly proceeding in a cosmopolitan planned and oriented way. We need a democratic cosmopolitan world government to reasonably do that.

Now examine the force of the standard criticism of world government – in reality a cluster of criticisms – that are conventionally thought to be compelling.[29] It was thought by Kant, among others, that a world government if strong would be tyrannical and if weak would be too vulnerable to internal attacks and uprisings turning into wars. Either way, a global government would not be viable or stable. But if we see the world government as arising through institutions (with a democratic aspiration) where increasingly large numbers of people come to see their problems linked to a lack of global governance and with that the need for such a government, we may well come to take a different view of the matter.

This very much needs explaining. Suppose, to make a start, we reform the United Nations along the following lines. We either abolish the Security Council or expand it and make it more representative and abolish veto powers for all of its members. This move would make the UN no longer hostage to U.S. power or to the power of other permanent members acting either individually or collectively. The General Assembly would not have such a subordinate role as it has now with such a change in the Security Council. The UN would finally be free of being captive of the Great Powers, particularly of the United States. With these changes, democratization would surely be furthered and the General Assembly would be greatly empowered. Such changes would, of course, be fiercely resisted by the

Great Powers – many say they would simply block them – but with the obvious democratic rationale for such changes, it very well might become increasingly difficult, and *perhaps* finally impossible, for the great powers to resist.

Moreover, to achieve global democracy and a world government, it would be crucially important and in accord with democratic procedures to reform the General Assembly itself. Suppose the General Assembly could be so reformed: a reform that would involve extensive reorganization. That, depending on how it was reorganized, would result in a considerable increase in global democracy. To this end, the General Assembly could be reformed so that it would clearly be sovereign over questions of war and peace, over questions of global justice, over questions of pollution and global warming – generally over cross-border environmental problems – and the like.

Many other questions could and would still be decided at a national or even at a more local level. *To that extent* there could be a divided sovereignty. Much legislation could and would be left to the national parliaments, which would not be eliminated on such a plan for world government. Education policy, health policy, language policy, and the like would remain a national prerogative. *Perhaps* even immigration policy should remain such a prerogative. The principal functions of the General Assembly would be issues that the nation-states cannot manage, namely, issues of intractable conflict between nation-states, issues of war and peace, most environmental issues which, analogously to bird migration, can know no borders, and issues of global justice which (by definition) are also issues without borders.

To achieve a genuine democratic structure, the representatives of the General Assembly should be individually elected by the world's nation-states and from competition between parties democratically constituted in those states. (It is done badly now in most national-states but it can be improved.) To handle the imbalance between the populations of the nation-states – Iceland is one thing; India is another – the number of representatives in the General Assembly from each state should, in one way or another, in part reflect the size of its population. Perhaps to avoid significant minorities within the individual states or groups of states, e.g., the Kurds, from never having an effective voice in the General Assembly or huge populations having too much of a voice, something analogous to proportional representation in nation-state legislatures should be worked out as well at the global level. And significantly large nations, like the Kurds, seeking to form a nation-state should somehow be given representation even if they do not have a nation-state of their own. And again, but differently, to democratically work out something equitable to all, given the great disparity in population between the different nations, there should be two elected chambers in the General Assembly similar to that of the Senate and the House of Representatives in the United States. The Secretary General should also be elected by the General Assembly for a determinate term from a list of candidates determined by and voted on by the General Assembly with no one being able to override or otherwise block that vote. This would help ensure the sovereignty of the General Assembly as well as the democratic legitimacy of the Secretary General. (Remember the United States's sorry role here.)

This, of course, is just a rough, amateurish sketch. Any such scheme for reforming the UN into a real democratically empowered world government would have to be thoroughly worked out and carefully examined and nuanced. But this amateurish sketch is sufficient to see something of how it could go, though its nuancing shouldn't be so cautious in its reforms, as many of the extant candidate reforms are, that nothing much would change.[30] My amateurish portrayal, however, does have something of the sketching out of what a genuinely democratic world government could look like. The details are much less important than to see that we can frame a world government, a governmental structure for a world-state or world federation that is maximally and cosmopolitanly democratic. The present UN, framed as it was in 1945, revealed a fear and distrust of democracy and a bias toward the great powers and indeed toward the greatest of them, i.e., the United States. It was framed to give them control. A world government (*pace* the standard objections) in reasonably short order would lead to a largely, though not completely, demilitarized (as well as a democratized) world.

Still, for a time, and perhaps for the foreseeable future there would be a need for the UN to have a military that is somewhat, though not much, stronger than a global police force. Where would it come from? If it came by the various countries voluntarily seconding soldiers from their own armed forces with various nations agreeing to contribute a certain number of troops, then those contributory nation-states, acting individually, could always withdraw their forces if they were displeased with the way the UN, through the authority of the General Assembly, was using them. They could decide they did not wish to have their troops so deployed, or rationalizing, claim they could not bear the expense of so deploying them, or that they wanted to use them differently elsewhere. The world government would in this important sense lack sovereignty, would be dependent on its constituent nation-states. Perhaps a better plan would be for the UN military force to be like that of many countries, namely, an all-voluntary force differing only in that it would be under direct UN control. The UN would set up recruiting stations all over the world and garner volunteers from many countries quite independently of the individual nation-states's direction or sanction, thus giving the UN's armed forces an international structure and an independence from nation-state control. There would be the problem of the great diversity of languages, but that could probably be solved by linguistically diverse regiments being under a unified, internationally determined command.

Where would the UN world government get the money for recruitment if it does not (as it does not now) have an independent tax base? It now relies on dues paid by the member nation-states but what if some members do not pay up? Who is going to make them pay? (Again, we see Hobbes's point about covenants without swords.) Remember the trouble when the United States refused to pay up? We seem not to be getting the kind of sovereignty we should want for a world government. But couldn't the UN come to tax the nation-states that make it up just as nation-states now collect taxes from their provinces? Again, this would no doubt be resisted by the great powers and some of the small nation-states as well. Would it violate the sovereignty of these nation-states great or small? But claiming that would be like saying that some provinces, being outvoted by other provinces in the same nation-state over some issue of interest to all of them and to the federal government as well, would violate the outvoted provinces' prerogatives of the nation-state in question. That relying on the vote of the representatives of the nation-states in the General Assembly has a democratic rationale that is so evident that it could not long be resisted, particularly if the amounts of taxation were modest. (If some provinces got out of order, that could make for Hobbesian problems too. But we get along in practice with the compliance of provinces, though some provinces with enough wealth can make problems, e.g., Alberta in Canada.)

I am confident that there are many more problems like the above that I have not foreseen, but this doesn't lead to the conclusion that the conception of world government – something like the one that I have set out – is impossible. Indeed something like it is possible and plausible. It is only that designing it more exactly is daunting and may very well need – indeed, certainly need – trial and error. But the desirability of attaining perpetual peace, a solution to environmental problems, the cutting back on the awful violence that plagues us, greatly relieving the extensive immiseration particularly in the South, and more generally attaining something like global social justice all make a world government increasingly mandatory and indeed desirable (and reasonably so) in our globalizing world with its global economy. (The increasing global economy with its increasing globalization also makes it increasingly necessary.) People must have had similar thoughts of impossibility when nation-states were coming into existence in our once-emerging, once-Westphalian, world. What is crucial is not the details of what I have said but the recognition that with the UN reformed – perhaps in somewhat different ways (perhaps even in radically different ways) than I have suggested – we could have a world government that was democratically empowered with a genuine ultimate sovereignty. I didn't say absolute or timeless sovereignty; nothing is written in stone. But it would not be the pseudo-sovereignty that makes the UN the creature of the Great Powers, principally the one Great Power. Moreover, there is no reason to think such a world government would be tyrannical or authoritarian. Our worries in this regard should instead be about the hyper-imperialism (the new U.S. imperialism) we have now without any democratic mandate or control.

IV

I have argued in previous sections that the secure achievement of political cosmopolitanism requires a world government or a world federation. But isn't that incompatible or at least in tension with my frequently defended liberal nationalism and my commitment to Quebec sovereignty?[31] It is neither. Samuel Scheffler, David Miller, Richard Miller, and Kok-Chor Tan have made compelling cases for there being compatriot priorities and the associative duties that go with them.[32] We are not sure (generally speaking) exactly when compatriot priorities override global ones and when they do not and, in turn, are overridden by global priorities. We are, however, confident that there are plain cases when compatriot priorities override global ones and vice versa.[33] But where do we draw the line? We do not know and perhaps there is no line to draw. That is a familiar problem in philosophy. Quine has shown us that we do not know where to draw the line between the analytic and synthetic either but, as he himself acknowledges, there are both analytic and synthetic sentences.[34] Similar things obtain for evaluative utterances and descriptive ones.[35] But we get along perfectly well in practice without a grasp of where to draw the line or even an understanding of how to coherently attempt to draw one.[36] Perhaps there is no line to be drawn, though, as Wittgenstein has shown us, we can always *stipulatively* for certain determinate purposes draw one. But this can be, and often is, a rather arbitrary and pointless business. Likewise, there is no criterion or criteria to be found which will tell us just when (particularly without a determinant context) compatriot priority obtains and when it doesn't or when a sentence is analytic or synthetic or when an utterance is evaluative or just descriptive. We know when I say "Hitler had a black moustache" or "Hitler painted" that I am *just* describing and when I say "Hitler had a black soul" or "Hitler became a demented monster" that I am evaluating but, at the same time in some way, describing. When I say "Bush went to Yale" I am just describing. When I say "Suprisingly, Bush went to Yale" I am both describing and evaluating, and if I say "Bush is a stupid bastard," I am again both evaluating and perhaps tendentiously, using thick evaluative (but also descriptive) words, saying something highly evaluative that still has some descriptive content. "Gandhi was a stupid bastard" is an intelligible English sentence but the slightest knowledge of Gandhi and the world reveals that it is utterly mistaken. Its descriptive content plus our knowledge of Gandhi does this. But it does both evaluate and have a descriptive content, just as does "Bush is a stupid bastard."

That we, in our own nations as parents, should give priority to our own children over similar children in other countries that have parents of approximately a wealth equal to ours is a plain enough case where compatriot partiality holds. Whether compatriot partiality holds or should hold in a battlefield situation where a doctor has to practice triage is more problematic. Should he practice it strictly according to the severity of the soldiers' wounds and chances of survival or should he attend first to compatriot soldiers and only after that to enemy soldiers? I doubt that there is any consensus on this. It is a contestable issue and it is *perhaps* unclear what the right thing to do is.[37]

With such considerations in the background, let us turn now to my take on liberal nationalism. In my conception of global government arising out of a distinctive strengthening of the UN General Assembly and a strengthened and greater democratization of the UN generally, there would be an important place for nation-states in relation to the UN. It would on my account be these nation-states that would elect representatives to the UN General Assembly to represent them and these nation-states would retain certain distinctive, though not overrideable, powers themselves. These nation-states, that is, would still have most of their normal powers and functions. They would make their own educational policy, health policy, language policy, etc., and collect taxes. They would no longer be allowed to have an army but only an extended police force and (even *de jure*) they would lose their ultimate Hobbesian sovereignty to the world government. (This is not quite as radical as it sounds as globalization is eroding it anyway.[38]) In some respects, the nation-states' relation to the world government would be like the relation of Swiss cantons to the Swiss federal government – but remember that the cantons are very powerful in Switzerland.

For liberal nationalists the people or peoples who live in a given territory should democratically determine their own state and with that state in place elect the government that the majority of people resident in that territory want, revealing their wants by how they vote. It should be the collective decision of the people or peoples – assuming they do not violate human rights – how they are to order their own public lives. However, if they vote to join the UN, then they must abide by its laws and regulations – something that often does not happen now – though it should be the case that their state can withdraw from the UN by a majority vote of that nation-state's citizens in a referendum specifically on that issue. But without that they must, once they have joined, obey its laws. (But who is to force them to do so? Again, the Hobbesian problem looms.)

Liberal nationalism is, moreover, not an ethnic nationalism rooting itself in ethnic origins. Rather, all of the permanent residents of the territory of a state or candidate state who claim to be members of that nation or nations making up that state or candidate state determine (usually by a simple majority vote) how that state is to be ordered. Whether a candidate state is to become a single-nation nation-state or to become a multinational nation-state, its permanent residents, whoever they are, become (if they wish it) citizens of that new nation-station. No such permanent residents of such a territory can be excluded. If they were not born in that territory, which is to become that new state, when they make the proper legal moves to gain citizenship when that state comes into existence, they *must* be granted citizenship in that emerging nation-state or (as it may be) that multi-nation nation-state (still a state unified by a common allegiance). When it becomes a state, they, if they were not born there, must be granted citizenship when they have made the open (and simple) proper legal moves to gain citizenship. People born there automatically have citizenship. The point is to exclude no one who is a permanent resident of the territory in question who wishes to become a citizen of that state. No one can be excluded because of his or her ethnic origins.

The rationale for such a liberal nationalism – itself a liberal rationale – is to make these permanent residents of that territory pledging allegiance or otherwise showing their commitment to that particular people or peoples on that territory *maîtres chez nous* within the limits of respecting the laws of the United Nations, laws established by the General Assembly. (The inclusion of "peoples" allows for the possibility for a nation-state to be a multinational nation-state. It allows for such a state to be made up of many peoples where these diverse peoples make a common commitment to live together in a unified state, though it could be a loosely unified federation of peoples.)

To be a nationalist in that sense (a familiar and widely accepted sense) does not to deny or otherwise eschew a loyalty or allegiance to a world government or for that matter to affirm it.[39] But a political cosmopolitan, if she thinks of what her cosmopolitanism comes to, will have a sense of unity with all of humankind, regarding each person in the world to be of equal moral worth and deserving of equal respect and concern and, where possible, understanding. But she will also recognize that all people are themselves a *particular* people.⁴⁰ They will have different attitudes to life and different ways of doing things, different ways of ordering their lives and with different commitments. In order to have any clarity concerning equal respect for people, a cosmopolitan must understand – at least to a degree – and respect what these different peoples are as *a particular people*. This equal respect, as with liberal tolerance, requires that all particular peoples themselves show such respect for others. And, of course, this respect for a particular people also goes down to the individuals who make up that people. A liberal nationalist can quite consistently with being a "one worlder" also be, and in my view should be, a *moral individualist*.⁴¹ However, in being tolerant we should not be *tolerant of intolerance*. Similarly, to have a respect for all others, we should not respect someone's disrespect of others. That does not mean they (their disrespectful views of and actions towards others aside) are not treated with respect themselves. We can and should respect a human being as a human being without respecting his *disrespectful* views. This can be, and indeed sometimes is, hard to do, but to be cosmopolitans, we must do it.

With this condition, then, a consistent cosmopolitan will, depending on their situation, either be a liberal nationalist or sympathetic to such nationalist causes where they are relevant. (Catalonia is one thing; Sweden is another. In Catalonia, there is a struggle to be recognized as a nation and to be a nation-state or nation as a part of a multi-nation nation-state. In Sweden there is not.) But as a liberal nationalist political cosmopolitan she will also (if she carefully thinks her political cosmopolitanism through) be a "one worlder" where the "one world" is to be democratically ordered. A cosmopolitan nationalist with a commitment to a world government is not an oxymoron.

One last word: there will be many circumstances where such a cosmopolitan will have to make tradeoffs between the weight she gives to compatriot priority considerations and compatriot neutral global moral considerations.⁴² Sometimes it will be reasonably evident that there is no right answer to be had and only a fanatic or someone philosophically confused or both would insist that there *must* be one. (We will not be like Henry Sidgwick and think there *must* always be one right answer to every moral question, though this is not at all to deny that there might be one right answer to *some* moral questions.) There are some situations, if our cosmopolitan is worth her salt, where she must give priority to global considerations. Suppose, for example, Quebec becomes independent and stably so and remains (as can be expected) a society of comparative wealth among the nation-states that political economists call the North (this includes New Zealand, Australia, and Singapore). Suppose that the North collectively agrees on something like Pogge's or Sachs's reforms concerning eradicating world poverty – something that could be carried out collectively in the North, if all nation-states in the North cooperate and where this could be done (as it could) without breaking the bank of any of these countries.[43] (Most people in these countries would not even notice the difference in their taxes.) Suppose we in Quebec want, on the model of some European countries, to introduce a regime of university education free of tuition. I take it that global poverty eradication, and doing our fair share to help achieve that, and a tuition-free university education would both be very good things if we reasonably can do them both. Suppose our government, wanting to do both, discovers that at that time it does not have the resources, even with a modest increase in taxes, to do so. It lacks, that is, the resources now to do its share in global poverty eradication and also to implement tuition-free university education. If this is the case – really the case – any consistent and committed cosmopolitan nationalist must conclude that global poverty eradication comes first and that the tuition-free university education must be put off until another day. This simply follows from a recognition of the comparative urgency – something that is not a formal matter – concerning the needs that are being addressed. (We should not be even Left libertarians here.) The very logic of moral cosmopolitanism (which a political cosmopolitan will take on board) takes it that all people are deserving of equal respect and concern and that the life of everyone matters and matters equally and that requires such an ordering of things in such a situation. (But remember I do not claim this is a conceptual truth.)

Moral cosmopolitanism is just the consequence of two things: (1) the firm recognition – or insistent claim – that every human being is of equal worth; and (2) a recognition in the light of (1), and the empirical facts on the ground, in the case of the comparative urgency of the need for global poverty eradication in contrast to the need for tuition-free universities. We could not be treating everybody as having equal worth without recognizing the greater urgency of such poverty eradication. (This is not a formal matter but a materially substantive normative matter.) We usually cannot have all the good things that come to the fore in most problematic situations, something John Dewey and Isaiah Berlin rightly stressed. Sometimes we must choose between goods, and sometimes, even when the choice is clear, given our range of choices, the choice still will be hard. That is just the way that the cookie crumbles in moral and political life. An ethical rationalism is itself not rational or reasonable. *Sometimes* what should or must be done is just a matter of reflective choice.[44] And sometimes not all people or even peoples will make the same choice.

Notes

1. Nussbaum, "Patriotism and Cosmopolitanism"; Scheffler, *Boundaries and Allegiances*; and Appiah, *Cosmopolitanism*.
2. Panitch and Leys, *The Imperial Challenge*; and Harvey, *The New Imperialism*.
3. Scheffler, "Immigration and the Significance of Culture," 105.
4. Appiah, *Cosmopolitanism*, 24–31 and 138–90.
5. Ibid.
6. Nussbaum, *Cultivating Humanity*.
7. Auerbach, *Mimesis*; Said: *Culture and Imperialism*; and *Humanism and Democratic Criticism*; and Brennan, *At Home in the World*.
8. Held, *Global Covenant*; and Archibugi et al., *Re-Imagining Political Community*.
9. Couture, "Liberals and Cosmopolitans"; and Couture, "Cosmopolitanism and the Compatriot Priority Principle."
10. Held, *Global Covenant*, 119–43; and Pogge, *World Poverty and Human Rights*, 168–95.
11. Rawls, *Lectures on the History of Political Philosophy*.
12. Nielsen, "World Government, Security, and Global Justice."
13. Pogge, "Moral Progress."
14. Rawls, *The Law of Peoples*; and Walzer, "Governing the Globe."
15. See here my "Globalization as a Tool for Imperialism."
16. Hägerström, *Inquiries into the Nature of Law and Morals*; and *Philosophy and Religion*.
17. Nielsen, *Globalization and Justice*; and "Globalization as a Tool for Imperialism."
18. Nye, *The Paradox of American Power*.
19. Panitch and Leys, *The Imperial Challenge*.
20. Johnson, *The Sorrows of Empire*.
21. Golub, "The Sun Sets Early on the American Century."
22. McNally, *Another World is Possible*.
23. Ignatieff, "The American Empire."
24. Nye, *The Paradox of American Power*.

25 Lemoine, in *Le Monde diplomatique*, 1.

26 For the distinction, see Scholte, "Global Capitalism and the State."

27 Ibid.

28 McNally, *Another World is Possible*.

29 Appiah, *Cosmopolitanism*, 163. See also Nye, *The Paradox of American Power*; and, more extensively, Walzer, "Governing the Globe."

30 See Archibugi et al., *Reimagining Political Community*; Falk, "The United Nations and Cosmopolitan Democracy"; and Held, "Democracy and the New International Order," for such modest proposals.

31 Nielsen, "Liberal Nationalism Both Cosmopolitan and Rooted"; "Liberal Nationalism, Liberal Democracies, and Secession"; "Le nationalisme cosmopolitique"; and *Globalization and Justice*.

32 Scheffler, *Boundaries and Allegiances*; D. Miller, "Cosmopolitanism: A Critique"; R. Miller, "Reasonable Partiality towards Compatriots"; and Tan, "Priority for Compatriots: Commentary on Globalization and Justice."

33 Couture and Nielsen, "Cosmopolitanism and the Compatriot Priority Principle."

34 Quine, "Two Dogmas in Retrospect."

35 H. Putnam, *The Collapse of the Fact/Value Dichotomy*.

36 Appiah, *Cosmopolitanism*.

37 I believe staunchly – speaking in my own voice – that there should be no compatriot priority there. But that, no doubt, is a contestable and contested issue. Still, I do not think it should be for a cosmopolitan and an egalitarian.

38 Nielsen, *Globalization and Justice*; and Scholte, "Global Capitalism and the State."

39 One worlders could consistently be non-nationalists or even anti-nationalists, but they can be, and often are, liberal nationalists. In my view, they should be liberal nationalists in Quebec, Wales, Scotland, or Catalonia and even in Ireland. I do not say that there is a place for that everywhere. It certainly was not so in what was once Yugoslavia.

40 Couture and Nielsen, "Introduction: Cosmopolitisme et particularisme."

41 Pogge, *World Poverty and Human Rights*, 192–94; and Scheffler, *Boundaries and Allegiances*.

42 Couture and Nielsen, "Introduction: Cosmopolitisme et particularisme."

43 Pogge, *World Poverty and Human Rights*; and Sachs, *The End of Poverty*.

44 The kind of *realpolitik* and geopolitical worries that have been nagging me come to the surface over presently alarming issues about the control and fate of the poles (and, most urgently, the Arctic) and loom for the future concerning outer space. See the important review article by Dominique Kopp, "Russia: The Polar Grab – Ultimate Struggle for Ultima Thule," 8–9.

Afterword

An Interview with Kai Nielsen on Political Philosophy

Interview conducted by Alexander Sager (AS)
and David Rondel (DR) in Montreal on June 1, 2010.

DR: Do you recall when you first regarded yourself as a leftist – when you first had this self-image of yourself as on the Left, and also how you came to think of yourself in that way? Is there any point in your life that you can recall where you may have been impressed with rightist political views in any way?

KN: I will answer the last part first. I've never been impressed by rightest views, but I've been impressed by liberal (*not* neo-liberal) views for a long time. I would have earlier regarded myself as a social democratic liberal – someone like John Dewey. I lived in the United States and foolishly thought we'd be like Sweden in thirty years. But even then, I went back and forth between social democratic views and more fully socialist views.

I can give you an impression of when I first got the sense that there was something that moved me left (I would never have so called it then) – that there was, that is, something rotten in Denmark. I grew up in a little Midwestern American town during the Great Depression where I saw, as a little boy, a number of things that left their mark on me. My parents did financially well during the Depression, as they had before and did after it. For example, we had a maid to pick up after us, particularly me. But across the ravine from our house lived a bunch of poor people and, as you know kids will do, I used to go home after school with some of my schoolmates to play ball with them. In one of the houses I visited, the only ball they had was something they had tied together with string. I remember that the house was unheated and the mother's face looked ravaged. There was almost no furniture. The father was away on the road looking for work. Many of the houses in our town were like that. But when I came home, I had a maid that picked up my clothes and books wherever I threw them. I had warmth and comfort and plenty to eat. I couldn't believe that this difference could be right. I realized then there was something wrong with the kind of society that would allow this. I had various awarenesses of this. Seeing, for example, people that worked on Work Projects Administration (the Roosevelt Administration's project for creating jobs), standing in lines leaning on their shovels. I remember asking my father (who was conservative, though I, in those days, never thought about this) as we drove by our big car – a predecessor of the Cadillac – "Who are these people?" And he said, "People hired by Roosevelt for the Works Project Administration. They could get real jobs if they wanted them. They don't have to live off the dole." It was experiences like this that impressed me and rooted what would become my turn to the left, later my firm socialism. If only my father would have read Upton Sinclair's *The Jungle*.

Another example, this one racial: One of my close schoolboy friends was black – a Negro, as we said then. One day after school, I invited him to come home with me to play. I noticed when we entered the house that our maid, who was Swedish, looked startled when she saw him. When he left, my mother came to me and said, "Don't ever bring George back here again." And my father, to stamp this in, called up George's father and told him not to allow George to come back.

These things stand out in my memory. But there were others like them. So I saw what would likely make many, who begin to think as they grow older, move to the left. And I moved to the left.

When I was a beginning undergraduate student in college, I was reading people like – just imagine it – good old Stalin. We used to call him Uncle Joe. I read a little of Stalin, more of Lenin, and a little more of Marx, though not systematically. It was during the Cold War and I was a freshman in what the Americans call college. I also began to read a lot of people who were attacking Marxists and I became, without abandoning my early feelings, much more of a social democrat as a result of this. Those are my earliest political influences as I neared adulthood. I guess social democrat or not, I always thought of myself as a socialist. But I was mixed up between being a socialist and a social democrat. I just wanted some kind of society that was rather more decent than what I saw in my world. I thought then that things need not be that bad.

DR: So hearing that account, one might have the impression that your parents didn't have that significant an impact on shaping your political world.

KN: I don't think they did. I didn't even think of my father as a conservative, though I realized much later that he was. I was fond of him. All he read was the *Chicago Tribune*, which then advertised itself as the world's greatest newspaper. My father was a Danish immigrant who came to New York City when he was fifteen. He didn't know a word of English then. They put him into the first grade in school and he hated it. What could he do? He couldn't speak any English and here he was with these little English-speaking kids. He was fifteen and they were five or six. He left school and just sort of made it on his own, as you could still do then.

My mother had a rather different background. She was Métis. Her mother came from Lac St. Jean, though she herself never spoke French. Her mother immigrated early to the United States before she could speak. I can illustrate in certain ways how different my mother was from my father. A few years before the Second World War, a friend of my father, who was his subordinate in an insurance company where my father was a superintendent, was invited to our summer home. This was during the Joe Louis/Max Schmeling boxing match. We were at our summer house, which had a big American flag on one wall and a big Danish flag on the other. This friend of my father, whom I called Uncle Percy, began to talk about Hitler – the Louis/Schmeling fight was a big German-American affair – and he said, "Well, there was one good thing Hitler did. He got after the Jews." My mother got up and walked out of the room and, after he had left, she told my father to never let Uncle Percy into the house again.

But I didn't have much sense of my parents as being political. My father, as conservative as he was, wanted me to become a corporate lawyer. I wanted to be a novelist! Even when I started studying quite different things, he always supported me, gave me money and I was never without anything.

He never pressed me to be a lawyer. So my parents, as I've said, had little influence on my political development.

DR: Moving ahead a little bit to when you started doing philosophy and thinking philosophically, do you recall when you first encountered Marx's work? Did it impress you then as it turned out to impress you later? If it did impress you then, what impressed you about it?

KN: It did impress me then. I didn't read *Capital* at first. I read the *Communist Manifesto* and things like that. Marx wanted a world where people stood as equals, wanted progress in the world, wanted capitalism overthrown, and was against religion and for the workers. That sort of thing impressed me. That was what I wanted too. For a long time afterwards, I had a struggle with myself. When people criticized the Soviet Union, I kept making excuses for the Soviet Union, saying that what we heard was American propaganda and that it can't be as bad in the Soviet Union as it was said to be. But things were certainly bad enough, particularly under Stalin. But I didn't believe the things I read about him then. Moreover, even before that, I was also reading people like Nietzsche and Dewey and some others. So Marx came along with others and *initially* had a short-run influence on me.

DR: As a graduate student, you were schooled in North Carolina pretty much exclusively both at Chapel Hill and then at Duke.

KN: I was, starting in my third year, an undergraduate at Chapel Hill. But I didn't begin at Chapel Hill. Perhaps I should tell you something about my beginning studies. It may reveal something about the reactions I came to have about religion. I first attended a little academy (St. Ambrose) – it was, as well as an academy, what the Americans call a college (undergraduate university). I went there because I wanted to play basketball and St. Ambrose had the best basketball team in town. I don't think my parents wanted me to go there because they had the usual prejudices, though not strong ones, against Catholics. But they let me go because they knew how much I wanted to play basketball there and that had nothing to do with religion. Moreover, at that time I had not the slightest interest in religion. After the war, I went back to St. Ambrose for two years of college before I transferred to the University of North Carolina. So my first college (university) was a Catholic school. There were two people who influenced me there. One was a priest who knew a lot about literature and talked about it in a really interesting way. The other was a layman who came from Montreal and had studied at the University of Toronto – at St. Michael's College – with Gilson and Maritain. His name was Frederich Flynn and he taught philosophy at this small Catholic college. You had to take a lot of philosophy in Catholic schools back then. Perhaps you still do. It was required and most of the students – most of them Catholics – hated it. Most of these courses at that school were unbelievably boring, taught by priests from scholastic manuals and most of these priests were not very interested in philosophy. I took a course from Flynn who taught Plato, Aristotle, and Aquinas. He was very different from the rest. When he talked about Aquinas, instead of just saying the proofs work, he said there were problems with them. And we talked about them and he found that I had an interest in these things. I was by then struggling with religion and he told me I should also read some Scotus, Ockham, and Maimonides and to read the philosophers themselves, not just the manuals. He impressed me and made me interested in philosophy. It was at this time that I also read Santayana and that had a secularizing effect on me. My previous wartime reading of Nietzsche and Dewey had a similar effect. At that time in my life, there were lots of conflicting currents tumbling around in me.

DR: Your graduate studies came at a pretty tumultuous time, particularly in the South of the United States. Can you say something about any recollections you might have about race relations in North Carolina at that time? And also, any kind of civil rights or political activism you might recall or might have participated in.

KN: I can tell you something about all of that. There was still segregation at that time. The University of North Carolina was not only segregated by race but by gender as well. There were only male students at UNC initially (except for graduate school). This was also the case when I taught at Hamilton College and Amherst College. I guess there are only two all-male schools left in the United States now, but back then there were a lot of them. But there was also racial segregation in North Carolina, including at the liberal

University of North Carolina. The University of North Carolina and Duke University had no black students at all. That was called "separate but equal." But that, of course, was not true.

By that time, I was sensitized to this, so I joined various challenging movements, particularly radical ones, though in the eyes of the establishment, they were all radical movements. It was a period during which I quickly became very radical. During a U.S. presidential race, Henry Wallace (not George Wallace), who had been vice president under Truman, formed a new party and ran for president. I joined a student movement supporting Wallace. (Wallace was a kind of social democrat but his party made the tactical mistake of accepting help from the American Communist Party and that finished them.) Paul Robeson, a black and prominent member of the Communist Party, was an articulate supporter of Wallace. I had seen Paul Robeson play the lead part in *Othello* in San Francisco during the war when I was still in the service. I remember responding then, "Jesus, what is this?" I was spellbound. We students at Chapel Hill arranged for Paul Robeson to come to campus to talk in support of Wallace and this third party. But he was a member of the Communist Party and by that time had been blacklisted. The university, after a lot of liberal dithering, finally said we could not meet in the lecture hall we had planned for and with their initial agreement. So we went to an empty lot that belonged to a gas station in downtown Chapel Hill that had closed for the evening. I introduced Robeson and he talked there. For that I got a cross burned in front of my house that night. Robeson has been a kind of hero of mine, besides being a wonderful singer and actor. People have told me that he was also a great football player at Princeton – something I didn't care about anymore. I believe he was what is called an All-American. He was a fighter for equality and all the way down an anti-racist and a good communist. He fought valiantly for a cause that slowly destroyed him. Tears come to my eyes when I think of him.

DR: Going forward a little bit, what about your opposition to American involvement in Vietnam?

KN: That is what really and permanently radicalized me. That's when I gave up the notion, "Oh, we'll be like Sweden if we just go steady and keep struggling." Pragmatists like Sidney Hook had an effect on me. Hook came to Chapel Hill while I was still an undergraduate there and made a very powerful case against the Soviet Union – or so it seemed to me then. With such influences, I moved more towards what would be called the left wing of the Democratic Party or towards a mild social democracy. But the Vietnam War changed me. I, Hilary Putnam, Noam Chomsky – a bunch of us – were on platforms all the time. I was always ambivalent because I wanted to study philosophy – I was teaching at NYU then – and I had to take a lot of my time demonstrating and speaking, though I don't regret that I did it for one moment. But I wanted to work at philosophy, too.

I was naïve then. I remember participating in a big demonstration in Washington – Chomsky spoke and Howard Zinn spoke to an enormous crowd with black and red flags of radical defiance flying. And I remember saying to myself, with joy in my heart, that this is the beginning of the end. How innocent I was. But, that naïveté aside, the Vietnam experience deeply influenced me and set me on a more radical – a more firmly socialist – course.

Only later, at Calgary, did I learn a lot about Marx. I realized the Political Science department there was full of reactionary Straussians. And so I said to myself, "Look, there isn't anyone else to teach Marx, so I will." I think the department was pretty surprised. I taught with Bob Ware, another radical who was an Oxford graduate – an American who got a D.Phil. from Oxford under, of all people, Gilbert Ryle. We jointly taught Marx until I retired from Calgary. (I should add that I didn't teach only these courses but also seminars on Rawls, Sidgwick, Wittgenstein, pragmatism, Habermas, and the like.) Together, Ware and I learned a hell of a lot about Marx and the Marxian tradition. We used to give a course we called "Marx and Engels" which was always just an introductory course. Then in the second term we would study some important Marxist figure or subject – I think the first time we taught Georg Lukács' *History and Class Consciousness*. I really learned a lot from this teaching. I learned a lot with my students and with Bob. But I never had any courses like this at all when I was a student myself. There weren't any such courses.

DR: You were talking a little bit about other anti-war intellectuals around the Vietnam era. And many of them – I'm thinking particularly here about

Chomsky – arrived at the judgment that anti-war resistance would be more effective to conduct from home. So Chomsky never left the United States – the same is true of Putnam and many, many others. So I'm wondering if you recall considering that argument – whether it would have been to the benefit of the anti-war movement to stay at home.

KN: I did stay at home during that time. At that time, NYU was, among the student body and *some* of the professors – my friend, Bertell Ollman, for example – a pretty radical place by North American standards. Many of the more radical students came to me for consultations as well as courses. They were trying to decide whether they should join the army and try to muck things up from inside or whether they should join resistance at home or go to Sweden or Canada or somewhere else. They talked to me a lot about that. And I advised them in various ways –ambivalently – but a lot of them, including me, felt we should stay, if we could, in the United States during the war. It was only in 1969–70, when things quieted down and the anti-war movement had evaporated, that I left the United States.

DR: Do you recall the thinking and the circumstances that ultimately led you to depart for Canada? And also, upon arrival in Calgary, what were your impressions of Canada?

KN: I was excited about going to Canada. I had an idea by then that people like David Barrett were making Canada a much more socialist-friendly place than the United States. There were some wild accounts in the United States about Canada. For example, that British Columbia under Barrett was becoming the Cuba of the North and a lot of ridiculous things like that. But I still had an idea that I was coming to a place that was more left wing, more radical, more open. Then, when I got to Calgary, I slowly came to realize that though the climate wasn't reactionary, at least not in the university, it was not radical. Calgary, to put it mildly, wasn't a socialist-friendly place. Yet, they didn't go on about anti-socialism as much as in the United States.

The philosophy faculty at Calgary was standardly liberal. Eastern Canadians at that time didn't like to go West (Vancouver apart) and that included Calgary. They thought it was a terrible thing. To go to Alberta, Saskatchewan, or Manitoba was like going to prison. They would have put themselves out in the wilds. I heard much later about a party at the University of Toronto that a friend of mine was at where some graduate students were talking about that crazy American who left NYU for Calgary. This was a time when they were building Canadian universities, new ones, and Calgary was one of them. They had a hard time getting Canadians to teach there. I didn't know anything about this when I first came. As a result, they had at that time in the philosophy faculty people from Britain, Germany, India – Ali Kazmi, who came later, was from Pakistan – as well as people from the United States. The staff wasn't particularly political, though some were – Bob Ware, a former American like me, for example. There were a lot of Brits who came from Oxford, and they were much more liberal than the ordinary population. So I thought it was a kind of liberation. But that was idealistic and naïve. I think of Canada now, and even of Quebec, as comprador nations of the United States (Quebec less than "English Canada").

DR: You mentioned a moment ago that you did stick around in the anti-war movement until the early 1970s at which point you said it was unbearable and impossible.

KN: It wasn't working anymore: there wasn't then any anti-war movement. But there were a lot of students – hippie types – who were wandering all over, hitchhiking all over the United States and Canada. There was a lot of this anti-establishment kind of thing. I had a colleague at Calgary – Shep Saslow – who got fired shortly afterwards. He thought of himself as political, but he was more concerned about smoking pot and joining his students in a pot circle. (The only time I ever tried pot was once with the "radical" students – they sat around in a circle and talked vaguely about life.) Most of the graduate students at that time at Calgary were American draft resisters, but many weren't like that. I don't know how many grad students the department had then, but I think maybe three quarters of them were American draft resisters and sometimes somebody from the UK, but there were almost no Canadians. A lot of the American students liked Calgary. They thought it was just like home – only the mailboxes were painted red.

DR: We've talked already about your growing up in a Midwestern town.

KN: Hick-town *par excellence*.

DR: So you have this American background. You are American-born and there are other intellectuals of your generation – I'm thinking in particular here of Richard Rorty – who have managed to retain a certain pride and love of the United States despite, of course, being critical of various atrocities and abuses of American power and so on. So someone like Rorty, for instance, will always supplement his critiques of American power with the stories of progressive visions of Emerson and Whitman and Dewey and so forth. Have you anything even resembling this kind of attenuated American pride and is it something even remotely important to you? Does your American background mean anything to you personally?

KN: Rorty and I are completely different in our circumstances. He, after all, lived close to NYC and he was practically a red diaper baby. He grew up with Sidney Hook – the radical young Sidney Hook – bouncing him on his knee. He had a completely different cultural background than I had. He was introduced to an intellectual and political elite early on. And, after all, he was only fifteen when he went to the University of Chicago. I didn't have any of that. I lived in a little town – more accurately, a cluster of towns that maybe were altogether 100,000 in population – situated between Iowa and Illinois on the Mississippi River. It was just a typical backward Midwestern place. I didn't hate it. I didn't know anything else. But I read a lot of literature my mother kept giving me and that I later sought out for myself and that gave me another sense of life. My father never read anything but the newspaper his whole life – the stock market columns, mainly. I read a lot. I only became anti-American during the Vietnam War, and even then, and still now, it wasn't against the American people but the American government and its compliant media. But I never had the attraction for America that Rorty had. I always thought it was too bad I hadn't been born in Europe, particularly Sweden. But that did not entail a hatred of the United States. Rather, just an indifference. I guess I am atypical. Eric Hobsbawm's fondness for the place always puzzled me, he being a deep Marxian. It seemed mainly about its jazz. When I was asked to teach American philosophy at Amherst, I didn't teach Emerson or Thoreau but the pragmatists with, for a counter-balance, a now-forgotten American philosopher, Alexander Johnson, who was an extreme empiricist. He even tried to make the logical constants denoting. After leaving the United States, I never felt any longing for it. There are certain places I like to see – the Oregon coast, New York City, Boston, Amherst, Chapel Hill – and certain other places I would like to visit, but I have no attachment to America, though, as I said, no dislike of Americans. I have a sadness concerning the cultural impoverishment that so many suffer from with no decent education. I hated, and still hate, American foreign policy. If I had been in Germany, I would have hated German foreign policy or *now* in Italy or France. But Rorty has a kind of love affair with America. I said to him about his book on America, "It's strange; you're a cosmopolitan, really a cosmopolitan. Why do you care about America so? It'd be nice if America became more like Europe."

DR: This is my last question before Alex will take over and I think it's a good segue from autobiography into some matters philosophical. This is a very sort of broad question, but I am wondering if you think there's an important connection or any connection at all between the kind of radical atheism that you defend and have defended for a long time – the thesis probably for which you are most famous, all things considered – and your politics?

KN: That's a good question. The connection is much more indirect. My first atheism – when I first drifted towards atheism – was not linked with politics at all. The little college I first went to was taught by Dominicans, but some – perhaps many – were often liberal by Catholic standards. I can remember seeing them on picket lines. I didn't have any sense at all about Cardinal [Francis Joseph] Spellman and all those incredible Catholic conservatives. I didn't see how conservative – even reactionary – many Catholics were or, rather, the Church with its hierarchy was. I had a kind of Santayana and Cardinal Newman picture of Catholicism. Remember, Santayana, after early retirement from Harvard, lived in a monastery with priest robes on, utter atheist that he was. But I didn't go that way or even Newman's way or, for something different, Maritain's way. I thought for a while that Catholicism was a nice dream – a fable, but still a nice dream. At first, I had much of Santayana's attitude. So I didn't link it as something in conflict with my politics, partly because of seeing my own professors/priests on the picket lines. I didn't then see what the Catholic Church was really like – though not all of the faithful, both clergy and lay persons, are like that. I'm now completely different, but that wasn't what moved me towards atheism or, for that matter, to radicalism. These were two quite separate things. I think what moved me politically was what I experienced as a boy and what I thought about it later when I read things like Upton Sinclair's *The Jungle* and John Dos Passos's *USA*. There was a thinker who probably influenced me more than any other very early on. He is completely forgotten now, but he ran for president in the United States. His name was Norman Thomas and he was hardly a socialist, though he thought he was. He proclaimed socialism. He was kind of a social democrat – not like New Labour, but like the earlier social democrats, like Olaf Palme in Sweden or Tommy Douglas in Canada. My radicalism had completely different roots than my atheism, though they later came to meld. Certainly, I have nothing but love and admiration for Father Berrigan, a priest made famous for his opposition to the Vietnam War and the U.S. intervention in Latin America – the cruel face of American imperialism.

AS: I'm going to begin by asking some follow-up questions. Speaking of religion, have you ever had an interest in or sympathy for Liberation Theology?

KN: No. I know a couple of liberation theologians – one quite well – and I like and respect them. But I would tell them, "Why do you bother with religion? Just go for politics." But I admire priests who resist – Father Berrigan, for example – particularly in Brazil or Italy or against the Nazi regime. I see them as comrades. I sometimes think that it would probably be much better if they just became secularists. But that's probably an ethnocentric and mistaken view on my part because maybe they are the only kind of people who could be successful in radical movements in certain countries and for certain people. Moreover, there are plenty of good and thoughtfully intelligent people who in one way or another are religious. For me, it is much more a theoretical matter. I don't see how people with any kind of education could be religious. Yet, some are. Moreover, I do not see with Kierkegaard why we should crucify our intellects and be religious (for him, of course, Christian). But that means I'm looking at religion *instrumentally*, and indeed I do. There is no attraction for me in Liberation Theology or any religion or theology. Theology is something that at best should disappear. But there are some intelligent people – though I think they are confused – that do not think this way.

AS: David was asking about your attachment or lack of attachment to the United States and I was wondering how that plays with your Quebec nationalism. You have written fairly extensively on cosmopolitanism and nationalism and argued that the two, in fact, do not conflict. Some might find it puzzling that you defend liberal nationalisms, but nonetheless do not personally have any deep attachment to any particular political community.

KN: I'll come to that last part a little later. You will see why. When I lived in the United States, particularly when I first became politically aware, I thought of nationalism as a disease – something to get rid of. I thought nationalism was something that people, when they became better educated, would forget. What turned me came much later, after I came to Canada – but my defence of nationalism wasn't connected to my living either in Canada or Quebec. It was actually an intellectual thing. I read Isaiah Berlin on Herder and Vico and I said to myself, "Ah, people do need local attachments – it's important to them. It's part of their culture and something that often is a deep part of their lives." I had earlier just thought people should forget about local attachments. But I read Berlin's account and I thought it was impressive, indeed compelling. So then I read Herder himself afterwards and found that a big disappointment. Berlin's better on Herder than Herder. Perhaps he manufactured his own Herder, which, I am told, was a typical thing for him to do. But he set out an account of things in this domain that was very attractive. So that started me to think about nationalism – or really basically about cultural identity and protection and the importance of language to a people. This was something in my time that you could easily forget about in the United States. Not, of course, just language period, but a particular language and how language – a particular language – was important to people (all people) and how it in part defined their approach to life. My earlier study of anthropology in graduate school helped me here. But my defence of nationalism came through no political orientation at all initially, but just my intellectual background from anthropology and from reading Berlin on Herder and other people broadly in sync with him.

But for the political attachments: Perhaps people think, "Ah, it's because of your partner that you became a Quebec nationalist." That had nothing to do with it. I mean she [Jocelyne Couture] tells me rather bitterly about the October Crisis days and yet, as a matter of fact, I had always admired Trudeau. I still admire him in a certain way, though I think he was very bad for Quebec. And the October Crisis and the War Measures Act deserve all the condemnation they can get. When I came to Quebec, I never felt any Canadian nationalism, nor did I when I lived outside of Quebec in Canada. I liked a lot of people in Quebec, as I liked a lot of people in other places where I've lived. A lot of my colleagues were completely alienated by Calgary. I never felt that way. I found it was a great place to hike in the mountains. It wasn't as crowded as it is now. But I don't think I'd like to be there now. I was never attracted to any Canadian nationalism. I thought – and still think – it is better to be a Canadian than an American, but Harper makes it increasingly difficult. What sustains me is the intellectual culture I am a part of and the books I read and films I see, the thinking I do and the considerations I have, and the interactions I have with people close to me, including pre-eminently my partner.

But when I came to Quebec having this background, I began to talk with a lot of people, most particularly with Jocelyne Couture and Michel Seymour, vis-à-vis nationalism and with that, along with my reading, I began to see the importance of sovereignty for Quebec and indeed for all people. It didn't abolish my internationalism or cosmopolitanism, but it nuanced it. I began to think about these matters and eventually to write about them. But the initial thing was just the importance for everyone of local attachments, along with, where this is possible for them, being cosmopolitans. I quickly saw how, if you were not an ethnic nationalist but a liberal nationalist, there was no incompatibility between cosmopolitanism and that kind of nationalism. Indeed, you could consistently be a radical (socialist) liberal nationalist.

AS: Do you feel much of an influence from later writers on nationalism – people like David Miller or Will Kymlicka?

KN: I tend to be not very sympathetic to communitarianism. I am sympathetic, like G. A. Cohen, to the notion and importance of community. But I have all the Rawlsian difficulties with it as well as the Marxian ones. I think there are interesting things in Kymlicka and in David Miller, but I see the conservative Oakeshott inside of communitarianism, including theirs. David Miller defends communitarianism about as well as anybody can, I think. He's extremely articulate, but I've always thought one shouldn't go that way and that he was rather ill-connected with a lot of empirical reality. It would have helped him to read and take to heart more Bertolt Brecht. Think of Brecht's *Keiner oder Alle*.

AS: Let's move on to more general questions about political philosophy. One thing you've said in a few writings is that you consider that the three major political philosophers are Aristotle, Hobbes, and Rawls. Why those three?

KN: Let me go at this indirectly. I had a shock on a train ride with G. A. Cohen. He asked me who the three most important political philosophers were. We first excluded Marx, great as he was, for not being a political philosopher. I said Aristotle, Hobbes, and Rawls. He said I was wrong. It was Plato, Hobbes, and Rawls. I always found, and still find, shocking as this might sound, Plato to be a great bore – except for the Gyges ring thing, which made me think about why be moral. I guess my anti-Platonism is deep, but Aristotle seems to have his feet on the ground *for the most part*. But, after reading Cohen's last big book, I now see and regret his attachment to Plato. Concerning Locke and Rousseau and other candidates, I was too much of an analytical philosopher to be able to read Rousseau decently and Locke's individualism put me off. I was never attracted to Hegel – I used to think he was a reactionary and, like Russell thought, a buffoon. But I've come to see that both are false. I now think of him as an obscurantist who was probably helpful in that he attuned philosophy to a sense of the importance of history. He brought a historicism – a global historicism – and challenged the *philosophia perennis* that ruled our philosophical life from Plato to Kant. I am sympathetic with that, as I regard myself as a historicist and a holist, but not a Hegelian holist. (I argue this in what I hope will be a future book, *Toward an Emancipatory Social Science*.) I think Hegel made us see the importance of time held in thought. I think that's marvellous, but why did he have to take so much jungle with him? Perhaps he couldn't help it – that was the tradition in which he was acculturated. My own feeling was that it was too bad Marx hadn't grown up in England.

AS: He probably would have been a liberal [laughing]. But with regard to Aristotle and Hobbes, do you feel you have any direct influence from Aristotle's politics or from Neo-Aristotelian thought or from Hobbes and Hobbesians?

KN: I like Hobbes for his tough-mindedness and his clarity. But I've never been attracted to Hobbes's contract theory – something that is central to his thought. I tried to take as little of that as possible from him or from Rawls. And Rousseau never affected me, nor did Locke. What attracts me to Hobbes is what he says about the state of nature, about the conditions of life, his hardness and clarity. That's what I really love. I came to that when I was teaching at Amherst where I had to teach in a Humanities course the historian – the first one in the West at least – Thucydides. He was required reading in that course. He fascinated me with his realism and political understanding. He struck me as more important than Plato and even Aristotle. Not surprisingly, Hobbes translated his *Peloponnesian War*. There's a side of me, it's actually a side of Marx as well, that takes political realism seriously. And Hobbes both exemplified and taught us political realism – much, but not all, of what we now regard as political realism. Not a bleeding morality, no political moralism. Marx inherited that. It came to me rather late in the day. And Bertolt Brecht stamped it in.

AS: What about Aristotle?

KN: Aristotle never influenced me as much as Hobbes, but I like his sense of practice, his sense of context, what he said about virtues. That was important to me. And he, unlike Plato, usually had his feet on the ground.

AS: Have you explored many Aristotelian themes in your own writing? I am wondering about connections to practical reason and the good reasons approach, or perhaps some of your ethical work.

KN: No. Remember – it must be strange for the two of you – but I grew up, came of age intellectually, in a time when logical positivism was really strong, at least in Anglo-Saxon and Scandinavian countries. (The Nazis had stamped it out in Germany and Austria, where it had its home.) It was just beginning to die down, but it had an enormous influence on me. Pragmatism came first for me and for my generation and for a lot of other Americans, but then, like many at the time, I said, "Ah, the positivists usefully cleaned it up." And for a long time I turned my attention away from the pragmatists with the thought that everything the pragmatists do the positivists can do better. But I no longer think this. My attitude now toward pragmatism is much like Rorty's.

With that shift in influence, I started to write my doctoral dissertation on the normative neutrality of metaethics. The emotive theory had an influence on me then. I still think of Charles Stevenson as a much more important thinker than is commonly recognized – something that now may seem like best-forgotten history. I came to think this in spite of my scholastic background, where my professor (Flynn) taught me how to read texts like Aristotle's and Aquinas's, which a lot of people don't know how to do anymore. When I came to the University of North Carolina, I was an English major. My honours thesis was on James Joyce, but I took a lot of philosophy courses. I was taught mainly by professors in what Santayana called "the genteel tradition" – they didn't know anything about analytic philosophy or care. But reading independently of my teachers, I went in a different direction. Dewey had prepared the way for that and logical positivism stamped it in.

Moreover, later on, some younger professors started to come to Duke when I was a graduate student there. They were mostly from Harvard, and they were all more or less Quineans and they also had a lot of Russell and the background of logical positivism. They influenced me. I thought at that time, "Well, look, why should we philosophers study Aristotle or Plato any more than physicists have to study Newton or Galileo?" And I remember preparing for my graduate exams. Like everyone else at that time, I had to take one on the history of philosophy. I did all right in logic and I did all right in epistemology and ethics. But I thought then, "Why should we read these old people?" I said to myself, "That just takes us backwards." So I read Father Copleston as the quickest way to find out about Leibniz and Hegel. And the department flunked me on that part of the exam – probably with good reason. The head of the department called me in and said, "You have to take some reading courses in the history of philosophy." But they did that stupidly. The first thing he assigned to me was Hegel's *Greater Logic*. I took a quick look at it and said to myself, "That man can't distinguish contraries from contradictories. Why should I read any more?" But they consoled me, "Keep reading, keep reading." Moreover, I could not see what the *Greater Logic* had to do with logic. I was later told that it had nothing to do with it, but that it is important all the same. I remained baffled and dismissive. Had they given me the *Phenomenology* or something of his writings on history, I might have gotten something out of it, though probably even then, my positivism was too engrained and would have blocked me. The other thing the head wanted me to do, at least seemingly irrelevantly, was to take a reading course with him on Whitehead. That seemed, and still seems, like a very strange way to teach history of philosophy. I read some Whitehead and it was *mildly* interesting, though turgid and obscure. I continued to think there was a better way to spend my time. But relevance to your point – I blocked out as much of the history of philosophy as I could in my dissertation writing and the beginning stages of my teaching. So I never did much, unfortunately, with Aristotle on practical reasoning, though I did something with, besides Toulmin and Baier, von Wright.

I started to work on my thesis with the emotivists and with Hare, whom I liked less than Stevenson, but still liked. Then I came upon Toulmin and, later, Baier. And Wittgenstein had come to influence me enormously. Perhaps the earlier influence of pragmatism paved the way for that. *Philosophical Investigations* hadn't been published yet when this influence started. One of my professors, one of the few older ones not in the genteel tradition, gave me his manuscript copy of the *Blue Book*. I read it in one sitting, the scales dropping from my eyes. I had been trying as background to my thesis to read people like Church, Carnap, and Reichenbach, and they, for the most part, bored me and didn't help at all. I had a hard time understanding Church, but I thought then from reading Russell and the positivists that logic was the key to philosophy. So I had to keep going at it. After the *Blue Book*, I dropped all that Russellian stuff about the foundational import of logic and about the normative neutrality of metaethics and moved in a Wittgensteinian direction, and the way I went about ethics was Toulminist, one of Wittgenstein's students, though he was also influenced by Collingwood. (By the way, as legend has it, Wittgenstein called Toulmin 'The Clown.' He, so the legend goes, had nicknames for his prize students. He called Anscombe, in a perfectly unconsciously sexist fashion, "Old Man.") And so I proceeded with what was then the main opposition to non-cognitivism – something I had earlier been captured by. I started to read the Good Reasons Approach and that's sort of how my dissertation developed, though I did not change my mind about Stevenson. Quite a bit of it is in my book, *Why be Moral?*

AS: So the third figure you listed is, of course, Rawls, whom you have written on a great deal and thought about a great deal. So I want to ask a series of questions about Rawls and your view of his place in twentieth-century and twenty-first-century political philosophy.

KN: The first thing about Rawls – I read his early *Philosophical Review* piece reviewing Toulmin and another reviewing a Swedish philosopher I admire (one of the great non-cognitivists), Axel Hägerström, and I thought vis-à-vis Rawls, "Ah, here's somebody to listen to." I'm talking about 1950 now. After that, Rawls began to write more extensively – it was 1958 when his classic "Justice as Fairness" was published. His work came to influence me a lot – "Justice as Fairness," of course, but "The Outline of a Decision Procedure for Ethics" as well. And they have continued to influence me down the years to his last major publication, "The Idea of Public Reason Revisited" (1995). I met Rawls early on and we spent an evening talking together. When I came to Amherst, I invited Rawls to give a talk there. Rawls used to be a stutterer. The paper he was reading at Amherst (later published) was called "The Sense of Justice." Halfway through it, he broke into such a stutter that we had to close the whole thing down. But "The Good Reasons Approach" was linked in my mind in a certain definitive way with Rawls, though for Rawls it was too consequentialist. I have always been ambivalent about that. But that is not to say that Rawls did not have an enormous influence on me.

AS: Do you think his influence on political philosophy since *A Theory of Justice* has been on the whole positive? I ask this because I want to ask about your philosophical commitments and some of the skeptical things you've said about the practice of political philosophy.

KN: I think the answer is yes and no – yes in certain respects and no in others. One of the last M.A. students I had at Concordia wrote about Rawls. He was a bright student, initially trained in orthodox economics. Among the questions I asked him during his M.A. exam were, "Do you think, as a result of Rawls, that the political climate generally and the political culture among intellectuals has advanced and that it in that respect Rawls's work has been instrumental in improving the political climate of our societies? Do you think things are better politically now than in 1950? Do you think Rawls has helped make things better or that the world around him has grown better because of his work since he started to write in 1950?" Rawls, as I see it, has had almost no influence on that political debate. He is too much into ideal theory, I guess, for that. He had incredible integrity and intelligence and so forth, and had a firm grasp on what a modernist moral point of view's structure is, but I thought (and he likely in some moods felt himself, though I don't know that he did) that his work had been in vain. His *Justice as Fairness: A Restatement* gives some suggestions on that. It has not in the sense that it carries on ably and innovatively in a theoretical tradition and that he has had his influence on the philosophical tradition. In that way he has certainly pushed things forward.

Related to what I have just been saying – you can seen how balkanized our intellectual culture has become. I read a big book called *Spectrum* by Perry Anderson, an able and non-*parti-pris* Marxist historian. In this carefully reasoned and carefully argued book, he has maybe forty pages devoted principally to the discussion of Rawls but also to a certain extent on Habermas and the relation between them. It's incredibly informed. He knows Rawls back and forth and Habermas as well, but it is mainly on Rawls that he concentrates his critical and acute expository attention. I found it brilliant. I looked it up in the philosophical literature about Rawls and nobody has read it. No philosopher I know of, except me, has ever gotten into it. It is not even cited in their bibliographies. This shows how balkanized and intellectually insulated our philosophical world has become. That wasn't so for Aquinas, Hobbes, Hume, Kant, or even for Hegel. Philosophers now aren't the cultural gods they once were. We have come down in the world.

AS: He had, I recall, a very critical essay in *The New Left Review* on Rawls, the Italian philosopher Bobbio, and Habermas – on the three of them.

KN: He was the editor of *The New Left Review* for a few years and that is where I first encountered his work. I didn't pay much attention to it at the time. It was an earlier version of what he came to write and explicate later. The reason I mentioned Anderson is because I think that Rawls's influence has been patchy and I think this is an unfortunate thing. If people paid more attention to him – and he had a wider intellectual critique by progressive intellectuals, including some public intellectuals – then the United States might have been a somewhat more progressive country and there would not have been any cultural or political space for a Tea Party. But maybe that gives too much weight to what public intellectuals can do anywhere! Remember: Rawls wrote the preface to the French translation of *A Theory of Justice* and said, "Well, I know on the Continent that you call me a welfare-state liberal. I'm not a welfare-state liberal. I'm what you would call in your context a social democrat. I think that the only plausible view that fits with mine is a liberal socialism or a property owning democracy." He never explained the latter very clearly. He was often thought of by the Left – take C. B. Macpherson, for example – to be a welfare-state liberal. Even I wrote an article about him saying – unfortunately and mistakenly – what a welfare-state liberal he was. And that was wrong, just plainly wrong. But that's how he's perceived and not only in the Anglo-Saxon world. Outside philosophy and legal theory and *some* political science, he's had almost no influence and certainly not one that catches the political orientation of his thought. Rawls, I fear, was too otherworldly.

AS: Why do you think that particular claim Rawls has made – that his theory is compatible in politics only to socialism or a property-owning democracy – has gotten so little attention from people writing on Rawls?

KN: I'm tempted to make what might be a *parti-pris* ideological, unfair remark. It is that our society is so bloody conservative, including most of its intellectuals – and that applies particularly to philosophers. Still, I don't know how to more generally and more properly answer your question. I would love to have someone who does intellectual history investigate the causes of that, if indeed it is so, and why it has gotten so little attention. After all, his preface was translated back from the French into English. And it would be interesting as well to see how and why so few French intellectuals took much notice. But this is the kind of work we philosophers do not do and indeed are not trained to do. It would be interesting to see whether it has had a different impact on the whole Continent than it has had in North America. I think it has been much the same in Germany, Italy, and Spain, as in France. But I don't know the answer to that and it would take a certain amount of research work in intellectual history. I would guess that Rawls's influence in politics has been minimal. There are a few Rawls specialists in those countries, and some very able ones, but my surmise is that they carry very little influence there. They are, in that respect, like our specialists on Gadamer or Schmitt.

AS: What about Rawls's methodology: the original position, and most particularly reflective equilibrium? This has influenced your work greatly. I wonder if you want to reflect a bit on the methodology of reflective equilibrium and its consequences for political philosophy.

KN: Yes, I have [reflected on it] and I will again. It has influenced me tremendously. I've picked from Rawls what I wanted for my purposes. I am not a historian of ideas. For Rawls, the original position as an instrument in a contractarianism is at least as important for him as his use of reflective equilibrium. I've never been caught, as I have already remarked, by his contractarianism or by any contractarianism. It always seemed to me that his ideal requirement that there has to be no disagreement at all was utterly unrealistic and, more importantly, it seemed to me to have no practical or intellectual value. When I first read about the original position, I was trying to figure out exactly what the original position was. As a methodological device, it seems to me to be useless.

A later essay of Rawls's – one which G. A. Cohen mentions only in a few words in his recent book and he rejects it utterly – "Justice as Fairness: Political not Metaphysical" – had a big influence on me as well as his presidential address. But I'm not a Rawls scholar. I greatly admire Rawls, and certain things of his which I've taken for my own purposes are, of course, of great importance to me. I hope I have not distorted them in using them. For example, consider his *wide* reflective equilibrium position; his coherentist position with "wide" as the important qualification. It can't be a *pure* coherentist position. With a pure coherentist position, you could make Christian Science have a coherentist justification. Note here and relevantly a remark about Cohen: Cohen has a long footnote where he says, "I take and examine Geoffrey McCord's conception of reflective equilibrium and that I have no trouble with." But that turns out to be *narrow* reflective equilibrium. And he says, just after his discussion about this, "When reflective equilibrium is used in a wider way, I leave it." That, I think, is telltale of his Platonism. He wants to have fact-insensitive values be the most crucial ones. But for me, that is not so and my reflective equilibrium is like Rawls's – a wide reflective equilibrium. And that does not lead to fact-insensitivity and it isn't compatible with a *pure* coherentism. Fact-sensitivity *pace* Cohen in morals is crucial.

AS: You've said in a number of publications that you think that the consequences of applying wide reflective equilibrium to political questions is that disciplinary boundaries disappear. There is no longer a particular capacity that political philosophers have that economists do not and so on.

KN: Exactly.

AS: That would seem to have a radical if not devastating effect on the profession. What do you think a philosophy department would look like in the future if we took this to heart?

KN: Do you mean the whole philosophy department or political philosophy?

AS: Let's talk about the whole philosophy department.

KN: I think the whole philosophy department would look very different. It has already become so marginalized that interesting political thought and discussion has to move or morph. It, like Classics, though for better reasons, in effect would disappear – or more probably, break up into several separate departments. Of course, I don't know if this will happen. If Rorty is right, philosophy, as it is, is becoming increasingly marginalized and should morph into quite different subjects. Philosophy, as we know it, would have a very small part in these new disciplines – some part to clarify things a bit but not much more than that. And that mainly comes to a cleaning of the Augean stable. Other than that clarifying work, it would morph into social geography, social anthropology, sociology, economics, history in general, and perhaps cognitive science. It would, that is, morph into a somewhat distinctive social science – what I call an emancipatory social science and social theory. That is what I hope will happen. Will it happen? I don't know. Perhaps my remarks are an old man's bad reaction, frustrated with a lot that goes for philosophy. I still read the philosophical journals, and sometimes there are good articles, but most of them, it seems to me, are dry and boring. They're going over things without much improvement, often in a somewhat different idiom, repeating what philosophers have been doing for years. Sometimes, though rarely, they break into something different, but often deal with something that is utterly trivial.

I still find people writing about the subject I laboured with in my *Why be Moral?* I spent a lot of time, perhaps wasted time, as Rorty thinks, writing about that question in an earlier phase of my work. I have come to realize, as Putnam does, and a lot of philosophers have taken it on now, that where you use, and unavoidably so, thick descriptions, you don't find any ability to untangle the normative from the non-normative. The two of them run together and this will have an effect on our inquiries. You can't, *contra* Hare, disentangle the factual for many, indeed most, of the normative things you want to say. Suppose I say, "You're being rude." Now, that's a normative remark but it's also a descriptive one. Someone might say, "Give me only the normative part and distinguish it." You can't do it. And once you realize that happens and you begin to take this to heart with all kinds of political considerations, political *philosophy* should start (though not just for this reason) to begin to disappear and become more generally political thought and social political studies. Most political studies departments used to call themselves political science departments; now, many more accurately call themselves political studies departments or just politics departments. I think that political philosophy will, or at least should, morph straightforwardly into political and social thought. It should not go around doing the peculiar philosophical things – metaphysical, epistemological, metapolitical – it does now. It will be in some considerable respects a different thing and the skills people will have will be different. Instead of people reading Church and Carnap, they'll study Durkheim and Weber. I never read them until late in my life and that was unfortunate and a big mistake on my part. I wasted precious time with Church and with Quine's *Methods of Logic*. Some might say that answers only to your interests and to those with your interests or with those interests broadly. But if your interests are in logic, it is a different matter. That is fair enough. But it in effect makes out what I think matters and what I think philosophy is, has been, and should morph into. Logic should become a special part of the mathematics department. Logicians should *not* be required to study Plato, Aristotle, Scotus, Descartes, Spinoza, Hegel, or Rawls, though they should know Quine, Kripke, and Wittgenstein.

AS: On a somewhat different topic, I am curious of your impression of how the university has changed during your time as a professor, how your experience differs from the experience of people graduating with PhDs today and how social, economic, and institutional factors have influenced this change.

KN: That's a lot and I can't answer all of it. I think universities have changed. For example, the professors who get jobs now – tenure-track jobs, at least – will usually be able to teach their specialty right away and they won't be so held down by enormous introductory courses or by teaching things that none of the senior professors want to teach. But you also have as part of the university system (and indeed functionally a very important part – one that takes in a lot of income and serves a lot of students) *lumpenprofessoriat* sessional instructors with enormous introductory courses, scant protection, and zero time for research. What is happening here is good for some people and bad for others. But it is also in crucial ways bad for the university structure in general – that is, if you don't think of it as a money-making operation. There are a lot of other things as well. There are things that are both better and worse at the same time, but the worse, I fear, grows larger.

When I was head of the department at NYU in the 1960s, I would have lunch with the dean and together we would decide, over lunch, the salaries of our colleagues in the Philosophy department – who would get raises and who would go up in rank. When Sidney Hook hired me while I was at Amherst College to come to NYU, we sat on the porch of a friend of his at Amherst and talked for two hours. I didn't even know I was being interviewed. Luckily, I didn't say anything pro-Marxist. Hook finally said, "Ok Kai, would you come to NYU next Fall?" And that was it. He didn't consult anyone. Paul Edwards said to me that I should come in the Fall to meet our new colleagues who, along with the old ones, didn't know of my hiring or often of anyone else's. It was very informal and that was nice in some ways. By contrast, when I was at Calgary, you had to go through long meetings of the whole Humanities division, though not about hiring, but there were things about tenure, ranking and salaries, etc. Hiring was done by the whole department in conjunction with the dean. The head couldn't do what Sidney Hook did at NYU. For many things, the heads of departments would meet for a week or two in consultative processes with the dean and there was endless bureaucracy. It is *probably* necessary in order to keep some fairness in the process. But it is also a pain in the ass for anyone who cares about intellectual life, who wants to get on with academic work. Perhaps people doing that kind of work should be pure administrators, but that has its plain downside, too. I don't know what to do about it. But it needs radical change and not just tinkering with.

AS: One thing I tell students who are thinking about going into graduate school is that, these days, graduate school is a professional degree. You have to look at it from a very early stage as a job where you are expected to be a member of the department, you're expected to publish …

KN: Even, shockingly, before you get your degree.

AS: Yes. And if you have ideals about a wonderful period in which you can read a lot of philosophy and think about things and use that as a period where you can consolidate your own views or think about what you want to think about, well, you probably shouldn't go to graduate school in these days … unless you are independently wealthy. Is that your sense as well of how it is these days? You have to start from basically the beginning being career-minded about it or you will either be a sessional instructor with part-time contracts or you will have to find something else to do.

KN: I think that's exactly right and it's criminal. When I went to Duke as a graduate student, I got a scholarship which was more or less automatically renewed unless you were making a big mess of things. I was the assistant to the Chair and sometimes when he was gone, though they wouldn't officially allow this at Duke, I taught for him. You didn't have to do a lot of paperwork or reports or grade yourself as you went along. It was true for both the professoriate and the graduate students. And I really had a free time to do the things you just said. Still, when sometimes people say, "We professors should make more money as some other privileged people do because we had to suffer all the way through graduate school," I think, even after all is said, it's a hell of a lot better to be going through graduate school than to be pumping gas or doing any kind of manual labour. When I went through, it was one of the best times of my life. Now it is in many ways terrible, though still not as terrible as pumping gas or working in construction or in a supermarket. In graduate school now, you have to constantly be preparing things. Much of it is a waste of time for everybody. You have to fill out a dossier for this and for that repeatedly. It was nothing like that when I went through graduate school. Sometimes it was hard to get jobs, but not as hard as it is now. But once you got one, you had in the olden days another disadvantage you typically do not have now when you came to teach. You ended up teaching what none of the established professors wanted to teach – what the *lumpenprofessoriat* teach now. But that was a temporary thing. You still had a lot of time to do your own research. In my time, you were often actually discouraged from publishing by many people – at least at the school where I taught. They said, "Don't publish now. Wait until you know what you want to say." The English, especially, even regarded it as vulgar to rush into print. That was, to be sure, a bit overstated, but it had a point. And some took the 'Don't publish now' slogan so much to heart that they never published.

AS: What about the increased privatization of universities and in many places, not all places, the withdrawal of government support and the demand that faculty members acquire grants?

KN: Bluntly, I think this is horrible. It wastes intellectuals' time. I never had to do this. The only grant I ever had in my life was when I was at Concordia.

Jocelyne [my partner] said, "I'm applying for a grant and I'll write one for you." I didn't want to take the time to apply for a grant and it wasn't necessary. But, due to her efforts, I got one anyhow. Now you have to get grants or you don't get promoted. Publishing papers and books is not enough. I think that is absolutely dreadful. Such matters should be – and could be – reversed. There was an editorial in *The Guardian Weekly* about taxes and that sort of thing regarding particularly the United States and how the Swedes had to pay more than Americans do in taxes. Then the article pointed out what Swedes got for their taxes. A lot of things in Sweden are free: university education, for example, and a whole lot of things like that. This is the way things should go and without a lot of policing and grant applications and the like. If we (taking the university and community as a whole) care about the intellectual life, there will be no such hoops, or at least very minimal ones. Some people, of course, will get grants that they don't deserve. But they do so now. There is an art in writing such applications. Artful phonies get through. Why go through such gymnastics? What does this have to do with the intellectual life or the maintaining of good universities?

AS: I have two final questions. One is a philosophical question and the other is a political question. The philosophical question is, in your judgment, what work in recent political philosophy do you think is going to endure?

KN: I would hope – though I don't know what to expect – the tradition of Rawls and Sen will endure if anything like philosophy endures. Cohen, I think, was a great articulator of historical materialism, both as an articulator of what it was in Marx and in developing it and modifying it. He made it clear once and for all that there were crucial things in Marx that could stand the closest rational scrutiny. But I think, contrary to my expectations, his moral and political philosophy is pretty close to being a disaster. I've read his last two books very carefully – the big one and the little one – and I say to myself, "How the devil does Jerry want this to contribute to socialism, which remained so important to him?" He was always a socialist and a Marxian one, too. Some people say he gave up fundamentalist Marxism. But he didn't give up what I call Marxianism – on analogy with Darwinism. Giving up fundamentalist Marxism was a good thing, even if he did it in his adult life.

I was a non-cognitivist for a long time. Whenever I hear people defend it – there are very subtle versions of non-cognitivism now – I think, and it's linked with my work on *Why be Moral?*, there is something there of importance that is hard to conceptualize correctly. You do not want to reduce (as has been done) non-cognitivism to a boo/hurrah account. You want to say it's something other than that. It is hard to give a proper articulation to it. It's all right to say that moral judgments are true or false. Indeed, it should be unproblematic. You can say mathematical judgments are true or false, or aesthetic judgments are true or false, but that's just a formal thing. But how do you warrantably assert, how can you establish, the truth of a fundamental moral judgment once you've granted that there can be one? (*Perhaps* something that it is a mistake to do.) There are people who call themselves moral realists. It doesn't seem to me that they have ever been able to resolve such an issue or show how our really basic moral judgments are warrantedly assertable and thus show their truth aptness. There is a deep place where something like a non-cognitivist thrust enters. That is – or so I believe – just how it has to be. I think, that is, that remains. But still I have just gestured at what *that* is. Maybe we will get a clearer articulation or maybe some people will fruitfully go back to Stevenson or to Gibbard. Gibbard probably has the most sophisticated statement of non-cognitivism on offer. Maybe that tradition will come back in a certain way, linked maybe with people like Sen, attracted to the methodological parts of Smith's *Theory of Moral Sentiments*. But you cannot, if you want to engage in the moral life, be just *observing* sentiments; you must *endorse* certain ones. A bad person could indeed write a good book on moral philosophy. But that is a different matter. You can't not engage in such endorsement if you want to be a moral agent – a decent human being. Maybe something like Smith's thing will come back. But I think the main influence that will remain will be Rawls and a whole group of people that work in that tradition. But philosophy will go in a more sociological and anthropological direction. It will also be more skeptical than Rawls (or for that matter Baier) that there is something that is *the* moral point of view, and it will be less hung up with ideal theory.

But I don't see many prospects for moral philosophy. I think it has had its day. I mean political moral philosophy. I think there will be political normative thought. Marx, for example, was contemptuous of moral *theory*. Whenever it was brought up, he would break into belly-laughs. People have said, "Therefore, he is against morality." But if you read *Capital* you will see it's full of passionate moral judgments and, for the most part, not judgments made without reason. So he was not against morality, any more than was Brecht, or against saying certain things are unjust or evil or vile. What he was suspicious about was moral *theories*, their relevance, and also about their ideological nature. Do we need moral philosophers? I share scepticism here with Marx. That is also a place where my pragmatism comes in. Does it make a practical difference whether we take certain positions in political philosophy, particularly in normative political philosophy? The real work seems to be done by social scientists, particularly historians like Eric Hobsbawm or Perry Anderson, or a person for all occasions like Tariq Ali. That seems to me where the action is. Indeed, scepticism isn't quite right about moral theory. Rejection is better. But that doesn't come to a rejection of morals or to a rejection of attempts to shape our world for the better and to seek a reasonable conception of what that would be.

AS: What about Habermas and the earlier critical theorists?

KN: I am glad you asked me that. I was once very influenced by Habermas, and one of the last seminars I gave was on Habermas and Rorty. I think political philosophy – and this might be too strong – might disappear and even, to put it normatively, will disappear. One of the projects I have is to go back to Rawls and Sen and some other people – perhaps Dworkin – and I want to ask what, if anything, is there in their work, work which is obviously important in some ways, for which someone needs some minimal philosophical training to grasp – that is, to learn some vocabulary and techniques that are not already in the repertoire of many non-philosophers (say, that of a lawyer, anthropologist, or some other well-educated person with some understanding of politics and its cultural life)? I am sceptical of this need for mastering philosophy's specialized vocabulary and techniques. But I think very little should remain of philosophy if that goes. But this goes with my rejectionism. Still, I'm not on the same side as Rorty who thinks philosophy will just become useless. I think there are still some points where the kind of clarification that analytic philosophers are adept at has a point – like, for example, the Putnam points about descriptions and evaluations, facts and values, as he put it. There is still some room for that. But that is cleaning the Augean stables and little, perhaps nothing, more. There will remain, of course, the history of ideas. But the *history* of philosophy is no more philosophy that then history of physics is physics – though this is not to say that the history of ideas is unimportant.

I don't think I ever urged anyone to go study philosophy. Some people will probably be obsessed with philosophy enough so that they will try to study it in some way and in effect go against my rejectionism. That will be something that will probably always obtain. But I think if you really care about politics and society, there are other things that you can better spend your time with. You learn more from literature about how life should be lived – more, for example, from reading *Middlemarch* than you do from studying John Stuart Mill, and I don't count John Stuart Mill as nothing. And you learn more from Tariq Ali, Mike Davis, or Eric Hobsbawm about how society is structured and how it should be ordered than from moral and political philosophers.

However, I have not answered your question about Habermas. I'll have a shot at it now. There was a time when I was taken by Frankfurt-style critical theory, including Habermas's attempt with the aid of contemporary analytic philosophy and contemporary sociology, to rationally reconstruct it. Prior to reading much of Habermas, I had been struck by parts of classical critical theory, particularly by Max Horkheimer's work and some things in Herbert Marcuse. Theodor Adorno, by contrast, who is typically thought to be the deepest of the classical critical theorists, was (and still is) a black box to me, except when he wrote jointly with Horkheimer, as in their wonderful *The Dialectics of the Enlightenment.* Thinking of what the Frankfurt School was trying to achieve and some of its particular attempts, it seemed to me an important project that some should clarify and develop, particularly in the way that Habermas developed it and even more so in the way that Raymond Geuss sanitized Habermas's account in Geuss's neglected but important book on Habermas and critical theory. However, after Habermas published his massive two volumes on communicative action, I began to grow less sympathetic to him. However, I think he has, and importantly, developed a central idea – a breakthrough in our accounts of rationality – in what he called 'communicative rationality.' Like instrumental rationality in its domain, communicative rationality in its domain is an important and unproblematic notion – a distinctive conception of rationality. However, it is not, as David Hume and Bertrand Russell mistakenly thought, that instrumental rationality what the whole of rationality. Both communicative rationality and instrumental rationality capture unproblematically something about rationality. Communicative rationality captures something of what Horkheimer, Marcuse, and much of rational philosophical tradition obscurely, problematically, and mystifyingly characterized as substantive rationality. But we need not have Habermas's vast and often obscure machinery for a clear and useful conception of communicative rationality. In short, Habermas is too much of a *philosophist* (to use G. A. Cohen's phrase). In the last seminars I gave, I set Habermas off on various topics (germane to both) against his analytical counterparts Rawls, Rorty, Davidson, and Brandom. And in all these cases I found Habermas wanting. With his 'Kantian pragmatism' – something that seems to me oxymoronic – he is at a great distance from critical theory. Habermas, unlike Rawls or Rorty, has sunk too much into the rationalist philosophical tradition – his vague talk of going 'post-metaphysical' to the contrary notwithstanding. I think in Habermas's and Rawls's seminal exchange in *The Journal of Philosophy* that Rawls generally has much the better of it. However, at one crucial point that very well *may* not be so. That is over their opposing conceptions of what it is to do moral philosophy. I hope to someday return to that, for I remain ambivalent here and it seems to be something that very much needs sorting out.

AS: I think it's fair to say that in recent years your vision of the world has become increasingly dystopian and pessimistic. You have compared the world, a number of times, to a pig sty.

KN: Yes, and when I think about global warming, to a global insane asylum. Those are two metaphors that I love and believe are quite apt for our condition.

AS: Do you see any hope in the near future or the far future, given things like environmental degradation and global warming and what currently looks like has turned into a global recession? Is there any hope on the horizon in your view?

KN: If I were a betting person, I would be incredibly pessimistic. I would have no hope. My view has grown darker and darker as my life goes on and as I read and study. We have, for example, the double-whammy – the mixed cocktail – of population growth and global warming. When I was born there were 2 billion people in the world; now, what is it, 7 or 8 billion?

AS: 6.5 billion, I think.

KN: It is predicted that by the middle of this century it will be 9 or 10 billion. At the same time, global warming will increase both desertification and flooding. Flooding will increase in places like Bangladesh. Desertification will increase in Africa. And nobody is doing anything about it seriously enough. In the 1960s, for example, when I went on a Vietnam war protest to Washington, there were great masses of people struggling against our condition and this was true in spades in Europe after the Second World War. There were political movements even in the United States, but also all over the world which were moving in what I would regard as a progressive direction. Socialism used to be thought by capitalists and their sympathizers to be a threat. Now it's a joke. So, things look very bad. But, after all, I'm an agent in the world; a human being struggling for some decency and respect and caring for human beings – all human beings. The things that Brecht so wanted. That's why you have the title for my book (*Pessimism of the Intellect, Optimism of the Will*) – from Gramsci, of course.[1] I would put it somewhat differently now. With me there is a pessimism – a growing deep pessimism. People often ask me, "How can you be a Marxian with such pessimism? How, with your historical materialism, can you be such a pessimist?" I think, *au contraire*, how can you not? I think – to go at this indirectly – Cohen is right about this. There will be change in the mode of production and eventually capitalism will disappear. But that it will be followed by socialism is not written in the stars. It may well be followed instead by a technological authoritarianism or some such dreadful thing. We don't know what will happen. So we can't, if we would be non-evasive, have the kind of optimism that many Marxists have had. I never had it, but I wasn't always as pessimistic as I am now. But this results from some specific things that have gone on and are going on in the world. We Marxians are not in a position to say history is on our side. I don't want you to change the title of the book but what I would speak of now is still the pessimism of the intellect; no longer of the *optimism* of the will but of the *determination* of the will. I think we will be defeated. But that, of course, and thank the non-existent God, is not certain. But this does not lessen but strengthens my determination to fight for socialism. It is the only way we can have a decent world – a morally tolerable world.

Maybe things won't be as disastrous about global warming as some people, including me, think. But it is going to be very bad. I have two grandchildren, 12 and 10, and they are bright and interesting and I think to myself, "Oh God, what kind of a horror of a world will they live in when they are my age – if they ever get to be my age?" Our times may very well be a picnic compared to theirs.

As Perry Anderson put it nicely, we socialists have been defeated – disastrously defeated. We, if we have our brains about us, must acknowledge that, but our head is not bowed. We are not like the coal miners returning to the pits at the end of *Germinal*. So we should struggle and soldier on. What other choice do we have? Should we just crawl into our holes? We are agents in the world, not just neutral observers in the world. So we have to struggle if we want to live with ourselves, but I wouldn't bet my farm that we'll win. I will not go in for betting at all. Neo-liberalism linked with conservatism has taken over and still is taking over the world even after our severe dip which really may not be over. We may have a double-dip neo-liberalism and the conservatism that goes with it. But it is beginning to crack badly. We talk about recession – it may well be a depression. Look at the levels of unemployment and how they are growing. We don't know how people will react if it goes on. I mean, we may, at least in the United States, get Tea Party people all over the place. And then things will get much worse, but people have been irrational before. But it is possible that there will be left movements developing again, or at least somewhat progressive movements, and it is possible that they may have some effect. Whether it is called socialism or not, I don't care. I call it, and not without reason, socialism. In fact, I would say something even worse: socialism is just the beginning stage of what Marx regarded as communism. And in saying that, I will be misunderstood by most people for they have a totally mixed up view of what communism is. I don't care much about whether it is called socialism, communism, or whatever. But I do care about radical change and see the necessity for it to be *now*. Yes, I have a kind of dystopia. The deepest moral urges in me make it imperative to fight back against our capitalist world and to not bow my head to evil – bow my head to the horrible world we have now with all its domination and indifference to misery.

Note

1   See the editors' introduction for a brief discussion of the title.

Selected Writings by Kai Nielsen

"The Functions of Moral Discourse." *Philosophical Quarterly* 7 (1957): 236–48.

"Justification and Moral Reasoning." *Methodos* 8, no. 33–34 (1957): 98–111.

"Good Reasons in Ethics." *Theoria* 24, no. 1 (1958): 9–28.

"The 'Good Reasons Approach' and 'Ontological Justifications' of Morality." *Philosophical Quarterly* 9, no. 35 (1959): 116–30.

"Dewey's Conception of Philosophy." *Massachusetts Review* 2 (1960): 110–34.

"Appraising Doing the Thing Done." *Journal of Philosophy* 57 (1960): 749–59.

"The Good Reasons Approach Revisited." *Archiv für Rechts- und Sozialphilosophie* 50 (1964): 455–84.

"Progress." *Lock Haven Review*, no. 7 (1965).

"Moral Truth." In *Studies in Moral Philosophy*, edited by Nicholas Rescher, 9–25. Oxford: Oxford University Press, 1968.

"Why There is a Problem About Ethics: Reflections on the Is and the Ought." *Danish Yearbook of Philosophy* 15 (1968): 68–96.

"Scepticism and Human Rights." *The Monist* 52, no. 4 (1968): 575–94.

"Reason and Sentiment: Skeptical Remarks about Reason and the Foundations of Morality." In *Rationality Today*, edited by Theodore Geraets, 248–79. Ottawa: University of Ottawa Press, 1970.

"On the Choice between Reform and Revolution." *Inquiry* 14, no. 1 (1971): 271–95.

"Principles of Rationality." *Philosophical Papers* 3, no. 2 (1974): 55–89.

"On Terrorism and Political Assassination." In *Assassination*, edited by Harold M. Zellner, 97–110. Cambridge, MA: Schenkman, 1974.

"Social Science and American Foreign Policy." In *Philosophy, Morality, and Public Affairs*, edited by Sydney Morgenbesser et al., 151–72. New York: Oxford University Press, 1974.

"Class Conflict, Marxism, and the Good-Reasons Approach." *Social Praxis* 2, no. 1–2 (1975): 89–112.

"On Philosophic Method." *International Philosophical Quarterly* 16, no. 3 (1976): 349–68.

"On Justifying Revolution." *Philosophy and Phenomenological Research* 37, no. 4 (1977): 516–32.

"The Priority of Liberty Examined." *Indian Political Science Review* 11, no. 1 (1977): 48–59.

"The Choice between Perfectionism and Rawlsian Contractarianism." *Interpretation* 6, no. 2 (1977): 132–39.

"Rawls and Classist Amoralism." *Mind* 86, no. 341 (1977): 19–30.

"Mill's Proof of Utility." In *New Dimensions in the Humanities and the Social Sciences*, edited by Harry Garvin, 110–23. Lewisburg, PA: Bucknell University Press, 1977.

"On the Very Possibility of a Classless Society: Rawls, Macpherson, and Revisionist Liberalism." *Political Theory* 6, no. 2 (1978): 191–208.

"Class and Justice." In *Justice and Economic Distribution*, edited by John Arthur and William H. Shaw, 225–45. Englewood Cliffs, NJ: Prentice-Hall, 1978.

"Why There Is a Problem about Ethics: Reflections on the Is and the Ought." *Danish Yearbook of Philosophy* 15 (1978): 68–96.

"Some Remarks on Philosophical Method." *Metaphilosophy* 9, no. 1 (1978): 23–26.

"Radical Egalitarian Justice: Justice as Equality." *Social Theory and Practice* 5 (1979): 209–26.

"On Deriving an Ought from an Is." *Review of Metaphysics* 32 (1979): 488–515.

"Some Theses in Search of an Argument: Reflections on Habermas." *National Forum* 59 (1979): 27–32.

"Impediments to Radical Egalitarianism." *American Philosophical Quarterly* 18, no. 2 (1981): 121–29.

"On Justifying Violence." *Inquiry* 24, no. 1 (1981): 21–57.

"Capitalism, Socialism, and Justice." In *And Justice for All*, edited by Tom Regan and Donald Van De Veer, 264–86. Totowa, NJ: Rowman & Littlefield, 1982.

"On Needing a Moral Theory: Rationality, Considered Judgments and the Grounding of Morality." *Metaphilosophy* 13, no. 2 (1982): 97–116.

"Political Violence and Ideological Mystification." *Journal of Social Philosophy* 13 (1982): 25–33.

"On the Need to Politicise Political Morality: World Hunger and Moral Obligation." In *Ethics, Economics and the Law*, edited by J.R. Pennock and J.W. Chapman, 253–67. New York: New York University Press, 1982.

"Global Justice and the Imperatives of Capitalism." *Journal of Philosophy* 80, no. 10 (1983): 608–10.

"On Taking Historical Materialism Seriously." *Dialogue* 22 (1983): 319–38.

"Global Justice, Capitalism, and the Third World." *Journal of Applied Philosophy* 1, no. 2 (1984): 228–41.

"Global Justice, Power, and the Logic of Capitalism." *Critica* 16, no. 48 (1984): 25–50.

"On Liberty and Equality: The Case for Radical Egalitarianism." *Windsor Yearbook of Access to Justice* 4 (1984): 121–42.

"Ideal and Non-Ideal Theory: How Should We Approach Questions of Global Justice?" *International Journal of Applied Philosophy* 2, no. 3 (1985): 33–41.

"If Historical Materialism Is True, Does Morality Totter?" *Philosophy of Social Sciences* 15 (1985): 389–407.

Equality and Liberty. Totowa, NJ: Rowman & Allanheld, 1985.

"On Finding One's Feet in Philosophy: From Wittgenstein to Marx." *Metaphilosophy* 16, no. 1 (1985): 1–11.

"Arguing for Equality." *Philosophic Exchange* 17 (1986): 5–23.

"Philosophy as Critical Theory." *Proceedings of the American Philosophical Association* 61st Annual Pacific Division Meetings (1987): 89–108.

"Cultural Identity and Self-Definition." *Human Studies* 10 (1987): 383–90.

"Undistorted Discourse, Ethnicity, and the Problem of Self-Definition." In *Ethnicity and Language*, edited by Winston A. Van Horne, 16–36. Madison, WI: The University of Wisconsin System, 1987.

"Survival and 'the Ecological Hypothesis'." In *Environmental Ethics*, edited by Raymond Bradley and Stephen Dugid, 135–75. Burnaby, BC: Institute for the Humanities; Simon Fraser University, 1987.

"Coming to Grips with Marxist Anti-Moralism." *Philosophical Forum* 18, no. 1 (1987): 1–22.

"Afterword: Feminist Theory – Some Twistings and Turnings." In *Science, Morality, and Feminist Theory*, edited by Marsha Hanen and Kai Nielsen, 383–418. Calgary: University of Calgary Press, 1987.

"Radically Egalitarian Justice." In *Legal Theory Meets Legal Practice*, edited by Anne Bayefsky, 53–69. Edmonton: Academic Printing and Publishing, 1988.

"In Defense of Wide Reflective Equilibrium." In *Ethics and Justification*, edited by Douglas Odegard, 19–38. Edmonton: Academic Publishers, 1988.

"World Government, Security, and Global Justice." In *Problems of International Justice*, edited by Steven Luper-Foy, 263–82. Boulder, CO: Westview Press, 1988.

"Justice, Equality, and Needs." *Dalhousie Review* 69, no. 2 (1989): 211–27.

"Equality of Condition and Self-Ownership." In *Ethics and Basic Rights*, edited by Guy Lafrance, 81–99. Ottawa: University of Ottawa Press, 1989.

Why Be Moral? Buffalo, NY: Prometheus Books, 1989.

"State Bureaucratic Socialism and Freedom." *Studies in Soviet Thought* 38, no. 4 (1989): 292–97.

"Afterword: Remarks on the Roots of Progress." In *Analyzing Marxism: New Essays on Analytical Marxism*, edited by Robert Ware and Kai Nielsen, 497–539: Calgary: University of Calgary Press, 1989..

Marxism and the Moral Point of View. Boulder, CO: Westview Press, 1989.

"The Concept of Ideology." *Rethinking Marxism* 2, no. 4 (1989): 146–74.

"State, Authority, and Legitimation." In *On Political Obligation*, edited by Paul Harris, 218–51. London: Routledge, 1990.

Ethics without God. Revised ed. Amherst, NY: Prometheus Books, 1990.

"Justice, Autonomy and Laissez Faire." *Windsor Yearbook of Access to Justice* 10 (1990): 400–421.

"The Very Idea of a Critical Theory." *Ratio* 5, no. 2 (1991): 124–45.

After the Demise of the Tradition: Rorty, Critical Theory and the Fate of Philosophy. Boulder, CO: Westview Press, 1991.

"Does a Marxian Critical Theory of Society Need a Moral Theory?" *Radical Philosophy* 59 (1991): 21–26.

"On the Status of Critical Theory." *Interchange* 23, no. 3 (1992): 265–84.

"Rights and Consequences: It All Depends." *Canadian Journal of Law and Society* 7, no. 1 (1992): 63–92.

"Engels." In *Encyclopedia of Ethics*, edited by Lawrence C. Becker, 306–9. New York: Garland Publishing, 1992.

"Global Justice, Capitalism, and the Third World." In *International Justice and the Third World*, edited by Robin Attfield and Barry Wilkins, 17–34. London: Routledge, 1992.

"Relativism and Wide Reflective Equilibrium." *The Monist* 76, no. 3 (1993): 316–31.

"Analytic Marxism Streamlined: A Minimal Program." *Brock Review* 2, no. 1 (1993): 79–89.

"Secession: The Case of Quebec." *Journal of Applied Philosophy* 10, no. 1 (1993): 29–43.

"Formalists and Informalists: Some Methodological Turnings." *Critica* 80, no. 73 (1993): 71–81.

"Analytical Marxism: A Form of Critical Theory." *Erkenntnis* 39 (1993): 1–21.

"Egoism and Relativism." In *Perspectives in Philosophy*, edited by Michael Boylan, 1–9. Fort Worth, TX: Harcourt Brace Jovanovich, 1993.

"Philosophy as Wide Reflective Equilibrium." *Iyyun* 32 (1994): 3–42.

"Philosophy within the Limits of Wide Reflective Equilibrium Alone." *Iyyun* 43 (1994): 3–41.

"Anti-Philosophy Philosophy." *Dialogue* 64 (1994): 149–58.

"Justice as a Kind of Impartiality." *Laval Théologique et Philosophique* 50 (1994): 511–39.

On Transforming Philosophy: A Metaphilosophical Inquiry. Boulder, CO: Westview Press, 1995.

"Reconceptualizing Civil Society for Now: Some Somewhat Gramscian Turnings." In *Toward a Global Civil Society*, edited by Michael Walzer, 41–67. Providence, RI: Berghahn Books, 1995.

"Wide Reflective Equilibrium without Uniqueness." *Iyyun* 45 (1996): 23–36.

Naturalism without Foundations. Amherst, NY: Prometheus Books, 1996.

"Radical Egalitarianism Revisited: On Going beyond the Difference Principle." *Windsor Yearbook of Access to Justice* 15 (1996): 121–60.

"There Is No Dilemma of Dirty Hands." *South African Journal of Philosophy* 15, no. 1 (1996): 1–7.

"Cultural Nationalism, Neither Ethnic nor Civic." *Philosophical Forum* 28, no. 1–2 (1996): 42–52.

"Naturalistic Explanations of Religion." *Studies in Religion* 26, no. 4 (1997): 441–66.

"Liberal Nationalism, Liberal Democracies, and Secession." *University of Toronto Law Journal* 48, no. 2 (1998): 253–95.

"Socialism and Nationalism." *Imprints* 2, no. 3 (1998): 208–22.

"Justice and the Modes of Production: Allen Wood's 'The Marxian Critique of Justice' Revisited." In *Norms and Values: Essays on the Work of Virginia Held*, edited by Joram G. Heber and Mark S. Halfon, 267–81. Lanham, MD: Rowman & Littlefield, 1998.

"Is Global Justice Impossible?" *Res Publica* 4, no. 2 (1998): 131–66.

"Cosmopolitanism, Universalism and Particularism in an Age of Nationalism and Multiculturalism." *Philosophic Exchange* (1998): 3–39.

"Taking Rorty Seriously." *Dialogue* 38, no. 3 (1999): 503–18.

"Cosmopolitan Nationalism." *The Monist* 82, no. 3 (1999): 446–68.

"Le Nationalisme cosmopolitique." In *Nationalité, Citoyenneté et Solidarité*, edited by Michel Seymour, 169–96. Montreal: Liber, 1999.

Naturalism and Religion. Amherst, NY: Prometheus Books, 2001.

"Moral Point of View." In *Encyclopedia of Ethics*, edited by Lawrence C. Becker and Charlotte B. Becker, 1141–45. New York: Routledge, 2001.

Globalization and Justice. New York: Humanity Books, 2003.

"Toward a Liberal Socialist Cosmopolitan Nationalism." *International Journal of Philosophical Studies* 11, no. 4 (2003): 437–63.

"On the Moral Justification of State Terrorism." *Osgoode Hall Law Journal* 41, no. 1–2 (2003): 427–44.

Atheism and Philosophy. Amherst, NY: Prometheus Books, 2005.

"Pragmatism as Atheoreticism: Richard Rorty." *Contemporary Pragmatism* 2, no. 1 (2005): 1–33.

Wittgensteinian Fideism? Suffolk, UK: SCM Press, 2005.

"Response to My Critics." *Economics and Philosophy* 22, no. 1 (2006): 147–58.

"Against Partition." *Dalhousie Review* 76, no. 2 (2006): 217–28.

"Globalization as a Tool for Imperialism." *Dalhousie Review* 76, no. 2 (2006): 183–93.

"Is to Understand to Forgive or at Least Not to Blame?" In *Judging and Understanding*, edited by Pedro A. Tabensky, 175–98. Aldershot, NH: Ashgate, 2006.

"Metaphilosophy, Pragmatism and a Kind of Critical Theory: Kai Nielsen and Richard Rorty." *Philosophical Papers* 36, no. 1 (2007): 119–50.

"Reply to Andrew Levine and David Schweickart on Marx and Marxism." In *Reason and Emancipation: Essays on the Philosophy of Kai Nielsen*, edited by Michel Seymour and Mathias Fritsch, 201–13. Amherst, NY: Humanity Books, 2007.

"Reply to Michel Seymour." In *Reason and Emancipation: Essays on the Philosophy of Kai Nielsen*, edited by Michel Seymour and Mathias Fritsch, 393–97. Amherst, NY: Humanity Books, 2007.

"On There Being Wide Reflective Equilibria: Why It Is Important to Put It in the Plural." *Windsor Yearbook of Access to Justice* 26, no. 2 (2009): 219–51.

"World Government: A Cosmopolitan Imperative." In *Cosmopolitisme : Enjeux et débats contemporains*, edited by Ryoa Chung and Geneviève Nootens, 119–49. Montreal: Presses de l'Université de Montréal, 2010.

Nielsen, Kai, and Steven Patten, eds. *Marx and Morality*. Guelph, ON: Canadian Association for Publishing in Philosophy, 1981.

Nielsen, Kai, and Roger A. Shiner, eds. *New Essays on Contract Theory*. Guelph, ON: Canadian Association for Publishing in Philosophy, 1977.

Bibliography

Ake, Christopher. "Justice as Equality." *Philosophy and Public Affairs* 5, no. 1 (1975): 69–89.

Allen, Derek. "The Utilitarianism of Marx and Engels." *American Philosophical Quarterly* 10, no. 3 (1973): 189–99.

———. "Is Marxism a Philosophy?" *Journal of Philosophy* 71, no. 17 (1974): 601–12.

———. "Reply to Brenkert's 'Marx and Utilitarianism'." *Canadian Journal of Philosophy* 6, no. 3 (1976): 517–34.

———. "Marx and Engels on the Distributive Justice of Capitalism." *Canadian Journal of Philosophy* supp. 7 (1981): 221–50.

Anderson, Elizabeth. *Value in Ethics and Economics*. Cambridge, MA: Harvard University Press, 1993.

———. "What Is the Point of Equality?" *Ethics* 109, no. 1 (1999): 287–337.

———. "Interview." *Imprints* 9, no. 1 (2005): 3–28.

Appiah, Kwame Anthony. "Cosmopolitan Patriots." In *For Love of Country*, edited by Joshua Cohen, 21–29. Boston: Beacon Press, 1996.

———. "The Multiculturalist Misunderstanding." *New York Review of Books* 44, no. 15 (1997): 30–36.

———. *Cosmopolitanism: Ethics in a World of Strangers*. New York: W.W. Norton, 2006.

Archibugi, Daniele. "From United Nations to Cosmopolitan Democracy." In *Cosmopolitan Democracy: An Agenda for a New World Order*, edited by Daniele Archibugi and David Held, 121–62. Oxford: Blackwell, 1995.

Archibugi, Daniele, David Held, and Martin Köhler, eds. *Re-Imagining Political Community: Studies in Cosmopolitan Democracy*. Cambridge: Polity Press, 1998.

Arneson, Richard. "Market Socialism and Egalitarian Ethics." In *Market Socialism*, edited by Pranab Bardhan and John Roemer, 281–97. Oxford: Oxford University Press, 1993.

———. "Why Justice Requires Transfers to Offset Income and Wealth Inequalities." *Social Philosophy and Policy* 19, no. 1 (2002): 172–200.

Arrighi, Giovanni. *The Long Twentieth Century: Money, Power, and the Origins of Our Times*. London: Verso, 1994.

Attfield, Robin, and Barry Wilkins, eds. *International Justice and the Third World*. London: Routledge, 1992.

Auerbach, Erich. *Mimesis: The Representation of Reality in Western Literature*. Princeton, NJ: Princeton University Press, 2003.

Baier, Annette. "The Need for More Than Justice." In *Science, Morality, and Feminist Theory*, edited by Marsha Hanen and Kai Nielsen, 41–56. Calgary: University of Calgary Press, 1987.

Barber, Benjamin. "Justifying Justice: Problems of Psychology, Politics, and Measurement." In *Reading Rawls*, edited by Norman Daniels, 292–318. Stanford: Stanford University Press, 1975.

———. "Constitutional Faith." In *For Love of Country*, edited by Joshua Cohen, 30–37. Boston: Beacon Press, 1996.

Barry, Brian. *The Liberal Theory of Justice*. Oxford: Clarendon Press, 1973.

———. "Nationalism." In *The Blackwell Encyclopedia of Political Thought*, edited by David Miller. Oxford: Blackwell, 1987.

———. *Liberty and Justice: Essays in Political Theory*. New York: Oxford University Press, 1991.

———. *Justice as Impartiality*. Oxford: Clarendon Press, 1995.

———. *Why Social Justice Matters*. Cambridge: Polity Press, 2005.

Bedau, Hugo. "Radical Egalitarianism." In *Justice and Equality*, edited by Hugo Bedau, 181–85. Englewood Cliffs, NJ: Prentice-Hall, 1971.

Beitz, Charles. *Political Equality*. Princeton, NJ: Princeton University Press, 1989.

———. "The Philosophy of International Relations." In *Routledge Encyclopedia of Philosophy*, edited by E. Craig, 826–33. London: Routledge, 1998.

Benhabib, Seyla, ed. *Democracy and Difference*. Princeton, NJ: Princeton University Press, 1996.

Benjamin, Alison. "Dollar a Week Bank Is Still a Success." *Guardian Weekly*, 19.06 2009.

Berlin, Isaiah. *Historical Inevitability*. London: Oxford University Press, 1954.

——. *Four Essays on Liberty*. Oxford: Oxford University Press, 1969.

——. *Vico and Herder: Two Studies in the History of Ideas*. London: Hogarth Press, 1976.

——. *Against the Current*. New York: Viking Press, 1980.

——. *Concepts and Categories*. Oxford: Oxford University Press, 1980.

——. *The Crooked Timber of Humanity*. New York: Alfred A. Knopf, 1991.

——. "Herder and the Enlightenment." In *The Proper Study of Mankind: An Anthology of Essays*, 359–435. New York: Farrar, Straus, and Giroux, 1998.

Bettelheim, Charles. "The Great Leap Backward." *Monthly Review* July–August (1978): 57–130.

Binns, Peter. "Anti-Moralism." *Radical Philosophy* 10 (1975).

Birnbaum, Norman. *Toward a Critical Sociology*. New York: Oxford University Press, 1971.

Blake, Michael. "Distributive Justice, State Coercion, and Autonomy." *Philosophy and Public Affairs* 30, no. 3 (2001): 257–96.

Boran, Idil. "Are Some of the Sailors in Neurath's Ship Moral Philosophers?" In *Reason and Emancipation: Essays on the Philosophy of Kai Nielsen*, edited by Michel Seymour and Matthias Fritsch, 261–70. Amherst, NY: Humanity Books, 2007.

Braybrooke, David. *Meeting Needs*. Princeton, NJ: Princeton University Press, 1987.

Brenkert, George. "Marx and Utilitarianism." *Canadian Journal of Philosophy* 5, no. 3 (1975): 421–34.

Brennan, Timothy. *At Home in the World: Cosmopolitanism Now*. Cambridge, MA: Harvard University Press, 1997.

Brighouse, Harry. "Against Nationalism." In *Rethinking Nationalism*, edited by Jocelyne Couture, Kai Nielsen, and Michel Seymour, 365–405. Calgary: University of Calgary Press, 1996.

Brinton, Crane. *The Anatomy of Revolution*. New York: Vintage Books, 1952.

Brock, Dan. "Quality of Life Measures in Health Care and Medical Ethics." In *The Quality of Life*, edited by Martha Nussbaum and Amartya Sen, 95–132. Oxford: Clarendon Press, 1993.

Buchanan, Allen. *Marx and Justice*. Totowa, NJ: Rowman & Littlefield, 1982.

———. *Secession*. Boulder, CO: Westview Press, 1991.

———. "What's So Special About Nations?" In *Rethinking Nationalism*, edited by Jocelyne Couture, Kai Nielsen, and Michel Seymour, 283–309. Calgary: University of Calgary Press, 1996.

———. "Theories of Secession." *Philosophy and Public Affairs* 22 (1997): 31–61.

———. "The Quebec Secession Issue: Democracy, Minority Rights, and the Rule of Law." In *Secession and Self-Determination*, edited by Stephen Macedo and Allen Buchanan, 238–71. New York: New York University Press, 2003.

Buchanan, Allen, Dan Brock, Norman Daniels, and Daniel Wilker. *From Chance to Choice: Genetics and Justice*. Cambridge: Cambridge University Press, 2000.

Calvert, Peter. "Revolution: The Politics of Violence." *Political Studies* 15, no. 1 (1967): 1–11.

Caney, Simon. *Justice beyond Borders: A Global Political Theory*. Oxford: Oxford University Press, 2005.

Chambers, Simone. "The Politics of Equality: Rawls on the Barricades." *Perspectives on Politics* 4, no. 1 (2006): 21–29.

Chavance, Bernard, ed. *Marx en Perspective*. Paris: Editions de l'Ecole des Hautes Etudes en Sciences Sociales, 1985.

Cheah, Pheng. "Introduction." In *Cosmopolitics*, edited by Pheng Cheah and Bruce Robbins, 20–44. Minneapolis: University of Minnesota Press, 1998.

———. "Given Culture: Rethinking Cosmopolitan Freedom in Transnationalism." In *Cosmopolitics*, edited by Pheng Cheah and Bruce Robbins, 240–328. Minneapolis: University of Minnesota Press, 1998.

Chomsky, Noam. "Notes on Anarchism." *New York Review of Books* 14, no. 10 (1970): 31–35.

———. "Trilateral's RX for Crisis: Governability Yes, Democracy No," *Seven Days*, 14 February 1977.

———. *Hegemony or Survival*. New York: Henry Holt, 2003.

———. "Simple Truths, Hard Problems: Some Thoughts on Terror, Justice and Self-Defence." *Philosophy* 80 (2005): 5–28.

Code, Lorraine. "Second Persons." In *Science, Morality, and Feminist Theory*, edited by Marsha Hanen and Kai Nielsen, 357–82. Calgary: University of Calgary Press, 1987.

Cohen, G.A. *Karl Marx's Theory of History: A Defence*. Oxford: Clarendon Press, 1978.

———. "Freedom, Justice and Capitalism." *New Left Review* 126 (1981): 3–16.

———. "Reply to Four Critics." *Analyse & Kritik* 5, no. 2 (1983): 195–221.

———. "Review of Wood's *Karl Marx*." *Mind* 92, no. 367 (1983): 442–45.

———. *History, Labour, and Freedom: Themes from Marx*. Oxford: Clarendon Press, 1988.

———. "On the Currency of Egalitarian Justice." *Ethics* 99 (1989): 906–44.

———. "Incentives, Inequality, and Community." In *The Tanner Lectures on Human Values*, 261–329. Salt Lake City: University of Utah Press, 1992.

———. "Equality of What? On Welfare, Goods, and Capabilities." In *The Quality of Life*, edited by Martha Nussbaum and Amartya Sen, 9–29. Oxford: Clarendon Press, 1993.

———. *Self-Ownership, Freedom, and Equality*. Cambridge: Cambridge University Press, 1995.

———. *If You're an Egalitarian, How Come You're So Rich?* Cambridge, MA: Harvard University Press, 2000.

———. *Rescuing Justice and Equality*. Cambridge, MA: Harvard University Press, 2008.

Cohen, Joshua. "G. A. Cohen: Marx's Theory of History." *Journal of Philosophy* 79, no. 5 (1982): 253–73.

———. "Democratic Equality." *Ethics* 99, no. 1 (1989): 727–51.

———. "A More Democratic Liberalism." *Michigan Law Review* 92 (1994): 1506–43.

———. "Review of Amartya Sen, *Inequality Reexamined*." *Journal of Philosophy* 92, no. 5 (1995): 275–88.

Cohen, Mitchell. "Rooted Cosmopolitanism." In *Toward a Global Civil Society*, edited by Michael Walzer, 223–30. Providence, RI: Berghahn Books, 1995.

Collier, Andrew. "Truth and Practice." *Radical Philosophy* 5 (1973).

———. "The Production of Moral Ideology." *Radical Philosophy* 9 (1974).

Collier, Paul. *The Bottom Billion: Why the Poorest Countries Are Failing and What Can Be Done About It*. New York: Oxford University Press, 2008.

Cooper, Wesley. "The Perfectly Just Society." *Philosophy and Phenomenological Research* 10 (1977): 46–55.

Copp, David. "Justice and the Difference Principle." *Canadian Journal of Philosophy* 4, no. 2 (1974): 229–40.

Corrigan, Philip, and Derek Sayer. "Moral Relations, Political Economy and Class Struggle." *Radical Philosophy* 12 (1975).

Couture, Jocelyne. "Liberals and Cosmopolitans." *Imprints* 3, no. 3 (1998): 156–67.

———. "Cosmopolitan Democracy and Liberal Nationalism." *The Monist* 82, no. 3 (1999): 491–515.

Couture, Jocelyne, Kai Nielsen, and Michel Seymour. "Afterword: Liberal Nationalism Both Cosmopolitan and Rooted." In *Rethinking Nationalism*, edited by Jocelyne Couture, Kai Nielsen, and Michel Seymour, 579–662. Calgary: University of Calgary Press, 1996.

Couture, Jocelyne, and Kai Nielsen. *Méta-Philosophie: Reconstructing Philosophy?* Calgary: University of Calgary Press, 1993.

———. "Cosmopolitanism and the Compatriot Priority Principle." In *The Political Philosophy of Cosmopolitanism*, edited by Gillian Brock and Harry Brighouse, 180–95. Cambridge: Cambridge University Press, 2005.

———. "Introduction: Cosmopolitisme et Particularisme." *Philosophiques* 34, no. 1 (2007): 3–16.

Craig, Gordon. "Hitler the Populist." *New York Review of Books* 4, no. 18 (1997): 20–23.

Crocker, Lawrence. "Equality, Solidarity and Rawls' Maximin." *Philosophy and Public Affairs* 6, no. 3 (1977): 262–66.

Crozier, Michel, et al, eds. *The Crisis of Democracy: Report on the Governability of Democracies to the Trilateral Commission*. New York: New York University Press, 1975.

Dahbour, Omar. "The Nation-State as a Political Community." In *Rethinking Nationalism*, edited by Jocelyne Couture, Kai Nielsen, and Michel Seymour, 311–43. Calgary: University of Calgary Press, 1996.

Dahrendorf, Rolf. *Essays in the Theory of Society*. Stanford, CA: Stanford University Press, 1968.

Daniels, Norman. "Equal Liberty and Unequal Worth of Liberty." In *Reading Rawls*, edited by Norman Daniels, 253–81. New York: Basic Books, 1975.

———, ed. *Reading Rawls*. New York: Basic Books, 1975.

———. "Equality of What: Welfare, Resources or Capabilities?" *Philosophy and Phenomenological Research* 40 (supplement) (1990): 273–96.

———. *Justice and Justification: Reflective Equilibrium in Theory and Practice*. Cambridge: Cambridge University Press, 1996.

———. "Democratic Equality: Rawls's Complex Egalitarianism." In *The Cambridge Companion to Rawls*, edited by Samuel Freeman, 241–76. Cambridge: Cambridge University Press, 2003.

———. "Nielsen and Rawls on Egalitarianism." In *Reason and Emancipation: Essays on the Philosophy of Kai Nielsen*, edited by Michel Seymour and Matthias Fritsch, 279–93. Amherst, NY: Humanity Books, 2007.

Darwall, Stephen. "Toward *Fin de Siècle* Ethics: Some Trends." In *Moral Discourse and Practice*, edited by Stephen Darwall, Allan Gibbard, and Peter Railton, 3–47. New York: Oxford University Press, 1997.

Davidson, Donald. *Inquiries into Truth and Interpretation*. Oxford: Clarendon Press, 1984.

Deming, Barbara. "Revolution and Equilibrium." In *Philosophy in the Age of Crisis*, edited by Eleanor Kuykendall, 203–222. New York: Harper & Row, 1970.

Deutscher, Isaac. *On Socialist Man*. New York: Merit Publishers, 1967.

Dewey, John. *Human Nature and Conduct*. Mineola, NY: Dover Publications, 2002.

———. *The Later Works of John Dewey, 1925–1953*. Edited by Jo Ann Boydston. Volume 11: 1935-1937, Essays, Liberalism and Social Action. Carbondale, IL: Southern Illinois University Press, 1987.

Dreben, Burton. "On Rawls and Political Liberalism." In *The Cambridge Companion to Rawls*, edited by Samuel Freeman, 316–46. Cambridge: Cambridge University Press, 2003.

Dworkin, Ronald. "The Original Position." *University of Chicago Law Review* 40, no. 3 (1973): 500–533.

———. *Taking Rights Seriously*. Cambridge, MA: Harvard University Press, 1977.

———. "Liberal Community." *California Law Review* 77, no. 3 (1979): 474–504.

———. "What Is Equality? Part 1: Equality of Welfare." *Philosophy and Public Affairs* 10 (1981): 185–246.

———. "What Is Equality? Part 2: Equality of Resources." *Philosophy and Public Affairs* 10 (1981): 283–345.

———. "What Is Equality? Part 4." *San Francisco Law Review* 22 (1987): 1–30.

———. "What Is Equality? Part 3." *Iowa Law Journal* 73 (1988): 1–54.

———. "Foundations of Liberal Equality." In *The Tanner Lectures on Human Values*, edited by G.B. Petersen, 3–119. Salt Lake City: University of Utah Press, 1990.

Easterly, William. *The White Man's Burden*. New York: Penguin, 2007.

Elliott, Gregory. "Balance-Sheets and Blueprints." *Radical Philosophy* 76 (1996): 41–43.

Elster, Jon. *Making Sense of Marx*. Cambridge: Cambridge University Press, 1985.

Engels, Friedrich. *Anti-Dühring*. New York: International Publishers, 1939.

Eshete, Andreas. "Contractarianism and the Scope of Justice." *Ethics* 85, no. 1 (1974): 38–49.

Falk, Richard. "World Revolution and International Order." In *Revolution*, edited by Carl J. Friedrich, 154–77. New York: Atherton Press, 1966.

———. *Ought, Reasons, and Morality*. Ithaca, NY: Cornell University Press, 1986.

———. "The United Nations and Cosmopolitan Democracy: Bad Dream, Utopian Fantasy, Political Project." In *Re-Imagining Political Community*, edited by Daniele Archibugi, David Held, and Martin Kohler, 308–31. Stanford, CA: Stanford University Press, 1998.

———. *The Declining World Order*. New York: Routledge, 2004.

Feinberg, Joel. "Economic Justice." In *Ethics in Perspective*, edited by Karsten J. Struhl and Paula Rothenberg, 420–29. New York: Random House, 1975.

Fine, Ben, and Elisa Valyenberge. "Correcting Stiglitz: From Information to Power in the World of Development." In *Socialist Register 2006: Telling the Truth*, edited by Leo Panitch and Colin Leys, 146–68. New York: Monthly Review Press, 2005.

Fletcher, Irving. "Karl Marx on Human Nature." *Social Research* 40, no. 3 (1973): 443–67.

Fletcher, Joseph. "Give If It Helps but Not If It Hurts." In *World Hunger and Moral Obligation*, edited by William Aiken and Hugh LaFollette, 103–14. Englewood Cliffs, NJ: Prentice-Hall, 1977.

Frankel, Boris. "Review Symposium of *Anarchy, State, and Utopia*." *Theory and Society* 3 (1976): 443–50.

Frankfurt, Harry. "Equality as a Moral Ideal." *Ethics* 98 (1987): 21–42.

Freeman, Alan, and Boris Kagarlitsky, eds. *The Politics of Empire*. London: Plato Press, 2004.

Freeman, Samuel. *Rawls*. New York: Routledge, 2007.

Fried, Marlene Gerber. "Marxism and Justice." *Journal of Philosophy* 71, no. 17 (1974): 612–13.

Friedmann, Harriet. "The Political Economy of Food: The Rise and Fall of the Post-War International Food Order." In *Marxist Inquiries*, edited by Michael Buraway and Theda Skocpol, 248–86. Chicago: University of Chicago Press, 1982.

Friedrich, Carl J. "An Introductory Note on Revolution." In *Revolution*, edited by Carl J. Friedrich, 3–9. New York: Atherton Press, 1966.

Galbraith, John Kenneth. *The Affluent Society*. New York: Mariner Books, 1998.

Gellner, Ernest. *Nations and Nationalism*. Ithaca, NY: Cornell University Press, 1983.

Geras, Norman. "On Marx and Justice." *New Left Review* 150 (1985): 47–89.

Geuss, Raymond. *The Idea of a Critical Theory: Habermas and the Frankfurt School*. Cambridge: Cambridge University Press, 1981.

Gilabert, Pablo. "The Duty to Eradicate Global Poverty: Positive or Negative?" *Ethical Theory and Moral Practice* 7 (2004): 537–50.

Goldmann, Lucien. "Is There a Marxist Sociology?" *Radical Philosophy* 1 (1972): 16–22.

Golub, Phillip. "The Sun Sets Early on the American Century." *Le Monde Diplomatique* (October 2007): 4–5.

Goodman, Nelson. *Fact, Fiction, and Forecast*. 4th ed. Cambridge, MA: Harvard University Press, 1979.

Graeber, David. *Direct Action: An Ethnography*. Edinburgh: AK Press, 2009.

Gramsci, Antonio. *Selections from the Prison Notebooks*. Edited and translated by Quintin Hoare and Geoffrey Nowell Smith. New York: International Publishers, 1971.

———. *Letters from Prison*, vol. 1. Edited by Frank Rosengarten and Raymond Rosenthal. New York: Columbia University Press, 2011.

Griffin, James. "Commentary on Dan Brock: Quality of Life Measures in Health Care and Medical Ethics." In *The Quality of Life*, edited by Martha Nussbaum and Amartya Sen, 133–39. Oxford: Clarendon Press, 1993.

Guerin, Daniel, and Mary Klopper. *Anarchism: From Theory to Practice*. New York: Monthly Review Press, 1970.

Habermas, Jürgen. "Richard Rorty's Pragmatic Turn." In *Rorty and His Critics*, edited by Robert Brandom, 31–55. Oxford: Blackwell, 2000.

———. *Truth and Justification*. Translated by Barbara Fultner. Cambridge, MA: MIT Press, 2003.

Hägerström, Axel. *Inquiries into the Nature of Law and Morals*. Translated by C.D. Broad. Stockholm: Almquist and Wiksells, 1953.

———. *Philosophy and Religion*. Translated by Robert Sandin. London: Allen and Unwin, 1964.

Hall, Everett. *Categorical Analysis*. Chapel Hill, NC: University of North Carolina Press, 1964.

Hampshire, Stuart. "A New Philosophy of the Just Society." *New York Review of Books* 24 (1972): 36–39.

Hanen, Marsha, and Kai Nielsen, eds. *Science, Morality, and Feminist Theory*. Calgary: University of Calgary Press, 1987.

Hardin, Garrett. "Lifeboat Ethics: The Case against Helping the Poor." In *World Hunger and Moral Obligation*, edited by William Aiken and Hugh LaFollette, 12–21. Englewood Cliffs, NJ: Prentice-Hall, 1977.

Harris, Paul, ed. *On Political Obligation*. London: Routledge, 1990.

Hart, H.L.A. *The Concept of Law*. Oxford: Clarendon Press, 1961.

Harvey, David. *The Condition of Postmodernity*. Cambridge, MA: Blackwell, 1990.

———. "Cosmopolitanism and the Banality of Geographical Evils." *Public Culture* 12, no. 2 (2000): 529–64.

———. "The 'New' Imperialism: Accumulation by Dispossession." In *Socialist Register 2004: The New Imperial Challenge*, edited by Leo Panitch and Colin Leys, 63–87. New York: Monthly Review Press, 2003.

———. *The New Imperialism*. New York: Oxford University Press, 2005.

Held, David. "Democracy and the New International Order." In *Cosmopolitan Democracy: An Agenda for a New World Order*, edited by Daniele Archibugi and David Held, 96–120. Oxford: Blackwell, 1995.

———. *Global Covenant*. Cambridge: Polity Press, 2004.

———. "Principles of Cosmopolitan Order." In *The Political Philosophy of Cosmopolitanism*, edited by Gillian Brock and Harry Brighouse, 10–27. Cambridge: Cambridge University Press, 2005.

Herder, Johann Gottfried. *Another Philosophy of History and Selected Political Writings*. Indianapolis, IN: Hackett, 2004.

Hiebert, Daniel. "Cosmopolitanism and the Local Level: The Development of Transnational Neighborhoods." In *Conceiving Cosmopolitanism*, edited by Steven Vertovic and Robin Cohen, 209–26. Oxford: Oxford University Press, 2003.

Hobsbawm, Eric. *Nations and Nationalism since 1780*. Cambridge: Cambridge University Press, 1990.

———. *Age of Extremes: The Short Twentieth Century 1914–1991*. London: Michael Joseph, 1994.

———. "Ethnicity, Migration and the Validity of the Nation-State." In *Toward a Global Civil Society*, edited by Michael Walzer, 235–40. Providence, RI: Berghahn Books, 1995.

———. "America's Imperialist Delusion." *Le Monde Diplomatique* 2003.

Hollis, Aidan, and Thomas Pogge. *The Health Impact Fund: Making New Medicines Accessible for All.* (Incentives for Global Health, 2008)

Holmstrom, Nancy. "Exploitation." *Canadian Journal of Philosophy* 7, no. 2 (1977): 353–69.

Honderich, Ted. *Three Essays on Political Violence*. Oxford: Blackwell, 1976.

Hook, Sydney. *Revelation, Reform and Social Justice*. Oxford: Blackwell, 1975.

Human Rights Watch. A Decade Under Chávez: Political Intolerance and Lost Opportunities for Advancing Human Rights in Venezuela. Accessed at: http://www.hrw.org/sites/default/files/reports/venezuela0908web.pdf (2008).

Hurka, Thomas. "Perfectionism and Equality." In *On the Track of Reason: Essays in Honor of Kai Nielsen*, edited by Rodger Beehler, David Copp, and Bela Szabados, 19–36. Boulder, CO: Westview Press, 1992.

Husami, Ziyad. "Marx on Distributive Justice." *Philosophy and Public Affairs* 8 (1978–79): 27–64.

Ignatieff, Michael. "How to Keep Afghanistan from Falling Apart: The Case for a Committed American Imperialism." *New York Times Magazine* July 26 (2002): 26–58.

———. "The American Empire: The Burden." *New York Times Magazine* January 5 (2003): 22–54.

Johnson, Chambers. *The Sorrows of Empire*. New York: Henry Holt, 2004.

Jones, Charles. *Global Justice: Defending Cosmopolitanism*. Oxford: Oxford University Press, 1999.

Kamenka, Eugene. "The Concept of a Political Revolution." In *Revolution*, edited by Carl J. Friedrich, 122–35. New York: Atherton Press, 1966.

Keat, Russell, and David Miller. "Understanding Justice." *Political Theory* 2, no. 1 (1974): 3–31.

Kopp, Dominique. "Russia: The Polar Grab – Ultimate Struggle for Ultima Thule," *Le Monde Diplomatique* September (2007): 8–9.

Korsgaard, Christine. *The Sources of Normativity*. Cambridge: Cambridge University Press, 1996.

Kumar, Chandra. "Progress, Freedom and Human Nature." *Imprints* 7, no. 2 (2003): 106–30.

Kymlicka, Will. *Liberalism, Community, and Culture*. Oxford: Clarendon Press, 1989.

———. *Multicultural Citizenship*. Oxford: Clarendon Press, 1995.

———. "Misunderstanding Nationalism." *Dissent* (1995): 130–37.

———. *Politics in the Vernacular*. Oxford: Oxford University Press, 2001.

Lambert, R. "Guataemala: A Private Business." *Le Monde Diplomatique* October (2007): 8–9.

Larmore, Charles. "The Moral Basis of Political Liberalism." *Journal of Philosophy* 96, no. 12 (1999): 599–625.

Lemoine, Maurice. "Up in Arms." *Le Monde Diplomatique* September, no. 1 (2007).

Lerner, Michael. "Marxism and Ethical Reasoning." *Social Praxis* 2 (1974): 63–89.

Levine, Andrew. *Arguing for Socialism*. London: Routledge and Kegan Paul, 1984.

———. "What Is a Marxist Today?" In *Analyzing Marxism: New Essays on Analytical Marxism*, edited by Robert Ware and Kai Nielsen, 29–58. Calgary: University of Calgary Press, 1989.

———. "Just Nationalism: The Future of an Illusion." In *Rethinking Nationalism*, edited by Jocelyne Couture, Kai Nielsen, and Michel Seymour, 345–63. Calgary: University of Calgary Press, 1996.

Lister, Andrew. "Reflective Equilibrium: Epistemological or Political?" *Windsor Yearbook of Access to Justice* 26, no. 2 (2008): 265–78.

Lomnitz, Claudio, and Rafael Sánchez. "United by Hate: The Uses of Anti-Semitism in Chávez's Venezuela." *Boston Review* July–August (2009), http://bostonreview.net/BR34.4/lomnitz_sanchez.php

Lukács, Georg. *History and Class Consciousness: Studies in Marxist Dialectics*. Translated by Rodney Livingstone. Berlin: Hermann Luchterhand, 1968.

Lukacs, John. *The Hitler of History*. New York: Alfred A. Knopf, 1997.

Lukes, Steven. "An Archimedean Point." *Observer* June 4 (1972).

——. "Relativism: Cognitive and Moral." *Proceedings of the Aristotelian Society*. Suppl. vol. 48 (1974): 165–89; 91–208.

Luper-Foy, Stephen, ed. *Problems of International Justice*. Boulder, CO: Westview Press, 1988.

MacFacquhar, R. "India: The Impact of Empire." *New York Review of Books* 44, no. 16 (1997): 26–32.

MacIntyre, Alasdair. "Breaking the Chains of Reason." In *Out of Apathy*, edited by E.P. Thompson, 195–240. London: Stevens and Sons, 1960.

——. *Three Rival Versions of Moral Inquiry*. Notre Dame, IN: Notre Dame University Press, 1990.

Macpherson, C.B. "Revolution and Ideology in the Late Twentieth Century." In *Revolution*, edited by Carl J. Friedrich, 139–53. New York: Atherton Press, 1966.

——. "Rawls's Models of Man and Society." *Philosophy of the Social Sciences* 3, no. 4 (1973): 341–47.

——. *Democratic Theory*. Oxford: Clarendon Press, 1979.

Mallet, Serge. *La Nouvelle Classe Ouvrière*. Paris: Seuil, 1962.

——. "Is There a Post-Industrial Revolution?" *Social Policy* 1, no. 2 (1970).

Marcuse, Herbert. "Ethics and Revolution." In *Ethics and Society*, edited by Richard T. De George, 133–48. Garden City, NY: Anchor Books, 1966.

Markovic, Mihailo. *The Contemporary Marx*. Nottingham, UK: Spokesman Books, 1974.

Martinez, Jenny S. "The Slave Trade on Trial." *Boston Review* 32, no. 5 (2007): 12–17.

Marx, Karl. "Critique of the Gotha Program." In *Karl Marx: Selected Writings*, edited by Lawrence H. Simon, 315–32. Indianapolis: Hackett, 1994.

———. "Theses on Feuerbach." In *Karl Marx: Selected Writings*, edited by Lawrence H. Simon, 98–101. Indianapolis: Hackett, 1994.

Marx, Karl, and Friedrich Engels. *The Marx-Engels Reader*. Edited by Robert C. Tucker. New York: W.W. Norton, 1978.

McBride, William. "Social Theory *Sub Specie Aeternitatis*." *Yale Law Journal* 81 (1972): 980–1003.

———. "The Concept of Justice in Marx, Engels, and Others." *Ethics* 85, no. 3 (1975): 204–18.

McCarthy, Thomas. *Ideals and Illusions*. Cambridge, MA: MIT Press, 1991.

McCloskey, H.J. "A Right to Equality?" *Canadian Journal of Philosophy* 6, no. 4 (1976): 625–42.

McDonald, Virginia. "Rawlsian Contractarianism: Liberal Equality or Inequality." In *New Essays on Contract Theory*, edited by Kai Nielsen and Roger Shiner, 71–94. Guelph: Canadian Association for Publishing in Philosophy, 1977.

McKerlie, Dennis. "Equality and Priority." *Utilitas* 6 (1994): 25–42.

McNally, David. *Another World Is Possible*. Winnipeg: Arbeiter Ring, 2002.

Melanson, Glen Vincent. "A Theory of Moral Personhood in the Thought of Karl Marx." PhD diss. University of Toronto, 1996.

Miller, David. "Democracy and Social Justice." *British Journal of Political Science* 8 (1977): 1–19.

———. "Secession and the Principle of Nationality." In *Rethinking Nationalism*, edited by Jocelyne Couture, Kai Nielsen, and Michel Seymour, 261–82. Calgary: University of Calgary Press, 1996.

———. *On Nationality*. Oxford: Oxford University Press, 1996.

———. "Justice and Global Inequality." In *Inequality, Globalization, and World Politics*, edited by Andrew Hurrell and Ngaire Woods, 187–210. Oxford: Oxford University Press, 1999.

———. "Cosmopolitanism: A Critique." *CRISSP* 5, no. 3 (2002): 80–85.

———. "Against Global Egalitarianism." *Journal of Ethics* 9 (2005): 55–79.

Miller, Richard. *Analyzing Marx*. Princeton, NJ: Princeton University Press, 1984.

———. "Cosmopolitan Respect and Patriotic Concern." In *The Political Philosophy of Cosmopolitanism*, edited by Gillian Brock and Harry Brighouse, 127–47. Cambridge: Cambridge University Press, 1995.

———. "Reasonable Partiality Towards Compatriots." *Ethical Theory and Moral Practice* 8, no. 1–2 (2005): 63–81.

Nagel, Thomas. *Mortal Questions*. New York: Cambridge University Press, 1979.

———. *The View from Nowhere*. New York: Oxford University Press, 1986.

———. *Equality and Partiality*. Oxford: Oxford University Press, 1991.

———. "The Problem of Global Justice." *Philosophy and Public Affairs* 33, no. 2 (2005): 113–47.

Neuman, Dominique. "Par Consention, le Canada Anglais devra reconnaîte du Québec." *Le Devoir* October 14 (1997).

Nevo, Isaac. "Is There a Widest Equilibrium?" *Iyyun* 45 (1996): 3–22.

———. "Reflective Equilibrium and the Contemplative Ideal of Knowledge." *Philo* 1, no. 2 (1998): 22–35.

Nisbet, Robert. "The Pursuit of Equality." *Public Interest*, no. 33 (1974): 103–20.

Norman, Richard. *Free and Equal*. Oxford: Oxford University Press, 1987.

———. *Studies in Equality*. Aldershot, UK: Avebury Press, 1995.

Nove, Alex. *The Economics of Feasible Socialism*. London: George Allen and Unwin, 1983.

Nowell-Smith, H. "A Theory of Justice?" *Philosophy of the Social Sciences* 3, no. 4 (1973): 315–29.

Nozick, Robert. *Anarchy, State, and Utopia*. New York: Basic Books, 1974.

Nussbaum, Martha. "Virtue Revised: Habit, Passion, and Reflection in the Aristotelian Tradition." *Times Literary Supplement* 9 (1992): 9–12.

———. "Patriotism and Cosmopolitanism." In *For Love of Country*, edited by Joshua Cohen, 3–17. Boston: Beacon Press, 1996.

———. "Reply." In *For Love of Country*, edited by Joshua Cohen, 134–44. Boston: Beacon Press, 1996.

———. *Cultivating Humanity*. Cambridge, MA: Harvard University Press, 1999.

———. *Frontiers of Justice*. Cambridge, MA: Harvard University Press, 2006.

Nussbaum, Martha, and Amartya Sen, eds. *The Quality of Life*. Oxford: Clarendon Press, 1993.

Nye, Joseph. *The Paradox of American Power*. Oxford: Oxford University Press, 2002.

O'Neill, Edward, and Onora O'Neill. "On Justice under Socialism." In *Ethics in Perspective*, edited by Karsten J. Struhl and Paula Rothenberg Struhl, 483–91. New York: Random House, 1976.

O'Neill, Onora. "Lifeboat Earth." In *International Ethics*, edited by Charles Beitz, 262–68. Princeton, NJ: Princeton University Press, 1985.

———. "Justice, Gender, and International Boundaries." In *International Justice and the Third World*, edited by Robin Attfield and Barry Wilkins, 50–76. London: Routledge, 1992.

———. *Towards Justice and Virtue*. Cambridge: Cambridge University Press, 1996.

Ohmae, Kenichi. *The End of the Nation State*. New York: Simon and Shuster, 1995.

———. *The Borderless World*. New York: Harper Collins, 1999.

Panitch, Leo, and Colin Leys, eds. *The Imperial Challenge*. London: Merlin Press, 2003.

Parfit, Derek. "Equality or Priority?" In *The Ideal of Equality*, edited by L. Pojman, 81–125. New York: Macmillan, 2000.

Peffer, Rodney. *Marxism, Morality, and Social Justice*. Princeton, NJ: Princeton University Press, 1990.

———. "Marxism, Moral Theory and Moral Truisms: A Response to Nielsen." *Radical Philosophy* 60 (1992): 30–35.

Pettee, George. *The Process of Revolution*. New York: Harper & Row, 1938.

———. "Revolution-Typology and Process." In *Revolution*, edited by Carl J. Friedrich, 10–33. New York: Atherton Press, 1966.

Phillips, Anne. *Which Equalities Matter?* Oxford: Polity Press, 1999.

Phillips, Derek. "The Equality Debate: What Does Justice Require?" *Theory and Society* 4 (1977): 247–72.

Pogge, Thomas. "Moral Progress." In *Problems of International Justice*, edited by Stephen Luper-Foy, 284–304. Boulder, CO: Westview Press, 1988.

———. "Cosmopolitanism and Sovereignty." In *Political Restructuring in Europe: Ethical Perspectives*, edited by C. Brown, 85–118. London: Routledge, 1994.

———. "An Egalitarian Law of Peoples." *Philosophy and Public Affairs* 23, no. 3 (1994): 195–224.

———. "The Bounds of Nationalism." In *Rethinking Nationalism*, edited by Jocelyne Couture, Kai Nielsen, and Michel Seymour, 463–504. Calgary: University of Calgary Press, 1996.

———. "Information and Priorities of Global Justice." In *Global Justice*, edited by Thomas Pogge, 1–23. Oxford: Blackwell, 2001.

———. *World Poverty and Human Rights*. Cambridge: Polity Press, 2002.

———. "Cosmopolitanism: A Defense." *CRISSP* 5, no. 3 (2002): 86–91.

Popper, Karl. *Conjectures and Refutations*. London: Routledge and Kegan Paul, 1969.

Prager, Carol. "Barbarous Nationalism and the Liberal International Order: Reflections on The 'Is,' The 'Ought' and The 'Can'." In *Rethinking Nationalism*, edited by Jocelyne Couture, Kai Nielsen, and Michel Seymour, 441–62. Calgary: University of Calgary Press, 1996.

Putnam, Hilary. *Realism with a Human Face*. Cambridge, MA: Harvard University Press, 1990.

———. *The Collapse of the Fact/Value Dichotomy*. Cambridge, MA: Harvard University Press, 2002.

———. *Ethics without Ontology*. Cambridge, MA: Harvard University Press, 2004.

Putnam, Robert. "E Pluribus Unum: Diversity and Community in the Twenty-First Century." *Scandinavian Political Studies* 30, no. 2 (2007): 137–74.

Quine, W.V.O. "Two Dogmas in Retrospect." *Canadian Journal of Philosophy* 21, no. 3 (1991): 265–74.

Quine, W.V.O., and J.S. Ullian. *The Web of Belief*. New York: Random House, 1978.

Ramonet, Ignacio. "Régimes Globalitaires." *Le Monde Diplomatique* January (1997).

———. "Silent Thought." *Le Monde Diplomatique* May 2006, no. 1 (2006).

Rapaport, Elizabeth. "Classical Liberalism and Rawlsian Revisionism." *Canadian Journal of Philosophy* Suppl. vol. 3 (1977): 95–119.

Rawls, John. "Distributive Justice." In *Philosophy, Politics, and Society*, edited by Peter Laslett and W.G. Runciman, 58–82. Oxford: Blackwell, 1967.

———. *A Theory of Justice*. Cambridge, MA: Harvard University Press, 1971.

———. "Some Reasons for the Maximin Criterion." *American Economic Review* 64 (1974): 141–46.

———. "Social Unity and Primary Goods." In *Utilitarianism and Beyond*, edited by Amartya Sen and Bernard Williams, 159–86. London: Cambridge University Press, 1982.

———. "Justice as Fairness: Political not Metaphysical." *Philosophy and Public Affairs* 14, no. 3 (1985): 223–51.

———. *Political Liberalism*. New York: Columbia University Press, 1993.

———. "The Idea of Public Reason Revisited." *University of Chicago Law Review* 64, no.3 (1997): 765–807.

———. *Collected Papers.* Edited by Samuel Freeman. Cambridge, MA: Harvard University Press, 1999.

———. *The Law of Peoples.* Cambridge, MA: Harvard University Press, 1999.

———. *Lectures on the History of Moral Philosophy.* Edited by Barbara Herman. Cambridge, MA: Harvard University Press, 2000.

———. *Justice as Fairness: A Restatement.* Edited by Erin Kelly. Cambridge, MA: Harvard University Press, 2001.

———. "For the Record." In *Philosophers in Conversation*, edited by S. Phineas Upham, 3–13. New York: Routledge, 2002.

———. *Lectures on the History of Political Philosophy.* Edited by Samuel Freeman. Cambridge, MA: Harvard University Press, 2007.

Reiman, Jeffrey. "Moral Philosophy: A Critique of Capitalism and the Problem of Ideology." In *The Cambridge Companion to Marx*, edited by Terrell Carver, 143–67. Cambridge: Cambridge University Press, 1991.

Roemer, John. *A Future for Socialism.* Cambridge, MA: Harvard University Press, 1994.

———. *Egalitarian Perspectives.* Cambridge: Cambridge University Press, 1994.

———. "A Future for Socialism." In *Equal Shares: Making Market Socialism Work*, edited by Erik Olin Wright, 7–39. London: Verso, 1996.

———. *Equality of Opportunity.* Cambridge, MA: Harvard University Press, 1998.

Rorty, Richard. *Philosophy and the Mirror of Nature.* Princeton, NJ: Princeton University Press, 1979.

———. *Consequences of Pragmatism.* Minneapolis: University of Minnesota Press, 1982.

———. *Contingency, Irony, and Solidarity.* Cambridge: Cambridge University Press, 1989.

———. *Objectivity, Relativism and Truth.* Cambridge: Cambridge University Press, 1991.

———. "Who Are We? Moral Universals and Economic Triage." *Diogenes* 173 (1996): 20–21.

———. "Idealization, Foundations, and Social Approaches." In *Democracy and Difference*, edited by Seyla Benhabib, 333–35. Princeton, NJ: Princeton University Press, 1996.

———. "Back to Class Politics." *Dissent* (Winter 1997): 31–34.

———. *Against Bosses, Against Oligarchies*. Charlottesville, VA: Prickly Pear Press, 1998.

———. *Achieving Our Country: Leftist Thought in Twentieth Century America*. Cambridge, MA: Harvard University Press, 1998.

———. *Truth and Progress*. Cambridge: Cambridge University Press, 1998.

———. *Philosophy and Social Hope*. London: Penguin, 1999.

———. "Response to Simon Thompson." In *Richard Rorty: Critical Dialogues*, edited by Matthew Festenstein and Simon Thompson, 51–54. Oxford: Blackwell, 2001.

———. "Philosophy as a Transitional Genre." In *Pragmatism, Critique, Judgment: Essays for Richard J. Bernstein*, edited by Seyla Benhabib and Nancy Fraser, 3–28. Cambridge, MA: MIT Press, 2004.

———. "Post-Democracy." *London Review of Books* 26, no. 7 (2004): 10–11.

———. *Take Care of Freedom and Truth Will Take Care of Itself*. Edited by Eduardo Mendieta. Stanford, CA: Stanford University Press, 2006.

———. "A Response to Kai Nielsen's Proposal for a Transformation of Philosophy." In *Reason and Emancipation: Essays on the Philosophy of Kai Nielsen*, edited by Michel Seymour and Matthias Fritsch, 122–30. Amherst, NY: Humanity Books, 2007.

Rosenstock-Huessy, Eugen. *Out of Revolution: Autobiography of Western Man*. Oxford: Berg Publishers, 1938.

Sachs, Jeffrey. *The End of Poverty*. New York: Penguin, 2005.

Said, Edward. *Culture and Imperialism*. New York: Random House, 1993.

———. *Reflections on Exile*. Cambridge, MA: Harvard University Press, 2001.

———. *Humanism and Democratic Criticism*. New York: Columbia University Press, 2004.

Scanlon, T.M. "Rawls' Theory of Justice." *University of Pennsylvania Law Review* 121 (1973): 1020–69.

———. "Preference and Urgency." *Journal of Philosophy* 72 (1975): 655–69.

———. "Rawls on Justification." In *The Cambridge Companion to Rawls*, edited by Samuel Freeman, 139–67. Cambridge: Cambridge University Press, 2003.

Scheffler, Samuel. "Conceptions of Cosmopolitanism." *Utilitas* 11, no. 3 (1999): 255–76.

———. *Boundaries and Allegiances*. Oxford: Oxford University Press, 2001.

———. "Immigration and the Significance of Culture." *Philosophy and Public Affairs* 35, no. 2 (2007): 93–125.

Scholte, Jan Aart. "Global Capitalism and the State." *International Affairs* 73 (1997): 427–52.

———. *Globalization: A Critical Introduction*. 2nd ed. New York: Palgrave Macmillan, 2005.

Schrecker, Paul. "Revolution as a Problem in the Philosophy of History." In *Revolution*, edited by Carl J. Friedrich, 34–52. New York: Atherton Press, 1966.

Schweickart, David. *Against Capitalism*. New York: Cambridge University Press, 1993.

———. *After Capitalism*. Lanham, MD: Rowman & Littlefield, 2002.

Sen, Amartya. "Equality of What?" In *The Tanner Lectures on Human Values*, 195–220. Salt Lake City: University of Utah Press, 1980.

———. *Poverty and Famines: An Essay on Entitlement and Deprivation*. Oxford: Clarendon Press, 1981.

———. *Inequality Reexamined*. Cambridge, MA: Harvard University Press, 1992.

———. *Development as Freedom*. New York: Anchor Books, 2000.

Seymour, Michel, Jocelyne Couture, and Kai Nielsen. "Introduction: Questioning the Ethnic/Civic Dichotomy." In *Rethinking Nationalism*, edited by Jocelyne Couture, Kai Nielsen, and Michel Seymour, 1–61. Calgary: University of Calgary Press, 1996.

Seymour, Michel, and IPSO (Intellectuals for the Sovereignty of Quebec). *Quebec Sovereignty: A Legitimate Goal*. Montreal: Fides, 1997.

Shapiro, Ian. *Democratic Justice*. New Haven, CT: Yale University Press, 1999.

Shue, Henry. "Liberty and Self-Respect." *Ethics* 85 (1975): 195–203.

———. "The Burdens of Justice." *Journal of Philosophy* 80, no. 10 (1983): 600–608.

Simpson, Evan. "Socialist Justice." *Ethics* 87, no. 1 (1976): 1–17.

Singer, Peter. *Practical Ethics*. London: Cambridge University Press, 1979.

———. *One World: The Ethics of Globalization*. New Haven, CT: Yale University Press, 2002.

Skillen, Tony. "Marxism and Morality." *Radical Philosophy* 8 (1974): 11–15.

Sklar, Martin. "Liberty and Equality, and Socialism." *Socialist Revolution* 7, no. 4 (1977): 92–104.

Sober, Elliott. "Testability." *Proceedings and Addresses of the American Philosophical Association* 73, no. 3 (1999): 47–76.

Stevenson, Charles. *Ethics and Language.* New Haven, CT: Yale University Press, 1944.

Stiglitz, Joseph. *Globalization and Its Discontents.* New York: W. W. Norton, 2002.

———. *Making Globalization Work.* New York: W.W. Norton, 2007.

Stojanovic, Svetozar. *Between Ideals and Reality.* New York: Oxford University Press, 1973.

Sunstein, Cass R. "Constitutionalism and Secession." *University of Chicago Law Review* 58 (1991): 633–70.

Tamir, Yael. "The Right to National Self-Determination." *Social Research* 58 (1991): 565–90.

———. *Liberal Nationalism.* Princeton, NJ: Princeton University Press, 1993.

Tan, Kok-Chor. "Justice and Personal Pursuits." *Journal of Philosophy* 100, no. 7 (2004): 331–62.

———. *Justice without Borders: Cosmopolitanism, Nationalism, and Patriotism.* Cambridge: Cambridge University Press, 2004.

———. "Priority for Compatriots: Commentary on Globalization and Justice." *Economics and Philosophy* 22 (2006): 115–23.

Taylor, Charles. "Interpretation and the Sciences of Man." *Review of Metaphysics* 25, no. 1 (1971): 3–51.

———. *Hegel.* Cambridge: Cambridge University Press, 1975.

———. *Hegel and Modern Society.* Cambridge: Cambridge University Press, 1979.

Taylor, Paul. "Utility and Justice." *Canadian Journal of Philosophy* 1, no. 3 (1972): 327–50.

Temkin, Larry. *Inequality.* New York: Oxford University Press, 1993.

Tolstoya, Tatyana. "Dreams of My Russian Summers." *New York Review of Books* 44, no. 18 (1997): 4–6.

Toulmin, Stephen. *Return to Reason.* Cambridge, MA: Harvard University Press, 2001.

Tucker, Robert C. *The Marxian Revolutionary Idea.* New York: W.W. Norton, 1969.

Vivanco, Jose Miguel, and Daniel Wilkinson. "Hugo Chávez Versus Human Rights." *New York Review of Books* 55, no. 17 (2008).

Waldron, Jeremy. "Minority Cultures and the Cosmopolitan Option." *University of Michigan Law Review* 25 (1992): 751–93.

Walzer, Michael. *Spheres of Justice*. New York: Basic Books, 1983.

———. "Governing the Globe." *Dissent* (2000): 44–52.

———. *Thinking Politically*. Edited by David Miller. New Haven, CT: Yale University Press, 2007.

Williams, Michael. "Rorty on Knowledge and Truth." In *Richard Rorty (Contemporary Philosophy in Focus)*, edited by Charles Guignon and David Hiley, 61–80. Cambridge: Cambridge University Press, 2003.

Wittgenstein, Ludwig. *On Certainty*. Translated by Denis Paul and G.E.M. Anscombe. New York: Blackwell, 1969.

———. *Philosophical Investigations*. Translated by G.E.M. Anscombe. Oxford: Blackwell, 1998.

Wolff, Robert Paul. *Understanding Rawls*. Princeton, NJ: Princeton University Press, 1977.

Wood, Allen. "The Marxian Critique of Justice." *Philosophy and Public Affairs* 1, no. 3 (1972): 224–82.

———. "Marx on Right and Justice: A Reply to Husami." *Philosophy and Public Affairs* 8, no. 3 (1979): 267–95.

———. "Doing Marx Justice." *Canadian Journal of Philosophy* Supplementary volume, 7. (1981): 251–68.

———. *Karl Marx*. London: Routledge and Kegan Paul, 1982.

———. "Marx and Equality." In *Issues in Marxist Philosophy*, edited by John Mepham and David Hillel-Ruben, 195–221. Brighton, UK: Harvester Press, 1982.

———. "Justice and Class Interests." *Philosophica* 33, no. 1 (1984): 9–32.

———. "Marx's Immoralism." In *Marx en Perspective*, edited by Bernard Chavance, 680–95. Paris: Editions de l'Ecole des Hautes Etudes en Sciences Sociales, 1985.

———. "Marx against Morality." In *A Companion to Ethics*, edited by Peter Singer, 511–24. Oxford: Blackwell, 1991.

———. "Marx." In *Encyclopedia of Ethics*, edited by Lawrence C. Becker, 763–69. New York: Garland Publishing, 1992.

———. "Attacking Morality: A Metaehical Project." In *On the Relevance of Metaethics: New Essays on Metaethics*, edited by Jocelyne Couture and Kai Nielsen, 221–49. Calgary: University of Calgary Press, 1995.

Worsley, Peter. *Marx and Marxism*. London: Tavistock, 1982.

Wright, Erik Olin. "A Compass for the Left." *New Left Review* 41, 2nd Series (2006): 93–126.

Wright, Erik Olin, ed. *Rethinking Socialism*. Special Issue of *Politics and Society* 22, no. 4 (1994).

Young, Gary. "Justice and Capitalist Production: Marx and Bourgeois Ideology." *Canadian Journal of Philosophy* 8, no. 3 (1978): 421–54.

———. "Doing Marx Justice." *Canadian Journal of Philosophy* suppl. 7 (1981): 251–68.

Young, Iris Marion. *Inclusion and Democracy*. Oxford: Oxford University Press, 2000.

Yunnus, Muhammad. *Banker to the Poor: Micro-Lending and the Battle against World Poverty*. New York, NY: Public Affairs, 2003.

Index

A

ability vs. will, 223–24, 227–28
abundance, 186, 200, 210, 214, 217–18, 222–23, 225, 248, 257, 270
academia, 425–26
    academic disciplines, xxxiv, 78–80, 82, 423–25
    privatization of, 427–28
    professionalization of, 426–27
analytic/synthetic distinction, 5, 8–9
analytic philosophy, 9, 12, 21, 417
Anderson, Elizabeth, 122n55
anti-representationalism, xiv, xxxviin13, 39n11
Aristotle, 244, 257, 415–16
atheism, 411–12
Augean stable cleaning, 21, 81, 83, 96–98, 102, 119-121n53, 122n55, 424, 430
Austin, J.L., 4
autonomy, 246–48, 257, 259, 302, 324–25, 338, 370n28. *See also* moral autonomy, freedom (political)

B

Barry, Brian, xliin83, 54, 77, 79, 107, 227, 267, 351, 352, 354
Berlin, Isaiah, xxix, 58, 95, 136, 310, 351, 399, 413–14
Boran, Idil, 43–44
boundary questions, 5
Brecht, Bertolt, 75, 191n35, 222, 229, 415–16, 433
Buchannan, Allen, 301–3, 313–15, 318–22, 325–26, 328–36, 339–42, 347-348n78

C

capitalism, xv–xvi, xix–xxiii, xxxiii, 26–27, 29–30, 118n38, 141. 160, 170, 181, 183–85, 191n38, 200, 214, 222, 228, 278, 283–85, 292–95, 404, 433
    authoritarian, 292–93, 296–97
    capitalist world order, xxviii, 84–85, 266, 269–71, 276–82, 288, 297, 380–81, 385–86, 388
    centres of, 293–94
    Japanese style, 284
    profits, xxviii, 203, 278, 283, 385–86
    resilience of, 285
    rich capitalist nations, 265, 302, 366
    welfare state, xx, 175, 217, 222, 295–96, 421
Carnap, Rudolph, 2, 36
carrying capacity of the world, 278
Chomsky, Noam, 4, 23–24, 148, 363
citizenship, 66, 174, 178, 306–7, 367, 371n45, 396
class, xv–xvi, xviii–xix, xxi, 29, 139, 141, 143, 161, 168–70, 172–75, 185, 187, 188n2, 199, 201, 217, 366
    consciousness, 141, 147
    conflict, 160
    middle class, 294–96
    possibility of classlessness, 181–84, 186, 191n38, 207–8
    vs. status, 210
    vs. strata, 171, 177, 183, 208–9, 217–18, 225
Cohen, G.A., xxii–xxiii, 13, 80, 216–17, 222–24, 228, 236–37, 415, 428

coherentism, xvi, 41–42, 54, 118n50, 156–57, 159, 423
communism. *See* socialism
communitarianism, 415
community, 310, 356, 358
   global, 273, 373–75, 379, 381
   moral, 184, 273
   political, xxxi, 303–6, 364, 413–15
compatibilism, 219, 240. *See also* free will
comprehensive analysis, 78–79
considered judgments, 46–47, 51–52, 106, 118n50, 159, 180, 330
consumerism, 75, 382
contextualism, xvi, 33, 36–37, 49, 51, 58, 106–7, 152, 154, 158
continental philosophy, 6, 7, 21
cosmopolitanism, xxvi, xxviii–xxxi, 309–10, 338, 349–52, 356, 360–62, 364, 368, 373–78, 379, 381, 389, 393, 396–99, 411, 413, 414
critical theory, xv–xvii, xxxvin3, xxxviiin22, 12, 15–22, 25–26, 76, 151, 163–64, 431
culture, xi, 10–11, 115, 293, 303–11, 314, 320, 331, 333–35, 337–38, 350, 353, 356, 358–59, 375, 413

D

Davidson, Donald, 5
demarcation problem, 16–17
demilitarization, 382–87, 391
democracy, xx–xxi, xxxi, 28, 66–68, 85, 101, 140, 191n38, 286–87, 302, 315, 362, 364, 367
   bourgeois, 140
   cosmopolitan, 379–80
   cynicism about, 362–63
   deliberative, xxxii, 60, 127
   democratic state diplomacy, 388
   liberal, xxiii, 30, 64, 67, 301–2, 307–9, 312, 315–24, 326, 340–41, 343–44, 366
   post-democracy, 85, 101
   rich capitalist, 27, 29, 362–63, 366
   social, 402–3, 412
   workplace, 364, 366
desert, 205–6, 215, 218–19
development projects, 87–88

Dewey, John, xi, xxii, 9–10, 19, 76, 80, 106–7, 245, 267, 287, 344, 404–5, 417
disability, 241, 258
discrimination, 66, 239, 316, 332–33
diversity, 350
division of labour, 169
   intellectual, 78, 83
Dworkin, Ronald, 235–37

E

economics, xxi, 78
   economic policy, 294
   modes of production, 127, 153–54, 156, 158–63, 386, 433
   multinational/transnational corporations, 84, 278–79, 385–86
   of food, 276–81
   See also moral-political-economic problems
education, 37, 105–6, 146
egalitarianism, xx, xvii–xxi, xxiv, 25–27, 45, 76, 107–8, 139, 145, 167–71, 173–75, 177–78, 182, 197, 209, 213–17, 226, 229, 253, 267, 286, 351, 353–55, 404, 406
   aspiration of, 231–33, 239, 242–43, 247, 259, 267, 275. 287, 293
   equal capability of functioning, 244, 257–58
   equal effective freedom, 215, 242, 244–47, 256–58
   equal satisfaction of needs, 245, 248–57
   equality of condition, 230, 232, 242–43, 254, 259–60
   equality of welfare, 234–42, 247, 255–56, 268
   equality of well-being, 244, 255
   maximization of well-being, 248, 255–56
   radical vs. liberal, 184, 186, 189n9, 193–95, 198, 200–201, 202, 205–8, 214, 259
   resource based, 235–37, 242, 247
   socialist, 216
   global xxvi, 87–88, 90
   vs. diversity, 229–30, 233, 243–45, 268
   vs. sufficientarianism, xxvi, 90, 105, 109, 175, 203, 254–254, 275–76
Enlightenment, the, 18, 31, 106, 110
Enlightenment rationalism, 18, 34–35, 310
entitlement, 215, 219–23, 281

environmental problems, 75, 84, 282–84, 388, 390, 393, 433
epistemology, 2, 20, 48, 80
essentialism, 39n39, 97, 244, 257
establishment, the, 126, 140, 142, 160, 199, 317, 406, 409
ethics, 114
  biomedical, 119-120n53
  emotive theory of, 3, 417–18
  ethical pluralism. *See* pluralism
  normative ethical theory, 108–9
  ethical principles, 112–13
  See also morality
exploitation, xxviii, 126, 169–70, 177, 183, 207–8, 232, 240, 265, 272, 278, 283–84, 296
experimental approach, 106–7

F

fach idioten (subject idiots), 78–79, 103
facism, 85, 101
fact/value distinction, xxxviiin20, 81, 95–97, 99, 122n55, 144, 157, 424, 430–31
fallibilism, xvi, 17, 23, 43, 69, 80, 107, 113, 118n50, 136, 162, 253
First Nations, 304–5, 307–8, 339, 357
foreign occupation, 85, 101
Foucault, Michel, 21–22
foundationalism, xvi, xxxviin14, 8–9, 11, 44, 69, 81, 153, 158
freedom (political), 127, 138–39, 141, 143–44, 161, 174, 208, 210, 223
  formal vs. effective, 246
  See also autonomy, moral autonomy
free will, 219. *See also* compatibilism

G

geopolitics, 382–85
global governance, xxxii, 90–92, 110, 349, 374, 379–82, 388–93, 395, 397
  divided sovereignty, 92, 380, 390
  global vs. national priorities, 394, 397–99, 400n37
  See also United Nations
global world federation. *See* global governance

globalization, 75, 84–85, 119-120n53, 380–81, 389, 393
  anti-globalization movement, xxvii
Goodman, Nelson, 53
'good reasons approach', xxxvin3, 8, 417, 419
Gadamer, Hans-Georg, 21–22
Gramsci, Antonio, xxv, xlin58, 16, 23, 29, 290, 363, 433, 441

H

Habermas, Jürgen, 22, 420, 430–32
happiness, 127, 133, 138–39, 141, 144, 161, 181, 238
Harvey, David, xxv, xlii, 39n12, 40n30, 79, 82, 99
health care, 121n53
Hegel, G.W.F., 32, 354, 415–18
heuristics, 107–8, 126, 232
historicism, xvi, 17–18, 38-39n6, 43, 106–7, 118n50, 141, 152, 154, 158, 415
Hobbes, Thomas, 92, 415–16
  sovereignty, 380
holism. *See* contextualism
homosexuality. *See* same-sex marriage
human nature, xxi, 37–38
human practices, xiii
human rights, xix, xxx, 73n50, 142, 145, 153, 221, 233–35, 312–14, 316, 319, 323, 327, 341, 351, 367, 377
humanitarian intervention, 85–86

I

ideal language, 2–3, 96
ideology, xx–xxi, 121n53, 138, 144–45, 159–60, 267, 297, 377
  critique of, 10, 19, 101
illiberal views, 46–48, 50, 52–53, 62–65, 70, 73n50
immigration, 88–89, 303, 306, 308, 337, 345n10, 367, 371n45, 390, 403
  protection of cultural identity, 88–89
  integration/accommodation, 89, 304
incentive, xviii, 215, 221–27
industrial society, 169–70
industrialization of developing world, 277–80

inequality, xxiv–xxv, 88–89, 103–4, 210, 216–17, 223–24, 227–29, 280, 295, 298. *See also* wealth disparity
international law, 314, 317, 320–21, 324–25, 340–43, 347-348n78
interpretative description, 87, 95–96, 102

J

journalism, 23–25, 113
justice, xix, xxi, 7, 10, 56, 60, 109, 118n50, 151–55, 185–87, 193, 213–15, 223–27, 234, 254, 271, 322
   as equality, 205–6
   circumstances of, 214, 218, 239
   distributive, xvii, xxvi, 89, 175, 195–97, 204, 235–40, 277
   global, xxiv, xxvi, xxviii–xxix, xlin55, 119n53, 265–68, 273, 275, 290, 393
   principles of, 112, 118n50, 162, 168, 173–76, 185, 192, 196–97, 201, 342–44, 352, 355, 367
   social/political, 112, 140–41, 159, 167, 169–73, 176, 178–80, 186, 193–96, 218, 221, 250, 272–73, 308
   socialist conception of, 168, 181
   theory of, 104, 157, 160–62, 220
   vs. justification, 190n24, 229
justification
   of belief, 18, 24, 41, 44, 46–55, 70, 71n6, 118n50, 157–58, 234
   of violence. *See* violence

K

Kant, Immanuel, 11, 19, 20, 25, 34, 48, 77, 91, 155, 184, 246, 256, 373, 380, 389, 421
Kymlicka, Will, 337, 356, 415

L

labour, 185, 196, 199, 243, 404
   extra remuneration, 225–26
language, xiii–xiv, 2–5, 12, 303, 306–7, 314, 333–35, 358–59, 413
   language-games, 49, 60, 96, 114
   philosophy of, 6

left-wing politics, xxv, 28, 30, 88, 90, 105, 131, 148, 193, 295, 382, 401–2, 407–9, 421, 434
Lewis, C.I., 2
liberalism, xi, xxxviin14, 44–45
   social, 351–52, 354–56, 361, 367
   See also Rawls (political liberalism)
liberal nationalism, xxix, xxxi, 306–7, 308, 331, 333, 335–37, 351–56, 362, 365–68, 393–96
   vs. ethnic nationalism, 306, 308, 395–96, 414
liberation, 142, 146
Liberation Theology, 412–13
liberty, 196. *See also* Rawls (liberty principle)
liberty vs. equality problem, 45
linguistics, 4
Lister, Andrew, 43–44
literature, 23, 113–14
logic, 2, 5
   philosophy of, 6

M

Macpherson, C.B., 131–32, 188n3
malnutrition, 269, 277, 279, 281, 283. *See also* poverty
Markovic, Mihailo, 207–10
Marcuse, Herbert, 131–32
   Revolution and Ethics, 138-139m 141–46, 147
Marx, Karl, 22, 78–79, 183, 188n2, 270, 297, 402, 404, 407, 428–30
   historical materialism, 29–30, 159
   Marxian theory, xv–xvi, xxii–xxiii, 16, 19, 29, 76, 151–52, 154, 156, 158–61, 163, 171, 286–87
   false consciousness, 184
   fundamentalist Marxism, 28
   Marxian vs. Marxist, xxxviin18, 286, 428
   proletariat, 22, 50, 278–79, 281, 285
mass media, 85, 87, 102
mathematics, 6
means of production, 169, 183, 185, 203. *See also* economics
means/ends interdependence, 245–48, 267–68, 287, 344
metaethics, 5, 80, 83, 95, 97, 416

metaphilosophy, xii–xv, xxv, xxxvin5, xxxviin16, 1, 15–17, 79, 81
metaphysics, xiii, xxxvin8, 2, 6, 20, 80–81, 83
military spending, 382–84
Miller, David, 303, 415
modernity, 53–54, 69, 234, 311, 326, 330–31, 335, 350, 352, 356, 358, 365, 369n22, 371n36
morality, xv, 18, 64, 93, 151–54, 157, 159–60, 187, 207, 227, 238–39, 320, 322, 327, 340, 429–30
  concreteness of, 354
  institutional, 339–40
  moral autonomy, 174, 178, 181–82, 184–87, 196
  moral equality, xix, 90, 107, 171, 173–76, 179, 202, 207, 220, 224, 233–34, 246, 273, 322, 353, 361–62
  moral evaluation, 96–97
  moral luck, 219–20
  moral philosophy, xxi, 3, 5, 7, 10, 19, 76–78, 80, 82–83, 154
  moral point of view, 106, 153, 156, 227, 232, 429
  moral preferences, 96–97
  moral reasoning, 103, 158, 172, 206, 249–50
  moral skepticism, 145
  moralism vs. critical morality, 163–64, 374
  sociology of, 155
  moral theory, 122n55, 157, 180, 429
  vs. ethics, 110–11
moral-political-economic problems, 76, 78, 81–84, 95, 97–98, 100, 102, 109, 112, 120n53, 145, 269. *See also* economics

N

nations, 302–4, 311, 313, 317–18, 321–22, 326, 329, 364
  homeland, 303–5, 309, 311, 321, 338, 358
  national identity, xxix–xxx, 302, 306, 309–12, 326, 328, 330–36, 350, 352, 356–61, 365, 369n22, 370n23, 371n36
  national minorities, 305–8, 315–16, 319, 324, 336–37, 367
  nation-states, xxxiii, 304, 307, 312, 318, 325–28, 338, 341, 351, 356–57, 364–66, 389–98

national self-determination, xxix–xxxii, 301–5, 311–12, 318–19, 321–29, 338–39, 354–55, 364–66, 395
  multi-nation states, 301, 308, 312, 320, 324–28, 338, 351, 356, 365–67
  post-national identity, 370n27
nationalism, 302, 304, 343, 349–50, 352, 364–65, 413. *See also* liberal nationalism
narrative philosophy, 19–20
needs, xix, 203, 205–6, 209, 215, 242, 248
  basic vs. adventitious, 250–54, 256–57
neo-conservatism, 87
neo-liberalism, 292, 366, 381
neo-Malthusianism, 269–71, 273–74, 281
Nietzsche, Friedrich, xvii, xxxviin14, 47, 49, 79, 188, 233, 404, 405
non-cognitivism, 429
normative judgments, 58
Nozick, Robert, xxxixn42, 104, 182, 214, 220, 224, 233, 271, 352

O

objectivity, xiii
  vs. intersubjectivity, 93, 102, 107
oppression, xi, xix, 126
ordinary language philosophy (Oxford Philosophy), 2–4

P

paternalism, 111–12, 199, 328, 339
Peirce, Charles Sanders, 33, 106
persecution, 316–17, 319
philosophy, 405
  history of, 418, 431
  limits of, 80–82, 93–94, 97–100, 102–4, 108–10, 113–16, 119–120n53
  methods of, 36, 79
  of mind, 6
  problem solving, 19
  purpose / role of, 1, 8–13, 16, 20–21, 25, 26, 31, 71–72n12, 73n49, 77, 100, 120n53
  professionalization of, 77–78
  vs. moral/ethical reflection, 114–15
  See also political philosophy

physical impossibility argument, 266, 268–70, 272–75, 281–82, 297
Plato, 415
pluralism, 42, 56, 59–60, 93–94, 112–13, 243–45, 331–33, 336
political activism, 405–6
political community, 304–6, 413
political impossibility argument, 266, 268–70, 282, 285–91, 297–98
political philosophy, xxii, xxxiv, xxxv, 7, 19, 77–78, 80–81, 415, 419–20, 422, 424, 428, 430
pollution. *See* environmental degradation
Popper, Karl, 141
   Utopia and Violence, 136–38, 142–44
   political rationalism, 137–38
population growth, 169, 282, 433
positivism, 101, 417–18
post-modernism, 26
poverty, xxiv–xxv, xlin54, 138–39, 258, 294–95
   global, xxxiii, 103–4, 108–9, 115–16, 117n38, 271–74, 276, 280, 393, 398
power differences, xix, 178, 186, 198–200, 202, 218, 223, 225, 227, 364
practical reason, 60
pragmatism, xxxii, xxxvin9, 2, 17, 122, 407, 417–18, 430, 432
preferences, 203–4, 235–40, 255
principle of sufficient reason, 158
progress, 128, 149n1
propaganda, 377, 383, 386, 388, 404
property, xx, xxiii
private ownership, 178
public intellectual, 32, 77–80, 82, 101, 103
public reason, 62, 67
Putnam, Hilary, xiii, xxxviin12, xxxviin20, 34, 95, 99, 407–8, 424, 430, 440n35

Q

Quebec nationalism, xxix–xxxii, 366–67, 413–14
Quine, W.V.O., 4–5, 54

R

racism, 88, 406
radical social transformation, 125–27, 134–35, 158, 434–35
   liberal vs. radical stance, 135–36
   motivating values of, 142
   positive vs. negative requirements, 126–27
   reform vs. revolution, 125–30, 133–36, 138, 143, 146–48, 161–62
   utilitarian considerations, 141–42, 145
   violence, 134, 142, 147
rationalism, 18, 56–59, 69, 153, 155–56, 187. *See also* "Enlightenment rationalism"
rationality, xv, 21, 54, 57, 93, 172, 180, 187
   communicative vs. instrumental, 431–32
Rawls, John, xviii–xxi, 8–11, 43–45, 49, 82, 167, 170–73, 177–78, 415, 419–23, 428
   A Theory of Justice, xx, 6–8, 168
   burdens of judgment, 55–57, 59, 67
   controversial philosophical positions, 47–49, 51, 59, 70, 108
   difference principle, xviii–xix, 168, 172, 176–82, 198, 200, 214–17, 224, 228–29, 233, 259, 267, 272–73
   ideal theory, xxi, xxvii, 214, 218, 259, 266–68, 322–23, 341–44, 420
   justice as fairness, 47, 71n8–9, 112, 196–97
   liberty principle, 172, 182, 196–98, 200–201, 245–46
   metaphysics. *See* controversial philosophical position
   on class, 183, 186, 189n9
   opportunity principle, 172, 174–75, 180–81, 242
   original position, 422
   overlapping consensus, 45, 47, 48
   political liberalism, 46, 48–50, 52, 54–56, 59–62, 64–71, 112–13, 364
   primary goods, 90, 198, 201, 203–4, 215, 242, 247, 256–58, 335, 353, 368–69n9
   reasonable comprehensive doctrine, 60–61, 63
   two moral powers, 56
realpolitik, 315, 321, 323–24, 327, 341, 355
reasonableness, 32, 42–43, 46, 54, 93–94, 110, 135, 137, 145, 157–58, 168, 232–33, 291
   Rortian vs. Rawlsian, 60–63, 65, 67, 70

reasonable disagreement, 55–59, 62–67
  compromise vs. violence, 136
recognition (political), 66, 252, 303, 307, 312, 331, 337
relativism, xiii, 154
religion, 18, 54, 63–65, 67–69, 73n50, 83, 336–37, 350, 359, 361, 404–5, 412–13
respect
  for persons, 66, 69, 112, 194–95. 197, 200, 302, 309, 329–30, 332, 352, 373, 397–98, 433
  for self, 168, 173, 177–78, 184–87, 194–95, 197–201, 210, 226, 246–47, 257, 309
revolution, 125, 127–30, 142–45, 162, 296
  connotations, 129–30
  "Great" revolutions, 130–31
  necessary conditions, 131
  overthrow of government, 134–35
  risk of authoritarian outcomes, 142
  socio-political, 131–34 139–40
  types of, 132
  violence, 127, 132, 134–35, 138, 139–41
  See also radical social transformation
right to secession, xxix–xxxi, 302, 311–14, 318–19, 321–23, 328, 341–44, 347–348n78, 365, 367, 395
  burden of proof, 301, 326
  institutional approach, 339–40
  just terms of succession, 313–14, 319
  Primary Right, 313–16, 318, 319–20, 324–26, 328, 329–31, 339–40
  Remedial Right Only, 313–16, 318, 319–20, 324, 328, 329
Roemer, John, xv, xxiii, xln50, 29, 152, 162, 286–88, 292–93, 296, 298
Rorty, Richard, xv, 8–11, 15–23, 25–37, 43–44, 48, 49, 51, 55, 60, 77, 273, 410
Russell, Bertrand, 65–67

S

same-sex marriage, 62–68
science
  scientism, 21, 33–34, 79, 144
  philosophy of, 6
secularism, 68–69
self-identity, 356–58, 360–61, 364

Sellars, Wilfrid, 5, 38n4
Sen, Amartya, 82, 244–45, 428
skepticism, xiii, 81–82
  about grand theory, 22, 27–29, 31, 35, 39n15
  Hume's mitigated, 17, 43, 51
  about philosophy's usefulness, 115, 120n53, 420–21, 429–31
  See also philosophy (role of)
slavery, 284
social acculturation, 37
social equality, 141
social goods, 202
social practices, 17–18, 34, 49, 153–54, 160, 163, 250
social reform, 125, 127–30, 133, 138, 148
  changing social arrangements, 130
  connotations, 128–29
  institutional improvements, 129–30
  See also radical social transformation
social sciences, 13, 77, 119n53, 156–57, 286
social theory, 10–13, 15–16, 19–26, 28, 30–32, 39n41, 43, 152
socialism, xix–xxiii, xxvii–xxviii, xxxi–xxxii, 26–27, 29–31, 39n24, 117n35, 147, 171, 182, 193, 208, 217, 259–60, 286, 298, 349, 361, 402–3, 406, 412, 421, 428, 433
  central planning, 29, 293
  command economy, 291–93
  market, xxi, xxiii, xxviii, xln50, 28–29, 162, 259, 287–93, 296
  decline of, xxv, 433–34
  global xxxii
  totalitarian 'communist' regimes, 28, 30, 142, 292–93, 296–97
  transition from capitalism, 30, 270, 285, 287–91, 293–98
  reputation in North America, 294
  right to equal share of goods, 196, 202, 204, 210
socialization, 307–8
sociology of knowledge, 159
state power, 56, 320
  repressive measures, 324

T

Taylor, Charles, 12
territorial integrity of states, 317, 320–22, 325, 341–42
terrorism, 117n34, 384, 387
theory/practice interrelation, 287, 290
tolerance, 59, 64, 375–77, 397, 403
truth, xiv–xv, 18, 51

U

United Nations, 91–92, 317, 380, 388, 396
    democratization of, 91–92, 389–91, 393, 395
    funding of, 392
    General Assembly, 91, 389–90, 392, 395–96
    military force of, 391–92
    Secretary General, 391
    Security Council, 91, 389
    sovereignty of, 92, 391–93
    See also global governance
United States, 85, 92, 98–99, 146, 279, 371n45, 384, 401, 403, 408, 410–11, 413
    American Communist Party, 406
    American philosophy, 410–11
    as police state, 101–2
    Afghanistan war, 100–101, 382–83
    client states, 98–100
    economic power, 385
    exploitive extraction, 99
    hard vs. soft power, 381, 385, 388
    media censorship, 102
    military superiority, 85, 382–83
    imperialism, xxvii–xxviii, 85–86, 98–100, 117n34, 119–120n53, 146, 374, 380–83, 387, 412
    Iraq war, 100–101, 382–83
    Occupy movement, 295
    Tea Party movement, 295, 421, 434
    Vietnam War, 6–7, 382, 406–12
utilitarianism, 145, 206
    utilitarian reasoning, 173, 179–81, 184, 206, 240–41, 249
utopianism, 90, 92, 130, 136–38, 144–45, 163, 287, 289, 315, 339, 373, 375

V

violence, xxx, 316–17, 321, 393
    justification of, 139–44, 156
    of the state, xxxii, 138–39, 146

W

warranted assertability, 51, 429
wealth disparity, 89–90, 103–4, 172–73, 179, 181–82, 185–86, 227, 271–72, 276, 279, 402. *See also* inequality
wealth distribution, xxxiii, xxxixn32, 104–5, 139, 143, 175, 187, 189n10, 196, 202, 209, 225–26, 271, 274–76, 298
Weber, Max, 78–79
Westphalian sovereignty, 90, 380, 388–89, 395
wide reflective equilibrium (WRE), xvi–xvii, xx, xxv, xxxvin3, 7, 21, 23, 33–38, 41–47, 52, 67, 69–70, 71n6, 73n49, 118n50, 120n53, 156–62, 180, 234, 238, 375, 422–23
    vs. narrow reflective equilibrium, 53, 423
Wittgenstein, Ludwig, 2–4, 9–10, 16, 83, 134, 418–19
    Philosophical Investigations, xi, 2
    philosophical therapy, 97–98, 100, 120n53, 122n55
    See also Augean stable cleaning
Wood, Allen, 151–56, 159–60, 163–65
world government. *See* global governance

www.ingramcontent.com/pod-product-compliance
Lightning Source LLC
Chambersburg PA
CBHW052009290426
44112CB00014B/2170